THE RESOURCEFUL TEACHER'S HANDBOOK 1994–5

MACMILLAN

First published 1994 by Pan Macmillan Ltd
Cavaye Place London SW10 9PG
and Basingstoke

Associated companies throughout the world

ISBN 0-333-61600-6

Copyright © Gill FitzHugh and The Marketing Department 1994

The right of Gill FitzHugh to be identified as the author of this
work has been asserted by her in accordance with the Copyright,
Designs and Patents Act of 1988.

All rights reserved. No reproduction, copy or transmission of this
publication may be made without written permission. No paragraph of
this publication may be reproduced, copied or transmitted save with
written permission or in accordance with the provisions of the Copyright
Act 1956 (as amended). Any person who does any unauthorised act in
relation to this publication may be liable to criminal prosecution and
civil claims for damages.

1 3 5 7 9 8 6 4 2

Every care has been taken in compiling the information contained in this publication but the
authors and publishers accept no responsibility for any error in detail, inaccuracy or
judgement whatsoever.

A CIP catalogue record for this book is available from
the British Library.

Typeset by Spottiswoode Ballantyne Ltd.

Printed and bound in Great Britain by
Cox & Wyman Ltd, Reading, Berkshire

THE RESOURCEFUL TEACHER'S HANDBOOK

CONTENTS

Foreword	v
Acknowledgements	vii
How to use	viii
Abbreviations	viii
Part 1: Visits In	1
Part 2: Visits Out	120
Part 3: Calendar of Events	568
Advertisers' Index	613
Comment Form	614

THE RESOURCEFUL TEACHER'S HANDBOOK

FOREWORD

The idea was conceived while teaching at North Westminster School when I started to organise a series of sixth form talks by visiting speakers from interesting and topical walks of life. The purpose was to fill gaps in the pupils' education, broaden their perspective and to excite and inspire them.

Throughout my professional teaching career I have tried to find ways to bring excitement and inspiration into learning. My abiding memory of school is the lessons which seemed interminably long and I think that this was the only time of my life when I have not thirsted for education. At the same time, I can recall the moments when I have been inspired and educated – when I've listened to a lecture, read an article, looked at a painting, listened to music, visited somewhere beautiful when my life was both changed and enhanced by the experience. I hope that this book will increase pupils' opportunities for moments such as these.

The book is for teachers and anyone responsible for the education and training of young people. It is to save the time which I wasted down blind alleys over the years when trying to organise speakers, to help fulfil the demanding targets of the National Curriculum, and to suggest new sources of material.

We plan to update *The Resourceful Teacher's Handbook* annually. Future editions will be greatly enhanced by teachers' contributions. As this is the first book there will undoubtedly be many gaps which we hope, with your input, to fill. If you feel able to comment on the content and quality of any visiting speaker or the value of a visit to any of the venues we have listed or can

THE RESOURCEFUL
TEACHER'S HANDBOOK

suggest new speakers and places to visit which you feel should be included, please do so. We also hope to expand the next edition with further sections so it will become even more comprehensive. Your comments and suggestions on extra areas that we should cover will be most welcome. A simple tear-out form can be found on page 614. Please take the time to fill it in and return it to me. Your contribution will, I know, prove invaluable.

ACKNOWLEDGEMENTS

I would like to thank all the people who helped compile this book. Sophie Eagar, Edmund Tyler and Antony Ifode did the initial research and I have relied totally on Davina Stewart for organising the material for me, Joyce and Jon Whowell for designing and constantly updating the computer systems, and Margaret Vallely for tireless work inputting the information.

I also owe an enormous debt to Michael Dickson and Shuna Kennedy, my associates, whose collaboration has made this publication possible.

Last, but not least, I must thank my husband William for hours of work and advice, the use of his computers and for the invaluable time of his FCM colleagues, Joyce and Margaret.

THE RESOURCEFUL TEACHER'S HANDBOOK

HOW TO USE

Visits In lists in alphabetical order organisations nationwide that can supply speakers to come and visit your school. There is a subject index at the end of the section to help you locate organisations that cover particular topics (e.g. animals, human rights, etc.).

Some organisations can supply speakers nationwide – others only cover a strictly local area. The geographical areas served are clearly indicated. Where the entry says 'any' geographical area, this means that the organisation will *try* to supply speakers to all parts of the country, but can't make any promises!

Costs of speakers vary widely. We have indicated whether expenses or fees are payable but, as policies can change, it's best to check with the organisation beforehand.

Abbreviations
KS1 Key Stage 1 (5–7 years)
KS2 Key Stage 2 (7–11 years)
KS3 Key Stage 3 (11–14 years)
KS4 Key Stage 4 (14–16 years)
NC National Curriculum

Visits Out lists by geographical region places of interest for school trips in England, Scotland, Wales and Northern Ireland. England has been divided into six regions covering:

London and the Southeast
Bournemouth, Brighton, Chatham, Colchester, Dover, Eastbourne, Guildford, Hertford, Isle of Wight, London, Luton, Margate, Newbury, Portsmouth, Reading, Southampton, Swindon, Tunbridge Wells, Welwyn, Winchester.

East Anglia
Bury St Edmunds, Cambridge, Chelmsford, Cromer, Ipswich, King's Lynn, Lowestoft, Norwich, Peterborough, Southend-on-Sea.

Midlands
Aylesbury, Banbury, Birmingham, Boston, Cheltenham, Crewe, Derby, Grantham, Leicester, Lincoln, Luton, Macclesfield, Northampton, Nottingham, Sheffield, Stafford, Stoke-on-Trent, Warwick.

Northeast
Darlington, Doncaster, Durham, Hartlepool, Hexham, Hull, Leeds, Newcastle, Rotherham, Scarborough, Sunderland, Wakefield, Whitby, York.

Northwest
Blackburn, Blackpool, Bradford, Carlisle, Chester, Huddersfield, Kendal, Keswick, Lancaster, Liverpool, Manchester, Penrith, Stockport, Wigan.

Southwest
Bath, Bristol, Bude, Exeter, Dorchester, Exeter, Ilfracombe, Launceston, Lyme Regis, Minehead, Newquay, Penzance, Plymouth, Salisbury, Torbay, Taunton, Wells, Weymouth.

Note
In *Visits Out*, 'NC Support' gives information suitable for A level and BTEC students as well as for younger children.

PART ONE

VISITS IN

Why arrange visits in?	3
Making the visit a success	4
How to find a speaker	7
Organisations A-to-Z	15
Subject Index	114

WHY ARRANGE VISITS IN?

Unquestionably it requires effort and imagination to arrange for visitors to come into school to give talks, run workshops, etc. This book is meant to relieve a teacher of at least some of the effort by saving them time researching where to find speakers. Teachers already have considerable worries about whether speakers will turn up, be on time, and do a good presentation when they are there. However, the potential for enhancement of the learning that goes on in schools is great when visitors are invited, because they are able to do the following:

- Provide outside stimulation for pupils.
- Provide specialist expertise in an area of education.
- Give an example of the rich variety of human experience and their unique response to it.
- Provide knowledge in an area not covered by the classroom teacher.
- Reveal the real issues and debates that are a part of any society.

The pupils learn from what the visitors have to say, and in addition, it teaches them social skills which include:

- Meeting and interacting with the visitors and learning to listen carefully and politely.
- Learning to ask questions in ways that produce relevant and full answers.
- Finding ways to probe the speaker and to disagree with them politely and firmly and perhaps to encourage them to look at issues differently.
- Thanking the visitor in an honest but caring way, knowing that coming to talk to the group has taken considerable time and effort on their part.

MAKING THE VISIT A SUCCESS

It is impossible to make all visits a success but following some basic rules will give a visit the best chance. These rules include: briefing the visitor clearly, planning the programme with input from the students, preparing the students and evaluating the visit.

BRIEFING THE VISITOR

It is very important that the visitor should know how to find the school, where to go and whom to ask for when they arrive, how large the group is and the age, ability, and relevant experience of the group. It is also important that the teacher should know whether the speaker requires any specialist equipment. It is essential to tell them the exact length of time with the students and to discuss how they want to arrange the presentation and whether they want pupils to participate during the presentation, or to wait till the end. If the visitor is giving a straight talk they very often like to be told when they should be winding up and either the teacher or a pupil could offer to do this five minutes before the end.

PLANNING THE PROGRAMME

Involving the students in deciding on whom to ask into school and planning the programme makes for a more successful programme. A teacher may also wish to choose people that he or she knows will add expertise and knowledge to the curriculum. A good way of enlisting pupils' involvement is to use the brainstorming technique. Use a flip chart or half a blackboard and ask each pupil to come up with a suggestion for a speaker and the reason for their choice. No idea is rejected, no one must interrupt or disagree, everyone must participate. When every idea has been written up then the class should decide which speakers to follow up and what they are going to be asked to talk about, and these ideas should be written up on the other side of the board or another page of the flip chart.

PREPARING THE PUPILS

The visit will have a much better chance of success if the pupils are carefully prepared beforehand about how to get the best out of the visitor. For example, they need to know that most speakers who come to schools, do so in a voluntary capacity. The visitor will go away with an impression of the school and they need to think about what gives them the impression and if it is what they want to convey. The pupils also need to think carefully beforehand about the questions that they want to ask the speaker and to make sure that at least one person is primed to ask the first question to prevent an embarrassing silence. The greater the number of pupils that can be encouraged to ask questions the better, rather than allowing the questions to be asked by one or two pupils only. It is important to encourage the pupils to ask open-ended questions rather than questions that can simply be answered in a word. They should prepare their questions clearly and do their best to make sure that the meaning of the question is clear. It is a good idea if a pupil introduces and thanks a speaker as this can make a useful initial training in public speaking.

EVALUATING THE TALK

Evaluation can be done by the pupils, teachers and the visitor themselves. It is very important that when pupils evaluate a talk they do so from a wide perspective and not simply look at the event from their own perspective.

Pupil Evaluation The following questions could be asked:

- Was it interesting?

- Did I or other members of the class learn anything worthwhile?
- If it was not interesting was it because the content was boring, irrelevant, incomprehensible or simply poorly presented?
- If it was poorly presented was it because the speaker's voice was unattractive or monotonous, too fast or too slow?
- Was it our fault that the talk was not better? Could we have made the speaker more at ease and relaxed?

A bad experience can also be a learning experience! A very good follow-up or preparation to inviting visitors in is to ask the students to do a short presentation themselves so that they start to learn the pitfalls.

Speaker Evaluation A speaker can be given a form to complete which will help a teacher to plan events in the future. The speaker could be asked questions about the preparations for the talk, the responses from the pupils, the levels and standards of the questions, whether any important areas of questioning were omitted and what impression the school and the pupils made on them.

HOW TO FIND A SPEAKER

Hours of time can be saved when teachers have even a small amount of knowledge about where and how to find speakers. Once a teacher knows where to *look*, it is then a matter of building up a talented local network to come into your school.

These speakers can provide pupils with a change from the routine teaching of professionals and can enrich young people with a whole variety of different views, ideas and experiences.

This section looks at how to find speakers from some of the wide variety of different sectors and it highlights some good examples. It also takes a look at some of the key issues that could be discussed with the pupils.

POLITICAL TALKS

National and European Government All the main political parties are listed in the speakers section and it should be possible to invite the sitting MP in to speak and the candidates or agents of the other parties. Members of the European Parliament are also willing to do talks in schools, though it will be necessary to plan the talk when they are available. There are also a number of organisations who will do talks on political issues. Charter 88 will talk on proportional representation, a Bill of Rights and freedom of information and the 300 group, which is campaigning for fairer representation of women in parliament, will discuss issues related to women in politics. The European Movement clarifies complex issues on Europe and gives excellent talks to schools.
Key issues: First past the post or proportional representation; the abolition of the House of Lords; fair representation of ethnic minorities and women; the balance of power between European, national and local government, Maastricht; should MPs be delegates or representatives?

VISITS IN

The Local Council A school can invite a local councillor in by phoning the Members Lobby of their local council and inviting in a councillor. They could ask the schools ward councillor if they want a general talk on the work of the council or the chair of a committee if they want a talk on a specific issue. They could also invite in a variety of people who work at the council such as a member of the housing department to talk on local housing and options for young people or an environmental officer to talk about the council's action on green issues.
Key issues: the relationship between central and local government; the council tax; compulsive competitive tendering; are the councils wasteful bureaucracies? When and how will councils cut themselves?

HEALTH TALKS

Talks on the Health Service The place where a school will go to find a speaker will depend on the nature of the talk wanted by the school. If the school wants a talk on the National Health Service then they should contact their nearest Community Health Council in England and Wales or the Scottish Association of Health Councils. These bodies are the public watch-dog over the Health Service and are meant to make sure that the service is working well. They frequently do presentations explaining how the service works though these vary from one body to another. Barnet Community Health Council has run school days for fifth and sixth formers to tell them about the CHC's role, their rights as a consumer and to give them a broad outline of how the service works. Their experience of these days is that the schools liked their visit round the hospital, but were not at all well informed about the system or health issues.
Key issues: the cost of health – Beveridge believed that the Health system would save money as everyone became healthier. Why was he wrong? Prevention or cure? National screening or exciting new operations?

VISITS IN

Talks on Health A school wanting a talk on a health issue should contact their local Health Education or Health Promotion Unit. These are listed under the name of the local Health Authority. The aim of the Health Education Authority and the Health Education Board for Scotland is to help people become more knowledgeable, better motivated, better able to acquire good health. A recent White Paper has highlighted five areas to concentrate on: coronary heart disease and stroke; cancer – initially lung, breast, cervical and skin; mental illness; HIV and AIDS and sexual health and accidents. They also wish to change behaviour in the following areas: tobacco smoking; diet and nutrition; alcohol consumption; blood pressure and the use of injectable drugs. The HEA publishes a number of wall sheets, leaflets, book and video resources that are available for purchase or hire. Many of these have been published very recently and are linked to the National Curriculum. If they are unavailable from your local bookshop or Health Education or Health Promotion Unit, then they can be requested from Customer Services, Health Education Authority, Mabledon Place, London WC1H 9TX. Tel 071-383 3833.

Talks on Drugs For information about drugs, the best organisation to approach is the school's nearest voluntary agency that is working with drug addicts and drug-related problems. Most of these will have an education officer, a development officer or even a fund raiser who will come and do a school talk. Some such as the Blenheim Project in London believe that the best way to teach is through drama workshops.
Key issues: should drugs be legalised? The impact and danger of heroine, LSD, ecstasy and crack; peer pressure; how to say 'No'; harm minimisation; the law.

Talks on AIDS The best way to find a speaker on AIDS is to contact the school's nearest voluntary agency. Not all of these provide speakers who go into schools but if a school is unable to find an organisation then they could contact the national AIDS Helpline on 0800 567 123 and ask for the nearest agency which will help. This body also publishes *The National Aids Annual* which gives up-to-date information.

Key issues: the spread of AIDS; how far has it spread to the heterosexual community? Prevention; confidentiality; living with AIDS.

Talks on Sex and Parenthood There are a number of organisations that provide speakers and help on issues related to sex and parenthood. A new body, listed in the Visits In section, is The Sex Education Forum, which is an umbrella body setting up a database covering the complete field of sex. An interesting organisation who are doing fascinating work in the field of parenthood is Exploring Parenthood, who can be contacted on 081-960 1678.
Key issues: one parent families; the right to life v. the right to abortion; peer pressure; sex and morality.

ACADEMIC TALKS FOR SIXTH FORMERS BY UNIVERSITY PROFESSORS

Some of the most exciting talks for sixth formers come from university professors who come into schools to talk about their specialist subjects. These can provide exciting tasters for pupils wishing to explore subjects further and have new doors opened for them. To contact these a school's best starting point is to ring their local university's Schools Liaison Officer. The addresses and phone numbers of all these are listed in the Visits In section under Universities (see page 98). Some universities have well-developed systems such as Lancaster University. The Schools Liaison Officer, Dr Colin Oldham, has produced a booklet of 156 possible lectures for schools! To show how interesting these can be the titles of some are listed below:

- Energy from Sea Waves and Other Natural Sources
- The Long Shadow of Chernobyl and its Aftermath
- Genetic Algebra
- Deterministic Chaos – Can We Be Certain of Anything?
- Why Social History is not 'History with the Politics left out': Social History in the 21st Century
- Understanding Industrial Misbehaviour

- Philosophy and Contemporary Issues
- Personal Relationships: the Action of Attraction
- Women in Islamic Societies
- The Emergence of Artificial Intelligence
- What is a Chair: the Questions of Design

Two specialist universities, the School of Oriental and African Studies and the School of Slavonic Studies, are excellent contacts for giving advice on how to find speakers to come and give talks on their areas of expertise and other resources. They not only can recommend the academics but also can recommend key charities to visit the school.

THE POLICE SERVICE

In 1993 the Police Schools Liaison Group brought out a new set of guidelines on Good Practice. This document is developed from the 1988 Code of Practice and takes account of the 1988 Education Reform Act and police policies and priorities. A new aspect of the 1993 guidelines is the role the police play in the National Curriculum. Traditionally the police have been involved in the area of personal and social education but today other areas of the curriculum have received contributions from the police. For example, using the costs associated with running and managing a police vehicle in Maths, participating in the CLASP Project on crime, law and society in History, and looking at urban regeneration and the removal of causes of disorder in Geography.

Head teachers and other relevant teachers should contact their local police commander or police community liaison officer to initiate discussion on what contribution police may be able to offer the school. Programmes and materials should be planned collaboratively. The Metropolitan Police produce a number of resources which include videos, role play resources and fact sheets. For details of these contact The Youth Affairs Branch: Room 636, New Scotland Yard, Broadway, London SW1H 0BG. Tel: 071-230 4216.

Key issues: Should there be more bobbies on the beat? Why is so little crime detected? Why are the statistics so different for fear of crime, unreported crime, crime and detected crime? Police and evidence; has the recent release of prisoners led to a loss of face in the Police Force? Police and racism.

THE FIRE SERVICE

Every fire brigade has its own schools education programme. Some send along a fire engine, some, such as the Tyne and Wear Metropolitan Fire Brigade, have a mobile classroom. Contact the local fire brigade to find out the service provided in your area. The London Fire Brigade has developed a comprehensive Fire Safety Curriculum for schools entitled 'Learn Not to Burn'. This has largely been developed on the Massachusetts Safety Education Program which is widely used throughout the USA. It has been adapted, with the assistance of London teachers, for use in this country in a way which makes it highly compatible with the teaching objectives of the new National Curriculum. From 1994 three volumes suited to Key Stages 1–3 will be available for purchase.

The first of the three packs to be produced was the pack for Key Stage 2. This pack is centred around a set of activities, each of which explores a theme related to fire safety and which are designed to encompass several core curricula topics at one time. The topics may be used independently, or in support of other teaching resources. Each activity is provided with a set of supporting teachers' notes describing the teaching objective and the way in which subject matter relates to the National Curriculum. The main emphasis in the pack is on pupil involvement and the encouragement of investigative learning. In addition the project provides material for Special Needs and mainstream children with sight, hearing or physical impairment. Contact The London Fire Brigade, Room 213, Queensborough House, 12–18 Albert Embankment, London SE1 7SD. Tel: 071-587 4580.

TEACHERS ASSURANCE

Whatever your needs ...

More income in retirement
Mortgages and personal loans
Motor insurance specially designed for teachers
Tax-free savings and investments
Competitive home and contents insurance
Protection against loss of income
Financial security for your dependants
Discount holidays and travel

... we can help

For sound advice on all your financial needs - without obligation - simply call

Freephone
0800 616 878

during normal office hours. At other times, an answerphone service is available. Simply leave your name and number, and we'll call you back the next working day.

The Teachers Assurance Marketing Group (members of which are members of Lautro and/or IMRO) comprises: Teachers Assurance Company Limited, a life assurance, pensions and investment company No. 314801; Teachers Provident Society, a registered Friendly Society No 372F; Sovereign Unit Trust Managers Limited No. 2072297, a member of the Association of Unit Trusts and Investment Funds. Teachers Assurance Company Limited is registered under the Consumer Credit Act 1974 Licence No 017601. Registered in England and Wales. Registered Office: 12 Christchurch Road, Bournemouth BH1 3LW. Telephone: Bournemouth (0202) 291111.

Your home is at risk if you do not keep up repayments on a mortgage or other loan secured on it.

RT9401

SCHOOL MINIBUSES FROM THE EXPERTS
Kirkham Minibuses
Custom Designed - Craftsman Built

Kirkham Minibuses can supply virtually any make of new minibus or a wide range of selected used vehicles up to four years old. Both new and used models are built to the same high quality incorporating luxury moquette trim seats, colour co-ordinated soft trim interior, anti slip one piece floor and the latest safety features.
All carry a twelve month warranty and are delivered painted and signwritten to your requirements with a wide range of options to meet your needs.

DEMONSTRATIONS, LOW COST FINANCE AND RENTAL PLANS ARE AVAILABLE

CONTACT
KIRKHAM MINIBUSES
**0772-683067 (Phone) 671162 (Fax)
Blackpool Road, Kirkham, Preston,
Lancashire PR4 2RE**

Computers and Dyslexia
Educational applications of new technology
Edited by CHRIS SINGLETON

•

Computer use is a powerful way of helping dyslexic learners of all ages. This latest book gives an overview of the best in new and current technology for dyslexia and special needs.

•

£10.95 plus £1.50 p & p. from

*Dyslexia Computer Resource Centre,
Dept. of Psychology, University of Hull,
Hull, HU6 7RX.*

Send S.A.E. for a list of publications and other resource materials for teachers.

By joining the **National Children's Bureau** you can gain immediate access to a vast pool of specialist knowledge through an influential network of childcare professionals.

NATIONAL CHILDREN'S BUREAU
The powerful voice of the child

Our Library and Information Service is probably the largest childcare information resource in the UK. Not only do we publish a wide range of books, but we also keep abreast of new developments in the form of training, conferences and seminars.

We now have a special membership for schools - to find out more and about the discounts you will enjoy as a member please call Jane Lewis, Membership Marketing Coordinator on 071-278 9441.

The National Children's Bureau is a registered Charity established for over 30 years.

VISITS IN
AFGHAN AID: AFGHANISTAN SUPPORT COMMITTEE

ACTIONAID
Registered Charity No 274467

Action Aid
- Kate Turner
- Action Aid Education, The Old Church House, Church Steps, Frome, Somerset. BA11 1PL
- 0373 452292 FAX 0373 453067

Works with some of the poorest communities in the world. Initiates village-development schemes in education, agriculture, health care, savings and credit. Also organises skills training and 'Sponsor-a-Child' scheme.

N C SUPPORT Yes. Action Aid produces resources on development issues for the National Curriculum and offers free visits from an Action Aid teacher. Further details and a catalogue available.
COSTS Donations accepted. No fee.
GEOGRAPHICAL AREAS SERVED
- Any

AGE OR KEY STAGE KS1 KS2 KS3 KS4 Sixth Form
SIZE OF GROUP 1–10 10–20 20–30 30+
NOTICE REQUIRED Four weeks.
DURATION OF PRESENTATION Forty minutes.
RESOURCES AVAILABLE
- Video
- Slides
- Worksheets
- Publications
- Displays
- Teacher's Notes

Action on Smoking and Health (ASH)
- Information Officer
- 109 Gloucester Place, London. W1H 3PH
- 071-935 3519 FAX 071-935 3463

Anti-smoking campaign set up in 1971. Alerts the public to the dangers of smoking and promotes policies to discourage it and reduce numbers of deaths caused by it. No speakers.

GEOGRAPHICAL AREAS SERVED
- Any

AGE OR KEY STAGE Sixth Form
RESOURCES AVAILABLE
- Publications
- Worksheets
- Displays
- Teacher's Notes

Advocacy Project
- Paul Oliver & Kate Smart
- Alone in London, 188 Kings Cross Road, London. WC1X 9DE
- 071-278 8304 FAX 071-837 7943

To help young, homeless people access social services support and accommodation through The Children Act.

GEOGRAPHICAL AREAS SERVED
- London
- S.E. England
- Any

AGE OR KEY STAGE KS4 Sixth Form
SIZE OF GROUP 1–10 10–20 20–30 30+
RESOURCES AVAILABLE
- Publications

Afghan Aid: Afghanistan Support Committee
- Jackie Wray
- 292 Pentonville Road, London. N1 9RN
- 071-278 2832

Aims to prevent further internal displacement of population, to increase Afghanistan's food production and to support refugee return. In addition Afghan Aid

AFGHAN AID: AFGHANISTAN SUPPORT COMMITTEE

operates a cross-border ambulance service and helps the disabled in refugee camps.

GEOGRAPHICAL AREAS SERVED
- Any

AGE OR KEY STAGE Sixth Form

SIZE OF GROUP 20–30 30+

NOTICE REQUIRED One month.

RESOURCES AVAILABLE
- Video
- Publications
- Slides
- Other

African, Caribbean and Asian Lawyers' Group
- Jerry Garvey
- Law Society House, 50–52 Chancery Lane, London. WC2A 1SX
- 071-242 1222

They provide practical assistance to people who wish to become solicitors or barristers.

GEOGRAPHICAL AREAS SERVED
- Any

AGE OR KEY STAGE KS4 Sixth Form

SIZE OF GROUP 10–20 20–30 30+

NOTICE REQUIRED Four weeks.

Age Concern
- Jane Tipley
- Age Concern (England), Astral House, 1268 London Road, London. SW16 4EJ
- 081-679 8000 FAX 081-679 6069

Age Concern England exists to provide care and enhanced quality of life to the 10 million-plus elderly people in the UK through campaigning, training and the provision of information and advice. It also provides local services through its 1000-plus local organisations.

N C SUPPORT It has a new range of schools' material which will provide teachers with ideas for ways of meeting the demands of the National Curriculum, especially in Technology, Geography and History, in ways that involve intergenerational contact. Available free: Key Stages 1, 2, 3 and 4.

GEOGRAPHICAL AREAS SERVED
- London
- S.E. England
- S.W. England
- East Anglia
- Midlands
- N.E. England
- N.W. England
- Scotland
- Wales
- Northern Ireland

AGE OR KEY STAGE KS1 KS2 KS3 KS4 Sixth Form

NOTICE REQUIRED Four weeks.

DURATION OF PRESENTATION By arrangement.

RESOURCES AVAILABLE
- Video
- Worksheets
- Publications
- Teacher's Notes

AHRTAG *see* Appropriate Health Resources & Technologies Group

Alcohol Concern
- Caroline Ray, Information Officer
- 275 Gray's Inn Road, London. WC1X 8QF
- 071-833 3471 FAX 071-278 2970

Alcohol Concern can put people in touch with local organisations which work with problem drinkers and which may provide speakers. They produce a directory of these services.

GEOGRAPHICAL AREAS SERVED
- Any

AGE OR KEY STAGE KS4 Sixth Form

SIZE OF GROUP 1–10 10–20 20–30 30+

RESOURCES AVAILABLE
- Publications

Alcoholics Anonymous
- General Service Officer
- PO Box 1, Stonebow House, Stonebow, York. YO1 2NJ
- 0904 644026 FAX 0904 629091

The organisation concentrates on group therapy, whereby members share experiences and gain strength and hope from each other so that they may solve their common problems and help others to recover from alcoholism.

N C SUPPORT Write to the above address. The staff will forward the letter to the relevant public information officer to arrange a visit.

COSTS No fee.

GEOGRAPHICAL AREAS SERVED
- Any

AGE OR KEY STAGE KS4 Sixth Form

SIZE OF GROUP 1–10 10–20 20–30 30+

NOTICE REQUIRED At least one month.

RESOURCES AVAILABLE
- Video
- Slides
- Publications

Amnesty International British Section
- Piers Bannister
- 99–119 Rosebery Avenue, London. EC1 4RE
- 071-278 6000 FAX 071-833 1510

Campaigns for the immediate and unconditional release of prisoners of conscience. Strives to end torture and the death penalty for all prisoners and works for fair and prompt trials for all political prisoners.

COSTS No fee.

GEOGRAPHICAL AREAS SERVED
- London
- S.E. England
- S.W. England
- East Anglia
- Midlands
- N.E. England
- N.W. England
- Scotland
- Wales
- Northern Ireland

AGE OR KEY STAGE KS3 KS4 Sixth Form

SIZE OF GROUP 30+

NOTICE REQUIRED One month.

RESOURCES AVAILABLE
- Video
- Publications
- Displays
- Other

Ancient Monuments Society
- Matthew Saunders
- St Ann's Vestry Hall, 2 Church Entry, London. EC4V 5HB
- 071-236 3934 FAX 071-329 3677

Founded in 1924 to save historic buildings of all ages and types. Covers all man-made structures of historic or architectural interest from all periods in all parts of the country.

GEOGRAPHICAL AREAS SERVED
- London

AGE OR KEY STAGE Sixth Form

VISITS IN
ANIMAL ABUSE, INJUSTICE & DEFENCE SOCIETY LTD

Animal Abuse, Injustice & Defence Society Ltd
- Gillian Egan
- 7 Castle Street, Towbridge, Kent. TN9 1BH
- 0732 364 5476

To campaign by all non-violent means for an end to animal abuse.

GEOGRAPHICAL AREAS SERVED
- S.E. England

AGE OR KEY STAGE KS3 KS4 Sixth Form

SIZE OF GROUP 20–30 30+

Anti-Apartheid Movement
- Information Officer
- 13 Mandela Street, London. NW1 0DW
- 071-387 7966 FAX 071-388 0173

Campaigning for a united, non-racial and democratic South Africa and the eradication of the legacies of apartheid.

COSTS Expenses.

GEOGRAPHICAL AREAS SERVED
- London
- S.W. England
- Midlands
- N.W. England
- Wales
- S.E. England
- East Anglia
- N.E. England
- Scotland

AGE OR KEY STAGE KS1 KS2 KS3 KS4 Sixth Form

SIZE OF GROUP 1–10 10–20 20–30 30+

NOTICE REQUIRED At least two weeks.

DURATION OF PRESENTATION Thirty minutes.

RESOURCES AVAILABLE
- Worksheets
- Publications
- Displays

Antiques Roadshow for Schools
- Jim Railton
- Nursery House, Chatton, Alnwick, Northumberland. ME66 5PY
- 06685 323

Visits schools to give in-house Antiques Roadshow events. Pupils bring in items of their own, which are displayed on a table in front of a specialist who talks about all the pieces as well as giving a general talk about antiques and the art world.

COSTS £50 plus travel expenses.

GEOGRAPHICAL AREAS SERVED
- N.E. England

AGE OR KEY STAGE KS4 Sixth Form

SIZE OF GROUP 20–30 30+

Anti-Slavery International
- David Ould, Campaigns and Fund Raising Assistant
- Stableyard, Broomgrove Road, London. SW9 9TL
- 071-582 4040 FAX 071-587 0573

The elimination of slavery in all its forms through research, awareness raising, lobbying and public campaigning. All of which supports the efforts of local groups with similar concerns.

COSTS Minimum to cover travel costs. Donation requested.

GEOGRAPHICAL AREAS SERVED
- London
- S.E. England

AGE OR KEY STAGE KS3 KS4 Sixth Form

SIZE OF GROUP 1–10 10–20 20–30 30+

NOTICE REQUIRED Preferably two months.

DURATION OF PRESENTATION Varies.

RESOURCES AVAILABLE
- Video
- Publications
- Displays
- Slides
- Teacher's Notes

Appropriate Health Resources & Technologies Action Group (AHRTAG)
☛ Information Officer
✉ 1 London Bridge Street, London. SE1 9SG
☎ 071-378 1403 FAX 071-403 6003

Supports primary healthcare programmes in developing countries by producing newsletters and other publications, and running an international health information resource centre and enquiry service which teachers can use.

AGE OR KEY STAGE Sixth Form

SIZE OF GROUP 20–30 30+

RESOURCES AVAILABLE
- Publications

Ark Trust
☛ Abbie Mycock
✉ 8 Bourdon Street, London. W1X 9HX
☎ 071-409 2638

Ark is a new environmental group which believes everyone can and must play a part in saving the planet. Ark helps people make simple but positive changes in their lifestyles which will contribute to safeguarding the environment, both locally and globally.

GEOGRAPHICAL AREAS SERVED
- London

AGE OR KEY STAGE Sixth Form

SIZE OF GROUP 20–30 30+

RESOURCES AVAILABLE
- Publications

Army Cadet Force Association
☛ Assistant General Secretary
✉ E Block, Duke of York's Headquarters, London. SW3 4RR
☎ 071-730 9733 FAX 071-730 8246

The ACF is sponsored by the Army and provides challenging military, adventurous and community activities. Its aim is to inspire young people to achieve success in life with a spirit of service to the Queen, their country and their local community. County ACFs can provide speakers.

N C SUPPORT The Gaining syllabus covers Map & Compass, Physical Fitness, Expedition Training, First Aid, Cadet & Community, Target Rifle Training.

COSTS Expenses.

GEOGRAPHICAL AREAS SERVED
- London
- S.W. England
- Midlands
- N.W. England
- Wales
- S.E. England
- East Anglia
- N.E. England
- Scotland
- Northern Ireland

AGE OR KEY STAGE Sixth Form

SIZE OF GROUP 10–20 20–30 30+

NOTICE REQUIRED One month.

Article 19
☛ Susan Hay
✉ 90 Borough High Street, London. SE1 1LL
☎ 071-403 4822 FAX 071-403 1943

Human Rights organisation founded to defend and advance the ideals embodied in Article 19 of the Universal Declaration of Human Rights on a worldwide basis.

N C SUPPORT No.

COSTS No fee.

GEOGRAPHICAL AREAS SERVED
- S.E. England

AGE OR KEY STAGE Sixth Form

SIZE OF GROUP 1–10 10–20 20–30 30+

NOTICE REQUIRED Four weeks.

DURATION OF PRESENTATION Varies.

ASH *see* Action on Smoking and Health

Aspirin Foundation
- Nick Henderson
- Henderson Group 1, Ryde House, Ripley, Surrey. GU23 6AT
- 0483 225398 FAX 0483 211043

Provides information about aspirin and aims to further the scientific study of aspirin.

N C SUPPORT Yes.

COSTS No fee.

GEOGRAPHICAL AREAS SERVED
- Any

AGE OR KEY STAGE Sixth Form

NOTICE REQUIRED Four weeks.

DURATION OF PRESENTATION One hour plus.

RESOURCES AVAILABLE
- Publications

ATD Fourth World
- Education Officer
- Education Department, 48 Addington Square, London. SE5 7LB
- 071-703 3231

An international voluntary human rights and peace organisation which works to provide aid and assistance to those in extreme poverty in all parts of the world.

N C SUPPORT Yes.

COSTS Donations requested.

GEOGRAPHICAL AREAS SERVED
- Any

AGE OR KEY STAGE KS1 KS2 KS3 KS4 Sixth Form

SIZE OF GROUP 1–10 10–20 20–30 30+

NOTICE REQUIRED Four to eight weeks.

DURATION OF PRESENTATION Up to half a day.

RESOURCES AVAILABLE
- Video
- Publications

Austrian Institute
- Librarian
- 28 Rutland Gate, London. SW7 0474
- 071-584 8654 FAX 071-225 0470

The Austrian Institute is willing to provide speakers to schools within Great Britain. Maps, booklets and videos can all be provided free of charge.

COSTS No fee.

GEOGRAPHICAL AREAS SERVED
- Any

AGE OR KEY STAGE KS3 KS4 Sixth Form

SIZE OF GROUP 30+

NOTICE REQUIRED One month.

RESOURCES AVAILABLE
- Publications
- Other
- Video

VISITS IN BARNARDO'S

AVERT
- Peter Kanabus
- 11–13 Denne Parade, Horsham, West Sussex. RH12 1JD
- 0403 210202 FAX 0403 211001

Funds research projects to understand more about HIV and its effects. AVERT research is conducted professionally in recognised medical establishments in various parts of the UK.

N C SUPPORT No.

COSTS Travelling expenses.

GEOGRAPHICAL AREAS SERVED
- Any

AGE OR KEY STAGE KS4 Sixth Form

NOTICE REQUIRED One to two months.

RESOURCES AVAILABLE
- Publications

Banking Information Service
- Jane Gibbins
- 10 Lombard Street, London. EC3V 9AT
- 071-626 9886 FAX 071-283 9655

BIS works on behalf of member banks to establish partnerships with education in order to increase knowledge and understanding of the banking industry and promote the work-related aspects of the curriculum.

N C SUPPORT National Curriculum targeted educational resources and a national team of full-time bank staff who undertake visits to schools and colleges.

COSTS Pricing policy for educational resources – a catalogue is available on request.

GEOGRAPHICAL AREAS SERVED
- London
- S.E. England
- S.W. England
- East Anglia
- Midlands
- N.W. England
- Wales
- N.E. England
- Scotland

AGE OR KEY STAGE KS3 KS4 Sixth Form

SIZE OF GROUP 1–10 10–20 20–30 30+

NOTICE REQUIRED At least four weeks due to operational needs of bank branches' departments.

RESOURCES AVAILABLE
- Publications

Barnardo's
- Marie De Vere
- Tanners Lane, Barkingside, Ilford, Essex. IG6 1QG
- 081-550 8822 FAX 081-551 6870

Originally Dr Barnado's and now Britain's largest voluntary child care charity, Barnado's helps children, young people and families facing disability or disadvantage.

N C SUPPORT No.

COSTS No fee. Fundraising only.

GEOGRAPHICAL AREAS SERVED
- Any

AGE OR KEY STAGE KS1 KS2 KS3 KS4 Sixth Form

SIZE OF GROUP 1–10 10–20 20–30 30+

DURATION OF PRESENTATION By arrangement.

RESOURCES AVAILABLE
- Publications
- Displays

BAYS *see* British Association for the Advancement of Science

BAYS

- Jackie Zammit
- Fortress House, 23 Savile Row, London. W1X 1AB
- 071-494 3326 FAX 071-734 1658

BAYS (British Association of Young Scientists), the national network of youth science clubs, aims to encourage and support all who interest young people in science and technology.

GEOGRAPHICAL AREAS SERVED
- Any

AGE OR KEY STAGE KS2 KS3 KS4

RESOURCES AVAILABLE
- Worksheets
- Publications
- Teacher's Notes

Birth Control Trust

- Amanda Callaghan
- 27-35 Mortimer Street, London. W1N 7RJ
- 071-580 9360 FAX 071-637 1378

Advances medical and sociological research in contraception, sterilisation and lawful termination of pregnancy; publishes results of research. Provides advice for women suffering physical or mental illness or distress resulting from unwanted pregnancy.

GEOGRAPHICAL AREAS SERVED
- London

AGE OR KEY STAGE Sixth Form

SIZE OF GROUP 1-10 10-20 20-30 30+

NOTICE REQUIRED One week.

RESOURCES AVAILABLE
- Other

Blackliners

- Trisha Plummer
- Eurolink Centre, 49 Effra Road, London. SW2 1BZ
- 071-738 7468 FAX 071-738 7945

Blackliners runs a helpline, provides care and support services to Black people of African, Asian or Caribbean descent. Education and training on HIV-related issues to voluntary and statutory agencies, community and youth groups.

COSTS £300 per day for one speaker. £100 per seminar workshop of one to one and a half hours. Fees negotiable for small community groups and groups without adequate funding.

GEOGRAPHICAL AREAS SERVED
- London
- East Anglia
- Scotland
- Wales
- Midlands
- N.E. England
- S.E. England
- S.W. England
- N.W. England
- Northern Ireland

AGE OR KEY STAGE Sixth Form

NOTICE REQUIRED At least one month, but may consider shorter notice.

RESOURCES AVAILABLE
- Publications

The Blenheim Project

- 7a Thorpe Close, London. W10 5XL
- 081-960 5599

A voluntary organisation that offers training, support, advice, information and counselling on drug issues. Runs talks and drama workshops for young people in London.

GEOGRAPHICAL AREAS SERVED
- London

AGE OR KEY STAGE **KS2 KS3 KS4 Sixth Form**

SIZE OF GROUP **20–30 30+**

RESOURCES AVAILABLE
- Publications

Blue Cross
- Information Officer
- Blue Cross Animal Welfare Society, Home Close Farm, Shilton Road, Burford, Oxon. OX18 4PF
- 0993 822651 FAX 0993 823083

Aims to encourage kindness to animals and give advice about good pet care. Twelve animal welfare centres, three animal hospitals and a clinic throughout the country. Particular emphasis on small animals and finding new homes for cats and dogs.

N C SUPPORT **No.**

COSTS **Donations welcome.**

GEOGRAPHICAL AREAS SERVED
- Any

AGE OR KEY STAGE **KS1 KS2 KS3 KS4 Sixth Form**

SIZE OF GROUP **1–10 10–20 20–30 30+**

NOTICE REQUIRED **Six months.**

DURATION OF PRESENTATION **One hour.**

RESOURCES AVAILABLE
- Slides
- Publications

Body Positive North East
- Al McDowell
- SIDA Centre, 12 Princes Square, Newcastle-upon-Tyne. NE1 8EG
- 091-261 8460

Registered charity providing education, training, direct services, support and advice to anyone infected, affected or interested in the issues surrounding HIV/AIDS.

GEOGRAPHICAL AREAS SERVED
- N.E. England

AGE OR KEY STAGE **Sixth Form**

SIZE OF GROUP **20–30**

NOTICE REQUIRED **One month.**

RESOURCES AVAILABLE
- Other

Boys' Brigade
- Brigade Secretary
- Feldon Lodge, Hemel Hempstead, Herts. HP3 0BL
- 0442 231681 FAX 0442 235391

Oldest Christian uniformed association for boys. Object is to provide a wide range of leisure-time activities for boys under Christian leadership with the purpose of drawing them into the Church.

N C SUPPORT **No.**

COSTS **No fee.**

GEOGRAPHICAL AREAS SERVED
- London
- S.W. England
- Midlands
- N.W. England
- Wales
- S.E. England
- East Anglia
- N.E. England
- Scotland
- Northern Ireland

AGE OR KEY STAGE **KS1 KS2 KS3 KS4 Sixth Form**

SIZE OF GROUP **1–10 10–20 20–30 30+**

NOTICE REQUIRED **By arrangement.**

RESOURCES AVAILABLE
- Publications

British Association for the Advancement of Science

- Mrs Smail
- 23 Savile Row, London. W1X 1AB
- 071-494 3326 FAX 071-734 1658

The British Association aims to promote science and technology to all sections of the community. The youth section provides support for the establishment of science clubs and Talking Science and lists speakers, organisations and groups who will give talks, demonstrations, etc.

N C SUPPORT Activities listed in BA Educational Publications are all linked to the National Curriculum.

COSTS Varies.

GEOGRAPHICAL AREAS SERVED
- London
- S.W. England
- Midlands
- N.W. England
- Wales
- S.E. England
- East Anglia
- N.E. England
- Scotland
- Northern Ireland

AGE OR KEY STAGE KS1 KS2 KS3 KS4 Sixth Form

SIZE OF GROUP 1–10 10–20 20–30 30+

NOTICE REQUIRED Varies.

DURATION OF PRESENTATION By arrangement.

RESOURCES AVAILABLE
- Publications

British Astronomical Association

- P Barber
- Burlington House, Piccadilly, London. W1V 9AG
- 071-734 4145

Junior membership is open to all persons interested in astronomy. There is a schools corporate membership. The BAA encourages all aspects of observational astronomy, circulates current astronomical information. Members will speak to schools on their specialist fields.

COSTS Expenses.

GEOGRAPHICAL AREAS SERVED
- London

AGE OR KEY STAGE Sixth Form

SIZE OF GROUP 1–10 10–20 20–30 30+

NOTICE REQUIRED Six weeks.

DURATION OF PRESENTATION By arrangement.

RESOURCES AVAILABLE
- Publications

British Atlantic Committee

- Alan Lee Williams, Director
- 154 Buckingham Palace Road, London. SW1W 9TR
- 071-730 3378 FAX 071-730 2278

Object is to educate the public on the aims of the Atlantic Treaty and to explain the UK's rights and responsibilities under the Treaty.

COSTS No fee.

GEOGRAPHICAL AREAS SERVED
- Any

AGE OR KEY STAGE Sixth Form

SIZE OF GROUP 1–10 10–20 20–30 30+

NOTICE REQUIRED Four weeks.

DURATION OF PRESENTATION Varies.

RESOURCES AVAILABLE
- Publications

British Computer Society
- Pam Bolwell
- PO Box 1454, Station Road, Swindon. SN1 1TG
- 0793 480269 **FAX** 0793 480270

Chartered professional body for IT and information systems. Aims to set and monitor standards in the industry and in education.

N C SUPPORT Local branches have Education Liaison Officers responsible for input to Education and Careers. The BCS Schools Committee publishes material for IT in support of the curriculum.

COSTS Speakers would normally expect expenses.

GEOGRAPHICAL AREAS SERVED
- London
- S.E. England
- Midlands
- Scotland
- N.W. England
- East Anglia
- S.W. England
- N.E. England
- Wales
- Northern Ireland

AGE OR KEY STAGE KS1 KS2 KS3 KS4 Sixth Form

NOTICE REQUIRED Depends on local branch.

RESOURCES AVAILABLE
- Worksheets
- Publications
- Teacher's Notes

British Defence and Aid Fund for Southern Africa
- Ethel de Keyser, Director
- 22 The Ivories, 6–8 Northampton Street, London. N1 2HX
- 071-354 1462 **FAX** 071-359 4875

Provides financial aid for the legal defence of Southern African political prisoners and the support of their families and dependants. Recently more concentration on the provision of aid.

COSTS Expenses.

GEOGRAPHICAL AREAS SERVED
- Any

AGE OR KEY STAGE KS4 Sixth Form

SIZE OF GROUP 1–10 10–20 20–30 30+

NOTICE REQUIRED Four weeks.

DURATION OF PRESENTATION Thirty minutes.

RESOURCES AVAILABLE
- Worksheets
- Publications
- Slides
- Displays

British Geological Survey
- Dr Brian J Taylor
- Keyworth, Nottingham. NG12 5GG
- 0602 363100 **FAX** 0602 363200

The British Geological Survey (BGS) is the UK's 'National Centre for Earth Science Information and Expertise'.

N C SUPPORT Provides talks/demonstrations that equate as closely as possible to the National Curriculum. Visits by prior appointment and strictly limited in 1994.

GEOGRAPHICAL AREAS SERVED
- Midlands
- Any

AGE OR KEY STAGE KS2 KS3 Sixth Form

SIZE OF GROUP 30+

NOTICE REQUIRED Four to six weeks.

DURATION OF PRESENTATION One to five hours for Key Stage 2; longer for other groups.

RESOURCES AVAILABLE
- Video
- Publications
- Displays

VISITS IN
BRITISH HUMANIST ASSOCIATION

British Humanist Association
- Mrs Anne Toy
- 14 Lamb's Conduit Passage, London. WC1R 4RH
- 071-430 0908 FAX 071-430 0908

The BHA is the national voice of humanism, concerned with moral issues from a non-religious viewpoint and with the establishment of a more open, just and caring society.

N C SUPPORT Material on spiritual and moral education, information on humanism as an ethical tradition as part of RE/PSE/Humanities work.

COSTS BHA has charitable status on the basis of its educational function. Speakers are voluntary, travelling expenses only required.

GEOGRAPHICAL AREAS SERVED
- London
- S.W. England
- Midlands
- N.W. England
- Wales
- S.E. England
- East Anglia
- N.E. England
- Scotland
- Northern Ireland

AGE OR KEY STAGE KS2 KS3 KS4 Sixth Form

SIZE OF GROUP 1–10 10–20 20–30 30+

NOTICE REQUIRED At least two weeks.

DURATION OF PRESENTATION By arrangement.

RESOURCES AVAILABLE
- Video
- Publications

British Mountaineering Council
- Derek Walker, General Secretary
- Crawford House, Precinct Centre, Booth Street East, Manchester. M13 9RZ
- 061-273 5835 FAX 061-274 3233

Representative body for all who take part in mountaineering activity. Mountain Leader Training Board trains teachers to take young people on the hills. Occasionally provides speakers.

N C SUPPORT Yes.

GEOGRAPHICAL AREAS SERVED
- Any

AGE OR KEY STAGE KS3 KS4 Sixth Form

NOTICE REQUIRED One month, numbers by arrangement.

RESOURCES AVAILABLE
- Publications

British Museum
- Education Officer
- Great Russell Street, London. WC1B 3DG
- 071-636 1555 x508 FAX 071-323 8515

Collections cover Egyptian, West Asiatic, Classical, Prehistoric, Romano-British, Oriental, Medieval and later periods. No speakers but educational services for use in schools include hire of videos and culture-specific packs.

N C SUPPORT The Anglo-Saxon video and the packs are related to the National Curriculum

GEOGRAPHICAL AREAS SERVED
- Any

AGE OR KEY STAGE KS1 KS2 KS3 KS4 Sixth Form

RESOURCES AVAILABLE
- Video
- Displays
- Worksheets

Free video loan, no speakers.

VISITS IN
BRITISH NUCLEAR FUELS

British Naturalists' Association
- J F Pearson, General Secretary
- 48 Russell Way, Higham Ferrers, Northants. NN9 8EJ
- 0933 314672 FAX 0933 314672

Objectives are to encourage schemes and legislation which protect wildlife and preserve natural beauty. Supports the promotion and maintenance of national parks, nature reserves, sanctuaries and conservation areas. Organises the Blakes Shield Annual Competition for Natural History/Conservation projects.

Competition of the Blake Shield is open to groups of young people 8–16 years with adult team leaders. It will be awarded to a Natural History/Conservation Project which may investigate a wood, pond, heath, etc, and observe plants, insects, animals and birds.

GEOGRAPHICAL AREAS SERVED
- London
- S.E. England
- S.W. England
- East Anglia
- Midlands
- N.E. England
- N.W. England
- Northern Ireland

AGE OR KEY STAGE **KS2 KS3 KS4**

RESOURCES AVAILABLE
- Publications

British Nuclear Forum
- Nigel Middlemiss
- 22 Buckingham Gate, London. SW1E 6LB
- 071-828 0116 FAX 071-828 0110

A trade association representing approximately 70 organisations engaged in funding, planning, building, operating and supplying services to the country's nuclear power industry.

COSTS **Expenses.**

GEOGRAPHICAL AREAS SERVED
- Any

AGE OR KEY STAGE **Sixth Form**

SIZE OF GROUP **1–10 10–20 20–30 30+**

NOTICE REQUIRED **Four weeks.**

DURATION OF PRESENTATION **Varies.**

RESOURCES AVAILABLE
- Publications

British Nuclear Fuels
- Enquiries
- Risley, Warrington, Cheshire. WA3 6AS
- 0925 832869 FAX 0925 832098

Manufactures and reprocesses nuclear fuel and disposes of nuclear waste.

N C SUPPORT **Yes.**

COSTS **No fee.**

GEOGRAPHICAL AREAS SERVED
- Any

AGE OR KEY STAGE **KS1 KS2 KS3 KS4 Sixth Form**

SIZE OF GROUP **1–10 10–20 20–30 30+**

NOTICE REQUIRED **Two weeks.**

DURATION OF PRESENTATION **One hour plus.**

RESOURCES AVAILABLE
- Video
- Slides
- Worksheets
- Publications
- Displays
- Teacher's Notes

VISITS IN
BRITISH PREGNANCY ADVISORY SERVICE

British Pregnancy Advisory Service
- Information Officer
- Austy Manor, Wootton Wawen, Solihull, West Midlands. B95 6BX
- 0564 793225 FAX 0564 794935

BPAS is a national, non-profit-making charity providing abortion advice and help, contraception, pregnancy testing and other related services.

N C SUPPORT Publication/leaflets available for those studying abortion for part of GCSE syllabus.

GEOGRAPHICAL AREAS SERVED
- Midlands
- Any

AGE OR KEY STAGE KS4 Sixth Form

SIZE OF GROUP 1–10 10–20 20–30 30+

NOTICE REQUIRED Four weeks.

DURATION OF PRESENTATION One hour.

RESOURCES AVAILABLE
- Publications

British Red Cross
- Jo Bradbury
- National Office, 9 Grosvenor Crescent, London. SW1X 7EJ
- 071-235 5454 FAX 071-245 6315

Gives studied and impartial care to people in need and crisis, in their homes and in the community, at home and abroad, in peace and in war. There is a Red Cross Youth organisation for 5–15 year olds. The National Office will tell schools whom to contact for resources and speakers.

N C SUPPORT Education packs linked to the National Curriculum for schools include a baby-sitting pack, Health Care, Safety, HIV & AIDS, International Understanding.

GEOGRAPHICAL AREAS SERVED
- Any

AGE OR KEY STAGE KS1 KS2 KS3 KS4 Sixth Form

NOTICE REQUIRED As much as possible.

DURATION OF PRESENTATION One period.

RESOURCES AVAILABLE
- Video
- Other
- Publications

British Refugee Council
- Jill Rutter, Education Officer
- 3 Bondway, London. SW8 1SJ
- 071-582 6922 FAX 071-582 9929

The Refugee Council provides practical support for refugees in Britain and campaigns on refugee issues throughout the world.

N C SUPPORT Publications for Key Stage 2, 3 and 4 for teachers of Geography, History, English.

COSTS Travel expenses. Donations appreciated.

GEOGRAPHICAL AREAS SERVED
- London
- S.E. England
- Midlands

AGE OR KEY STAGE KS1 KS2 KS3 KS4 Sixth Form

SIZE OF GROUP 10–20 20–30 30+

NOTICE REQUIRED Six weeks.

DURATION OF PRESENTATION Thirty minutes.

RESOURCES AVAILABLE
- Video
- Slides
- Worksheets
- Publications
- Displays
- Teacher's Notes

British Southern Slav Society
☞ John Burns, Secretary
✉ 121 Marsham Street, Westminster, London. SW1P 4LX
☎ 071-828 2762

Non-political charitable society promoting cultural and economic contacts and understanding between the UK and all the countries of the former Yugoslavia. They have expertise in the political situation.

COSTS Negotiable, but expenses required.

GEOGRAPHICAL AREAS SERVED
- London
- S.W. England
- Midlands
- N.W. England
- Wales
- S.E. England
- East Anglia
- N.E. England
- Scotland

AGE OR KEY STAGE KS4 Sixth Form

SIZE OF GROUP 1–10 10–20 20–30 30+

NOTICE REQUIRED Preferably four weeks.

DURATION OF PRESENTATION By arrangement.

RESOURCES AVAILABLE
- Publications

British Trust for Conservation Volunteers
☞ Andrea Mannings
✉ 36 St Mary's Street, Wallingford, Oxon. OX10 0EU
☎ 0491 39766 FAX 0491 39646

Undertakes practical conservation work and aims to educate people in general on conservation principles in practice. Eleven regions and over 400 local groups. Conservation training programmes organised for members.

N C SUPPORT Yes.

COSTS No fee.

GEOGRAPHICAL AREAS SERVED
- Any

AGE OR KEY STAGE KS1 KS2 KS3 KS4 Sixth Form

SIZE OF GROUP 1–10 10–20 20–30 30+

NOTICE REQUIRED Four weeks.

DURATION OF PRESENTATION Varies.

RESOURCES AVAILABLE
- Publications

Brook
ADVISORY CENTRES

NHS, funded contraception and counselling centres for teenagers. Free and confidential. Under 16s welcome.

School visits to Centres can be arranged as part of the PSHE programmes.

Sex education resources also produced for use in schools. Free catalogue available.

For more information ring 071.708.1234 or write to Brook Advisory Centres, National Office, 153a East Street, London SE17 2SD. Brook will be moving in 1994. Please check after April 1994.

Brook Advisory Centre
☞ Alison Hadley
✉ 153a East Street, London. SE17 2SD
☎ 071-708 1234 FAX 071-708 1390

Nineteen centres throughout the country offer young people free, confidential birth control advice and supplies, and help with emotional and sexual problems.

N C SUPPORT Most recent publications identify curriculum areas with which the material may be used. Publications catalogue available.

COSTS Donation appreciated. Some branches request £20–£50.

GEOGRAPHICAL AREAS SERVED
- London

AGE OR KEY STAGE KS3 KS4 Sixth Form

SIZE OF GROUP 1–10 10–20

NOTICE REQUIRED As much as possible.

DURATION OF PRESENTATION Varies.

RESOURCES AVAILABLE
- Video
- Publications
- Worksheets
- Teacher's Notes

The Building Experience Trust

- Nigel Frost
- PO Box 217, Cambridge. CB4 1EA
- 0223 65378

Independent registered charity, collaborating with other professionals to promote the study of and campaign for Built Environment education in schools as a process of learning. Pupils work as individuals, then into groups using simple materials to produce large constructions. Workshops presented by multidisciplined trained and practised 'Animateurs'.

N C SUPPORT Provide 'hands-on' workshops which develop practical skills, provide knowledge of Built Environment concepts, relevant to National Curriculum Technology, Art, History, Natural Science, Humanities and Geography.

COSTS Two two-hour workshops per day at the school, fee £220.

GEOGRAPHICAL AREAS SERVED
- London
- East Anglia
- S.E. England
- Midlands

AGE OR KEY STAGE KS2 KS3

SIZE OF GROUP 30+

CAFOD (Catholic Fund for Overseas Development)

- Regional Organiser, Schools Section
- Romero Close, Stockwell Road, London. SW9 9TY
- 071-733 7900 FAX 071-274 9630

CAFOD is the official development agency of the Catholic Church in England and Wales. It works in 75 countries of the south and supports over 1000 projects. Its education work in schools seeks to raise awareness about the causes of poverty and injustice in the world so as to bring about change.

N C SUPPORT Development Education resource materials link into National Curriculum Attainment Targets and RE programmes as well as cross-curricular themes.

COSTS No fee.

GEOGRAPHICAL AREAS SERVED
- London
- S.W. England
- Midlands
- N.W. England
- Wales
- S.E. England
- East Anglia
- N.E. England
- Scotland

AGE OR KEY STAGE KS1 KS2 KS3 KS4 Sixth Form

SIZE OF GROUP 1–10 10–20 20–30 30+

CAMPAIGN AGAINST THE ARMS TRADE

NOTICE REQUIRED Approximately half to one term.

DURATION OF PRESENTATION Half to one day.

RESOURCES AVAILABLE
- Video
- Worksheets
- Teacher's Notes
- Slides
- Publications
- Displays
- Other

Cambridge AIDS Helpline
- Toni Elkins
- PO Box 257, Cambridge. CB2 3AY
- 0223 359857

Provides care and support to people living with HIV/AIDS in Cambridgeshire and aims to heighten people's awareness around the issues of HIV/AIDS and related issues.

GEOGRAPHICAL AREAS SERVED
- East Anglia

AGE OR KEY STAGE KS3 KS4 Sixth Form

SIZE OF GROUP 1–10 10–20 20–30 30+

NOTICE REQUIRED Two months if possible (sometimes we can respond more quickly).

RESOURCES AVAILABLE
- Video
- Displays
- Publications
- Other

Campaign Against Censorship
- Mrs Hayward
- c/o 25 Middleton Close, Fareham, Hants. PO14 1QN
- 0329 284471

Upholds the right to obtain and impart knowledge; advocates freedom of ownership, and freedom for creative artists to present their perceptions, interpretations and ideas.

COSTS Expenses.

GEOGRAPHICAL AREAS SERVED
- S.E. England

AGE OR KEY STAGE KS4 Sixth Form

SIZE OF GROUP 1–10 10–20 20–30 30+

NOTICE REQUIRED Four weeks.

DURATION OF PRESENTATION Varies.

RESOURCES AVAILABLE
- Publications

Campaign Against the Arms Trade
- Information Officer
- 11 Goodwin Street, London. N4 3HQ
- 071-281 0297 FAX 071-281 0297

Committed to ending the international arms trade and Britain's involvement in it. Long-term objectives include the conversion of military industry to civil uses.

COSTS Expenses.

GEOGRAPHICAL AREAS SERVED
- London

AGE OR KEY STAGE Sixth Form

SIZE OF GROUP 1–10 10–20 20–30 30+

NOTICE REQUIRED Four weeks.

DURATION OF PRESENTATION Varies.

RESOURCES AVAILABLE
- Video
- Worksheets
- Displays
- Slides
- Publications
- Teacher's Notes

Campaign for a Smoke Free Environment *see* Cleanair

VISITS IN
CAMPAIGN FOR FREEDOM OF INFORMATION

Campaign for Freedom of Information
- Maurice Frankel
- 88 Old Street, London. EC1V 9AR
- 071-253 2445

A campaigning organisation which aims to eliminate unnecessary official secrecy and to give people legal rights to information which affects their lives.

COSTS Expenses.

GEOGRAPHICAL AREAS SERVED
- S.E. England

AGE OR KEY STAGE Sixth Form

SIZE OF GROUP 1–10 10–20 20–30 30+

NOTICE REQUIRED Three weeks.

DURATION OF PRESENTATION One hour plus.

RESOURCES AVAILABLE
- Publications

Campaign for Nuclear Disarmament (CND)
- John Handelaar
- Youth CND, 162 Holloway Road, London. N7 8DQ
- 071-607 3616 FAX 071-700 2357

Campaigns for the unilateral abandonment by the UK of nuclear weapons and nuclear bases. Conducts a public information campaign.

COSTS Expenses.

GEOGRAPHICAL AREAS SERVED
- Any

AGE OR KEY STAGE KS3 KS4 Sixth Form

SIZE OF GROUP 1–10 10–20 20–30 30+

NOTICE REQUIRED Four weeks.

DURATION OF PRESENTATION Varies.

RESOURCES AVAILABLE
- Worksheets
- Publications
- Displays
- Teacher's Notes

Campaign for Press & Broadcasting Freedom
- Jo Treharne
- 8 Cynthia Street, London. N1 9JF
- 071-278 4430 FAX 071-837 8868

Works for greater diversity in ownership and content of the media, proper public regulation of media operators, equal opportunity for groups discriminated against; development of industrial democracy within press and broadcasting, reform of legislation on secrecy, and enshrinement of principles of free access to the media.

COSTS Expenses and donations welcome.

GEOGRAPHICAL AREAS SERVED
- London
- S.W. England
- N.E. England

AGE OR KEY STAGE KS4 Sixth Form

RESOURCES AVAILABLE
- Publications

Campaign for Research into Human Reproduction
- Ann Humphrey
- 27–35 Mortimer Street, London. W1N 7RJ
- 071-436 4528 FAX 071-637 1378

The Campaign for Research into Human Reproduction (PROGRESS) aims to support and protect controlled research into the earliest stages of human development and the prevention of infertility, miscarriage, and congenital handicap. Also involved in activities of an educational nature.

COSTS Expenses. No fee.

GEOGRAPHICAL AREAS SERVED
- S.E. England

AGE OR KEY STAGE Sixth Form

SIZE OF GROUP 1–10 10–20 20–30 30+

NOTICE REQUIRED Four weeks.

DURATION OF PRESENTATION One hour plus.

RESOURCES AVAILABLE
- Publications

Cancer and Leukaemia in Childhood Trust (CLIC) UK

- Felicity Hanley, Executive Assistant
- CLIC House, 11–12 Fremantle Square, Cotham, Bristol. BS6 5TL
- 0272 244333

Support and provision of excellence of care. National funds used to help organisations in the regions to improve services/facilities for childhood cancer patients and families.

GEOGRAPHICAL AREAS SERVED
- London

AGE OR KEY STAGE KS3 KS4 Sixth Form

SIZE OF GROUP 1–10 10–20 20–30 30+

RESOURCES AVAILABLE
- Worksheets
- Publications
- Displays

Cancer Research Campaign

- Jean King
- 10 Cambridge Court, London. NW1 4JL
- 071-224 1333 FAX 071-487 4310

Raises funds to be distributed as grants to support research into the causes and treatment of cancer.

N C SUPPORT Yes.

GEOGRAPHICAL AREAS SERVED
- Any

AGE OR KEY STAGE KS1 KS2 KS3 KS4 Sixth Form

SIZE OF GROUP 10–20 20–30 30+

RESOURCES AVAILABLE
- Video
- Teacher's Notes
- Publications

Care for the Wild

- Johanna Gibbon
- 1 Ashfolds, Horsham Road, Rusper, West Sussex. RH12 4QX
- 0293 871596 FAX 0293 871022

Campaigns against activities which endanger wildlife and distributes information to its supporters and campaigners.

COSTS Expenses or donation.

GEOGRAPHICAL AREAS SERVED
- London
- S.E. England

AGE OR KEY STAGE KS3 KS4 Sixth Form

SIZE OF GROUP 1–10 10–20 20–30 30+

NOTICE REQUIRED Four weeks.

DURATION OF PRESENTATION Varies.

RESOURCES AVAILABLE
- Video
- Slides
- Worksheets
- Publications
- Displays
- Teacher's Notes

VISITS IN
CATHEDRAL CAMPS

Cathedral Camps
- Shelley Bent
- 16 Glebe Avenue, Flitwick, Bedfordshire. MK45 1HS
- 0525 716237

Aims to preserve, conserve and repair cathedrals. Work is conducted by volunteers, sometimes with the aid of professional conservers on special projects.

COSTS **No fee.**

GEOGRAPHICAL AREAS SERVED
- Any

AGE OR KEY STAGE **Sixth Form**

SIZE OF GROUP **1–10 10–20 20–30 30+**

NOTICE REQUIRED **Four weeks.**

DURATION OF PRESENTATION **One period.**

RESOURCES AVAILABLE
- Video
- Slides

Catholic Fund for Overseas Development *see* CAFOD

Catholic Institute for International Relations
- Phil Bloomer/Tony Williams
- 22 Coleman Fields, London. N1 7AF
- 071-354 0883

Third World charity working to overcome poverty and injustice in the Third World. Education and information work and overseas programme to help people to become self-reliant.

N C SUPPORT **Specialist areas: Latin America, South Africa, the Philippines.**

GEOGRAPHICAL AREAS SERVED
- London
- Any

AGE OR KEY STAGE **Sixth Form**

SIZE OF GROUP **10–20 20–30 30+**

Central America Human Rights Committee
- Information Officer
- 83 Margaret Street, London. W1N 7HB
- 071-631 4200

Inform about, and campaign against, abuses of human rights in Central America. Publish a bi-monthly magazine.

N C SUPPORT **Talks as and where possible on Central America.**

GEOGRAPHICAL AREAS SERVED
- London

AGE OR KEY STAGE **KS3 KS4 Sixth Form**

SIZE OF GROUP **10–20 20–30 30+**

Centre for Alternative Technology
- Education Officer
- Llwyngwern Quarry, Machynlleth, Powys, Wales. SY20 9AZ
- 0654 702400 FAX 0654 702782

Demonstration and education centre which promotes practical ideas and gives information on technologies which do not damage the environment.

N C SUPPORT **Yes.**

COSTS **£30 per hour.**

GEOGRAPHICAL AREAS SERVED
- Any

AGE OR KEY STAGE **KS1 KS2 KS3 KS4 Sixth Form**

VISITS IN
THE CHILDREN'S SOCIETY

SIZE OF GROUP 1–10 10–20 20–30 30+

NOTICE REQUIRED Six months.

DURATION OF PRESENTATION Varies.

RESOURCES AVAILABLE
- Video
- Worksheets
- Publications
- Slides
- Teacher's Notes

Charter 88
☞ Gail Warden
✉ Exmouth House, 3–11 Pine Street, London. EC1R 0JH
☎ 071-833 5813 FAX 071-833 5895

Citizens' movement for constitutional reform which would include Freedom of Information, a fair voting system, reform of the Houses of Commons and Lords, a written constitution and a Bill of Rights.

N C SUPPORT
Citizenship/Politics/Sociology. Charter 88 has been the basis of many lectures throughout Britain and appears on some syllabuses.

COSTS Travelling expenses.

GEOGRAPHICAL AREAS SERVED
- London
- S.W. England
- Midlands
- N.W. England
- Wales
- S.E. England
- East Anglia
- N.E. England
- Scotland
- Northern Ireland

AGE OR KEY STAGE KS3 KS4 Sixth Form

SIZE OF GROUP 20–30

NOTICE REQUIRED At least six weeks.

DURATION OF PRESENTATION One hour plus.

RESOURCES AVAILABLE
- Publications

Chaucer Heritage Trust
☞ Philippe Wibrotte
✉ 22 St Peter's Street, Canterbury, Kent. CT1 2BQ
☎ 0227 470 379 FAX 071-229 0635

Promotes the life, times and works of Geoffrey Chaucer to the general public and schools.

N C SUPPORT Talks and dramatisations on all aspects of Geoffrey Chaucer. Resource material available.

COSTS Fees or expenses depend on type of programme.

GEOGRAPHICAL AREAS SERVED
- London
- S.E. England

AGE OR KEY STAGE KS4 Sixth Form

SIZE OF GROUP 1–10 10–20 20–30 30+

NOTICE REQUIRED Three months.

RESOURCES AVAILABLE
- Publications

The Children's Society
☞ Marian Ferguson, Schools and Youth Organiser
✉ Edward Rudolf House, Margery Street, London. WC1X 0JL
☎ 071-837 4299 FAX 071-837 0211

The Children's Society is an independent voluntary organisation guided by Christian principles, operating 130 projects in England and Wales ranging from family centres to special refuges for young runaways.

N C SUPPORT Education of Citizenship (Key Stage 4). 'Spotlight' packs support National Curriculum Key Stage 4 (free). Spotlight on 'Family

VISITS IN THE CHILDREN'S SOCIETY

Centres', 'Homeless Families', 'Young Runaways', 'Leaving Care', 'History of the Society'.

COSTS No fee but a fundraising event appreciated.

GEOGRAPHICAL AREAS SERVED
- London
- S.E. England
- S.W. England
- East Anglia
- Midlands
- N.E. England
- N.W. England
- Wales

AGE OR KEY STAGE KS4 Sixth Form

SIZE OF GROUP 1–10 10–20 20–30 30+

NOTICE REQUIRED Three weeks.

DURATION OF PRESENTATION By arrangement.

RESOURCES AVAILABLE
- Video
- Slides
- Worksheets
- Publications
- Displays
- Teacher's Notes

Christian Aid

☞ Jean Harrison (Secondary Schools Educational Advisor), Ruth Leavis (Children's Advisor)
✉ PO Box 100, London. SE1 7RT
☎ 071-620 4444 FAX 071-620 0719

A major relief and development organisation committed to strengthening the poor. At present it works where the need is greatest in more than 70 countries. Funds Third World relief work, development, medical and social services, and industrial and trade training.

N C SUPPORT Resources support the National Curriculum, particularly Geography, RE and cross-curricular themes and dimensions.

COSTS Travel expenses. Fee optional.

GEOGRAPHICAL AREAS SERVED
- London
- S.E. England
- S.W. England
- East Anglia
- Midlands
- N.E. England
- N.W. England
- Scotland
- Wales
- Northern Ireland

AGE OR KEY STAGE KS1 KS2 KS3 KS4 Sixth Form

SIZE OF GROUP 10–20 20–30 30+

NOTICE REQUIRED As much as possible.

DURATION OF PRESENTATION Twenty minutes plus.

RESOURCES AVAILABLE
- Video
- Slides
- Worksheets
- Publications
- Displays
- Teacher's Notes
- Other

Issues of International Trade

Use simulations to enhance your teaching

Market Trading - explores the complex issues of European single market legislation and its impact on Third World countries. £1.00. Age 16+. Playing time 90 Minutes.

The Trading Game - looks at how possession of raw materials or technology affects national prosperity. £1.00. Age 14+. Playing time 90 minutes.

A Fair Deal? - a computer simulation to enable understanding of economic factors influencing development and trade. (Available for Archimedes, RM Nimbus/PC compatible or IBM/IBM compatible computers - please state which version required.) £35.00. Age 14+. Playing time two and a half hours (does not need continuous play).

The Paper Bag Game - explores the difficulties of trying to survive without social security. How many paper bags do you have to produce? 50p. Age 9+. Playing time 45 minutes.

Order from Customer Services, Christian Aid, PO Box 100, London SE1 7RT. Tel: 071 620 4444 or 071 928 0710 (24 hr ansaphone)

Christian Aid
Registered Charity No 258003

VISITS IN COMMON LORE

Christian Impact
- Ernest Lucas, Education Division
- St Peter's Church, Vere Street, London. W1M 9HP
- 071-629 3615

Courses on Christian ethics; current issues and application of Christian faith to the present day.

GEOGRAPHICAL AREAS SERVED
- London
- S.E. England

AGE OR KEY STAGE Sixth Form

SIZE OF GROUP 10–20 20–30 30+

Church Action on Poverty
- Paul Goggins
- Central Buildings, Oldham Street, Manchester. M1 1JT
- 061-236 9321

An ecumenical organisation which aims to educate people, especially in the churches, about the causes and extent of poverty in Britain. Campaigns for changes which assist the least well-off.

COSTS No fee.

GEOGRAPHICAL AREAS SERVED
- Any

AGE OR KEY STAGE Sixth Form

SIZE OF GROUP 1–10 10–20 20–30 30+

NOTICE REQUIRED Three months.

DURATION OF PRESENTATION By arrangement.

RESOURCES AVAILABLE
- Video
- Displays

Cleanair: Campaign for a Smoke Free Environment
- Mr Mullick
- 33 Stillness Road, London. SE23 1NG
- 081-690 4649

Campaigns to restore the basic human right to breathe clean air.

GEOGRAPHICAL AREAS SERVED
- Any

AGE OR KEY STAGE KS3 KS4 Sixth Form

SIZE OF GROUP 20–30 30+

RESOURCES AVAILABLE
- Publications
- Other

Commission for Racial Equality
- Margaret Michie
- Elliot House, 10–12 Allington Street, London. SW1E 5EH
- 071-828 7022 FAX 071-630 7605

Home Office funded. Works closely with the 87 Racial Equality Councils of the UK. RECs aim to eliminate racial discrimination, to promote equality of opportunity between different racial and ethnic groups. Staff from the local RECs will contribute to the debate on racial issues.

GEOGRAPHICAL AREAS SERVED
- London
- Any

AGE OR KEY STAGE Sixth Form

RESOURCES AVAILABLE
- Publications

Common Lore
- Judith Lawson/Andy Russell
- Unit 301, The Small Business Centre, 444 Brixton Road, London. SW9 8GJ
- 071-738 5051

The promotion and education of story-telling arts through performances and workshops.

N C SUPPORT Workshops can be tailormade to suit the curriculum but are particularly relevant to English and Music. Resource pack for primary teachers.

COSTS Speakers £75–£200 plus VAT.

GEOGRAPHICAL AREAS SERVED
- London
- Any

AGE OR KEY STAGE KS1 KS2 KS3 KS4 Sixth Form

SIZE OF GROUP 1–10 10–20 20–30 30+

Commonwealth Human Ecology Council (CHEC)
- Secretary
- 57–58 Stanhope Gardens, London. SW7 5RF
- 071-373 6761 FAX 071-318 1439

Aims to encourage the growth of organisations concerned with human ecology in the Commonwealth. Develops research into field techniques in Commonwealth countries which apply human ecology principles.

N C SUPPORT Yes.

COSTS Expenses.

GEOGRAPHICAL AREAS SERVED
- Any

AGE OR KEY STAGE KS3 KS4 Sixth Form

SIZE OF GROUP 1–10 10–20 20–30 30+

NOTICE REQUIRED Two months.

DURATION OF PRESENTATION One hour plus.

RESOURCES AVAILABLE
- Publications

Commonwealth Institute
- Karen Fields
- Kensington High Street, London. W8 6NQ
- 071-603 4535 x224

Works in the field of education with the 50 Commonwealth countries.

N C SUPPORT Has an 'Artists in Education' programme whereby Commonwealth artists visit schools from a multi-disciplinary background. The programme is cross-curricular and can be tailor-made to suit the school.

COSTS £650 + VAT for a week. £150 + VAT for a day.

GEOGRAPHICAL AREAS SERVED
- London
- Any

AGE OR KEY STAGE KS1 KS2 KS3 KS4 Sixth Form

NOTICE REQUIRED At least half a term.

RESOURCES AVAILABLE
- Video
- Slides
- Publications

Community Education Development Centre
- Phil Street
- Lyng Hall, Blackberry Lane, Coventry. CV2 3JS
- 0203 638660 FAX 0203 681161

CEDC is the national centre for the furtherance and promotion of community education and achieves its objectives through training, projects, publications and consultancy services.

N C SUPPORT CEDC aims to support schools develop a community-active National Curriculum through encouraging schools to link the delivery of the curriculum to

VISITS IN COMPASSION IN WORLD FARMING

community resources and opportunities.

COSTS £360 per day plus travel and subsistence.

GEOGRAPHICAL AREAS SERVED
- London
- S.E. England
- S.W. England
- East Anglia
- Midlands
- N.E. England
- N.W. England
- Scotland
- Wales
- Northern Ireland

AGE OR KEY STAGE KS1 KS2 KS3 KS4 Sixth Form

SIZE OF GROUP 1–10 10–20 20–30 30+

NOTICE REQUIRED One month, but can respond to shorter notice.

RESOURCES AVAILABLE
- Video
- Worksheets
- Displays
- Teacher's Notes
- Publications

Community Service Volunteers (CSV) Advisory Service
☞ Executive Officer, CSV Education
✉ 237 Pentonville Road, London.
☎ 071-278 6601

CSV Advisory Service supports schools and colleges in developing a National Curriculum with the closest possible links within the community.

N C SUPPORT Yes.

GEOGRAPHICAL AREAS SERVED
- London
- S.E. England
- S.W. England
- N.E. England
- Midlands
- East Anglia
- N.W. England
- Scotland
- Wales
- Northern Ireland

AGE OR KEY STAGE KS1 KS2 KS3 KS4 Sixth Form

DURATION OF PRESENTATION Half day.

RESOURCES AVAILABLE
- Video
- Publications
- Worksheets
- Teacher's Notes

Compassion in World Farming
☞ Gill Wright
✉ 20 Lavant Street, Petersfield, Hants. GU32 3EW
☎ 0730 264208

Aims to educate the consumer about how food is produced. Campaigns for the abolition of factory farming, for mandatory standards of animal welfare and a ban on international export of live animals.

COSTS Expenses.

GEOGRAPHICAL AREAS SERVED
- London
- S.E. England
- S.W. England
- East Anglia
- Midlands
- N.E. England
- N.W. England
- Scotland
- Wales
- Northern Ireland

AGE OR KEY STAGE KS3 KS4 Sixth Form

SIZE OF GROUP 30+

NOTICE REQUIRED Preferably one month.

DURATION OF PRESENTATION Varies.

RESOURCES AVAILABLE
- Video
- Slides
- Worksheets
- Publications
- Displays
- Teacher's Notes

VISITS IN
CONSCIENCE PEACE TAX CAMPAIGN

Conscience Peace Tax Campaign
- Malcolm Reid
- 6 Endsleigh Street, London. WC1H 0DX
- 071-739 5088 FAX 071-739 5088

Objectives are to persuade Parliament to introduce legislation allowing people conscientiously opposed to war to have the military part of their taxes devoted to peace building. Speaks on: Legal Studies, History, RE, Philosophy and Politics.

COSTS No fee.

GEOGRAPHICAL AREAS SERVED
- Any

AGE OR KEY STAGE Sixth Form

SIZE OF GROUP 10–20

NOTICE REQUIRED Two weeks.

DURATION OF PRESENTATION One period plus.

RESOURCES AVAILABLE
- Slides
- Publications
- Teacher's Notes

Conservation Trust
- Penny Pitty, Education Officer
- George Palmer Site, Northumberland Avenue, Reading, Berks. RG2 7PW
- 0734 868442 FAX 0734 314051

Aims to provide independent information about the global environment to people of all ages. Concerned with all aspects of the environment: population, resources, sustainability and ecology.

COSTS Expenses.

GEOGRAPHICAL AREAS SERVED
- Any

AGE OR KEY STAGE KS1 KS2 KS3 KS4 Sixth Form

NOTICE REQUIRED Four weeks.

DURATION OF PRESENTATION One period.

RESOURCES AVAILABLE
- Slides
- Publications
- Teacher's Notes

The Conservative Party
- Martin Mins, Youth Officer
- Conservative Central Office, 32 Smith Square, London. SW1P 3HH
- 071-222 9000 FAX 071-222 1135

Talks on the history and current policies of the Conservative Party can be arranged through local branches.

COSTS No fee.

GEOGRAPHICAL AREAS SERVED
- Any

AGE OR KEY STAGE Sixth Form

NOTICE REQUIRED Two weeks.

DURATION OF PRESENTATION Thirty minutes.

RESOURCES AVAILABLE
- Video
- Displays

Contact A Family
- Parent Advisors
- 16 Strutton Ground, London. SW1P 2HP
- 071-222 2695 FAX 071-222 3969

Aims to encourage mutual support between families who have children with disability or special needs. Coordinates a nationwide network of local groups.

COSTS Expenses.

GEOGRAPHICAL AREAS SERVED
- S.E. England

NOTICE REQUIRED Four weeks.

DURATION OF PRESENTATION By arrangement.

RESOURCES AVAILABLE
- Publications

Cooperation for Development
- Michelle Scully
- 21 Germain St, Chesham, Bucks. HP5 1LB
- 0494 775557 FAX 0494 791376

Project-funding non-government organisation supporting self-help initiatives and community development in the Third World.

N C SUPPORT No, but hope to develop this area.

COSTS Expenses and donation appreciated.

GEOGRAPHICAL AREAS SERVED
- London
- S.E. England
- Any

AGE OR KEY STAGE KS1 KS2 KS3 KS4 Sixth Form

SIZE OF GROUP 1–10 10–20 20–30 30+

NOTICE REQUIRED Two months.

RESOURCES AVAILABLE
- Video
- Slides
- Worksheets
- Publications
- Other
- Teacher's Notes

Council for British Archaeology
- Peter Halkon, Education Officer
- The King's Manor, York. YO1 2EP
- 0904 433925

Aims to promote the study and safeguarding of the British historical environment and to improve public awareness of archaeology in Britain.

COSTS Expenses only. No fees.

GEOGRAPHICAL AREAS SERVED
- N.E. England

AGE OR KEY STAGE KS1 KS2 KS3 KS4 Sixth Form

DURATION OF PRESENTATION One hour plus.

RESOURCES AVAILABLE
- Publications

Council for National Parks
- Amanda Nobbs, Director
- 246 Lavender Hill, London. SW11 1LJ
- 071-924 4077 FAX 071-924 5761

Aims to ensure the conservation and protection of the 10 national parks and to provide information on the parks for the public.

N C SUPPORT Recently published a new education pack aimed at GCSE and A-level teachers and students working in subjects such as Geography, Environmental Studies, General Studies, History and Science. Also cross-curricular and vocational work. There are 22 fact sheets on different topics and 12 park profiles.

GEOGRAPHICAL AREAS SERVED
- Any

AGE OR KEY STAGE KS3 KS4 Sixth Form

RESOURCES AVAILABLE
- Publications

Council for the Advancement of Arab–British Understanding

- Maria Holt
- 21 Collingham Road, London. SW5 0NU
- 071-3273 8414 FAX 071-835 2088

Educational and lobby organisation which attempts to promote better understanding about the Arab world among British people, including MPs, journalists, teachers and students.

COSTS Expenses.

GEOGRAPHICAL AREAS SERVED
- London
- S.E. England
- S.W. England
- East Anglia
- Midlands

AGE OR KEY STAGE KS3 KS4 Sixth Form

SIZE OF GROUP Any number.

NOTICE REQUIRED As much as possible.

RESOURCES AVAILABLE
- Video
- Slides
- Publications

Council of Christians and Jews

- Education Department
- 1 Dennington Park Road, London. NW6 1AX
- 071-794 8178 FAX 071-431 3500

Exists to educate Christians and Jews to appreciate each other's distinctive beliefs and to recognise areas of common ground. Combats anti-Semitism and other forms of discrimination.

N C SUPPORT Yes.

COSTS Expenses.

GEOGRAPHICAL AREAS SERVED
- Any

AGE OR KEY STAGE KS1 KS2 KS3 KS4 Sixth Form

NOTICE REQUIRED Three weeks.

DURATION OF PRESENTATION By arrangement.

RESOURCES AVAILABLE
- Video
- Teacher's Notes
- Publications

Crusaders

- Dr Alan Kerbey
- 2 Romeland Hill, St Albans, Herts. AL3 4ET
- 0727 855422 FAX 0727 848518

Crusaders is a dynamic inter-denominational Christian Youth Movement committed to bringing the life-changing good news of Jesus to today's young people through youth groups, holiday programmes and active teaching materials. Crusaders run an increasing number of extra-curricular youth groups in schools whose basis is to promote the personal and social development of young people from a Christian perspective.

COSTS Expenses and by negotiation.

GEOGRAPHICAL AREAS SERVED
- London
- S.E. England
- S.W. England
- East Anglia
- Midlands
- N.E. England
- N.W. England
- Scotland
- Wales

AGE OR KEY STAGE KS3 KS4 Sixth Form

SIZE OF GROUP 20–30 30+

NOTICE REQUIRED One to two months.

Cruse Bereavement Care
☞ Hilary Belton, Information Officer
✉ Cruse House, 126 Sheen Road, Richmond, Surrey. TW9 1UR
☎ 081-940 4818 FAX 081-940 7638

Cruse offers free help to all bereaved people through its 194 local branches, by providing both individual and group counselling; opportunities for social contact and practical advice. A list of related publications and newsletters is also available. Help is open to anyone who has lost someone close to them through death. The Cruse Bereavement Line (081-332 7227) provides a direct link to a counsellor.

N C SUPPORT Yes.

COSTS No fee.

GEOGRAPHICAL AREAS SERVED
- London
- S.E. England
- S.W. England
- East Anglia
- Midlands
- N.E. England
- N.W. England
- Scotland
- Wales
- Northern Ireland

AGE OR KEY STAGE KS1 KS2 KS3 KS4 Sixth Form

NOTICE REQUIRED Two weeks.

DURATION OF PRESENTATION Varies.

RESOURCES AVAILABLE
- Worksheets
- Publications
- Displays

CSV *see* Community Service Volunteers

Marie Curie Memorial Foundation
☞ Ms T Cooper
✉ 25 Belgrave Square, London. SW1X 8QG
☎ 071-235 3325

Aims to investigate and allay the disease of cancer and to promote the welfare of cancer patients and their families by means of professional and lay education.

N C SUPPORT Work pack for primary schools. Book on life and work of Marie Curie.

GEOGRAPHICAL AREAS SERVED
- London
- S.E. England
- S.W. England
- East Anglia
- Midlands
- N.E. England
- N.W. England
- Scotland
- Wales
- Northern Ireland

AGE OR KEY STAGE KS3 KS4 Sixth Form

SIZE OF GROUP 10–20 20–30 30+

RESOURCES AVAILABLE
- Video
- Worksheets
- Slides
- Teacher's
- Publications
- Notes

Cyclists' Touring Club
☞ David Wey
✉ Cotterell House, 69 Mead Row, Godalming, Surrey. GU7 3HS
☎ 0483 417217 FAX 0483 426994

Britain's largest national cycling organisation; a network of local groups with speakers who will give talks in schools. Advice on proficiency. Student information on request. Local LTC groups, via ESCA (English Schools Cycling

Association), may provide local help/contact.

COSTS Expenses.

GEOGRAPHICAL AREAS SERVED
- Any

AGE OR KEY STAGE KS1 KS2 KS3 KS4 Sixth Form

NOTICE REQUIRED One month.

DURATION OF PRESENTATION By arrangement.

RESOURCES AVAILABLE
- Displays

Democratic Left
- Helen Taylor
- 6 Cynthia Street, London. N1 9JF
- 071-278 4443 FAX 071-278 4425

The successor to the Communist Party of Great Britain, the Democratic Left aims to enable its members to contribute to the development of a popular movement for socialism which is 'democratic, humane and green'.

COSTS Expenses.

GEOGRAPHICAL AREAS SERVED
- Any

AGE OR KEY STAGE Sixth Form

NOTICE REQUIRED Four weeks.

DURATION OF PRESENTATION Forty minutes.

RESOURCES AVAILABLE
- Publications

The Design Council
- The Education Officers (primary or secondary)
- 28 Haymarket, London. SW1Y 4SU
- 071-839 8000 FAX 071-925 2130

Acts as information source on UK design; aims to ensure UK businesses understand the importance of design and its strategic role in achieving success in competitive markets. Has an extensive slide library.

COSTS Fee and expenses.

GEOGRAPHICAL AREAS SERVED
- Any

AGE OR KEY STAGE KS1 KS2 KS3 KS4 Sixth Form

SIZE OF GROUP 1–10 10–20 20–30 30+

DURATION OF PRESENTATION Varies.

RESOURCES AVAILABLE
- Slides

Resourceful Development

Frustrated by lack of stimulating resources on development issues?

Want to promote alternative and positive images of the South?

Need help and support to increase global awareness within national curriculum guidelines?

The Development Education Association, through a network of national development agencies and over 40 local resource centres, provides access to materials, advice and training.

Development Education Association

29-31 Cowper Street   London EC2A 4AP
Tel 071 490 8108

VISITS IN
DEVELOPMENT EDUCATION ASSOCIATION

Development Education Association
- Sandy Henderson
- 29–31 Cowper Street, London. EC2A 4AP
- 071-490 8108 FAX 071-490 8123

The Development Education Association promotes development education through its members and beyond. It acts as a network of support and coordination for the Development Education movement in Britain. Support is given by referring enquiries to people who can help more in their locality. See local Development Education Association bodies below.

COSTS **No fees. SAE requested.**

GEOGRAPHICAL AREAS SERVED
- London
- S.W. England
- Midlands
- N.W. England
- Wales
- S.E. England
- East Anglia
- N.E. England
- Scotland
- Northern Ireland

AGE OR KEY STAGE **KS1 KS2 KS3 KS4 Sixth Form**

RESOURCES AVAILABLE
- Video
- Worksheets
- Publications

Aylesbury Development Education Centre
- Pauline Roby
- Elmhurst County Middle School, Dunsham Lane, Aylesbury. HP20 2DB
- 0296 395185

Bangor World Education Project
- Sheila Bennell
- Welsh National Centre for Religious Education UCNW, Deiniol Road, Bangor. LL57 2UU
- 0248 351151 x2947

Bath Development Education Centre
- Paddy Nisbett
- 12a Westgate Street, Bath. BA1 1BQ
- 0225 313274

Belfast One World Centre
- Pauline Jones
- 4 Lower Crescent, Belfast. BT7 1NR
- 0232 241879

Birmingham Development Education Centre
- Ina Clason
- Gillette Centre, 998 Bristol Road, Selly Oak, Birmingham. B29 6LE
- 021-472 3255

Bournemouth Development Education Centre
- Angela Joynson
- East Dorset Professional Education Centre, 40 Lowther Road, Bournemouth. BH8 8NA
- 0202 296071 x228

Brighton Worldwise
- Jacky Kulkarni
- Brightelm Centre, North Road, Brighton. BN1 3LA
- 0273 821220

Bristol Education for Action in Development
- Liz Small
- 84 Colston Street, Bristol. BS1 5BB
- 0272 230458

VISITS IN

DEVELOPMENT EDUCATION ASSOCIATION

Cambridge Centre for Environment and Development Education
- Charlie Nurse
- The Harambee Centre, 110 Regent Street, Cambridge. CB2 1DP
- 0223 358116

Canterbury World Development Education Group
- Marian Walter
- The Canterbury Centre, St Alphege Lane (Off Palace Street), Canterbury. CT1 2EB
- 0227 7665522

Chard South Somerset Development Education Centre
- Tony Smith
- Maulin Cottage, Winsham, Chard. TA20 4PA
- 0460 30551

Chelmsford One World Resource Centre
- Tony Bender
- c/o UNICEF, 1-3 Broomfield Road, Chelmsford. CM1 1SZ
- 0245 354375

Cheltenham Centre for World Development Education
- Alex Hawkins
- 13 Priory Terrace, Cheltenham. GL52 6DS
- 0242 520969

Cleveland Development Education Centre
- Averil Newsam
- Bracken Hoe School, Martin Road, Middlesbrough. TS4 3RX
- 0642 300821

Colchester Pamoja Environment Information Centre
- The Administrator
- Colchester Sixth Form College, North Hill, Colchester. CO1 1SN
- 0206 794078

Cumbria Development Education Centre
- Jean Crosbie
- Charlotte Mason College, Keswick, Ambleside. LA22 9BB
- 0539 433066

Derby Rainbow Centre
- Cliff James
- 88 Abbey Street, Derby. DE22 3SQ
- 0332 298185/766025

Derry Development Education Centre
- Rosemary Vaughan
- 15 Pump Street, Derry. BT48 6JG
- 0504 269183

Dudley One World Resource Centre
- Frank Wilson
- Hillcrest School & Community College, Simms Lane, Netherton, Dudley. DY2 0PB
- 0384 457799

Dundee One World Centre
- Ken Mather
- 5 Victoria Street, Dundee. DD4 6EG
- 0382 454603

Edinburgh Scottish DEC
- Linda Grey
- Old Play House Close, Institute of Education, Moray House, Holyrood Road, Edinburgh. EH8 8AQ
- 031-557 3810

VISITS IN
DEVELOPMENT EDUCATION ASSOCIATION

Exmouth Centre for International Studies
- Roger Morgan
- Meadowlea House, 86 Littleham Road, Exmouth. EX8 2QT
- 0395 264902

Hampshire Development Education Centre
- Pat Francis
- Mid Hants Professional Centre, Elm Road, Winchester. SO2 5AG
- 0962 856106

Hull Development Education Centre
- Ben Ballin
- c/o David Lister School, Rustenberg Street, Hull. HU9 2PR
- 0482 786488

Lancashire Development Education Centre
- Julie Downs
- Global Education Centre, 37 St Peter's Square, Preston. PR1 7BX
- 0772 252299

Leamington Spa
- Richard Wright
- Warwickshire World Studies Centre, Manor Hall, Sandy Lane, Leamington Spa. CV32 6RD
- 0926 413719

Leeds Development Education Centre
- Nigel West
- 151–153 Cardigan Road, Leeds. LS6 1LJ
- 0532 784030

Leicester World Development Centre
-
- 10a Bishop Street, Leicester. LE1 6AF
- 0533 540957

Llanidloes
- Jenny Morrison
- Powys Environment and Development Education Centre, 12 Great Oak Street, Llanidloes. SY18 6BU
- 0551 22731

London Humanities Education Centre
- Margaret Burr
- The Professional Centre, English Street, London. E3 4TA
- 081-981 0183

London LONDEC
- Sarbjit Johal
- Instrument House, 205-207 King's Cross Road, London. WC1X 9DB
- 071-713 7907

Malvern Third World Centre
- Isla Williams
- 22 Church Street, Malvern. WR14 2AY
- 0684 565796

Manchester Development Education Project
- Anne Strachan
- c/o Manchester Metropolitan University, 801 Wilmslow Road, Didsbury, Manchester. M20 8RG
- 061-445 2495

Marlborough Brandt Group Third World Education Centre
- Sam Woodhouse
- St John's Lower School, Chopping Knife Lane, Marlborough. SN8 2AU
- 0672 514078

VISITS IN
DEVELOPMENT EDUCATION ASSOCIATION

Milton Keynes World Development Education Centre
- Debbie Greaves
- Block A, Bridgewater Hall, Stantonbury Campus, Stantonbury, Milton Keynes. MK14 6BN
- 0908 310951

Norfolk Education & Action Development Centre
- Chantal Finney
- 38–40 Exchange Street, Norwich, Norfolk. NR2 1AX
- 0603 610993

North Staffordshire Development Education Centre
- Jane Glen
- Newcastle-under-Lyme College, Liverpool Road, Newcastle-under-Lyme. ST5 2DF
- 0782 711455

Nottingham Mobile Unit for Development Issues
- Lis Martin
- School of Education, University of Nottingham, University Park, Nottingham. NG7 2RD
- 0602 514485

Oxford Development Education Centre
- Pippa Bobbett
- East Oxford Community Centre, 44b Princess Street, Oxford. OX4 1DD
- 0865 790490

Reading International Support Centre
- Martin Mikhail
- 103 London Street, Reading. RG1 4QA
- 0734 586692

Sheffield Education Development Centre
- Rob Unwin/Dee Tossell
- Woodthorpe School, Woodthorpe Road, Sheffield. S13 8DD
- 0742 656662

Wheathampstead Education Centre
- John Burden
- Butterfield Road, St Albans. AL4 8PY
- 0582 830372

World Education Development Group
- Marion Walter/Tom Andrews
- The Canterbury Centre, St Alphage Lane, Canterbury, Kent. CT1 2EB
- 0227 766552

Dickens Fellowship
- Dr David Parker, Curator
- 48 Doughty Street, London. WC1N 2LF
- 071-405 2127

Charles Dickens' house; tours can be arranged for school parties. The house also acts as the HQ for the Dickens Fellowship which has branches throughout the world and can provide speakers.

COSTS **Expenses and fees by arrangement.**

GEOGRAPHICAL AREAS SERVED
- London
- S.E. England

AGE OR KEY STAGE **KS3 KS4 Sixth Form**

NOTICE REQUIRED **Two weeks.**

DURATION OF PRESENTATION **By arrangement.**

RESOURCES AVAILABLE
- Publications

Down's Syndrome Association

- Information Officer
- 155 Mitcham Road, London. SW17 9PG
- 081-682 4001 FAX 081-682 4012

Offers information, advice, support and counselling to those with Down's Syndrome, their families, carers, interested professionals and others. Nineteen branches and 75 groups throughout the country.

COSTS **No fees.**

GEOGRAPHICAL AREAS SERVED
- Any

AGE OR KEY STAGE **KS1 KS2 KS3 KS4 Sixth Form**

NOTICE REQUIRED **Four weeks.**

DURATION OF PRESENTATION **Varies.**

RESOURCES AVAILABLE
- Publications

The Duke of Edinburgh Award

- Richard White
- Gulliver House, Madeira Walk, Windsor, Berks. SL4 1EU
- 0753 810753

The Award is a progressive programme of practical, cultural and adventurous leisure-time activities designed to encourage pupils' personal and social development.

GEOGRAPHICAL AREAS SERVED
- Any

AGE OR KEY STAGE **KS4 Sixth Form**

SIZE OF GROUP **1–10 10–20 20–30 30+**

RESOURCES AVAILABLE
- Video
- Worksheets
- Displays
- Other
- Slides
- Publications
- Teacher's Notes

Eastern Health and Social Services Board

- Health Promotion Unit
- 12–22 Linenhall Street, Belfast. BT2 8BS
- 0232 321313

The Health Promotion Unit organises speakers to visit schools to discuss good health practices.

GEOGRAPHICAL AREAS SERVED
- Northern Ireland

AGE OR KEY STAGE **KS1 KS2 KS3 KS4 Sixth Form**

Eating Disorders Association

- Information Officer
- Sackville Place, 44 Magdalen Street, Norwich, Norfolk. NR3 1JU
- 0603 621414 FAX 0603 664915

Independent self-help organisation which offers information and advice through telephone helplines, guidelines, newsletters and a national network of self-help groups for anorexics.

COSTS **Expenses.**

GEOGRAPHICAL AREAS SERVED
- Any

AGE OR KEY STAGE **KS3 KS4 Sixth Form**

NOTICE REQUIRED **Four weeks.**

DURATION OF PRESENTATION **Varies.**

RESOURCES AVAILABLE
- Video
- Publications

VISITS IN EDUCATIONAL COMPUTER CENTRE

Educational Computer Centre
- Hilary Pitts
- Noak Hill Centre, Noak Hill Road, Harold Hill, Romford, Essex. RM3 7JW
- 0708 349115 FAX 0708 343467

The Educational Computer Centre provides a holistic IT support service including curriculum, technical and administrative IT.

N C SUPPORT The Centre provides support for the use of IT within technology and across all subjects.

COSTS Cost dependent on the individual's requirements.

GEOGRAPHICAL AREAS SERVED
- S.E. England

AGE OR KEY STAGE KS1 KS2 KS3 KS4 Sixth Form

SIZE OF GROUP 1–10 10–20 20–30 30+

NOTICE REQUIRED Generally at least one month.

DURATION OF PRESENTATION One period.

RESOURCES AVAILABLE
- Publications

Embassy of Israel
- Information Department
- 2 Palace Green, London. W8 8QB
- 071-957 9500 FAX 071-957 9555

Offices in Glasgow, Manchester, Cardiff and Birmingham so they can provide speakers for schools whatever the location.

COSTS No fee.

GEOGRAPHICAL AREAS SERVED
- Any

SIZE OF GROUP 30+

NOTICE REQUIRED Two months.

RESOURCES AVAILABLE
- Publications

Electoral Reform Society of Great Britain and Ireland
- Enid Lakeman
- 6 Chancel Street, London. SE1 0UU
- 071-928 1622

Objectives are to introduce proportional representation to the UK by means of the single transferable vote.

COSTS Expenses only. No fees.

GEOGRAPHICAL AREAS SERVED
- Any

AGE OR KEY STAGE Sixth Form

NOTICE REQUIRED Two weeks.

Embassy of the Czech Republic
- Mrs R Calabkova, Cultural Attaché
- 26 Kensington Palace Gardens, London. W8 4QY
- 071-243 1115

The Czech Centre (Cultural and Information Centre of the Czech Republic) can help with arranging trips. The Centre is able to organise the whole visit (accommodation, transport, cultural activities, tickets, excursions, etc). A new Czech Centre is soon to be established at 30 Kensington Palace Gardens, London W8 4QY, telephone 071-243 7981. Fax 071-727 9589.

COSTS Postage only for information.

GEOGRAPHICAL AREAS SERVED
- London
- Any

RESOURCES AVAILABLE
- Video
- Slides
- Publications
- Other

The Engineering Council
- Tony Miller
- 10 Maltravers Street, London. WC2R 3ER
- 071-240 7891 FAX 071-240 7517

The Engineering Council organises the Neighbourhood Engineers Scheme which establishes teams of engineers and teachers to aid teaching of the National Curriculum in secondary schools.

N C SUPPORT Participating engineers support Technology and other subjects where required. WISE (Women into Science and Engineering) campaign vehicles visit schools.

COSTS No fee.

GEOGRAPHICAL AREAS SERVED
- Any

AGE OR KEY STAGE KS3 KS4 Sixth Form

RESOURCES AVAILABLE
- Publications
- Displays
- Other
- Teacher's Notes

English Folk Dance & Song Society
- Carolyn Robson, Education Officer
- 2 Regents Park Road, London. NW1 7AY
- 071-284 0534

Preserves and makes known English folk dances, songs and other folk music, and encourages the practice of traditional forms. Promotes study of the origins, development and traditional practice of English folk dances, songs and music and their relationships with those of other countries.

GEOGRAPHICAL AREAS SERVED
- London

AGE OR KEY STAGE KS3 KS4 Sixth Form

RESOURCES AVAILABLE
- Publications
- Teacher's Notes
- Other

The Environment Council
- Ms R Adatia
- 80 York Way, London. N1 9AG
- 071-278 4736 FAX 071-837 9688

Forum for individuals and organisations working towards solutions to environmental problems. Centre for distribution of information on the environment and related issues.

GEOGRAPHICAL AREAS SERVED
- Any

AGE OR KEY STAGE Sixth Form

RESOURCES AVAILABLE
- Publications

VISITS IN ENVIRONMENTAL INVESTIGATION

Environmental Investigation Organisation
- Patrick Alley
- 2 Pear Tree Court, London. EC1R 0DS
- 071-490 7040 FAX 071-490 0436

Undercover investigators obtain film, photographic and documentary evidence of environmental abuse. Evidence is used to lobby for legislative change at inter-governmental level. Campaigns include whales and dolphins, elephants, rhinos, wild birds, forests.

COSTS Travel expenses essential. Donations welcome.

GEOGRAPHICAL AREAS SERVED
- Any

AGE OR KEY STAGE KS3 KS4 Sixth Form

SIZE OF GROUP 1–10 10–20 20–30 30+

NOTICE REQUIRED One month.

RESOURCES AVAILABLE
- Video
- Slides
- Publications

The European Movement
- Stephen Woodard
- 158 Buckingham Palace Road, London. SW1W 9TR
- 071-824 8052 FAX 071-824 8124

The European Movement works for the development of the European Community into a larger, more effective and more democratic European Union. Seeks popular support for this objective.

COSTS No fee. Expenses sometimes required for speakers.

GEOGRAPHICAL AREAS SERVED
- Any

AGE OR KEY STAGE KS3 KS4 Sixth Form

SIZE OF GROUP 1–10 10–20 20–30 30+

NOTICE REQUIRED At least four weeks.

DURATION OF PRESENTATION One period plus.

RESOURCES AVAILABLE
- Video
- Slides
- Publications

Family Educational Trust
- Valerie Riches, Director
- Wicken, Milton Keynes. MK19 6BU
- 0908 57234 FAX 0908 57331

Provides educational aids for parents, policy-makers, teachers and others which convey social, medical and personal benefits of stable family life.

N C SUPPORT Yes.

COSTS Expenses.

GEOGRAPHICAL AREAS SERVED
- S.E. England

AGE OR KEY STAGE KS4 Sixth Form

NOTICE REQUIRED Four weeks.

DURATION OF PRESENTATION By arrangement.

RESOURCES AVAILABLE
- Video
- Publications

Farming and Wildlife Advisory Group
- Richard Knight, National Adviser
- National Agricultural Centre, Stoneleigh, Kenilworth. CV8 2RX
- 0203 696699 FAX 0203 696760

The Farming and Wildlife Advisory Group unites wildlife and landscape conservation with farming and forestry.

VISITS IN THE FEDERATION OF WORKER WRITERS

COSTS Initially travelling and overnight expenses.

GEOGRAPHICAL AREAS SERVED
- London
- S.E. England
- S.W. England
- East Anglia
- Midlands
- N.E. England
- N.W. England

AGE OR KEY STAGE Sixth Form

SIZE OF GROUP 1–10

NOTICE REQUIRED Two months.

RESOURCES AVAILABLE
- Video
- Publications

The Fawcett Society
☛ Charlotte Burt
✉ 40–46 Harleyford Road, London. SE11 5AY
☎ 071-587 1287 FAX 071-793 0451

Campaigners for equality between the sexes since 1866. Talks relating to women's roles, lives and history. They mainly visit places in London but often arrange for speakers to talk in other areas.

GEOGRAPHICAL AREAS SERVED
- London
- Any

AGE OR KEY STAGE KS4 Sixth Form

SIZE OF GROUP 1–10 10–20 20–30 30+

NOTICE REQUIRED As much as possible.

RESOURCES AVAILABLE
- Publications

Federal Trust
☛ Judy Keep
✉ 158 Buckingham Palace Road, London. SW1W 9TR
☎ 071-259 9990

Primarily a research group on European issues. Education programme consists of a summer school for young people and a London-based discussion group.

GEOGRAPHICAL AREAS SERVED
- London

AGE OR KEY STAGE KS4 Sixth Form

RESOURCES AVAILABLE
- Video
- Publications

The Federation of Worker Writers and Community Publishers
☛ Tim Diggles
✉ c/o 23 Victoria Park Road, Stoke-on-Trent. ST6 6DX
☎ 0782 822327

Aims to make writing and publishing accessible for all through training, networking, distribution, empowerment. Poetry, oral history, novel writing, publishing and working across generations.

COSTS Varies, but at least £50 per half day.

GEOGRAPHICAL AREAS SERVED
- London
- S.E. England
- S.W. England
- Midlands
- N.E. England
- N.W. England

AGE OR KEY STAGE KS1 KS2 KS3 KS4 Sixth Form

SIZE OF GROUP 10–20

NOTICE REQUIRED One or two months.

RESOURCES AVAILABLE
- Worksheets
- Teacher's Notes
- Publications

VISITS IN THE FRENCH EMBASSY

The French Embassy
- ☛ Information Office
- ✉ Cultural Service, 23 Cromwell Road, London. SW7 2EL
- ☎ 071-838 2055

The French Embassy provides a number of educational services to schools including Study Visits (language courses and recreational activities – above address). Book loans from Institut Français, Mrs Roe (Tel: 071-589 6211). Requests for speakers: Alliance Française (Tel: 071-723 6439).

Comenius Centres are situated throughout the UK and offer teachers a wide range of services. Campus 2000, a computer link-up between British & French schools, enables pupils to access a huge variety of information on France (Tel: 0442 237812).

COSTS Contact the various educational services.

GEOGRAPHICAL AREAS SERVED
- Any

AGE OR KEY STAGE KS1 KS2 KS3 KS4 Sixth Form

SIZE OF GROUP 1–10 10–20 20–30 30+

RESOURCES AVAILABLE
- Publications
- Other

Friends of Israel Education Trust
- ☛ John Levy
- ✉ 25 Lyndale Avenue, London. NW2 2QB
- ☎ 071-435 6803

Non-denominational foundation established to generate critical interest in the history, cultures and peoples of Israel and the Middle East in order to fashion practical links between Great Britain and Israel.

COSTS No formal charge; contributions gratefully accepted.

GEOGRAPHICAL AREAS SERVED
- Any (except N. Ireland)

AGE OR KEY STAGE KS4 Sixth Form

SIZE OF GROUP 20–30 30+

NOTICE REQUIRED Two months preferably.

RESOURCES AVAILABLE
- Video
- Slides
- Worksheets
- Publications
- Other

Friends of the Earth
- ☛ Education Officer
- ✉ Education Section, 26–38 Underwood Street, London. N1 7JQ
- ☎ 071-490 1555 FAX 071-490 0881

Friends of the Earth Trust is a registered charity committed to the conservation and protection of the environment through research, information and education. They have a national network of over 300 local groups who may be able to respond to teachers' requests to do presentations in schools. Any interested teachers can find out details of their local group by calling our central office.

N C SUPPORT Publishes a range of educational materials suitable for Key Stages 2, 3 and 4.

COSTS Small charge to cover printing and administrative costs.

GEOGRAPHICAL AREAS SERVED
- London
- S.E. England
- S.W. England
- East Anglia
- Midlands
- N.E. England
- N.W. England
- Scotland

VISITS IN

GOETHE INSTITUTE

- Wales
- Northern Ireland

AGE OR KEY STAGE KS1 KS2 KS3 KS4 Sixth Form

SIZE OF GROUP 10–20 20–30 30+

RESOURCES AVAILABLE
- Video
- Worksheets
- Publications
- Teacher's Notes

Gallery Scene for Children
- Gill Bennun/Carole Sylvester
- 1 Albert Terrace, London. NW1
- 071-722 5079 FAX 081-297 2130

Aims to open children's eyes to the magic and mystery of paintings through slide lectures and guided tours. Special programmes for children are aimed at stimulating their interest and encouraging their participation in the classroom and in major art galleries and museums. Familiar with all the major collections, and accustomed to speaking to large audiences of all ages, either with slides or in the galleries.

GEOGRAPHICAL AREAS SERVED
- London
- S.E. England

AGE OR KEY STAGE KS1 KS2 KS3 KS4 Sixth Form

SIZE OF GROUP 10–20 20–30

NOTICE REQUIRED As much as possible.

DURATION OF PRESENTATION One hour plus questions.

RESOURCES AVAILABLE
- Slides

Georgian Group
- Dr Steven Parissien
- 37 Spital Square, London. E1 6DY
- 071-377 1722

Aims to save Georgian buildings, monuments, parks and gardens where necessary by encouraging their appropriate repair or restoration and the protection and improvement of their setting and to stimulate public knowledge of Georgian architecture.

GEOGRAPHICAL AREAS SERVED
- Any

AGE OR KEY STAGE Sixth Form

SIZE OF GROUP 10–20 20–30 30+

RESOURCES AVAILABLE
- Other

Goethe Institute
- R. Homrighausen
- 50 Princes Gate, Exhibition Rd, London. SW7 2PH
- 071-411 3431 FAX 071-581 0974

Aims to promote better understanding, closer contacts, interchange and co-operation through: cultural events and projects, library and information services, teacher liaison for German as a foreign language, German language courses

N C SUPPORT The Goethe Institute offer a speaker service at the Goethe Institute on topics relevant to the National Curriculum

GEOGRAPHICAL AREAS SERVED
- London
- Any

AGE OR KEY STAGE KS2 KS3 KS4 Sixth Form

SIZE OF GROUP 10–20

VISITS IN
GOETHE INSTITUTE

NOTICE REQUIRED 2 months.

RESOURCES AVAILABLE
- Video
- Other
- Displays
- Worksheets
- Publications
- Teacher's Notes

Green Alliance
- Karen Crane
- 49 Wellington Street, London. WC2E 7BN
- 071-836 0341 FAX 071-240 9205

Independent organisation concerned with environmental policy. Aims to introduce an ecological perspective into politics. Recently has concentrated on analysing and influencing the direction of environmental policy.

COSTS Expenses.

GEOGRAPHICAL AREAS SERVED
- Any

AGE OR KEY STAGE KS4 Sixth Form

SIZE OF GROUP 30+

NOTICE REQUIRED Four weeks.

DURATION OF PRESENTATION One period.

RESOURCES AVAILABLE
- Publications

The Green Party
- John Bishop
- 10 Station Road, London. SW12 9AZ
- 081-675 6701 FAX 081-675 4434

Emphasis placed on its role as a genuine political party rather than an environmental pressure group. Talks in schools occasionally given about green politics and the role of the Green Party.

COSTS Expenses.

GEOGRAPHICAL AREAS SERVED
- Any

AGE OR KEY STAGE Sixth Form

NOTICE REQUIRED Four weeks.

DURATION OF PRESENTATION One hour plus.

RESOURCES AVAILABLE
- Video
- Slides
- Displays

Greenpeace
- Public Information Coordinator
- Canonbury Villas, London. N1 2PN
- 071-354 5100 FAX 071-696 0014

An international, independent environmental pressure group. Aims to protect animals and the environment by peaceful direct action. It campaigns against nuclear power and nuclear weapons, pollution, and threats to wildlife.

COSTS No fee.

GEOGRAPHICAL AREAS SERVED
- London

AGE OR KEY STAGE KS3 KS4 Sixth Form

SIZE OF GROUP 1–10 10–20 20–30 30+

DURATION OF PRESENTATION One hour.

RESOURCES AVAILABLE
- Slides
- Displays

Guide Dogs for the Blind
- Alison Radevsky, Fundraising Department
- Hillfields, Burghfield, Reading, Berks. RG7 3YG
- 0734 835555 FAX 0734 835211

Breeds and trains guide dogs and instructs visually impaired people in their safe use. Other services and facilities for visually impaired people are available.

COSTS No fee. Expenses and/or donation welcome.

GEOGRAPHICAL AREAS SERVED
- London
- S.E. England
- S.W. England
- East Anglia
- Midlands
- N.E. England
- N.W. England
- Scotland
- Wales
- Northern Ireland

AGE OR KEY STAGE **KS1 KS2 KS3 KS4 Sixth Form**

NOTICE REQUIRED As much as possible.

DURATION OF PRESENTATION By arrangement.

RESOURCES AVAILABLE
- Video
- Displays
- Publications

Health Education Authority
- Fiona Martin, Library & Information Department
- Hamilton House, Mabledon Place, London. WC1H 9TX
- 071-383 3833 FAX 071-413 0339

The stated mission of the Health Education Authority is 'to help the people of England to become more knowledgeable, better motivated, and more able to acquire and maintain good health'.

N C SUPPORT The Health Education Authority will provide speakers for schools (local HEAs and Health Promotion Units are listed under the name of the local Health Authority). The HEA also publishes a wide range of books and video resources for the professional, student and general market.

COSTS Contact your local HEA or HPU for details. Many of its publications are free to educational establishments.

GEOGRAPHICAL AREAS SERVED
- London
- S.E. England
- S.W. England
- East Anglia
- Midlands
- N.E. England
- N.W. England
- Scotland
- Wales
- Northern Ireland

AGE OR KEY STAGE **KS1 KS2 KS3 KS4 Sixth Form**

NOTICE REQUIRED Contact local HEA.

RESOURCES AVAILABLE
- Video
- Publications
- Other
- Teacher's Notes

Health Education Board for Scotland
- George Pringle
- Woodburn House, Canaan Lane, Edinburgh. EH10 4SG
- 031-447 8044 FAX 031-452 8140

Works to promote better health. They have lists of the individual Health Boards and corresponding education departments, each of which provides individual services.

GEOGRAPHICAL AREAS SERVED
- Scotland

AGE OR KEY STAGE **KS1 KS2 KS3 KS4 Sixth Form**

Health Unlimited
- Pam Rumfritt
- 3 Stamford Street, London. SE1 9NT
- 071-928 8105 FAX 071-928 7736

Founded in 1983 by a small group of health professionals who had worked abroad with refugees. Aids communities and civilians who are not assisted by other agencies. Speakers to schools depend on availability in particular area.

COSTS Expenses only. No fee.

GEOGRAPHICAL AREAS SERVED
- Any

AGE OR KEY STAGE KS3 KS4

NOTICE REQUIRED Four weeks.

DURATION OF PRESENTATION Varies.

RESOURCES AVAILABLE
- Publications

Hearing Dogs for the Deaf
- The Administrator
- London Road, Lewknor, Oxford. OX9 5RY
- 0844 353099

Hearing Dogs for the Deaf train rescued or unwanted dogs to alert severely, profoundly or totally deaf people, by touch, to everyday household sounds, e.g.: doorbell, smoke alarm, alarm clock, etc, thereby providing independence and companionship. Speakers according to availability.

GEOGRAPHICAL AREAS SERVED
- Any

AGE OR KEY STAGE KS1 KS2

Help the Aged
- Schools Programme
- St James's Walk, London. EC1R 0BE
- 071-253 0253 FAX 071-895 1407

Help the Aged is a charity which works to improve the quality of life of elderly people in the UK and internationally, particularly those who are frail, isolated or poor.

N C SUPPORT Cross-curricular/topic-based education packs.

COSTS No fees charged for schools participating in the full educational and fundraising programme.

GEOGRAPHICAL AREAS SERVED
- Any

AGE OR KEY STAGE KS1 KS2 KS3 KS4 Sixth Form

SIZE OF GROUP 30+

RESOURCES AVAILABLE
- Worksheets
- Teacher's Notes

High Commission for Pakistan
- Education Attaché
- 40 Lowndes Square, London. SW1X 9JN
- 071-235 2044/2195 FAX 071-416 8417

Provides speakers for schools anywhere within the UK. Also provides information and gives help with arranging visits to Pakistan.

COSTS Expenses.

GEOGRAPHICAL AREAS SERVED
- Any

SIZE OF GROUP 1–10 10–20 20–30 30+

NOTICE REQUIRED Two months.

RESOURCES AVAILABLE
- Video

Historic Churches Preservation Trust
- Schools Education Officer
- Fulham Palace Road, London. SW6 6EA
- 071-736 3054

VISITS IN

Gives grants and interest-free loans to churches to aid restoration work. Especially helps churches not aided by English Heritage. Programme of lectures and events throughout the country.

N C SUPPORT **No.**

COSTS **Expenses.**

GEOGRAPHICAL AREAS SERVED
- **Any**

AGE OR KEY STAGE **KS3 KS4 Sixth Form**

NOTICE REQUIRED **Four weeks.**

DURATION OF PRESENTATION **One hour.**

RESOURCES AVAILABLE
- Slides
- Displays

Howard League for Penal Reform
- Frances Crook
- 708 Holloway Road, London. N19 3NL
- 071-281 7722 FAX 071-281 7722

Liaises with prisons, campaigns on issues like suicides and the plight of young people in prison, conducts research on all aspects of the penal system and provides an information service.

GEOGRAPHICAL AREAS SERVED
- London
- S.E. England

AGE OR KEY STAGE **KS3 KS4 Sixth Form**

NOTICE REQUIRED **Twelve weeks.**

DURATION OF PRESENTATION **By arrangement.**

RESOURCES AVAILABLE
- Video
- Displays
- Teacher's Notes

Hunger Project Trust
- The Education Officer
- 140 Cornwell Road, London. SW7 4HA
- 071-373 9003 FAX 071-373 5134

Campaigns to assist in the eradication of world hunger and starvation and to make the issue of hunger a priority on the international political agenda. Major public information campaign.

COSTS **Expenses only. No fees.**

GEOGRAPHICAL AREAS SERVED
- **S.E. England**

AGE OR KEY STAGE **KS3 KS4 Sixth Form**

NOTICE REQUIRED **Six weeks.**

DURATION OF PRESENTATION **One hour plus.**

RESOURCES AVAILABLE
- Publications
- Teacher's Notes

Imperial Cancer Research Fund
- Central Office
- PO Box 123, Lincoln's Inn Fields, London. WC2A 3PX
- 071-242 0200

Europe's largest independent cancer research institute. Conducts over one-third of all cancer research in the UK. Work in schools mainly involves developing fund-raising projects. Contact Central Office to find nearest local branch.

GEOGRAPHICAL AREAS SERVED
- **Any**

AGE OR KEY STAGE **KS1 KS2 KS3 KS4 Sixth Form**

SIZE OF GROUP **1–10 10–20 20–30 30+**

DURATION OF PRESENTATION One period.

RESOURCES AVAILABLE
- Publications
- Displays

Industrial Society
- Roger Opie, Head of Education
- Quadrant Court, 49 Calthorpe Road, Edgbaston, Birmingham. B15 1TH
- 021-454 6769 FAX 021-456 2715

Objective is to help organisations become more efficient and more customer orientated. Runs training courses and conferences on employee-related issues and advises and assists organisations in all sectors. Does presentations at schools.

N C SUPPORT Yes.

GEOGRAPHICAL AREAS SERVED
- Any

AGE OR KEY STAGE KS4 Sixth Form

SIZE OF GROUP 10-20 20-30 30+

RESOURCES AVAILABLE
- Video
- Publications

Institute for the Study of Drug Dependence
- Information Officer
- 1 Hatton Place, London. EC1N 8ND
- 071-430 1991 FAX 071-404 4415

ISDD is Britain's national resource on the misuse of drugs and houses the world's largest library on this topic. Do not visit schools but may be able to advise on groups which do.

N C SUPPORT Guidelines for schools on drugs in the curriculum. Apply for brochure.

GEOGRAPHICAL AREAS SERVED
- Any

RESOURCES AVAILABLE
- Video
- Publications
- Displays

Institute of Data Processing Management
- Ian Rickwood
- IDPM House, Ruxley Corner, Sidcup, Kent. DA14 5HR
- 081-308 0747

Prepared to talk to sixth formers about career opportunities and have a number of branches throughout the country.

COSTS No fee.

GEOGRAPHICAL AREAS SERVED
- Any

AGE OR KEY STAGE KS4 Sixth Form

SIZE OF GROUP 1-10 10-20 20-30 30+

DURATION OF PRESENTATION Varies.

RESOURCES AVAILABLE
- Publications

Institute of Physics
- Cathy Wilson
- 47 Belgrave Square, London. SW1X 8QX
- 071-235 6111 FAX 071-259 6002

Stated aims are to promote the advancement and dissemination of education in the science of physics. Now also sees itself as a scientific, professional and campaigning force.

N C SUPPORT Yes.

COSTS Expenses.

GEOGRAPHICAL AREAS SERVED
- Any

NOTICE REQUIRED By arrangement.

VISITS IN
KENYA HIGH COMMISSION

DURATION OF PRESENTATION By arrangement.

RESOURCES AVAILABLE
- Video
- Publications

Institute of Race Relations
- Information Officer
- 2–6 Leeke Street, London. WC1X 9HS
- 071-837 0041

Will provide material and information for use in schools on race-related issues.

GEOGRAPHICAL AREAS SERVED
- Any

AGE OR KEY STAGE KS4 Sixth Form

RESOURCES AVAILABLE
- Video
- Publications
- Displays

Intermediate Technology Development Group
- Sheela Hammond, Education Unit
- Myson House, Railway Terrace, Rugby
- 0788 560631 FAX 0788 540270

ITDG seeks to support and encourage teachers to incorporate, in various curricular areas, appropriate technology and development issues into the classroom. Will give talks wherever possible.

GEOGRAPHICAL AREAS SERVED
- Any

AGE OR KEY STAGE Sixth Form

SIZE OF GROUP 20–30 30+

RESOURCES AVAILABLE
- Video

Japanese Embassy
- Rhian Williams
- Education Section, 101–104 Piccadilly, London. W1V 9FN
- 071-637 4934

The Japanese Embassy has a limited speaker service for schools. A free slide and video loan service. Write for 'Resources at a Glance'.

N C SUPPORT Geography pack for Key Stage 3, workshops Key Stages 3 and 4.

GEOGRAPHICAL AREAS SERVED
- London
- Any

AGE OR KEY STAGE KS3 KS4 Sixth Form

SIZE OF GROUP 20–30 30+

NOTICE REQUIRED At least two months.

RESOURCES AVAILABLE
- Video
- Slides
- Other

Kenya High Commission
- Education Attaché
- 45 Portland Place, London. W1N 4AS
- 071-636 2371

Provides speakers for schools all over the UK. Maps, books, videos and posters can all be provided free of charge to schools.

COSTS No charge for materials.

GEOGRAPHICAL AREAS SERVED
- Any

AGE OR KEY STAGE KS1 KS2 KS3 KS4 Sixth Form

SIZE OF GROUP 1–10 10–20 20–30 30+

NOTICE REQUIRED Two weeks.

RESOURCES AVAILABLE
- Video
- Publications
- Displays

VISITS IN KIDSCAPE

Kidscape
- Florence Rothman
- 152 Buckingham Palace Road, London. SW1W 9TR
- 071-730 3300 FAX 071-730 7081

A registered charity providing teaching resources and training on child sexual abuse prevention and bullying.

N C SUPPORT PSE and cross-curricular themes on education for citizenship.

COSTS £190 per half day, £290 per full day + VAT and expenses.

GEOGRAPHICAL AREAS SERVED
- London
- S.E. England
- East Anglia
- Midlands
- N.W. England

AGE OR KEY STAGE KS1 KS2 KS3 KS4

SIZE OF GROUP 1–10 10–20 20–30 30+

NOTICE REQUIRED At least one month.

RESOURCES AVAILABLE
- Worksheets
- Publications
- Other
- Teacher's Notes

The Labour Party
- Ms F Williamson
- 150 Walworth Road, London. SE17 1JT
- 071-701 1234 FAX 071-234 3300

Talks in schools about the history of the Labour Party and its role in politics can be arranged through local party organisations.

COSTS No fee.

GEOGRAPHICAL AREAS SERVED
- London
- S.E. England
- S.W. England
- East Anglia
- Midlands
- N.E. England
- N.W. England
- Scotland
- Wales
- Northern Ireland

AGE OR KEY STAGE KS3 KS4 Sixth Form

SIZE OF GROUP 1–10 10–20 20–30 30+

NOTICE REQUIRED Four weeks.

RESOURCES AVAILABLE
- Video
- Publications
- Displays

The Suzy Lamplugh Trust
- Hilary Clifford
- 14 East Sheen Avenue, London. SW14 8AS
- 081-392 1839 FAX 081-392 1830

Through research, education and training the Trust is seeking a safer society and enables people to help themselves to go about their daily lives with increased confidence and without fear. Limited capacity to supply speakers.

N C SUPPORT Careers Education and Guidance needs for Key Stage 4. On request, various packages available.

GEOGRAPHICAL AREAS SERVED
- Any

AGE OR KEY STAGE KS4 Sixth Form

SIZE OF GROUP 10–20 20–30

NOTICE REQUIRED Two months.

RESOURCES AVAILABLE
- Video
- Worksheets
- Publications
- Teacher's Notes

Law Centres Federation
☞ Head Office
✉ Duchess House, Warren Street, London. W1P 5DB
☎ 071-387 8570

There are 55 law centres in England. They will send speakers out to schools to talk on legal issues. Ring or write to the Law Centres Federation to find the name of your nearest centre.

COSTS Expenses.

GEOGRAPHICAL AREAS SERVED
● Any

AGE OR KEY STAGE KS3 KS4 Sixth Form

SIZE OF GROUP By arrangement.

NOTICE REQUIRED By arrangement.

DURATION OF PRESENTATION By arrangement.

RESOURCES AVAILABLE
● Publications

League Against Cruel Sports
☞ Kevin Flack, Information Officer
✉ 83–87 Union Street, London. SE1 1SG
☎ 071-407 0979 FAX 071-403 4532

Campaigns for the protection of wildlife.

N C SUPPORT Supplies an information pack for schools (GCSE level) on animal welfare.

COSTS No fee.

GEOGRAPHICAL AREAS SERVED
● Any

AGE OR KEY STAGE KS2 KS3 KS4 Sixth Form

SIZE OF GROUP 10–20 20–30 30+

NOTICE REQUIRED Eight weeks.

DURATION OF PRESENTATION By arrangement.

RESOURCES AVAILABLE
● Video
● Publications
● Slides
● Teacher's Notes

Leicestershire AIDS Support Services
☞ Gordon Warren, Training Development Officer
✉ The Michael Wood Centre, 53 Regent Road, Leicester, Leics. LE1 6YF
☎ 0533 559995 FAX 0533 559979

The major voluntary organisation in Leicestershire providing services to all people affected by HIV/AIDS. Promotes positive sexual health and is a premier training organisation in the HIV/AIDS field.

N C SUPPORT Supports HIV/AIDS education, sexual health, sex education and personal and social educational work from a range of perspectives: medical, scientific, and particularly social.

COSTS Fees (if charged) are always flexible, realistic and sensitive, depending upon whom they are working with and the type of work involved. Services generally free, particularly in Leicestershire.

GEOGRAPHICAL AREAS SERVED
● Midlands

AGE OR KEY STAGE KS3 KS4 Sixth Form

SIZE OF GROUP 1–10 10–20 20–30 'Smaller' groups (less than 30 approx.) preferred, but can adapt for larger group audiences.

NOTICE REQUIRED The longer the better, if possible about 2-3 weeks.

RESOURCES AVAILABLE
● Video
● Publications
● Other

VISITS IN LIBERTY

Liberty
- Information Officer
- 21 Tabard Street, London. SE1 4LA
- 071-403 3888 FAX 071-407 5354

Previously the National Council for Civil Liberties. Objectives are to defend and extend civil liberties within the UK and to ensure the fair administration of justice. Campaigns for freedom of speech.

COSTS Expenses only. No fee.

GEOGRAPHICAL AREAS SERVED
- Any

AGE OR KEY STAGE Sixth Form

SIZE OF GROUP 1–10 10–20 20–30 30+

NOTICE REQUIRED Four weeks.

DURATION OF PRESENTATION By arrangement.

RESOURCES AVAILABLE
- Publications

LIFE (Save the Unborn Child)
- Nuala Scarisbrick
- LIFE House, New Bond Terrace, Leamington Spa. CV32 GEA
- 0926 421587

Pregnancy and abortion counselling, housing for homeless mothers, education and publishing on all LIFE issues. Talks in schools.

N C SUPPORT Video, leaflets, factsheets for years 9–13.

COSTS No fee.

GEOGRAPHICAL AREAS SERVED
- London
- Scotland
- S.E. England
- N.E. England
- N.W. England
- East Anglia
- Midlands
- S.W. England
- Wales
- Northern Ireland

AGE OR KEY STAGE KS2 KS3 KS4 Sixth Form

SIZE OF GROUP 1–10 10–20 20–30 30+

NOTICE REQUIRED One week.

DURATION OF PRESENTATION By arrangement.

RESOURCES AVAILABLE
- Video
- Displays
- Slides
- Publications
- Worksheets
- Teacher's Notes

Living Earth International Ltd
- Information Officer
- The Old Laundry, Ossington Buildings, Moxon Street, London. W1M 3JD
- 071-487 3661 FAX 071-487 3662

An educational charity which concentrates on working with schools and local communities to provide information, expertise and practical help on environmental issues. Initiated and runs a number of projects in both the UK and abroad.

COSTS Expenses and fee.

GEOGRAPHICAL AREAS SERVED
- Any

AGE OR KEY STAGE Sixth Form

NOTICE REQUIRED Six weeks.

DURATION OF PRESENTATION Varies.

RESOURCES AVAILABLE
- Worksheets
- Displays
- Publications
- Teacher's Notes

VISITS IN
LONDON STOCK EXCHANGE

Lloyd's of London
- Judy Sizeland
- One Lime Street, London. EC3M 7HA
- 071-327 5733 FAX 071-327 5642

Lloyd's of London, the world's most important insurance market, had its origins in a 17th-century coffee house and now insures anything from footballers' legs to space satellites. Provides resources which can back up a talk by a Lloyd's underwriter or member of Lloyd's.

AGE OR KEY STAGE Sixth Form

RESOURCES AVAILABLE
- Video
- Slides
- Publications
- Teacher's Notes

Lokabandhu
- David Powell
- London Buddhist Centre, 51 Roman Road, Bethnal Green, London. E2 0HU
- 081-981 1225

Teaches Buddhist meditation techniques to all who are interested in promoting the Buddhist spiritual path.

N C SUPPORT Information packs available free; teachers' packs on various topics available at a cost of approximately £5 each.

COSTS No fee. Donations welcome.

GEOGRAPHICAL AREAS SERVED
- London

AGE OR KEY STAGE KS1 KS2 KS3 KS4 Sixth Form

SIZE OF GROUP 1–10

NOTICE REQUIRED Two weeks.

RESOURCES AVAILABLE
- Publications
- Teacher's Notes

London Fire Brigade
- Malcolm Kelly
- Room 208, Queensborough House, Albert Embankment, London. SE1
- 071-587 4580

Fire and Civil Defence Authority.

N C SUPPORT 'Learn not to Burn' schools programme is designed to fit in with the National Curriculum and is not additional to it.

COSTS £30 per copy of each volume.

GEOGRAPHICAL AREAS SERVED
- London

AGE OR KEY STAGE KS1 KS2 KS3

RESOURCES AVAILABLE
- Worksheets
- Teacher's Notes

London Stock Exchange
- The Information Officer
- 19th Floor, Old Broad Street, London. EC2N 1HP
- 071-797 1000 FAX 071-588 4561

The floor of the Stock Exchange can no longer be visited but schools can approach a local stockbroker to come and do a talk in their schools. Lists of stockbrokers can be obtained from the above address.

The stock market produces ten booklets on the Stock Exchange, its history, how to buy and sell shares and a video called 'An Introduction to The Stock Market'. The publishing department is in Old Broad Street, London EC2N 1HP. Telephone: 071-797 3631.

GEOGRAPHICAL AREAS SERVED
- London

AGE OR KEY STAGE KS4 Sixth Form

RESOURCES AVAILABLE
- Video
- Publications

London Wildlife Trust
- Gina Oliver
- 80 York Way, London. N1 9AG
- 071-278 6612 FAX 071-837 8060

Aims to protect and improve London's natural environment, develop awareness and understanding amongst all sections of the community and campaign to protect London's green and wild spaces for future generations.

N C SUPPORT All programmes and publications are tailored to the National Curriculum and the Trust provides fun and useful INSET programmes on the environment as well as a mobile unit: Wildlife on Wheels.

COSTS No fee.

GEOGRAPHICAL AREAS SERVED
- London

AGE OR KEY STAGE KS1 KS2 KS3 KS4 Sixth Form

SIZE OF GROUP 30+

NOTICE REQUIRED Two months for visits.

RESOURCES AVAILABLE
- Slides
- Other
- Publications
- Teacher's Notes

Making Choices Project
- Karl Berger/Paul Patterson
- c/o Saferworld, 82 Coulston Street, Bristol. BS1 5BB
- 0272 276435 FAX 0272 253305

The Making Choices Project promotes an accreditable learning approach for empowering young people to build decision-making skills and apply them to address challenges facing themselves, their community and their country.

N C SUPPORT The 'choices' approach that this project promotes supports all Key Stage 4 core subject areas. Current materials are particularly linked with Key Stage 4 English, History and Geography.

COSTS Travelling expenses. Fees negotiable.

GEOGRAPHICAL AREAS SERVED
- London
- S.W. England
- Midlands
- N.W. England
- Wales
- S.E. England
- East Anglia
- N.E. England
- Scotland

AGE OR KEY STAGE KS4 Sixth Form

SIZE OF GROUP 1–10 10–20 20–30 30+

NOTICE REQUIRED Two weeks.

Mammal Society
- Gill Crane, Information Officer
- Department of Zoology, University of Bristol, Woodland Road, Bristol. BS8 1UG
- 0272 272300

Aims to promote the study of mammals by professional biologists and amateurs. Can send speakers very occasionally.

N C SUPPORT Produces a booklet, 'Mammalaction Project Book', and factsheets on 18 different mammals, for 7–11 year olds (£3 and 50p p&p).

GEOGRAPHICAL AREAS SERVED
- S.W. England

AGE OR KEY STAGE **KS3 KS4** Sixth Form

RESOURCES AVAILABLE
- Publications

Marine Conservation Society
- Information Officer
- 4 Gloucester Road, Ross-on-Wye, Herefordshire. HR9 5BU
- 0989 66017

Aims to ensure the protection of the marine environment from pollution and the conservation of Britain's sea and seashore.

N C SUPPORT Educational Resources have full curriculum guidance for England and Wales and are being prepared for Scotland.

COSTS £190 per day and travel expenses of 20p per mile.

GEOGRAPHICAL AREAS SERVED
- Any

AGE OR KEY STAGE **KS3 KS4** Sixth Form

SIZE OF GROUP **10–20 20–30 30+**

NOTICE REQUIRED As long as possible.

DURATION OF PRESENTATION Varies.

RESOURCES AVAILABLE
- Publications
- Displays
- Worksheets
- Teacher's Notes

MENCAP
- Richard Capewell
- 115 Golden Lane, London. EC1Y 0TJ
- 071-696 5581

MENCAP is the major charity concerned with people with learning disabilities (mental handicap) and can often arrange for local speakers, particularly parents, to talk to schools about the reality of disability.

COSTS Donations welcome.

GEOGRAPHICAL AREAS SERVED
- London
- S.W. England
- East Anglia
- Midlands

AGE OR KEY STAGE **KS1 KS2 KS3 KS4** Sixth Form

SIZE OF GROUP **1–10 10–20 20–30 30+**

NOTICE REQUIRED As much as possible.

RESOURCES AVAILABLE
- Publications

Metropolitan Police Service
- Inspector Paul Wotton
- Youth Affairs Branch, Room 927 Broadway, New Scotland Yard, London. SW1H 0BG
- 071-230 4216 FAX 071-230 4214

A copy of the Service's Statement of Common Purpose and Values is available. The Schools Involvement Programme forms part of this Statement. The aims are to promote an awareness among young people of (1) how to protect themselves and each other, (2) the role of the police in the community and (3) people's related rights, responsibilities, expectations and obligations in society, i.e. Health Education and Education for Citizenship.

COSTS No fee within London. Outside London local police officers should be available.

GEOGRAPHICAL AREAS SERVED
- London

AGE OR KEY STAGE **KS1 KS2 KS3 KS4** Sixth Form

SIZE OF GROUP **1–10 10–20 20–30 30+**

VISITS IN
METROPOLITAN POLICE SERVICE

NOTICE REQUIRED Preferably pre-planned – period of notice negotiable.

RESOURCES AVAILABLE
- Video
- Publications
- Displays
- Worksheets
- Teacher's Notes

Mexican Embassy
- Raul Ortiz
- 42 Hertford Street, London. W1Y 7TF
- 071-499 8565 FAX 071-495 4035

Provides speakers to schools all round Britain. Also provides maps, books (on loan), videos (on loan), slides (on loan), posters, postcards and leaflets.

COSTS Expenses.

GEOGRAPHICAL AREAS SERVED
- Any

SIZE OF GROUP 10–20

NOTICE REQUIRED Two months.

RESOURCES AVAILABLE
- Video
- Slides
- Publications
- Other

MIND
- Information Officer
- 22 Harley Street, London. W1N 2ED
- 071-637 0741 FAX 071-323 0061

Promotes the preservation of mental health and assists in giving relief to and rehabilitating people suffering from mental disorder or emotional distress. Promotes the study of and research into mental illness. Local MIND groups are autonomous and some see education as a priority and send speakers. Produces a pack called 'Insight' for all ages and abilities. The BBC have produced a study guide called 'Madness'.

GEOGRAPHICAL AREAS SERVED
- Any

RESOURCES AVAILABLE
- Publications
- Displays

MINORITY RIGHTS GROUP

MRG publishes teaching packs and reports on minority issues. Recent examples are:

- Voices From Somalia, Kurdistan and Eritrea (dual language books)
- Bangladesh is My Motherland (information for teachers)
- We Have Always Lived Here: The Maya of Guatemala (active learning pack)
- First They Came For The Jews: The Legacy of Pastor Niemoller (educational pack)

(Please send for catalogue. See entry below)

MRG, 379 Brixton Rd, London SW9 7DE
Credit card orders: 071 978 9498

Minority Rights Group
- Rachel Warner
- 379 Brixton Road, London. SW9 7DE
- 071-738 6295 FAX 071-978 9498

International charity working to secure justice for minority groups who are suffering discrimination, and for the peaceful co-existence of communities. MRG runs an information service for teachers and pupils on minority topics as well as racism and prejudice. Please write with A4 SAE to Rachel Warner.

N C SUPPORT Over 80 reports available on minority groups worldwide. MRG's education project publishes packs, booklets and leaflets linked to the NC Key Stages at primary and secondary levels.

Movement for the Ordination of Women
- Caroline Davis/Jenny Standage
- Napier Hall, Vincent Street, London. SW1P 4NJ
- 071-834 2736 FAX 071-834 7238

Campaigning organisation to get the priests' (Ordination of Women) measure through Parliament and promulgated by the General Synod so that women can be priests in the Church of England. They can arrange for speakers locally.

AGE OR KEY STAGE Sixth Form

SIZE OF GROUP 30+

NOTICE REQUIRED By arrangement.

RESOURCES AVAILABLE
- Video
- Publications

Museum of Mankind
- Education Officer
- Burlington Gardens, London. W1X 2EX
- 071-323 8043

Ethnography department of the British Museum. Collections come from the indigenous cultures of Africa, Australia and the Pacific Islands, North and South America and certain parts of Asia and Europe.

N C SUPPORT No speakers but the Museum has videos called 'Living Arctic' and 'Paper Magic' (on Mexico) which can be loaned free to schools for a period of two weeks.

RESOURCES AVAILABLE
- Video
- Publications
- Displays
- Worksheets
- Teacher's Notes

Museum of the Moving Image (MOMI)
- Education Officer
- South Bank, London. SE1 8XT
- 071-928 3535

The history of film and television. Social significance of the moving image in the twentieth century. Also covers animation, advertising and the film and TV industry.

N C SUPPORT Try to link their work to the National Curriculum.

COSTS Expenses.

GEOGRAPHICAL AREAS SERVED
- London
- S.E. England

AGE OR KEY STAGE KS2 KS3 KS4 Sixth Form

SIZE OF GROUP 20–30

NOTICE REQUIRED As much as possible.

DURATION OF PRESENTATION One hour.

RESOURCES AVAILABLE
- Publications

National Abortion Campaign
- Leonora Lloyd
- Wesley House, 4 Wild Court, London. WC2B 5AU
- 071-405 4801 FAX 071-430 2036

Campaigning group for the right of women to choose whether to

VISITS IN

NATIONAL ABORTION CAMPAIGN

continue or terminate a pregnancy; opposed to any attempt to restrict this. Emphasis on good sex education for all children.

N C SUPPORT **No.**

COSTS **Expenses.**

GEOGRAPHICAL AREAS SERVED
- Any

AGE OR KEY STAGE **KS4 Sixth Form**

SIZE OF GROUP **1–10 10–20 20–30 30+**

NOTICE REQUIRED **Two weeks.**

DURATION OF PRESENTATION **One hour.**

RESOURCES AVAILABLE
- Publications
- Teacher's Notes
- Displays

National AIDS Helpline

☏ 0800 567 123

Questions about AIDS? Call the National AIDS Helpline: to talk to an advisor call 0800 567 123; for free leaflets call 0800 555 777. All calls are free of charge from anywhere in the UK. Can give a school details of their nearest voluntary agency from where they can find a speaker.

GEOGRAPHICAL AREAS SERVED
- Any

AGE OR KEY STAGE **KS4 Sixth Form**

SIZE OF GROUP **1–10 10–20 20–30 30+**

National AIDS Trust

☞ Information Officer/Policy Development Officer
✉ 6th Floor, 80 Newington Causeway, London. SE1 6EF
☏ 071-972 3200 FAX 071-972 2885

An independent voluntary organisation whose purpose is to promote a wider understanding of AIDS and to initiate, develop and support efforts designed to prevent the spread of HIV. Can direct schools towards local AIDS organisations who might send speakers. Has produced a paper called 'Living for Tomorrow' following work done consulting young people about AIDS and HIV.

RESOURCES AVAILABLE
- Video
- Publications

National Anti-Vivisection Society

☞ Jan Creamer
✉ 261–263 Goldhock Road, London. W12 9PE
☏ 081-846 9777 FAX 081-846 9712

The NAVS campaigns for an end to experiments on live animals by means of public education, political lobbying, publicity campaigns and scientific reports to change the law on animal experiments.

COSTS **No fee.**

GEOGRAPHICAL AREAS SERVED
- London
- Midlands
- N.E. England
- N.W. England

AGE OR KEY STAGE **KS2 KS3 KS4 Sixth Form**

NOTICE REQUIRED **Talks possible at short notice but very early request preferred.**

DURATION OF PRESENTATION **By arrangement.**

RESOURCES AVAILABLE
- Video
- Worksheets
- Publications
- Displays
- Other
- Teacher's Notes

NATIONAL CAMPAIGN FOR FIREWORK REFORM

National Association for Environmental Education
- Jacky Donnolly
- Wolverhampton Polytechnic, Walsall Campus, Gorway, Walsall. WS1 3BD
- 0922 31200

Association of teachers, lecturers and others concerned with education and the environment. Members include representatives from all disciplines involved in environmental education.

N C SUPPORT Yes.

COSTS Expenses.

GEOGRAPHICAL AREAS SERVED
- Any

AGE OR KEY STAGE KS1 KS2 KS3 KS4 Sixth Form

SIZE OF GROUP 1–10 10–20 20–30 30+

NOTICE REQUIRED Eight weeks.

DURATION OF PRESENTATION Varies.

RESOURCES AVAILABLE
- Worksheets
- Publications

National Association of Volunteer Bureaux
- Information Officer
- St Peter's College, College Road, Saltley, Birmingham. B8 3TE
- 021-327 0265 FAX 021-327 3696

NAVB supports a network of 250 volunteer bureaux. Bureaux help people wishing to volunteer to find suitable volunteering placements. Bureaux also promote good volunteer practice.

N C SUPPORT Volunteer bureaux staff may be able to contribute to the curriculum via talks covering issues relating to helping, volunteering and social activism.

COSTS Contact local bureau for information. It is unlikely that fees will be charged.

GEOGRAPHICAL AREAS SERVED
- London
- S.W. England
- Midlands
- N.W. England
- Wales
- S.E. England
- East Anglia
- N.E. England
- Scotland
- Northern Ireland

AGE OR KEY STAGE KS1 KS2 KS3 KS4 Sixth Form

NOTICE REQUIRED Contact local bureau for information.

RESOURCES AVAILABLE
- Video
- Displays
- Publications
- Worksheets
- Teacher's Notes

National Campaign for Firework Reform
- Noel Tobin
- 18 Long Acre, London. WC2E 9PA
- 071-836 6703

Objective is to amend the 1875 and 1976 Explosives Acts; to introduce legislation restricting fireworks to holders of licences aged over 18, essentially for properly organised firework displays; to ban shop sales of fireworks.

GEOGRAPHICAL AREAS SERVED
- London

AGE OR KEY STAGE KS3 KS4 Sixth Form

RESOURCES AVAILABLE
- Publications
- Other

National Caving Association
- John Cliffe, Training Coordinator
- 45 Gwernyfed Avenue, Three Cocks, Brecon, Powys. LD3 0RT
- 0497 847575

Federation of five Regional Councils of Caving Clubs, together with five other well-recognised organisations. Local clubs can affiliate to their Regional Council.

N C SUPPORT Provides a list of people who give lectures on aspects of caving throughout the world. Many of these lectures are linked to subjects in the National Curriculum. The school should contact the speaker direct from the list.

COSTS Fee negotiable plus expenses.

GEOGRAPHICAL AREAS SERVED
- Wales

NOTICE REQUIRED Depends on individual speakers and day of week.

RESOURCES AVAILABLE
- Video
- Publications

National Federation of City Farms
-
- 93 Whitby Road, Brislington, Bristol. BS4 3QF
- 0272 719109

The development of vacant land for the use of the local community to offer educational and recreational facilities to the entire community regardless of age, sex or race.

AGE OR KEY STAGE KS3 KS4 Sixth Form

RESOURCES AVAILABLE
- Publications

National Secular Society
- The Secretary
- 702 Holloway Road, London. N1 3NL
- 071-272 1266

Campaigns for the promotion of free thought, civil liberties and rational ethics. Works for a wide range of social reform: minority rights, racial and sexual equality and voluntary euthanasia, amongst others.

COSTS Expenses.

GEOGRAPHICAL AREAS SERVED
- Any

AGE OR KEY STAGE Sixth Form

NOTICE REQUIRED Two weeks.

DURATION OF PRESENTATION By arrangement.

RESOURCES AVAILABLE
- Publications

National Society for Education in Art and Design
- J Steers
- 7a High Street, Corsham, Wiltshire. SN13 0ES
- 0249 714825 FAX 0249 716138

The National Society for Education in Art and Design is the leading national authority, combining professional subject association and trade union functions, which represents every facet of art, craft and design in education.

N C SUPPORT Can provide publications and talks relevant to all sectors of education regarding the structure and position of art, craft and design within the education system.

COSTS Officers of the society charge £75 per lecture/talk plus expenses.

VISITS IN
NONSUCH (HISTORY & DANCE)

Other one-day INSET presentations are negotiable.

GEOGRAPHICAL AREAS SERVED
- East Anglia

AGE OR KEY STAGE **KS1 KS2 KS3 KS4 Sixth Form**

SIZE OF GROUP **10–20 20–30 30+**

RESOURCES AVAILABLE
- Publications

National Society for the Prevention of Cruelty to Children (NSPCC)
- Young NSPCC (Schools Dept)
- 67 Saffron Hill, London. EC1N 8RS
- 071-242 1626 **FAX** 071-831 9562

Aims to prevent children from suffering significant harm as a result of ill-treatment. Protects children at risk from ill-treatment and helps children overcome the experience of cruelty.

COSTS **No fee.**

GEOGRAPHICAL AREAS SERVED
- Any

AGE OR KEY STAGE **KS1 KS2 KS3 KS4 Sixth Form**

SIZE OF GROUP **1–10 10–20 20–30 30+**

DURATION OF PRESENTATION **By arrangement.**

RESOURCES AVAILABLE
- Worksheets
- Publications
- Displays

New Assembly of Churches
- Reverend C Jones MBE
- 15 Oldbridge Road, Balham, London. SW12 8PL
- 081-637 0595

Works with young people at risk of offending, and provides support for the families where appropriate.

COSTS **Expenses.**

GEOGRAPHICAL AREAS SERVED
- London

AGE OR KEY STAGE **KS3 KS4**

SIZE OF GROUP **10–20**

Nonsuch (History & Dance)
- Peggy Dixon
- 16 Brook Drive, London. SE11 4TT
- 071-735 8353

The Company has been in existence for 26 years and is a registered educational charity. It can provide workshops on specific periods from the 12th to the 19th century and talks on cultural aspects of each period, specifically illustrated by dance, a performance with contemporary words and dance from a specific period, or as a review of court dance.

N C SUPPORT **Nonsuch has done workshops in several London schools. Specific topics include Tudor England: History Key Stage 2.**

COSTS **Costs depend on what is required and the number of personnel needed.**

GEOGRAPHICAL AREAS SERVED
- London
- S.E. England

AGE OR KEY STAGE **KS2 KS3 KS4 Sixth Form**

SIZE OF GROUP **20–30 30+**

VISITS IN
NORTHERN HEALTH AND SOCIAL SERVICES BOARD

The Northern Ireland Chest, Heart and Stroke Association
- The Administrator
- 21 Dublin Road, Belfast. BT2 7HB
- 0232 320184

Organises speakers to visit schools to discuss its aims.

GEOGRAPHICAL AREAS SERVED
- Northern Ireland

Northern Ireland Health & Social Services Board
- Central Health Promotion Department
- 2 George Street, Ballymena. BT43 5AP
- 0266 46021

The Health Promotion Department organises speakers to visit schools to discuss good health practices.

GEOGRAPHICAL AREAS SERVED
- Northern Ireland

AGE OR KEY STAGE Sixth Form

Outward Bound Trust
- Dawn Christmas
- Chestnut Field, Regent Place, Rugby. CV21 2PJ
- 0788 560423 FAX 0788 541069

The Outward Bound Trust offers a choice of open enrolment and tailor-made programmes in personal development and teamwork skills at five national centres. All specialist equipment and clothing is provided.

N C SUPPORT Programmes can be designed to enhance the development and communication, problem-solving and personal and social skills in support of the National Schools Curriculum.

COSTS No fee for visiting the school for a talk regarding our courses.

GEOGRAPHICAL AREAS SERVED
- London
- S.W. England
- Midlands
- N.W. England
- Wales
- S.E. England
- East Anglia
- N.E. England
- Scotland
- Northern Ireland

AGE OR KEY STAGE KS4 Sixth Form

SIZE OF GROUP 1–10 10–20 20–30 30+

NOTICE REQUIRED As much as possible; at least two weeks.

RESOURCES AVAILABLE
- Video
- Publications
- Slides
- Displays

Oxfam
- Youth and Education Officer
- 274 Banbury Road, Oxford. OX2 7DZ
- 0865 311311 FAX 0865 311311

Oxfam is a development agency providing emergency relief in times of crisis but its main concern is long-term sustainable development. It offers advice, training and support to teachers to enable them to bring an international dimension to their work with young people. Advice and a catalogue freely available.

N C SUPPORT Oxfam specialist staff can advise teachers of all age groups. It provides resources, INSET training, curriculum development support, one-off sessions, etc.

COSTS Varies from region to region.

VISITS IN
PORTUGUESE EMBASSY

Oxfam working with teachers
Teaching about world development? Oxfam offers:

PUBLICATIONS – a wide selection of books, pamphlets, posters and videos
CATALOGUE OF RESOURCES – a free guide to over 180 materials
TRAINING AND SUPPORT – provided by locally-based specialist education staff

Additional support includes **speakers** and an **Enquiry Service**

For more information about how Oxfam can work with the resourceful teacher, write to Supporter Services, Oxfam, 274 Banbury Road, Oxford, OX2 7DZ or telephone 0865 311311. Or contact your local Oxfam office which is listed in the telephone directory.

Working for a Fairer World

Registered charity no. 202918

GEOGRAPHICAL AREAS SERVED
- Any

AGE OR KEY STAGE **KS1 KS2 KS3 KS4 Sixth Form**

SIZE OF GROUP **1–10 10–20 20–30 30+**

NOTICE REQUIRED **Varies from region to region.**

RESOURCES AVAILABLE
- Video
- Worksheets
- Displays
- Slides
- Publications
- Teacher's Notes

Population Concern
☛ Fiona Barr
✉ 231 Tottenham Court Road, London. W1P 9AE
☎ 071-631 1546 **FAX** 071-436 2143

An independent charity with population and development programmes in developing countries and an advocacy programme in the UK which aims to raise awareness and create a better understanding of population-related issues.

GEOGRAPHICAL AREAS SERVED
- London

AGE OR KEY STAGE **KS3 KS4 Sixth Form**

SIZE OF GROUP **10–20**

NOTICE REQUIRED **At least two months.**

RESOURCES AVAILABLE
- Video
- Publications
- Worksheets
- Displays

The Portman Group
☛ The Education Officer
✉ 20 Wimpole Street, London. W1M 7AA
☎ 071-499 1010

Produces material on strength of drinks, drink-driving. Established by large drink producers with the aim of reducing alcohol misuse. Register of alcohol education materials. Speakers can be arrrranged if available.

GEOGRAPHICAL AREAS SERVED
- Wales
- Any

AGE OR KEY STAGE **KS4 Sixth Form**

SIZE OF GROUP **1–10 10–20 20–30 30+**

NOTICE REQUIRED **One month.**

RESOURCES AVAILABLE
- Publications
- Other

Portuguese Embassy
☛ Eugenio Lisboa, Cultural Counsellor
✉ 11 Belgrave Square, London. SW1X 8PP
☎ 071-235 5331

VISITS IN
PORTUGUESE EMBASSY

From time to time provides speakers for schools but the resources available at the Embassy do not cater for systematic supply. Loan of slides and videos to teachers.

COSTS No fee for schools within and near London if personnel is available.

GEOGRAPHICAL AREAS SERVED
- London

AGE OR KEY STAGE KS1 KS2 KS3 KS4 Sixth Form

NOTICE REQUIRED At least two months.

RESOURCES AVAILABLE
- Video
- Slides

Prince's Youth Business Trust
- Jan Reid, PRO
- 5 Cleveland Place, London. SW1 6JJ
- 071-321 6500 FAX 071-839 6494

Helps young people aged 18–29 to set themselves up in business with grants and loans and business advice. Regional offices will send speakers into schools to talk about enterprise and setting up businesses.

GEOGRAPHICAL AREAS SERVED
- Any

AGE OR KEY STAGE Sixth Form

SIZE OF GROUP 10–20 20–30 30+

Prison Reform Trust
- Diana Ruthven
- 59 Caledonian Road, London. N1 9BU
- 071-278 9815 FAX 071-838 5543

PRT is a small, charitable organisation which works to educate the public about the prison system, promote the use of alternatives to custody and lobby to improve prison conditions.

COSTS Expenses.

GEOGRAPHICAL AREAS SERVED
- London
- S.E. England
- Any

AGE OR KEY STAGE KS3 KS4 Sixth Form

NOTICE REQUIRED At least one month.

RESOURCES AVAILABLE
- Worksheets
- Publications

Pro-Dogs National Charity
- Lesley Scott Ordish
- Rocky Bank, 4 New Road, Ditton, Maidstone, Kent. ME20 6AD
- 0732 848 499

Aims to promote a higher standard of dog ownership and a better understanding of people towards dogs. Originated the PAT visiting scheme whereby members take suitable, friendly dogs on regular visits to people in hospitals and homes for children and the elderly.

GEOGRAPHICAL AREAS SERVED
- S.E. England

AGE OR KEY STAGE KS1 KS2 KS3

RESOURCES AVAILABLE
- Publications

Project Trust
- Mr Jake Lloyd-Smith
- The Hebridean Centre, Ballyhough, Isle of Coll, Argyll. PA78 6TE
- 08793 444 FAX 08793 357

Project Trust is a charity which sends school leavers abroad to Africa, Asia and Latin America for twelve-month work placements between school and university.

COSTS No fee. No expenses.

GEOGRAPHICAL AREAS SERVED
- Any

AGE OR KEY STAGE Sixth Form

SIZE OF GROUP 1–10 10–20 20–30 30+

NOTICE REQUIRED Four to six weeks.

RESOURCES AVAILABLE
- Video
- Displays

ProShare Education
- Pam Mapes, Director, Education
- Library Chambers, 13–14 Basinghall Street, London. EC2V 5BQ
- 071-600 0984 FAX 071-600 0947

ProShare is committed to the provision of formal and informal education in personal financial management. Runs the National Investment Programme for Schools (16–19 years of age), a competition which offers pupils the opportunity to invest in companies and to learn about the nature of and need for personal investment choices. A list of stockbrokers who could be invited into schools can be requested.

GEOGRAPHICAL AREAS SERVED
- London
- Any

AGE OR KEY STAGE Sixth Form

RESOURCES AVAILABLE
- Publications

Rainer Foundation
- Angela Richardson
- 89 Blackheath Hill, London. SE10 8TJ
- 081-691 0874 FAX 081-691 4326

Works with young people in trouble. Services are for young offenders and young homeless people.

N C SUPPORT Material would be useful for all social context teaching as well as sex education/childcare.

COSTS Expenses. Donation welcome.

GEOGRAPHICAL AREAS SERVED
- London
- S.E. England
- Midlands

AGE OR KEY STAGE KS3 KS4 Sixth Form

SIZE OF GROUP 1–10 10–20 20–30 30+

RESOURCES AVAILABLE
- Video
- Slides
- Publications

Rare Breeds Survival Trust
- Mrs Pat Cassidy, Public Relations
- National Agricultural Centre, Kenilworth, Warwickshire. CV8 2LG
- 0203 696551 FAX 0203 696706

Aims are the preservation and conservation of rare and endangered species of British farm animals. Encourages farmers and smallholders to keep and breed animals on the Trust's priority list.

N C SUPPORT Yes.

COSTS Travel expenses at least 30p a mile.

GEOGRAPHICAL AREAS SERVED
- Midlands
- Any

AGE OR KEY STAGE KS1 KS2 KS3 KS4 Sixth Form

NOTICE REQUIRED One term.

DURATION OF PRESENTATION By arrangement.

VISITS IN
RARE BREEDS SURVIVAL TRUST

RESOURCES AVAILABLE
- Slides
- Publications
- Teacher's Notes

Rationalist Press Association
☛ The Secretary
✉ 88 Islington High Street, London. N1 8EW
☎ 071-226 7251

Publishing organ of the humanist movement. Produces publications on all subjects of interest to the general cause of free thought. Also organises lectures, conferences, meetings and debates and public opinion surveys.

COSTS Expenses.

GEOGRAPHICAL AREAS SERVED
- Any

AGE OR KEY STAGE Sixth Form

NOTICE REQUIRED Two weeks.

DURATION OF PRESENTATION By arrangement.

RESOURCES AVAILABLE
- Publications

Research into Ageing
☛ Mrs Elizabeth Mills
✉ Baird House, 15-17 St Cross Street, London. EC1N 8UN
☎ 071-404 6878 FAX 071-404 6878

Funds medical research into ailments suffered by elderly people. Speakers occasionally available.

GEOGRAPHICAL AREAS SERVED
- London

AGE OR KEY STAGE Sixth Form

SIZE OF GROUP 10-20 20-30 30+

RESOURCES AVAILABLE
- Video

Aled Richards Trust
☛ Lynne Reay
✉ 2 Hetling Court, Bath. BA1 1SH
☎ 0225 444347

The Aled Richards Trust is a voluntary agency which provides services to people affected by HIV infection throughout Avon, West Wiltshire and East Somerset.

N C SUPPORT They are able to give talks which are linked to the National Curriculum. This needs to be discussed with teachers prior to the event.

COSTS Travelling expenses and a donation.

GEOGRAPHICAL AREAS SERVED
- S.W. England

AGE OR KEY STAGE KS3 KS4 Sixth Form

SIZE OF GROUP 1-10 10-20 20-30 30+

NOTICE REQUIRED Two months.

The Roman Society
☛ Dr Helen Cockle
✉ 31-34 Gordon Square, London. WC1H 0PP
☎ 071-387 8157

Founded in 1910 as the leading society for those interested in the study of Rome and the Roman Empire. Its scope covers Roman history, archaeology, literature and art down to AD700. They have a list of speakers and lecturers.

N C SUPPORT The schools committee gives small grants for text books.

COSTS Expenses.

VISITS IN

ROYAL NETHERLANDS EMBASSY

GEOGRAPHICAL AREAS SERVED
- Any

AGE OR KEY STAGE Sixth Form

SIZE OF GROUP 1–10 10–20 20–30 30+

NOTICE REQUIRED By arrangement.

DURATION OF PRESENTATION One hour plus.

RESOURCES AVAILABLE
- Slides
- Publications

Royal Danish Embassy
- Mrs N Bigbie
- 55 Sloane Street, London. SW1X
- 071-333 0200 FAX 071-333 0270

Provides speakers for schools.

COSTS Expenses.

GEOGRAPHICAL AREAS SERVED
- London

SIZE OF GROUP 1–10 10–20 20–30 30+

NOTICE REQUIRED Two weeks.

RESOURCES AVAILABLE
- Video
- Publications
- Slides
- Other

Royal Institute of British Architects
- Frances Mills, Education Assistant
- Educational & Professional Services, 66 Portland Place, London. W1N 4AD
- 071-580 5533 FAX 071-255 1541

Refers teachers to appropriate regional offices to find speakers to talk on architectural subjects.

GEOGRAPHICAL AREAS SERVED
- Any

AGE OR KEY STAGE KS1 KS2 KS3 KS4 Sixth Form

Royal National Lifeboat Institution
- Heather Deane
- West Quay Road, Poole, Dorset. BH15 1HZ
- 0202 671133 FAX 0202 670128

Exists to save lives at sea. Provides a 24-hour rescue service adequate to cover search and rescue requirements up to 50 miles out from the coast of the UK and the Republic of Ireland.

COSTS Expenses.

GEOGRAPHICAL AREAS SERVED
- S.W. England

AGE OR KEY STAGE KS1 KS2 KS3 KS4 Sixth Form

NOTICE REQUIRED Two weeks.

DURATION OF PRESENTATION Thirty minutes.

RESOURCES AVAILABLE
- Video
- Worksheets
- Publications
- Teacher's Notes
- Displays

Royal Netherlands Embassy
- Press & Cultural Affairs Department
- 38 Hyde Park Gate, London. SW7 5DP
- 071-584 5040 FAX 071-581 0053

Provides speakers for schools within the Greater London area. Also provides free maps, videos, slides and posters.

COSTS No fee.

GEOGRAPHICAL AREAS SERVED
- London

AGE OR KEY STAGE KS2 KS3 KS4 Sixth Form

SIZE OF GROUP 1–10 10–20 20–30 30+

NOTICE REQUIRED One month.

RESOURCES AVAILABLE
- Video
- Displays
- Other
- Publications
- Slides

Royal Society for the Prevention of Accidents
- Safety Education Adviser
- The Priory, Cannon House, Queensway, Birmingham. B4 6BS
- 021-200 2461

Aims to prevent accidents on the roads, in the home, in leisure pursuits, in commerce, industry and agriculture by educational means. Speakers on safety can be found at a school's local council offices.

GEOGRAPHICAL AREAS SERVED
- Any

AGE OR KEY STAGE KS1 KS2 KS3 KS4 Sixth Form

RESOURCES AVAILABLE
- Publications

Royal Society for the Prevention of Cruelty to Animals *see* RSPCA

Royal Society for the Protection of Birds (RSPB)
- Education Officer
- Education Department, The Lodge, Sandy, Beds. SG19 2DL
- 0767 680551

Aims are the conservation of birds and their habitats. The society manages 113 bird reserves, monitors the threat to birds from changing land use, and examines alleged offences against the Wildlife and Countryside Act.

COSTS Expenses.

GEOGRAPHICAL AREAS SERVED
- Any

AGE OR KEY STAGE KS1 KS2 KS3 KS4 Sixth Form

RESOURCES AVAILABLE
- Publications
- Displays
- Worksheets
- Teacher's Notes

RSPCA
- Head of Education
- The Causeway, Horsham, West Sussex. RH12 1HG
- 0403 264181

Objective is to promote kindness and to prevent cruelty to animals. Two hundred and fifty Inspectors in England and Wales to investigate cases of animal abuse. Monitors developments in farming, wildlife care and the use of animals in research.

N C SUPPORT New resources aimed at teaching the National Curriculum and animal welfare. Ten education officers in England and Wales who offer in-service training visits, advice and resources.

COSTS No fee.

GEOGRAPHICAL AREAS SERVED
- S.E. England
- Any

AGE OR KEY STAGE KS1 KS2 KS3 KS4 Sixth Form

NOTICE REQUIRED At least one term.

DURATION OF PRESENTATION One hour.

RESOURCES AVAILABLE
- Video
- Worksheets
- Displays
- Other
- Slides
- Publications
- Teacher's Notes

VISITS IN
SAMARITAN YOUTH PROJECTS (NORTH LONDON)

St John Ambulance
- Ann Cable
- 1 Grosvenor Crescent, London. SW1X 7EF
- 071-235 5231 FAX 071-235 0796

A voluntary organisation providing first aid, support and care services within the community. It teaches first aid and allied subjects and has an extensive youth section.

N C SUPPORT A teachers' pack on St John Ambulance in Victorian Britain (applicable to Key Stage 2).

COSTS Generally free though expenses and/or a donation would be appreciated and this is down to local negotiation.

GEOGRAPHICAL AREAS SERVED
- London
- S.E. England
- S.W. England
- East Anglia
- Midlands
- N.E. England
- N.W. England
- Scotland
- Wales
- Northern Ireland

AGE OR KEY STAGE KS1 KS2 KS3 KS4 Sixth Form

SIZE OF GROUP 20–30

NOTICE REQUIRED Preferably four weeks.

DURATION OF PRESENTATION Varies.

RESOURCES AVAILABLE
- Publications

The Salvation Army
- Mrs Major Sylvia Dalziel
- Schools/Colleges Department, The Salvation Army, 101 Queen Victoria Street, London. EC4P 4EP

Charitable/religious organisation in the UK. It is second only to the government as a provider of social services.

N C SUPPORT Resource packs for teachers and students relating to the GCSE curriculum, including Salvation Army history, worship, funding, social services and viewpoints.

COSTS No fee.

GEOGRAPHICAL AREAS SERVED
- London
- S.E. England
- S.W. England
- East Anglia
- Midlands
- N.E. England
- N.W. England
- Scotland
- Wales
- Northern Ireland

AGE OR KEY STAGE KS3 KS4 Sixth Form

SIZE OF GROUP 1–10 10–20 20–30

RESOURCES AVAILABLE
- Video
- Slides
- Other
- Teacher's Notes

Samaritan Youth Projects (North London)
- Outreach Officer
- 40 Queens Road, Bounds Green, London. N11 2QU
- 081-889 6888

Visits schools and gives them an understanding of the Samaritan Movement, so that they are aware that there is somewhere they can go and talk in total confidence 24 hours a day.

GEOGRAPHICAL AREAS SERVED
- London

VISITS IN

SAMARITAN YOUTH PROJECTS (NORTH LONDON)

AGE OR KEY STAGE KS2 KS3 KS4 Sixth Form

NOTICE REQUIRED As long as possible.

Samaritan Youth Projects (South London)
- Outreach Officer
- 362 New Cross Road, London. SE16 6AG
- 081-692 5228

To meet as many young people as possible in their school environments and to give them an understanding of the Samaritan Movement.

GEOGRAPHICAL AREAS SERVED
- London

AGE OR KEY STAGE KS2 KS3 KS4 Sixth Form

NOTICE REQUIRED As long as possible.

The Samaritans
- Outreach Officer
- 10 The Grove, Slough, Berks. SL1 1QT
- 0753 532713 FAX 0753 819004

A voluntary organisation which provides 24-hour confidential emotional support to the despairing and suicidal. Each branch has a talks officer who will talk to schools. Please write or ring with a request. Teachers' resource packs about how to approach problems available. Schools project pack.

COSTS No fee.

GEOGRAPHICAL AREAS SERVED
- Any

RESOURCES AVAILABLE
- Worksheets
- Publications
- Other

Save the Children Education Unit
- Don Harrison
- 17 Grove Lane, London. SE5 8RD
- 071-703 5400 FAX 071-793 7467

An international development agency which aims to make a reality of children's rights through practice and influence in the UK, Europe and developing countries.

N C SUPPORT Curriculum targeted learning materials and teacher education programmes.

COSTS Workshop fees and travel expenses welcome.

GEOGRAPHICAL AREAS SERVED
- London
- Scotland
- Any

AGE OR KEY STAGE KS1 KS2 KS3 KS4 Sixth Form

SIZE OF GROUP 1–10 10–20 20–30 30+ Small groups preferred.

NOTICE REQUIRED Adequate time for advance planning.

DURATION OF PRESENTATION By arrangement.

RESOURCES AVAILABLE
- Video
- Slides
- Worksheets
- Publications
- Displays
- Teacher's Notes

School Play Productions Ltd
- David Wenden
- 15 Inglis Road, Colchester, Essex. CO3 3HU
- 0206 549111 FAX 0206 766944

A business especially created to promote theatrical works for performance by schools. Also provides workshops and lectures and runs a help and advice service.

N C SUPPORT Workshops can be tailored to meet a school's needs and the requirements of the National Curriculum.

COSTS Workshops from £85 per half day. Scripts and scores from £2.50.

GEOGRAPHICAL AREAS SERVED
- East Anglia

AGE OR KEY STAGE KS1 KS2 KS3 KS4 Sixth Form

SIZE OF GROUP 20–30 30+

RESOURCES AVAILABLE
- Worksheets

Schoolworks
- Peter Trevitt
- 20 St James Street, London. W6 9RW
- 081-741 7437 FAX 081-741 2307

Schoolworks offers a series of curriculum-based 'hands-on' science exhibitions available to schools on their premises. The equipment is easy to use. Clear comprehensive literature is provided for teachers.

N C SUPPORT Each exhibition addresses strands from the Science curriculum, drawing from the programmes of study in levels 1–6. The equipment has good educational value for years 1–7.

COSTS Charges are made which vary depending on regional organisers in London. In London charges are £70 + VAT for the first day, and £40 + VAT per day thereafter, all inclusive.

GEOGRAPHICAL AREAS SERVED
- London
- S.W. England
- Midlands
- N.W. England
- S.E. England
- East Anglia
- N.E. England
- Scotland
- Wales
- Northern Ireland

AGE OR KEY STAGE KS1 KS2

SIZE OF GROUP 30+

RESOURCES AVAILABLE
- Worksheets
- Displays
- Other
- Teacher's Notes

Scottish Association of Health Councils
- 5 Leamington Terrace, Edinburgh. EH10 4JW
- 031-229 2344 FAX 031-228 2344

The watchdog for the National Health Service of Scotland. List of all the local Health Councils and the chair and vice chair and staff who could be contacted if a school wanted a talk on the working of the NHS and patients' rights.

GEOGRAPHICAL AREAS SERVED
- Scotland

AGE OR KEY STAGE Sixth Form

Scottish Nuclear Limited
- David Beveridge
- 3 Redwood Crescent, Peel Park, East Kilbride. G74 5PR
- 03552 62626

Scottish Nuclear is Scotland's nuclear generating company producing 50% of the electricity requirement.

GEOGRAPHICAL AREAS SERVED
- Scotland

AGE OR KEY STAGE KS2 KS4

SIZE OF GROUP 1–10 10–20 20–30 30+

NOTICE REQUIRED One week.

RESOURCES AVAILABLE
- Video

SEX EDUCATION FORUM

Sex Education Forum
- Caroline Ray, Information Officer
- 8 Wakeley Street, London. EC1V 7QE
- 071-278 9441 FAX 071-278 9512

The Sex Education Forum is an umbrella body consisting of national organisations involved directly or indirectly in sex education. It is setting up a database of organisations and projects in the field of sex education. Although unable to supply speakers for schools itself, may be able to suggest local contacts.

GEOGRAPHICAL AREAS SERVED
- London
- Any

Shape London
- Guy Evans
- 1 Thorpe Close, London. W10 5XL
- 081-960 9245 FAX 081-968 1674

Shape has local offices in five London boroughs where staff work with local authorities, arts organisations and voluntary groups to ensure that people with disabilities can achieve equal opportunity in the arts.

N C SUPPORT Heart 'n' Soul is a musical group of people with learning difficulties who run drama workshops for 15–19 year olds with severe learning difficulties. The workshop leaders also work with the GCSE drama group on the theme of positive images of disadvantaged people through the medium of drama which was then filmed on video.

COSTS Varies. Contact the Shape office for details.

GEOGRAPHICAL AREAS SERVED
- London

AGE OR KEY STAGE KS1 KS2 KS3 KS4 Sixth Form

SIZE OF GROUP 1–10 10–20 20–30 30+

NOTICE REQUIRED By arrangement.

RESOURCES AVAILABLE
- Video
- Publications
- Other

The Shape Network
- The Chair
- c/o East Midlands Shape, 27a Belvoir Street, Leicester. LE1 6FL
- 0533 552933

The network services all broadly work to improve and increase access and involvement of disabled, elderly and other under-represented groups in all aspects of the arts. This can be through practical arts workshops in institutional settings, training courses or festivals, etc. Many art forms are covered including drama, dance, music and puppetry as well as most kinds of visual art.

COSTS Contact your nearest Shape service or write to the above address.

GEOGRAPHICAL AREAS SERVED
- Midlands
- Any

AGE OR KEY STAGE KS1 KS2 KS3 KS4 Sixth Form

SIZE OF GROUP 1–10 10–20 20–30 30+

NOTICE REQUIRED Depends on activities. Contact the above.

RESOURCES AVAILABLE
- Video
- Publications
- Other

Shelter: National Campaign for the Homeless
- Mark Henstock
- 88 Old Street, London. EC1
- 071-253 0202

A charity with cross-party support which campaigns nationally for homeless people. It advises and assists all political parties and the government in understanding housing issues. It sends speakers when available.

N C SUPPORT A free schools pack for key stages 2–4 is available. It contains five lessons.

GEOGRAPHICAL AREAS SERVED
- Any

AGE OR KEY STAGE KS4 Sixth Form

SIZE OF GROUP 10–20 20–30 30+

NOTICE REQUIRED As much as possible.

RESOURCES AVAILABLE
- Video
- Publications
- Displays

Social and Liberal Democratic Party
- The Information Unit
- 4 Cowley Street, London. SW1P 3NB
- 071-222 7999 FAX 071-799 2170

1992 manifesto included emphasis on electoral reform, the environment, education and progress towards a 'fully integrated, federal and democratic Europe'.

COSTS Expenses.

GEOGRAPHICAL AREAS SERVED
- Any

AGE OR KEY STAGE KS3 KS4 Sixth Form

SIZE OF GROUP 1–10 10–20 20–30 30+

NOTICE REQUIRED Four weeks.

DURATION OF PRESENTATION One hour.

RESOURCES AVAILABLE
- Publications
- Displays

Society for Cooperation in Russian and Soviet Studies
- Information Department
- 320 Brixton Road, London. SW9 6AB
- 071-274 2282

Aims to promote cultural relations between the peoples of the UK and republics of the former USSR. Sends speakers according to availability.

GEOGRAPHICAL AREAS SERVED
- Any

AGE OR KEY STAGE KS3 KS4 Sixth Form

Society for the Promotion of Hellenic Studies
- Dr Lyn Rodley
- 31–34 Gordon Square, London. WC1H 0PP
- 071-387 7495

Founded in 1879 to advance the study of Greek Language, Literature, History, Art and Archaeology in the Ancient, Byzantine and Modern periods. List of speakers and lecturers.

N C SUPPORT Small grants are given to schools for text books and other resources.

COSTS Expenses.

GEOGRAPHICAL AREAS SERVED
- Any

AGE OR KEY STAGE Sixth Form

NOTICE REQUIRED Four weeks.

Society for the Protection of Unborn Children (SPUC)
- ☞ Paul Tully, Development Officer
- ✉ 7 Tufton Street, London. SW1P 3QN
- ☎ 071-222 5845 **FAX** 071-222 0630

Campaigns against the 1967 Abortion Act. Provides information to raise public awareness on the nature of abortion.

COSTS No fee.

GEOGRAPHICAL AREAS SERVED
- Any

AGE OR KEY STAGE Sixth Form

NOTICE REQUIRED Two weeks.

DURATION OF PRESENTATION Thirty minutes plus.

RESOURCES AVAILABLE
- Video
- Slides
- Publications

Society for Underwater Technology
- ☞ Commander D R Wardle
- ✉ 76 Mark Lane, London. EC3R 7JN
- ☎ 071-481 0750 **FAX** 071-481 4001

Aims are to advance the study of the ocean, further the proper economic and sociological use of the oceans and the earth beneath the oceans, and to assist the exchange of information between workers in underwater academic research.

RESOURCES AVAILABLE
- Publications

DURATION OF PRESENTATION One period plus.

RESOURCES AVAILABLE
- Slides
- Publications

Soil Association
- ☞ Eric Booth
- ✉ The Organic Food & Farming Centre, 86 Colston Street, Bristol. BS1 5BB
- ☎ 0272 290661 **FAX** 0272 252504

To develop understanding of ecological land use and of the links between soil, plants, animals and people. Founded in 1946 it is well known for the symbol scheme for organic food.

N C SUPPORT Relevant in Science, Geography. Food and Farming are particularly suitable for cross-curricular topics.

COSTS By arrangement with local groups of the Soil Association.

GEOGRAPHICAL AREAS SERVED
- London
- S.E. England
- S.W. England
- East Anglia
- Midlands
- N.E. England
- N.W. England
- Scotland
- Wales
- Northern Ireland

AGE OR KEY STAGE KS1 KS2 KS3 KS4 Sixth Form

SIZE OF GROUP 20–30 30+

NOTICE REQUIRED Varies.

RESOURCES AVAILABLE
- Publications
- Teacher's Notes
- Displays

SOS Children's Villages UK
- ☞ Christina Barnes, Deputy Director
- ✉ 32 Bridge Street, Cambridge. CB2 1UJ
- ☎ 0223 65589

Aims to promote loving care and a secure future for homeless, orphaned and abandoned children throughout the world.

VISITS IN
SPANISH EMBASSY EDUCATION OFFICE

N C SUPPORT SOS features in the Geography National Curriculum Key Stage 2 Attainment Target 2 of the LADAKH Activity Pack published by the Geographical Association.

GEOGRAPHICAL AREAS SERVED
- Any

AGE OR KEY STAGE KS2 KS3

South East Pharmaceutical Industry Group
- Mrs Bonny Green
- Henderson Group 1, Ryde House, Ripley, Surrey. GU23 6AT
- 0483 225398 FAX 0483 211043

Group of eight companies based in Kent and Sussex which aims to provide information about the pharmaceutical industry in the region. Schools programme maintained and panel of speakers available.

N C SUPPORT Yes.

GEOGRAPHICAL AREAS SERVED
- S.E. England

AGE OR KEY STAGE KS3 KS4 Sixth Form

NOTICE REQUIRED Four weeks.

DURATION OF PRESENTATION One hour plus.

RESOURCES AVAILABLE
- Publications
- Teacher's Notes

South Place Ethical Society
- The Secretary
- Conway Hall, 25 Red Lion Square, London. WC1R 4RL
- 071-242 8032

Cultural social organisation with the objective of the study and dissemination of ethical principles, the cultivation of a rational and humane life, and the advancement of education in related fields.

GEOGRAPHICAL AREAS SERVED
- London
- S.E. England
- S.W. England
- East Anglia
- Midlands
- N.E. England
- N.W. England
- Scotland
- Wales
- Northern Ireland

AGE OR KEY STAGE Sixth Form

NOTICE REQUIRED Four weeks.

DURATION OF PRESENTATION By arrangement.

RESOURCES AVAILABLE
- Publications

Southern Health and Social Services Board
- Area Health Promotion Department
- Tower Hill, Armagh. BT61 9DR
- 0861 52262

The Area Health Promotion Department organises speakers to visit schools to discuss good health practices.

GEOGRAPHICAL AREAS SERVED
- Northern Ireland

AGE OR KEY STAGE KS4 Sixth Form

Spanish Embassy Education Office
- Dr Enrique Wulff
- 20 Peel Street, London. W8 7PD
- 071-727 2462 FAX 071-229 4965

The Spanish Embassy Education Office is developing its support for the teaching of Spanish as a foreign language at all levels in the UK, at a

VISITS IN SPANISH EMBASSY EDUCATION OFFICE

time when the establishment of a foreign language as a foundation subject in the National Curriculum provides a powerful impulse to language teaching in this country. Increasing the range of contexts in which Spanish is taught, these projects may be connected to an international programme, or place emphasis on another curriculum area such as Business or Technology. Staffing support is provided in the particular school running the project.

COSTS Free loan system for audio and video cassettes and magazines for teachers. Please write direct to the above concerning costs of courses for teachers of Spanish and speakers for schools.

GEOGRAPHICAL AREAS SERVED
- Any

AGE OR KEY STAGE KS1 KS2 KS3 KS4 Sixth Form

SIZE OF GROUP 10–20 20–30 30+

NOTICE REQUIRED At least one month.

RESOURCES AVAILABLE
- Video
- Teacher's Notes
- Publications

Student Community Action Development Unit (SCADU)
- Julie Christie & Kelly Drake
- Oxford House, Derbyshire Street, London. E2 6HG
- 071-739 9001 FAX 071-729 0435

SCADU funds 130 SCA groups nationwide which run projects with local community and voluntary groups.

COSTS Expenses and a fee by negotiation.

GEOGRAPHICAL AREAS SERVED
- London

AGE OR KEY STAGE Sixth Form

SIZE OF GROUP 1–10 10–20 20–30 30+

NOTICE REQUIRED One to two months.

RESOURCES AVAILABLE
- Worksheets
- Publications

Survival International
- Alison Sanders
- 310 Edgware Road, London. W2 1DY
- 071-723 5535 FAX 071-723 4059

Survival International is a worldwide movement to support tribal peoples. It stands for their right to decide their own future and helps them protect their lands, environment and way of life.

COSTS £50–£100.

GEOGRAPHICAL AREAS SERVED
- London

AGE OR KEY STAGE KS1 KS2 KS3 KS4 Sixth Form

SIZE OF GROUP 20–30 30+

NOTICE REQUIRED Four weeks.

DURATION OF PRESENTATION One hour.

RESOURCES AVAILABLE
- Video
- Slides
- Publications
- Displays
- Worksheets
- Teacher's Notes

Sussex AIDS Centre
- Janet Finn
- PO Box 17, Cavendish Street, Brighton. BN2 5NQ
- 0273 608511

They offer training and support to the community through their

VISITS IN TALKING SCIENCE PLUS

helpline, direct care and education. (These are the major functions of SAC).

COSTS Fee for private/independent schools only.

GEOGRAPHICAL AREAS SERVED
- S.E. England

AGE OR KEY STAGE Sixth Form

SIZE OF GROUP 30+

NOTICE REQUIRED Two to three months.

RESOURCES AVAILABLE
- Video
- Publications
- Worksheets
- Other

Tailormade Tour of London
☛ Richard Tames
✉ 76 Regent Square, Bruce Road, London. E3 3HW
☎ 081-981 2732 FAX 081-981 2732

'Stroll-on' guided walks and coach minibus tours designed to order, on historical themes. Also available in French/Spanish/Japanese. The guide is a Cambridge graduate, qualified 'blue badge' guide and author of 'A Traveller's History of London'.

N C SUPPORT Can be geared to National Curriculum History (e.g. Victorians/World War II/Islam).

COSTS Depends on preparation required. Normally £150 per day.

GEOGRAPHICAL AREAS SERVED
- London
- East Anglia

AGE OR KEY STAGE KS3 KS4 Sixth Form

NOTICE REQUIRED Normally one week.

RESOURCES AVAILABLE
- Worksheets
- Teacher's Notes

Talking Point in the Biological Sciences
☛ Manager
✉ 58 Great Marlborough Street, London. W1V 1DD
☎ 071-287 2595

A free lecture service which aims to bring schools into contact with speakers actively involved in biological and medical research. Talks are aimed mainly at GCSE, A-level and Highers (Scotland) students.

COSTS Expenses.

GEOGRAPHICAL AREAS SERVED
- Any

AGE OR KEY STAGE KS3 KS4 Sixth Form

DURATION OF PRESENTATION By arrangement.

Talking Science Plus
☛ Jane Mole
✉ Fortress House, 23 Savile Row, London. W1X 1AB
☎ 071-494 3326 FAX 071-734 1658

Talking Science Plus is part of The British Association which aims to promote Science and Technology to all sections of the community. Talking Science Plus lists speakers, organisations and groups who will give talks, demonstrations, etc.

GEOGRAPHICAL AREAS SERVED
- Any

AGE OR KEY STAGE KS1 KS2 KS3 KS4 Sixth Form

SIZE OF GROUP 1–10 10–20 20–30 30+

NOTICE REQUIRED Varies.

RESOURCES AVAILABLE
- Worksheets
- Teacher's Notes
- Publications

VISITS IN TEEN CHALLENGE UK

Teen Challenge UK
- Rachel McNamee
- Teen Challenge Outreach Centre, Stoke Road, Shelton, Stoke-on-Trent, Staffs. ST1 4DQ
- 0269 842718

Christian group campaigning against drugs.

COSTS Donation requested.

GEOGRAPHICAL AREAS SERVED
- Any

AGE OR KEY STAGE KS3 KS4 Sixth Form

NOTICE REQUIRED Two weeks.

DURATION OF PRESENTATION Varies.

Terrence Higgins Trust
- Frankie Lynch
- 52–54 Gray's Inn Road, London. WC1X 8JU
- 071-831 0330 FAX 071-242 0121

THT was the first organisation to produce popular leaflets about AIDS. The Trust provides a number of services, including a Helpline, a Legal Line, an Advice Centre and a Prisoners' Link.

COSTS £25 per hour.

GEOGRAPHICAL AREAS SERVED
- Any

AGE OR KEY STAGE KS3 KS4 Sixth Form

NOTICE REQUIRED Four weeks.

DURATION OF PRESENTATION Varies.

RESOURCES AVAILABLE
- Worksheets
- Publications
- Displays

Thames Valley Police
- Inspector A W Holman
- The Old Police Station, Chinnor Road, Thame, Oxon. OX9 3LN
- 0296 396376 FAX 0296 396380

Structured schools programme. Talking to and with young people about personal safety, the police role and crime.

N C SUPPORT All themes are cross-curricular but aimed towards Citizenship.

GEOGRAPHICAL AREAS SERVED
- S.E. England

AGE OR KEY STAGE KS1 KS2 KS3 KS4 Sixth Form

Third World First
- Luis Revecl
- 232 Cowley Road, Oxford. OX4 1UH
- 0865 245678 FAX 0865 200179

National organisation founded in 1969 by students within Oxfam. Since 1976 it has been an independent NGO. It combines education about the root causes of poverty with raising funds for projects in the Third World and in Britain.

COSTS Expenses.

GEOGRAPHICAL AREAS SERVED
- Any

AGE OR KEY STAGE Sixth Form

SIZE OF GROUP 10–20 20–30 30+

NOTICE REQUIRED Four weeks.

DURATION OF PRESENTATION By arrangement.

RESOURCES AVAILABLE
- Publications

The 300 Group
- Catherine Mulgan
- 3rd Floor, 19 Borough High Street, London. SE1 9SE
- 071-357 6660 FAX 071-357 6632

An all-party campaign to get more women into parliament, local government and public life. They are especially keen to stimulate interest in politics among girl students.

GEOGRAPHICAL AREAS SERVED
- Any

AGE OR KEY STAGE KS4 Sixth Form

SIZE OF GROUP 1–10 10–20 20–30 30+

NOTICE REQUIRED Preferably at least one month.

RESOURCES AVAILABLE
- Publications
- Other

The Tibet Society: The Tibet Relief Fund of the UK
- Margo Pallus, Sponsorship Secretary
- Olympia Bridge, 70 Russell Road (Westside), Kensington, London. W14 8YL
- 071-603 7764

Supports the right to self-determination and independence of the people of Tibet. Promotes the course of Tibetan independency to assist those Tibetans who have fled the country and promotes understanding of Tibetan history, culture and religion.

GEOGRAPHICAL AREAS SERVED
- Any

AGE OR KEY STAGE KS4 Sixth Form

SIZE OF GROUP 10–20 20–30 30+

RESOURCES AVAILABLE
- Publications

The Tree Council
- Robert Osborne, Director
- 35 Belgrave Square, London. SW1X 8QN
- 071-235 8854 FAX 071-235 2023

Its purpose is to promote tree planting and care throughout the UK. It is an umbrella organisation for all other organisations involved in the planting and protection of trees and runs an annual tree campaign and a national tree week.

N C SUPPORT Schools pack planned.

COSTS No fee.

GEOGRAPHICAL AREAS SERVED
- Any

AGE OR KEY STAGE KS1 KS2 KS3 KS4 Sixth Form

SIZE OF GROUP 10–20 20–30 30+

NOTICE REQUIRED As much as possible.

RESOURCES AVAILABLE
- Publications
- Slides

Turning Point
- Katie Smith, Regional Adviser (South)
- New Look House, 101 Backchurch Lane, London. E1 1LU
- 071-702 1458

Helps people with drink/drugs and mental health problems. Runs day centres, community centres. Speakers may be available to visit schools.

N C SUPPORT For details ring Northern area: Sheila Radcliffe 061 832 3417; Central area: Tricia Wilcockson 0602 691263. Southern area: Katie Smith 071 702 1458.

GEOGRAPHICAL AREAS SERVED
- Any

AGE OR KEY STAGE KS3 KS4 Sixth Form

VISITS IN TURNING POINT

SIZE OF GROUP 1–10 10–20 20–30 30+

NOTICE REQUIRED At least one month.

Tyne & Wear Metropolitan Fire Brigade
- Divisional Officer Phillips
- Fire Brigade, Fire Service Headquarters, Pilgrim Street, Newcastle-upon-Tyne. NE99 1HR
- 091-232 1224 FAX 091-222 1110

Local Authority fire brigade providing full emergency service and fire safety advice to the community.

N C SUPPORT Fire safety introduction follows a number of National Curriculum areas. Mobile classroom which visits schools.

COSTS No fee.

GEOGRAPHICAL AREAS SERVED
- N.E. England

AGE OR KEY STAGE KS1 KS2

SIZE OF GROUP 1–10 10–20

NOTICE REQUIRED At least one week.

UK Band of Hope
- Martin Perry, Education Coordinator
- 25f Copperfield Street, London. SE1 0EN
- 071-928 0848

Main objectives are to encourage young people to avoid alcohol and drugs and to lead healthy lives.

N C SUPPORT Yes.

COSTS No fee.

GEOGRAPHICAL AREAS SERVED
- Any

NOTICE REQUIRED Four weeks.

DURATION OF PRESENTATION One period.

RESOURCES AVAILABLE
- Worksheets
- Publications
- Displays
- Teacher's Notes

The Ulster Cancer Foundation
- The Administrator
- 40–42 Eglantine Avenue, Belfast. BT9 6DX
- 0232 663281

The Ulster Cancer Foundation organises speakers to visit schools to discuss its work.

GEOGRAPHICAL AREAS SERVED
- Northern Ireland

UNAIS United Nations Association International Service
- Michelle Kendrick
- Hunter House, 57 Goodramgate, York. YO1 2LS
- 0904 647799 FAX 0904 652353

UNAIS promotes long-term development by recruiting skilled and qualified workers to work in locally initiated projects in Latin America, West Africa and the Middle East.

GEOGRAPHICAL AREAS SERVED
- N.E. England
- N.W. England

AGE OR KEY STAGE KS4 Sixth Form

SIZE OF GROUP 10–20 20–30 30+

RESOURCES AVAILABLE
- Publications

VISITS IN
UNDERSTANDING DISABILITIES EDUCATION TRUST

unicef

UNICEF, the United Nations Children's Fund, always puts children first.

Contact us today for a copy of our free catalogue. We have a range of education materials designed to help you bring the world into your classroom, while meeting the demands of the National Curriculum.

Our order form will put you in touch with one of our specially trained Education Representatives, who will run active sessions for your pupils about **UNICEF**, children's rights, food, water or teaching about a locality in an economically developing country.

Or write to us for details about our annual school event, National Non-uniform Day, for which a free poster and booklet are produced every year.

**UNICEF, 55 Lincoln's Inn Fields, London WC2A 3NB.
Tel: 071 405 5592**

UNICEF (UK)
- Heather Jarvis
- 55 Lincoln's Inn Fields, London. WC2A 3NB
- 071-405 5592 FAX 071-405 2332

UNICEF, the United Nations Children's Fund, is the world's largest organisation working for children. The UK office is an advocate for children's rights in the UK and engages in education, information and fundraising.

N C SUPPORT Our education resource staff help teachers meet the demands of the National Curriculum. We also have a network of volunteers who can assist teachers in schools.

COSTS Free.

GEOGRAPHICAL AREAS SERVED
- London
- S.E. England
- East Anglia
- N.W. England
- Wales
- Midlands
- Scotland
- Northern Ireland

AGE OR KEY STAGE KS1 KS2 KS3 KS4 Sixth Form

SIZE OF GROUP 1–10 10–20 20–30 30+

NOTICE REQUIRED The longer the better, but we always try to meet schools' requirements.

RESOURCES AVAILABLE
- Video
- Publications
- Slides
- Other

Understanding Disabilities Education Trust
- Mary Anne Grant
- Weydon School, Weydon Lane, Farnham, Surrey. GU9 8UG
- 0252 733167 FAX 0252 734306

VISITS IN

UNDERSTANDING DISABILITIES EDUCATION TRUST

Disability awareness teaching packs for schools and students aged sixteen and over. The programme includes four videos and supporting teaching notes and incorporates visits by disabled guests. Schools and colleges arrange local speakers.

N C SUPPORT National Curriculum Links with English AT 1–3, Science AT 1–4, Mathematics AT 1–4 and Geography AT 1 and 5. The education pack also contains information on Technology, Physical Education and RE.

COSTS Local speakers may require expenses.

GEOGRAPHICAL AREAS SERVED
- Any

AGE OR KEY STAGE **KS2 KS3 KS4 Sixth Form**

SIZE OF GROUP **30+**

NOTICE REQUIRED **Three weeks.**

RESOURCES AVAILABLE
- Video
- Other
- Teacher's Notes

Understanding Industry

- A. Wood
- 59–65 Upper Ground, London. SE1 9PQ
- 071-620 0735 **FAX** 071-928 0578

Understanding Industry links business and education through participative courses led by local managers. Each session covers a different aspect of commercial life.

N C SUPPORT UI is developing specific programmes designed to act as a resource for GNVQ at levels 2 and 3 – especially Business Manufacturing and Management.

COSTS UI charges schools at an agreed rate which is renewed annually. GNVQ courses are currently £80–£100 per session.

AGE OR KEY STAGE **KS4**

SIZE OF GROUP **20–30**

NOTICE REQUIRED **Eight to twelve months.**

RESOURCES AVAILABLE
- Video
- Worksheets
- Other
- Slides
- Teacher's Notes

ARO Highland Region
- David Charnley
- Education Centre, Castle Street, Dingwall. IV15 9U
- 0349 63441

ARO Tamar
- Jenny Rhodes
- Tamar EBP, Derriford Road, Plymouth. PL6 8BH
- 0752 768799

Avon
- Tony Comer
- Orchard Lodge, Northfields, Lansdown Bath. BA1 5TN
- 0225 423808

Ayrshire
- Jim Clark
- 52 Ben Wyvis Drive, Hawkhead Estate, Paisley. PA2 7LB
- 041-887 5280

Bedfordshire
- Lawrence Hurn
- 5 Elger Close, Biddenham, Bedford. MK40 4AU
- 0234 364251

Berkshire & South Bucks
- Geoff Cavell
- Spade Oak Bungalow, Spade Oak, Reach Bourne End. SL8 5RQ
- 06285 24851

VISITS IN
UNDERSTANDING INDUSTRY

Berkshire (West)
- Margaret Coleman
- Silver Trees, Cold Ash Hill, Cold Ash, Newbury. RG16 9PW
- 0635 868328

Birmingham
- Malcolm Davis
- 47 Shipton Road, Sutton Coldfield, West Midlands. B72 1NR
- 021-355 3157

Birmingham
- Bob Noyce
- Oak Tree Cottage, 6 Nine Days Lane, Redditch, Worcs. B98 7TE
- 052785 2757

Brighton
- Maureen Dickson
- 79 Surrenden Road, Brighton, East Sussex. BN1 6PQ
- 0273 504478

Cheshire
- Andrew Morton
- 6 Pinewood Bowdon, Altrincham, Cheshire. WA14 3JQ
- 061-928 8712

Cheshire & South Manchester
- David Alderton
- 37 Badger Road, Tytherington, Macclesfield, Cheshire. SK10 2EW
- 0625 428565

Cornwall
- Anne Shaw
- Rosehill, Zelah, Truro, Cornwall. TR44 9HH
- 0872 540362

Derbyshire (North)
- Carol Knock
- 42 Brookside Bar, Chesterfield. S40 3PJ
- 0246 568224

Devon & Dorset
- Peter Hill
- Garden House, Bonfire Lane, Woodbury, Devon. EX5 1HT
- 0395 232559

Durham
- Lesley McHugh
- 45 Thorntons Close, Pelton, Durham. DH2 1QQ
- 091-370 1089

Dyfed
- Alun Stephens
- Delfryn, Henfwlch Road, Carmarthen, Dyfed. SA33 5EJ
- 0267 211324

Essex
- George Lawrence
- Lyndhurst New Road, Ingatestone, Essex. OM4 0HH
- 0277 355451

Glamorgan (Mid)
- Carol Wood
- 45 Jubilee Crescent, Mid Glamorgan. CF31 3AU
- 0656 669457

Glamorgan (South)
- Clive Westwood
- 51 Pasturton Avenue, Pontcanna, Cardiff. CF1 9HL
- 0222 342824

Glamorgan (West)
- Dez Corkhill
- Livewire Business Centre, Ysguborfach Street, Swansea. SA1 2DD
- 0222 813261

Grampian
- John Gough
- Heatherlea, Montrose Road, Inverbervie. DD10 0PJ
- 0561 361 082

VISITS IN
UNDERSTANDING INDUSTRY

Greater Manchester
- Neville Lingard
- Marton Bank Farm, Whitegate Road, Marton, Winsford, Cheshire. CW7 2PU
- 0606 556234

Greater Manchester (North)
- Deirdre Watson
- 8 Triminham Drive, Bury, Lancs. BL8 1HB
- 061-764 8440

Gwent
- Janice Cook
- 4 Bridge Street, Usk, Gwent. NP5 1BG
- 0291 672985

Hereford & Worcester
- Stan Browning
- The Hawthorns, Blackwell, Near Bromsgrove. B60 1BN
- 021-445 5048

Herts
- Geoffrey Dale
- 16 Palfrey Close, St Albans, Herts. AL3 5RE
- 0727 857665

Kent (East)
- James Stacey
- Hardicot House, Kingsdown Road, Walmer, Kent. CT14 8AW
- 0304 373867

Kent (East)
- Keith Crocker
- 12 Birch Tree Drive, Emsworth, Hants. PO10 7RT
- 0243 374455

Lancashire & Cumbria
- Ron Harrison
- 20 Carleton Avenue, Simonstone, Burnley, Lancs. BB12 7JA
- 0282 772081

London
- Peter Gummer
- Enterprise House, 59-65 Upper Ground, London. SE1 9PQ
- 071-620 0735

London
- Anthony Wood
- 59-65 Upper Ground, London. SE1 9PQ
- 071-620 0735

London (South & SE)
- Kay Stone
- 1 Ravensbury Road, St Paul's Cray, Orpington, Kent. BR5 2NR
- 0689 834 621

London (West & NW)
- Earl Goodwin
- 50 West Drayton Avenue, West Drayton, Middlesex. UB7 7QB
- 0895 442679

Lothian
- Christine Hewitt
- 101 Inverleith Row, Edinburgh. EH3 5NJ
- 031-552 2937

Maidenhead & District
- Martin Leach
- 11 Birch Close, Teddington, Middlesex. TW11 8BJ
- 081-943 0194

Manchester TEC
- Anna Brown
- 48 Beacon View, Marple, Stockport. SK6 6PX
- 061-427 2402

Merseyside & North Wales
- William Sutton
- 40 Westwood Road, Birkenhead. L43 9RQ
- 051-652 4573

VISITS IN
UNITED NATIONS ASSOCIATION

Norfolk
- D Campbell Miles
- The Dormers, Ipswich Road, Upper Tasburgh, Norfolk. NS15 1NS
- 0508 470115

Northamptonshire
- Frank Gartside
- Picts Hill House, Barnwell, Oundle, Peterborough. PE8 5QB
- 0832 273303

Nottinghamshire & Lincolnshire
- Sheila Hobden
- 163 Harrow Road, Wollaton Park, Notts. NG8 1FL
- 0602 288439

Oxfordshire
- Joyce Vallis
- 6 Church Street, Ducklington, Oxon. OX8 7UG
- 0993 779984

Shropshire & Walsall
- John Evans
- 19 Wells Road, Penn, Wolverhampton. WV4 4BQ
- 0902 340648

Solihull & Warwickshire
- Derek Baker
- 10 Clyde Road, Dorridge, Solihull, West Midlands. B93 8BD
- 0564 774375

Strathclyde
- David Millar
- 86 Eastwoodmains Road, Giffnock, Glasgow. G46 6PW
- 041-638 8601

Suffolk
- Roger James
- Theberton Grange, Suffolk. IP16 4PR
- 0728 830625

Surrey, SW London & N Hampshire
- Keith Ayres
- Pinelea Seymour Road, Headley Down, Hants. GU35 8JU
- 0428 714 573

Wiltshire & Somerset
- Alec Beck
- MDEC, Vallis House, Robins Lane, Frome, Somerset. BA11 1EG
- 0373 452000

Wolverhampton & Staffordshire
- Cherry Walton
- 63 Suckling Green Lane, Codsall, West Midlands. WV8 2BT
- 0902 842100

Yorkshire (North)
- Rosemary Ward
- 15 The Drive, Roundhay, Leeds, Yorks. LS8 1JF
- 0532 665036

Yorkshire (South)
- Pearl Shaw
- 22 Hope Street, Manor Road, Ossett. WF5 0LP
- 0924 262857

Yorkshire (West)
- John & Hilary Ball
- 2 The Beeches, Holden Lane, Baildon, Yorks. BD17 6HZ
- 0274 594879

United Nations Association
- Education Officer
- 3 Whitehall Court, London. SW1A 2EL
- 071-930 5893 **FAX** 071-930 5893

Objectives are to campaign for the implementation of the United Nations Charter in UK policy and to provide information to the wider public on the principles and activities of the UN.

N C SUPPORT **Yes.**

COSTS **Expenses.**

GEOGRAPHICAL AREAS SERVED
- Any

AGE OR KEY STAGE **KS4 Sixth Form**

SIZE OF GROUP **20–30 30+**

NOTICE REQUIRED **Two weeks.**

DURATION OF PRESENTATION **One hour plus.**

RESOURCES AVAILABLE
- Video
- Slides
- Displays
- Worksheets
- Publications

Universities

The following universities have schools' liaison officers who may be able to arrange a speaker.

Anglia Polytechnic University
- Student Recruitment Manager
- East Road, Cambridge. CB1 1PT
- 0223 63271

Aston University
- Coordinator Schools Liaison
- Aston Triangle, Birmingham. B4 7ET
- 021-359 3611 x4812

Bangor Normal College of Higher Education
- Admissions Officer
- Bangor, Gwynedd. LL57 2PX
- 0248 370171

Bath College of Higher Education
- Careers Adviser
- Newton Park, Bath. BA2 9BN
- 0225 873701

Bedford College of Higher Education
- Schools Liaison Officer
- Cauldwell Street, Bedford. MK42 9AH
- 0234 345151

Bishop Grosseteste College
- The College Registry
- Lincoln. LN1 3DY
- 0522 527734 x284

Bolton Institute of Higher Education
- Schools & Colleges Liaison Officer
- Deane Road, Bolton. BL3 5AB
- 0204 28851 x3817

Bournemouth University
- Schools Liaison Officer
- Fern Barrow, Poole, Dorset. BH12 5BB
- 0202 524111

Bradford & Ilkley Community College
- Admissions Tutor
- Great Horton Road, Bradford, West Yorkshire. BD7 1AY
- 0274 751610

Bretton Hall
- Admissions Co-ordinator
- West Bretton, Wakefield, West Yorkshire. WF4 4LG
- 0924 830261

Bristol: University of the West of England
- Admissions Officer
- Frenchay Campus, Coldharbour Lane, Frenchay, Bristol. BS16 1QY
- 0272 763809

Brunel University
- Head of Liaison Centre
- Education Liaison Centre, Uxbridge, Middlesex. UB8 3PH
- 0895 274000

VISITS IN UNIVERSITIES

Buckinghamshire College
- Marketing Department
- Queen Alexandra Road, High Wycombe, Bucks. HP11 1QU
- 0494 522141 x205

Canterbury Christ Church
- Admissions Officer
- Canterbury. CT1 1QU
- 0227 7822490

Cardiff Institute of Higher Education
- Schools & Colleges
- PO Box 377, Llandaff Centre, Western Avenue, Cardiff. CF5 2SG
- 0222 551111

Charing Cross & Westminster Medical School
- Admissions Officer
- The Reynolds Building, St Dunstans Road, London. W6 8RP
- 081-846 7202

Cheltenham & Gloucester College of Higher Education
- Gill Thatcher
- PO Box 220, The Park, Cheltenham, Gloucestershire. GL50 2QF
- 0242 532872

Chester College of Higher Education
- Marketing Officer
- Cheyney Road, Chester. CH1 4BJ
- 0244 375444 x2241

City University
- Senior Assistant Registrar
- Northampton Square, London. EC1V 0HB
- 071-447 8016

Colchester Institute
- Marketing Manager
- Sheepen Road, Colchester. CO3 3LL
- 0206 761660

College of St Mark & St John
- Public Relations
- Derriford Road, Plymouth. PL6 8BH
- 0752 777188

Courtauld Institute of Art
- Secretary to the Registrar
- Somerset House, The Strand, London. WC2R 0RN
- 071-873 2645

Coventry University
- Education Liaison Officer
- Priory Street, Coventry. CV1 5FB
- 0203 8368614

Cranfield Institute of Technology
- Faculty Information Officer
- Faculty of Military Science, Shrivenham, Swindon. SN6 8LA
- 0793 785434/5

Cranfield Institute of Technology
- Student Recruitment Executive
- Faculty of Agriculture & Engineering, Silsoe, Bedford. MK45 4DT
- 0525 860428

Crewe & Alsager College
- Admissions & Marketing Tutor
- Crewe, Cheshire. CW1 1DU
- 0270 500661 x2138

De Montfort University
- Director of Schools & College Liaison
- Leicester, The Gateway, Leicester. LE1 9BH
- 0533 577359

De Montfort University
- General Manager
- Milton Keynes, Hammerwood Gate, Kents Hill, Milton Keynes. MK7 6HP
- 0908 834905

VISITS IN UNIVERSITIES

Doncaster College
- Head of Client Services
- Waterdale, Doncaster. DN1 3EX
- 0302 322122

Edge Hill College of Higher Education
- Head of Admissions
- St Helen's Road, Ormskirk, Lancashire. L39 4QP

Glasgow Caledonian University
- Education Officer
- Cowcaddens, Glasgow, Strathclyde. G4 0BA
- 041-331 3332

Goldsmith's College
- Assistant Registrar
- New Cross, London. SE14 6NW
- 081-692 7171

Gwent College of Higher Education
- Director of Marketing
- College Crescent, Caerleon, Gwent. NP6 1XJ
- 0633 430088

Heriot-Watt University
- Education Liaison Officer
- James Watt Centre, Riccarton, Edinburgh. EH14 4AS
- 031-451 3450

Heythrop College
- Information Officer
- Kensington Square, London. W8 5HQ
- 071-580 6941

Homerton College
- Admissions Secretary
- Cambridge. CB2 2PH
- 0223 411141

Imperial College of Science Technology & Medicine
- Schools Liaison Officer
- South Kensington, London. SW7 2AZ
- 071-589 5111

Jordanhill Faculty of Education
- Registrar
- University of Strathclyde, Southbrae Drive, Glasgow. G13 1PP
- 041-950 3000

Keele University
- Schools Liaison Officer
- Keele, Staffordshire. ST5 5BG
- 0782 621111

King Alfred's College
- Admissions Officer
- Sparkford Road, Winchester, Hampshire. SO22 4NR
- 0962 841515

King's College London
- Schools & Colleges Liaison Officer
- Cornwall House Annex, Waterloo Road, London. SE1 8TX
- 071-872 3003

King's College School of Medicine and Dentistry
- Administrative Assistant
- Bessemer Road, London. SE5 9PJ
- 071-274 6222

Kingston University
- Recruitment Liaison Officer
- Penrhyn Road, Kingston upon Thames, Surrey. KT1 2EE
- 081-549 7410 x251

Lancaster University
- Schools Liaison Officer
- Lancaster. LA1 4YA
- 0524 593724

VISITS IN UNIVERSITIES

Leeds Metropolitan University
- Schools Liaison Officer
- Calverley Street, Leeds. LS1 3HE
- 0532 832600/3018

Liverpool Institute of Higher Education
- Schools Liaison Officer
- Woolton Road, Liverpool. L16 8ND

Liverpool John Moores University
- Schools Liaison Officer
- Rodney House, Liverpool. L3 5UX
- 051-231 4110

London Guildhall University
- Schools & Colleges Liaison Officer
- 31 Jewry Street, London. EC3N 2EY
- 071-320 3058

The London Hospital Medical School
- Admissions Officer
- Turner Street, London. E1 2AD
- 071-377 7000

London School of Economics and Political Science
- Information Officer
- Houghton Street, London. WC2A 2AE
- 071-955 7122

London University
- Information Officer
- Birkbeck College, Malet Street, London. WC1E 7HX
- 071-631 6581

Loughborough University of Technology
- Senior Assistant Registrar
- Loughborough, Leicestershire. LE11 3TU
- 0509 263171

LSU College of Higher Education
- Auriel Samuelsen
- The Avenue, Southampton. SO9 5HB
- 0703 228761

Luton College of Higher Education
- Schools Liaison Officer
- Park Square, Luton. LU1 3JU
- 0582 401401

Manchester Metropolitan University
- Educational Adviser
- All Saints, Manchester. M15 6BH
- 061-247 3492

The Medical College of St Bartholomew's Hospital
- Admissions Officer
- West Smithfield, London. EC1A 7BE
- 071-601 8834

Middlesex University
- Education Liaison Officer
- White Hart Lane, London. N17 8HR
- 081-362 5913

Moray House Institute of Education
- Assistant Principal
- Heriot-Watt University, Holyrood Campus, Holyrood Road, Edinburgh. EH8 8AQ
- 031-556 8455

Napier University
- Student Recruitment Officer
- 219 Colinton Road, Edinburgh. EH14 1DJ
- 031-455 4358

Nene College of Higher Education
- Geoffrey Middleton
- Moulton Park, Northampton. NN2 7AL
- 0604 791179

VISITS IN UNIVERSITIES

Newman & Westhill Colleges
- Schools Liaison Officers
- Birmingham. B32 3NT
- 021476 1181

North Cheshire College
- Information Officer
- Padgate Campus, Fearnhead Lane, Warrington. WA2 0DB
- 0925 814343

North East Wales Institute
- Admissions Office
- NEWI Plas Coch, Mold Road, Clwyd, Wrexham. LL11 2AW
- 0978 290666

North Riding College
- Senior Tutor
- University College Scarborough, Filey Road, Scarborough, North Yorkshire. YO11 3AZ
- 0732 362392

Norwich City College
- Education Liaison Officer
- Ipswich Road, Norwich. NR2 2LJ
- 0603 6600011 x277

Nottingham Trent University
- Schools Liaison Officer
- Burton Street, Nottingham. NG1 4BU
- 0602 486540

Oxford Brookes University
- Communications Officer
- Headington, Oxford. OX3 0BP
- 0865 819554

Queen Mary & Westfield College
- Schools Relations Officer
- Mile End Road, London. E1 4NS
- 071-975 5314

Queen's University Belfast
- Admissions Officer
- Belfast. BT7 1NN
- 0232 245133 x3079

The Robert Gordon University
- Schools Liaison Officer
- Schoolhill, Aberdeen. AB9 1FR
- 0224 633611

Roehampton Institute
- Schools Liaison Officer
- Roehampton Lane, London. SW15 5PU
- 081-392 3147

Royal Free Hospital Medical School
- Admissions Officer
- Rowland Hill Street, London. NW3 2PF
- 071-794 0500

Royal Holloway College
- Schools & International Liaison Officer
- Egham Hill, Egham, Surrey. TW20 0EX
- 0784 443025

Royal Veterinary College
- The Registrar
- Royal College Street, London. NW1 0TU
- 071-387 2898 x391

St David's University College
- Schools Liaison Officer
- Lampeter, Dyfed. SA48 7ED
- 0570 423751

St George's Hospital Medical School
- Admissions Officer
- Cranmer Terrace, Tooting, London. SW17 0RE
- 081-672 9944

St Martin's College
- Marketing Manager
- Lancaster. LA1 4JD
- 0542 63446 x320

VISITS IN UNIVERSITIES

St Mary's College of Higher Education
- School Liaison Officer
- Strawberry Hill, Twickenham. TW1 4SX
- 081 892 0051 x209

St Mary's Hospital Medical School
- Admissions Secretary
- Norfolk Place, Paddington, London. W2 1PG
- 071-723 1252

School of Oriental & African Studies
- Educational Liaison Officer
- Thornhaugh Street, Russell Square, London. WC1H 0XG
- 071-637 2388

The School of Pharmacy
- The Registrar
- 29–39 Brunswick Square, London. WC1N 1AX
- 071-753 5827

School of Slavonic & East European Studies
- Registry Assistant
- Malet Street, London. WC1E 7HU
- 071-637 4934

Sheffield Hallam University
- Education Liaison Co-ordinator
- Pond Street, Sheffield. S1 1WB
- 0742 532504

South Bank University
- Schools Liaison Officer
- 103 Borough Road, London. SE1 0AA
- 071-815 6717

Southampton Institute of Higher Education
- Schools Liaison Officer
- East Park Terrace, Southampton. SO9 4WW
- 0703 319380

Staffordshire University
- Educational Liaison Officer
- College Road, Stoke on Trent. ST4 2DE
- 091-515 2922

Swansea Institute of Higher Education
- Careers Adviser
- Mount Pleasant, Swansea. SO9 4WW
- 0792 469004 x2213

Thames Valley University
- Schools Liaison Officer
- Slough Campus, Wellington Street, Slough. SL1 1YG
- 0753 697614

Thames Valley University
- Schools Liaison Officer
- St Mary's Road, Ealing, London. W5 5RF
- 081-231 2267

Trinity and All Saints College
- Publicity & Recruitment
- Brownberrie Lane, Horsforth, Leeds. LS18 5HD
- 0532 584341

Trinity College
- The Registrar
- Carmarthen, Dyfed. SA31 3EP
- 0267 237971/2/3

United Medical & Dental Schools of Guy's & St Thomas's Hospitals
- Undergraduate Admissions Officer
- St Thomas's Campus, Lambeth Palace Road, London. SE1 7EH
- 071-992 8013

University College London
- Schools & Colleges Liaison Officer
- Gower Street, London. WC1E 6BT
- 071-380 7108

VISITS IN UNIVERSITIES

University College of North Wales
- Assistant Registrar
- Bangor, Gwynedd. LL57 2DG
- 0248 351151

University of Aberdeen
- Schools Liaison Officer
- University Office, Regent Walk, Aberdeen, Scotland. AB9 1FX
- 0224 272090/1

University of Bath
- Assistant Registrar
- Claverton Down, Bath. BA2 7AY
- 0225 826826

University of Birmingham
- Schools Recruitment & Schools Liaison
- Birmingham. B15 2TT
- 021-414 3344

University of Bradford
- Schools/Overseas Liaison Officer
- Richmond Road, Bradford. BD7 1DP
- 0274 383080/1/2

University of Brighton
- Education Liaison Officer
- Mithras House, Lewes Road, Brighton. BN2 4AT
- 0273 642603

University of Bristol
- Student Recruitment Officer
- Senate House, Bristol. BS8 1TH
- 0272 303030

University of Buckingham
- Schools Liaison Officer
- Buckingham. MK18 1EG
- 0280 814080

University of Cambridge
- Administrative Secretary CIAO
- Applications Office, Kellet Lodge, Tennis Court Road, Cambridge. CB2 1QJ
- 0223 333304

University of Central England in Birmingham
- Recruitment Officer
- Perry Barr, Birmingham. B42 2SU
- 021-331 6269

University of Central Lancashire
- The Admissions Secretary
- Preston. PR1 2HE
- 0772 201201

University of Derby
- Assistant Marketing Officer
- Kedleston Road, Derby. DE22 1GB
- 0332 47181

University of Dundee
- Schools Liaison Service
- Dundee. DD1 4HN
- 0382 23181 x4160

University of Durham
- Information Officer
- St Cuthbert's Society, 12 South Bailey, Durham City. DH1 3EE
- 091-374 3463

University of East Anglia
- Senior Administrative Assistant
- Norwich. NR4 7TJ
- 0603 56161 x2201

University of East London
- Head of Schools & Colleges Liaison Unit
- Longbridge Road, Dagenham, Essex
- 081-590 7722 x2049

University of Edinburgh
- Director Schools Liaison Service
- Old College, South Bridge, Edinburgh. EH8 9YL
- 031-650 4360

University of Essex
- Schools Liaison Officer
- Wivenhoe Park, Colchester. CO4 3SQ
- 0206 872991/2002

VISITS IN UNIVERSITIES

University of Exeter
- Schools Liaison Officer
- Exeter, Devon. EX4 4QJ
- 0392 263035

University of Glamorgan
- Head of External Relations
- Llanwit Road, Treforest, Pontypridd, Mid Glamorgan. CF37 1DL
- 0443 482484

University of Glasgow
- Director Schools & Colleges Liaison Service
- Glasgow. G12 8QQ
- 041-339 8855 x4263

University of Greenwich
- Schools & Colleges Liaison Officer
- Wellington Street, Woolwich, London. SE18 6PF
- 081-316 8140/8000

University of Hertfordshire
- UK Development Manager
- College Lane, Hatfield, Herts. AL10 9AB
- 0707 284458

University of Huddersfield
- Information & Liaison Officer
- Queensgate, Huddersfield. HD1 3DH
- 0484 422288/2282

University of Hull
- Schools Liaison Officer
- Hull. HU6 7RX
- 0482 440550

University of Humberside
- Education Liaison
- Cottingham Road, Hull. HU6 7RT
- 0482 440550

University of Kent at Canterbury
- Head of Undergraduate Recruitment Services
- Canterbury, Kent. CT2 7NZ
- 0227 764000

University of Lancaster
- Information Officer
- Faculty of Teacher Education & Training, Ambleside, Cumbria. LA22 9BB
- 05394 33066

University of Leeds
- Schools Liaison Officer
- Leeds. LS2 9JT
- 0532 333995

University of Leicester
- Assistant Registrar
- University Road, Leicester. LE1 7RH
- 0533 522674

University of Liverpool
- Clerical Officer
- PO Box 147, Liverpool. L69 3BX
- 051-794 3212

University of London
- Public Relations Officer
- Senate House, Malet Street, London. WC1E 7HU
- 071-636 8000

University of Manchester
- Schools Liaison Officer
- Oxford Road, Manchester. M13 9PL
- 061-275 2056

University of Manchester
- Executive Officer
- Institute of Science and Technology, PO Box 88, Manchester. M60 1QD
- 061-200 4022/4023

VISITS IN UNIVERSITIES

University of Newcastle upon Tyne
- Assistant Registrar
- 6 Kensington Terrace, Newcastle upon Tyne. NE1 7RU
- 091-222 6121

University of North London
- Marketing & Communications Officer
- 166–220 Holloway Road, London. N7 8DB
- 071-607 2789

University of Northumbria
- Education Liaison Officer
- Ellison Building, Ellison Place, Newcastle upon Tyne. NE1 8ST
- 091-235 8265

University of Nottingham
- Schools Liaison Officer
- University Park, Nottingham. NG7 2RD
- 0602 486540

University of Oxford
- Secretary Oxford College Admissions Office
- Wellington Square, Oxford. OX1 2JD
- 0865 270207

University of Paisley
- Public Relations Officer
- High Street, Paisley. PA1 2BE
- 041-848 3334

University of Plymouth
- Schools Liaison Officer
- Drake Circus, Plymouth. PL4 2UP
- 0752 233985

University of Portsmouth
- Information Officer
- University House, Winston Churchill Avenue, Portsmouth. PO1 2UP
- 0705 843435

University of Reading
- Director of Schools & College Liaison
- Whiteknights, Reading. RG6 2AH
- 0734 318619

University of Salford
- Schools Liaison Officer
- Salford, Greater Manchester. M5 4WT
- 061-745 5976

University of Southampton
- Administrative Assistant
- Highfield, Southampton. SO9 5NH
- 0703 593726

University of St Andrews
- Director Schools Liaison Service
- Old Union Building, North Street, St Andrews, Fife. KY16 9AJ
- 0334 76161 x473

University of Stirling
- Director Schools & Colleges Liaison Service
- Stirling. FK9 4LA
- 0786 67046

University of Strathclyde
- Head Schools & Colleges Liaison Service
- Glasgow. G1 1XQ
- 041-552 4400 x2391

University of Sunderland
- Careers Adviser
- Chester Road, Sunderland, Tyne and Wear. SR2 7EE
- 091-515 2922

University of Surrey
- Schools Liaison Officer
- Guildford, Surrey. GU2 5XH
- 0483 509192

University of Sussex
- Assistant Registrar
- Sussex House, Falmer, Brighton, Sussex. BN1 9RH
- 0273 678416

VISITS IN URBAN WILDLIFE TRUST

University of Teesside
- Schools & Colleges Liaison Officer
- Middlesbrough, Cleveland. TS1 3BA
- 0642 342275

University of Ulster
- Admissions Officer
- Coleraine, Co Londonderry. BT52 1SA
- 0265 44141 x4562

University of Wales
- Schools Liaison Officer
- PO Box 2, Aberystwyth, Dyfed. SY23 2AX
- 0970 622065

University of Wales Cardiff
- Schools Liaison Officer
- Cathays Park, PO Box 921, Cardiff. CF1 3XQ
- 0222 874455

University of Wales College of Medicine
- Deputy Secretary
- Heath Park, Cardiff. CF4 4XN
- 0222 742027

University of Wales Swansea
- Schools Liaison Officer
- Singleton Park, Swansea. SA2 8PP
- 0792 205784

University of Warwick
- Schools Liaison Officer
- Coventry. CV4 7AL
- 0203 523648

University of Westminster
- Schools & Colleges Liaison Officer
- Corporate Communications Office, 309 Regents Street, London. W1R 8AL
- 071-911 5000 x2016

University of Wolverhampton
- Schools Liaison Officer
- Molineux Street, Wolverhampton. WW1 1SB
- 0902 432674

University of York
- Senior Admissions Tutor
- Heslington, York. YO1 5DD
- 0904 432674

West London Institute
- Schools Liaison Officer
- Borough Road, Isleworth, Middlesex. TW7 5DU
- 081-891 0121

West Sussex Institute of Higher Education
- Marketing Officer
- The Dome, Upper Bognor Road, Bognor Regis, West Sussex. PO21 1HR
- 0243 865581 x306

Westminster College
- Publicity Officer
- Oxford. OX2 9AT
- 0865 247644

Worcester College Of Higher Education
- Dr M A Richards
- Henwick Grove, Worcester. WR2 6AJ
- 0905 748080

Wye College
- The Registrar
- Ashford, Kent. TN25 5AH
- 0233 812401x490

Urban Wildlife Trust
- Peter Shirley
- Unit 213, Jubilee Trades Centre, 130 Pershore Street, Birmingham. B5 6ND
- 021-666 7474 FAX 021-622 4443

West Midlands group which campaigns to protect and improve sites of wildlife value; also promotes ideas combining nature and recreation. Carries out practical landscaping projects and monitors planning applications.

COSTS Fees and expenses by negotiation.

GEOGRAPHICAL AREAS SERVED
- Midlands

AGE OR KEY STAGE KS1 KS2 KS3 KS4 Sixth Form

SIZE OF GROUP 1–10 10–20 20–30 30+

RESOURCES AVAILABLE
- Publications

The Vegetarian Society
☞ Glynne Steele
✉ Parkdale, Dunham Road, Altrincham, Cheshire. WA14 4QG
☎ 061-928 0793 FAX 061-926 9182

The Vegetarian Society of the UK campaigns to increase the number of vegetarians through education relating to human health, the environment and animal cruelty. National network of school speakers available.

N C SUPPORT Various leaflets and publications.

COSTS Expenses.

GEOGRAPHICAL AREAS SERVED
- Any

AGE OR KEY STAGE KS1 KS2 KS3 KS4 Sixth Form

SIZE OF GROUP 1–10 10–20 20–30 30+

NOTICE REQUIRED By arrangement.

DURATION OF PRESENTATION One hour.

RESOURCES AVAILABLE
- Video
- Publications
- Worksheets
- Teacher's Notes

Voluntary Euthanasia Society
☞ John Oliver
✉ 13 Prince of Wales Terrace, London. W8 5PG
☎ 071-937 7770

Aims to achieve a change in the law so that an adult person suffering from a severe illness for which no relief is known is able to receive an immediate painless death, if that is his or her expressed wish.

GEOGRAPHICAL AREAS SERVED
- London
- S.W. England
- Midlands
- N.W. England
- Wales
- S.E. England
- East Anglia
- N.E. England
- Scotland

AGE OR KEY STAGE KS3 KS4 Sixth Form

RESOURCES AVAILABLE
- Publications

Voluntary Service Overseas
☞ Publicity Officer
✉ 317 Putney Bridge Road, London. SW15 2PG
☎ 081-780 2266 FAX 081-780 1326

Aims to help Third World development by providing volunteers with the skills to make a practical contribution. Volunteers are at least 20 years old and are sent abroad in response to requests from developing countries.

COSTS Expenses.

VISITS IN WATERAID

GEOGRAPHICAL AREAS SERVED
- London
- Any

AGE OR KEY STAGE Sixth Form

NOTICE REQUIRED Three to four weeks.

DURATION OF PRESENTATION One hour plus.

RESOURCES AVAILABLE
- Publications

Volunteer Missionary Movement
☛ Madeline Hair
✉ Comboni House, London Road, Sunningdale, Ascot, Berks. SL5 0JX
☎ 0344 875380 FAX 0344 875280

An international Catholic Church movement which works in projects linked with local churches overseas. Involved in schools, hospitals, rural health centres, technical institutions and community development programmes. VMM enables Christian men and women to share their lives and skills in Africa.

N C SUPPORT Yes.

COSTS Donations appreciated.

GEOGRAPHICAL AREAS SERVED
- London
- S.E. England
- S.W. England
- East Anglia
- Midlands
- N.E. England
- N.W. England
- Scotland
- Wales

AGE OR KEY STAGE Sixth Form

NOTICE REQUIRED Two to three months.

DURATION OF PRESENTATION One period.

RESOURCES AVAILABLE
- Video
- Slides
- Publications
- Displays
- Other

War on Want
☛ Caroline Winchurch
✉ 37–39 Great Guildford Street, London. SE1 0ES
☎ 071-620 1111

Campaigns against world poverty and seeks to identify and eliminate the causes of poverty.

COSTS Expenses welcome.

GEOGRAPHICAL AREAS SERVED
- London
- S.E. England
- Midlands

AGE OR KEY STAGE KS3 KS4 Sixth Form

SIZE OF GROUP 1–10 10–20 20–30 30+

NOTICE REQUIRED One month.

DURATION OF PRESENTATION Tailor-made presentation for school. By arrangement.

RESOURCES AVAILABLE
- Video

WaterAid
☛ Schools Information Officer
✉ 1 Queen Anne's Gate, London. SW1H 9BT
☎ 071-233 4800 FAX 071-233 3161

A Third World charity specialising in the provision of clean, safe water and sanitation to the poorest communities in Africa and Asia.

COSTS Expenses.

GEOGRAPHICAL AREAS SERVED
- London

AGE OR KEY STAGE KS3 KS4 Sixth Form

DURATION OF PRESENTATION Forty minutes.

Wellbeing

- 🕮 Vivienne Parry
- ✉ 27 Sussex Place, Regent's Park, London. NW1 4SP
- ☎ 071-262 5337 **FAX** 071-724 7725

Medical research charity funding work nationwide for the better health of women and their babies.

N C SUPPORT Pregnancy/birth-related topics for Child Development.

COSTS No fee, but a donation appreciated.

GEOGRAPHICAL AREAS SERVED
- London
- S.E. England
- East Anglia

AGE OR KEY STAGE KS4 Sixth Form

SIZE OF GROUP 1–10 10–20 20–30 30+

NOTICE REQUIRED One month.

RESOURCES AVAILABLE
- Other

West Midlands Police

- 🕮 Sergeant Tony Ayers
- ✉ Community Services Department, Lloyd House, Colmore Circus Queensway, PO Box 52, Birmingham. B4 6NQ
- ☎ 021-626 5351

West Midlands Police Officers working with schools with the aim of promoting good citizenship, informing about the law/rights and responsibilities, making young people aware of dangers and encouraging crime prevention.

N C SUPPORT Volumes of educational resources supported by a network of trained School Liaison Officers. Citizenship/PSE/English and other areas covered.

COSTS Most of the services are free of charge. Resources are free to West Midlands schools in first instance, with further copies available on non-profit basis.

GEOGRAPHICAL AREAS SERVED
- Midlands

AGE OR KEY STAGE KS1 KS2 KS3 KS4 Sixth Form

SIZE OF GROUP 1–10 10–20 20–30 30+

NOTICE REQUIRED By arrangement.

RESOURCES AVAILABLE
- Video
- Slides
- Worksheets
- Publications
- Displays
- Teacher's Notes

Western Health & Social Services Board

- 🕮 Health Promotion Department
- ✉ Beech Villa, Gransha Hospital, Clooney Road, Londonderry. BT47 1TF
- ☎ 0504 860261

The Health Promotion Department organises speakers to visit schools to discuss good health practices.

GEOGRAPHICAL AREAS SERVED
- Northern Ireland

AGE OR KEY STAGE KS4 Sixth Form

VISITS IN
WOMEN INTO INFORMATION TECHNOLOGY (WIT)

Whizz-Kidz
The movement for non-mobile children

Why not get on the move for Whizz-Kidz and help change disabled childrens lives. Did you know that thousands of children in the UK rely almost all the time upon their parents, children in wheelchairs have to wait until someone is ready to push them.

By helping Whizz-Kids you will be helping to pay for a special powered or lightweight wheelchair so that non-mobile children can get around under their own steam. We'll let you know exactly who'll get the chair, why its needed and, hopefully arrange for you to meet. You'll realise then just what a difference a new pair of wheels can make.

Help us to keep kidz whizzing.

(P.S. Thank you for sending me the tricical. I can play in the playground with my frens and go to the common when we have our Natcher lesson. It is fun. Love Imogden Aged 10).

Tel: 071-233 6600
Reg Charity No: 802872

Whizz-Kidz
- Alicia Crossley
- 215 Vauxhall Bridge Road, London. SW1V 1EN
- 071-233 6600 FAX 071-233 6611

A national children's charity which aims to improve the quality of life and mobility of disabled children by providing adapted lightweight powered and sports wheelchairs.

COSTS For train journeys to Scotland and other long distances expenses are appreciated. Talks are free.

GEOGRAPHICAL AREAS SERVED
- London
- S.E. England

AGE OR KEY STAGE KS1 KS2 KS3 KS4 Sixth Form

NOTICE REQUIRED One month.

RESOURCES AVAILABLE
- Slides
- Other

Women into Information Technology (WIT)
- Ellen Neighbour
- Campaign Office, Concept 2000, 250 Farnborough Road, Farnborough, Hants. GU14 7LU
- 0252 528329 FAX 0252 528178

A consortium of IT manufacturers and users, supported by the Department of Trade and Industry, WIT campaigns to raise the proportion of women and girls in IT-related careers.

N C SUPPORT National Curriculum links with Intermediate Technology.

COSTS Expenses may be charged depending on location.

GEOGRAPHICAL AREAS SERVED
- London
- S.E. England
- S.W. England
- East Anglia
- Midlands
- N.E. England
- N.W. England
- Scotland
- Wales

AGE OR KEY STAGE KS1 KS2 KS3 KS4 Sixth Form

SIZE OF GROUP 1–10 10–20 20–30 30+

NOTICE REQUIRED As much as possible, but would do our best to accommodate.

DURATION OF PRESENTATION Varies.

RESOURCES AVAILABLE
- Publications
- Slides
- Worksheets
- Teacher's Notes

VISITS IN
YOUNG EXPLORERS TRUST

Young Explorers Trust
- Ted Grey, Company Secretary
- Stretton Cottage, Wellow Road, Ollerton, Newark. NG22 9AX
- 0623 861027

Aims to promote safe expeditioning for young people.

COSTS Expenses.

GEOGRAPHICAL AREAS SERVED
- London
- S.E. England
- S.W. England
- East Anglia
- Midlands
- N.E. England
- N.W. England
- Scotland
- Wales
- Northern Ireland

AGE OR KEY STAGE KS3 KS4 Sixth Form

SIZE OF GROUP 1–10 10–20 20–30 30+

NOTICE REQUIRED Four weeks.

DURATION OF PRESENTATION By arrangement.

RESOURCES AVAILABLE
- Video
- Slides
- Publications
- Displays

understand the need for sound, sensible conservation.

N C SUPPORT Fact sheet information, environmental discovery courses and lectures designed with National Curriculum requirements in mind.

COSTS School lectures (at the moment restricted to Home Counties) no fee. Postal information also free (SAE requested). Environmental Discovery course: fees available on request.

GEOGRAPHICAL AREAS SERVED
- London
- S.E. England

AGE OR KEY STAGE KS1 KS2 KS3 KS4 Sixth Form

SIZE OF GROUP 1–10 10–20 20–30 30+ (Maximum of forty for Educational Discovery courses.)

NOTICE REQUIRED Varies but several weeks preferable.

DURATION OF PRESENTATION One period plus.

RESOURCES AVAILABLE
- Publications
- Video
- Slides
- Worksheets
- Other

Young People's Trust for Environment & Nature Conservation
- Miss Sally Webster
- 8 Leapale Road, Guildford, Surrey. GU1 4JX
- 0483 39600 FAX 0483 301992

A charity dedicated to the education of young people in all matters relating to the world's natural resources and to helping them

Zewell Visitors Centre, Sizewell Power Station
- Mrs Sally Caton
- Nuclear Power plc, Nr Leiston, Suffolk. IP16 4UR
- 0728 642139 FAX 0728 642146

Public information centre looking at all areas of nuclear power and associated subjects. The environment is a big part of this with

VISITS IN
ZEWELL VISITORS CENTRE

one field study classroom, wildlife, beach and woodland area. Send speakers to talk about careers in the Nuclear industry.

GEOGRAPHICAL AREAS SERVED
- S.E. England

AGE OR KEY STAGE **KS3 KS4 Sixth Form**

SIZE OF GROUP **30+**

NOTICE REQUIRED **Four to five weeks.**

RESOURCES AVAILABLE
- Worksheets
- Publications
- Teacher's Notes

THE RESOURCEFUL TEACHER'S HANDBOOK

SUBJECT INDEX

Animals
(*See also* ENVIRONMENT & CONSERVATION)
Animal Abuse, Injustice & Defence Society	18
Blue Cross	23
Care for the Wild	33
Compassion in World Farming	39
Guide Dogs for the Blind	56
Hearing Dogs for the Deaf	58
League Against Cruel Sports	63
Mammal Society	66
National Anti-Vivisection Society	70
National Federation of City Farms	72
Pro-Dogs National Charity	76
Rare Breeds Survival Trust	77
Royal Society for the Protection of Birds	80
RSPCA	80

Art & Architecture & Antiques
Ancient Monuments Society	17
Antiques Roadshow for Schools	18
Building Experiences Trust	30
The Design Council	44
Georgian Group	55
Historic Churches Preservation Trust	58
National Society for Education in Art and Design	72
The Roman Society	78
Royal Institute of British Architects	79
Society for the Promotion of Hellenic Studies	85

Art Galleries & Museums
British Museum	26
The Design Council	44
Gallery Scene for Children	55
Museum of Mankind	69
Museum of the Moving Image	69
Royal Institute of British Architects	79

Business & Industry
Banking Information Service	21
Industrial Society	60
Lloyd's of London	65
London Stock Exchange	65
Prince's Youth Business Trust	76
ProShare Education	77
Understanding Industry	94

Children & Young People
Barnardo's	21
The Children's Society	35
Contact a Family	40
Family Educational Trust	52
Kidscape	62

VISITS IN SUBJECT INDEX

Making Choices Project	67
National Society for the Prevention of Cruelty to Children	73
New Assembly of Churches	73
Rainer Foundation	77
The Salvation Army	81
Save the Children Education Unit	82
SOS Children's Villages UK	86
UNICEF (UK)	93
Whizz-Kidz	111

Classic Civilisations

The Roman Society	78
Society for the Promotion of Hellenic Studies	85

Community Education

Community Education Development Centre	38

Development Education

Development Education Association	45

English

Chaucer Heritage Trust	35
Common Lore	37
Dickens Fellowship	48
The Federation of Worker Writers and Community Publishers	53
School Play Productions Ltd	82
Making Choices Project	66
The Federation of Worker Writers and Community Publishers	53

Environment & Conservation

Ark Trust	19
British Naturalists' Association	27
British Trust for Conservation Volunteers	29
Cathedral Camps	34
Centre for Alternative Technology	34
Cleanair	37
Commonwealth Human Ecology Council	38
Conservation Trust	40
Council for British Archaeology	41
Council for National Parks	41
The Environment Council	51
Environmental Investigation Organisation	52
Farming and Wildlife Advisory Group	52
Friends of the Earth	54
Green Alliance	56
Greenpeace	56
Intermediate Technology Development Group	61
Living Earth International Ltd	64
London Wildlife Trust	66
Marine Conservation Society	67
National Association for Environmental Education	71
National Federation of City Farms	72
Society for Underwater Technology	86
Soil Association	86
Survival International	88
The Tree Council	91
UNAIS	92
Urban Wildlife Trust	107
Young People's Trust for the Environment & Nature Conservation	112

Equal Opportunities

Age Concern	16
Commission for Racial Equality	37
The Fawcett Society	53
Help the Aged	58
Institute of Race Relations	61
Movement for the Ordination of Women	69
Shape London	84
The Shape Network	84
The 300 Group	91
Women into Information Technology	111

Fire, Police, Rescue & Safety

London Fire Brigade	65
Metropolitan Police Service	67
Royal National Lifeboat Institution	79
Royal Society for the Prevention of Accidents	80
The Suzy Lamplugh Trust	62
National Campaign for Fireworks Reform	71
Thames Valley Police	90

VISITS IN
SUBJECT INDEX

Tyne & Wear Metropolitan Fire
  Brigade 92
West Midlands Police 110

Health & Medical
Action on Smoking & Health 15
Alcohol Concern 16
Alcoholics Anonymous 17
Aspirin Foundation 20
AVERT 21
Birth Control Trust 22
Blackliners 22
The Blenheim Project 22
Body Positive North East 23
British Pregnancy Advisory Service 28
British Red Cross 28
Brook Advisory Centre 29
Cambridge AIDS Helpline 31
Campaign for Research into Human
  Reproduction 32
Cancer & Leukaemia in Childhood Trust
  UK 33
Cancer Research Campaign 33
Cruse Bereavement Care 43
Marie Curie Memorial Foundation 43
Down's Syndrome Association 49
Eastern Health & Social Services
  Board 49
Eating Disorders Association 49
Guide Dogs for the Blind 56
Health Education Authority 57
Health Education Board for Scotland 57
Health Unlimited 57
Hearing Dogs for the Deaf 58
Imperial Cancer Research Fund 59
Institute for the Study of Drug
  Dependence 60
Leicestershire AIDS Support Services 63
LIFE 64
MENCAP 67
MIND 68
National Abortion Campaign 69
National AIDS Helpline 70
National AIDS Trust 70
The Northern Ireland Chest, Heart &
  Stroke Association 74
Northern Ireland Health and Social
  Services Board 74
The Portman Group 75
Research Into Ageing 78
Aled Richards Trust 78
Royal Society for Prevention of
  Accidents 80
St John Ambulance 81
Samaritan Youth Projects (N. London) 81
Samaritan Youth Projects (S. London) 82
The Samaritans 82
Scottish Association of Health
  Councils 83
Sex Education Forum 84
Shape London 84
The Shape Network 89
Society for the Protection of Unborn
  Children 86
Southern Health & Social Services
  Board 87
Sussex AIDS Centre 88
Talking Point in the Biological
  Sciences 89
Teen Challenge UK 90
Terrence Higgins Trust 90
Turning Point 91
UK Band of Hope 92
The Ulster Cancer Foundation 92
Understanding Disabilities Education
  Trust 93
The Vegetarian Society 108
Voluntary Euthanasia Society 108
Wellbeing 110
Western Health & Social Services
  Board 110

Housing & Poverty
Advocacy Project 15
Church Action on Poverty 37
Rainer Foundation 77
Salvation Army 81
Shelter 85
SOS Children's Villages UK 86
War on Want 109

History
Chaucer Heritage Trust 35

SUBJECT INDEX

Nonsuch (History & Dance)	73
Tailormade Tour of London	89

Human Rights

Amnesty International	17
Anti-Apartheid Movement	18
Anti-Slavery International	18
Article 19	19
ATD Fourth World	20
British Defence & Aid Fund for Southern Africa	25
British Red Cross	28
British Refugee Council	28
Campaign Against the Arms Trade	31
Catholic Institute for International Relations	34
Central America Human Rights Committee	34
Institute of Race Relations	61
Liberty	64
Survival International	88
The Tibet Society	91

International

Austrian Institute	20
British Atlantic Committee	24
British Southern Slav Society	29
Commonwealth Institute	38
Council for the Advancement of Arab-British Understanding	42
Council of Christians and Jews	42
Embassy of Israel	50
Embassy of the Czech Republic	50
The European Movement	52
Federal Trust	53
The French Embassy	54
Friends of Israel Education Trust	54
Goethe Institute	55
High Commission for Pakistan	58
Japanese Embassy	61
Kenya High Commission	61
Mexican Embassy	68
Portuguese Embassy	75
Royal Danish Embassy	79
Royal Netherlands Embassy	79
Society for Co-operation in Russian & Soviet Studies	85
Society for the Promotion of Hellenic Studies	85
Spanish Embassy Education Office	87
The Tibet Society	91
United Nations Association	97

Law & Justice

African, Caribbean & Asian Lawyers' Group	16
British Defence & Aid Fund for Southern Africa	25
Howard League for Penal Reform	59
Law Centres Federation	63
Liberty	64
New Assembly of Churches	73
Prison Reform Trust	76
Rainer Foundation	77

Media

Campaign against Censorship	31
Campaign for Freedom of Information	31
Campaign for Press & Broadcasting Freedom	31

Outdoor & Leisure

Army Cadet Force Association	19
Boys' Brigade	23
British Mountaineering Council	26
Crusaders	42
Cyclists' Touring Club	43
The Duke of Edinburgh Award	49
National Caving Association	72
Outward Bound Trust	74
Young Explorers Trust	112

Performing Arts

English Folk Dance & Song Society	51
Nonsuch (History & Dance)	73
The Young National Trust Theatre	112

Politics

Campaign Against Censorship	31
Campaign Against the Arms Trade	31
Campaign for Freedom of Information	32
Campaign for Nuclear Disarmament	32
Charter 88	35
Conscience Peace Tax Campaign	40
The Conservative Party	40

SUBJECT INDEX

Democratic Left 44
Electoral Reform Society of Great Britain
   and Ireland 50
Green Alliance 56
The Green Party 56
The Labour Party 62
Social & Liberal Democratic Party 85
300 Group 91
United Nations Association 97

Religion & Ethics
British Humanist Association 26
Christian Impact 37
Council of Christians and Jews 42
Crusaders 42
Lokabandhu 65
National Secular Society 72
New Assembly of Churches 73
Rationalist Press Association 78
The Salvation Army 81
South Place Ethical Society 87

Science & Technology
BAYS 22
British Association for the Advancement
   of Science 24
British Astronomical Association 24
British Computer Society 25
British Geological Survey 25
British Nuclear Forum 27
British Nuclear Fuels 27
Educational Computer Centre 50
The Engineering Council 51
Institute of Data Processing
   Management 60
Institute of Physics 60
Schoolworks 83
Scottish Nuclear Ltd 83
Society for Underwater Technology 86
Soil Association 86
South East Pharmaceutical Industry
   Group 87
Talking Point in the Biological
   Sciences 89
Talking Science Plus 89
Women into Information Technology 111

Third World Development
Action Aid 15
Afghan Aid 15
Appropriate Health Resources &
   Technologies Action Group 19
ATD Fourth World 20
CAFOD (Catholic Fund for Overseas
   Development) 30
Catholic Institute for International
   Relations 34
Christian Aid 36
Cooperation for Development 41
Health Unlimited 57
Help the Aged 58
Hunger Project Trust 59
Intermediate Technology Development
   Group 61
Oxfam 74
Population Concern 75
Save the Children Education Unit 82
SOS Children's Villages UK 86
Third World First 90
UNAIS 92
War on Want 109
Water Aid 109

Universities
Universities – schools liaison officers 98

Voluntary Work
Community Service Volunteers 39
National Association of Volunteer
   Bureaux 71
Project Trust 77
St John Ambulance 81
Student Community Action Development
   Unit 88
Voluntary Service Overseas 108
Volunteer Missionary Movement 109

PART TWO

VISITS OUT

Planning and organising a school visit out	**121**
A look at major providers	**126**
Who pays for trips: the legal position	**131**
Transport	135
Accidents and Insurance	139
Organisations by area	
England	**146**
London and the South East	146
East Anglia	268
Midlands	295
North East	333
North West	396
South West	434
Northern Ireland	**473**
Scotland	**491**
Wales	**526**

VISITS OUT

PLANNING AND ORGANISING A SCHOOL VISIT OUT

Clearly the main wish of a teacher taking out a school party is that the visit should be successful both in terms of the organisation and in the educational value of the visit. This chapter looks at ways to ensure a trip's success and a teacher's legal, financial and health and safety responsibilities. It also looks at the recommendations made by teachers' unions and educational authorities.

THE TEACHER'S LEGAL RESPONSIBILITY: IN LOCO PARENTIS

The common law doctrine of 'in loco parentis' applies to teachers taking visits out. This means that teachers are expected to act towards their pupils as caring parents would towards their child, bearing in mind that it is very different looking after 20 pupils than looking after a family.

LEADERSHIP OF THE PARTY

One teacher must be identified as leader of the party and this named person must be clear to all those involved. On some trips a headteacher may participate but not be the person responsible: this must be made clear to everyone on the trip! The NUT recommend that for larger and longer trips there should be a deputy leader and this too should be known to all concerned.

PLANNING THE VISIT

A large number of places that can be visited grant free pre-visits for teachers, and some schools and LEAs make financial provision for these. Alternatively the costs of a pre-visit can be borne in the total costs for the actual visit.

A pre-visit is very useful in establishing whether or not it is worth using the official guide. Today many places to visit have highly trained education officers, a majority of whom are ex-teachers, and if this is so it might well be best to hand over the teaching to them. In addition to visiting the place a teacher will also be able to plan the route, timing, facilities, and transport arrangements.

SCHOOL AND LEA POLICIES AND GUIDELINES FOR SCHOOL VISITS

Schools and LEAs have guidelines covering the following which clearly need to be adhered to and will probably include:
- Consultation procedures.
- Codes of conduct: supervision levels, health and safety and discipline.
- Guidelines for criteria for what qualifies as a school visit.
- Planning procedures.
- Financial and insurance requirements.
- Aims and objectives of the visit and how these are to be met, including preparation for the visit, educational value of the visit, and follow up and evaluation.

CONSULTATION

Parents, Head Teachers, other relevant teachers such as Heads of Year, Heads of House, Form teachers may have to be consulted according to the school's policy. Governors are responsible for the approval and monitoring of school visits which involve an overnight stay.

It is not strictly necessary to have parents/guardians consent for visits that are in school hours and are just to the local museum or library. For longer school trips it is essential to have written consent from them and to give them details about the trip and it is also important to know whether their child has any dietary or religious requirements and medical needs and, if

VISITS OUT

necessary, for them to give teachers the authorisation to administer medicine. It may be necessary to ask parents for an address and telephone number for emergency contact.
The essential information for school trips is:
- The name and address of the place(s) to be visited.
- The name of the teacher in charge, the staff contact at school, and contact number for evenings and weekends, if this is necessary.
- The time and place of departure and return, and arrangements for collecting and leaving the pupils.
- Methods of travel.
- Details of activities and arrangements for supervision.
- Make-up of the party (age range and sex) and whether there are children with special needs or health problems
- Financial arrangements which should include details of deposit, payment, recommended pocket money and details of a breakdown of costs.
- Insurance – what is and what is not included.
- Clothing.

SUPERVISION AND RECOMMENDED LEVELS OF SUPERVISION

There is no legislation concerning supervision and supervision levels, but schools, local education authorities and unions have recommended levels. Clearly the age, distance and length of travel, responsibility, experience and capability of the pupils and accompanying adults and the activity will determine the supervision levels. The Association of Teachers and Lecturers recommends there should be two adults accompanying any group of up to 20 students and for groups of over 20 there should be one adult for every 10 students. For mixed groups of any size there should be one male and one female teacher. For younger pupils higher levels of supervision are frequently recommended. In one LEA the following minimum levels are required for junior pupils:
- Two teachers and one responsible adult or further teacher for up to 30 pupils.

VISITS OUT

- Three teachers and one responsible adult or further teacher for 31–50 pupils.
- For each additional 10 one teacher and one further responsible adult.
- For infants a ratio of 1:4 adult to child is the minimum level.

USING NON-TEACHERS FOR SUPERVISION

A number of local authorities make recommendations about the use of adults other than teachers and they usually recommend that they should:

- Take part in the planning and be well informed about the arrangements for the visit.
- Be aware of the discipline and conduct expected by the leader of the visit.
- Be acceptable to the organiser and/or head or deputy head.
- Be willing to take responsibility for the safety and discipline of pupils.

Leaders of the visit should be aware of the regulations about notifying the authorities of the names of any non-employees they are taking on a visit for insurance purposes. It is mandatory for any person who has 'substantial access' to children to disclose any criminal background and it may be necessary to ask for this or even to do a police check. DES Circular 4/86 explains the legal position.

ORGANISING THE FINANCES

Costing a visit This is clearly one of the first things to be done particularly in view of the Charging for School Activities regulations. Details of these regulations are covered in the section Who Pays for Trips (see page 131). The obvious fixed costs will be admission charges, transport, meals and insurance. Further allowance should be made to cover the preliminary planning, administration costs, telephone and postage and a 10% contingency cost. Teachers should not forget VAT! This may be reclaimable via the LEAs' arrangement with the Inland Revenue.

VISITS OUT

Raising money If a teacher wishes to take a school trip and money is the prohibitive factor then a number of avenues can be pursued:
- Many local authorities will make provision for pupils in need.
- *The Educational Grants Directory* published by The Directory of Social Change gives details of educational grants.
- The Directory of Social Change and the Charity Aid Foundation have other publications with details of grants made by charities.
- The local Round Table or Rotary Club may help and some local Chambers of Commerce will give advice on companies to approach.
- The School Journey Association can supply members with funds for needy pupils.
- Teachers and Parent Teacher Associations sometimes fundraise for their own trips, by running fairs, sales, sponsored events, discos etc.

Responsibility for the money If a teacher agrees to collect the money they are responsible for it while it is in their possession, and will have to make good the amount if it is lost, or stolen, or unaccounted for. Professional associations and unions may insure members against cash losses on school premises as LEAs are reluctant to pay for these.

Keeping accounts Schools normally have a special account for school visits and instructions for keeping records and receipts. The teacher and the pupil must keep a record of every transaction. Final accounts need to be prepared at the end of the trip.

FINAL DETAILS BEFORE SETTING OFF

Teachers should make sure that they bring the following with them:
- A full list of party members, with their home addresses and phone numbers.

VISITS OUT

- A copy of the letters confirming essential arrangements.
- Consent forms for medical authorisations.
- Insurance details and claims forms.
- Details of the itinerary.
- First-aid kit.

FURTHER INFORMATION FROM:

Out of School published by The Association of Teachers and Lecturers, 7 Northumberland Street, London WC2N 5DA Tel: 071-930 6441 (cost: £1 to non-members).
Beyond the Classroom published by The National Union of Teachers, Hamilton House, Mabledon Place, London WC1H 9BD.
The Educational Grants Directory from The Directory of Social Change, Radius Works, Back Lane, London NW3 1HL Tel: 071-435 8171.
Charity Aid Foundation, 48 Pembury Road, Tonbridge, Kent TN9 2JD.

MAJOR PROVIDERS

The National Trust, the National Trust for Scotland, English Heritage, Welsh Historic Monuments and Historic Scotland are major providers each with an educational policy for their properties. These properties are identified in the reference section.

THE NATIONAL TRUST

The National Trust was set up at the end of the nineteenth century but it was not till the late 1970s that education became one of its main objectives. Today there are people in the regional

VISITS OUT

offices with responsibility for education, who aim to identify a handful of properties, in each region, of country houses and areas of countryside and coastline that are suitable for the development of educational resources. They then work closely with the local inspectorate to develop work linked to the National Curriculum. Local teachers are involved in the production of materials and when these are developed INSET courses are set up for teachers. Increasingly study bases are set up which are staffed by both paid and voluntary staff.

There has been a huge growth in the use of National Trust properties by school children and, in particular, primary students who account for 70% of the 500,000 pupils who visit properties annually. The National Trust also runs the Young National Trust Theatre which was set up in 1977 and tours eight National Trust properties each year working with over 7,000 school children aged from 8 to 16. It is heavily oversubscribed, so those wishing to take pupils should book early. Education Group Members receive priority mailing.

VISITING A NATIONAL TRUST PROPERTY

The Trust likes schools to book well in advance by telephoning or writing to the administrator of the property with details about the visit. There is generally a reduction of 50% for all school pupils under 16 when accompanied by a teacher. It is essential for there to be an adult-to-pupil ratio of 1:10 at all times. They particularly like teachers to make a preliminary visit to plan the specific activities and the timing. They also stress that photography is not allowed inside the properties.

EDUCATION GROUP MEMBERSHIP

The Trust runs a corporate membership scheme which gives a school free access to every Trust property. Over 5,000 schools are corporate members of the National Trust. Membership costs are dependent on the size of the school:
- up to 50 on role   £14 per annum

- 51–100   £29
- 101–200   £35
- 201–500   £40
- over 501   £45
- adult education £60

THE GUARDIANSHIP SCHEME

The National Trust runs 12 guardianship schemes in the UK. These are essentially partnership schemes between local National Trust properties and schools. They were started in the mid-1980s and are not sited on the Trust's major sites but on local sites where a link is made between a school and the warden of a property. Generally this is made between one school and one property but in some cases more schools are involved. For example in Northern Ireland at Strangford Lough, 12 schools, both Catholic and Protestant, are involved and are part of a guardianship scheme which is also part of the Northern Ireland scheme called Education for Mutual Understanding (EMU).

The pupils participating in these schemes are called Countryside or Coastal Guardians depending on the location. They have the opportunity to undertake a range of activities linked to the National Curriculum such as practical conservation work, monitoring, observation and recording. The National Trust staff and school teachers work closely together to set up the scheme and plan the best mixture of 'hands on' conservation work and field work study to be done in the areas adopted. A timetable of school visits is organised depending on the amount of time a warden has available and the school timetable.

ENGLISH HERITAGE

English Heritage was created by Parliament in 1984 to protect the countryside and encourage people to understand and enjoy England's architectural and archaeological heritage. They give

VISITS OUT

advice on, and grants for, conservation and are the government's principal expert adviser on the historic environment. They also manage over 375 of England's greatest historic properties which are open to the public.

ENGLISH HERITAGE EDUCATION SERVICE

English Heritage has an Education Service to help teachers at all levels make better use of the historic environment. Whatever subject is being taught, at any level from Key Stage 1 to GCSE or even adult education, the range of over 375 historic properties and teaching resources can offer teachers the help they need to make the most of the past. Their Education Service includes Regional Education officers who are all ex-teachers with considerable experience in schools, teacher training, archaeology and museums. They are sensitive to teachers' needs and can offer professional help and advice to plan your work.

PROVISION OF FREE EDUCATIONAL VISITS

Among the historic properties managed by English Heritage are most of those places which feature as landmarks in England's history – from prehistoric and Roman sites to medieval castles, great abbeys, historic houses, agricultural and industrial monuments. At many properties there is normally a charge for public entry. However educational group visits to all English Heritage historic properties are absolutely free, provided teachers book in advance. Teachers can also make a free exploratory visit to a property to plan a group visit, at which point English Heritage site custodians can offer information and help. Their properties are spread throughout the country from Hadrian's Wall to Cornwall and Kent, so there's bound to be one within visiting range of your school.

At some properties English Heritage provide Education Centres for school groups to use. These are marked in the *Resourceful Teacher's Handbook* entries. These are intended as bases for the exploration of the site and equipped with a range of materials. There is a Free Educational Visits booklet which contains full details of how to book a free visit along with a complete list of all English Heritage properties and a booking form. To obtain a free copy write to English Heritage Education Services, Keysign House, 429 Oxford Street, London W1R 2HD or ring 071-973 3442/3.

NATIONAL CURRICULUM

The National Curriculum recommends visits to historic sites and English Heritage's Free Educational Visits Scheme offers an ideal opportunity to include visits in programmes of work. Almost every aspect of the curriculum can be explored at their properties. They can be used not only for studying History but also linked to other subjects as varied as English, Maths, Science, Technology, Geography and Music. English Heritage has produced a wide range of National Curriculum teachers' guides and videos to give teachers plenty of stimulating ideas. To find out more about them send for a free copy of their *Resources* catalogue from Keysign House, 429 Oxford Street, London W1R 2HD.

RESOURCES

English Heritage produce a range of resource material offering practical teaching ideas including books, videos, posters, slide packs and computer software. They all suggest teaching strategies for using the historic environment. Their 'Education on Site' series of books for instance includes titles such as *Learning from Objects*, *Storytelling* and *Using Listed Buildings*, as well as *Using Abbeys* and *Using Historic Houses* and National Curriculum subject books such as *Maths* and *Science*.

They have produced handbooks for teachers for over 30 of their historic properties which are intended to help teachers plan a visit. These combine historical background with a variety of study approaches, documentary sources and activity sheets for

VISITS OUT

classroom and on-site work, together with practical information about the site. There is a wide range of videos which introduce sites and resources, encouraging investigative learning approaches by looking at the physical evidence of the past. Many can be linked to visits to historic sites, either as part of preparation or follow-up, and some are specifically aimed at teacher training like 'Teaching on Site' series. Over 40 titles are available and they can all be borrowed by teachers on two weeks' free loan.

COURSES AND EVENTS

English Heritage education officers arrange and teach a variety of courses for teachers often in association with Local Education Authorities, the Department for Education or museum services. At some sites each year they arrange special educational events, often with the involvement of experts such as musicians and storytellers, for visiting educational groups.

FURTHER INFORMATION FROM:

The National Trust Education Office: 36 Queen Anne's Gate, London SW1H 9AS Tel: 071-222 9251.
The National Trust for Scotland, 5 Charlotte Square, Edinburgh EH2 4DU Tel: 031-226 5922.
English Heritage, Keysign House, 429 Oxford St, London W1R 2HD Tel: 071-973 3000.
Cadw: Welsh Historic Monuments, Brunel House, 2 Fitzalan Rd., Cardiff CF2 1UY Tel: 0222 465511.
Historic Scotland, 20 Brandon St., Edinburgh EH3 5RA Tel: 031-244 3101.

WHO PAYS FOR TRIPS: THE LEGAL POSITION

Until the 1988 Education Act it had been the practice to charge parents for school trips. However this practice was challenged in

VISITS OUT

1986 by the Ombudsman for Local Government and led to changes which were incorporated in the new Act.

THE EDUCATION REFORM ACT 1988: CHARGES FOR SCHOOL ACTIVITIES

The changes introduced by the Act were intended to simplify the procedures but in reality have made them more complicated. The rules were based on the following principles:
- To maintain the right to free education.
- To ensure that activities offered by schools during or mainly during school hours are free.
- To enable schools to *invite* voluntary contributions from parents.

THE RIGHT TO FREE VISITS

No charges may be made for the following:
- Any visit that is part of a syllabus for a public examination.
- Any visit that is part of the statutory National Curriculum.

THE RIGHT TO FREE VISITS DURING SCHOOL HOURS

There is a general principle that activities provided wholly or mainly in school hours are free. School hours mean during school day but *excluding* the lunch break which is not part of official school hours. A day visit is deemed to be in school hours if 50% or more of the whole time spent on the activity, including travelling time, occurs during school hours.

VISITS OUT

THE OPTION FOR SCHOOLS TO INVITE VOLUNTARY CONTRIBUTIONS FROM PARENTS

Charges can only be made if more than 50% of the school visit (including travelling time) takes place outside school hours. It can then be looked at as an 'optional extra' and charges can be made to cover the following: pupil travel costs, materials, books, other equipment and non-teaching costs.

Voluntary contributions can be invited but pupils cannot be chosen to go on a visit because their parents or guardians can afford to pay. In some areas LEAs have a policy which ensures that no pupil is excluded from going on a school visit for financial reasons. LEAs have delegated the budget to schools welfare funds to cover this need. The cost of charging for some pupils cannot be passed on to the parents of other pupils participating in the activity. There cannot be any element of subsidy.

RESIDENTIAL VISITS

Parents can be charged the cost of board and lodging for any residential visit which takes place in or outside school hours. Exceptions are made in the case of parents whose parents are in receipt of Income Support or Family Credit. These parents must have the charges remitted if the trip is part of the National Curriculum, or a public examination syllabus, or within school hours.

The Act says that if a residential visit takes place inside school hours no other charges must be levied. They have a complicated formula, based on half days within a school session, to determine whether or not the trip takes place within school hours. If the time spent on the visit is over 50% of half days then no charge can be made except for the residential charge. All travelling time must be excluded in the calculation. A half day morning session is any time from 0.01–12.00 hours and an afternoon session is 12.00–24.00 hours. A period is deemed as a session if at least

VISITS OUT

50% or more of that session is taken up. This means that if a school misses five school sessions and nine half days, no charge can be made but if they miss four school sessions and nine half days charges can be made for the full cost of the visit.

POLICY STATEMENT ON CHARGING FOR OPTIONAL SCHOOL ACTIVITIES

The 1988 Act requires LEAs or governing bodies of grant-maintained and independent schools to draw up a statement on the policy on charging and remissions and without this policy they are not allowed to make charges. A governing body can decide to subsidise, or remit in full, charges levied by an LEA.

SCHOOL TRIPS ORGANISED BY 'THIRD PARTIES'

The 1988 Act introduced a new form of arrangement for school trips which allowed for a 'third party' to organise school trips and charge parents direct, in or out of school time on a commercial basis. A third party is deemed to be an organisation other than an LEA or a school, such as a travel company or an organisation which receives school parties. Here again the rules are complicated and it is clear that the government does not want schools to liaise with travel companies and to act as agents for them and to use this as a method of getting round the rules. The DES circular 2/89 makes it clear that these third party provisions should not be the norm, and should happen only in exceptional circumstances. The rules which apply if these third party trips are organised are:
- The third party must negotiate directly with the parents.
- Parents who wish their children to participate must inform the school and get permission to be absent.
- Teachers who wish to participate in the visit must apply for leave of absence.

The 1981 Education Regulations allow parents to take their children out of school for two weeks a year on holidays or visits such as this. Teachers who go on these third party visits need to ensure that the trips are properly organised, that the insurance cover is adequate and that there is a personal liability for teachers, as the normal LEA cover will not apply. They also need to clarify whether or not they will be paid during the school trip.

The Chairman of the School Journey Association says that to his knowledge they have not been asked to organise these third party trips and the Association of Teachers and Lecturers, having considered the problems of these third party trips, recommend their members not to participate.*

FURTHER INFORMATION FROM:

The Department of Education Circular 2/89 *The Education Reform Act 1988: Charges for School Activities.*
* Association of Teachers and Lecturers booklet: *Charging for School Activities.*

TRANSPORT

Cost, convenience and safety are the three predominant factors to be taken into consideration when planning a school trip. This section looks at the different forms of transport available taking into account these considerations.

TRAVEL BY CAR

Small groups may be taken on trips using staff's and parents' cars and this could be a cheap, convenient and safe way to travel. However it is essential that teachers transporting pupils on a school visit should check their insurance. A teacher's insurance policy should cover the vehicle for business purposes and should, ideally, be comprehensive. If they are using a family car, which is a business car for their partner, it will not automatically cover students on a school journey. If parents' cars are being used, they too need to be adequately insured and roadworthy. Parents should be informed that teachers' and other parents' cars are being used.

TRAVEL BY MINIBUS

Again, if the group is not too large, the most convenient, safe and cheap way to travel might be in the school or local authority minibus. The 1985 Transport Act allows voluntary groups and schools to charge for passenger transport providing that the minibus is covered by a permit and no overall profit is made. Minibuses designed to carry 9–16 passengers need a small bus permit. Since 1987, individual permits are not linked to specific vehicles; instead applicants are issued with a disc which can be used on any vehicle. The driver of a minibus is personally responsible for making sure that the minibus is fit to drive and it needs to be routinely checked. In addition it is subject to spot checks for roadworthiness and the number of passengers must not exceed the seating capacity.

TRAVEL BY BUS OR COACH

Generally it is cheaper per person to travel by bus or coach than by train with the additional advantage that there is no restriction to BR timetables. However for buses and coach travel, as for other industries, market forces are the key to travel costs. The industry has been deregulated and today the same operator may be the owner of both the bus and the coach company. Competition counts and so it is wise for a school to ask for two or three quotes and not to book their trip on Derby Day! If a school does not have a satisfactory company whom they normally use and have no success from *Yellow Pages*, they could contact the Bus and Coach Council for advice.

The size of group and length of journey will determine whether to use a minibus, bus or coach. The following is a rough guide:
- 8–16 on the trip   minibus
- 17–35   midibus or coach
- Approximately 50   coach

VISITS OUT

- Around 60   single decker bus
- Around 70   double decker bus

More young people can be fitted on a bus where three pupils under 14 are allowed on a double seat. However a coach is both more comfortable and safer for a longer distance. Safety is clearly important and two pressure groups: BUSK (Belt up School Kids) and ACSIC (Action for Child Safety in Coaches) are campaigning for safety belts to be compulsory in coaches. Nevertheless if trips are well supervised and children seated during journeys, they should be safe. Modern coaches are fitted with energy-absorbing seats to protect passengers in case of an accident and seats in exposed positions are now fitted with seat belts. It is advisable for one teacher to sit near the driver and for another teacher to sit near the emergency exit for optimum supervision in the event of emergencies.

TRAVEL BY TRAIN

Train may be the best form of travel if the visit is to the centre of a city, where parking is difficult, although inevitably it means first getting to the station. Trains are sometimes quicker, more available, and more convenient to organise. Group travel tickets are limited and schools are advised to book early. Discount is available on savers, super savers, network away breaks, cheap day returns, standard single, open return fares and standard day singles and returns. When groups of ten or more fare-paying passengers travel fares will be reduced by 25% (note – journeys over different lines qualify for different discounts). A further advantage is that 16 or 17-year-old pupils will only be charged the child fare and also qualify for the 25% reduction. Schools can either ring British Rail to organise their trip or alternatively approach an organisation such as School Rail (St Albans Travel Service, 4a Spencer Street, St Albans, Herts AL3 5EQ Tel: 0727 834 475). School Rail provides a service to school teachers all over Britain travelling with groups, offering the same discounts as British Rail, but also provides the additional service of designing package tours to suit the requirements of individual teachers and the National Curriculum.

VISITS OUT

For those parties travelling through London, the cost of the underground between mainline stations is included in the ticket. If the school's destination is in Central London, British Rail include underground tickets for a small extra charge.

GROUP DAY TICKETS IN LONDON

A group day ticket can be purchased by any group of more than ten travelling in London and this entitles them to travel anywhere on the Underground or Docklands Light Railway, under-18s travelling at the child rate. There is no need to pre-book or fill in any forms. Tickets can be issued at the time of travel or up to seven days in advance. They can be purchased at any Underground Ticket Office or from London Transport Commercial Office, 55 Broadway, London SW1H 0BD Tel: 071-918 3921.

TRAVEL ARRANGEMENTS BY THE SCHOOL JOURNEY ASSOCIATION

The School Journey Association organises travel from anywhere in the UK to any destination by coach, train, scheduled or charter flights for members of the organisation. Membership costs UK schools £5 plus VAT for five years. It is a charity and its profits are ploughed back into the organisation and any surplus may be used to help disadvantaged children travel. They have a brochure with details of their trips and services. The SJA has two youth hotels for the accommodation of school groups situated in Clapham South, open all year with no surcharges for the high season. A choice of bed & breakfast with or without packed lunch and dinner is available and for every ten places one is free. As a guideline for prices, under 16-year-olds are charged £11 plus VAT per day (1993 price).

FURTHER INFORMATION FROM:

Bus and Coach Council: Sardinia House, 52 Lincoln's Inn Fields, London WC2A 3LZ Tel: 071-831 7546.

VISITS OUT

The School Minibus and the Law: a free leaflet from the Association of Teachers and Lecturers, 7 Northumberland Street, London WC2N 5DA.
An Introduction to Basic Minibus Driving, published by The Royal Society for the Prevention of Accidents.
The School Journey Association, 48 Cavendish Road, London SW12 0DG Tel: 081-675 6636.
London Travel Information Service: 071-222 1234.

ACCIDENTS AND INSURANCE

ACCIDENTS

Accidents can happen even when all sensible precautions have been taken. The best any teacher can do is to anticipate likely problems and be prepared. A teacher is only held responsible if they are shown to be negligent. There are seldom any grounds for taking action against a teacher. Where an allegation is made any following claim will be made against the Education Authorities, that is the local education authorities, or the governors of private schools. Most Education Authorities give support to teachers who are accused of negligence. Teachers' unions and professional associations also support them.

HEALTH AND SAFETY REGULATIONS

The Health and Safety at Work Act 1974 requires local education authorities or governing bodies to have regard to the health and safety of all persons including non-employees affected by their activities (ref. section 3 [1]). This by definition covers pupils on visits out. The Act does provide for action to be taken against teachers if an accident occurs to a pupil in their charge but in practice prosecutions are very rare. They may be taken out by the Health and Safety Executive's own inspectors or by, and with the consent of, the Director of Public Prosecutions. Where they have taken place there tends to have been gross disregard of a code of practice or a specific instruction from an inspector.

VISITS OUT

The United Kingdom has introduced new regulations to comply with the new European Community Health and Safety at Work Directives. The Management of Health and Safety at Work Regulations 1992 which came into force in January 1993 require employers to make a written risk assessment of their activities and to introduce risk control measures and inform employees of these measures. The Health and Safety Executive has produced a helpful booklet explaining this regulation.

INSURANCE

Pupils do not need insurance for their time at school. A teacher organising a school trip should ensure whether or not they need to take out a special insurance with their local education authority or person responsible within the school. The Department of Education advises teachers to take out insurance if the trip may be hazardous. All schools will have employers' liability and public liability policies which will have been taken out by the LEA or governing body or proprietor, and today these bodies are expected also to have insured the voluntary participation of teachers working in non-directed time. The precise terms of the cover may differ and the costs of insurance may be delegated as part of a statutory scheme of local management of schools, but they should cover capital benefits for death or injury and indemnification against third-party claims which would include claims by pupils or their parents. Any cover that is missing should be taken out by the organiser.

Teachers should consider whether they need the following to be covered by insurance:
- Loss of, or damage to, personal equipment.
- Public liability of the responsible authority covering claims for negligence.
- Third-party liability covering claims against the responsible authority and its employees.
- Personal accident cover for groups (leaders, volunteer helpers and pupils).
- Medical treatment.

VISITS OUT

- Transport and passenger liability.
- High risk activities.
- Damage or loss to hired equipment.
- Transport, accommodation and other expenses in case of emergency.
- Compensation against cancellation and delay.
- Failure or bankruptcy of the travel company.
- Legal advice in the case of accidents.

The new 1992 EC Travel Directive on package tours says that organisers of trips can be liable if the trip falls through and the company becomes bankrupt. This Directive only refers to overnight trips which are sold inclusive of accommodation, transport and some training. The school will be responsible for funding the money back to the parents. Schools should ensure that they are not vulnerable to this regulation either by ensuring that they are covered by the LEA, or by retaining any payments in a separate account until the contract has been completed by taking out insurance.

LOSS OF PROPERTY

Loss of cameras and clothing are one of the commonest hazards on a school trip and it is important to clarify whether or not there is an insurance policy for parents, and to state that the organiser takes no responsibility for property lost.

PROCEDURE TO FOLLOW WHEN ACCIDENTS HAPPEN

When accidents happen – even minor ones – the following procedure is recommended:
- Give first aid or obtain the help of someone who can. But only give it if you are sure it is correct.
- Call for professional medical help or an ambulance if necessary.
- Stop any activity being carried on by the other pupils unless you are sure that they are properly supervised.
- Ensure that the pupil receives all the medical aid that is necessary.

VISITS OUT

- Inform the parents or guardians.
- Report the incident to the Head or Deputy giving *factual* details of the name of the pupil, year, class or tutor group, time and place of the accident, the nature of the injury, the first aid that was given and who gave it and the name of the person responsible for the pupil. *At this stage no further reports should be given and no opinion about the cause of the accident expressed orally or verbally.*
- For serious accidents members of unions or professions should contact them as soon as possible.

RESOURCEFUL TEACHERS NEED THE BEST RESOURCES

At Routledge we publish the most timely and authoritative work from experts in the world of education. Used widely by teachers and managers, our comprehensive list of education books explores the issues and debates surrounding schooling today.

Committed to developing the list at every opportunity, Routledge is widely respected as the number one publisher in the following subject areas:

- Primary and Secondary Teaching
- Educational Management
- Special Education
- Professional Development

Find out more about how Routledge can help you to develop whole school policies alongside effective teaching practices.

*Call our customer hotline to request a FREE copy of the latest **Education in Practice** catalogue on 0264 342897 – You'll find full details of all books in the above areas, plus many, many more.*

ROUTLEDGE

VISITS OUT

NATIONAL SOCIETY'S RE CENTRE
23 KENSINGTON SQUARE
LONDON W8 5HN
TEL: 071 937 4241

The RE Centre houses a large reference collection of books currently available for religious and moral education, and for loan to members, videos, tapes, posters and artefacts. We also offer a limited range of publications for sale.

Opening Hours: Monday - Friday 9.30am - 4.30pm.

For further information, a programme of courses and membership details, please contact the Centre or phone to arrange a visit.

THE CENTRAL SCHOOL
OF SPEECH AND DRAMA

Principal: Robert S. Fowler, MA (Oxon), LGSM, FRSA.

APPLICATIONS ARE NOW BEING INVITED FOR THE FOLLOWING PART-TIME EVENING COURSES COMMENCING EARLY OCTOBER 1994:

ADVANCED DIPLOMA IN MEDIA EDUCATION - New for 1994

DIPLOMA IN DRAMA EDUCATION

MA in ARTS EDUCATION (DRAMA)

The above courses would be suitable for qualified teachers from a range of sectors and disciplines, however, this would not be a prerequisite for entry. Students may be admitted without these qualifications if it is established that they can benefit from the course.

For further information, application form and Prospectus, please send an A4, stamped-addressed envelope marked with the course title to: Linda Roe, Marketing Coordinator, The Central School of Speech and Drama, Embassy Theatre, 64 Eton Avenue, London, NW3 3HY. Tel: 071 722 8183.

(In conjunction with Hampshire County Council Education Authority)

Announce the launch of

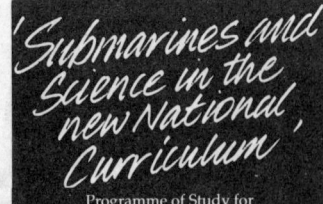

Programme of Study for Attainment Targets 24

Send for further information or send £2.00 (inclusive of postage) for your Teacher Pack to:
Royal Navy Submarine Museum
Haslar Jetty Road, Gosport, Hampshire. PO12 2AS

VISITS OUT

SPORTSPAGES

Specialist Sports Bookshops

For the best range of new sports books in the UK, come to the specialists; we stock more books and videos on more sports than any other bookshop, plus a huge range in the physical education/sports studies area.

Write, fax, or phone for our lists, and details of our
mail order service.

SPORTSPAGES	SPORTSPAGES
Caxton Walk	Barton Square
94-96 Charing Cross Rd	St Ann's Square
London WC2H OJG	Manchester M2 7HA
Phone: 071 240 9604	Phone: 061 832 8530
Fax: 071 836 0104	Fax: 061 832 9391

SPORTSPAGES - THE BOOKSHOPS THAT TAKE SPORT SERIOUSLY

CORNWALL OUTDOORS
CORNWALL COUNTY COUNCIL
OUTDOOR EDUCATION CENTRES

...for your next residential visit......

Why not come to one of our four multi-activity centres set in the heart of Cornwall's countryside?
- Individually designed outdoor education and field study programmes to meet your budget requirements.
- Comfortable and fully equipped accommodation.
- Full range of quality outdoor activities ranging from the maritime to the moorland with qualified and caring instruction.
- Open all year round.

Further details and free brochure can be obtained by contacting:

Kate Sargeant
Cornwall Outdoors
Cornwall County Council
Dalvenie House, County Hall
Truro, Cornwall
Tel: 0872 74282 Ext. 4402

SCOTTISH SCHOOLS

For the latest free Health Education Videos, Films and Booklets.

Contact:
Training Resources,
SCET,
74 Victoria Crescent Road,
Glasgow, G12 9JN.

Tel: 041-334 9314
Fax: 041-334 6519

VISITS OUT
LONDON & THE SOUTH EAST

Accademia Italiana
- Sarah Burles, Education Officer
- 24 Rutland Gate, London. SW7 1BB
- 071-839 3321 FAX 071-589 5187

The Accademia Italiana was established in 1987 as a registered arts charity to promote and develop closer cultural links between Italy and the UK through a programme of high quality loan exhibitions (up to eight exhibitions per year). These exhibitions focus on different aspects of Italian art and design and range from Pompeiian frescoes to contemporary sculpture. To accompany each of these exhibitions there is a full education programme which changes according to each exhibition.

N C SUPPORT Programmes for schools include gallery talks, workshops, study days and other events, whilst the broader programme includes regular lecture series and symposiums encouraging new research. Groups wishing to specialise in a particular aspect of Italian art and culture can be accommodated at any time subject to prior arrangement. Mailing list: regular information on forthcoming exhibitions in a termly newsletter, together with details of workshops, teachers' evenings, resource packs and other information. To join please write, giving name and school/college address, telephone number and any special area of interest, age group or special need.

OPENING Tuesday to Saturday 10.00am–5.30pm, Wednesday 10am–8.00pm, Sunday 2.00pm–5.30pm.

COST For details of schools programmes, workshops, study days and other events contact Sarah Burles, Education Officer, on 071-225 3474.

DISABLED FACILITIES Disabled access by prior arrangement with the administrator.

DIRECTIONS Tube: Knightsbridge or South Kensington. Bus: 9, 10, 52 (request stop at top of Rutland Gate); 14, 19, 22, 137, 137a (stop at Knightsbridge). Coach: setting-down point at the top of Rutland Gate.

Alfriston Clergy House
- The Administrator
- The Tye, Alfriston, Polegate, East Sussex. BN26 5TL
- 0323 870001

The first building acquired by the National Trust; a 14th-century priests' house, thatched and half-timbered; medieval hall, exhibition room and two other rooms shown; garden open to visitors.

N C SUPPORT National Curriculum links with History and Science.

DISABLED FACILITIES None.

DIRECTIONS Four miles northeast of Seaford, just east of B2108, in Alfriston village, adjoining The Tye and St Andrews Church. Bus: Southdown 726 Eastbourne to Brighton (passing close BR Polegate & Seaford); Brighton Buses A2 Brighton to Newhaven (Tel: 0273 478007). BR: Berwick two and a half miles.

VISITS OUT
LONDON & THE SOUTH EAST

Amberley Museum
- Howard Stenning
- Amberley, Arundel, West Sussex. BN18 9LT
- 0798 831370 **FAX** 0798 831831

Working museum showing the industrial history of southeast England, with working craftsmen, narrow-gauge railway, early motor buses, stationary engines, historic buildings and many other exhibits and displays.

N C SUPPORT Services of Education Officer, teachers' handbook and other material available.

ANNUAL OR ONE OFF EVENT Programme of events available on request.

OPENING End March to end October: Wednesdays to Sundays (daily during school holidays) 10.00am.

CATERING Tea room and picnic areas.

COST Children £1.50, one staff member free for every ten pupils (1993 prices).

DISABLED FACILITIES All exhibition areas accessible by wheelchair. Toilets both in car park and in museum site.

DIRECTIONS On B2139 midway between Arundel and Storrington. Immediately adjacent to Amberley station.

Anne of Cleves House
- Mr S Watts
- 52 Southover High Street, Lewes, East Sussex
- 0273 474610

A house of the late fifteenth or early sixteenth century. A Wealden timber-framed building, now a museum of local history.

N C SUPPORT Education project headquarters located in house: organisers T Barenam and C Shelley (Tel: 0273 486 6959).

OPENING Easter to November: Monday to Saturday 10.00am–5.00pm, Sunday 2.00pm–5.00pm. Will open other times for groups.

CATERING Tea/coffee, biscuits.

COST Children 80p, adults £1.60. Group rates (20 or more): children 60p, adults £1.20. Combined ticket with Lewes Castle available.

DISABLED FACILITIES None.

DIRECTIONS Well signposted throughout Lewes.

Appuldurcombe House
- The Head Custodian
- Wroxall, Isle of Wight. PO38 3EW
- 0983 852 484

The bleached shell of a fine 18th-century baroque-style house standing in a rolling green landscape in its own ornamental grounds, landscaped by 'Capability' Brown.

OPENING All year round. Pre-booking is essential.

DISABLED FACILITIES Parking. Wheelchair access (quarter of a mile uphill from car park). Dogs allowed on leads.

DIRECTIONS Half a mile west of Wroxall off B3327 (OS map 196; ref SZ 543800). Bus: Southern Vectis 2A Newport to Ventnor, 16B Ryde to Ventnor (Tel: 0983 62264). BR: Shanklin three and a half miles. Ferry: Ryde (Wightlink) 11 miles.

VISITS OUT
LONDON & THE SOUTH EAST

Apsley House
- J Miller
- The Wellington Museum, 149 Piccadilly, Hyde Park Corner, London. W1V 9FA
- 071-499 5676 FAX 071-493 6576

First Duke of Wellington's London Palace housing his superb collection of paintings with masterpieces by Velazquez, his great services in porcelain and silver-gilt, plate, sculpture, swords and batons, orders and medals and other Wellington memorabilia.

ANNUAL OR ONE OFF EVENT Waterloo week (June, when open), Christmas festival (concerts, historic dance recreation, theatre, guided tours).

CATERING None.

COST Free for pre-booked school parties. Pre-booked parties of 12 or more: children £1.00, adults £2.00, £1.00 concessionary.

DISABLED FACILITIES Wheelchair available, but few steps.

DIRECTIONS On Hyde Park Corner beside the tube station.

The Archbishops' Palace & Heritage Centre
- Rosamunde Bell, Education Officer
- Palace Gardens, Mill Street, Maidstone, Kent. ME15 6YE
- 0622 754497 FAX 0622 602193

Beautiful 14th-century palace overlooking the river Medway. Recently restored, it includes restaurant, shop, conference facilities and an excellent Heritage Centre which celebrates the turbulent history of the Medieval Palace.

N C SUPPORT English Civil War artefact handling sessions and brass rubbing workshops are available by prior arrangement with the Education Officer.

ANNUAL OR ONE OFF EVENT Regular programme of activities and living history events each year.

OPENING Monday to Sunday 10.30am–5.30pm (last admission 4.00pm), closed Christmas Day and Boxing Day.

CATERING Excellent restaurant, fully licensed, open daily 10.30am–4.00pm.

COST Pre-booked schools rate: £1.00 per child, one adult free for every ten children. (Ticket includes visit to Carriage Museum.)

DISABLED FACILITIES Wheelchair access to Heritage Centre only, not palace or restaurant.

DIRECTIONS Centre of Maidstone, by the river.

Arundel Museum & Heritage Centre
- Miss A English
- 61 High Street, Arundel, West Sussex. BN18 9AJ
- 0903 882344

The museum is on two floors and has nine galleries covering different subjects from Roman sites to a small country town in the Victorian age. It also features superb models.

N C SUPPORT Key Stage 2, Invaders and Settlers: Romans, Anglo-Saxons, Vikings. Victorian Britain. Ships and Seafarers (The Port of Arundel).

VISITS OUT
LONDON & THE SOUTH EAST

OPENING Easter to October: weekends and bank holidays. End of May to beginning of September: Tuesday to Friday 11.00am–1.00pm and 2.00pm–5.00pm (closed Sunday morning).

CATERING None.

COST Children 25p, adults £1.00, Senior Citizens 50p (adults free when accompanying a group). Free visit for teachers looking round before bringing children.

DISABLED FACILITIES None.

The Ashridge Estate
- The Administrator
- Ringshall, Berkhamsted, Herts
- 0494 28051

The Ashridge estate covers some six square miles in Hertfordshire and Buckinghamshire, running along the main ridge of the Chiltern Hills from Ivinghoe Beacon to Berkhamsted; it comprises 4000 unspoilt acres of open spaces, commons and woodlands; the main focal point is the granite monument erected 150 years ago to the third Duke of Bridgewater; wildlife is well represented.

N C SUPPORT National Curriculum links with Science and Geography. Teachers' pack.

DISABLED FACILITIES In monument area, on monument drive and to Information Centre. Adapted WC. Special parking near Information Centre. Self-drive battery-powered vehicles available free of charge from Information Centre; advance booking advisable.

DIRECTIONS Between Northchurch and Ringshall just off B4506, three miles north of A41. Bus: Monument: Aylesbury Bus 27 from BR Tring, alight Aldbury, half a mile; Beacon: 612 Aylesbury to Luton (passing close BR Aylesbury and Luton). BR: Monument: Tring; Beacon: Cheddington.

Athelstan Museum
- Roberta Prince
- Town Hall, Cross Keys, Malmesbury, Wilts
- 0666 822143

Local history collection, costume, lace, early fire engine, bicycles, coins. The local railway featured in photographs. Also photographs, prints and drawings of the town.

N C SUPPORT Contact with local schools in the area. Schoools by arrangement with Curator. Demonstrations of lacemaking by arrangement.

ANNUAL OR ONE OFF EVENT Various travelling exhibitions.

OPENING Summer. Tuesday to Saturday: 10.30am–12.30pm and 1.00pm–3.00pm. Hours extended most days to 4.30pm by volunteers (summer only). Winter: Wednesday, Friday and Saturday 1.00pm–3.00pm only.

CATERING None.

COST Free.

DISABLED FACILITIES Access for people with disabilities (downstairs only).

DIRECTIONS Malmesbury is situated near the A429 Chippenham to Cirencester Road between Chippenham and Cirencester.

VISITS OUT
LONDON & THE SOUTH EAST

Atwell Wilson Motor Museum
- Richard or Hazell Atwell
- Downside, Stockley Lane, Calne, Wilts. SN11 0NF
- 0249 813119

There are over 50 exhibits in the museum including cars, motor bikes, antique lawnmowers, etc., ranging from 1924 to 1989.

N C SUPPORT None.

OPENING 1 April to 31 October Monday to Thursday 10.00am–5.00pm, Sunday 11.00am–5.00pm. 1 November to 31 March Monday to Thursday 10.00am–4.00pm, Sunday 11.00am–4.00pm. Open Good Friday.

CATERING None at present, but 'we could get a caterer in if needed'.

COST Children 75p, adults £1.50, Senior Citizens £1.00 (including VAT).

DISABLED FACILITIES Yes.

DIRECTIONS Turn right off A4 going from Calne to Marlborough, just out of Calne, into Stockley Lane.

Avon Tyrrell Youth Clubs UK
- Philip Robson
- Bransgore, Hants. BH23 8EE
- 0424 672347

A residential centre for groups in the New Forest. Vast range of activities and environmental opportunities available.

N C SUPPORT Environmental Studies, Geography, History.

OPENING All year round.

CATERING Catered or self-catering.

COST Self-catering from £14.00 per week, full board from £101.00 per week.

DISABLED FACILITIES Excellent.

DIRECTIONS Six miles from Christchurch.

Badsell Park Farm
- Christine Greaves
- Matfield, Tonbridge, Kent. TN1 7EN
- 0892 832549 FAX 0892 833436

'Darling Buds'-style fruit farm (strawberries, apples, pears). Has large animal park and fancy fowl house. Almost all animals are tame and touchable.

N C SUPPORT School pack provided to all school visitors. Aimed at children 5–12 yrs of age. Informative animal section.

ANNUAL OR ONE OFF EVENT Sheep Shearing Day and demonstrations of spinning and weaving.

OPENING All year round: daily 10.00am–5.30pm.

CATERING Cafe for teas, coffees, soft drinks, sandwiches, all day breakfasts, etc.

COST Children 3 years and over £2.50, adults £3.00, Senior Citizens £2.50, under 3s free.

DISABLED FACILITIES Toilet and wide gates.

DIRECTIONS Just off A228 (formerly the B2015).

VISITS OUT
LONDON & THE SOUTH EAST

The Bank of England Museum
- Information Officer
- The Public Liaison Group, Threadneedle Street, London. EC1R 8AH
- 071-601 4878

Housed within the Bank of England itself, right at the heart of the City of London, the Museum traces the history of the Bank from its foundation by Royal Charter in 1694 to the high-tech world of modern banking. There are gold bars dating from ancient times to the modern market bar, plus coins and banknotes. The Bank Stock Office, a late 18th-century banking hall by Sir John Soane, has been reconstructed and interactive videos give the opportunity of looking behind the doors of the nation's bank.

N C SUPPORT A variety of presentations is available for both economics-based and general interest groups. These are suitable for a wide range of ages and for those with special needs. Films and slide shows suitable for different age groups can be viewed.

ANNUAL OR ONE OFF EVENT The Bank of England celebrates its 300th birthday in 1994.

OPENING Winter: Monday to Friday 10.00am–5.00pm. Summer (Good Friday to end September): Monday to Friday 10.00am–5.00pm, Sunday and public holidays 11.00am–5.00pm. Also open on the day of the Lord Mayor's Show. Closed Christmas Day, Boxing Day and New Year's Day. (Tel: 071-601 5792.)

COST Free.

DISABLED FACILITIES The Museum welcomes disabled visitors and tries to overcome the limitations of historic buildings which do not give easy access for the less able-bodied. Appreciate prior notice of an intended visit if possible.

DIRECTIONS Entrance is in Bartholomew Lane. Tube: Bank (Northern/Central line). Docklands Light Railway: Waterloo and City. BR: Liverpool Street, Fenchurch Street, Cannon Street (weekdays only). Bus: 6, 8, 9*, 11, 15*, 21*, 22, 22B, 25, 43, 76, 133, 149*, 501* (*weekdays only).

Bankside Gallery
- Judy Dixey
- 48 Hopton Street, London. SE1 9JN
- 071-928 7521 FAX 071-928 2820

Gallery exhibiting works of art on paper. Five regular shows and mixed themed shows: historical and contemporary.

OPENING Phone for details.

DISABLED FACILITIES Yes.

DIRECTIONS Left along south side of Blackfriars Bridge.

The Banqueting House
- The Head Custodian
- Whitehall, London. SW1A 2ER
- 071-930 4179

From the days of Henry VIII till its destruction by fire in 1689, the great Palace of Whitehall was the sovereign's main London residence. The only part to survive that fire was the Banqueting House, a lone

VISITS OUT
LONDON & THE SOUTH EAST

testament to the splendours of a regal past.

N C SUPPORT 'A Building as Historical Evidence' in the Resource Book for Teachers will help prepare for investigating the building's design and decoration as evidence of the ideology of the Stuart monarchs. Refer to 'A Visit for Art Historians' for a suggested programme for older pupils. Also the special use of space and shape can be explored in relation to the Banqueting House's function in Stuart times. Make use of information technology in the programme.

There is a C17 London Trail which includes the Banqueting House and is suited to children aged ten and over. Teacher's Resource Book: also useful to sixth form and students in tertiary education. There are also on-site sessions for schools which include Stuart dance; costumes and masques available during summer term.

OPENING Pre-booked parties of school schildren and students in full-time education on curriculum-related visits are eligible for free admission to the Banqueting House. Free admission cannot include weekends or bank holidays. Teachers may also make a free planning visit on request.

CATERING There are no lunchroom facilities for schools. In fine weather St James's Park, which is a short walk away, could be used for picnics.

COST Monday to Saturday 10.00am–5.00pm (last admission 4.30pm), closed Sunday, 24–26 December, 1 January, Good Friday, other public holidays and at short notice for Government functions.

DISABLED FACILITIES No access for wheelchairs to the Hall which is up a flight of approximately 35 steps.

DIRECTIONS Nearest tube: Westminster, Embankment, Charing Cross. BR: Charing Cross.

Barbican Art Gallery
- Christine Stewart
- Barbican Centre, London. EC2Y 8DS
- 071-638 4141 FAX 071-628 0364

Barbican Art Gallery opened in 1982 and is owned, funded and managed by the Corporation of London, occupying two floors (levels eight and nine) within the Barbican Centre. Each year the gallery has between four and six temporary exhibitions, along with a selection of works by Sir Matthew Smith from the Corporation of London's collection. The Gallery's exhibition programme of 19th- and 20th-century art includes regular photographic exhibitions.

N C SUPPORT The Schools' Programme includes practical workshops with specific reference to syllabus requirements. Regular information on forthcoming exhibitions, exhibition guides, education notes (produced for certain exhibitions) and details of Schools' Programme.

OPENING Monday and Wednesday to Saturday 10.00am–6.45pm, Tuesday 10.00am–5.45pm, Sunday and bank holidays 12.00 noon–6.45pm.

VISITS OUT
LONDON & THE SOUTH EAST

CATERING Education Room: bookable free for use by groups Monday to Friday 10.00am–4.00pm.

COST For details of Schools' Programme workshops and other events contact Christine Stewart.

DISABLED FACILITIES Access is on the level via main lifts to gallery entrance on level eight. Inside the gallery there is a staircase to level nine and a service lift. Please ask a gallery warder if you wish to use the service lift. For details of the Centre's facilities for those with disabilities, including free parking, ring 071-638 4141 and ask for the Information Desk.

DIRECTIONS Tube and BR: Moorgate, Barbican, St Paul's, Bank, Liverpool Street, Farringdon, St Paul's Thameslink, Cannon Street (not all these stations open every day). On foot: follow signs and yellow lines from Barbican and Moorgate tube stations to Centre. Coach: setting down and picking up only in Silk Street.

Basingstoke Canal Centre
- Visitor Manager
- Mytchett Place Road, Mytchett, Surrey. GU16 6DD
- 0252 370073 FAX 0252 371758

Exhibition of the history and wildlife of the Basingstoke Canal.

N C SUPPORT Teachers' pack and worksheet available. Phone for details.

OPENING Tuesday to Sunday 10.00am–4.30pm.

CATERING Classroom and servery available for use.

COST Exhibition: £1.00 per person (includes guidebook). Boat trips: £1.00. Accompanying adults free.

DISABLED FACILITIES Wheelchair access and toilets and showers.

DIRECTIONS Coach access to Centre from A321 at Mytchett via Mytchett Lake Road.

Bateman's Burwash
- The Administrator
- Etchingham, East Sussex. TN19 7DS
- 0435 882302

Rudyard Kipling's home, 1902–36; built by a local ironmonger in 1634. Kipling's rooms and study as they were during his lifetime; garden; watermill grinds corn for flour; alongside is one of the oldest working water-driven turbines in the world, installed by Kipling; his 1928 Rolls-Royce is on show in its original garage.

N C SUPPORT Teachers' resource book; children's guide. National Curriculum links with Science, Technology, History and English.

DISABLED FACILITIES The mill is not suitable for wheelchair users, but ground floor of house and garden are accessible; there are routes which avoid the steps. Adapted toilet in car park.

DIRECTIONS Half a mile south of Burwash (A265); approached by road leading south from west end of the village or north from Woods Corner (B2096). Bus: RDH/Autopoint 318 Hurst Green to Heathfield (passing BR Etchingham) (Tel: 0273 478007). BR: Etchingham three miles.

VISITS OUT
LONDON & THE SOUTH EAST

Battle Abbey
- The Head Custodian
- Ticket Office, High Street, Battle, East Sussex. TN33 0AD
- 0424 773792

Visitors can explore the actual battlefield of Hastings, stand where Harold's men stood and see where William the Conqueror's horsemen turned the tide of battle and won the day. The abbey was founded c.1070 by William to atone for the bloodshed, with the high altar built on the very spot where King Harold fell. The magnificent 14th-century gatehouse is now open to the public, housing a new museum which traces the history of the site from the Battle of Hastings onwards.

OPENING All year round. Good Friday or 1 April (whichever is earlier): Tuesday to Sunday 10.00am–6.00pm, plus Mondays in winter. Abbot's Hall open to public during school summer holidays only.

DISABLED FACILITIES Personal stereo tour available for the partially sighted, those in wheelchairs or with learning difficulties. Accessible but there are some steps.

DIRECTIONS At south end of Battle High Street (OS Map 199; ref TQ 749157). Bus: Hastings Buses/Maidstone and District 4/5 Maidstone to Hastings (Tel: 0634 832666). BR: Battle half a mile.

Battle Museum of Local History
- Mrs A M Swann
- Langton Memorial Hall, High Street, Battle, East Sussex. TN33 0JL
- 0424 773116

The Museum contains a display of artefacts and pictorial records illustrating the development of the town of Battle from 1066 to the present day, and the occupation of the land by temporary settlers prior to the Battle of Hastings.

N C SUPPORT Short talks on subjects specified by schools, artefact handling sessions and conducted tours of this small museum can be provided by prior arrangement.

OPENING Easter to end September: Monday–Saturday, 10.00am–1.00pm and 2.00pm–5.00pm. Sunday 2.00pm–5.00pm. 1 October to Easter: by arrangement.

CATERING None.

COST £12 for first group (of up to 25 children), £8.00 for each successive group.

DISABLED FACILITIES None.

DIRECTIONS The museum is situated upstairs at the rear of the Langton Hall, which is in Battle High Street opposite the Post Office and facing the Abbey Green.

Battle Town Model
- Mrs K Field
- The Almonry, High Street, Battle, East Sussex. TN33 0EA
- 0424 772727

Scale model of conservation area of Battle in Medieval Hall House with garden. Light and sound commentary. Shop and restaurant.

N C SUPPORT Key Stage 2, Local history supplement. Key Stage 3, Interpretations AT2.

OPENING Easter to end September: Monday to Saturday 10.00am–

VISITS OUT
LONDON & THE SOUTH EAST

5.00pm, Sunday 12.00 noon–5.00pm. 1 October to Easter: Monday to Saturday 10.00am–4.00pm, Sunday 12.00 noon–4.00pm.

CATERING Restaurant on site.

COST Children 70p, adults £1.00, Senior Citizens 70p, family £3.00. School parties 70p, accompanying adults free.

DISABLED FACILITIES None.

DIRECTIONS North end of Battle High Street, on left by zebra crossing.

Bayham Abbey
- The Head Custodian
- The Dower House, Lamberhurst, Kent. TN3 8BE
- 0892 890381

These riverside ruins are of a house of 'white' canons, founded c.1208 and preserved in the 18th century, when its surroundings were landscaped to create the delightful setting in which visitors find the ruins today.

OPENING Good Friday or 1 April (whichever is earlier) to 30 September: daily 10.00am–6.00pm.

DISABLED FACILITIES No access.

DIRECTIONS One and three quarter miles west of Lamberhurst off B2169 (OS Map 188; ref TQ 651366). Bus: Warrens 256 BR Tunbridge Wells to Wadhurst (Tel: 0800 696996). BR: Frant four miles.

Bekonscot Model Village
- Barry Newman
- Warwick Road, Beaconsfield, Bucks. HP9 2PL
- 0494 672919

A miniature world where time has stood still for over 60 years. An ideal place to bring junior children. A unique teaching aid showing rural England in the 1930s.

N C SUPPORT Education pack available on request.

OPENING 12 February to 31 October: 10.00am–5.00pm

CATERING Refreshment kiosk.

COST Group rates: children £1.20, adults £2.40.

DISABLED FACILITIES Toilets. Exhibition on flat ground.

DIRECTIONS Junction 2 M40. BR: direct line Marylebone to Beaconsfield.

Bethnal Green Museum of Childhood
- P Kinsey or A Burton
- Cambridge Heath Road, London. E2 9PA
- 081-980 3204

The national collection of toys, games, puppets, etc. Also displays devoted to the social history of childhood.

N C SUPPORT Study sessions bookable in advance only.

OPENING Monday, Thursday and Saturday 10am–5.30pm, Sunday 2.30pm–5.30pm, closed Friday.

CATERING Picnic facilities.

COST Free.

DISABLED FACILITIES Please phone in advance.

DIRECTIONS Tube: Bethnal Green. Bus: 8, 253.

VISITS OUT
LONDON & THE SOUTH EAST

Bexhill Museum
- Brenda Mason, Curator
- Egerton Road, Bexhill-on-Sea, East Sussex. TN39 3JV
- 0424 211769

Small friendly museum with local history and important natural history displays. Geology and dinosaur remains. Adjacent to Egerton Park.

N C SUPPORT Cross-curricular activities a speciality. Will help make activities to complement programmes of study, particularly History, Geography, Science, Technology to Key Stage 3.

OPENING Tuesday to Friday 10.00am–5.00pm, Saturday and Sunday 2.00pm–5.00pm, closed Monday except bank holidays.

CATERING None.

COST Free if pre-booked, otherwise 25p, under 13s free.

DISABLED FACILITIES Access for wheelchair. Toilets close by.

Bexhill Museum of Costume and Social History
- Mrs P Bullock or Mrs M Rymer
- Upper Sea Road, Manor Gardens, Bexhill Old Town. TN40 1RL
- 0424 210045

Display of costume, toys and social history memorabilia from 18th century.

N C SUPPORT Displays of Victorian clothes and artefacts with some 'hands-on' opportunities to learn about them.

ANNUAL OR ONE OFF EVENT Changing displays annually.

OPENING Usually April to November: Monday to Friday 10.30am–5.30pm weekdays, Saturday and Sunday 2.00pm–5.00pm. Other months school parties by prior arrangement.

CATERING Cafes nearby; picnic opportunities in surrounding manor gardens.

COST Children 50p, adults £1.00, Senior Citizens 70p, teachers free.

DISABLED FACILITIES Easy access.

DIRECTIONS A quarter of a mile north from Bexhill Station. Junction Upper Sea Road and High Street, Bexhill.

Bignor Roman Villa
- Charlotte Compton, Curator
- Bignor, Pulborough, West Sussex. RH20 1PH
- 07987 259

The Roman Villa is situated in a superb rural setting to the north of the South Downs, only one mile from the South Downs Way. The mosaic floors, discovered in 1811, are some of the finest in Britain and they are displayed under cover. The Museum also contains many interesting artefacts found on the site during excavations, and these tell the story of the Villa over the years.

OPENING March to May: Tuesday to Sunday and bank holidays 10.00am–5.00pm. June to September: daily 10.00am–6.00pm. October: Tuesday to Sunday 10.00am–5.00pm.

CATERING A cafeteria serves tea, coffee and light snacks. Free picnic area for visitors to Roman Villa.

COST Children (under 16s) £1.15, adults £2.25, Senior Citizens £1.50. Group rates (parties of ten or more): children (under 16s) 95p, adults £1.80, Senior Citizens £1.50, one teacher free for every ten pupils. Guided tour: £7.50 per group (up to about 30 people).

DISABLED FACILITIES Yes.

DIRECTIONS Off A283, Stane Street.

Birdworld
- Janet Newman
- Holt Pound, Farnham, Surrey. GU10 4LD
- 0420 22992 **FAX** 0420 23715

Best bird collection in the country. Incubation research centre with lots of rare baby birds in the breeding season. Penguin island, seashore walk, indoor tropical walk. Picnic and play area. New Jenny Wren farm.

N C SUPPORT All children are given a coloured question booklet. Also available: teachers' packs on specialised topics such as eggs, legs and feet, beaks; bird language, flight, senses, fossil birds, etc.

OPENING Summer: 9.30am–6.00pm. Winter: 9.30am–4.00pm.

CATERING Cafeteria (seats 100). Pizza and chips snack bar in picnic area.

COST Children £1.65, adults £2.55 (1993 prices).

DISABLED FACILITIES Solid flat paths. Wheelchairs available. Special toilet facilities.

DIRECTIONS Three miles south of Farnham on the A325.

Bishop's Waltham Palace
- The Head Custodian
- Bishop's Waltham, Hants. SO3 1DH
- 0489 892460

The medieval seat of the Bishops of Winchester once stood in an enormous park. There are still wooded grounds surrounding the mainly 12th- and 14th-century remains visitors can see today. They include the Great Hall and three-storey tower, as well as the moat which once surrounded the palace. The round floor of the Dower House is furnished as a 19th-century farmhouse, with an exhibition on the powerful Winchester Bishops on the first floor.

OPENING All year round. Good Friday or 1 April (whichever is earlier) to 30 September: daily 10.00am–6.00pm. October to Maundy Thursday or 31 March (whichever is earlier): Tuesday to Sunday 10.00am–4.00pm. Closed 24–26 December and 1 January.

DISABLED FACILITIES Wheelchair access to grounds only.

DIRECTIONS In Bishop's Waltham (OS Map 185; ref SU 552173). Bus: Hampshire Bus 69 Winchester to Southsea (Tel: 0962 852352), Solent Blue Line 48A/C from Eastleigh (Tel: 0703 226235). BR: Botley three and a half miles.

Bocketts Farm Park
- James or Jane Gowing
- Young Street, Fetcham, Leatherhead, Surrey. KT22 9DA
- 0372 363764

Set in beautiful countryside on the North Downs this working family farm, with old and modern breeds of animals, has outdoor paddocks and a large covered area with many friendly animals. Picnic and play areas.

VISITS OUT
LONDON & THE SOUTH EAST

N C SUPPORT Teachers' pack available with many worksheets geared to the National Curriculum. Guided tours for schools based on 'The Farming Year' and Agriculture in the Environment.

ANNUAL OR ONE OFF EVENT Lambing of 400 ewes from two weeks before Easter to end of Easter holidays.

OPENING Daily (except Christmas Day and two and a half weeks in January) 10.00am–6.00pm.

CATERING Tea rooms serving homemade lunches and cream teas in beautiful 18th-century barn.

COST Children £1.50, adults £2.00. Group rate: children £1.35, adults £1.85.

DISABLED FACILITIES Toilet. Mainly flat terrain for easy access to farm park.

DIRECTIONS Off Fetcham roundabout on A246 south of Leatherhead, five minutes from M25 junction 9.

Bodiam Castle
- Mr George Bailey
- Bodiam, East Sussex. BN32 3UA
- 0580 830436

Voted one of the 'top six castles for kids'. Bodiam Castle is the most popular example of English heritage south of the Tower of London. Built by Royal Licence of October 1385 'for the defence of the adjacent country and the resistance of our (the King's) enemies', this exciting castle blocked the River Rother from incursions by the French, who had burned Rye and Winchelsea. It remains the outstanding example of medieval military architecture.

N C SUPPORT Two Education Rooms, housed within the northeast tower and designed to link closely with the targets and themes in the National Curriculum, can be booked by schools for either a morning or afternoon session. School children can use the many 'hands-on' resources available, to experience what it was like to live in a medieval castle.

OPENING November to March Tuesday to Sunday 10.00am–sunset. April to October: daily 10.00–5.30pm.

CATERING Tea room. Burger bar.

COST Children £1.30; adults £2.50.

DISABLED FACILITIES Yes.

DIRECTIONS A28 to Ashford. A268 Northiam. A229 Hawkhurst.

Booth Museum of Natural History
- John Cooper
- 194 Dyke Road, Brighton. BN1 5AA
- 0273 552586 FAX 0273 563455

Displays include the famous Booth collection of British birds, butterflies and other insects, skeletons, fossils and minerals, as well as temporary displays and a museum shop.

N C SUPPORT Supported by the educational staff of Brighton Borough Council's Royal Pavilion and Museums Division, of which the museum is a part. Classes, loans, teaching packs.

ANNUAL OR ONE OFF EVENT A regularly produced events leaflet is available on request.

OPENING Monday to Saturday 10.00am–5.00pm, closed Thursday, Sunday 2.00pm–5.00pm.

CATERING None.

COST Free.

DISABLED FACILITIES Access for wheelchairs at rear of building; all public areas on one floor.

DIRECTIONS One and a half miles north of Brighton on the Dyke Road, close to the A27.

Bowles Outdoor Centre
- Mrs B Rudkin
- Eridge Green, Tunbridge Wells. TN3 9LW
- 0892 665665 FAX 0892 669556

A residential outdoor centre offering multi-activity educational courses, including skiing, rock climbing and canoeing. Accommodation for 72. Highest professional standards to BS5750 quality standard.

N C SUPPORT An ideal way to meet the PE curriculum requirement for an element of 'outdoor adventurous activity'. Suitable for primary or secondary schools.

OPENING All year round, subject to prior booking.

CATERING Fully catered.

COST £132 plus VAT for 5 days residential; £72–£88 per group of 12 per half day non-residential.

DISABLED FACILITIES Disabled visitors are welcome but the centre is not yet geared up for wheelchair disabled.

DIRECTIONS Signposted from the A26, between Tunbridge Wells and Crowborough.

Box Hill
- The Administrator
- Surrey
- 0306 885502

Over 1000 acres of chalk downland and woodland; a designated country park, an Area of Outstanding Natural Beauty and a Site of Special Scientific Interest; rich plant life and interesting geological features; historical and literary associations.

N C SUPPORT National Curriculum links with Science, Geography and Environmental Education. Teachers' pack.

DISABLED FACILITIES Summit area including shop and takeaway accessible. Special parking behind takeaway. Wheelchair path to viewpoint. Adapted WCs near NT shop. Braille guide.

DIRECTIONS One mile north of Dorking, two and a half miles south of Leatherhead on A24. Bus: Epsom Buses 551 Dorking to Box Hill; 551 Dorking to Box Hill (passing BR Betchworth). BR: Boxhill/Westhumble half a mile.

Brambles Wildlife Park
- Mrs S Todd
- Herne Common, Herne Bay, Kent. CT6 7LQ
- 0227 712379

Twenty acres of natural woodland. Adventure playground. Animals varying from rabbits to wildcats, ponies to wallabies. Indoor garden with frogs etc. Gift shop.

OPENING Easter to end October: daily 10.00am–5.00pm (last admission 4.15pm).

CATERING Cafeteria.

COST Children £1.40, adults £2.20, Senior Citizens £1.80. Group rates: children £1.00, adults £1.20.

VISITS OUT
LONDON & THE SOUTH EAST

DISABLED FACILITIES All access is sloped. Toilet facility.

DIRECTIONS Situated on A291 between Herne Bay and Canterbury.

Brighton Museum and Art Gallery
- Richenda McNaughton
- Church Street, Brighton. BN1 1VE
- 0273 713262 FAX 0273 779108

Houses displays of Art Nouveau and Art Deco, furniture and decorative art; fashion; Old Master and modern paintings; Sussex archaeology and history of Brighton; Ethnography and musical instruments; pottery and porcelain; also frequent temporary exhibitions.

N C SUPPORT Offers Victorian handling sessions, which teachers run independently of the Education Officer. Supports History AT3 Key Stage 1 and Key Stage 2 Victorian Britain. Also offers handling sessions on archaeology/Stone Age, gothic costume, toys, Egyptians, worksheets and slide packs.

ANNUAL OR ONE OFF EVENT Sixth-form study days, usually in connection with temporary exhibitions, on an art theme.

OPENING Monday to Saturday 10.00am–5.30pm, Sunday 2.00pm–5.00pm, closed Wednesday.

COST Free.

DISABLED FACILITIES Ground-floor access only (stairs to toilets in basement and up to cafe on first floor). Nearest toilets in Royal Pavilion or Pavilion Gardens.

DIRECTIONS Half a mile from Brighton Station adjacent to Royal Pavilion.

Brighton Sea Life Centre
- Katherine Mercer
- Marine Parade, Brighton. BN2 1TB
- 0273 604234 FAX 0273 681840

A display of British marine fish in tanks designed to look like their natural habitat and the longest walk in Europe through an underwater tunnel with sharks and stingrays.

N C SUPPORT Two work books in line with Key Stages 1 and 2 of the National Curriculum; ages 4–7 and 8–12 with teachers' notes and three work cards and notes for over 12s.

ANNUAL OR ONE OFF EVENT Special kids entertainments during Easter and Summer holidays.

OPENING Early part of season: 9.00am–10.00am. Later part of season: daily 9.00am–6.00pm.

CATERING Restaurant serves hot and cold food.

COST Children £3.25, adults £4.25, Senior Citizens £3.75, students £3.25, schools £32.25, people with disabilities £2.80. Groups: children £2.75, adults £3.75, students £2.75.

DISABLED FACILITIES Ramps, wheelchair access, adapted toilets.

DIRECTIONS Opposite Palace Pier on Brighton seafront.

British Museum
- Education Service
- Great Russell Street, London. WC1B 3DG
- 071-323 8043

The British Museum is one of the great museums of the world,

VISITS OUT
LONDON & THE SOUTH EAST

showing objects from prehistoric times to the present day.

N C SUPPORT For Key Stage 2 History the Museum offers INSET on Roman Britain, Greeks, Anglo Saxons, History of Writing, all linked to schools' TV and radio. The Assyrians exhibition introduces new teaching resources as do the recently opened Sackler Galleries for Mesopotamia including the Assyrians. For Geography teaching at all Key Stages the Museum is collaborating with the 'Learning through Action' team at the Museum of Mankind (see separate listing). Also National Curriculum links with Religion and Art.

ANNUAL OR ONE OFF EVENT For a list of planned events for the academic year write to the Education Service of the Museum.

OPENING All visits must be booked, however small the group and whatever age. All educational visits are scheduled to try and avoid overcrowding of specific galleries, some of which are enormously popular. Before phoning read the leaflet 'Planning Your Visit to the British Museum', which is available from the Education Service.

CATERING School lunch room must be booked at least one term in advance. Cafe and restaurant at the end of Room 2 cannot accommodate large groups.

COST Free. All teacher study days are also free.

DISABLED FACILITIES Can make special arrangements for people with disabilities when booked in advance.

DIRECTIONS Contact the Education Section concerning drop-off points, entrances, etc.

Broadstairs Youth Hostel
- Richard Bell
- Thistle Lodge, 3 Osborne Road, Broadstairs, Kent. CT10 2AD
- 0843 604121 FAX 0843 604121

Mid-Victorian villa, accommodating up to 37 in clean, simple comfort at value-for-money prices. Historic traditional seaside resort with strong Dickensian links. Nearby Channel Ferry and medieval Sandwich.

N C SUPPORT Contact Manager for details. Nearby are Thanet Technical College, Kent School of English and Hilderstone College for Performing Arts.

ANNUAL OR ONE OFF EVENT Dickens Festival second week in June (0843 861045).

OPENING All year round: daily. Booking is necessary in winter. Daytime access by arrangement.

CATERING Self-catering groups a speciality (well-equipped kitchen available) but continental breakfasts/lunchpacks also available.

COST Per night: under 18s £4.60, adults £6.90 (1993 prices); with sole-use rental during winter at good discounts.

DISABLED FACILITIES No.

DIRECTIONS Broadstairs is on the coast, two miles north of Ramsgate Ferry-Port, on extreme tip of Kent. Broadstairs railway station is 100 yards from the Youth Hostel.

VISITS OUT
LONDON & THE SOUTH EAST

Brunel Exhibition Rotherhithe
- N G De Salis
- Brunel Engine House, Tunnel Road, London. SE16 4LF
- 081-318 2489

Within the original engine house in Tunnel Road, Rotherhithe, the exhibition commemorates the world's first subaqueous tunnel built by Sir Marc and Isambard K Brunel between 1825 and 1843.

N C SUPPORT Industrial Archaeology, Victorian Civil Engineering.

ANNUAL OR ONE OFF EVENT Guided tours and lectures.

OPENING First Sunday of the month 12.00 noon–4.00pm. Otherwise by arrangement.

COST Adults £1.50, Concessions 50p. No group discounts.

DIRECTIONS Tube: Rotherhithe (East London line). BR: New Cross, New Cross Gate then East London Line. Bus: Waterloo Station to London Bridge, Peckham P11; Liverpool Street to London Bridge, Lewisham 47; Euston to Greenwich, 188. Docklands Light Railway: Shadwell then East London line.

Buckinghamshire Railway Centre
- C Taylor
- Quainton Road Station, Station Road, Quainton, Aylesbury, Bucks. HP22 4BY
- 0296 655720 FAX 0296 655450

A working railway museum.

N C SUPPORT A comprehensive collection covering the major development of the railways over the last 140 years which can be linked to History and Technology.

OPENING Monday to Friday 10.00am–5.00pm, weekends and bank holidays 11.00am–6.00pm. Steam operation is Easter to October: Sunday; June to August: Wednesday.

COST Special rates for schools and group visits. Please telephone.

DISABLED FACILITIES The majority of the Centre is accessible, including toilets, refreshments, etc.

DIRECTIONS Take A41 Banbury Road out of Aylesbury and follow brown tourist signs.

Butlin's Southcoast World
- Robert Lee
- Bognor Regis, West Sussex. PO21 1JJ
- 0243 822445 FAX 0243 824902

Day visits with a difference. Enjoy the sub-tropical waterworld, funfair, games complex, boating lake, feature film, outdoor funpool, Wizzy's World and Wizzy's Kingdom, both ideal for children under five feet tall, and much more.

N C SUPPORT Workbooks available on request.

OPENING April to October: daily 10.00am.

CATERING Full range available; pre-paid discounted menus available to schools.

COST Main season admission from £5.99 and special schools' discount of £2 per pupil when booked and paid in advance. Please check for 1994 prices/discounts.

VISITS OUT
LONDON & THE SOUTH EAST

DISABLED FACILITIES Most areas accessible to wheelchairs.

DIRECTIONS A259 into Bognor Regis. Day customer entrance is situated on the sea front.

Cabaret Mechanical Theatre
- Sarah Alexander
- 33-34 The Market, Covent Garden, London. WC2E 8RE
- 071-379 7961 FAX 071-240 3198

An exciting and unique experience where over 70 machines come to life at the touch of a button.

N C SUPPORT Very useful and imaginative module for CDT courses.

OPENING Tuesday to Saturday 10.00am–6.30pm. Monday 12.00 noon–6.30pm. Sunday 11.00am–6.30pm.

CATERING None.

COST Children under 5 free, adults £1.75, students £1.00. Family (two adults and up to three children) £4.25. Concessions available.

DISABLED FACILITIES None.

DIRECTIONS Lower Courts, Covent Garden market.

Cabinet War Rooms
- Liz Newton
- Clive Steps, King Charles Street, London. SW1A 2AQ
- 071-930 6961 FAX 071-839 5897

The emergency underground accommodation provided to protect the Prime Minister and the British Government against air attack during World War II.

N C SUPPORT Programme of free illustrated talks linked to the History National Curriculum; project sheets; free sound guides available in a special version for children.

OPENING 10.00am–6.00pm (last admission 5.15pm).

CATERING No catering facilities but visitors can eat packed lunches in the Conference Room.

COST Schools: children £1.50, one teacher per ten pupils free, £3.00 for additional adults.

DISABLED FACILITIES Toilet. Lift down to Museum. Accessible throughout to disabled visitors.

DIRECTIONS Tube: Westminster (Circle and District lines). BR: Charing Cross.

Calshot Activities Centre
- David Evans
- Calshot Spit, Fawley, Southampton. SO4 1BR
- 0703 892077 FAX 0703 891267

Residential and non-residential courses for children aged nine upwards. Accommodation for 150. Ideal location on the shores of the Solent and near the New Forest. Outdoor and adventure education, field studies at Key Stages 2–3. Fully approved by British Canoe Union and Royal Yachting Association.

N C SUPPORT Teachers' pack, including video, on request.

VISITS OUT
LONDON & THE SOUTH EAST

OPENING All year round.

CATERING Yes.

COST £125 for five-day residential, £70 for weekends.

DISABLED FACILITIES Limited.

DIRECTIONS From M27 on to M271, then A35 and on to A326 signposted Fawley.

Calshot Castle
- The Head Custodian
- Calshot Spit, Fawley, Southampton. SO4 1BR
- 0703 892023

Henry VIII built this coastal fort in an excellent position, commanding the sea passage to Southampton. The fort houses an exhibition and recreated pre-World War I barrack room.

OPENING Good Friday or 1 April (whichever is earlier) to 30 September: daily 10.00am–6.00pm.

DIRECTIONS On spit, two miles south-east of Fawley off B3053 (OS Map 196; ref SU 488025). Bus: Solent Blue Line X9, 39 Southampton to Calshot (passes BR Southampton) to within one mile (Tel: 0703 226235).

Camden Arts Centre
- Laurie Peake or Mandy Prowse
- Arkwright Road, London. NW3 6DG
- 071-435 2643 FAX 071-794 3371

Camden Arts Centre is North London's major centre for contemporary and 20th-century art. With a lively programme of exhibitions and extensive studio facilities the Centre is uniquely placed to offer extended provision to schools in the shape of general visits, workshops and longer-term projects with artists-in-residence at the Centre.

N C SUPPORT The Centre offers schools skill-based projects in its pottery, printmaking, painting and sculpture studios through half-day or whole-day workshops, using a combination of discussion-based and practical activities.

ANNUAL OR ONE OFF EVENT News-sheets giving details of exhibitions and workshops, etc. are produced every seven weeks. Please write for details.

OPENING Tuesday to Thursday 12.00 noon–8.00pm, Friday to Sunday 12.00 noon–6.00pm, closed Monday. School groups: Tuesday to Friday from 10.00am. Usual workshop hours 10.00am–12.00 noon and 1.00pm–3.00pm.

CATERING Space to eat sandwiches is available if arranged in advance.

COST All events are free to school groups. Maximum 15 places per workshop. Groups with special needs are given extra planning time and professional support is brought in where necessary.

DISABLED FACILITIES The Centre regrets that access to the galleries and toilets is difficult with a steep flight of stairs to both. Staff are available to assist visitors who use wheelchairs if notified in advance.

DIRECTIONS Tube: Finchley Road, Hampstead. BR: Finchley Road and Frognal. Bus: 13, 82, 113.

LONDON & THE SOUTH EAST

Canterbury Heritage Museum
- Ms Marit Hendriks
- Stour Street, Canterbury, Kent
- 0227 452747 FAX 0227 455047

Set in a breathtaking medieval building, this award-winning new attraction is an absorbing experience of the city's 2000-year history and its treasures. Computer, hologram and audio-visual techniques. New Rupert Bear Gallery.

N C SUPPORT Roman resource pack for teachers. Loan boxes are available, e.g. Roman, Medieval Pottery, Canterbury at War resource pack.

OPENING Monday to Saturday 10.30am–5.00pm (last admission 4.00pm). June to end October: also Sunday 1.30pm–5.00pm (last admission 4.00pm).

COST Children 70p, adults £1.40, concessions £1.00. Discount of 10% for groups of ten or more.

DISABLED FACILITIES Access to ground floor only.

DIRECTIONS By road: A2 then Central Car Parks. BR: Canterbury East and West stations are within walking distance.

The Canterbury Tales
- Mark Allen
- St Margaret's Street, Canterbury, Kent. CT1 2TG
- 0227 454888 FAX 0227 765584

A breathtaking recreation of medieval life, on a 40-minute 'pilgrimage'. A selection of Chaucer's colourful stories are brought vividly to life by characters from the Tales, using light, sounds and smells!

N C SUPPORT Resource pack available, meeting needs of National Curriculum as part of a Local History/Geography study at Key Stage 2 or Key Stage 3 and following the core study unit of Medieval Realms.

OPENING March to October: daily 9.30am–5.30pm. November to February: Sunday to Friday 10.00am–4.30pm, Saturday 9.30am–5.30pm.

CATERING Coffee shop.

COST Prices on application. One adult free for every ten children.

Capel Manor Horticultural & Environmental Centre
- Pat Webb, Courses Officer
- Bullsmore Lane, Enfield, Middx. EN1 4RQ
- 0992 763849 FAX 0992 717544

Capel Manor is one of the country's leading horticultural and environmental centres and offers school visits to the farm, gardens or environmental centre or a combination to suit schools' needs.

N C SUPPORT All education programmes are linked to the National Curriculum. Details of all programmes are available on request. Several publications are also available. Please ask for the publications list.

ANNUAL OR ONE OFF EVENT Various shows and events take place throughout the year.

OPENING Gardens: April to October: daily 10.00am–5.00pm. November to March: Monday to Friday only 10.00am–4.30pm. Farm: April to October: weekends and school holidays 1.00pm–5.30pm. Environmental Education Centre: pre-booked groups only.

CATERING Refreshments normally available in the gardens. No catering facilities at the farm or Environmental Education Centre.

COST Children £1.00, adults £2.00, concessions £1.50. For environmental day visits for primary schools led by experienced staff (includes a farm visit): children £4.50, accompanying teachers free.

DISABLED FACILITIES Access and toilets on both sites.

DIRECTIONS Junction 25 of the M25. Travel south down the A10 and follow the signs to Capel Manor.

Carisbrooke Castle
- The Head Custodian
- Newport, Isle of Wight. PO32 1XY
- 0983 522107

The castle dates from Norman times and is best known as the prison of Charles I in 1647–8. There are some seven acres of castle and earthworks to explore, including the impressive gatehouse, the delightful chapel and the keep, and visitors can also see donkeys working a 16th-century wheel to pull water from a well. The Governor's Lodge houses the island's County Museum.

OPENING All year round. Good Friday or 1 April (whichever is earlier) to 30 September: daily 10.00am–6.00pm, plus Monday in winter.

CATERING Restaurant/cafe (normally open summer season only).

DISABLED FACILITIES Wheelchair access grounds and lower levels only.

DIRECTIONS One and a quarter miles southwest of Newport (OS Map 196; ref SZ 486877). Bus: Southern Vectis 91A from Newport in summer, otherwise 1B/C, 7/A, 16 from Newport and Yarmouth to within quarter of a mile (Tel: 0983 62264). BR: Ryde Esplanade nine miles. Ferry: West Cowes (Red Funnel).

Carlyle's House
- Mrs G A Elwes, Custodian
- 24 Cheyne Row, London. SW3 5HL
- 071-352 7087

18th-century house belonging to the National Trust. Contains furniture, portraits, personal relics, etc. of the period. Readings of Victorian poets, from the writings of Thomas Carlyle, take place in the drawing room.

N C SUPPORT A Victorian personality, in a Victorian setting: the interior has remained unchanged for close on 100 years. Historical quiz available.

ANNUAL OR ONE OFF EVENT A specialist house for those interested in history and houses. Carlyle was a historian and philosopher: The 'True Sage of Chelsea'.

DISABLED FACILITIES None.

DIRECTIONS Between Kings Road, Chelsea, and The Embankment, off Oakley Street. Nearest tube: South Kensington, Sloane Square. Bus: 239, 11, 19, 22, 49.

VISITS OUT
LONDON & THE SOUTH EAST

Chartwell
- The Administrator
- Westerham, Kent. TN16 1PS
- 0732 866368

Home of Sir Winston Churchill from 1924: the rooms, left as they were in his lifetime, evoke his career and interests, with pictures, maps, documents and personal mementoes; a museum of his many gifts and uniforms; terraced gardens and lake with black swans; garden studio containing many of Churchill's paintings.

N C SUPPORT National Curriculum links with Science, Art and History. Children's guide.

DISABLED FACILITIES Telephone the Administrator for special parking; ground floor accessible; small lift to first floor; garden difficult. Adapted toilet in coach park.

DIRECTIONS Two miles south of Westerham, fork left off B2026 after one and a half miles. Bus: London & Country 320 BR Bromley N to Westerham (passing BR Bromley S); 410 Reigate to Westerham (passing BR Oxted); Kentish Bus 483 Sevenoaks to Westerham (passing BR Sevenoaks) (Tel: 0800 696996). BR: Edenbridge four miles.

Chaucer Heritage Trust
- Philippe Wibrotte
- Chaucer Heritage Centre, 22 St Peter's Street, Canterbury, Kent. CT1 2BQ
- 0227 470379 FAX 071-2290635

Promotes the life, times and works of Geoffrey Chaucer for the general public and schools.

N C SUPPORT Talks and dramatisations on all aspects of Geoffrey Chaucer. Key Stage 4 and sixth form. Resource material is available.

ANNUAL OR ONE OFF EVENT Annual conferences: Easter Pilgrimage, and July London and Canterbury Festivals; exhibitions, concerts, illustrated talks, theatre ('Canterbury Tales' in Nevill Coghill's modern version (with or without music), small, medium and large productions), fairs and commemorative services (Southwark Cathedral).

OPENING School parties can visit festival events in London and Canterbury. Easter Pilgrimage (London to Canterbury). Information available from above address three months before events.

COST Fees or expenses depend on type of programme.

Chelsea Physic Garden
- Dawn Sanders
- 66 Royal Hospital Road, London. SW3 4HS
- 071-352 5646 FAX 071-376 3910

One of the oldest botanic gardens in Britain. Particularly specialises in medicinal plants. New this year: world medicine garden area.

N C SUPPORT Education pack available at £2.50 if purchased at garden or £4.50 mail order. Pack covers a variety of topics with National Curriculum links.

OPENING Schools: Monday to Friday by prior arrangement (Thursday and Friday are particularly good times).

VISITS OUT
LONDON & THE SOUTH EAST

CATERING No catering facilities.

COST Free.

DISABLED FACILITIES Toilets are generally accessible.

DIRECTIONS Tube: Sloane Square. Ten minutes walk from BR: Battersea Park and walk via Albert Bridge.

Chessington World of Adventure
- Brian Sedgley
- Chessington, Surrey. KT9 2NE
- 0372 729560 FAX 0372 725050

Chessington World of Adventures offers an opportunity for pupils to learn about conservation through education. Free education talks on animals by their keepers. Free Teachers' Open Days.

N C SUPPORT Teachers' booklets available free for National Curriculum Key Stages 1 and 2, project booklet for Upper Primary and Lower Secondary, GCSE problem-solving for Geography and Biology and Design and Technology in preparation.

OPENING Term-time: Monday to Saturday daily 10.00am. Theme Park 2.00pm season April to October, remainder of the year 2.00pm only.

CATERING Two restaurants, plus numerous fast food and healthy snacks available all over the park.

COST Term-time: £4.50. July: £6.00. One teacher free for every ten pupils.

DISABLED FACILITIES Guide for people with disabilities available on request.

DIRECTIONS CWOA is situated 12 miles from London on the A243, only two miles from both the A3 and M25 junction 9. Free coach and car park.

Chichester District Museum
- Susan Fullwood
- 29 Little London, Chichester, West Sussex. PO19 1PB
- 0243 784683

Displays tell the story of the people and area of the Chichester district. Major strengths are archaeology, especially Roman, geology and local social history. There is also a programme of temporary exhibitions.

N C SUPPORT The museum runs an artefact loan service for schools. This has been brought into line with the National Curriculum requirements. Also a teachers' handbook on the use of museums by schools.

OPENING Tuesday to Saturday 10.00am–5.30pm.

CATERING None.

COST Free.

DISABLED FACILITIES Wheelchair access to ground floor gallery.

DIRECTIONS Little London is a turning off East Street opposite McDonalds (which can't be missed).

Chiddingstone Castle
- Custodian
- Nr Edenbridge, Kent. TN8 7AD
- 0892 870347

One of the historic houses of Kent, formerly the seat of the Streatfields. Rebuilt in the Castle style by William Atkinson c.1805. Denys Eyre Bower made it his home in 1955, bringing his famous collection here. Stuart and Jacobite historical, Japanese lacquer and swords, Egyptian antiquities, Buddhist art. Left to the nation on Bower's death in 1977.

N C SUPPORT Key Stage 1: background on social, domestic and historical change; Key Stage 2: English history, Stuarts. Antiquity: Egypt, Japanese art. Religion: Buddhism. Changes in building, architecture and furnishing. Aims to fire the child's imagination. Older children: collections offer specialised information.

OPENING Open to parties of 20 or more at any time of the year, by arrangement.

CATERING Children generally prefer to bring a picnic. They can use the grounds if fine, or there is cover if wet. Tea, coffee, soft drinks and cakes can be provided.

COST Parties of 20 or more: children £1.50, helpers and teachers free (1993 price).

DISABLED FACILITIES Most of ground floor on one level. Easy stairs to first floor.

DIRECTIONS Off the B2027 at Bough Beech. Accessible from M25 to A21.

The Children's Farm
- Mrs J A Farrant
- Great Knelle Farm, Beckley, Rye, East Sussex. TN31 6UB
- 0797 260250 FAX 0797 260347

Traditional working farm. Watch the dairy experience, make butter and cream. Feed the lambs during March and April. Cows, sheep and pigs. Puppet show, tractor ride, talking scarecrow.

N C SUPPORT The Dairy Experience, school rooms, guided tours with valuable information on farms.

ANNUAL OR ONE OFF EVENT Lamb feeding in March and the beginning of April. Sheep shearing first two weeks in June. Hop picking August and September.

OPENING 10.30am–5.30pm.

CATERING Farmhouse breakfasts, lunches and snacks and milkbar by the playground.

COST Group bookings £3.00 per head. Guided tours include tractor ride, puppet show and milkshake. General public: children £2.50, adults £3.50, Senior Citizens £2.50.

DISABLED FACILITIES Toilets. Ramps and concrete to all shops. Wheelchair available to arrivals.

DIRECTIONS A21 to Flimwell, left to Hawkhurst. Straight on till A268 on left signed to Rye. (Just off the A28 near the village of Northiam).

Chiltern Open-Air Museum
- Janet Ahlberg
- Newland Park, Gorelands Lane, Chalfont St Giles, Bucks. HP8 4AD
- 0494 875542

Museum of buildings, rescued from demolition and re-erected in beautiful countryside. Historic buildings include medieval barn, Victorian toll house, Edwardian toilet, 1940s prefab. Additional attractions: Iron Age house, nature trail.

N C SUPPORT Themed visits: Homes through the Ages, Victorian Britain, Medieval Realms, Building Materials, Food and Farming. Key Stage 1 days and GCSE coursework

VISITS OUT
LONDON & THE SOUTH EAST

programmes. Individual programmes devised with schools include work experience, Technology, History A-Level.

OPENING All year round. Monday to Friday 9.00am–5.00pm. All school parties must be booked.

COST Children £2.50, accompanying adults free.

DISABLED FACILITIES Toilet. Braille guidebook, map and labels; taped guide.

DIRECTIONS Signposted on leaving junction 17 of the M25. Signposted from A413 Chalfont St Giles.

Chisenhale Gallery
- Juliet Dean
- 64–84 Chisenhale Road, London. E3 5EZ
- 081-981 4518

Founded in 1980 by a group of resourceful artists, Chisenhale has expanded dramatically over the past 12 years, and now houses not only a large community of artists but also a gallery committed to the promotion of innovative contemporary art, and an Education Workshop.

N C SUPPORT The Education Workshop runs a year-round programme of activities which are targeted in particular at schools, colleges and community groups. The organisation's aim is to increase people's awareness and enjoyment of contemporary art, with an emphasis placed on active rather than passive involvement.

ANNUAL OR ONE OFF EVENT Examples of the education programme include studio and gallery visits, artists' talks, practical workshops relating to the exhibitions, training sessions and long-term projects. These are devised in close consultation with schools, other relevant organisations and individuals so as to meet the particular educational needs of each group. These activities take place both in the Education Space and in the form of 'outreach' work in borough-wide venues such as schools, colleges and community centres.

OPENING Wednesday to Sunday 1.00pm–6.00pm. The Gallery is closed for approximately two weeks in between exhibitions.

COST Admission to all exhibitions is free. A small charge is made for workshops.

DISABLED FACILITIES Level access and toilet. Newly renovated Education Space with access for people with disabilities.

DIRECTIONS Tube: Mile End, Bethnal Green. Bus: 8, 106, D6, D77 (evenings and Sundays only) to Roman Road.

Chiswick House
- The Head Custodian
- Burlington Lane, Chiswick, London. W4
- 081-995 0508

One of the first English Palladian villas, built c.1725 for Lord Burlington and internationally renowned. The interior decoration is by William Kent, as are the beautiful Italianate gardens, with classical statues and neoclassical temples. Both house and gardens are undergoing extensive restoration. There is an exhibition on the ground floor with a film telling the story of the house and gardens.

OPENING All year. Good Friday or 1 April (whichever is earlier) to 30 September: daily 10.00am–6.00pm. Closed 26 December and 1 January.

CATERING Picnic facilities.

DISABLED FACILITIES Wheelchair access to exterior and ground floor only.

DIRECTIONS Bus: LT 190, 290 Hammersmith to Richmond; E3 Greenford to Chiswick (Tel: 071-222 1234). BR: Chiswick half a mile. Tube: Turnham Green one mile.

Cholderton Rare Breeds
- Mrs Pam Sydenham
- Farm Park, Amesbury Road, Cholderton, Salisbury, Wilts. SP4 0EW
- 0980 64438

A touching experience with animals from our history. 50 or more breeds of endangered farm animals and poultry and 50 or more breeds of rabbit. Lots under cover. Nature trail with badger sett and lots more.

N C SUPPORT Various expert talks geared to age group and subject. On booking, a pack including History and Information on the Animals, worksheets and colouring sheets is sent.

OPENING Easter to end October: daily 10.00am–6.00pm.

CATERING Cafeteria, picnic areas. Under cover if wet.

COST Special school rates: children £1.35, adults and teachers £2.50, one teacher free per 25 children.

DISABLED FACILITIES Most areas are accessible. No special toilets.

DIRECTIONS Just off A338, nine miles north of Salisbury; or A303, six miles west of Andover (Brown signs).

Chuffa Trains
- Bryan Rising
- Railmania Museum, 82 High Street, Whitstable, Kent. CT5 1AZ

The Museum houses an impressive collection of railway artefacts, memorabilia and model trains. These are used to tell the history of British railways over the centuries. Particular emphasis is given to the Canterbury and Whitstable Railway, which opened in 1830.

N C SUPPORT Lectures with slides are given on the Canterbury and Whitstable Railway and also other historic developments and events in the history of Britain's rail network. Subjects supported in the National Curriculum are: Science, History, Geography, Technology and Maths.

OPENING Monday to Friday 10.00am–3.00pm, Saturday 10.00am–5.00pm.

CATERING None.

COST Children 75p, adults £1.50, Senior Citizens £1.00.

DISABLED FACILITIES None.

DIRECTIONS Follow M2 until junction 7, take A299 Thanet Way to Whitstable, turn left at Long Reach roundabout down Borstal Hill and into the High Street. Museum is next to and above the Nationwide Building Society.

VISITS OUT
LONDON & THE SOUTH EAST

Church Farmhouse Museum
- Gerrard Roots
- Greyhound Hill, London. NE4 4JR
- 081-203 0130

Seventeenth-century farmhouse, in a small public garden. Reconstructed 14th-century kitchen, dining room and scullery. Continuous programme of temporary exhibitions (local/social history, decorative arts). Parties should be of no more than 30 people. Booking essential.

N C SUPPORT The museum has a large collection of 19th- and early 20th-century domestic material which can be made available to schools (contact the curator).

OPENING Monday to Thursday 10.00am–5.00pm, Saturday 10.00am–1.00pm and 2.00pm–5.30pm, Sunday 2.00pm–5.30pm, closed Friday.

CATERING None.

COST Free.

DISABLED FACILITIES Access is extremely difficult.

DIRECTIONS Off Watford Way (A41), Hendon. Bus: 113, 143, 183, 240. Tube: Hendon Central. BR: Hendon.

Cissbury Ring
- Nicola Creed, Regional Public Affairs Manager
- National Trust Regional Office, Polesden Lacey, Dorking, Surrey. RH5 6BD
- 0372 453401

Second largest Iron Age hillfort in the country; 60 acres enclosed: highest point 600 feet above sea level; dates from c.250 BC; contains sites of about 250 neolithic flint mines dating from c.2500 BC; splendid views on clear days to Beachy Head and the Isle of Wight, including seascape, townscape and mainly cultivated downland.

N C SUPPORT National Curriculum links with History, Geography and Environmental Education.

CATERING Restaurant.

DISABLED FACILITIES All showrooms and parts of garden accessible; some fairly firm gravel paths. Disabled drivers may park near shop, restaurant and house with permission of the Administrator. Adapted WC near restaurant. Rose and lavender gardens. Braille guide to house.

DIRECTIONS Five miles northwest of Dorking, two miles south of Great Bookham, off A246 Leatherhead to Guildford road. Bus: London & Country 433 from BR Guildford & BR Dorking, summer Sunday; 408 Guildford to West Croydon. BR: Boxhill and Westhumble, two miles; Bookham two and a half miles.

City Museum
- Christopher Spendlove
- Museum Road, Old Portsmouth, Hants. PO1 2LJ
- 0705 296905 FAX 0705 875276

'The Story of Portsmouth' exhibition uses objects, paintings, audio-videos and costume figures/sound effects in a series of room settings to show life in Portsmouth from the 17th century to the 1950s.

N C SUPPORT History Key Stage 2: CSUs on Tudor and Stuart times. Victorian Britain: Britain since 1930. Key Stage 2: SSU on Local History.

Key Stage 3: The Era of the Second World War. Geography ATs 2 and 4: Understanding Places and Human Geography. Art Craft and Design AT2: Study of Original Works of Art.

OPENING Daily 10.30am–5.30pm. Closed 24–26 December).

CATERING None.

COST Schools and other educational establishments in Great Britain free if booked in advance. Foreign language schools 51p per pupil. Teachers free.

DISABLED FACILITIES Complete access for people with disabilities, including toilet. Loan of wheelchair available.

DIRECTIONS By road: follow signposting to City Museum from M27/M275 into Portsmouth (look for the symbol (M) on the brown signposts).

The Clipper Ship Cutty Sark
- J Bowen
- King William Walk, Greenwich, London. SE10 9HT
- 081-858 3445 FAX 081-853 3589

Only surviving tea clipper, with displays chronicling the building and life of the ship. Also a large collection of merchant ship figureheads.

N C SUPPORT Guided tours on 'Ships and Seafarers', 'Explorers' and 'Victorians'. Teachers' guide and children's activity book.

OPENING Monday to Saturday 10.00am–6.00pm, Sunday and Good Friday 12.00 noon–6.00pm (October to March closes 5.00pm).

CATERING Evening functions by arrangement.

COST Adults £3.25, concessions £2.25, family £8.00. Groups: adults £2.60, concessions £1.80.

DISABLED FACILITIES Access to middle deck, stairlift to lower deck, no access to top deck.

DIRECTIONS Intersection of A200 and A206. BR: Greenwich from London Bridge, Charing Cross and Waterloo. Frequent riverboat service.

Clandon Park
- The Administrator
- West Clandon, Guildford, Surrey. GU4 7RQ
- 0483 222482

Built in early 1730s for the 2nd Lord Onslow by the Venetian architect Giacomo Leoni; two-storeyed marble hall; Onslow family pictures and furniture; Gubbay collection of porcelain, furniture and needlework; old kitchens, Queen's Royal Surrey Regimental Museum; garden with parterre, grotto and Maori House.

N C SUPPORT National Curriculum links with History and Art.

OPENING Write to or telephone the administrator of the house, giving preferred date and time, the size and age of the group, and the main purpose of the visit.

COST Usually there is a reduction of around 50% for children aged 16 and under when accompanied by their teacher. Schools' Corporate Members are admitted free. However, please note that there may be a small charge for any additional educational facilities or activities.

DISABLED FACILITIES Parking near the front of the house for disabled drivers only; disabled visitors may be set down at the house. Adapted toilet on lower ground floor; ramp to garden. Braille guide.

DIRECTIONS At West Clandon on A247, three miles east of Guildford; if using A3 follow signposts to Ripley to join A247 via B2215. Bus: Blue Saloon 532 BR Bookham to Guildford (passing BR Clandon). BR: Clandon one mile.

Colne Valley Park Groundwork Trust
- Martin Healey
- Denham Country Park, Colne Valley Park Centre, Denham, Uxbridge, Middx. UB9 5PG
- 0895 832662 FAX 0895 833552

The Colne Valley Park Groundwork Trust is an environmental charity working in partnership with business, public authorities and communities in order to achieve sustainable environmental improvement.

N C SUPPORT The Trust supports the aims of the National Curriculum through a number of local and national projects. These projects link schools with industry, farms and other cross-curricular themes. Farmlink, linking schools and farms. Greenlink, linking schools and industry. Bulb campaign and other national projects.

OPENING Monday to Friday 9.00am–5.30pm.

CATERING No catering facilities.

COST Normally donations at the discretion of the school.

DISABLED FACILITIES Available.

DIRECTIONS Denham roundabout, off A40.

Commonwealth Institute
- Schools' Reception
- Kensington High Street, London. W8 6NQ
- 071-603 4535 FAX 071-602 7374

The Commonwealth Institute is the centre for Commonwealth education and culture in Britain, promoting knowledge and understanding of the Commonwealth through its permanent exhibitions on the 50 Commonwealth countries, cultural programmes and a diverse Education Programme which offers a unique range of workshops for schools, teachers' seminars and conferences.

N C SUPPORT A free copy of the Education Programme and a publications' mail order list is available from Marketing and Publicity, ext. 305. Curriculum resource pack and other specialist services are available from the Education and Curriculum Section, ext. 254, 284. A multi-media resource loan scheme and reference library are offered by the Commonwealth Resource Centre, ext. 501.

ANNUAL OR ONE OFF EVENT Commonwealth Day is celebrated on the second Monday in March and the Institute hosts a lively cultural and educational programme which schools can participate in. For further details, please contact the Schools' Reception, ext. 283.

VISITS OUT
LONDON & THE SOUTH EAST

OPENING Please ring for details.

CATERING Commonwealth Brasserie, schools' dining room bookable in advance, ext. 283.

COST Under 5s free. Discount of 10% for groups of ten or more. Special school rates.

DISABLED FACILITIES Toilets, lift, assistance. Visitors with impaired mobility welcome. Please call in advance for assistance, ext. 283.

DIRECTIONS Tube: High Street Kensington, Holland Park, Olympia, Earl's Court.

Commonwork Land Trust
- Margaret Williams
- Bore Place, Chiddingstone, Edenbridge, Kent. TN8 7AR
- 0732 463255 FAX 0732 740264

An educational trust enabling people of all ages and abilities to explore the world in which they belong. Educational, arts and environmental activities are offered, drawing on resources on site: 500-acre farm, biogas digester and hand-made brickworks.

N C SUPPORT INSET courses for teachers. Primary School Support Project: effective ways to work towards a better sense of community in school and off-site for teachers and children, especially special needs groups. Activities offered link with attainment targets in Science, Geography, History, Technology and Art.

OPENING All year round.

CATERING Self-catering or catering.

COST Varies: on average £3.00 per visit for activities.

DISABLED FACILITIES Wheelchair access to educational spaces.

DIRECTIONS Commonwork is 20 minutes from junction 5 of the M25 onto A21 towards Edenbridge. Follow directions for Cuddinglingstone Causeway, third turning on right and follow signposts to Bore Place.

Courtauld Institute Galleries
- Julia Weiner, Schools' Events Organiser
- Somerset House, Strand, London. WC2R ORN
- 071-873 2526/2538

In 1990 the Courtauld Institute Galleries moved to Somerset House, a premier Neo-classical building designed by Sir William Chambers and former home of the Royal Academy of Arts. The Permanent Collections range from the 13th century to the present day and include the world famous collection of Impressionist and Post-Impressionist paintings bequeathed by Samuel Courtauld. Among the artists represented in this collection are Manet, Monet, Cézanne, Gauguin and Toulouse Lautrec. The Education Officer can arrange talks on any aspect of the collection for school groups for a small fee; lectures on Impressionism and Post-Impressionism are particularly popular. Please give at least one month's notice. Also half-term and holiday workshops for kids aged 7–11 on various subjects including visit to the Galleries and practical workshop. For further details contact Sarah Phillips at above address.

VISITS OUT
LONDON & THE SOUTH EAST

N C SUPPORT Workshops for Key Stages 1 and 2 formulated to fulfil Attainment Targets of the National Curriculum for Art and Design. Pack on Impressionism for French teachers. Guided visits for GCSE and A-Level Art and Design and History of Art students.

OPENING Galleries: Monday to Saturday 10.00am–6.00pm, Sunday 2.00pm–6.00pm, closed 24–26 December and 1 January but open over Easter.

CATERING Cafe on lower ground floor. Classroom for primary school workshops which acts as lunch room.

COST Admission to the Galleries is free for all students under 18 in groups. Adults £3.00. Concessions £1.50. Free to all University of London staff and pupils and members of NAC.

DISABLED FACILITIES Enter by the West service door. Wheelchairs are available at the entrance, and parking can be arranged for minibuses if advance notice is given.

DIRECTIONS Nearest tube: Temple, Covent Garden. BR: Charing Cross, Waterloo. Bus: 1, 4, 6, 9, 11, 13, 15, 68, 77A.

Crafts Council
- The Education Section
- 44a Pentonville Road, London. N1 9BY
- 071-278 7700 FAX 071-837 6891

The Crafts Council is the national body for promoting the crafts in England and Wales. Its Education Section offers a range of educational activities and facilities covering the whole spectrum of the crafts.

The Crafts Council has an Education Workshop which is used for a range of activities to promote greater understanding of the crafts, including craftspeople in residence, practical workshops for adults and pupils and school holiday workshops. There are opportunities to handle new materials and tools, experiment with a range of working techniques, exercise critical judgement through looking at and handling finished artefacts and pieces in the making, and develop a conceptual vocabulary.

N C SUPPORT INSET provision for teachers includes Curriculum Development conferences, craft study days and practical workshop sessions to develop craft skills in a range of disciplines.

OPENING Tuesday to Saturday 11.00am–6.00pm, Sunday 2.00pm–6.00pm, closed Monday.

COST Please apply direct for details.

DISABLED FACILITIES Wheelchair access to Gallery and Education Workshop.

DIRECTIONS Tube: Angel (two minutes). Bus: 4, 19, 30, 38, 43, 56, 73, 153, 171, 171a, 196, 224, 263a, 279, 279a.

Cuming Museum
- Caroline Ellis
- 155–157 Walworth Road, London. SE17 1RS
- 071-701 1342

Southwark's history from Roman times to the present together with worldwide collections on the Cuming family and annual special exhibition.

N C SUPPORT Series of events based on specific aspects of the History curriculum.

OPENING 10.00am–5.00pm Tuesday to Saturday

CATERING None.

COST Free.

DISABLED FACILITIES Difficult for people with mobility problems: one flight of stairs.

DIRECTIONS Tube/BR: Elephant & Castle quarter of a mile. Bus: 12, 35, 40, 45, 68, 171, 176, P5.

Darwin Museum
- Mrs Morris
- Downe House, Luxted Road, Downe, Kent. BR6 7JT
- 0689 859119

Home of Charles Darwin from 1842 until his death in 1882. The Museum houses memorabilia from the voyages of HMS Beagle and the old study in which he wrote *The Origin of the Species*. Garden is under restoration to original plan.

N C SUPPORT In preparation. Teachers should contact the Curator for details.

ANNUAL OR ONE OFF EVENT Special activities can be arranged.

OPENING Wednesday to Sunday and bank holiday Mondays 1.00pm–6.00pm (last admission 5.30pm). Closed mid-December, January and February.

CATERING None.

COST Children £1.00, adults £2.50, students £1.50, Senior Citizens £1.50. No discount.

DISABLED FACILITIES Ground floor exhibits and level garden paths.

DIRECTIONS By public transport: BR to Bromley South, then 146 bus to Downe Village (no service on Sunday). From there a short walk (quarter mile) along Luxted Road. By car: via A21 from London to Bromley, then A233 south toward Biggin Hill; or via Orpington (A224); signposted.

D-Day Museum & Overlord Embroidery
- Christopher Spendlove
- Clarence Esplanade, Southsea, Hants. PO5 3NT
- 0705 296905 FAX 0705 875276

The magnificent 'Overlord Embroidery', 34 panels telling the complete story of the D-Day operation, with personal soundguide, audio-visual show; scenes and sounds from life in wartime Britain. Join the landing craft on the beach with military vehicles.

N C SUPPORT History Key Stage 2: CSU 4 Britain since 1930. History Key Stage 3: CSU 5 The Era of the Second World War.

ANNUAL OR ONE OFF EVENT Annual Military Vehicle Rally in May/June. Contact Visitor Services Officer for details.

OPENING Daily 10.00am–5.30pm. Closed 24–26 December.

CATERING None.

COST Special Education Group rates.

DISABLED FACILITIES Complete access, including toilets. Loan of wheelchairs available.

DIRECTIONS By road: follow signposting to D-Day Museum from M27/M275 or M27/A2030 into Portsmouth (look for the symbol (M) on the brown signposts).

Deal Castle
- The Head Custodian
- Victoria Road, Deal, Kent. CT14 7BA
- 0304 372762

Crouching low and menacing, the huge, rounded bastions of this austere fort, built by Henry VIII, once carried 119 guns. It is a fascinating castle to explore, with long, dark passages, battlements, and a huge basement with an exhibition on England's coastal defences.

OPENING All year round. Good Friday or 1 April (whichever is earlier) to 30 September: daily 10.00am–6.00pm.

DISABLED FACILITIES Personal stereo available for the partially sighted, those with learning difficulties. Wheelchair access to the courtyards and ground floor only.

DIRECTIONS Southwest of Deal town centre (OS Map 179; ref TR 378521). Bus: from surrounding areas (Tel: 0800 696996). BR: Deal half a mile.

Denmans Garden
- M J Neve
- Denmans Lane, Fontwell, Nr Arundel, West Sussex. BN18 0SU
- 0243 542808 FAX 0243 544064

Unique 20th-century three and a half acre garden, artistically planted and forming vistas of colours, shapes and textures which create all-year interest. Majestic trees, flowering shrubs, rare plants nurtured by John Brookes.

N C SUPPORT None.

OPENING All year round: daily 9.00am–5.00pm, including bank holidays, closed Christmas Day.

CATERING Garden cafe 10.00am–5.00pm: coffees, teas, lunches, cream teas, homemade cakes and savouries.

COST Children over 5 years £1.25, adults £2.25, Senior Citizens £1.85, Groups of 15 or more £1.65.

DISABLED FACILITIES Double doors to garden cafe. No steps or steep slopes in garden.

DIRECTIONS Six miles east of Chichester, six miles west of Arundel. Adjacent Fontwell Racecourse. Denmans Lane is off A27 eastbound.

Design Museum
- Alex Adie, Education Department
- Butler's Wharf, Shad Thames, London. SE1 2YD

The Design Museum is the first museum of its kind in the world. Through regular changing exhibitions and displays, which include cars, furniture, domestic appliances, cameras and graphics, and the educational activities, the Design Museum offers an accessible introduction to the role of design in our everyday lives.

N C SUPPORT The schools' programme provides workshops

VISITS OUT
LONDON & THE SOUTH EAST

and materials for primary, secondary, further and higher education students. A teachers' broadsheet and sample worksheets are available on request.

OPENING Museum: daily 10.30am–5.30pm. Library: Tuesday to Friday 10.30am–5.30pm. Closed for lunch 1.30pm–2.30pm.

CATERING No designated school picnic area. Cafe on the ground floor of the Museum.

COST All pre-booked college groups receive a discount if studying on state-funded courses: 50p without activity, half-hour introduction £1.00, half-day workshop £1.50, full-day workshop £2.50.

DISABLED FACILITIES Lift available to all floors. Wheelchair access to the Library and Lecture Theatre.

DIRECTIONS The Design Museum is south of the river by Tower Bridge. Tube: Tower Hill (District/Circle line), walk over Tower Bridge; London Bridge (Northern line and BR), walk along Tooley Street.

Charles Dickens' Birthplace
- Christopher Spendlove
- 393 Old Commercial Road, Portsmouth, Hants. PO1 4QL
- 0705 296905 FAX 0705 875276

Charles Dickens was born in 1812. The small terraced house has been restored, decorated and furnished in Regency style appropriate to the time of his parents and includes the couch on which he died.

N C SUPPORT English Key Stage 3 Charles Dickens.

OPENING Special openings at Christmas and, Charles Dickens' birthday, 7 February. Contact above for details.

CATERING None.

COST Schools and other educational establishments in Great Britain free if booked in advance. Foreign language schools 51p per pupil. Teachers free.

DISABLED FACILITIES Not accessible to people with disabilities.

DIRECTIONS By road: follow signposting to Charles Dickens' Birthplace from M27/M275 into Portsmouth (look for the symbol (M) on the brown signposts).

The Dickens House
- Dr D Parker
- 48 Doughty Street, London. WC1N 2CF
- 071-405 2127 FAX 071-831 5175

Charles Dickens's home while he was working on *The Pickwick Papers*, *Oliver Twist* and *Nicholas Nickleby*, 48 Doughty Street provides displays of books, manuscripts, pictures, furniture, personal possessions, etc.

N C SUPPORT Relevant to Key Stage 2 core study unit on Victorian Britain. Joint Curriculum pack in preparation.

OPENING Monday to Saturday 10.00am–5.00pm.

CATERING No catering facilities.

COST Children under 16 £1.00, students of 16 or more £2.00.

DISABLED FACILITIES None.

DIRECTIONS Off Gray's Inn Road and Guildford Street.

VISITS OUT
LONDON & THE SOUTH EAST

Diocesan Education Resource Centre
- Rachel Head
- The Education Centre, The Cathedral, Staghill, Guildford, Surrey. GU2 5UP
- 0483 450423 FAX 0483 4504224

A resource lending library of books, videos and equipment for use in religious education in schools and parish, catering for all ages.

OPENING Monday to Thursday 9.30am–5.00pm.

CATERING None.

COST No membership fee; hire of videos: £1.00 per week.

DISABLED FACILITIES Yes.

DIRECTIONS First building on left as visitors approach the cathedral.

The Dove Narrowboat Project
- David Scoffield
- Meanwhile Gardens, 156 Kensal Road, London. W10 5BN
- 081-969 3069

A voluntary group running a canal narrowboat as a low-cost resource for community organisations, schools and families. Carries 12 passengers on day trips in the London area. Can include visit to the London Canal Museum in day-trip itinerary.

OPENING Day trips at times between 9.00am and 5.00pm to suit groups' needs. All year including weekends.

CATERING Fully equipped kitchen available on board.

COST Annual membership £10.00, day hire £55.00.

DISABLED FACILITIES Wheelchair access via ramp from towpath. Lift between rear deck and open-plan cabin. Toilet.

DIRECTIONS Mooring adjacent to office at Meanwhile Community Gardens.

Dover Castle
- The Head Custodian
- The Keep, Dover, Kent. CT16 1HH

Dramatically located on the white cliffs overlooking the English Channel, man and nature have combined to make this one of Western Europe's most impressive medieval fortresses. Its history is alive with reminders of a glorious past from the Iron Age to World War II. The great medieval keep towers to 95 feet and has walls up to 21 feet thick. There is also a rare Roman lighthouse, the remarkably restored Saxon church of St Mary of Castro, and ancient earthworks and tunnels, dating back to 1216. It was from this amazing complex of tunnels and wartime operation rooms, concealed in the white cliffs beneath Dover Castle, that the Dunkirk evacuation was masterminded in 1940.

N C SUPPORT Teachers' Handbook in preparation.

ANNUAL OR ONE OFF EVENT At some sites each year there are special educational events, often with the involvement of experts such as musicians and storytellers, for visiting educational groups.

OPENING All year round. Good Friday or 1 April (whichever is earlier) to 30 September: Tuesday to Sunday 10.00am–4.00pm. 1 October to Maundy Thursday or 31 March (whichever is earlier): 10.00am–

VISITS OUT
LONDON & THE SOUTH EAST

4.00pm. Closed 24–26 December and 1 January.

CATERING Restaurant/cafeteria.

COST Student groups and school parties are admitted free to English Heritage properties, but should book in advance through the relevant Regional Office.

DISABLED FACILITIES Wheelchair access to courtyard and grounds; some very steep slopes.

DIRECTIONS On east side of Dover (OS Map 179; ref TR 326416). Bus: East Kent 90 from BR Dover Priory (Tel: 0800 696996). BR: Dover Priory one and a half miles.

Dover Gaol
- Kim Morton, Education Officer
- Dover Town Hall, Biggin Street, Dover, Kent
- 0304 242766

A reconstructed Victorian courtroom and gaol where models using the high-tech talking heads technology tell their stories.

N C SUPPORT A chance to experience Victorian life. A resource pack using written and photographic evidence is available.

ANNUAL OR ONE OFF EVENT One-day Victorian Festival in November.

OPENING Summer: Monday to Saturday 10.00am–4.30pm, Sunday 2.30pm–4.30pm. Winter: Wednesday to Sunday 10.00am–4.30pm.

CATERING Room available for eating packed lunch in, if requested prior to booking.

COST Children £1.70, accompanying adults free.

DISABLED FACILITIES Lift facilities for disabled.

DIRECTIONS On Main Street inside Dover Town Hall.

Dover Museum
- Kim Morton, Education Officer
- Market Square, Dover, Kent. CT16 1PB
- 0304 201066 FAX 0304 241186

A three-floor local history and archaeology museum which is a rich source for schools looking for history study and local study material.

N C SUPPORT Opportunities exist for work in many areas of the National Curriculum, including Art, English, Geography, History, Science and Technology. A range of worksheets and loan packs are available.

ANNUAL OR ONE OFF EVENT A regular programme of special days for schools is organised every term.

OPENING 28 March to 8 November: daily 10.00am–6.00pm. 9 November–27 March: daily 10.00am–5.00pm.

CATERING Cafeteria; room available for eating packed lunch.

COST School children 65p, accompanying adults free.

DISABLED FACILITIES Full lift facilities for disabled.

DIRECTIONS In centre of town, adjacent to White Cliffs Experience.

Education at Beaulieu
- Graham Carter
- The National Motor Museum, Beaulieu, Hants. SO42 7ZN
- 0590 612345 FAX 0590 612624

Residential opportunities at the Out of Town Centre link to educational programmes in National Motor Museum, historic buildings and the countryside. Day visits also welcome. Details on request.

N C SUPPORT Services can be matched to a wide range of National Curriculum Attainment Targets (e.g. History Key Stage 2, Transport, Environment). Foreign language talks and tours.

OPENING Daily (except Christmas Day). Hours vary according to season.

CATERING Brabazon Restaurant and cafeteria.

COST Group rate (min. 15): children £3.75, adults £5.65.

DISABLED FACILITIES Yes.

DIRECTIONS M27 westbound, M271 (junction 3) to Southampton, A326 and follow signs.

Emmetts Garden

☛ The Administrator
✉ Ide Hill, Sevenoaks, Kent. TN14 6AY

Five-acre hillside garden, one of the highest in Kent; noted for its collection of rare trees and shrubs; spring and autumn colours; additional parts of garden now open and restoration work in progress.

N C SUPPORT National Curriculum links with Science and Geography. Teachers' pack; tree trail.

DISABLED FACILITIES Most of the garden is accessible; golf buggy (seats three) available from car park to ticket hut only; wheelchairs available for garden. Adapted WC.

DIRECTIONS One and a half miles south of A25 on Sundridge to Ide Hill Road, one and a half miles north of Ide Hill off B2042, leave M25 at exit 5, then four miles. Bus: Nu-Venture 404 from BR Sevenoaks, alight Ide Hill, one and a half miles. BR: Sevenoaks four and a half miles, Penshurst five and a half miles.

ENGLISH HERITAGE

National Curriculum Support
Almost every aspect of the curriculum can be explored at English Heritage properties. They can be used not only for studying History but linked to other subjects as varied as English, Maths, Science, Technology, Geography and Music. English Heritage has produced a wide range of National Curriculum teachers' guides and videos to give plenty of stimulating ideas. Write to English Heritage Education Service, Keysign House, 429 Oxford Street, London W1R 2HD, for a free copy of the resources catalogue.

Annual or one-off event At some sites each year there are special educational events, often with the involvement of experts such as musicians and storytellers, for visiting educational groups.

Cost Student groups and school parties are admitted free to English Heritage properties, but should book in advance through the relevant Regional Office.

See individual entries for all other information.

Appuldurcombe House

VISITS OUT
LONDON & THE SOUTH EAST

Battle Abbey
Bayham Abbey
Bishop's Waltham Palace
Calshot Castle
Carisbrooke Castle
Chiswick House
Deal Castle
Farnham Castle Keep
Fort Brockhurst
Hurst Castle
Jewel Tower
Kenwood
Lullingstone Roman Villa
Marble Hill House
Medieval Merchant's House
Osborne House
Pevensey Castle
Portchester Castle
Rangers House
Richborough Castle
Rochester Castle
St Augustine's Abbey
Upnor Castle
Walmer Castle
Westminster Abbey
Wolvesey Old Bishops Palace
Yarmouth Castle

English National Opera

- Rebecca Meitlis, Co-Director
- (The Baylis Programme), London Coliseum, St Martin's Lane, London. WC2N 4ES
- 071-836 0111 ext. 354 **FAX** 071-379 5530

The Baylis Programme plays a vital role in the framework of English National Opera. Established in 1985, the Programme has created a unique repertoire of schemes and projects which enable people from the widest possible community to extend the meaning of, and get to grips with, opera. Planning for the department is done annually with a projected sketchy plan for three and five years ahead.

N C SUPPORT The Programme has worked in all areas of the National Curriculum in the past. The Programme offers workshops and creative activities in schools, other venues and occasionally at their rehearsal studios in West Hampstead. The aim is to improve the ability to provide INSET activities in the light of LMS and they offer written materials where possible and appropriate. They run two youth opera groups: Live Wires 9–14 years, Saturday mornings; and Live Culture 15–30 years, Thursday evenings and occasional Sundays. These are creative and lively groups who devise their own music-theatre. Contact the Baylis Programme for more information.

COST Contact the Baylis Programme for details.

DISABLED FACILITIES They do not run specific projects for disabled children at the moment though no one is specifically excluded.

DIRECTIONS Studios are situated in West Hampstead.

The English Wine Centre

- Christopher Ann
- Alfriston Roundabout, East Sussex. BN26 5QS
- 0323 870164 **FAX** 0323 870005

A small vineyard, English Wine Museum is situated in beautiful countryside; with 17th-century oak barn and seven boules pitches.

N C SUPPORT Interesting tours and tastings of non-alcoholic drinks for under 18s.

VISITS OUT
LONDON & THE SOUTH EAST

ANNUAL OR ONE OFF EVENT English Wine and Regional Food Festival with entertainment in September.

OPENING All year round. Monday to Saturday 10.00am–5.00pm, Sunday 12.00 noon–3.00pm. Closed 24 December to 2 January.

COST There are a number of different tours, some lasting one and a quarter hours, others four hours, with lunch, tour and tastings included. Please write for details.

DISABLED FACILITIES Toilets and ramp entrances where it is necessary. Site is level.

DIRECTIONS Twenty yards off the A27 at the Alfriston roundabout between Eastbourne and Lewes.

Epping Bury Farm Centre
- Doug Hosie
- Upland Road, Epping, Essex. CM16 5SA
- 0992 578400

Rare Breeds Farm Centre. Cattle, sheep, pigs, goats, poultry, pets corner. Many in barns for all-weather visits. Nature trail, lake, stream, picnic sites, play areas.

N C SUPPORT 'The Ideal Open Air Classroom', a 20-minute talk on any farming or conservation topic, is included for all school visits when requested. Teacher information sheets available.

OPENING All year: daily 9.30am–8.30pm.

CATERING Cafe. DIY barbecue (no charge). Indoor/outdoor picnic facilities.

COST Farm: children £1.25, adults £2.00. Adventure Barn: children £2.00. Farm and Barn: 10% discount on groups of 12 or more; children £2.75, teachers free.

DISABLED FACILITIES Flat. Ramp access to all buildings and pens.

DIRECTIONS M25 to M11, north. First exit (seven) Roundabout B1393 signposted Epping. Two miles turn right into Upland Road, signposted Epping Green. In Upland Road, two miles on the left.

Eurotunnel Exhibition Centre
- Visits Coordinator
- St Martin's Plain, Folkestone, Kent. CT19 4QD
- 0303 270111 FAX 0303 270212

Free catalogue with over 20 educational publications and a description of the exhibition as an educational visit. Offers practical workshops and presentations: primary, secondary and FHE.

N C SUPPORT A learning context for Science, Technology, Geography, Environmental Education, French and German language learning, European dimension, staff development activities.

ANNUAL OR ONE OFF EVENT 1994 is the year 'Le Shuttle' services begin.

OPENING Summer: daily 10.00am–6.00pm. Winter: daily 10.00am–5.00pm.

CATERING French-style cafe, picnic area.

COST Group rate (over 10 persons): children up to 16 £1.30, adults £2.50 (1993 prices).

DISABLED FACILITIES Lift to first floor, ramps, limited access to observation tower.

DIRECTIONS Junction 12 M20: free parking.

N C SUPPORT A learning context for Science, Technology, Geography, Environmental Education, French and German language learning, European dimension, staff development activities.

ANNUAL OR ONE OFF EVENT 1994 "Le Shuttle" services begin.

OPENING Summer: daily 10.00am–6.00pm. Winter: daily 10.00am–5.00pm.

CATERING French-style cafe, picnic area.

COST Group rate (over 10 persons): Children up to 16 £1.30, adults £2.50 (1993 prices).

DISABLED FACILITIES Lift to first floor, ramps, limited access to observation tower.

DIRECTIONS Junction 12 M20: free parking.

The Fan Museum
- Mrs H Alexander
- 12 Crooms Hill, Greenwich, London. SE10 8ER
- 081-305 1441 FAX 081-293 1889

The world's only fan museum. The collection of over 2000 items is housed in restored Georgian townhouses. Apart from mounting exhibitions, the Museum carries out research and conservation.

N C SUPPORT The Museum offers curriculum-based programmes, a 'hands-on' 'Study Collection' and a comprehensive library for research students.

OPENING Tuesday to Saturday 11.00am–4.30pm, Sunday 12.00 noon–4.30pm, closed Monday.

CATERING Visiting adult groups can have tea or coffee and light refreshments for a small fee by prior arrangement.

COST Children £1.50, adults £2.50, Senior Citizens and people with disabilities £1.50, families £7.50.

DISABLED FACILITIES Lift to all floors. Wheelchair ramps on front steps. Toilet.

DIRECTIONS BR: from Charing Cross, Waterloo East, London Bridge and Cannon Street. Bus: 1, 177, 180, 185, 188, 286.

Farnham Castle Keep
- The Head Custodian
- Castle Hill, Farnham, Surrey. GU6 0AG
- 0252 713393

Used as a fortified manor by the medieval Bishops of Winchester, this motte and bailey castle has been in continuous occupation since the 12th century. Visitors can see the large shell-keep enclosing a mound in which are massive foundations of a Norman tower.

OPENING Summer season. Good Friday or 1 April (whichever is earlier) to 30 September: daily 10.00am–6.00pm.

DIRECTIONS Half a mile north of Farnham town centre on A287 (OS Map 186; ref SU 839474). Bus: from surrounding areas (Tel: 0483 605757). BR: Farnham three-quarters of a mile.

VISITS OUT
LONDON & THE SOUTH EAST

Fenton House
- Joy Ashby
- National Trust, Windmill Hill, Hampstead, London. NW3 6RT
- 071-435 3471 **FAX** 071-435 3471

Seventeenth-century merchant's house, containing collections of porcelain, needlework, furniture, paintings, early keyboard instruments and with a beautiful walled garden.

ANNUAL OR ONE OFF EVENT Regular concerts. Annual outdoor theatre.

DISABLED FACILITIES None.

DIRECTIONS Tube: Hampstead (Northern line). Holly Hill opposite, 300 yards to 'Golden Gates' entrance.

Finkley Down Farm Park
- Mrs J Waters
- Andover, Hants. SP11 6NF
- 0264 352195

The farm offers a comprehensive range of different breeds of all farm animals and poultry including children's pets and many baby animals during the season. Gift shop.

N C SUPPORT Worksheets available.

CATERING Cafeteria serving light refreshments including ice cream, sweets, tea, coffee, etc. There is also a play and picnic area.

COST Children £1.50, adults £2.50, one adult free for every ten children (1993 prices).

DISABLED FACILITIES All areas accessible for wheelchairs. Toilet.

DIRECTIONS Signposted from A303. Follow signs around Ring Road A3093 for two miles.

Fishbourne Roman Palace
- The Secretary
- Salthill Road, Fishbourne, Chichester, West Sussex. P19 3QR
- 0243 785859 **FAX** 0243 539266

The remains of a large first-century palatial structure, under a modern cover building. Fine collection of mosaics; hypocausts; replica dining room. Also a museum and Roman garden.

N C SUPPORT Free audio-visual programme and background talk. Hour-long artefact handling and role-play sessions in the education workshop. This facility costs £30 per session, maximum 35 children per session.

OPENING 14 February to 12 December. March, April, October: daily 10.00am–5.00pm. May to September: daily 10.00am–6.00pm. February, November, December: daily 10.00am–4.00pm. Remainder of year: Sunday only 10.00am–4.00pm.

CATERING Cafeteria serving hot and cold food, snacks and drinks. The cafeteria is closed during the winter months.

COST Children £1.50, adults £3.40, students and Senior Citizens £2.70, family ticket (two adults and two children) £8.00. Adult groups (20 and above booked parties): £2.70. School parties: children £1.50, one adult free with every ten children, additional adults £2.70.

DISABLED FACILITIES Reduced admission charge: £2.70 (blind/partially sighted £1.50). Access is easy for wheelchairs, with ramps and walkways and custom-built toilet facilities. Free taped guided tours available for blind and partially sighted visitors. Small handling collection on request.

DIRECTIONS The museum is sited half a mile west of Chichester to the north of the A259, off Salthill Road, signposted from Fishbourne village. Access from the north is signposted from the A286. BR: within five minutes walking distance Fishbourne station.

Floating Point Science Theatre
- Steve Mesure
- 23 Ribston Close, Bromley. BR2 8LS
- 081-462 6441

Theatrical performances in schools using mime, physical theatre, drama and audience participation to teach science and technology.

N C SUPPORT The shows are devised to reach attainment targets in the Science and Teaching Curricula as well as addressing targets from the Maths, English and Geography Curricula. FPST tours schools in all regions.

OPENING To be arranged with school.

COST £130 + VAT per show if touring the area. £400 + VAT per day.

DIRECTIONS Contact the office for directions.

Fort Alpherst
- Mr J Loudwell
- Dock Road, Chatham, Kent. ME4 4HB
- 0634 847747

Britain's finest Georgian Fortress. Comprising a tunnel complex, surface features, ditches, revetments, magazines, barracks and redoubts. The fortifications provide excellent views of the Medway towns and the secluded corners provide ideal backdrops for period re-enactment centred on garrison life c.1815.

OPENING Daily 10.30am–5.00pm.

CATERING Light snacks, tea, coffee.

COST For groups: £2.50 and £1.50; discount of 5% for groups of 15–25, of 7.5% for groups of 26–35 and of 10% for groups of 36 or more.

DISABLED FACILITIES Limited.

DIRECTIONS A231 Chatham to Gillingham.

Fort Brockhurst
- The Head Custodian
- Gunner's Way, Elson, Nr Gosport, Hants. PO12 4DS
- 0705 581059

This was a new type of fort, built in the 19th century to protect Portsmouth with formidable firepower. Largely unaltered, the parade ground, gun ramps and moated keep can all be viewed. An exhibition illustrates the history of Portsmouth's defences. There is an Educational Centre at Fort Brockhurst. This is equipped with audio-visual, printed and relica sources appropriate to the property, which teachers can use themselves. This Centre can be booked in advance through English Heritage.

OPENING All year round. From Good Friday or 1 April (whichever is earlier) to 30 September: daily 10.00am–6.00pm. 1 October to Maundy Thursday or 31 March

VISITS OUT
LONDON & THE SOUTH EAST

(whichever is earlier): Tuesday to Sunday 10.00am–4.00pm. Closed 24–26 December and 1 January.

DISABLED FACILITIES Wheelchair access to grounds and ground floor only.

DIRECTIONS Off A32, in Gunner's Way, Elson on north side of Gosport (OS Map 196; ref SU 596020). Bus: Provincial 1–7, 37 Fareham to Gosport Ferry (passes BR Fareham, also Gosport Ferry links with BR Portsmouth and Southsea) (Tel: 0705 586921). BR: Fareham three miles.

Forty Hall Museum
- John Griffin
- Forty Hill, Enfield, Middlesex. EN2 9HA
- 081-363 8196 FAX 081-361 9098

A local history museum, housed in a 1629 mansion and set in parkland. It has a teaching/loan collection for projects, and a meeting room is available for schools' use. A teachers' pack is available.

OPENING Thursday–Sunday: 11.00am–5.00pm.

COST Admission free.

DISABLED FACILITIES Access to ground floor, toilets, parking, cafe.

DIRECTIONS Off the A10, close to M25/A10 Junction 25. BR: Gordon Hill, Turkey Street, Enfield Town, Enfield Chase.

Close to M25 and A10

FORTY HALL MUSEUM

Forty Hill, Enfield, Middx. EN2 9HA.
A 1629 mansion set in rolling parkland.
Temporary exhibitions, permanent galleries of local history.
cafe and parking.

* Meeting room available.
* Teaching/Loan Collection for project work.
* Teaching pack material available from April 1994.

Open Thursday - Sunday 11am-5pm
Tuesday and Wednesday.
group visits can be booked.

Admission FREE.
For more information
☎ 081-363 8196

Freud Museum
- Ivan Ward
- 20 Maresfield Gardens, London. NW3 5SX
- 071-435 2002 FAX 071-431 5452

Home of Sigmund Freud, founder of psychoanalysis, who lived, worked and died here. Outstanding feature is Freud's study and library with his famous couch and his antiquity collection. Exhibitions and archive film.

N C SUPPORT Educational packs available in 1994 on the history of medicine and on the Victorians. Educational Officer available for school group tours and discussions.

OPENING Wednesday to Sunday 12.00 noon–5.00pm.

CATERING None.

COST Adults £2.50, students £1.50. Concessions available. Special student group tours £2.00 each.

DISABLED FACILITIES The main part of the museum is on the ground floor which is accessible for people with disabilities. There are no other facilities.

DIRECTIONS Tube: Finchley Road five minutes (signposted) walk. Maresfield Gardens is off Fitzjohn's Avenue.

Gatwick Zoo
- Terry Thorpe
- Charlwood, Surrey. RH6 6EG
- 0293 862312

A modern zoo with animals in large enclosures, many of which are walk-through; landscaped grounds; tropical houses; education facilities. Animals include monkeys, meerkats, flamingos, parrots and penguins. Gift shop.

N C SUPPORT Teachers' notes, worksheets, guides.

OPENING March to end October: daily 10.30am–6.00pm. Winter: weekdays 10.30am–4.00pm.

CATERING Cafe, picnic tables.

COST Children (3–14 years) £2.50, adults £3.50. Discount of 10% for schools visits of 20 or more.

DISABLED FACILITIES Full access. Toilets.

DIRECTIONS From A23 and A217 just north of Gatwick Airport, follow signs to Charlwood and Zoo.

Gaveston Hall Youth Centre
- C Morris
- Nuthurst, Horsham, West Sussex. RH13 6RF
- 0403 891431 FAX 0403 891439

School journey, field study and recreation centre set in 100 acres of park, with woodland and streams, nature trail, classrooms, pond dipping and sports facilities including swimming, football, tennis, etc. Accommodation for approximately 100.

OPENING All year round.

CATERING Three meals are provided: breakfast, packed lunch and supper. The menu is varied to meet the needs of the younger generation. A tuck shop is available on request and there is a staffroom with TV, kettle and fridge. All prices include full board and recreation facilities.

COST Weekly (seven nights): £85.00 plus VAT. Monday to Friday (four nights): £52.00 plus VAT. Daily rate: £14.50 plus VAT.

DIRECTIONS The nearest town is Horsham, approximately five miles away. BR: regular train service Horsham to Victoria direct (approximately 1 hour).

Geffrye Museum
- Vicky Woollard
- Kingsland Road, London. E2 8EA
- 071-739 9893 FAX 071-729 5647

A small museum, housed in 18th-century almshouses, displaying English domestic interiors from 1600 to 1950s. The ten rooms represent the front parlour with furniture, fittings and personal ornaments.

VISITS OUT
LONDON & THE SOUTH EAST

N C SUPPORT A fully professional team, which offers class teaching in the room sets, INSET training, student training and Twilight session. Written suggestions for classwork.

ANNUAL OR ONE OFF EVENT Projects for schools each term involving practical activities.

OPENING Tuesday to Saturday 10.00am–5.00pm, Sunday 2.00pm–5.00pm, closed Monday (except bank holidays) 2.00pm–5.00pm.

CATERING Small coffee bar (not for school parties). Lunch room for packed lunches.

COST Free.

DISABLED FACILITIES Access. Toilets.

DIRECTIONS North of Liverpool Street station. Shoreditch end of the Kingsland Road (A10).

Godalming Museum

- Museum Full-Time Officer
- 109A High Street, Godalming, Surrey. GU7 1AQ
- 0483 426510

Alive, busy and welcoming local history museum featuring exhibitions chronicling Godalming's development, industries and personalities; small, walled garden in the style of Gertrude Jekyll; local studies reference library; shop.

N C SUPPORT Offers talks (tailored to groups' needs) at the Museum, plus quiz on personalities (the Woollen Industry).

ANNUAL OR ONE OFF EVENT Annual Christmas collage competition for schools.

OPENING Summer: Tuesday to Saturday 10.00am–5.00pm. Winter: Tuesday to Saturday 10.00am–4.00pm.

CATERING Soft drinks and biscuits available if arranged in advance; use of meeting room.

COST Free.

DISABLED FACILITIES Ramps (temporary, folding) available up to entrance. Access restricted to ground floor.

DIRECTIONS On High Street opposite The Pepperpot.

Goethe Institute

- B Homrighausen
- 50 Princes Gate, Exhibition Road, London. SW7 2PH
- 071-4113431 FAX 071-581 0974

Fosters mutual understanding, closer contacts, interchange and co-operation through cultural events and projects, library and information service. Teacher liaison for German as a Foreign Language, German language courses.

N C SUPPORT The Goethe Institute offers short talks (at the Institute) on topics relevant to the National Curriculum. Publicity material also free.

ANNUAL OR ONE OFF EVENT Contact the Institute for details.

OPENING Contact the Institute for details.

COST Free.

DIRECTIONS Tube: South Kensington.

VISITS OUT
LONDON & THE SOUTH EAST

Gosport Ferry Ltd
- Diane Wright
- South Street, Gosport, Hants. PO12 1EP
- 0705 524551 FAX 0705 524802

A fascinating trip around all the historic sites of Portsmouth Harbour, aboard large all-weather vessels. Live commentary given. Trips last approximately one hour.

N C SUPPORT Teachers' pack available to tie in with National Curriculum (Key Stages 1 and 2).

OPENING Trips can be arranged to suit school timetable.

CATERING Solent Enterprise has refreshment facilities available. Small boats do not.

COST Children £2.00, one teacher free for every eight children (1993 prices).

DISABLED FACILITIES Ferries and Solent Enterprise can acccommodate up to 20 wheelchairs. No toilet on board.

DIRECTIONS Junction 11 of M27. A32 into Gosport. Follow signs for ferry.

Guildhall Museum
- M I Moad, Curator
- High Street, Rochester, Kent. ME1 1PY
- 0634 848717

Conservancy board wing illustrates themes of Victorian/Edwardian life in the Medway towns.

OPENING All year round: daily 10.00am–5.30pm (last admission 5.00pm), closed Christmas Day, Boxing Day and Good Friday.

COST Free.

DIRECTIONS West end of Rochester High Street, near the bridge.

Guinness World of Records Exhibition
- Mike Tickner
- Trocadero, Piccadilly Circus, London. W1V 7FD
- 071-439 7331 FAX 071-494 1266

Brings to life thousands of the spectacular facts, feats and records from the world famous *Guinness Book of Records*.

N C SUPPORT Educational Resource pack covering Key Stages 2 and 3 and features all core and most fundamental subjects in a variety of curricular approaches (available free on request).

OPENING Daily (except Christmas Day) 10.00am–10.00pm.

CATERING Catering facilities available within the Trocadero Centre.

COST Children £3.50, adults £5.50, students £4.20. Group rates: children £2.75, adults £4.25, students £3.75.

DISABLED FACILITIES Lifts. Toilet.

DIRECTIONS Tube: Piccadilly Circus. BR: Charing Cross.

Gunnersbury Park Museum
- Sue McAlpine
- Popes Lane, London. W3 8LQ
- 081-992 1612 FAX 081-752 0686

Neo-classical mansion once home of the Rothschilds, with original kitchens. Changing social history displays feature carriages, costume, local history and special exhibitions.

N C SUPPORT Interpretative offices offers full programme of activities to schools adapted to National Curriculum. Also 'Meet the Butler/Housekeeper' sessions in the

VISITS OUT
LONDON & THE SOUTH EAST

Victorian kitchens. Some education packs and museum publications available. Member of WLMA replica costume scheme.

ANNUAL OR ONE OFF EVENT Special activity weeks on changing subjects.

OPENING Winter: daily 1.00pm–4.00pm. Summer: daily 1.00pm–5.00pm. Two schools' sessions daily (morning and afternoon).

CATERING Cafe in park. Also park benches under cover.

COST Free public access. Free education facilities for London boroughs of Ealing and Hounslow schools, except for special events and kitchens visits. All others £1.00 per head.

DISABLED FACILITIES Galleries on ground floor. Ramps. Large print exhibition texts.

DIRECTIONS Tube: Acton Town. Intersection of North Circular Road and M4.

Hackney City Farm
- Jonathan Edwards
- 1a Goldsmiths Row, London. E2 8QA
- 071-729 6381

Farm animals, gardens and fields; pottery and textiles.

N C SUPPORT Hatching in schools, Science back-up, possibilities for Art, Geography, History, Local History. Work experience.

ANNUAL OR ONE OFF EVENT Seasonal events including sheep and wool fair, country fair, pig racing, Christmas Fête, etc.

OPENING Tuesday to Sunday 10.00am–4.30pm, closed Monday.

CATERING Cafe offering light refreshments open during farm opening hours.

COST Free. Guided tours: £15.00. Free to members (£25.00 per year).

DISABLED FACILITIES Full access to all ground floor inside and out. Toilet, induction loop, facilities for sight-impaired; taped guides.

DIRECTIONS Bus: 6, 35, 48, 55. Tube: Bethnal Green, Old Street. BR: Cambridge Heath.

Hampstead Museum
- Christopher Wade, Hon. Curator
- Burgh House, New End Square, London. NW3 1LT
- 071-431 0144

Small museum in 1703 building displaying local history of Hampstead, including writers and artists such as Constable. (Run by volunteers.)

OPENING Wednesday to Sunday 12.00 noon–5.00pm, closed Good Friday and Christmas Day.

COST Free. Donations welcome.

DISABLED FACILITIES Limited.

DIRECTIONS Tube: Hampstead (Northern line).

Hampton Court Palace
- The Education Officer
- East Molesey, Surrey. KT8 9AU
- 081-781 9790/1

Hampton Court has been the home of monarchs since the 16th century and is still used today by the Royal Family for State occasions and major functions. In 1514 Cardinal Wolsey ordered building to begin on the Palace and in 1525 he presented it to King Henry VIII in a vain attempt to retain his favour.

N C SUPPORT Key Stage 2 'Tudor and Stuart Times' (CSU2) or Key Stage 3 as part of 'Crowns, Parliaments and Peoples' (CSU3). The Tudor Kitchens for 'Food and Farming' Key Stage 2 and the Royal Collection of Paintings for 'The Italian Renaissance' Key Stage 3. Use the design and decoration of the Palace for the study of size, shape, angles, straight lines, numbers and patterns. Read 'A Teacher's Guide to Maths & Historic Environment' for some good ideas.

A Teachers' Information Pack is in preparation. There are also free teachers' notes and pupils' trails for the Tudor Kitchens, notes on Technology and Methodology sheets on 'Making Sense of Buildings' and 'Looking at Paintings'.

OPENING Palace and Maze: mid-March to mid-October: Tuesday to Sunday 9.30am–6.00pm, Monday 10.15am–6.00pm. Mid-October to mid-March: Tuesday to Sunday 9.30am–4.30pm, Monday 10.15am–4.30pm. Gardens 7.00am–9.00pm.

CATERING There is a small lunch room, accommodating approximately 30, which can be booked.

COST Pre-booked parties of school children and students under the age of 18 in full-time education on curriculum-related visits are eligible for free admission to the Palace between September and April. Teachers may also make a free planning visit on request, any day of the week except Sunday.

DISABLED FACILITIES Disabled access to gardens and courtyards; one small step into Tudor Kitchens, the Tudor Wine Cellar has steps down but can be viewed from the door; the State Apartments on the first floor are accessible to groups of up to ten disabled people. Please ask for details.

DIRECTIONS The Palace and Gardens are situated on the north side of Hampton Court Bridge. BR: Hampton Court Station (direct from Waterloo). Bus: 111, 131, 216, 267, 431, 461, 511, 513, 531. Boat: Enquiries to Thames Passenger Launches (Tel: 071-930 0921) to Turks Launches (Tel: 081-546 2434).

Haringey Museum Service

☞ Penny Wheatcroft
✉ Brule Castle, Lordship Lane, London. N17 8NU
☎ 081-808 8772 FAX 081-808 4118

Historic building in park, Tudor manor house extensively rebuilt. Contains displays of local history, postal history, art gallery.

N C SUPPORT Education Officer. Handling collections available.

OPENING Thursday to Sunday 1.00pm–5.00pm. Pre-booked school parties may visit at other times.

COST Free.

DISABLED FACILITIES Permanent exhibitions are on the ground floor, fully accessible. No lifts.

DIRECTIONS At junction of Lordship Lane and Brule Grove. BR Brule Grove ten minutes. Bus: 123, 243.

VISITS OUT
LONDON & THE SOUTH EAST

Harting Down
- Nicola Creed, Regional Public Affairs Manager
- National Trust Regional Office, Polesden Lacey, Dorking, Surrey. RH5 6BD
- 0372 453401

Common of 550 acres, set within the Sussex Downs Area of Outstanding Natural Beauty; extensive views over the Weald to the north and to the coast; exceptionally rich in flowering plants; good evidence of evolving land use.

N C SUPPORT National Curriculum links with Science, Geography and Environmental Education.

DISABLED FACILITIES Contact the Administrator for access details.

Hastings Museum
- The Curator
- Cambridge Road, Hastings, East Sussex. TN34 1ET
- 0424 721202

Paintings, ceramics, Sussex pottery, Sussex ironwork, new local wildlife and dinosaur galleries, Oriental, Islamic and Australasian art, the Dutbar Hall (Indian palace) temporary exhibition programme.

N C SUPPORT Worksheets and information sheets available. School visits welcome.

OPENING All year: Monday to Friday 10.00am–5.00pm, Saturday 10.00am–1.00pm and 2.00pm–5.00pm, Sunday 3.00pm–5.00pm.

COST Admission free.

DIRECTIONS Immediately after Hastings Sports Centre on the main A21 into Hastings.

Hastings Sea Life Centre
- Nikki Hasell
- Rock-A-Nore Road, Hastings, East Sussex. TN34 3DW
- 0424 718776 FAX 0424 718757

At Hastings Sea Life Centre education and enjoyment go hand in hand for children of every age. Educational staff bring to life the fascinating underwater world and its amazing inhabitants as students experience close encounters with creatures of the deep.

N C SUPPORT Educational resources and talks given by our educational staff provide unrivalled opportunities for youngsters to experience local marine life first hand. An endless range of subjects can be studied. Teachers' resource packs and pupil work booklets are available, tailored to the National Curriculum for specific age groups. Special preliminary visits for teachers, please contact for further details.

OPENING 10.00am–5.00pm (later in summer holidays).

CATERING Breakers coffee shop.

COST Children £2.45, adults £2.45, one teacher free for every ten pupils.

DISABLED FACILITIES Adapted toilets and access to all displays except Underwater Tunnel, where there are several steps. Staff will assist.

DIRECTIONS Follow the signs to the Old Town, and Hastings Sea Life Centre is adjacent to the Shipwreck Heritage Centre.

VISITS OUT
LONDON & THE SOUTH EAST

Hastings Tourism & Leisure Department
- Barbara Browning
- 5 Robertson Terrace, Hastings, East Sussex. TN34 1JE
- 0424 442122 FAX 0424 716411

Visit the Smugglers' Adventure; Sealife Centre; 1066 story of Hastings Castle, the Embroidery; Shipwreck Heritage Centre. The Central Booking Service books all these for you with just one telephone call.

N C SUPPORT The Smugglers' Adventure, the Sealife Centre and the Central Booking Service all offer education packs.

OPENING The Shipwreck Heritage Centre can be opened for group bookings. All others: daily all year round.

CATERING Yes.

COST All attractions offer group discounts. Ask for a copy of group travel guide.

DISABLED FACILITIES Yes.

Hatfield House
- Colonel Douglas McCord
- Hatfield, Herts. AL9 5NQ
- 0707 262823 FAX 0707 275719

Celebrated Jacobean house (1611) and Old Palace (1497). Childhood home of Elizabeth I. Extensive Great Park, with nature trails, small adventure play area, national collection of model soldiers; kitchen exhibition (1833); delightful gardens; gift and garden shops.

N C SUPPORT School guided tours; 'Tudor and Stuart Times', Key Stage 2, Study Unit 2; 1833 Kitchen Exhibition, Key Stage 2, Study Unit 3, 'Domestic Life'; Interactive nature trail supported by Teacher's Handbook, Key Stages 2 and 3 in Science, Geography, History and Mathematics.

ANNUAL OR ONE OFF EVENT Living Crafts: one of the biggest and longest-established Craft Fairs in Europe, held in the grounds of Hatfield House in May.

OPENING 25 March to 10 October: park 10.30am–8.00pm; gardens 11.00am–6.00pm; house guided tours Tuesday to Friday 12.00 noon–4.00pm, Saturday 12.00 noon–4.30pm.

CATERING Restaurant open as gardens, outdoor and indoor picnic facilities.

COST House, gardens and exhibitions: children £3.00 (group £2.50), adults £4.50, Senior Citizens and groups £3.70. Park and Gardens: £2.50 and £1.70.

DISABLED FACILITIES Full access to house (lift and ramps) for individual wheelchairs, access to gardens, restaurant and park. Toilets.

DIRECTIONS On A1000, entrance opposite Hatfield BR Station. Seven miles north of Exit 23, signed from exit 4 on A1(M), two miles away.

The Hawk Conservancy
- Mrs H Smith
- Weyhill, Andover, Hants. SP11 8DY
- 0264 773750 FAX 0264 773772

Largest bird-of-prey centre in the south of England. School flying demonstration at 12.00 noon on weekdays, when children are permitted to hold a bird.

VISITS OUT
LONDON & THE SOUTH EAST

N C SUPPORT Worksheets available.

OPENING March to last Sunday in October: daily 10.30am–4.00pm (last admission; 5.00pm in summer).

CATERING Picnic area. Cafe serving hot and cold meals.

COST School groups: children £1.50, one adult free for every ten children, additional adults £3.00 (1993 prices). Must be pre-booked.

DISABLED FACILITIES Toilets. Special area for wheelchairs at flying ground.

DIRECTIONS Just off A303, three and a half miles west of Andover (well signposted).

Hayward Gallery
- Gilane Tawadros, Art Education Officer
- South Bank Centre, London. SE1 8XZ
- 071-921 0886 FAX 071-928 0063

Art Gallery. *Box office: 960*

N C SUPPORT Teachers' packs, *4249* teachers' days, children's guides/workshops, special private views for teachers.

OPENING Daily 10.00am–6.00pm, Tuesday and Wednesday until 8.00pm.

CATERING Catering available in Royal Festival Hall.

COST Variable; special group rates are available for parties of ten or more.

DISABLED FACILITIES Welcome people with disabilities. It is advisable to telephone on 071-928 3144 to ensure that the visit is as straightforward as possible.

DIRECTIONS Situated on the south bank of the Thames, the Hayward Gallery is part of the South Bank Centre, and lies between the Royal National Theatre and Royal Festival Hall. Nearest tube: Embankment. Nearest BR: Waterloo. Bus to Waterloo Bridge (request stop). Riverbus to Festival Pier.

Hertfordshire Police Schools Programme
- WPc Sally Flint
- County Headquarters, Stanborough Road, Welwyn Garden City, Herts. AL8 6XF
- 0707 331177 FAX 0707 331177

Seven Schools Liaison Officers give presentations on safety, crime, drugs and police in the community, mainly secondary year and upwards but can assist with JMI Levels. Duke of Edinburgh covered, school panels and Crime Prevention based projects. Available to schools within the Hertfordshire Police District.

ANNUAL OR ONE OFF EVENT Annual youth events covering various topics with workshops.

COST Free.

DIRECTIONS Information from WPc Flint (Youth Crime Prevention Officer) on extension 1550.

Hever Castle
- Jan Roberts
- Hever, Edenbridge, Kent. TN8 7NG
- 0732 865224 FAX 0732 866796

Thirteenth-century double-moated castle with beautiful Tudor interior. Once the home of Anne Boleyn. Restored by the Astor family at the beginning of this century. Grounds

VISITS OUT
LONDON & THE SOUTH EAST

include a maze and adventure playground.

N C SUPPORT Ideal visit for schools studying Tudors as part of the National Curriculum. There is a permanent costume exhibition in the castle featuring Henry VIII and Anne Boleyn.

ANNUAL OR ONE OFF EVENT Jousting tournaments on Saturday afternoons in June, July and August.

OPENING March to November. Gardens 11.00am–6.00pm. Castle 12 noon–6.00pm. Last admission 5.00pm. Private guided tours can be booked outside normal opening times.

CATERING Two self-service restaurants serve hot and cold food and drink.

COST Castle and garden group rates, children (5–16 years) £2.30, adults £4.40, students (17–19 years) £3.20.

DISABLED FACILITIES The ground floor of the Castle is accessible for wheelchairs and all of the garden is ramped.

DIRECTIONS Three miles southeast of Edenbridge off B2026, between Sevenoaks and East Grinstead.

The Historic Dockyard
- Jane Middleton
- Chatham, Kent. ME4 4TE
- 0634 812551 FAX 0634 826918

Eighty-acre site: an 18th-century/early 19th-century river dockyard, telling the story of ship construction up to 1964. Achieved through a lively mix of museum, gallery, commercial tenants and working craftsmen.

N C SUPPORT Friendly and professional education service, providing on-site facilities and resource material (general and specific). Assistance in planning visits/projects: other support available. Free preliminary visit for teachers.

ANNUAL OR ONE OFF EVENT A number of special events take place each year.

OPENING End October to end March: Wednesday, Saturday and Sunday. April to October: Wednesday to Sunday.

CATERING Restaurant and tea shop. Covered picnic area available. Outdoor picnic area.

COST Rates on application.

DISABLED FACILITIES Access guide, toilets.

DIRECTIONS Convenient location: good access from A2/M2. Tourist signs from main roads to visitor entrance.

HMS Belfast Museum Ship
- Sarah Hogben
- Morgan's Lane, Tooley Street, London. SE1 2JH
- 071-407 6434 FAX 071-403 0719

Europe's largest preserved World War II warship. HMS Belfast uses all seven decks to recreate the conditions of life onboard for up to 1000 sailors from 1939 to 1963.

N C SUPPORT Free teachers' information pack including sample worksheets, mini poster and exercise suggestions. Free preliminary visit for teachers, illustrated talks and a variety of films available to all pre-booked groups.

OPENING 2 November to 19 March: daily 10.00am–4.30pm. 20 March to 31 October: daily 10.00am–6.00pm. Closed 24–26 December and 1 January. Educational facilities only available on weekdays.

CATERING Walrus Cafe on board serves sandwiches and snacks. Packed lunch area open to pre-booked groups and seats 24.

COST Groups of ten or more: children £1.60, adults £3.20, Senior Citizens/students £2.40, one teacher free per ten pupils.

DISABLED FACILITIES Wheelchair lift on to deck. Ramp to upper deck. Limited access around ship. Two decks only.

DIRECTIONS BR: London Bridge. Tube: London Bridge, Monument or Tower Hill. Bus: any to London Bridge. Coach Park off Tooley Street.

Hobbs Cross Open Farm
- Jennie Smith
- Theydon Garnon, Epping, Essex. CM16 7NY
- 0992 814764 FAX 081-501 2327

A working open livestock farm giving educational tours; including pigs, cattle, sheep, hens, etc. Tours can be tailored to suit specific topics. Also farm/gift shop.

N C SUPPORT Specific topics can be covered, including textiles, reproduction, living things, the environment, growth, food chain, food production.

OPENING Daily 9.00am–5.00pm, closed Christmas week.

CATERING Restaurant and picnic facilities on site.

COST Children £2.00, adults £2.50. Groups of 25 or more: children £1.50, adults £2.00.

DISABLED FACILITIES Ramps into pens, toilet, coach/car park right up to entrance.

DIRECTIONS Junction 26 on M25 then follow brown tourist signs.

Horniman Museum
- Vivien Golding
- 100 London Road, Forest Hill, London. SE23 3PG
- 081-699 1872 FAX 081-291 5506

A term-time service for booked groups of 30 (max.) students of thrice-daily talks and handling sessions on the museum collections. The collections are ethnographic, Ethnical Musical Instruments and Natural History (new aquarium).

N C SUPPORT All the booked sessions cover relevant areas of the National Curriculum. Teachers' notes can also be sent out to interested groups on a number of NC areas.

OPENING Monday to Saturday 10.30am–5.30pm, Sunday 2.00pm–5.30pm.

CATERING Small cafe (Philip Moore) for the general public. Seating and tables for booked school groups (60 places).

COST Free.

DISABLED FACILITIES Everywhere except the North Hall Balcony (insects and fossils). Toilets etc.

DIRECTIONS BR: Forest Hill five minutes walk. A number of buses pass the Museum.

VISITS OUT
LONDON & THE SOUTH EAST

Howletts & Port Lympne Wild Animal Parks
- Terrylee Cox
- Bekesbourne, Nr Canterbury, Kent. CT4 5EL
- 0227 721286 FAX 0227 721853

Wild animal parks specialising in the care and breeding of endangered animals with the eventual aim of returning them to safe areas in the wild.

N C SUPPORT Primary and secondary education packs based on the National Curriculum as a guide. Worksheets and information incorporating relevant levels of notes that may be met by a visit to the parks.

OPENING Winter: 10.00am–4.00pm. Summer: 10.00am–5.00pm.

CATERING At both parks there are large covered restaurants offering a wide range of food and drink, as well as several ice cream/snack kiosks open during summer months.

COST Children £4.40, adults £6.50, school parties (during term time only) £2.25.

DISABLED FACILITIES Howletts is the smaller park and mostly level, and is therefore recommended for wheelchair access.

DIRECTIONS Howletts is located at Bekesbourne, three miles southeast of Canterbury, and is clearly signposted from the A2. Port Lympne lies between Sellindge and Hythe: follow M20, take Exit 11 on to A20 and follow the signs.

Hughenden Manor
- The Administrator
- High Wycombe, Bucks. HP14 4LA
- 0494 32580

Bought in 1847 by Disraeli; contains many Disraeli relics, including furniture, pictures and books; an extensive park.

N C SUPPORT National Curriculum links with Technology, Art, History and Science. Teachers' notes and resource material.

DISABLED FACILITIES Ground floor and grounds only. Special car parking arrangements. Adapted WC. Braille and taped guides.

DIRECTIONS One and a half miles north of High Wycombe; on west side of the Great Missenden Road (A4128). Bus: Wycombe Bus 323/4 High Wycombe to Aylesbury (passing close BR High Wycombe). BR: High Wycombe two miles.

Hurst Castle
- The Head Custodian
- c/o Yarmouth Castle, Quay Street, Yarmouth, Isle of Wight. PO41 0PB

Hurst Castle was one of the most sophisticated fortresses built by Henry VIII, and later strengthened in the 19th and 20th centuries, to command the narrow entrance to the Solent. There is an exhibition in the castle, and two huge 38-ton guns from the fort's armaments.

OPENING Summer season. Good Friday or 1 April (whichever is earlier) to 30 September: daily 10.00am–6.00pm.

CATERING Restaurant/cafe April and May: weekends only; June to September: daily.

DIRECTIONS On Pebble Spit south of Keyhaven. Best approached by ferry from Keyhaven (OS Map 196; ref SZ 319898). Bus: Wilts and Dorset 123/4 Bournemouth to Lymington (passes BR New Milton) to within two and a half miles, or one mile to ferry (Tel: 0202 673555). BR: Lymington Town four and a half miles to Keyhaven, six and a half miles to Fort.

Ightham Mote

- The Administrator
- Ivy Hatch, Sevenoaks, Kent. TN15 0NT
- 0732 810378

A beautiful medieval moated manor house with important later additions; features include great hall, old chapel and crypt c.1340; Tudor chapel, drawing room with Jacobean fireplace and frieze. Seven rooms furnished in Victorian style. Exhibition showing conservation and restoration work.

N C SUPPORT National Curriculum links with History and Art. Children's guide.

DISABLED FACILITIES Garden, courtyard, Great Hall, tea pavilion and part of shop only; woodland walk; special parking, apply to ticket kiosk. Adapted WC.

DIRECTIONS Six miles east of Sevenoaks, off A25, and two and a half miles south of Ightham, off A227. Bus: Maidstone & District 222/3 BR Borough Green to BR Tunbridge Wells; Nu-Venture 67/8 Sevenoaks to Plaxtol (passing BR Sevenoaks), on both alight Ivy Hatch.

Imperial War Museum

- Anita Ballin, Education Officer
- Lambeth Road, London. SE1 6HZ
- 071-416 5000 FAX 071-416 5374

The Imperial War Museum tells the story of war in the 20th century, both at the front line and on the home front.

N C SUPPORT A wide range of activities are offered for pupils aged 8–18, including study sessions, films, lectures and sixth-form conferences; all pertinent to the National Curriculum.

ANNUAL OR ONE OFF EVENT Teachers' courses every July.

OPENING 10.00am–6.00pm.

CATERING Cafe and schools' lunch room.

COST Group rate (10 or more): children £1.70, adults £3.35. Pre-booked school parties free (two weeks in advance).

DISABLED FACILITIES Toilets, lifts to all floors.

DIRECTIONS Tube: five minutes walk from Lambeth North, Elephant and Castle.

International Doll & Toy Collection

- Mr & Mrs L Pickering
- 4–6 Orange Street, Canterbury, Kent. CT1 2JA
- 0227 785008

Britain's only ethnic doll and toy museum, displaying authentic dolls and dolls houses from around the world. It also houses working model railways, teddy bears, dioramas, etc. Museum shop.

N C SUPPORT Quiz sheets; guided tours if requested.

OPENING Daily 10.00am–5.00pm.

COST Children (4–14 years) £1.80, adults £2.30, groups over 20 are offered 10% discount.

DISABLED FACILITIES Wheelchair users welcome.

DIRECTIONS One minute from the Cathedral in the High Street.

International Study Centre
- Sandy Montgomery
- Herstmanceux Castle, Hailsham, East Sussex. BN27 1RP
- 0323 833413 FAX 0323 832562

The Centre will be opening in September 1994. The grounds are open to the public from July to end of September.

ANNUAL OR ONE OFF EVENT Science and arts events throughout the year.

OPENING 11.00am–6.00pm.

CATERING Restaurant.

COST Children £1.50, adults £2.50, concessions £2.00, groups £1.50.

DISABLED FACILITIES The restaurant, toilets and gardens are accessible.

DIRECTIONS Off the Worthing Road between Pevensey and Boreham Street.

Institute of Contemporary Art
- Kim Sweet, Education Officer
- The Mall, London. SW1Y 5AH
- 071-930 0493 FAX 071-837 0051

The Education Department at the ICA works in collaboration with the cinema, exhibitions and live arts departments on an annual programme of events including practical workshops, gallery talks, student screenings and after-performance discussions.

N C SUPPORT The education programme is devised in collaboration with schools as a means of providing specific support for National Curriculum requirements. The majority of the current education programme is aimed at and devised for an audience of 16 years plus.

OPENING Monday to Saturday 12.00 noon–1.00pm, Sunday 12.00 noon–11.00pm. Galleries: daily 12.00 noon–7.30pm, Tuesday 12.00 noon–9.00pm.

CATERING Cafeteria: Monday to Saturday 12.00 noon–3.00pm and 5.30pm–11.00pm, Sunday 12.00 noon–9.00pm.

COST Under 14s free, student concessions. Day membership £1.50. Concession rate for educational groups of ten or more to all activities £1.00.

DISABLED FACILITIES Access limited. Toilet.

DIRECTIONS Tube: Charing Cross, Piccadilly Circus. BR: Charing Cross.

Isle of Wight Steam Railway
- T Hastings
- The Railway Station, Havenstreet, Isle of Wight. PO33 4DS
- 0983 882204

A rare chance to sample travel in a real vintage train. The line captures the unique atmosphere of old island railways and regularly uses engines

VISITS OUT
LONDON & THE SOUTH EAST

and rolling stock dating back to the 1870s and earlier. Havenstreet is the headquarters of the railway and focal point of its activities. There are workshops, a well-stocked souvenir shop and cafeteria.

N C SUPPORT The Data Pack, which is copyright waived, is acclaimed as one of the leaders in its field and, to quote the *Times Educational Supplement*, is 'no mere tick and see worksheet'. The Pack, which is a joint production with the IW Teachers' Centre, is designed in loose-leaf format and contained in a plastic wallet so that teachers may extract what they feel is appropriate for their students' programmes of study. (Price £3.50 plus £1.20 p&p. Payment with order please.)

OPENING School package available all operating days 25 March to 22 July inclusive. Advance booking essential.

CATERING Cafe in Haverstreet.

COST Return: children (5–15 years) £2.80, adults £3.50. This includes audio-visual presentation and full round-trip from Havenstreet Station. The rates apply to school groups of ten or more and are available for a complete round-trip for which seats will be reserved. Applicable 25 March to 22 July only. Teachers: one free with every ten paying pupils.

DISABLED FACILITIES Telephone or write to the Station Manager.

DIRECTIONS By car: from all parts of the island, head for Ryde and then follow the sign to Havenstreet and the Steam Railway. Public transport: from the mainland the most convenient route to the Railway is by Wightlink ferry from Portsmouth Harbour to Ryde, and then by 'Island Line' train to Smallbrook Junction.

Jewel Tower
- The Head Custodian
- c/o Chapter House, Westminster Abbey, London. SW1P 3PE
- 071-222 2219

Built *c.*1365 to house the personal treasures of Edward III and formerly part of the Palace of Westminster, it was used to house valuables which formed part of the king's 'wardrobe', and subsequently as a storehouse and government office. There is an exhibition, 'Parliament Past and Present'.

OPENING All year. Good Friday or 1 April (whichever is earlier) to 30 September: daily 10.00am–6.00pm. 1 October to 31 March: Tuesday to Sunday 10.00am–4.00pm. Closed 24–26 December and 1 January. Pre-booking essential. Liable to be closed at short notice.

DISABLED FACILITIES None.

DIRECTIONS Opposite south end of Houses of Parliament (Victoria Tower). Bus: frequent from surrounding areas (Tel: 071-222 1234). BR: Charing Cross three-quarters of a mile; Victoria and Waterloo, both one mile. Tube: Westminster quarter of a mile.

Jewish Museum
- Jennifer Marin
- Woburn Street, Tavistock Square, London. WC1H 0EP
- 071-388 4525

VISITS OUT
LONDON & THE SOUTH EAST

Outstanding collection of Jewish ceremonial art and historical objects. Special exhibits explaining Jewish religious practice.

N C SUPPORT Worksheets for primary and secondary age-groups, talks and audio-visual programmes.

OPENING Tuesday, Wednesday and Thursday 10.00am–4.00pm, Sunday and Friday 10.00am–4.00pm (10.00am–12.45pm in winter), closed bank holidays and Jewish holidays.

COST Telephone for details.

DISABLED FACILITIES Full access.

DIRECTIONS Nearest tube: Euston, Euston Square, Russell Square.

Dr Johnson's House
- Curator
- 17 Gough Square, London. EC4A 3DE
- 071-353 3745

Memorial to 18th-century lexicographer in the house where he compiled the first definitive English dictionary. Prints of distinguished contemporaries and relics.

OPENING October to April: Monday to Saturday 11.00am–5.00pm. May to September: Monday to Saturday 11.00am–5.30pm. Closed Sunday and bank holidays.

CATERING None.

COST Student rate £1.50.

DISABLED FACILITIES None.

DIRECTIONS Off Fleet Street (signposted).

Juniper Hall Field Studies
- John Beddington
- Council Centre, Dorking, Surrey. RH5 6DA
- 0306 883849 FAX 0306 742627

A Field Centre which is part of a network of Field Studies Council study centres and provides tailor-made courses in environmental topics to suit schools' curriculum needs.

N C SUPPORT Courses can be designed to suit all Key Stages on a day or residential basis. There is a long tradition of A-Level provision with specialist courses in Geography and Biology. INSET provision and student courses available.

OPENING Season begins at the end of January and finishes at the beginning of December.

CATERING Fully catered courses are offered as part of the package.

COST Full costs available on application.

DISABLED FACILITIES Limited special facilities are available.

DIRECTIONS The Centre is five minutes from Dorking on the A24. BR: every half hour from either Victoria or Waterloo.

Keats House
- Mrs C M Gee
- Keats Grove, London. NW3 2RR
- 071-794 6829 FAX 071-794 6829

Home of John Keats (poet); contains relics of Keats and his circle. Keats Memorial Library has 8000 volumes.

OPENING April to October: Monday to Friday 10.00am–1.00pm and

VISITS OUT
LONDON & THE SOUTH EAST

2.00pm–6.00pm, Saturday 10.00am–1.00pm and 2.00pm–5.00pm, Sunday and bank holidays 2.00pm–5.00pm. November to March: Monday to Friday 1.00pm–5.00pm, Saturday 10.00am–1.00pm and 2.00pm–5.00pm, Sunday 2.00pm–5.00pm.

CATERING None.

COST Free. Guided tour: £2.00 (by appointment only). Audio tour: £1.00.

DISABLED FACILITIES None.

The Keeping Gallery
- Renate Keeping
- 16 Church Road, Shortlands, Kent. BR2 0HP
- 081-460 7679

A Gallery and Resource Centre showing original children's book illustrations by Charles Keeping, also lithographs by him of old London stablings, and soft sculpture. Watercolours etc. on very extensive show in six rooms.

N C SUPPORT Guided tour for parties of school children, junior, senior and college students with explanations, and background of the work.

OPENING By appointment, according to demand.

CATERING Light refreshments, e.g. tea, coffee, soft drinks; can adapt to demand for food.

COST Prices on application.

DISABLED FACILITIES None.

DIRECTIONS BR: Shortlands or Bromley South (20 minutes from Victoria).

Kent & East Sussex Railway
- Dr G Sivian
- Tenterden Town Station, Tenterden. TN30 6HE
- 0580 765 155

A private railway operated by steam locomotives with vintage carriages.

N C SUPPORT Relevant for National Curriculum studies in History (especially Victorian times), Geography and Science.

ANNUAL OR ONE OFF EVENT Details on application.

OPENING Daily 10.00am–6.00pm. Trains operate daily in June, September and weekends in winter.

CATERING Yes.

COST Children £1.00, or £3.00 to include full educational package.

DISABLED FACILITIES Yes. Toilets.

DIRECTIONS In station road, off Tenterden High Street.

Kentish Town City Farm
- Angela Rose
- 1 Cressfield Close, Off Grafton Road, London. NW5 4BN
- 071-916 5420

Farmyard with pigs, goats, cows, sheep, horses and various poultry. Classroom facilities and full-time education worker, various activities on offer, such as dairying, spinning and weaving, animal care, etc.

N C SUPPORT Worksheets available based on National Curriculum Science and Geography for Key Stages 1–5.

OPENING Tuesday to Sunday 9.30am–5.30pm.

COST Guided tour: children 65p. Other activities range from 75p to £1.00. Entrance free to groups visiting if no tour required.

DISABLED FACILITIES Wheelchair access and toilets for disabled. (Wildlife and sensory garden planned for 1995).

DIRECTIONS BR: Gospel Oak (North London line). Tube: Chalk Farm, Kentish Town (Northern line).

Kenwood

- The Head Custodian
- The Iveagh Bequest, Kenwood, Hampstead Lane, London. NW3 2JR
- 081-348 1286

Standing in splendid grounds on the edge of Hampstead Heath, Kenwood contains the most important private collection of paintings ever given to the nation. There is a selection of Old Masters, among the finest a *Self Portrait* by Rembrandt and paintings by British artists such as Turner, Reynolds and Gainsborough. The outstanding neoclassical house itself was remodelled by Robert Adam (1764–73), who created the magnificent Library.

N C SUPPORT Teachers' Handbook in preparation. An Education Centre has been provided for study use by school parties. These are equipped with audio-visual, printed and replica sources appropriate to the property which teachers can use themselves. Education Centres can be booked in advance. For more information, please contact the English Heritage Education Service, Keysign House, 429 Oxford Street, London W1R 2HD.

ANNUAL OR ONE OFF EVENT Lakeside concerts held in the summer.

OPENING All year. Good Friday or 1 April (whichever is earlier) to 30 September: daily 10.00am–6.00pm. 1 October to 31 March: plus Mondays in winter, 26 December and 1 January.

CATERING Restaurant/cafeteria, picnic areas.

DISABLED FACILITIES Access to ground floor only. Toilets.

DIRECTIONS Bus: LT 210 BR Finsbury Park to Golders Green (Tel: 071-222 1234). BR: Hampstead Heath one and a half miles. Tube: Highgate one mile.

Kensington Palace

- The Education Officer
- State Apartments & Court Dress Collection, Kensington, London. W8 4PX
- 071-937 9561

Decorations, paintings and furniture reflect the style and splendour of Court life. The King's Grand Staircase, the rich decor of Queen Mary II's Bedchamber and the Duchess of Kent's lavish Dressing Room evoke the elegance of times past. Visiting the young Princess Victoria's Bedroom reminds us of her excitement as she was awakened to the news that she was to be Queen.

N C SUPPORT The State Apartments and Royal Ceremonial Dress Collection are especially useful resources for History, English and Art and Design although they do have uses in other curriculum areas. Storytelling sessions are relevant to History Study Units which include the Greeks and the Romans (Key Stage 3) and Victorian Britain (Key Stage 2).

There is a large Education Room which can accommodate 35; a handling collection of costume accessories and fabric types, pottery and a range of teachers' notes which include background information for the replica costume and handling collections and suggestions on how they may be used within the curriculum.

OPENING Summer: Monday to Saturday 9.00am–5.30pm, Sunday 11.00am–5.30pm (last admission 4.45pm). Winter: Monday to Saturday 9.00am–5.00pm, Sunday 11.00am–5.00pm (last admission 4.15pm).

CATERING Packed lunches may be eaten in the Education Room. Please book in advance.

COST Pre-booked parties of school children and students in full-time education on curriculum-related visits are eligible for free admission to the Palace. Free admission cannot include weekends or bank holidays. Teachers may also make a free planning visit on request.

DISABLED FACILITIES Access to gardens and, with three small steps up, to ground floor (Court Dress Collection); there are 31 shallow stairs in three flights up to the State Apartments and steep steps down to the Education Room so access is very limited, although disabled visitors may be able to manage with their own assistant. Please ring to discuss individual requirements.

DIRECTIONS Bus: Bayswater Road 12, 88. Tube: Queensway, Notting Hill Gate (both Central line), High Street Kensington (District/Circle line).

Kew *see* Royal Botanic Gardens

Kew Bridge Steam Museum
- Derek Gooding
- Green Dragon Lane, Brentford-upon-Thames, Middx. TW8 0EN
- 081-452 8567

Victorian waterworks with world's largest collection of water-pumping beam engines (1820–1910). History of London's water supply, popular with schools as thematic cross-curricular support venue. Key Stages 2–4.

N C SUPPORT Science, History, Technology, Maths, Geography, Art, pollution, Industrial Revolution, problem solving, Design, the 'Steam Age'. Full educational support (pre-booking is essential), minimum teaching time 90 minutes (video support also shows engines in detail).

ANNUAL OR ONE OFF EVENT Twice-yearly special 'Steaming Days for Schools' (May and November) with 45-minute introductory lectures by museum education officer.

OPENING Option 1: stand-alone teaching 11.00am-5.00pm. Option 2: any time by prior arrangement (full teacher support). Option 3: engines working and educational support.

CATERING Eating areas if booked in advance. No catering during the week. Students responsible for cleaning up tea room after use.

COST Weekday 1993 prices. Option 1: normal entrance less 10% group discount for 12 or more; adults £1.70, students 90p. Option 2: £45 for up to 30 students (extras £2.50 each). Option 3: from £98.75.

DISABLED FACILITIES Reasonably good access for wheelchairs to enter museum and 'Hall of Steam' but five stairs to oldest engine; and 14 stairs in three stages (6,5,3) to world's largest beam engine.

DIRECTIONS The museum entrance in Green Dragon Lane is 100 yards from the north end of Kew Bridge. BR: Kew Bridge (Waterloo line). Tube: South Ealing, then bus.

Kew Palace

- The Education Officer
- Kew Gardens, Kew Road, Richmond-upon-Thames, Surrey. TW7 3AB
- 081-781 9790/91

The house was built in 1631 and acquired by the Crown in 1781 and is one in a series of royal houses in the area used initially by members of the royal household. In 1802 King George and Queen Charlotte, together with their 15 children, moved into Kew Palace. The interior of the Palace has been restored to try to re-create the house's character, and the life of the royal residents, between 1802–18.

N C SUPPORT At History Key Stage 2 it is an ideal resource for supplementary study units 'Domestic Life, Families and Childhood'; Art and Design: working drawings of the facades of the Palace can be translated back in the classroom through various media, e.g. lino prints, batik, collage, paint, pen, etc. Mathematics: explore shapes and patterns on the palace's exterior; and PSE/curricular elements: use the ceiling images for classroom discussion about the delights or otherwise that the senses can bring. There is an undercroft furnished with slatted tables and benches accommodating approximately 30 for use as a schools' base. It is intended for use by teachers with their classes to develop their own work whilst visiting the Palace.

OPENING Kew Palace: April to September: daily 11.00am–5.30pm. Queen Charlotte's cottage: April to September: weekends and bank holidays only 11.00am–5.30pm.

CATERING Packed lunches may be eaten in the undercroft. Pre-booking essential.

COST Pre-booked parties of school children and students in full-time education on curriculum-related visits are eligible for free admission to Kew Palace. Free admission cannot include weekends or Bank Holidays. Teachers may also make a free planning visit on request.

DISABLED FACILITIES Ground floor only (four shallow steps at entrance: help is available to negotiate these).

DIRECTIONS Bus: 27, 65, 90B; also 237, 267 to Kew Bridge one and a half miles from Palace. BR and Tube: Kew Gardens (North London line) and Kew Bridge. Boat: Kew Pier (from Westminster Bridge), enquiries to Thames Passenger Launches (Tel: 071-930 0921).

VISITS OUT
LONDON & THE SOUTH EAST

Knebworth House Gardens & Park
- Mrs J Birch
- The Estate Office, Knebworth, Herts. SG3 6PY
- 0438 812661 FAX 0438 811908

Home of the Lytton family since 1490. The house and gardens stand in 250 acres of deer park. Large adventure playground with 'Fort Knebworth', British Raj exhibition.

N C SUPPORT Seventeen educational worksheets have been produced with curriculum guidelines. Props, toys and activities are available to school parties to cover Tudors and Stuarts, Victorians and the British Raj.

OPENING April to October, for pre-booked groups of 20 or more.

CATERING Full cafeteria service available, or picnic areas.

COST Group rates. House, gardens, park, playground: children £2.80, adults £3.20; park and playground only: children and adults £2.00. Two adults free with the first 20 in the group, plus one additional adult free with each extra 20.

DISABLED FACILITIES Very limited.

DIRECTIONS Thirty miles north of London at junction 7 of the A1(M). Direct access from junction 7.

Lauderdale House
- Jenny Tolerton
- Waterlow Park, Highgate Hill, London. N6 5HG
- 081-348 8716 FAX 081-348 4293

Lauderdale House Society is a charity which runs Lauderdale House as a community arts centre. There are Saturday morning children's shows, children's after-school workshops and concerts.

ANNUAL OR ONE OFF EVENT The House can be hired out for social events, concerts, exhibitions, workshops, meetings and conferences. There is a continuous programme of events throughout the year.

OPENING Opening times vary according to events taking place.

CATERING The Lauderdale Restaurant (closed Mondays except bank holidays): telephone 081-341 4807.

COST Please apply for leaflet containing information on costs per hour/day/week. Information on any event open to the public can be included on the Lauderdale House monthly 'What's On' sheet.

DISABLED FACILITIES Ground floor fully accessible to the disabled (gallery, performance space, workshop, restaurant and toilet).

DIRECTIONS Tube: Archway (Northern line). Bus: 143, 210, 271 (to the house); 41, 134, 27, C11, C12, 43, 17, 263 (to Archway).

Leeds Castle
- Nigel Philpott
- Maidstone, Kent. ME17 1PL
- 0622 765400 FAX 0622 735616

Known as 'the loveliest Castle in the world'; home to a Saxon royal family. Rebuilt in stone by the Normans and beautifully enriched by Henry VIII.

N C SUPPORT An education pack consisting of Discovery Sheets (six) for children and accompanying teachers' notes is available free of charge. Relevant to National Curriculum. Leeds can provide help with students studying marketing and tourism.

OPENING March to October: daily 10.00am–5.00pm. November to March: 10.00am–3.00pm. Closed Christmas Day. Private visits can be arranged at other times.

COST Group rate (min. 20): children £2.80, students £3.50 (Castle additional £1.00), one adult free per group.

DISABLED FACILITIES Leeds warmly welcomes visitors with disabilities. A new leaflet summarising the facilities is available.

DIRECTIONS Located four miles east of Maidstone in Kent at junction 8 of the M20. Midway between London and the Channel Ports.

Leighton House
- Julia Findlater
- 212 Holland Park Road, London. W14 8LZ
- 071-602 3316 FAX 071-371 2467

Purpose-built studio house belonging to the Victorian painter Lord Leighton, with spectacular Arab Hall incorporating brick tiles of c.16th and 17th centuries. Collections include furniture, ceramics and paintings by Leighton and his contemporaries.

N C SUPPORT Teachers' resource pack dealing with Key Stages 1 and 2 available at a cost.

OPENING Monday to Saturday 11.00am–5.30pm.

CATERING None.

COST Museum free, guided tours £1.50 (minimum group of 15).

DISABLED FACILITIES None. House has four steps to front door and two flights of wide stairs to upper floor.

DIRECTIONS Tube: High Street Kensington, then bus 9, 10, 27, 28, 33, 49.

Lewes Castle & Museum
- Helen Poole
- Barbican House, 169 High Street, Lewes, East Sussex. BN7 1YE
- 0273 486290 FAX 0273 486990

Lewes Castle, one of the oldest in England, stands opposite the Museum of Sussex Archaeology, which displays prehistory to 1485. The Lewes Living History model brings Victorian Lewes to audio-visual life.

N C SUPPORT Displays have been changed to meet National Curriculum topics, particularly Invaders and Settlers and Medieval Realms.

ANNUAL OR ONE OFF EVENT Holiday activities for children and adults. Details available on request.

OPENING Lewes Castle and Museum of Sussex Archaeology: Monday to Saturday 10.00am–5.30pm, Sunday 11.00am–5.30pm. Anne of Cleves House Museum: Monday to Saturday 10.00am–5.30pm, Sunday 2.00pm–5.30pm.

CATERING None.

COST Lewes Castle and Museum: children £1.25, adults £2.50. Group rate (if booked 48 hours in advance): children £1.00, adults £2.00.

DISABLED FACILITIES Poor: castle is on a steep hill and both museums have a great many steps.

VISITS OUT
LONDON & THE SOUTH EAST

Lewisham Local History Centre
- A J Wait
- Manor House, Old Road, London. SE13 5SY
- 081-852 5050 FAX 081-297 0927

Archives and local history collections (books, pamphlets, photographs, maps) for London Borough of Lewisham.

N C SUPPORT Talks given to classes and groups, on localities within borough and topics such as World War II.

OPENING Monday, Thursday and Saturday 9.30am–5.00pm, Tuesday 9.30am–1.00pm and 2.00pm–8.00pm.

CATERING None at present building.

COST Schools within the Borough of Lewisham free.

DISABLED FACILITIES None at present building.

Lincolsfield Activity Centre
- Jenny Lewis
- Bushey Hall Drive, Bushey, Herts. WD2 2ER
- 0923 233841 FAX 0923 213055

Accommodation for groups of up to 60 children. Also available: classroom, arts and crafts room, TV lounge, kitchen, dining hall, games room and pre-arranged visits and activities (send for details).

N C SUPPORT Key Stages 1 and 2 covered: Pond and Plant and Insect Life. Opportunities for English, Maths and Geography work at Key Stages 1 and 2.

OPENING All year round: Monday to Friday 9.00am–4.00pm (24-hour answerphone).

CATERING Catering staff (Centre Catering) or self-catering kitchen available.

COST £48 per head, one teacher free with every ten children. Fully inclusive catering.

DISABLED FACILITIES Access to residential area.

DIRECTIONS Two minutes off M1. Junction 5 to Harrow, right at roundabout and half a mile along A4008 to Bushey; right at roundabout to Bushey Hall Drive.

Linley Sambourne House Museum
- Sheila Ayres
- 18 Stafford Terrace, London. W8 7BH
- 081-994 1019

A unique surviving example of a late Victorian townhouse, the home of Linley Sambourne, a leading 'Punch' illustrator, with original fixtures and furniture and pictures by Sambourne and his friends.

N C SUPPORT Key stage 2 and GCSE groups welcome. Historical workbook for teachers and children available.

OPENING March to October: Sunday 2.00pm–5.00pm. Wednesday 10.00am–5.00pm. Closed November to February.

CATERING No catering facilities.

COST Children under 16 and accompanying adults £1.50. Must book in advance.

DISABLED FACILITIES Not suitable for disabled as there are six flights of stairs and the only public toilet is at the top of the third flight.

DIRECTIONS Tube: Kensington High Street five minutes. Bus: 9, 9A, 10, 27, 28, 31, 49, 52, 70, C1.

Little Holland House
- Valary Murphy
- 40 Beeches Avenue, Carshalton Beeches, Surrey
- 081-770 4781 FAX 081-770 4777

The home of Frank Dickinson (1874–1961), artist, designer and craftsman. The Grade II listed interior contains hand-made furniture, paintings and craft objects. Made by Dickinson following the ideals of Ruskin and Morris.

N C SUPPORT Guided tours available outside normal opening hours.

OPENING First Sunday of the month, and Sunday and Monday of bank holiday weekends 1.30pm–5.30pm, closed Christmas and New Year.

CATERING None.

COST Guided tour for groups: children under 18 £1.00, one teacher free for every ten pupils; adults £2.00, one person free for every ten.

DISABLED FACILITIES Access to ground floor only. No toilet facilities suitable for wheelchair access.

DIRECTIONS BR: Carshalton Beaches 30 minutes. On B278. No off-street parking available.

Livesey Museum
- Nicola Boyd
- 682 Old Kent Road, London. SE15 1JF
- 071-639 5604

The Livesey is a children's museum presenting a lively and varied programme of 'hands-on' exhibitions for the under 12s, their schools, families and carers.

N C SUPPORT Exhibitions are normally cross-curricular and tied in to Key Stages 1 and 2.

ANNUAL OR ONE OFF EVENT Normally one exhibition per year.

OPENING During exhibitions: Monday to Saturday 10.00am–5.00pm.

CATERING None, but courtyard where packed lunches may be eaten.

COST Free.

DISABLED FACILITIES Toilets. Access for wheelchairs to ground floor and courtyard.

DIRECTIONS Bus: 21, 53, 172, 177, 78, P11, P13. Nearest tube: Elephant and Castle, New Cross, New Cross Gate, Surrey Quays. Museum is opposite Kentucky Fried Chicken near Gas Works.

Living World
- David Rushen
- Seven Sisters Country Park, Exceat, Seaford, East Sussex. BN25 4AD
- 0323 870100

Mainly invertebrate exhibition of living creatures, e.g. butterflies, caterpillars, bees, ants, snails, locusts, plus sea life amphibians and reptiles. Ova, larvae and pupae for sale by mail order.

VISITS OUT
LONDON & THE SOUTH EAST

N C SUPPORT Mini-beast handling experience at the school and slide show on mini-beasts. Ranger service for school trips to living world on the country park. Assorted subjects.

ANNUAL OR ONE OFF EVENT Mini-beast handling experience every Wednesday during summer holidays.

OPENING Mid-March to end October: Monday to Friday 10.00am–5.00pm. Winter: daily 10.00am–5.00pm.

CATERING Cafeteria in adjacent building.

COST Children £1.40, adults £2.20, Senior Citizens £1.40. Groups of 20 or more: children £1.20, teachers free.

DISABLED FACILITIES All parts of the exhibition can be reached by wheelchair. Toilets outside.

DIRECTIONS In Cuckmere Valley. A259, two miles east of Seaford, five miles west of Eastbourne.

London Brass Rubbing Centre
- Patricia Dodwell
- The Crypt, St Martin-in-the-Fields Church, Trafalgar Square, London. WC2N 4JJ
- 071-437 6023

Knights, kings, ladies and merchants provide links with History, Craft and Social Studies in Medieval Realms. Material and instruction provided for successful brass rubbing.

N C SUPPORT Teachers' notes. Historical data in guide book. All free. Indispensable adjunct to Medieval Realms Key Stage 3.

OPENING Monday to Saturday 10.00am–6.00pm, Sunday 12.00 noon–6.00pm, closed 25, 26 December and 1 January.

CATERING Cafe on site.

COST Contact the Administrator.

DISABLED FACILITIES Wheelchair lift (phone first).

DIRECTIONS Entrance in Duncannon Street, adjacent to Trafalgar Square.

The London Butterfly House
- Julian Burgess
- Syon Park, Brentford, Middx. TW8 8JF
- 081-560 0378 FAX 081-560 0378

A large tropical garden under glass with many beautiful free-flying butterflies from around the world. Also Insect City (scorpions, giant spiders, etc.) and unique wildlife gift shop.

N C SUPPORT Supply education packs with worksheets and can accommodate educational talks.

OPENING British winter time: 10.00am–3.30pm. British summer time: 10.00am–5.00pm.

CATERING Cafeteria within the park (one minute walk).

COST School groups: children 2–15 years £1.20, one adult/teacher for every six children £1.20, extra adults/teachers £1.80.

DISABLED FACILITIES Wheelchairs easy access. Carers free.

DIRECTIONS Just off junction two of the M4.

VISITS OUT
LONDON & THE SOUTH EAST

The London Canal Museum
- The Curator
- 12–13 New Wharf Road, King's Cross, London. N1 9RT
- 071-713 0836

The London Canal Museum tells the story of the development of London's canals, from the early days as an important trade route, to today's more leisurely pursuits. Learn about the cargoes and canal crafts, about the people who strove to make a living from canals, and the horses that pulled the boats.

N C SUPPORT There is a classroom that can be booked in advance by school parties. A number of exhibits related to London's industrial heritage can be linked to the National Curriculum.

OPENING Tuesday to Sunday 10.00am–4.30pm. Open all bank holidays except 24–26 December, 1 and 2 January. Last admissions are 45 minutes before closing time. School parties and groups by arrangement.

COST Children £1.25, adults £2.50, Senior Citizens/concessions £1.25. Group rates available.

DISABLED FACILITIES Ring for details.

DIRECTIONS Tube: King's Cross, St Pancras. BR: King's Cross, King's Cross Thameslink, St Pancras. Bus: 10, 14, 14A, 17, 18, 30, 45, 46, 63, 73, 74, 214, 221, 259, C12.

The London Dungeon
- Feisal Khalif
- 28–34 Tooley Street, London. SE1 2SZ
- 071-403 0606 FAX 071-378 1529

World-famous horror museum presenting a historically authentic portrayal of the darker side of European history.

N C SUPPORT Education pack covering various History study units from Key Stages 2 and 3 History.

OPENING Daily 10.00am–4.30pm.

COST Children (14 and under) £4.00, adults £6.00, students £5.00. Groups: children £3.25, adults £4.50, students £4.00.

DISABLED FACILITIES Excellent.

DIRECTIONS Tube: London Bridge.

London Planetarium
- Teresa Grafton
- Marylebone Road, London. NW1 5LR
- 071-486 1121 FAX 071-465 0862

Space trail exhibition with planetary models and interactive video. Talks under the dome for schools and public astronomy shows.

N C SUPPORT AT4 Astronomy, live talks on weekdays in term time for all Key Stages. Teachers' packs free with booking. Recorded shows throughout every day. Occasional lectures on other educational subjects; Sky this Month (monthly talk).

OPENING 10.00am–5.00pm (longer hours in holidays). Schools programmes 10.45am. Public shows every 40 minutes from 12.20pm.

CATERING Cafe. Very limited provision for packed lunches (must book in advance).

VISITS OUT
LONDON & THE SOUTH EAST

COST On application.

DISABLED FACILITIES No wheelchairs in Planetarium but children may be carried in (maximum three).

The London Toy & Model Museum
- Hamish MacGillivray, Curator
- 21–23 Craven Hill, London. W2 3EN
- 071-262 9450 FAX 071-724 9111

A wonderful journey through a children's world of dolls, cars, planes, trains, teddies, penny toys and much more, including garden railway and merry-go-round. A fun-filled day of entertainment. Redevelopment of Museum facilities scheduled in 1994.

N C SUPPORT 'Hands-on' facilities available Wednesday and Thursday to tie in with National Curriculum. Source pack available.

OPENING Tuesday to Saturday 10.00am–5.30pm Sunday and bank holidays 11.00am–5.30pm.

CATERING Catering facilities limited to soft drinks etc.

COST Groups of ten or more need to be booked in advance and will receive 10% discount.

DISABLED FACILITIES Limited: some ramps. It is advisable to confirm visit with Museum to decide best access.

DIRECTIONS Tube: Paddington or Lancaster Gate. BR: Paddington.

London Transport Museum
- Stephen Allen
- Covent Garden, London. WC2E 7BB
- 071-379 6344 FAX 071-836 4118

The Museum tells the story of London's transport, its impact on the capital and the people who have used it. The Museum has recently undergone extensive refurbishment.

N C SUPPORT The Education Service offers advice and resources to teachers as well as activities and workshops. Contact Education Service for more details.

ANNUAL OR ONE OFF EVENT None.

OPENING Daily 10.00am–6.00pm (last admission 5.45pm).

CATERING Cafeteria attached to the Museum. School lunch room will be available.

COST Group discounts available (contact Education Service for details).

DISABLED FACILITIES Toilets. Good access throughout.

DIRECTIONS In the heart of London's Covent Garden. Tube: Covent Garden or Charing Cross. BR: Charing Cross.

London Waterbus Co.
- The Manager
- 58 Camden Lock Place, London. NW1 8AF
- 071-482 2550/2660

Canal boat trips between Camden Lock and Little Venice along the Regent's Canal. Trips can be arranged to include lock demonstrations or a visit to London Zoo.

N C SUPPORT The Regent's Canal is an educational resource offering a practical opportunity for children to learn about many subjects including History, Maths and Science,

Technology, Arts and Design and Geography.

OPENING April to September: daily 10.00am–5.00pm. October: daily 10.30am–4.30pm. November to March: Saturday and Sunday, weekday in winter by arrangement.

CATERING No catering facilities.

COST Normal fares reduced to group rate of 10–15% for groups booked in advance.

DISABLED FACILITIES None.

DIRECTIONS For Little Venice: Warwick Avenue tube, Paddington BR. For Camden Lock: Camden Town tube, Camden Road BR.

London Zoo
- Ms Vicente Timperley
- Regent's Park, London. NW1 4RY
- 071-722 3333 FAX 071-483 4436

A leading centre for the conservation of endangered species. Over 680 species, including elephants, apes, penguins, cats, reptile house, aquarium and invertebrates.

N C SUPPORT Wide-ranging programme of activities, including project packs, tours, illustrated talks, 'hands-on' and discovery centre. Brochure available. INSET courses.

ANNUAL OR ONE OFF EVENT Special Needs Children's Day (date to be decided).

OPENING March–September: daily 10.00am–5.30pm. October–February: daily 10.00am–4.00pm.

CATERING Self-service restaurant. Hot and cold lunches for schools at special rate (pre-booked). Covered picnic area.

COST Reduced rate for schools: children 4–15 yrs £3, 16 and over £4, one adult free per ten paying children.

DISABLED FACILITIES Toilets. Access to all but two animal houses. Special Needs Education Officer.

DIRECTIONS In Regent's Park. Nearest tube: Camden Town or Baker Street, then 274 bus.

Longdown Dairy Farm
- Annette Todhunter
- Longdown, Nr Southampton, Ashurst, Hants. SO4 4UH
- 0703 293326 FAX 0703 293376

A modern, working dairy farm. School groups are given a free guided tour, watch the afternoon milking, feed and touch young animals and learn about modern farming methods.

N C SUPPORT Teachers' pack explains the workings of the farm and suggests ideas for pre-visit preparation and post-visit project work.

OPENING Easter to end October: 11.00am–5.00pm. School groups may visit out of season, and from 10.00am, by arrangement.

CATERING Extensive picnic area.

COST Group rates: (minimum 15) children (3–4 years) £1.00, children (5–14 years) £2.00, adults £3.00, one teacher free for every 15 children (1993 prices).

DISABLED FACILITIES All areas accessible. Toilet.

DIRECTIONS Off A35, between Southampton and Lyndhurst.

Gestetner Tour of Lord's

Lord's Tours
- Nikolaus Stewart
- Marylebone Cricket Club, Lord's Ground, London. NW8 8QN
- 071-266 3825 FAX 071-289 9100

Regular guided tours of Lord's ground include the Long Room, MCC Museum, real tennis court, mound stand, indoor school. It traces both the social development and history of the MCC, and the history of cricket in general.

N C SUPPORT Related subject areas: History, Sociology, PE, Sport/Leisure Studies, Architecture. All school tours are tailored to meet specific needs.

OPENING Every day except major match days. Tours normally start at noon and 2.00pm. Schools can negotiate preferred times.

COST Children £3.00, adults £4.00. In groups of 25 plus – children £3.50 adults £4.95.

DISABLED FACILITIES Toilets, lifts (to most areas).

DIRECTIONS Situated on St John's Wood Road, north of Baker Street between A41 (Finchley Road) and A5 Edgware Road. Underground: St John's Wood.

Lullingstone Roman Villa
- The Head Custodian
- Lullingstone Lane, Eynsford, Kent. DA4 0JA

Some splendid mosaic tiled floors can be seen among the remains of this large country villa, which has been extensively excavated in recent years. Four distinct periods of building have been identified as well as one of the earliest private Christian chapels.

N C SUPPORT Teachers' Handbook in preparation.

OPENING All year round. Good Friday or 1 April (whichever is earlier) to 30 September: daily 10.00am–6.00pm. 1 October to 31 March: 10.00am–4.00pm. Closed 24–26 December and 1 January. Pre-booking is essential.

DIRECTIONS Half a mile southwest of Eynsford off A225 (OS Map 177; ref TQ 529651). BR: Eynsford three-quarters of a mile.

Maidstone Museum & Art Gallery
- Rosamunde Bell, Education Officer
- St Faith's Street, Maidstone, Kent. ME14 1LH
- 0622 754497 FAX 0622 602193

Housed in the Tudor Chillington Manor, the Museum and Art Gallery is one of the finest outside London and contains outstanding collections, some of national importance.

N C SUPPORT Curriculum-based artefact handling sessions and related creative activities are always available. Many areas are covered, including Ancient Egypt, Victorians,

Anglo-Saxons, Romans' Medieval, World War II, etc.

ANNUAL OR ONE OFF EVENT Young Archaeologists' Day; Living History Events; regular programme of holiday activities.

OPENING Monday to Saturday 10.30am–5.30pm, Sunday 2.00pm–5.00pm, closed Christmas Day and Boxing Day.

CATERING One drinks/snack dispensing machine.

COST Admission free. Small charge for creative activities and events.

DISABLED FACILITIES Wheelchair access to ground floor only.

DIRECTIONS Maidstone Town Centre, two minutes from railway station.

Marble Hill House
- The Head Custodian
- Richmond Road, Twickenham, Middx. TW1 2NL
- 081-892 5115

A magnificent Thames-side Palladian villa built 1724–29 and set in 66 acres of parkland. The Great Room, recently restored, has lavish gilded decoration and architectural paintings by Panini. The house also contains an important collection of early Georgian furniture.

OPENING All year. Good Friday or 1 April (whichever is earlier) to 30 September: daily 10.00am–6.00pm. Plus Mondays in Winter, 26 December and 1 January.

CATERING Restaurant/cafe (normally open summer season only).

DISABLED FACILITIES Wheelchair access to exterior and ground floor only. Toilets.

DIRECTIONS Bus: frequent from surrounding areas (Tel: 071-222 1234). BR: St Margaret's half a mile. Tube: Richmond one mile.

Marwell Zoological Park
- Clare Sulston
- Colden Common, Nr Winchester, Hants. SO21 1JH
- 0962 777407 FAX 0962 777511

Marwell is a charitable trust dedicated to the conservation of threatened species. Set in 100 acres of Hampshire countryside, the park is home to over 120 animal species.

N C SUPPORT The Education Service offers short sessions and day courses in its Education Centre for ages 3–20, 'hands-on' opportunities and resource materials for teachers and children; all in support of the National Curriculum.

OPENING 10.00am–6.00pm (dusk in winter).

CATERING Restaurant and kiosks.

COST School rates: children £2.50 for entry plus 40p for Education Centre visit (1993 prices).

DISABLED FACILITIES Paths and toilets for disabled.

DIRECTIONS Just off M3, six miles south of Winchester.

Marx Memorial Library
- Tish Newland
- 37a Clerkenwell Green, London. EC1R 0DU
- 071-253 1485

Independent subscription library (registered charity) in historic building. Resource for History, Sociology, Economics, Political

Studies. Georgian building originally charity school. Lenin's office, fresco to view. Books, pamphlets, periodicals, pictures.

N C SUPPORT Can supply speakers to schools or have groups in the lecture hall. Social, Political or Economic History in particular. Life and times of Karl Marx etc.

OPENING Monday 1.00pm–6.00pm, Tuesday to Thursday 1.00pm–8.00pm, Saturday 10.00am–1.00pm. Visits at other times (from 10.30am) by arrangement.

CATERING None. Cafe next door.

COST Group visits £1.00 per head. School parties are just requested to give a donation.

DISABLED FACILITIES Access to ground floor by ramp.

DIRECTIONS Tube: Farringdon. Bus: 55, 63, 221, 243, 259, 505, Clerkenwell Road or Farringdon Road.

Mechanical Music & Doll Collection
- Mrs E Jones
- Church Road, Portfield, Chichester, West Sussex. PO19 4HN
- 0243 785421

Guided tours during which mechanical instruments are demonstrated, e.g. music boxes, street pianos, barrel organs, orchestrations, fair organs, etc. Many beautiful dolls (1830–1930). Other fine Victorian artefacts are on display.

N C SUPPORT Toys and dolls. Sounds and music. Victorians.

OPENING School visits any day throughout year. Telephone for details.

CATERING None.

COST School parties: children 75p (min. £22.50).

DISABLED FACILITIES Easily accessible for wheelchairs.

DIRECTIONS One mile east of Chichester city centre, off A27.

Medieval Merchant's House
- The Head Custodian
- 58 French Street, Southampton, Hants. SO1 0AT
- 0703 221503

The life of a prosperous merchant in the Middle Ages is vividly evoked by the brightly painted cabinets and chests, and colourful wall hangings authentically recreated for this faithfully restored 13th-century townhouse, originally built as a shop and home for wine merchant John Fortin.

OPENING All year round. Good Friday or 1 April (whichever is earlier) to 30 Sepember and 1 October to 31 March: daily 10.00am–6.00pm. Winter: Tuesday to Sunday 10.00am–4.00pm. Closed 24–26 December and 1 January. Pre-booking is essential.

DISABLED FACILITIES Suitable for disabled people (one step). Dogs on leads allowed.

DIRECTIONS Quarter of a mile south of city centre just off Castle Way (between High Street and Bugle Street) (OS Map 196; ref SU 419112). Bus: Southampton Citybus 17A/B, 27 from BR Southampton (Tel: 0703 553011). BR:

VISITS OUT
LONDON & THE SOUTH EAST

Southampton three-quarters of a mile.

Merton Abbey Mills
- John Hawks
- Merantun Way, London. SW19 2RD
- 081-543 9608 FAX 081-540 1145

Craft village created out of disused Victorian printing factory, which once printed Liberty's silks. School parties visit the waterwheel (alternative power exhibition) and the remains of the 900-year-old Chapter House of Merton Priory (archaeological relic).

OPENING Short guided tour by arrangement during weekdays.

CATERING Tea shop, pizza restaurant, pub.

COST Free.

DISABLED FACILITIES Toilet. Ramp.

DIRECTIONS Merantun Way is A24 at Colliers Wood (South Wimbledon) opposite Savacentre Hypermarket.

Mudchute Park & Farm
- Rob Eager
- Pier Street, London. E14 9HP

The Mudchute Park and Farm is a 32-acre public park, consisting of a working farm, a horse-riding stables, areas designated for natural wildlife and large tracts of open parkland.

N C SUPPORT The Mudchute has a 'Nature and Environment Study Centre' with an on-site teacher who provides structured activities linked to Science, Geography, Maths, Art, History and English in the National Curriculum.

ANNUAL OR ONE OFF EVENT Environment Week (May), National Tree Week (November), Lambing (March).

OPENING Daily (including bank holiday weekends) 9.00am–5.00pm.

CATERING Picnic tables for packed lunches. Cafe serving hot and cold meals. Souvenir and sweet shop.

COST Classroom and on-site teacher £1.60 per child per day. Classroom only £1.20 per child per day.

DISABLED FACILITIES Access to most buildings. Toilet in main stable building. Wheelchair access to fields.

DIRECTIONS Vehicular access via Pier Street. Pedestrian access through Asda Supermarket car park.

Museum of Artillery
- S C Walter, Curator
- Repository Road, London. SE18 4BJ
- 081-316 5402 FAX 081-316 5402

The collection of artillery was started in 1778 by Capt. William Congreve RA at Woolwich Arsenal. Col. Sir William Congreve succeeded his father. Needing more space for the collection, he persuaded the Prince Regent to give the largest of the six tent-like buildings designed by John Nash for the reception of the Allied Sovereigns at Carlton House in 1814. This was erected on its present site in 1820 and is now known as the Rotunda.

N C SUPPORT Many examples of artillery from the 14th and 15th centuries to World War II. Of relevance to students of History and Technology.

VISITS OUT
LONDON & THE SOUTH EAST

OPENING April to end October: Monday to Friday 12.00 noon–5.00pm, Saturday 1.00pm–5.00pm, Sunday 1.00pm–5.00pm. November to end March: Monday to Friday 12.00 noon–4.00pm, Saturday 1.00pm–4.00pm, Sunday 1.00pm–4.00pm.

CATERING Cold-drink machine.

COST Free.

DISABLED FACILITIES Yes.

DIRECTIONS Telephone the Curator for a copy of the leaflet illustrated with a map of the area.

Museum of Farnham
- Mrs Ruth Watson
- 38 West Street, Farnham, Surrey. GU9 7DX
- 0252 71594

Newly refurbished local history museum, with displays on Arts & Architecture, Town Life, Transport and Change in the Countryside. Special temporary exhibitions and related activities; local studies history; shop; garden.

N C SUPPORT Loans service (c. 400 objects), talks and handling sessions on National Curriculum History themes and termly schools' newsletter offered within schools' affiliation scheme; special activities linked to exhibitions.

OPENING Tuesday to Saturday 10.00am–5.00pm.

CATERING Tea, coffee or squash sold by prior arrangement; groups are welcome to eat their packed lunches in the garden.

COST Free.

DISABLED FACILITIES Disabled access to front and rear; fully equipped toilet.

DIRECTIONS Nearest parking: The Hart. From The Hart turn right along West Street and the Museum is at No. 38.

Museum of Fulham Palace
- M Poliakoff
- Bishops Avenue, London. SW6 6EA
- 071-736 3233

Tudor building with Georgian additions and Victorian chapel. Grounds include a herb garden. Museum tells the story of the buildings, the garden history, archaeology and the bishops of London.

N C SUPPORT Ideal for cross-curricular work but in particular History, Geography and Leisure and Tourism. Teachers' pack available £2.95. Special school visits by appointment.

ANNUAL OR ONE OFF EVENT Special sessions using replica Victorian costume mid-May to mid-June.

OPENING Wednesday to Sunday 2.00pm–5.00pm. Winter: 1.00pm–4.00pm. Schools must book.

CATERING None.

COST London Borough of Hammersmith and Fulham schools free, others £30 per visit.

DISABLED FACILITIES No adapted toilet. The Museum is totally accessible, audio tours for the blind and for people with learning difficulties.

DIRECTIONS Coaches must not enter the Palace site but should park in

Bishops Avenue (off Fulham Palace Road).

Museum of London
- Joanna Ball
- London Wall, London. EC2Y 5HN
- 071-600 3699 FAX 071-600 1058

The collections display the history of London and the lives of Londoners from prehistoric times to the present day through archaeological and historical items of significance.

N C SUPPORT None

OPENING Tuesday to Saturday 10.00am–6.00pm (last admission 5.30pm), Sunday 12.00 noon–6.00pm (last admission 5.30pm), closed every Monday except bank holidays (10.00am–6.00pm). Prior booking usually two months in advance is required for all groups.

CATERING The licensed restaurant and coffee shop provide hot and cold meals, snacks and drinks in pleasant surroundings.

COST Three-month ticket: adults £3.00, concessions £1.50, family £7.50 (maximum two adults). Annual ticket: £6.00, concessions £3.00. Under fives free. School and full-time college parties free if booked 4 days in advance. Discount of 50% for adult education parties if booked in advance.

DISABLED FACILITIES All parts of the Museum are accessible by wheelchair: lifts and ramp connect all floors. Toilets. Wheelchairs available. Please contact the Press & Public Relations Office, ext. 240, for details of road access and parking. Tape guides and braille sheets available for partially sighted and blind visitors.

DIRECTIONS The Museum is situated at the junction of London Wall, Aldersgate Street and St Martins-Le-Grand. The main entrance is located on the pedestrian highwalk. Nearest tube: Barbican, St Paul's, Moorgate, Bank. Bus: Museum of London 4, 279a, 172; St Paul's 8, 11, 15, 22b, 23, 25, 26, 501.

Museum of Mankind
- British Museum Education Service
- Burlington Gardens, London. W1X 2EX
- 071-323 8043

The ethnographic collections of the British Museum. Interactive programmes run by the 'Learning through Action' team are involved in a number of exhibitions.

N C SUPPORT Teachers' pack available. Exhibitions linked to a number of National Curriculum subjects. Contact the Education Service for publications.

OPENING Monday to Saturday 10.00am–5.00pm, Sunday 2.30pm–6.00pm.

CATERING Cafe.

COST Free.

DISABLED FACILITIES Contact the Education Service.

VISITS OUT
LONDON & THE SOUTH EAST

DIRECTIONS Contact the Education Service.

Museum of the Order of St John
- Francesca Alden
- St John's Gate, St John's Lane, London. EC1M 4DA
- 071-253 6644 FAX 071-490 8835

Sixteenth-century Gatehouse and 12th-century crypt belonging to the medieval order of St John. The Museum houses many treasures of the Knights Hospitallers and of St John Ambulance.

N C SUPPORT Teachers' resource pack for History Key Stage 2: 'St John Ambulance in Victorian Britain' is available. Tour of Gatehouse and crypt with worksheets. Object handling sessions available. The Museum collections are available as resources.

ANNUAL OR ONE OFF EVENT Tours of the building on Tuesday, Friday and Saturday 11.00am–2.30pm.

OPENING Monday to Friday 10.00am–5.00pm, Saturday 10.00am–4.00pm, closed bank holiday Mondays.

CATERING Weather permitting, the cloister and garden are available; indoor refreshments facilities by arrangement.

COST Donations welcome.

DISABLED FACILITIES Toilet. The Museum rooms are on the ground floor but the rest of the building is only via flights of stairs.

DIRECTIONS Tube: Farringdon five minutes walk.

The Musical Museum
- The Chairman
- 368 High Street, Brentford, Middx. TW8 0BD
- 081-560 8108 FAX 081-560 8108

Large collection of automatic musical instruments from 1880–1930 demonstrated. Wonderful mixture of mechanics and music for all tastes.

N C SUPPORT Ideal visit to cover many cross-curricular issues: Physics, Music, Power and Social History.

ANNUAL OR ONE OFF EVENT Series of specialist concerts on Saturday evenings.

OPENING April to October: Saturday and Sunday 2.00pm–5.00pm. July to August: Wednesday to Friday 2.00pm–4.00pm. Party visits at other times.

CATERING None.

COST Children £2.00, adults £2.80. Party visit £70.00 for up to 60 people.

DISABLED FACILITIES None.

DIRECTIONS Next to Kew Bridge.

The National Gallery
- The Education Officer
- Trafalgar Square, London. WC2N 5DN
- 071-839 3321 FAX 071-930 1681

The National Gallery collection consists of around 2600 Western European paintings dating from about 1250–1920. The display of the collection is divided chronologically into four areas: the Sainsbury Wing (1250–1510), West Wing (1510–

1600), North Wing (1600–1700) and East Wing (1700–1920). Most of the paintings are on show most of the time.

N C SUPPORT The Education Department offers a range of services for teachers, primary and secondary school groups and students. These include teachers' courses, INSET days and free talks on any aspect of the collection for school groups. These talks can be on specific periods such as the Italian Renaissance, on general themes such as Looking at Paintings or on topics, for example, Water, Colour and Light or the Human Figure. Links with subjects across the curriculum: History, Maths and Science, for example.

OPENING Monday to Saturday 10.00am–6.00pm, Sunday 2.00pm–6.00pm. Closed 1 January, Good Friday, May Day, 24, 25 and 26 December. Minimum number for a booked group is ten, maximum number is 30. At least three weeks' notice is required but more at busy times of the year.

CATERING Booked school groups are requested to come in through the Orange Street Entrance where the schools' cloakroom and sandwich rooms are situated. The two sandwich rooms, where pupils can eat packed lunches, are available only to groups which have booked a Gallery talk and must be reserved in advance.

COST For bookings, up-to-date information on additional Education Department events and Services for Schools leaflets call on 071-389 1744/1743.

DISABLED FACILITIES The Orange Street Entrance and Sainsbury Wing Entrance are at street level and have lifts to all floors. Wheelchairs are available on request.

DIRECTIONS Nearest tube: Trafalgar Square.

National Maritime Museum

- Dr Margarette Lincoln
- Romney Road, Greenwich, London. SE10 9NF
- 081-858 4422 FAX 081-312 6632

The world's largest collection of maritime artefacts. Oil paintings, ship models, historical and modern galleries all tell the story of Britain and the sea and much of the rest of the world as well. Research facilities.

N C SUPPORT The Museum's collections support work in History, Science (Astronomy), Technology and Art.

OPENING Monday to Saturday 10.00am–5.00pm, Sunday 2.00pm–5.00pm.

CATERING Schools' lunch room available (autumn and spring terms only) on first come first served basis.

COST Key Stage 1 pupils free, Key Stages 2 and 3 £1.50 per pupil, one adult free for every ten pupils. Free repeat visits for 12 months after date of first visit.

DIRECTIONS From M25 to junction two (A2) to Greenwich.

VISITS OUT
LONDON & THE SOUTH EAST

National Museum of Cartoon Art
- Paul Gravett
- 183 Eversholt Street, London. NW1 1DD
- 071-388 4326 FAX 071-388 4326

Two galleries exhibiting original cartoons, caricatures and comic strips from the time of Hogarth to the present.

N C SUPPORT Exhibitions are related to Art, Media Studies and History.

OPENING Monday to Friday 12.00 noon–6.00pm, Thursday 12.00 noon–7.00pm. School visits can be arranged at other times on weekdays.

CATERING None.

COST Free. Donations welcome.

DISABLED FACILITIES Wheelchair access at rear.

DIRECTIONS BR/Tube: Euston. Bus: 168 and 253 stop outside. Located opposite 'Carriage' pub.

National Portrait Gallery
- The Education Officer
- St Martin's Place, London. WC2H 0HE
- 071-306 0055 FAX 071-306 0056

The National Portrait Gallery was founded in 1856 to collect the likenesses of famous British men and women. Today the collection constitutes a unique record of the men and women who created (and are still creating) the history and culture of the nation. There are oil paintings, watercolours, drawings, miniatures, sculpture, caricatures, silhouettes and photographs.

N C SUPPORT The Education Department helps both organised groups and individual visitors make the most enjoyable and beneficial use of the Gallery. We provide a direct-teaching service, with sessions tailored to meet schools' needs, supported by printed material as appropriate. The Gallery's commitment to encouraging the practice of portraiture is evident in the programme of school and adult practical workshops and holiday activities.

ANNUAL OR ONE OFF EVENT Talks introduce a selection of works (the Gallery's choice or agreed after discussion with schools) and highlight what can be derived from them on different levels. Workshops begin with a short introductory talk, then move on to practical advice and instruction as appropriate. Specific projects can be worked on in the studio when this alternative space is needed.

OPENING Monday to Friday 10.00am–5.00pm, Saturday 10.00am–6.00pm, Sunday 2.00pm–6.00pm. Closed New Year's Day, Good Friday, May Day bank holiday, Christmas Eve, Christmas Day and Boxing Day. Please ring at least six weeks before to discuss the requirements of the intended visit.

CATERING There is no lunch room.

COST Admission to the Gallery is free except for some special exhibitions. Group rates are always available. Inclusion on the mailing list is also free.

DIRECTIONS Tube: Leicester Square, Charing Cross, Piccadilly Circus.

VISITS OUT
LONDON & THE SOUTH EAST

National Postal Museum
- S L Goron
- King Edward Building, King Edward Street, London. EC1A 1LP
- 071-239 5420 FAX 071-600 3021

The history of British postage and foreign stamps from the original Penny Black up to the very latest issues.

ANNUAL OR ONE OFF EVENT Exhibitions on postal themes held annually. Telephone for details of events.

OPENING Monday to Friday 9.30am–4.30pm.

COST Free.

DISABLED FACILITIES Please telephone Museum for details. No facilities for people with disabilities but we can help with wheelchairs.

NATIONAL TRUST

Opening Times Write or telephone the administrator of the house, give preferred day and time, the size and age of the group, and the main purpose of the visit. *The National Trust Handbook* contains further relevant information.

Cost Unless otherwise stated in the *Handbook*, there is a reduction of around 50% for children aged 16 and under, when accompanied by their teacher. Education Group Members are admitted free. However, please note that there may be a small charge for any additional educational facilities or activities.

See individual entries for all other information.

Alfriston Clergy House
The Ashridge Estate
Bateman's Burwash
Bodiam Castle
Box Hill
Carlyle's House
Chartwell
Cissbury Ring
Emmetts Garden
Fenton House
Harting Down
Hughenden Manor
Ightham Mote
The Needles Battery
Osterley Park
Seven Sisters
South Downs
Sutton House
Witley Centre
The Young National Trust Theatre

The Natural History Museum
- Visitor Resources
- Cromwell Road, London. SW7 5BD
- 071-938 9090 FAX 071-938 8881

A huge range of exciting exhibits can be used to cover many areas of the National Curriculum, particularly the Earth and Life Sciences.

N C SUPPORT A range of activity sheets available from Key Stage 1 to sixth form. Guided tours for children 6–11. Discovery Centre bookable by school groups of 7–11-year-olds. Teachers' pack.

ANNUAL OR ONE OFF EVENT Many.

OPENING Monday to Saturday 10.00am–5.50pm. Sunday 11.00am–5.50pm.

CATERING Sandwich area with small snack bar.

VISITS OUT
LONDON & THE SOUTH EAST

COST Free to pre-booked groups from British schools in full-time education.

DISABLED FACILITIES Access to most of the Museum available.

DIRECTIONS South Kensington tube and subway link. Bus: 74, 14, 30, 45, 49, 264, C1.

Natural History Museum (Southsea)
- Christopher Spendlove
- Cumberland House, Eastern Parade, Southsea, Hants. PO4 9RF
- 0705 296905 FAX 0705 875276

Wildlife dioramas and geology of the Portsmouth area, full-size reconstruction of dinosaur 'Iguanadon'. Formation of the earth and Ice Age audio-visual displays. Freshwater aquarium and British, European and tropical butterflies flying free.

N C SUPPORT Science AT2 'The Variety of Life', AT3 'Processes of Life', AT4 'Evolution', AT16 'The Earth and Space'. Geography AT2 'Knowledge and Understanding of Places' (particularly level 14), AT3 Physical Geography (particularly levels 4 and 5).

OPENING Daily 10.30am–5.30pm. Closed 24–26 December.

CATERING None.

COST Schools and other educational establishments free if booked in advance. Foreign language schools 51p per pupil. Teachers free.

DISABLED FACILITIES Access for people with disabilities is difficult, with five steps to the museum entrance. Ground-floor displays include the Aquarium and sections of the Geology Gallery.

DIRECTIONS By road: follow signposting to Natural History Museum from M27/A2030 into Portsmouth (look for the symbol (M) on the brown signposts).

The Needles Battery
- The Administrator
- West Highdown, Totland Bay, Isle of Wight. PO39 OJH
- 0983 754772

Palmerstonian fort, built in 1862; 250 feet above sea level, 200 ft tunnel to spectacular view of Needles Rocks and lighthouse; two original gun barrels mounted on carriages in the parade ground.

N C SUPPORT National Curriculum links with History and Geography. Restored laboratory; exhibition on the history of the Headland; children's exhibition; interpretation boards throughout the property explain how the old and new batteries functioned.

DISABLED FACILITIES Not recommended to visitors with disabilities.

DIRECTIONS At Needles Headland, west of Freshwater Bay and Alum Bay. Bus: Southern Vectis 42 Yarmouth to Needles, May to October only; otherwise any service to Alum Bay. Ferry: Yarmouth.

Netley Abbey
- The Head Custodian
- 1 Abbey Hill, Netley, Southampton, Hants. SO3 5FB
- 0732 778000

Extensive ruins of a 13th-century Cistercian abbey, converted in

Tudor times for use as a house, in a peaceful and beautiful setting.

OPENING Summer season: daily 10.00am–4.00pm. Winter: weekends only 10.00am–4.00pm. Pre-booking essential.

COST Children 90p, adults £1.20, concessions 60p.

DISABLED FACILITIES Wheelchair access. Dogs allowed on leads.

DIRECTIONS In Netley, four miles south-east of Southampton, facing Southampton Water (OS Map 196; ref SU 453089). Bus: Southampton Citybus 16/A. BR: Southampton to Hamble line (Tel: 0703 553011), Netley station one mile.

New Forest Butterfly Farm
- Annette Todhunter
- Longdown, Ashurst, Nr Southampton, Hants. SO4 4UH
- 0703 292166 FAX 0703 293376

Indoor tropical jungle, with butterflies and moths from all over the world flying freely. Insectarium, woodland walk, dragonfly ponds, picnic area, adventure playground, shops and wagon rides.

N C SUPPORT Teachers' pack explains metamorphosis, and the reason for setting up the farm. It includes pre- and post-visit suggestions for topics.

OPENING Easter to end October: 10.00am–5.00pm.

CATERING Self-service restaurant; ice creams; extensive picnic area.

COST Group rates (minimum 15): children (3–4 years) £1.00, children (5–14 years) £2.20, adults £3.20, one teacher free for every 15 children (1993 prices).

DISABLED FACILITIES All areas (apart from woodland walk) accessible by wheelchair. Toilet.

DIRECTIONS Off A35, between Southampton and Lyndhurst.

New Forest Owl Sanctuary
- Bruce Berry, Director
- Crow Lane, Crow, Ringwood. BH24 1EA
- 0423 476487

Lectures at 11.00am, 1.00pm and 4.00pm in the Lecture Hall and, weather permitting, flying of larger birds of prey in the field at 12.00 noon, 2.00pm and 4.00pm.

N C SUPPORT Sheet for children up to age 9 years.

OPENING Daily 10.00am–5.00pm.

CATERING Cafe for light refreshments. Shop with gifts.

COST Children up to 13 years £1.50, adults £2.50, Senior Citizens £1.50. No discount for groups.

DISABLED FACILITIES Toilets. Ramp for cafe. All walkways are concrete paths.

DIRECTIONS Contact the Sanctuary for directions.

Newham City Farm
- Sarah Scott
- Custom House, King George Avenue, London. E16 3HR
- 071-476 1170

A working urban farm with community involvement and opportunities for 'hands-on' activities. A wide range of farm

VISITS OUT
LONDON & THE SOUTH EAST

animals including shire horse, dairy cows, donkey, llama and wallabies. Indoor classroom facilities are available.

N C SUPPORT Education/interpretation officer. Materials, publications, worksheets. Guided tours, practical, 'hands-on' experience and studies.

ANNUAL OR ONE OFF EVENT Newham City Farm Spring Festival, first bank holiday in May.

CATERING Picnic area, indoor eating facilities, kitchen available to groups, small kiosk.

COST Contact farm for details.

DISABLED FACILITIES Accessible entrances, pathways and toilet facilities.

DIRECTIONS Bus: D2, 262. BR: Custom House North. Tube: East Ham, Plaistow.

News International Exhibitions
- Tricia Neill
- PO Box 495, Virginia Street, London. E1 9XY
- 071-782 6872 FAX 071-782 6870

News International tours of a newspaper plant.

N C SUPPORT The Schools' Fair, supported by a free seminar programme.

ANNUAL OR ONE OFF EVENT The Schools' Fair (annual event) is held at the Business Design Centre, Islington. It is targeted exclusively at 16-plus school leaver age group looking for long-term career counselling, advice on Higher Education course choice and exciting opportunities in training and employment now and in the future in both the UK and abroad. 22, 23, 24 June 10am–4.30pm.

OPENING By arrangement. There is a waiting list for visits.

CATERING Catering facilities.

COST Free.

DISABLED FACILITIES Yes.

DIRECTIONS In Wapping near Tower Bridge.

Florence Nightingale Museum
- Kate Prinsley
- 2 Lambeth Palace Road, London. SE1 7EW
- 071-620 0374

Comprehensive display on the life and work of Florence Nightingale (1820–1910) featuring personal possessions, dress and uniform, a scutari lamp, lifesize model of hospital ward and 20-minute audio-visual show.

N C SUPPORT Ideal for Key Stage 2, core study unit 3 'The Victorians', Health, Women, 19th-century social conditions: notes and questionnaires. Mary Seacole teachers' pack available.

OPENING Tuesday to Sunday 10.00am–6.00pm, closed Monday.

CATERING Cafeteria/packed lunch area available across car park in St Thomas's Hospital.

COST 1993 prices: standard £2.50, student concession £1.50. Groups of 11 or more: students 90p, teachers free.

DISABLED FACILITIES Toilet. Wheelchair access.

VISITS OUT
LONDON & THE SOUTH EAST

DIRECTIONS On the site of St Thomas's Hospital in the main car park. Tube: five minutes from Westminster or Waterloo. BR: Waterloo.

Old Operating Theatre Museum & Herb Garret

- Kevin Hude, Director
- 9a St Thomas's Street, London. SE1 9RY
- 071-955 4791

Fascinating historical interior in attic of Baroque church, used as herb garret and the oldest operating theatre in Britain. Displays on medieval monastery, hospitals of St Thomas, Guy's and herbal medicine.

N C SUPPORT Each group receives a free talk tailored to the National Curriculum from curatorial staff.

ANNUAL OR ONE OFF EVENT Special herbal medicine exhibition.

OPENING Daily (except Monday) 10.00am–4.00pm.

COST Children £1.50, adults £2.00. School groups £1.00.

DISABLED FACILITIES Access by spiral staircase only.

DIRECTIONS Tube/BR: London Bridge two minutes signposted walk.

Old Royal Observatory

- Dr Margarette Lincoln
- Greenwich Park, London. SE10 9NF
- 081-858 4422 FAX 081-312 6632

On this site astronomers have worked since 1676 to plot the stars. Students can stand astride Longitude 0 degrees, see many fascinating clocks and see how these sciences have progressed to the modern day.

N C SUPPORT The Museum's collections support work in History, Science (Astronomy), Technology and Art.

OPENING Apply for details.

CATERING Schools' lunch room available (autumn and spring terms only).

COST Key Stage 1 pupils free, Key Stages 2 and 3 £1.50 per pupil, one adult free for every ten pupils. Free repeat visits for 12 months after date of first visit.

Osborne House

- Monument Manager
- Royal Apartments, York Avenue, East Cowes, Isle of Wight. PO32 6JY
- 0983 200022

Queen Victoria's seaside home was built at her own expense in 1845 and designed by Thomas Cubitt. The house itself is an Italianate villa with two tall towers. The apartments and rooms contain mementoes of royal travels abroad, sometimes incorporated into the decor. Visitors will see intricate Indian plaster decoration, furniture made from deer antlers and over 400 works of art, pictures and pieces of furniture.

OPENING Summer season: daily; grounds 10.00am–6.00pm, house 10.00am–5.00pm (last admission 4.00pm). October: daily; house and grounds 10.00am–5.00pm (last admission 4.00pm). Pre-booking is essential.

VISITS OUT
LONDON & THE SOUTH EAST

CATERING Restaurant/cafeteria.

DISABLED FACILITIES Wheelchair access to exterior and ground floor only, vehicles with disabled passengers may set them down at house entrance before returning to car park.

DIRECTIONS One mile southeast of East Cowes (OS Map 196; ref SZ 516948). Bus: Southern Vectis 4 Ryde to East Cowes, 5 Newport to East Cowes (Tel: 0983 523831). BR: Ryde Esplanade seven miles. Ferry: East Cowes (Red Funnel) one and a half miles; Fishbourne (Wightlink) four miles; Ryde (Wightlink) seven miles.

Osterley Park
- The Administrator
- Isleworth, Middx. TW7 4RB
- 081-560 3918

Elizabethan mansion transformed by Robert Adam in 1760–80; Adam decoration and furniture; 140 acres of parkland.

N C SUPPORT National Curriculum links with History, Geography, Science, Technology and Environmental Education. Study centre, resource book and children's leaflet.

DISABLED FACILITIES House and park accessible. Special parking arrangements when the house and tea-room are open. Adapted WC in park. Park is level, easily accessible; three powered vehicles available Wednesday, Thursday and Sunday 2.00pm–5.00pm in summer. Stair lift gives access to house. Braille guide.

DIRECTIONS Access via Thornbury Road on north side of A4 between Gillette Corner and Osterley tube station; M4, junction 3. Bus: LT H91 Hounslow to Hammersmith, to within half a mile, except Sunday. BR: Syon Lane. Tube: Osterley, (Piccadilly line).

Overlord Embroidery *see* D-Day Museum

Painshill Park
- Mr M Singleton
- Education Trust, Portsmouth Road, Cobham, Surrey. KT11 1JE
- 0932 866743

This evocative and stimulating 18th-century landscape garden is open for day visits from school groups of all ages. There is an Education Centre and teaching staff are on site.

N C SUPPORT The Trust has produced a number of workpacks and trails covering a variety of subjects and linked to the National Curriculum.

OPENING All year round. Special visits and times by arrangement, including holidays and weekends.

CATERING Picnic benches, Education Centre.

DISABLED FACILITIES Virtually the whole park is accessible. Toilets adapted, Ramp to Education and Visitor Centres.

DIRECTIONS Painshill Park is on the A245 near to the junction with the A3 (Cobham side) and can be reached via M25 junction 10.

Palace of Westminster
- Mrs Chris Weeds
- Parliamentary Education Unit, Room 20G, 1 Derby Gate, London. SW1A 2DG
- 071-219 4750 FAX 071-219 5839

Tours include visits to both the House of Commons and the House of Lords. Gallery visits are possible when House is in session.

N C SUPPORT Educational material can be supplied on request from individual students or teachers/group leaders (written or telephone requests welcomed).

ANNUAL OR ONE OFF EVENT Autumn visits programme for 11–13-year-old students held in September and October each year includes video, question session and tour.

OPENING In session: Monday to Thursday morning, Friday from 3.00pm. In recess: certain mornings depending on which recess.

CATERING None.

COST £18 per group of up to 16.

DISABLED FACILITIES Lifts. Toilets. Parking may be arranged at certain times.

DIRECTIONS Directly opposite Westminster tube.

Pallant House Gallery Trust
- D E Coke, Curator
- Pallant House, 9 North Pallant, Chichester, West Sussex. PO19 1TJ
- 0243 774557 FAX 0243 536038

Restored and furnished Queen Anne townhouse with a superb collection of mainly British 20th-century art including Moore, Piper, Hitchens, Nash, Sutherland, Geoffrey Freeman Bow Porcelain collection.

N C SUPPORT Teachers' resource pack published in 1993.

ANNUAL OR ONE OFF EVENT Changing exhibitions throughout the year.

OPENING Tuesday to Saturday 10.00am–5.30pm. (last admission 4.45pm).

COST £1.00 per pupil.

DISABLED FACILITIES Wheelchair access to Exhibition Gallery only.

DIRECTIONS Follow tourist signs in town.

House & Gardens, Pulborough, West Sussex

Beautiful Elizabethan House with 11 acres of fine gardens.

Private guided school groups on Wednesday and Thursday mornings from Easter until October each year.

FREE ACTIVITY SHEET FOR EACH CHILD

Church; Picnic Area; Shop; Children's Play Area; Large Car & Coach Park; Brick & Turf Maze;

Enquiries: 0903 744888

VISITS OUT
LONDON & THE SOUTH EAST

Parham House & Gardens
- Pat Kennedy
- Parham Park, Pulborough, West Sussex. RH20 4HS
- 0903 742021

Elizabethan House with Great Hall, Long Gallery, etc. Furnished with period furniture, paintings and needlework. Eleven acres of gardens with miniature stone Wendy House and children's play area.

N C SUPPORT History–Elizabethan. Free activity sheet for guided school groups.

OPENING Easter Sunday–First Sunday in October: Wednesdays and Thursday morning private guided tours; Wednesday, Thursday, Sunday and bank holiday afternoons – gardens 1.00–6.00pm.

COST Guided School groups: £2.50 per person (minimum of 30).

DIRECTIONS Main gate mid-way between Pulborough and Storrington on A283 road. Four-and-a-half miles from A24 and A29 roads.

Paultons Park
- Anne Ruffell
- Ower, Nr Romsey, Hants. SO51 6AL
- 0703 814455 FAX 0703 813025

Family leisure park with many educational opportunities, including exotic birds, wildfowl, mazes (hedge and mirror), nursery rhymes, pets, corner, dinosaurs, animals, village life. Romany museums.

N C SUPPORT Teachers' pack containing factsheets and worksheets is free.

OPENING Mid-March to October.

CATERING Self-service restaurant, tearooms, refreshment kiosks for packed lunches, hot meals, etc. Discounts for pre-booked catering.

COST Special rates for schools.

DISABLED FACILITIES Three toilets. All the paths are flat and most are tarmacked. Facilities for wheelchairs in restaurant.

DIRECTIONS Just off Exit 2 of M27.

Pevensey Castle
- The Head Custodian
- Pevensey, East Sussex. BN24 5JP
- 0323 762604

This medieval castle includes the remains of an unusual keep enclosed within its walls, which originally date back to the fourth-century Roman fort Anderida.

N C SUPPORT Teachers' Handbook in preparation.

OPENING All year round: Good Friday or 1 April (whichever is earlier) to 30 September: daily 10.00am–6.00pm. 1 October to Maundy Thursday or 31 March (whichever is earlier): Tuesday to Sunday 10.00am–4.00pm. Closed 24–26 December and 1 January.

CATERING Restaurant/cafe.

DISABLED FACILITIES None.

DIRECTIONS In Pevensey (OS Map 199; ref TQ 645048). Bus: Eastbourne buses 28, Southdown 6A/C, Hastings Buses 799 from Eastbourne (Tel: 0273 478007). BR: Pevensey and Westham or Pevensey Bay, both half a mile.

VISITS OUT
LONDON & THE SOUTH EAST

The Photographers' Gallery
- The Education Officer
- 5 & 8 Great Newport Street, London. WC2H 7HY
- 071-831 1772 FAX 071-836 9704

The Photographers' Gallery opened in 1971 as the first independent gallery in Great Britain devoted entirely to professional photography. The exhibition programme presents 21 shows per year in four galleries. These range from contemporary developments in photography to historical surveys and offer new perspectives on key figures from the past and present.

N C SUPPORT The education programme consists of a regular series of lectures, panel discussions and photographers/artists-in-residence. Practical workshops for schools encourage critical engagement with our exhibitions. Events and support material for teachers play an increasingly important part in the programme.

Where support in the form of guided discussions is required, teachers should discuss their needs with the Education Officer beforehand. A Teachers' Information Pack accompanies most main exhibitions. Copies are available free at Teachers' Events or on visits to the relevant exhibition. Inclusion on the Education Mailing List is currently free.

OPENING Tuesday to Saturday 11.00am–7.00pm. Other times by arrangement with the Education Officer.

COST Free.

DISABLED FACILITIES Ground-floor galleries and bookshop are accessible for wheelchairs. No toilet.

DIRECTIONS Tube: Leicester Square, Charing Cross. Bus: 24, 29, 176 to Charing Cross Road.

Planet Earth Garden Paradise
- Mr Eddie Knapp
- Avis Road, Newhaven, East Sussex. BN9 0JH
- 0273 512123 FAX 0273 513985

History of the world from 4500 million years ago to the present day: fossils, minerals, crystals, dinosaurs, Rise of Life, Early Civilisations, Early Explorers, Destruction of the Rainforests and much more.

N C SUPPORT National Curriculum Guide, Teachers' Guide, worksheets, Key Stages 1–4.

OPENING All year round. March to October: daily 10.00am–5.30pm. November to February: daily 10.00am–4.30pm.

CATERING Coffee shop (seats 120) and indoor picnic facilities.

COST Group rates from £1.99.

DISABLED FACILITIES Full facilities for disabled, including toilets, level or ramped areas, etc.

DIRECTIONS Signposted off A26 and A259.

Plashet Zoo
- Ken Tansley
- Plashet Park, Plashet Grove, London. E12
- 081-503 5994

VISITS OUT
LONDON & THE SOUTH EAST

A collection of farm and small unusual animals including waterfowl, aviary birds, tropical butterfly house, Shetland ponies, rabbits and guinea pigs.

N C SUPPORT General education leaflet available.

OPENING Winter: daily (except Monday) 10.00am–4.00pm. Summer: daily (except Monday) 10.00am–5.00pm.

COST Free.

DISABLED FACILITIES Accessible.

DIRECTIONS Tube: East Ham. Bus: D2.

Polka Theatre for Children
- Education Officer
- 240 The Broadway, London. SW19 1SB
- 081-543 3741 FAX 081-542 7723

Leading children's theatre with performances for schools and a wide range of educational support activities, workshops for schools and teachers, National Curriculum material, etc. Winner (twice) of London Fringe Awards. Free teacher preview evenings for every production.

N C SUPPORT Each production supported by teachers' pack with information relating the play to the National Curriculum Key Stages and ATs, cross-curricular information and suggestions for follow-up work.

OPENING Performance times vary. Contact the ticket office.

CATERING Polka Cafe. Packed lunch facilities and interval refreshments available. Please book in advance.

COST Ticket prices from £2.80 (preview price). Discounts for schools. Free tickets for teachers.

DISABLED FACILITIES Wheelchairs welcome. Signed performances. Braille brochure available. Also full Special Needs programme.

DIRECTIONS Tube: Wimbledon (District line), South Wimbledon (Northern line). BR: Wimbledon. By car/coach on main bus route.

Port Lympne Wild Animals Parks see Howletts and Port Lympne

Portchester Castle
- The Head Custodian
- Castle Street, Fareham, Portchester, Hants. PO16 0QW
- 0705 378291

A residence for kings and a rallying point for troops, the history of this grand castle stretches back for nearly 2000 years. There are Roman walls, the most complete in Europe, substantial remains of the royal castle and an exhibition which tells the story of Portchester.

N C SUPPORT An Education Centre has been provided for study use by school parties. This is equipped with audio-visual, printed and replica sources appropriate to the property, which teachers can use themselves. The Education Centre can be booked in advance. For more information, please contact the English Heritage Education Service, Keysign House, 429 Oxford Street, London W1R 2HD. Teachers' Handbook in preparation.

VISITS OUT
LONDON & THE SOUTH EAST

OPENING All year round. Pre-booking essential.

DISABLED FACILITIES Wheelchair access to grounds and lower levels only.

DIRECTIONS On south side of Portchester off A27 (OS map 196; ref SU 625046). Bus: Red Admiral 65/A, 67 Fareham to Southsea to within quarter of a mile. BR: Portchester one mile.

Portsmouth Sea Life Centre
- Alicia Wall
- Clarence Esplanade, Southsea, Portsmouth, Hants. PO5 3PB
- 0705 734461 FAX 0795 294443

Experience the marvels of a deep-sea dive, without getting wet. Thousands of astonishing sea creatures are featured in spacious displays which re-create their natural habitats. Displays include the recently added Shark Encounter.

N C SUPPORT Educational workbooks for 5–7 and 8–12-year-olds. Work cards for 12–16-year-olds. Interactive talks tailored to the curriculum and different age groups. Educational certificates for each pupil (including free second visit).

OPENING Winter: 10.00am–6.00pm. Summer: 10.00am–9.00pm.

COST Children £2.25, one adult free with every ten children, additional teachers £2.25. Discount for disabled.

DISABLED FACILITIES Toilets, ramps and doorways.

DIRECTIONS Take the M275 and follow the signs to Southsea. Brown tourist board signs direct all the way.

Preston Manor
- Richenda McNaughton
- Preston Park, Brighton, Sussex. BN1 6SD
- 0273 603005 FAX 0273 779108

Edwardian country house with reconstructed servants' quarters.

N C SUPPORT 'Situations Vacant' Victorian servants' role-play and guided tours with opportunities for 'hands-on' work tailored to National Curriculum needs.

OPENING Tuesday to Saturday 10.00am–5.00pm, Sunday 2.00pm–5.00pm, closed Monday except bank holidays.

CATERING None.

COST Admission fee varies. Cheap rate applies between 10 October and 28 February.

DISABLED FACILITIES None. Wheelchair access difficult.

DIRECTIONS Located at the corner of Preston Grove and London Road, A23. Bus: 5 from town centre.

Quarry Farm Rural Experience
- Angela Swart, Administrator
- Bodiam, East Sussex. TN32 5XD
- 0580 830670

Quarry Farm is an agricultural educational farm, with a collection of steam tractor engines and farming bygones. Displays on the Farmers' Year, Farm Animals, Woods and Wildlife.

ANNUAL OR ONE OFF EVENT Annual Country Steam Fayre.

OPENING Weekends, bank holidays, daily during school holidays

VISITS OUT
LONDON & THE SOUTH EAST

10.00am–5.00pm. Any day for group bookings.

CATERING Restaurant, licensed bar, lunches, cream teas, dinners.

COST Children £1.50, adults £3.00, Senior Citizens and disabled £1.50. Discount of 10% on groups of ten and over.

DISABLED FACILITIES Well laid out paths. Toilets.

DIRECTIONS Follow sign off A28, A21, A268 or B2244 (formerly A229) to Bodiam. Quarry Farm is half a mile south of the village.

Queen Elizabeth Country Park
- Sarah Evans
- Visitors Centre, Gravel Hill, Horndean, Waterlooville, Hants. PO8 0QE
- 0705 595040 FAX 0705 592409

On the South Downs; comprising traditional chalk downland contrasting with broadleaf and conifer woodland. Evidence of man's influence past and present, a place of outstanding beauty.

N C SUPPORT Geography, History, CDT, Art, Maths, English. Both guided and self-guided activities. Free teachers' information pack. Various support notes. Plenty of opportunity for 'hands-on' experience.

OPENING School bookings taken all year round. Visitor Centre: January to February: Sunday only 10.00am to dusk. March to October: 10.00am–6.00pm. November to December: Saturday and Sunday only 10.00am to dusk.

CATERING Picnic tables and barbecue sites.

COST Self-guided: free. Car parking charge. Guided: children 85p. For one hour's activity £15.00 minimum charge and £1.50 per child. For two hours activity £20.00 minimum charge.

DISABLED FACILITIES Toilets and two easy access trails.

DIRECTIONS Along the A3, 15 miles north of Portsmouth, four miles south of Petersfield.

The Queen's Gallery
- Miss Julie Grist
- Buckingham Palace, London. SW1A 1AA
- 071-930 4832 FAX 071-930 9781

The Queen's Gallery was opened in 1962 to hold exhibitions featuring works of art from the Royal Collection, one of the finest art collections in the world.

OPENING Tuesday to Saturday 10.00am–5.00pm. Sunday 2.00pm–5.00pm.

CATERING None.

COST Children under 17 £1.20, adults £2.50, Senior Citizens £1.80, family £6.00. Discount of 10% for pre-paid, pre-booked groups (must pay at least two weeks in advance).

DISABLED FACILITIES It is better to ring in advance and discuss the visit as access is limited.

DIRECTIONS Tube: Victoria; turn right into Buckingham Palace Road, then five-minute walk.

VISITS OUT
LONDON & THE SOUTH EAST

The Queen's House
- Dr Margarette Lincoln
- Romney Road, London. SE10 8NF
- 081-858 4422 FAX 081-312 6632

This royal palace for a Stuart Queen has been restored to the bright colours of the court in 1662. Built by Inigo Jones it also demonstrates the mathematical basis of his classical style. Beautiful marine paintings.

N C SUPPORT The museum's collections support work in History, Science (Astronomy), Technology and Art.

CATERING Schools' lunch room available (autumn and spring terms only).

COST Key Stage 1 pupils free, Key Stages 2 and 3 £1.50 per pupil, one adult free for every ten pupils. Free repeat visits for 12 months after date of first visit.

DIRECTIONS From M25 to junction two (A2) go to Greenwich.

Queen's Royal Surrey Regimental Museum *see* Clandon Park

Ragged School Museum
- Pauline Plumb
- 46–48 Copperfield Road, London. E3 4RR

The Museum is in a Victorian canalside warehouse converted by Dr Barnardo to serve as a ragged school 1877–1908. A recreated classroom is used for role-play Victorian lessons, and displays look at pupils' lives.

N C SUPPORT Worksheets and teachers' notes explore links for Key Stages 1 and 2 in Maths, Science, Geography and History. The Victorian Lesson USII, CSU3. Museum visit CSU4.

OPENING Wednesday and Thursday 10.00am–5.00pm, first Sunday of the month 2.00pm–5.00pm.

CATERING Cafe open to public but can be used by schools for packed lunches.

COST Museum: free. Victorian lesson: £1.00.

DISABLED FACILITIES Not accessible for wheelchairs. Lesson suitable for children with special needs.

DIRECTIONS Tube: Mile End ten minutes walk. Parking outside Museum.

Rangers House
- The Head Custodian
- Chesterfield Walk, Blackheath, London. SE10 8QX
- 081-853 0035

A handsome red-brick villa built *c.*1700 on the edge of Greenwich Park, with a splendid bow-windowed gallery. It houses a remarkable series of Jacobean portraits and a collection of musical instruments.

OPENING All year. Good Friday or 1 April (whichever is earlier) to 30 September: daily 10.00am–6.00pm.

DISABLED FACILITIES Wheelchair lift available.

DIRECTIONS Bus: LT 53 Oxford Circus to Plumstead (Tel: 071-222 1234). BR: Maze Hill half a mile.

VISITS OUT
LONDON & THE SOUTH EAST

Rare Breeds Centre
- Mrs M E Hanlon
- Highlands Farm, Woodchurch, Ashford, Kent. TN26 3RJ
- 0233 861493 **FAX** 0233 861457

Ninety-acre farm with 55 breeds of rare farm animals and poultry, run by people with learning disabilities. Opportunity to experience animals close at hand. Woodland walks and tractor rides.

N C SUPPORT Worksheets in preparation, please enquire. Clipboards available. Talks on Genetics, Working with People with Disabilities, and Invader Animals are given on site.

ANNUAL OR ONE OFF EVENT Living History: Anglo Saxon Village May 1994. Experience life as an Anglo Saxon.

OPENING Summer: 10.30am–5.30pm. Winter: 10.30am–4.30pm.

CATERING Restaurant, snacks, picnic areas.

COST Schools: children 50p, adults £2.25, one teacher free for every ten pupils (1993 prices).

DISABLED FACILITIES Excellent. All areas level access or ramps. Toilets. Woodland trails difficult.

DIRECTIONS On B2067 Hamstreet to Tenterden road. M20 Junction 10, follow A2070 to Hamstreet.

Richborough Castle
- The Head Custodian
- Richborough, Sandwich, Kent. CT13 9JW

This fort and township date back to the Roman landing in AD43. The fortified walls and the massive foundations of a triumphal arch which stood 80 feet high still survive.

OPENING All year round. Good Friday or 1 April (whichever is earlier) to 30 September: daily 10.00am–6.00pm. 1 October to Maundy Thursday or 31 March (whichever is earlier): Tuesday to Sunday 10.00am–4.00pm. Closed 24–26 December and 1 January.

DISABLED FACILITIES Wheelchair access.

DIRECTIONS One and a half miles north of Sandwich off A257 (OS Map 179; ref TR 324602). BR: Sandwich two miles. Riverbus (summer season only) from Highway Marine, Sandwich (Tel: 0304 613925).

Robin Hood's Rest
- Francis McLennan
- 61 Lincolnsfield Centre, Bushey Hall Drive, Bushey, Herts. WD2 2ER
- 0923 818 786 **FAX** 0923 213 055

Pets' Corner: rare breed centre with over 1000 animals and birds. Rare breed poultry collection. Information Centre, shop, woodlands.

N C SUPPORT Key Stages 1 and 2 covered.

OPENING All year round: 10.00am to dusk, closed Monday.

CATERING Cafe 12.00 noon–6.00pm.

COST Children 30p, adults 50p, Senior Citizens 30p.

DISABLED FACILITIES Access to cafe and Pets' Corner.

DIRECTIONS Two minutes off M1. Junction 5 to Harrow, right at roundabout and half a mile along

A4008 to Bushey; turn right at roundabout to Bushey Hall Drive.

Rochester Castle
- The Head Custodian
- The Keep, Rochester-upon-Medway, Kent. ME1 1SX
- 0634 402276

Built in the 11th century to guard the point where the Roman road of Watling Street crossed the River Medway, the size and position of this grand Norman bishop's castle, founded on the Roman city wall, eventually made it an important royal stronghold for several hundred years. The keep is truly magnificent, over 100 feet high and with walls 12 feet thick. At the top visitors will be able to enjoy fine views over the river and surrounding city of Rochester.

OPENING All year round. Good Friday or 1 April (whichever is earlier) to 30 September: daily 10.00am–6.00pm. 1 October to 31 March: Tuesday to Sunday 10.00am–4.00pm. Closed 24–26 December and 1 January.

COST Student groups and school parties are admitted free to English Heritage properties, but should book in advance through the relevant Regional Office.

DISABLED FACILITIES None.

DIRECTIONS By Rochester Bridge (A2) (OS Map 178; ref TQ 742686). Bus: from surrounding areas (Tel: 0800 696996). BR: Rochester half a mile.

Roman Museum
- Marit Hendriks
- Butchery Lane, Canterbury, Kent
- 0227 452747 FAX 0227 455047

A new museum in the city centre. Underground in the levels of Roman Canterbury. Main features include the remains of a Roman townhouse with fine mosaics. Finds from excavations in the Roman town.

N C SUPPORT 'Hands-on' area with task cards and a Roman pack for teachers.

OPENING Monday to Saturday 10.30am–5.00pm (last admission 4.00pm). June to end October: also Sunday 1.30pm–5.00pm (last admission 4.00pm).

COST Children 70p, adults £1.40, concession £1.00. Discount of 10% for groups of ten or more.

DISABLED FACILITIES Good access.

DIRECTIONS By road: A2 then central car parks. BR: Canterbury East and West stations are within walking distance.

Roman Painted House
- Brian Philip
- New Street, Dover, Kent. CT17 9AJ
- 0374 203279

Major Roman townhouse (within large cover building) with in situ Roman wall paintings, hypocaust system and later late-Roman fort wall and bastion.

N C SUPPORT Extensive graphic display with finds on Roman Dover, 'Touch table', recorded commentaries, videos, 'reconstructed heads' display, special talks to schools by prior arrangement, publications.

OPENING April to October: daily (except Monday) 10.00am–5.00pm. Open for school visits in winter by prior arrangement.

VISITS OUT
LONDON & THE SOUTH EAST

CATERING None.

COST Children 50p, adults £1.50, staff/adults with school groups free.

DISABLED FACILITIES Access to ground floor only, where there are two clear viewing panels. Stair to lower floor.

DIRECTIONS Close to Market Square: New Street is small road opposite the parish church in Cannon Street.

Romney, Hythe & Dymchurch Railway
- Derek Smith
- New Romney Station, New Romney, Kent. TN28 8PL
- 0679 62353 FAX 0679 63591

World's smallest public railway at 13.5 miles; one-third full-size steam and diesel railway running from Hythe to Dungeness across Kent's historic Romney Marsh.

N C SUPPORT In preparation.

ANNUAL OR ONE OFF EVENT Steam Diesel Gala (in May). New Romney Bus Rally (in June).

OPENING March and October: weekends only. Easter to end September: daily.

CATERING Cafe (seats 60) at New Romney Station, cafe (seats 70) at Dungeness and various picnic areas.

COST Depends on length of journey. Schools travel at one-third the adult rate and one teacher travels free for every ten children.

DISABLED FACILITIES Limited.

DIRECTIONS M20 to Junction 11. Follow signs for Hythe or A259 to New Romney.

The Royal Academy of Arts
- The Education Officer
- Burlington House, Piccadilly, London. W1V 0DS
- 071-494 5763 FAX 071-434 0837

The Royal Academy of Arts, founded in 1758, is the oldest Fine Arts Institution in Great Britain. It is an independent organisation, run by and for artists, and is best known today for its major international loan exhibitions and its annual Summer Exhibition of contemporary art. The exhibitions policy is broad and ranges from historical retrospectives of individual artists and specific movements to extensive surveys of art from a variety of cultures.

N C SUPPORT Services for schools consist of In-House and Outreach programmes. There are specific programmes for teachers and their students in conjunction with each exhibition. The In-House programmes put emphasis on providing teachers with the background material they need for their pupils. The Outreach programme encourages individuals to take the initiative in discovering their creative potential and increases awareness about the integral nature of artistic theory and practice.

Teachers' lectures and private views take place as soon as possible after the opening of an exhibition and packs of background material for teachers are available free of charge on application to the department. In addition, an Annual Teachers' Conference is held at the end of the summer term which highlights forthcoming shows in

VISITS OUT
LONDON & THE SOUTH EAST

order to facilitate preparation and to inspire links to coursework in schools. Students are also catered for through a range of Study Days, Workshops and Guide Sheets as well as talks.

OPENING Daily 10.00am–6.00pm.

COST Entry rates for pre-booked school parties vary for each exhibition: 11–18 yrs approximately £2.00–£2.50, under 11s £1.00. For enquiries about Outreach please contact Paula Kitt on 071-494 5730.

DISABLED FACILITIES The building is totally accessible to wheelchair users.

DIRECTIONS Nearest tube: Piccadilly Circus.

Royal Air Force Museum
- John Edwards
- Grahame Park Way, London. NW9 5LL
- 081-200 1763

Seventy full-size aeroplanes displayed under cover illustrating the story of flight from the time of the Wright brothers to the present day.

N C SUPPORT Illustrated talks, handling sessions, activity sheets for Key Stages 2 and 3 History. GCSE sessions, assistance with projects and 'flight' topics. Education centre, lunch room, picnic facilities, flight simulator.

ANNUAL OR ONE OFF EVENT Annual 'Flight Activities' week in August. Regular exhibitions.

OPENING Daily 10.00am–6.00pm.

CATERING Restaurant on site.

DISABLED FACILITIES All parts of Museum accessible to wheelchairs.

DIRECTIONS Easy access via M1 (Junction four), A1 and M25.

Royal Armouries
- Curator or Frank Bartlett
- Fort Nelson, Down End Road, Fareham, Hants. PO17 6AN
- 0329 233734 FAX 0329 822092

Fort Nelson is one of a ring of forts built in the 1860s to defend Portsmouth from a possible French assault by land. A fine specimen of Victorian Military Architecture.

N C SUPPORT Groups are taken on a guided tour and can focus on: Life in a Victorian Fort; How to defend the Fort against attack; The development of Artillery; Science-based 'hands-on' activity, moving heavy guns with pulleys and ropes.

ANNUAL OR ONE OFF EVENT There are special themed events throughout the season: Romans through to Modern Artillery.

OPENING Schools can visit any day of the week 10.30am–4.30pm.

CATERING Picnic on the ramparts or book hot/cold snacks and drinks in the cafe.

COST Schools free.

DISABLED FACILITIES Well-equipped to deal with tours of people with disabilities.

DIRECTIONS Leave M27 at junction 11. Follow yellow signs for Fort Nelson. Maps on request.

VISITS OUT
LONDON & THE SOUTH EAST

The Royal Artillery
- J J Starr, Curator
- Regiment Museum, Old Royal Military Academy, London. SE18 4DN
- 081-781 5628

This museum tells the story of the Royal Regiment of Artillery from its formation in 1716 to the present day.

N C SUPPORT None.

OPENING Monday to Friday 12.30pm–4.30pm.

CATERING Ring for details.

COST Free.

DISABLED FACILITIES None. Museum housed on upper floors of building with no elevator facilities.

Royal Botanic Gardens
- Laura Ponsonby
- Kew, Richmond, Surrey. TW9 3AB
- 081-332 5612 FAX 081-332 5610

The country's foremost botanical garden, created in the mid-18th century. Its attractions include the Orangery and 10-storey Chinese Pagoda. In-Service Training for Teachers (INSET): courses are by arrangement; subjects include Geography, History, Technology, Environmental Studies, Music, etc. Teacher placement. 'Topic Days': mainly Key Stages 1 and 2 for children.

N C SUPPORT INSET on 'Plants Across the Curriculum' courses or by arrangement (see above). Teachers' Handbook (KS2) available. Advisory service for teachers. Limited number of guided tours available for A-Level groups.

OPENING From 9.30am. Closing times vary from 4.00pm to 6.30pm on weekdays and from 4.00pm to 8.00pm on Sundays and Public Holidays, depending on the time of sunset. The Kew Gardens Gallery, Marianne North Gallery and glasshouses open at 9.30am and the Sir Joseph Banks Building at 10.00am. Closed 4.45pm weekdays and 5.45pm Sundays.

CATERING The Pavilion Restaurant (self-service cafeteria), the Orangery Restaurant (cold carvery lunches and a selection of afternoon teas) and the Kew Bakery (snacks and drinks). For general enquiries contact the Manager, Pavilion Restaurant, on 081-332 5186.

COST All those in full-time education free entry to Kew. Topic Days: £1.00. INSET: £21.00 plus VAT full day, £12.50 plus VAT half day.

DISABLED FACILITIES Wheelchairs can be borrowed from the Main Gate and Victoria Gate; it is advisable to book them in advance. Please telephone 081-332 5121.

DIRECTIONS Bus: 65, 237, 267, 391. Nearest BR: Kew Bridge and Kew Gardens (North London line). Tube: Kew Gardens (District line). River motor vessels run between Westminster and Hampton Court, calling at Kew Pier, near Kew Bridge, during the summer months.

The Royal London Hospital Museum & Archive
- Jonathan Evans
- The Royal London Hospital, Whitechapel, London. E1 1BB
- 071-377 7000 FAX 071-377 7677

VISITS OUT
LONDON & THE SOUTH EAST

Museum of health care: permanent exhibition on the story of the Royal London Hospital from 1740 to the present day looks at work of pioneers like Dr Barnardo and Edith Cavell; collection of nursing uniforms and equipment.

N C SUPPORT Teachers' pack with several other museums of health and medicine. Slide and photographs collection (Thames: hospitals, nursing, medical history). Videos and publications for sale.

ANNUAL OR ONE OFF EVENT The Royal London Street Tour (Saturday afternoon in late June each year).

OPENING Monday to Friday 10.00am–4.30pm.

CATERING Available in Alexandra House (in Hospital garden). Snack bar in Out Patients Department (opposite Museum)

COST Free. Groups: school children 50p, others £1.50.

DISABLED FACILITIES Wheelchair access (one six-inch step). Toilets in Alexandra House and Out Patients Department.

DIRECTIONS Museum is in basement of St Augustine with St Philip's Church, Newark Street (behind main hospital building in Whitechapel Road).

The Royal Mews
- Miss Julie Grist
- Buckingham Palace, London. SW1A 1AA

The Royal Mews is the home of the Queen's magnificent gilded and polished State Carriages and Coaches, as well as of their horses and equipage. There is also a display of photographs and other items of interest.

OPENING Telephone for details. 5 January to 23 March: 12.00 noon–4.00pm. 29 March to 29 September: 12.00 noon–4.00pm. 5 October to 21 December: 12.00 noon–4.00pm. Last admission 3.30pm.

CATERING None.

COST Children under 17 £1.20, adults £2.50, Senior Citizens £1.80, family £6.00. Discount of 10% for pre-paid groups.

DIRECTIONS Tube: Victoria; turn right into Buckingham Palace Road, then five-minute walk.

The Royal Museum & Art Gallery and Buffs Regimental Gallery
- Ms Marit Hendriks
- High Street, Canterbury, Kent. CT1 2JE
- 0227 452747 FAX 0227 455047

The city's picture collection, including the T S Cooper Gallery for England's leading Victorian animal painter; special exhibitions gallery with regular art events; the Buffs Regimental Gallery telling the story of one of England's oldest infantry regiments.

N C SUPPORT Teachers' idea sheets are available for some exhibitions.

OPENING Monday to Saturday 10.00am–5.00pm.

COST Free.

DISABLED FACILITIES None.

DIRECTIONS By road: A2 then Central Car Parks. BR: Canterbury East and West stations are within walking distance.

VISITS OUT
LONDON & THE SOUTH EAST

Rural Life Centre
- H Jackson
- Reeds Road, Tilford, Farnham, Surrey. GU10 2DL
- 0252 792300

Collection of displays on all aspects of past village life, arboretum picnic areas, souvenir shop, cafe, woodland walk.

N C SUPPORT Special exhibition on 1930s and World War II, wheelwright talks, blacksmith demonstrations.

ANNUAL OR ONE OFF EVENT Rustic Sunday in July: Craft demonstrations and Country Fair.

OPENING April to end September: Wednesday to Sunday and bank holidays 11.00am–6.00pm.

CATERING Cafe serves light meals, ices, etc.

COST Children £1.25, adults £2.50, Senior Citizens £2.00. Groups over 20 are offered 10% discount and two teachers go free.

DISABLED FACILITIES Toilets. Ramps to buildings.

DIRECTIONS From Farnham, 219 Stagecoach service. Brown tourist signs from Tilford and Frensham A287.

Rye Art Gallery
- Miranda Leonard
- Ockman Lane, East Street, Rye, East Sussex. TN31 7JY
- 0797 223218

Two galleries, Stormont Studio and Easton Rooms, showing a continuous programme of historical and contemporary exhibitions of fine art and craft, with a connecting courtyard with views over Romney Marsh.

N C SUPPORT Workshops, questionnaires, tours and thematic work can be provided for the specific curriculum requirements of schools consulting in advance.

ANNUAL OR ONE OFF EVENT All round programme of workshops. Annual Children's Art Exhibition in February. Please write for details.

OPENING Daily 10.30am–5.00pm. Stormont Studio closed Tuesdays (booking advised).

CATERING None.

COST Free.

DISABLED FACILITIES None.

DIRECTIONS Through Land Gate to top of High Street. Easton Rooms entrance 107 High Street.

Rye Harbour Nature Reserve
- Dr Barry Yates
- 2 Watch Cottages, Nook Beach, Winchelsea, East Sussex. TN36 4LU
- 0797 223862

Coastal nature reserve with three birdwatching hides overlooking pools. Good variety of sea birds all year and many wildflowers in May and June.

N C SUPPORT Information leaflet available on enclosure of sae.

OPENING Information Centre at Rye Habour: April to September: 10.00am–5.00pm. Reserve always open.

DISABLED FACILITIES Toilet for people with disabilities and one birdwatching hide accessible to wheelchairs.

DIRECTIONS Two miles southeast of Rye in East Sussex.

Rye Museum
- Mrs M H Bird
- Rye Castle, Rye, East Sussex. TN31 7HH
- 0797 226728

Thirteenth-century stone tower, built to defend Rye, overlooking rivers and Romney Marsh. Local history of Rye and district, shipbuilding, pottery, topographical model of coastal changes.

N C SUPPORT Geographical/historical changes of Romney Marsh area. Maritime and shipbuilding. Castle and prison pottery.

OPENING April to November: daily 10.30am–5.30pm.

CATERING None.

COST Children (under 16s) 50p, (over 16s) 80p, adults £1.50, students £1.00. Groups of ten or more: 40p.

DISABLED FACILITIES Not suitable.

DIRECTIONS Centre of town, near church. Coach park near station, easy walking distance.

Rye Town Model
- The Administrator
- Rye Heritage Centre, Strand Quay, Rye, East Sussex. TN31 7AY
- 0797 226696

Relive 700 years of historical events of the ancient town of Rye, brought to life by the fascinating Sound and Light experience; also a historical storyboard exhibition, shop and Tourist Information.

OPENING Daily 10.00am–5.00pm. Winter weekends or by arrangement throughout the year for groups.

CATERING None.

COST £1.00 per person, group leaders or teachers free.

DISABLED FACILITIES Wheelchair access.

DIRECTIONS From Rye Station walk up Station Approach, turn right at T-junction and follow road signs marked Tourist Information. Heritage Centre is situated on the A259.

St Augustine's Abbey
- The Head Custodian
- Longport, Canterbury, Kent. CT1 1TF

Founded in 598, this was one of the earliest monastic sites in southern England. Here you will find remarkable remains of the foundations of the original sixth-century churches, the Norman church and medieval monastery.

OPENING All year round. Good Friday or 1 April (whichever is earlier) to 30 September: daily 10.00am–6.00pm. 1 October to Maundy Thursday or 31 March (whichever is earlier): Tuesday to Sunday 10.00am–4.00pm. Closed 24–26 December and 1 January.

DISABLED FACILITIES Wheelchair accessible but there are some steps.

DIRECTIONS In Longport, quarter of a mile east of Cathedral Close (OS Map 179; ref TR 154578). Bus: from surrounding areas (Tel: 0800

VISITS OUT
LONDON & THE SOUTH EAST

696996). BR: Canterbury East and West, both three-quarters of a mile.

St Mary's Church
- The Rector
- St Mary Church Street, London. SE16 4JE
- 071-231 2465

Georgian parish church (1715) on an ancient site. Part of riverside conservation area. Interesting furnishings, and links with the Pilgrim Fathers (1620). Famous organ (1764).

OPENING Daily 7.00am–6.00pm.

CATERING Churchyard quad for picnics; lavatories and kitchen available.

COST Free.

DISABLED FACILITIES Ramps only.

DIRECTIONS Off the roundabout at the entrance to the Rotherhithe Tunnel (signpost to church).

St Paul's Cathedral
- Rory Milligan, Visits Officer
- St Paul's Churchyard, London. EC4M 5AD
- 071-248 4128 FAX 071-248 3104

A national monument, an international centre of religion and an outstanding example of Wren's work. Unique in mosaic decoration, its full-length crypt and its galleries; particularly the whispering gallery.

N C SUPPORT No formal support as yet, but willing to assist in any way they can.

OPENING Monday to Saturday 8.30am–4.00pm.

CATERING None.

COST UK schools parties admitted free. If booked, a guide is also available free. Galleries: £1.00.

DISABLED FACILITIES Wheelchair access. Toilets.

DIRECTIONS Tube: St Paul's (Central line).

School Journey Association
- Miss Julie Coakley
- 48 Cavendish Road, London. SW12 0DG
- 081-675 6636 FAX 081-673 8763

Voluntary non-profit-making charity assisting schools with insurance, travel in the UK and Europe, London school hotels, language courses.

ANNUAL OR ONE OFF EVENT Isle of Man tours with National Curriculum orientation May 1994 and yearly (refer IOM Tourist Board), from £65.00.

OPENING Office: Monday–Friday 9.30am–4.30pm.

CATERING Full.

COST London hotel (1993 discounted): £19.00 per night full board, £11.00 B&B (under 16).

DISABLED FACILITIES None.

DIRECTIONS Tube: Clapham South. Cavendish Road is part of South Circular Road.

Science Museum
- Education Unit
- Exhibition Road, London. SW7 2DD
- 071-938 8222

Devoted to the history and contemporary practice of science, technology and medicine. Includes

VISITS OUT
LONDON & THE SOUTH EAST

Launch Pad and Flight Lab interactive galleries, Food for Thought, Exploration of Space, Flight and Land Transport.

N C SUPPORT Term-time programme of teachers' courses, free events for children and INSET days, all related to National Curriculum. Range of teachers' resource materials available.

ANNUAL OR ONE OFF EVENT Many events. Newsletter produced each term with details.

OPENING Monday to Saturday 10.00am–6.00pm, Sunday 11.00am–6.00pm.

CATERING Schools' lunch room available for booking, other picnic areas open to schools but not bookable.

COST Free admission for prebooked educational groups and teachers on planning visits.

DISABLED FACILITIES Museum can cater for visitors with disabilities. Groups should state special needs on booking form.

DIRECTIONS Tube: South Kensington.

Serpentine Gallery

- Vivien Ashley, Educational Organiser
- Kensington Gardens, London. W2 3XA
- 071-402 0343 FAX 071-402 4103

The Serpentine Gallery puts on changing exhibitions of British and international modern and contemporary art. The innovative programme encompasses painting, sculpture, installation, video and photography, as well as the annual staging of performance events. Artists range from those of international stature, such as Claus Oldenburg, Paula Rego, Andy Warhol, Leonora Carrington, Richard Deacon and Ivor Hitchens, to up-and-coming young practitioners just out of art school.

The Gallery, with its intimate scale and friendly atmosphere, is ideal for introducing young people to 20th-century art. Very near the Serpentine lake, it has four large and beautifully proportioned rooms with French windows leading out into the surrounding parkland.

N C SUPPORT One-day events for older school students and shorter workshops for younger pupils take place during every show. Through a combination of discussion and practical work students explore some of the ideas in the exhibition, and develop their understanding of 20th-century art. These workshops, which take account of recent curriculum developments, are led by practising artists and take place in the gallery in front of the artworks. An intensive two-week summer school is designed for sixth form students every July.

OPENING Daily 10.00am–6.00pm.

CATERING None. Park can be used for picnics.

COST Free to LEA schools.

DISABLED FACILITIES The galleries and bookshop are accessible by wheelchair. Accessible toilets nearby.

DIRECTIONS Tube: Lancaster Gate, South Kensington, Knightsbridge. Bus: 9, 10, 52 south of the park; 12, 94 north of the park.

VISITS OUT
LONDON & THE SOUTH EAST

Seven Sisters
- Regional Education Officer
- The National Trust Regional Office, The Estate Office, Scotney Castle, Lamberhurst, Tunbridge Wells, Kent. TN3 8JN

The Trust owns 1,172 acres along this stretch of the South Downs; a variety of landscapes, including farmland and water meadow at Frog Firle Farm, chalk downland at Crowlink and coastline at Birling Gap.

N C SUPPORT National Curriculum links with Geography and Science. Teachers' pack.

DISABLED FACILITIES Contact the Administrator for access details.

DIRECTIONS On application.

Shell Grotto
- W Heigl
- Grotto Hill, Margate, Kent. CT9 2BU
- 0843 220008

The only underground Shell Temple in the world. An ancient Shell Temple, accidentally discovered in 1835. It has been open to the public since 1837 and its origin is still a mystery. Millions of shells have been used to decorate the 2000 square feet of winding passages with exquisite mosaic designs.

OPENING April to October: Monday to Friday 10.00am–5.30pm, Saturday and Sunday 10.00am–4.00pm.

CATERING None.

COST Children under 12 50p, adults £1.00. Group discount 10%.

DISABLED FACILITIES Access to gift shop, but Shell Grotto not suitable (narrow stairs).

DIRECTIONS Grotto Hill off Northdown Road, Margate.

Smugglers' Adventure
- Anne Donnelly
- St Clements Caves, West Hill, Hastings, East Sussex. TN34 3HY

Set in over an acre of subterranean caverns and passages, the centre includes an exhibition, museum, video theatre and adventure walk, as well as over 50 lifesize figures, push buttons and dramatic sound and lighting.

N C SUPPORT Free Primary and Secondary education packs available. Free preliminary visits for teachers.

OPENING Winter: 11.00am–4.30pm (last admission). Summer: 10.00am–5.30pm (last admission).

CATERING Special school rates for parties of 10 or more. Smugglers' Adventure: Children/adults £1.95. 1066 Story (Hastings Castle): children/adults £1.20. Combined (both venues): children/adults £2.95. At each venue one adult/teacher is admitted free for every ten children.

COST None.

DISABLED FACILITIES None.

DIRECTIONS Hastings is 62 miles from London. The major road route is the A21, which links with the M25. BR: frequent trains run from London Victoria and Charing Cross. Coach:

VISITS OUT
LONDON & THE SOUTH EAST

National Express operate regular daily services from Victoria.

Southampton Hall of Aviation
- The Curator
- Albert Road South, Southampton. SO1 1FR
- 0703 635830

Not just a collection of aeroplanes but the story of 26 local aircraft companies. On display are 16 aircraft, some unique, some historic, and all relevant to the Solent area.

N C SUPPORT Displays are ideal for those studying topics such as Transport (flight), History of Aviation, World War II in the air and on the home front, Science and Technology, Power units including gas turbine.

ANNUAL OR ONE OFF EVENT Various events, usually evening lectures.

OPENING Tuesday to Saturday 10.00am–5.00pm, Sunday 12.00 noon–5.00pm, Monday (during school holidays only) 10.00am–5.00pm.

CATERING None available but numerous cafes at nearby Ocean Village.

COST Children (5–15 years) £1.50, adults £2.50, students/Senior Citizens £2.00. Group rates: children £1.00, adults £2.00, one adult free per ten children.

DISABLED FACILITIES Lift and ramps; all floors accessible. Toilets.

DIRECTIONS Follow signs: Docks, Old Town to Ocean Village and Hall of Aviation.

The South Bank Centre
- Acting Director of Education
- Royal Festival Hall, London. SE1 8XX
- 071-921 0848 FAX 071-928 0063

The South Bank Centre comprises the Royal Festival Hall, Queen Elizabeth Hall and the Hayward Gallery. A range of educational events and resources are available for all ages across different art forms: dance, music, visual arts, literature.

N C SUPPORT Teachers' packs and courses relating to art, music and dance as well as different subject areas in the National Curriculum are organised throughout the year.

OPENING Please ring the box office for details on 071-928 8800.

CATERING A range of cafeterias and restaurants are available in the Royal Festival Hall and Hayward Gallery.

COST Group discounts are available for schools and colleges. Please ring the box office.

DISABLED FACILITIES The South Bank Centre welcomes people with disabilities. For full access information, please ring on 071-921 0639.

DIRECTIONS The South Bank Centre lies between and either side of Waterloo and Hungerford Bridges. Bus to Waterloo. Tube: Waterloo or Embankment. BR: Waterloo.

South Downs
- Geoff Sully
- Slindon Estate Yard, Slindon, Arundel, West Sussex. BN18 0RP
- 0243 65554 FAX 0245 65711

VISITS OUT
LONDON & THE SOUTH EAST

Wonderful examples of well-managed countryside, including Cissbury Ring, Slindon Village and Estate, Harting Down and Woolbeding Common.

N C SUPPORT Guided trails for Harting and Slindon Village, Guardianship booklets for Harting, Woolbeding and Cissbury. National Curriculum guidance in all publications. Orienteering and guided walks.

ANNUAL OR ONE OFF EVENT Oak Apple Day in May. Other educational activities on offer.

DIRECTIONS On application.

South London Gallery
- Valerie Chang
- 65 Peckham Road, London. SE5 8UH
- 071-703 6120 FAX 071-252 4730

Provides programmes of art activities which fit in with the National Curriculum and meet the needs of young people. They will be designed to broaden knowledge and skill, enhance perception and understanding of contemporary art and provide opportunities to meet and learn from professional artists.

N C SUPPORT Targeted at primary level (7–11), secondary level (12–18), Art and Design BTech foundation course (18 plus). 25 places for each workshop. Special courses can be arranged for sixth form groups (talks, workshops), to assist with their development of visual literacy and to link in with course work.

OPENING Tuesday to Friday 11.00am–6.00pm, Thursday 11.00am–7.00pm, Saturday and Sunday 2.00pm–6.00pm. Bank holiday weekends.

COST Negotiable. For average group of 25–30 students £15–£20 contribution.

DISABLED FACILITIES None.

DIRECTIONS Tube: Oval, Vauxhall or NewCross then bus 36. Bus: 12, 36, 171, P3. Parking: side street opposite the gallery.

Southsea Castle
- Christopher Spendlove
- Clarence Esplanade, Southsea, Hants. PO5 3PA
- 0705 296905 FAX 0705 875276

Built by Henry VIII in 1545 to protect the coasts from foreign invasion. Displays a variety of artillery, military history of Portsmouth; audio-visual show/reconstructed scenes showing life in the Castle; underground tunnels.

N C SUPPORT History Key Stage 2: CSU 2 Tudor and Stuart Times. History Key Stage 2: SSU Local History. Resource pack available.

ANNUAL OR ONE OFF EVENT Henry VIII and his Court at Southsea Castle, a celebration on the weekend nearest his birthday (28 June). Contact above for details.

OPENING March to October: 10.00am–5.30pm.

CATERING Self-service cafe (seats 30) for snacks/beverages only.

COST Schools and other educational establishments in Great Britain free if booked in advance. Foreign language schools 51p per pupil. Teachers free.

VISITS OUT
LONDON & THE SOUTH EAST

DISABLED FACILITIES Access limited to the courtyard and ground floor galleries. Special wheelchair available on loan.

DIRECTIONS By road: follow signposting to Southsea Castle from M27/A2030 into Portsmouth (look for the symbol (M) on the brown signposts).

Spitalfields Farm
- Ellie Horne
- Weaver Street, London. E1 6HJ
- 071-247 8762

Education, recreation and learning activities. Summer play scheme, regular lectures and fundraising events.

N C SUPPORT Covers all aspects of environmental education and tailors services to the specific projects of schools. Provides work experience placements all year round.

OPENING Tuesday to Sunday 9.00am–6.00pm.

COST £50.00 per year or pay by visit depending on service required, e.g. 30p per head.

DISABLED FACILITIES Access and adapted toilet.

DIRECTIONS Nearest tube: Shoreditch, Whitechapel and Bethnal Green.

Spitting Image Rubberworks
- Dawn Baker
- Cubbitts Yard, James Street, London. WC2E 8PA
- 071-240 0393 FAX 071-240 0719

Tour starts in workshop: experience life behind the scenes, how the puppets are made and current developments. Then show with over 30 characters. Plenty of interactive displays and puppets.

N C SUPPORT Schools activity pack supplied. Rubberworks is a useful tool in Technology, Art and Design and Media Studies. Will appeal to both boys and girls.

OPENING Tuesday to Friday 11.00am–5.30pm, Saturday and Sunday 11.00am–6.30pm, Monday during school holidays.

CATERING None.

COST Children £2.95, adults £3.95. Groups (ten people): under 16s £2.00, 16 and over £2.50.

DISABLED FACILITIES Access to all parts of building.

DIRECTIONS Tube: Covent Garden turn right out of station and right again after 100 metres.

Staunton Country Park
- R Cleaver
- Middle Park Way, Havant, Hants. PO9 5HB
- 0705 453405 FAX 0705 498156

The Ornamental Farm and Gardens are the focus of this historic park. The farm contains a wide range of livestock, while the gardens include a huge Victorian-style glasshouse which is full of exotic plants.

N C SUPPORT A touch-screen computer facility provides historical and other educational material for visitors. Teacher liaison and support is available if pre-arranged with park staff. Contact the officer for details.

ANNUAL OR ONE OFF EVENT A number of special events are organised every year. Please phone the Park office for details.

OPENING Summer: daily 10.00am–6.00pm. Winter: daily 10.00am–4.30pm.

CATERING Refreshments available. Group bookings essential.

COST Group rates: children £1.70, adults £2.00.

DISABLED FACILITIES Toilet, level paths, wheelchair available on request.

DIRECTIONS Off B2149, Havant to Horndean road. Accessible from A3(M) or A27: follow the brown tourist road signs.

Story of Telecommunications
- Claire Beswick
- 145 Queen Victoria Street, London. EC4V 4AT
- 071-248 7444 FAX 071-236 5464

The BT Museum is a 'hands-on', fun way for children and parents to learn the history and look to the future of telecommunications aided by video material and worksheets.

N C SUPPORT During a visit, National Curriculum attainment targets can be achieved in the following subjects: Maths (2, 4, 5); Science (1, 3, 4); English (1–5); History (1, 3); Geography (1, 2, 4); Art (1, 2); Technology (1, 2, 4).

ANNUAL OR ONE OFF EVENT Special opening on Lord Mayor's Show Day, second Saturday in November, 10.00am–5.00pm.

OPENING Monday to Friday 10.00am–5.00pm, closed bank holidays and weekends.

CATERING None.

COST Free.

DISABLED FACILITIES Very basic. No toilet facilities for people with disabilities. To move between floors involves going outside.

DIRECTIONS Next to Blackfriars tube and BR station.

Summer Music
- Murray Gordon
- 22 Gresley Road, London. N19 3JZ
- 071-272 5664

Organisers of music weekends and day courses for cellists, string quartets, guitarists, singers (choral and solo). Tai Chi, flautists, pianists summer school, and general music summer school.

ANNUAL OR ONE OFF EVENT Residential summer school in August for orchestras, choirs, opera, oratorio, lieder, conducting, composing, early music, contemporary music, etc.

CATERING Full board.

COST £100 plus VAT for summer school.

DISABLED FACILITIES Yes.

DIRECTIONS Contact Murray Gordon for directions.

Superchoice Adventure
- Lloyd Smith
- 191 Freshfield Road, Brighton. BN2 2YE
- 0273 676467 FAX 0273 676290

Superchoice Adventure operate adventure courses, educational school tours and information technology courses at eight coastal locations in England and Wales.

VISITS OUT
LONDON & THE SOUTH EAST

N C SUPPORT All courses and tours are driven by the needs of the National Curriculum Key Stages 2–4.

OPENING All year round. Apply for details.

CATERING Full-board catering provided at all locations.

COST Tariff sheets available. Prices start from £14.00 plus VAT per day.

DIRECTIONS Return travel to school by coach.

Sutton House
- Carole Mills
- 2 & 4 Homerton High Street, London. E9 6JQ
- 081-986 2264 FAX 081-985 5628

Tudor brick house, built 1535. In continuous use, front elevation modernised 1700, house divided 1740, half remained family house, other half became series of private schools. Three rooms hung with original panelling. Two rooms with 18th-century panelling. Bought by National Trust in 1938.

HQ of Young National Trust Theatre, Theatre in Education Co. serving whole of England.

N C SUPPORT Education programme initiated in 1988 and reconstructed in line with the National Curriculum in 1992. Actively used by local schools, Key Stages 1, 2 and 3. New education programme and education room recently made available. Tudor, 18th-century and Victorian aspects.

CATERING Cafe/bar seating 32 not open Monday or Tuesday but space can be used those days for eating packed lunches.

DISABLED FACILITIES Wheelchair access to ground floor only.

DIRECTIONS BR: Hackney Central. Bus: 38, 22b, 253, 55. Corner of Sutton Place, Urswick Road, Homerton High Street.

Tate Gallery
- The Education Department
- Millbank, London. SW1P 4RG
- 071-821 1313 FAX 071-931 7512

The Tate Gallery houses the national collection of British painting from the 16th century to the present day. It is also the national gallery for modern art, encompassing painting and sculpture made in Britain, Europe, America, and other countries associated with the European tradition in this century. In addition, the collection includes watercolours and modern prints executed after 1945. The Clore Gallery houses paintings, watercolours, drawings and sketchbooks by J M W Turner.

N C SUPPORT Each term the Education Department offers a wide variety of participatory activities for groups of pupils aged 4–18. These include interactive gallery talks, workshops and study days relating to the permanent collection and temporary exhibitions. Courses for teachers and teachers in training are also offered. There is no charge for this service. For further details, please contact the Education Department on 071-821 1313.

ANNUAL OR ONE OFF EVENT It is the Tate Gallery's policy to change displays, bringing forward different aspects of the permanent collection in an annual cycle. Three major loan exhibitions and smaller temporary exhibitions are also offered each year.

OPENING Monday to Saturday 10.00am–5.50pm, Sunday 2.00pm–5.50pm. Advance booking of all groups is essential. Ideally a group should number 10–30 pupils.

CATERING There is a schools cloakroom area with a few tables for picnic lunches, lockers and toilets.

COST Free.

DISABLED FACILITIES The Gallery is wheelchair accessible.

DIRECTIONS Nearest tube: Pimlico (Victoria Line). Bus: 77a and 88 stop outside the Gallery. There are two NCP coach parks in the area and a small one near the Tate. Parking meters are also available.

Thorpe Park
- Group Sales
- Staines Road, Chertsey, Surrey. KT16 8PN
- 0932 569393 FAX 0932 566367

One of Britain's favourite family leisure attractions, with over 100 rides, shows and attractions, including Loggers Leap, one of Britain's highest log flume rides, raging rapids on Thunder River.

N C SUPPORT A range of worksheets produced by education consultants relating to aspects of the National Curriculum. Several subjects cater for four age groups.

OPENING April to end October: 10.00am–5.00pm (6.00pm during school summer holidays).

CATERING Thorpe Park offers a superb variety of diners, e.g. a floating Chinese restaurant, Pizza Hut Express, Potbellies Family Diner, Fish 'n' Chips, French Cafe, Burger King, as well as a number of kiosks selling ice cream, popcorn, etc., situated around the park.

COST Children £8.95, adults £9.95. Prepaid 14 days in advance: children £4.00, adults £6.00.

DISABLED FACILITIES Easy access to all main rides via ramps. Toilet.

DIRECTIONS Thorpe Park is situated on the A320 between Staines and Chertsey. Junction 11 or 13 of the M25.

Tower Hill Pageant
- Booking Coordinator
- 1 Tower Hill Terrace, London. EC3N 4EE
- 071-709 0081 FAX 071-702 3656

Travel in a time-car through 2000 years of London's history; see, hear and even smell the past. Plus see the waterfront FINDS Museum, with over 1000 medieval and Roman artefacts.

N C SUPPORT Work based on the Pageant can develop skills in the following areas of the National Curriculum: History, Historical Sources, English, Mathematics, Science, Technology and Geography.

OPENING April to October: 9.30am–5.30pm. November to March: 9.30am–4.30pm.

CATERING Snack bars on Tower Hill Terrace.

COST Prices on application. One adult admitted free for every ten children.

VISITS OUT
LONDON & THE SOUTH EAST

DISABLED FACILITIES Suitable for wheelchair access. Phone to book in advance.

DIRECTIONS Located next to the Tower of London. Nearest tube: Tower Hill.

Towner Art Gallery & Local History Museum
- Catherine Tonge
- Eastbourne, East Sussex. BN20 8BB
- ☎ 0323 411688 FAX 0323 648182

An 18th-century house set in gardens and housing an important collection of 20th-century British Art. Also Victorian and earlier paintings. Lively temporary exhibition programme. Museum features development at Eastbourne from the Stone Age.

N C SUPPORT Towner staff are pleased to discuss individual requirements. Teachers' packs available for some exhibitions.

ANNUAL OR ONE OFF EVENT Events and/or workshops with most major exhibitions. Children's Club once a month.

OPENING Wednesday to Saturday 10.00am–5.00pm, Sunday and bank holiday Monday 2.00pm–5.00pm, closed 24–26 December, 1 January and Good Friday.

COST Children, students and group leaders free, Eastbourne Resident's Card Holders free, adults £2.00, concessions £1.40.

DISABLED FACILITIES Access to ground floor only.

DIRECTIONS On main A259 road out of Eastbourne towards Brighton, opposite Safeway.

Tyrwhitt Drake
- Rosamunde Bell, Education Officer
- Museum of Carriages, Mill Street, Maidstone, Kent. ME15 6YE
- ☎ 0622 754497 FAX 0622 602193

Housed in the superb timbered stable buildings of the Archbishops' Palace, the Museum contains one of the finest collections of horse-drawn carriages in the country.

N C SUPPORT Many displays relevant to the History, Geography and Technology curricula at Key Stages 1, 2 and 3.

OPENING Monday to Sunday 10.30am–5.30pm (last admission 4.00pm), closed Christmas Day and Boxing Day.

CATERING None.

COST Free to all holders of a ticket for the Archbishops' Palace and Heritage Centre. Pre-booked school party rate for Carriage Museum only: children 50p, one adult free for every ten children.

DISABLED FACILITIES Wheelchair access to ground floor only.

DIRECTIONS Centre of Maidstone, opposite the Archbishops' Palace and Heritage Centre.

Upnor Castle
- The Head Custodian
- High Street, Upper Upnor, Nr Strood, Rochester, Kent. ME2 4XG
- ☎ 0634 718742

This well-preserved 16th-century gun fort was built to protect Queen Elizabeth I's warships. However, in 1667 it failed to prevent the Dutch navy, which stormed up the Medway destroying half the English fleet.

VISITS OUT
LONDON & THE SOUTH EAST

OPENING Good Friday or 1 April (whichever is earlier) to 30 September: daily 10.00am–6.00pm. Pre-booking is essential.

DISABLED FACILITIES Wheelchair access to grounds only.

DIRECTIONS At Upnor on unclassified road off A228 (OS Map 178; ref TQ 758706). Bus: Maidstone and District 197 from BR Chatham; otherwise 190–4 Chatham to Hoo, alight Wainscott, then one mile (Tel: 0634 832666). BR: Strood two miles.

Vauxhall City Farm
- Hilary Eastwood
- Vauxhall City Farm, 24 St Oswalds Place, London . SE11 5JE
- 071-582 4204

Vauxhall City Farm offers recreational and educational opportunities to a variety of both individuals and groups. There is a selection of farm animals, ponds, and a small herb garden.

N C SUPPORT Groups of school children are welcome, linking practical observation with classroom projects.

ANNUAL OR ONE OFF EVENT Annual Open Day in May/June. The animals are at the Lambeth Country Show each year.

OPENING Tuesday to Thursday, Saturday and Sunday 10.30am–5.00pm, closed Monday and Friday.

COST Free. Guided tours: 50p (minimum group of ten).

DISABLED FACILITIES Two toilets and easy access onto the farm.

DIRECTIONS Near Vauxhall station. Entrance in Tyers Street off Kennington Lane.

Vestry House Museum
- Local Studies Officer
- Vestry Road, London. E17 9NH
- 081-509 1917

Eighteenth-century workhouse and local history museum. Displays include 19th-century police cell; the Bremer car c.1984; special temporary exhibition; school classroom and garden.

N C SUPPORT Schools' loan boxes and travelling displays. Archives and Local History library.

ANNUAL OR ONE OFF EVENT Temporary exhibitions programme.

OPENING Monday to Friday 10.00am–1.00pm and 2.00pm–5.30pm, Saturday 10.00am–1.00pm and 2.00pm–5.00pm.

CATERING Packed lunches may be eaten in the Museum classroom, by prior arrangement (maximum of 35 children).

COST Free.

DISABLED FACILITIES Limited access to ground floor.

DIRECTIONS BR: Walthamstow Central (British Rail Eastern Region) five minutes walk. Tube: Walthamstow (Victoria line).

Victoria & Albert Museum
- The Education Department
- London. SW7 2RL
- 071-938 8636 FAX 071-938 8661

The Victoria & Albert Museum is the national museum of art and design.

VISITS OUT
LONDON & THE SOUTH EAST

The Museum houses collections of British, European, American, Far Eastern, Islamic and South Asian art, craft and design including dress, textiles, watercolours, furniture, armour and tapestry. Some galleries are devoted to British and European artefacts from the Middle Ages to the present; others, like the Nehru Gallery of Indian Art and the T T Tsui Gallery of Chinese Art, contain displays of objects from one particular culture.

N C SUPPORT The Schools' Section of the Education Department was re-established in autumn 1991. The Museum has a policy of developing publications and INSET programmes that will enable teachers to make effective independent use of the collections and temporary exhibitions. Direct teaching by Schools' Section staff and freelancers will be part of the development process for publications and will target different galleries or themes each year. There is a South Asian Art Education Officer who works with schools.

ANNUAL OR ONE OFF EVENT Forthcoming shows in the programme of temporary exhibitions include: Pugin, 19th-century architect of the Palace of Westminster; young British ceramicists; and Gates of Mystery, an exhibition of Russian icons. For further information on lecture courses for teachers please contact the Education Department.

OPENING Monday 12.00 noon–5.50pm, Tuesday to Sunday 10.00am–5.50pm. All school groups must book in advance. Enquiries should be made initially by telephone on 071-938 8638.

CATERING There is a lunch room which can be booked (maximum capacity 40).

COST There is no charge for school groups visiting the permanent collections and there is a special concessionary rate for groups visiting large temporary exhibitions. Smaller exhibitions are often free.

DISABLED FACILITIES There is independent wheelchair access to most of the Museum. If bringing pupils in wheelchairs please contact the Education Department to discuss requirements.

DIRECTIONS Tube: South Kensington.

£50 = talk max 25

Walmer Castle
- The Head Custodian
- Kingsdown Road, Deal, Kent. CT1 1TF

This is one of the many forts built along the south coast by Henry VIII, and has since been transformed into an elegant stately home. As the residence of the Lords Warden of the Cinque Ports, Walmer was much used by the Duke of Wellington, and is still used today by HM the Queen Mother. Rooms used by Her Majesty, including the dining room and drawing room, are open to visitors, as are those once used by Wellington, who died here. The delightful castle gardens should not be missed.

OPENING Good Friday or 1 April (whichever is earlier) to 30 September: 10.00am–6.00pm. Closed January and February when Lord Warden is in residence.

VISITS OUT
LONDON & THE SOUTH EAST

DISABLED FACILITIES Personal stereo available for the hard of hearing. Wheelchair access to courtyard and garden only.

DIRECTIONS On coast south of Walmer (OS Map 179; ref TR 378501). Bus: from surrounding areas (Tel: 0800 696996). BR: Walmer one mile.

The Walter Rothschild Geography and Science Physical Education Museum
- Sarah Ferri
- Akeman Street, Tring, Herts. HP23 6AP
- 0442 824181 FAX 0442 890693

Hertfordshire's most unusual Museum was founded by the second Baron Rothschild and is famous for its magnificent collection of animals. Rare, beautiful and bizarre species in a unique Victorian setting.

N C SUPPORT The Museum is suitable for a wide range of National Curriculum activities.

OPENING Monday to Saturday 10.00am–5.00pm, Sundays 2.00pm–5.00pm.

CATERING Drinks and snacks machines only.

COST Children (5–17 years) £1.00, adults £2.00, concessions £1.00, free to pre-booked school parties.

DISABLED FACILITIES Limited: access to ground floor only. Toilet.

DIRECTIONS Tring is on the A41 between Berkhamsted and Aylesbury. The Museum is in Akeman Street, a turning off the High Street.

Wellington Riding
- Suzanne Green
- Basingstoke Road, Heckfield, Hants. RG27 0LJ
- 0734 326308 FAX 0734 326661

Equestrian centre providing training facilities for novice and advanced children and adults in the disciplines of dressage, show jumping and cross country for pleasure and career purposes.

N C SUPPORT Horse and land management. Career training and leisure industry.

OPENING Daily 9.00am–5.30pm.

CATERING Light refreshments and hot and cold meals available in restaurant.

COST Children (up to 16 years) £10.99 per lesson, adults and students £14.50 per lesson. Discounts for groups.

DISABLED FACILITIES Facilities for disabled riders.

DIRECTIONS Located on the A33 midway between Reading and Basingstoke, 20 minutes from Junction 11 of M4.

Wembley Stadium Tours
- Charlie McCracken
- Wembley Stadium, Middx. HA9 0DW
- 081-902 8833 FAX 081-903 5733

Behind-the-scenes tour of Wembley Stadium. Highlights include: Event Control Room; England Changing Rooms; Film Show; Players' Tunnel; Royal Box; Land Train; Climb the 39 steps and lift 'The Cup'.

VISITS OUT
LONDON & THE SOUTH EAST

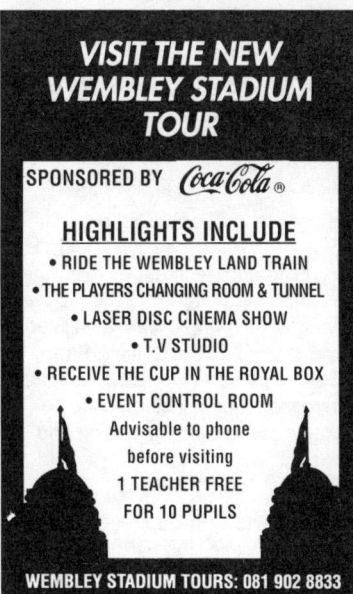

N C SUPPORT Historical building: ten-minute film shows history of stadium since built in 1922. World-famous sporting venue.

OPENING April to September: 10.00am–4.00pm. October to March: 10.00am–3.00pm. Closed on major event days.

COST Group discount for 20 or more; one teacher free per ten pupils.

DISABLED FACILITIES Venue not suitable for people with disabilities: many steps.

DIRECTIONS Just off North Circular Road. Nearest tube: Wembley Park.

Wesley's Chapel
- L A Dyson
- 49 City Road, London. EC1Y 1AU
- 071-253 2262 FAX 071-608 3825

Wesley's Chapel, House and Museum of Methodism (1778) where the founder of Methodism lived and died.

OPENING Monday to Saturday 10.00am–4.00pm.

COST Children £1.50, adults £3.00, Senior Citizens £1.50. Discount of 10% for groups.

DISABLED FACILITIES Lift etc. Toilets.

DIRECTIONS Between Moorgate and Old Street tube stations.

Westminster Abbey
- The Head Custodian
- Chapter House, Pyx Chamber and Abbey Museum, London
- 071-222 5897

The Chapter House, built by the royal masons in 1250 and faithfully restored in the 19th century, contains some of the finest examples of medieval English sculpture to be seen. The building is octagonal, with a central column, and still has its original floor of glazed tiles. Its uses have varied, but in the 14th century it was used as a meeting place for the Benedictine monks of the abbey, and also for Members of Parliament. The 11th-century Pyx Chamber now houses the Abbey treasures.

OPENING All year. Good Friday or 1 April (whichever is earlier) to 30 September: daily 10.00am–6.00pm. 1 October–31 March: plus Mondays. Liable to be closed at short notice on state occasions.

DISABLED FACILITIES None.

DIRECTIONS Approach either through the Abbey or through Dean's Yard

West Gate Museum

- Ms Marit Hendriks
- St Peter's Street, Canterbury, Kent
- 0227 452747 FAX 0227 455047

One of England's finest medieval gates, built as part of the city defences in the 1320s. Visitors can see cells, a collection of arms, armour and other items, as well as panoramic views of the city from the battlements.

N C SUPPORT Teachers' notes to help plan, support and follow-up a visit to the West Gate Museum. Worksheet for History Key Stage 3.

OPENING Monday to Saturday 11.00am–12.30pm and 1.30pm–3.30pm.

COST Children 30p, adults 60p, concessions 40p. Discount of 10% for groups of ten or more.

DISABLED FACILITIES None.

DIRECTIONS By road: A2 then central car parks. BR: Canterbury East and West stations are within walking distance.

The Whitbread Hop Farm

- Louise Walker
- Beltring, Paddock Wood, Kent. TN12 6PY
- 0622 872068 FAX 0622 872630

Boasts the largest group of Victorian oasthouses, housing museums on hop farming, nature trail, shire horses, birds of prey. A popular family outing.

N C SUPPORT Exhibitions and events of interest to those studying Science, e.g. Animal Activity Packs available from the wardens; Technology and History, with reference to The Hop Story Exhibition which has been designed using modern technology to create an authentic insight into the lives and times of the people who have lived and worked on the Beltring Farm. Visitors can also view various craft demonstrations, including the potter's wheel, firing, glazing and decoration.

ANNUAL OR ONE OFF EVENT Various special events throughout the year. The Whitbread Hop Farm presents a full and exciting array of Special Weekend Events, from Classic Car Shows to Hot Air Balloon Meets and from open-air concerts to firework displays.

OPENING Summer: 10.00am–6.00pm (last admission 5.00pm). Winter: 10.00am–4.00pm (last admission 3.00pm).

CATERING Roundels restaurant serves anything from snacks to three-course meals.

COST Children £3.00, adults £4.50, Senior Citizens and registered disabled £3.00, under 5s free. Discount of 10% for groups of 30 or more.

DISABLED FACILITIES Disabled visitors are very welcome, but facilities are limited due to the historic architecture.

DIRECTIONS On the A228 (formerly the B2015).

VISITS OUT
LONDON & THE SOUTH EAST

Whitechapel Art Gallery
- Lucy Dawe Lane or Fiona Furness
- Whitechapel High Street, London. E1 7QX
- 071-377 5015 FAX 071-377 1685

Architecturally stunning gallery showing temporary exhibitions of 20th-century art. (No collection.) Full range of educational activities in support of each exhibition.

N C SUPPORT Special preview and wet sessions for teachers, two-hour workshops for schools daily at 2.00pm (maximum 15), all suiting National Curriculum requirements. GCSE Saturday classes.

ANNUAL OR ONE OFF EVENT May/June 1994 Whitechapel Open and open studios: opportunity for many collaborations between schools and local artists.

OPENING Tuesday and Thursday to Sunday 11.00am–5.00pm, Wednesday 11.00am–8.00pm, closed Monday.

CATERING Cafe in gallery for lunch and snacks.

COST Workshops free to local schools. Free admission to exhibitions. Small charge for INSET (£2.00).

DISABLED FACILITIES Level access. Lift to all floors. Adapted toilet. Special talks and tours for deaf and visually impaired visitors. Ring for details.

DIRECTIONS Tube: Aldgate East. Bus: 5, 15, 15A, 25, 40, 67, 78, 253, ten minutes Liverpool Street station.

White Cliffs Experience
- Kim Norton, Education Officer
- Market Square, Dover, Kent. CT16 1PB
- 0304 214566 FAX 0304 212057

A series of dramatic, academically researched visual and audio displays on the Romans, Channel crossings and World War II, together with Roman, Saxon and Norman archaeological sites.

N C SUPPORT A visit to the White Cliffs Experience can be a truly cross-curricular event. A range of photocopiable resource packs and worksheets are available.

ANNUAL OR ONE OFF EVENT Three-day Roman Festival in June provides a chance for school children to experience life as a Roman.

OPENING 28 March to 8 November: 10.00am–5.00pm (last admission). 9 November to 14 February: 10.00am–3.00pm (last admission).

CATERING Cafeteria and room for eating sandwiches.

COST Schools: children £2.10, one adult free for every ten pupils, extra adults £4.25.

DISABLED FACILITIES Full access for people with disabilities, including toilet.

Whitehall
- Pat Jackson
- 1 Malden Road, Cheam, Sutton, Surrey. SM3 8QD
- 081-643 1236 FAX 081-770 4777

Timber-framed house built c.1500, featuring displays on Henry VIII Nonsuch Palace, medieval Cheam pottery and Cheam school, plus changing exhibitions.

N C SUPPORT Guided tours available tailored to various themes. Full-day or part-day visits available to include history walk and visit to Lumley Chapel's Tudor memorials.

VISITS OUT
LONDON & THE SOUTH EAST

ANNUAL OR ONE OFF EVENT 'Birthday Party' in June. Cheam Charter Fair outdoors every 15 May.

OPENING April to September: Tuesday to Friday and Sunday 2.00pm–5.30pm, Saturday 10.00am–5.30pm. October to March: Wednesday, Thursday and Sunday 2.00pm–5.30pm, Saturday 10.00am–5.30pm, bank holiday Mondays 2.00pm–5.00pm.

CATERING Tea room with home-made cakes.

COST Children 40p, adults 75p. Groups (outside normal opening hours) 25p, one teacher free for every ten children.

DISABLED FACILITIES Not suitable for wheelchairs or people with mobility impairment.

DIRECTIONS On A2043; pay and display car park close by. BR: Cheam five minutes walk.

Whitstable Museum & Gallery
- Helen Evans
- Oxford Street, Whitstable, Kent. CT5 1DB
- 0227 276998

A coastal museum exploring the seafaring traditions of the town, with special features on divers, shipbuilders and oyster fishers. Gallery with regularly changing special exhibitions.

N C SUPPORT Teachers' information packs: 'Whitstable and the Sea' and 'Victorian Whitstable'. Special exhibition activity sheets.

ANNUAL OR ONE OFF EVENT Special exhibitions, please ask for details.

OPENING Daily (except Wednesday and Sunday) 10.30am–1.00pm and 2.00pm–4.00pm.

COST Free.

DISABLED FACILITIES Special wheelchair entrance.

DIRECTIONS By road: A290 from Canterbury; A299 from Faversham or Herne Bay. BR: Whitstable from London and Margate, ten minutes walk.

Wickham Vineyard
- Caroline Charnley
- Botley Road, Shedfield, Southampton. SO3 2HL
- 0329 834042 FAX 0329 834907

This commercial vineyard offers both self-guided and group tours around the vineyard and winery, plus a nature trail through ancient woodland and wetlands. Picnic areas, toilets and shops on site.

OPENING May to September: Monday to Saturday 10.30am–5.30pm, Sunday 12.00 noon–3.00pm. Other dates and times by prior arrangement.

CATERING Picnic area with soft drinks and snacks available (please request).

COST £1.50 per person.

DISABLED FACILITIES Toilets. Access to winery.

DIRECTIONS Wickham Vineyard is exactly halfway between Botley and Wickham on the A334. Junction 7 of M27 from west, junction 10 of M27 from east.

VISITS OUT
LONDON & THE SOUTH EAST

Wildfowl & Wetlands Trust
- Jane Lovering
- Mill Road, Arundel, West Sussex. BN18 9PB
- 0903 883355

A fascinating centre where children can come 'nose to beak' with a variety of swans, ducks and geese from around the world. Full education service available.

N C SUPPORT Offers a range of educational programmes tailored to support the National Curriculum, particularly Science AT2. There is scope for work on Geography, Art, English and Drama. Range of courses on Freshwater Ecology for GCSE and A-Level groups.

OPENING April to September: daily 9.30am–5.30pm. October to March: daily 9.30am–4.30pm. Closed Christmas Day.

COST School party rate: children £1.30, adults £2.80, one adult free for every ten children.

DISABLED FACILITIES All areas accessible by wheelchair. Toilet. Braille guidebooks available.

DIRECTIONS One mile north of Arundel town centre. Signposted from A27 and A29.

William Morris Gallery
- Liz Woods, Assistant Keeper
- Lloyd Park, Forest Road, London. E17 4PP
- 081-527 3782

Childhood home of William Morris, Victorian designer, craftsman, thinker, containing permanent displays relating to his life and work. Also Pre-Raphaelite paintings and material relating to Arts and Crafts Movement. Temporary exhibition programme.

N C SUPPORT National Curriculum material currently being developed. Talks and activities available by arrangement. Please telephone for more information and to discuss requirements.

OPENING Tuesday to Saturday 10.00am–1.00pm and 2.00pm–5.00pm, first Sunday of the month 10.00am–12.00 noon and 2.00pm–5.00pm.

COST Free. Donations welcome.

DISABLED FACILITIES Access to ground floor (Morris displays); temporary ramp available. Telephone for more information.

DIRECTIONS Victoria line either to Walthamstow Central then 15 minutes walk or buses 97, 34, 215, 275; or to Blackhorse Road then bus 123. By road: A503.

The Wimbledon Lawn Tennis Museum
- Mrs P Newell
- Church Road, Wimbledon, London. SW19 5AE
- 081-946 6131 FAX 081-944 6497

From the lawns of Victorian England to the glamour and the glitter of the world's top professional tournaments, the story of lawn tennis unfolds.

OPENING Tuesday to Saturday 10.30am–5.00pm, Sunday 2.00pm–5.00pm, closed Monday, public holidays and three days prior to championships.

CATERING Tea room, serving morning coffee, light lunches, afternoon tea. Schools' room available for picnics etc., August to May.

COST Children under 16 £1.00, adults £2.00, Senior Citizens, students (with valid card) £1.00. Pre-booked groups of 20 or more receive 10% discount.

DISABLED FACILITIES Disabled access to tea room and Museum. Toilet.

DIRECTIONS From central London take the A3 Portsmouth Road to Tibbet's corner, at the underpass turn left towards Wimbledon. The entrance is in Church Road in the grounds of the All England Lawn Tennis Club.

Wimbledon Windmill Museum
- N Plastow
- Windmill Road, Wimbledon Common, London. SW19 4NL
- 081-947 2825

The story of windmills and windmilling in pictures, models and the machinery and tools of the trade, housed in the Windmill on Wimbledon Common, built in 1817.

N C SUPPORT Teachers' notes on Science, Technology, History and Local History, free to visiting schools or £1.50 including postage. Talks, lectures and video in museum.

OPENING Public opening weekend afternoons only. School parties and group visits at any time by prior booking.

CATERING Snacks and hot and cold meals.

COST Children 50p, accompanying adults free (minimum charge £5.00).

DISABLED FACILITIES Access difficult.

DIRECTIONS Midway between Wimbledon and Putney off A219. Parking for cars and coaches. Bus: 93 from Wimbledon or Putney.

Witley Centre
- Geoff Sully
- Haslemere Road, Whitley, Godalming, Surrey. GU8 5QA
- 0428 683207 FAX 0428 683207

An outstanding educational centre providing audio-visual introduction, cloakrooms, eating areas, toilets. The centre has an interpretative display, lecture room, educational area and is set in over 300 acres of diverse habitat.

N C SUPPORT Works closely to facilitate schools' needs with respect to the National Curriculum, GCSE and 'A' level. Visits are carefully coordinated and prior consultation is recommended.

DISABLED FACILITIES Wheelchair available, with access to self-guided nature trail.

DIRECTIONS Signposted from the A3, one mile south of Milford.

Wolvesey Old Bishops Palace
- The Head Custodian
- College Street, Winchester, Hants. SO23 9NB
- 0962 854766

The fortified palace of Wolvesey was the chief residence of the Bishops of Winchester and one of the greatest of all medieval buildings in England. Its extensive ruins still reflect the importance and immense wealth of the Bishops of Winchester, occupants of the richest See in medieval England. Wolvesey was

VISITS OUT
LONDON & THE SOUTH EAST

frequently visited by medieval and Tudor monarchs and was the scene of the wedding feast of Philip of Spain and Mary Tudor in 1554.

OPENING Summer season. Good Friday or 1 April (whichever is earlier) to 30 September: daily 10.00am–6.00pm.

DISABLED FACILITIES Wheelchair access.

DIRECTIONS Quarter of a mile southeast of Winchester Cathedral, next to the Bishop's Palace; access from College Street (OS Map 185; ref SU 484291). Bus: from surrounding areas (Tel: 0962 852352). BR: Winchester three-quarters of a mile.

Woods Mill Countryside Centre
- S C Webster, Manager
- Sussex Wildlife Trust, Woods Mill, Wenfield, West Sussex
- 0273 492630 FAX 0273 494500

Fifteen-acre nature reserve with woodland, lake meadow, ponds and hedgerows. Visits are for a whole day with use of a classroom led by Education Officers. Courses for teachers on a variety of topics. Details available on request.

N C SUPPORT Studies are directly related to Attainment Targets in Science, Maths, Geography and History. Please contact the Centre for details of target levels and subject matter.

OPENING Easter to October: Tuesday to Thursday for school visits.

CATERING Groups are required to bring their own lunches.

COST £3.00 per pupil per day; minimum charge £70, non-returnable deposit £40.00.

DISABLED FACILITIES By special arrangement as facilities are limited.

DIRECTIONS Situated on the A2037 one mile south of Henfield at the junction with Horn Lane, entrance is 100 yards up Horn Lane.

World Education Development Group (WEDG)
- Tom Andrews or Marion Walter
- The Canterbury Centre, St Alphege Lane, Canterbury, Kent. CT1 2EB
- 0227 766552 FAX 0227 766118

Teachers' and students' resource centre with materials for loan or sale: books, slides, videos, simulation games, resource boxes. Speaker service/youth worker. Send sae and particular requirements to above address.

N C SUPPORT Advice on materials for Interfaith RE. Geography, Humanities, Maths and Science on the themes of the wider world, environmental issues, human rights and justice.

ANNUAL OR ONE OFF EVENT Festival of Schools. Workshops in music, dance, drama, crafts and an exhibition in February.

OPENING Wednesday to Saturday 10.30am–5.00pm.

CATERING Tea, coffee; light lunches.

COST Membership of library £5.00 per annum.

DISABLED FACILITIES Access to building no problem. Toilet three minutes away.

VISITS OUT
LONDON & THE SOUTH EAST

DIRECTIONS In the centre of Canterbury just off Palace Street. Nearest car park in St Radigunds.

Worthing Museum & Art Gallery
- Dr Sally White, Curator
- Chapel Road, Worthing, West Sussex. BN11 1HP
- 0903 239999 FAX 0903 236552

Collections strong on local archaeology and history, costume, toys and dolls, English paintings and glass. Frequent special exhibitions.

N C SUPPORT Liaise closely with teachers to tackle curriculum-led projects related to the collections.

OPENING April to September: Monday to Saturday 10.00am–6.00pm. October to March: Monday to Saturday 10.00am–5.00pm.

CATERING None.

COST Free.

DISABLED FACILITIES The building is fully accessible: ramps, lift, toilet, wheelchair.

DIRECTIONS On A24 close to town centre, next door to Town Hall.

Yarmouth Castle
- The Head Custodian
- Quay Street, Yarmouth, Isle of Wight. PO41 0PB
- 0983 760678

This last addition to Henry VIII's coastal defences was completed in 1547 and is, unusually for its kind, square with a fine example of an angle bastion. It was garrisoned well into the 19th century. It houses exhibitions of paintings of the Isle of Wight and photographs of old Yarmouth.

OPENING Summer season. Good Friday or 1 April (whichever is earlier) to 30 September: daily 10.00am–6.00pm. Pre-booking is essential.

DISABLED FACILITIES Wheelchair access to ground floor only. Dogs allowed on leads.

DIRECTIONS In Yarmouth, adjacent to car ferry terminal (OS Map 196; ref SZ 354898). Ferry: Yarmouth (Wightlink) adjacent.

YMCA Day Camps
- Julia Rankin or John Weston
- 640 Forest Road, London. E17 3DZ
- 081-520 5599

YMCA Day Camps run activity holiday schemes for 5–15-year-olds in the M25 region throughout the school summer and Easter holidays. Free transportation is provided and quality childcare guaranteed.

OPENING Office: all year 9.00am–5.00pm. Camp: school summer and Easter holidays 9.30am–4.30pm.

COST Negotiable.

DIRECTIONS Three camp sites in Harefield, Middlesex, Hainault in Essex and Westerham in Kent. Full details available from the Day Camps Office.

Young Designers Centre
- Information Officer
- Design Council, 28 Haymarket, London. SW1Y 4SU
- 071-839 8000 ext. 4392 FAX 071-925 2130

VISITS OUT
LONDON & THE SOUTH EAST

A national centre displaying design from schools and colleges. Includes permanent and thematic exhibitions. Information/Resource Service, specialist bookshop. Provides opportunities to explore design processes, including research, use of materials, model-making, presentation.

N C SUPPORT Teachers' packs available prior to visits. Free slide loan service for teachers and students, free information sheets and careers-related literature. Design Council Education Publications catalogue.

ANNUAL OR ONE OFF EVENT Thematic exhibitions. Computer Aided Design May to October 1994.

OPENING Monday to Saturday 10.00am–6.00pm. Sunday and bank holidays 1.00pm–6.00pm. (Telephone enquiries Monday to Friday 1.30pm–5.30pm.)

CATERING None.

COST Free.

DISABLED FACILITIES Lift available.

DIRECTIONS Tube: Bakerloo or Piccadilly line to Piccadilly Circus, Northern or Piccadilly line to Leicester Square. Bus: 1, 3, 6, 9, 13, 15, 88, 159, 228. Northbound buses stop in Lower Regent Street, southbound buses stop in Haymarket.

The Young National Trust Theatre

- Sally Woodhead, Administrator
- Sutton House, 2 & 4 Homerton High Street, London. E9 6QJ
- 081-986 0242

The Young National Trust Theatre is the National Trust's professional Theatre-in-Education company. Established in 1977, the YNTT tours eight National Trust properties each year, working with well over 7000 school children aged from 8–16.

Theatre-in-Education brings drama-based programmes into primary and secondary schools or, in the YNTT's case, into National Trust houses. The YNTT's programmes use 'participation' as a key learning method.

N C SUPPORT Participation in YNTT performances can help pupils from Key Stage 2 upwards to develop historical understanding. Performances are set in periods which are required for National Curriculum History programmes of study, and can be used to further knowledge and understanding of History (AT1). The Theatre's work is also closely allied to English AT1, speaking and listening. Involvement in a performance meets several of the requirements of the PE curriculum (AT2) and involves a wide variety of musical styles.

DISABLED FACILITIES Dependent on venue. Contact the administrator for further details.

DIRECTIONS Contact the administrator.

VISITS OUT
EAST ANGLIA

Anglesey Abbey
- Graham Moran
- The National Trust, Lode, Cambs. CBS 9GS
- 0223 811200

Anglesey Abbey consists of a Visitors' Centre (restaurant, shop, plant centre), the Abbey itself and 100 acres of gardens (with statues). The house has collections of silver, clocks, tapestries, paintings.

N C SUPPORT The Abbey could be visited in conjunction with several areas of the National Curriculum; Art, History, etc.

CATERING Restaurant.

DISABLED FACILITIES Access to house fairly limited; but grounds very good; also two wheelchairs; two self-drive electric wheelchairs.

DIRECTIONS Anglesey Abbey and Gardens are situated in the village of Lode, on the B1102, six miles north-east of Cambridge (signposted from A45).

Audley End House and Park
- The Head Custodian
- Saffron Walden, Essex
- 0799 522399

A palatial Jacobean country mansion set in magnificent parklands landscaped by 'Capability' Brown. Thirty rooms are on view, including reception rooms by Robert Adam, with a fascinating collection of paintings and period furniture.

OPENING Summer season only: Wednesday to Sunday and bank holidays 1.00pm–6.00pm; park and gardens 12.00 noon–6.00pm (last admission 5.00pm).

CATERING Restaurant, gift shop, garden centre. Picnics welcome.

DISABLED FACILITIES Substantial ground floor area and gardens accessible to wheelchair users.

DIRECTIONS One mile west of Saffron Walden on B1383 (M11 exits 8, 9 (northbound only), and 10 (OS Map 154; ref TL 525382). Bus: Hedingham 50 from BR Audley End, Eastern National 301 Bishops Stortford to Saffron Walden, Sovereign Bus 699 from Stevenage to Saffron Walden (Tel: 0245 492211). BR: Audley End one and a half miles.

Banham Zoo
- Mrs Julie Austin
- The Grove, Banham, Norfolk. NR16 2HE
- 095 387 771 FAX 095 387 445

A collection of rare and endangered species worldwide. Watch the gracefulness of penguins swimming underwater in 'World of Penguins'. Hear Perky Parrot's story about rainforests and conservation worldwide.

ANNUAL OR ONE OFF EVENT Various animal theme weeks/months.

OPENING Daily (except Christmas Day and Boxing Day) 10.00am–6.30pm (or dusk if earlier).

CATERING Parrot Pavilion Food Hall in Zoo. Pantiles Bistro and Coffee Shop in Appleyard Court across the road.

COST Children £3.50, adults £5.50. Senior Citizens £4.00. Groups of 15 or more: children £2.50, under fives free, adults £3.50, Senior Citizens £2.50.

VISITS OUT
EAST ANGLIA

DISABLED FACILITIES All areas of the zoo are accessible. Toilets. Free wheelchair loan available.

DIRECTIONS Banham is situated between Attleborough and Diss on the B1113 Norwich to Bury St Edmunds road.

Berney Arms Windmill

- The Head Custodian
- c/o Mr & Mrs Hewitt, Claire Cottage, 37 Station Road North, Belton, Norfolk. NR31 9NG
- 0493 700605

A wonderfully situated marsh mill, one of the best and largest remaining in Norfolk, with seven floors, making it a landmark for miles around. It was in use until 1951.

OPENING Summer season. Good Friday or 1 April (whichever is earlier) to 30 September: daily 10.00am–6.00pm.

DIRECTIONS Three and a half miles northeast of Reedham on north bank of River Yare. Accessible by boat, by train to Berney Arms station (quarter of a mile walk) or by footpath from Halvergate (three and a half miles) (OS Map 134; ref TG 465051). BR: Berney Arms quarter of a mile.

Blakeney Point

- The Administrator
- Warden's Residence, 35 The Cornfield, Langham, Holt, Norfolk. NR25 7DQ
-

Three and a half mile sand and shingle spit; summer home for more than eleven species of breeding birds including common and sandwich tern, oystercatcher and ringed plover; common seal colony; exhibition in Old Boathouse; bird-hides.

N C SUPPORT Teachers' resource book and special guided tours for pre-booked school parties. Telephone the National Trust Regional Office on 0263 733471.

DISABLED FACILITIES Contact the warden.

DIRECTIONS Contact the warden.

Bradwell Field Studies & Sailing Centre

- Mrs A Johnson
- Bradwell Waterside, Southminster, Essex. CM0 7QY
- 0621 776256 FAX 0621 776378

Overlooking the river Blackwater, the Centre offers accommodation for 40 students and six staff. The building is centrally heated with full toilet, shower and drying facilities.

Day and residential courses week, mid-week and weekend.

N C SUPPORT National Curriculum at all levels in Geography, Science and Physical Education.

OPENING All year.

CATERING Fully catered.

COST Residential: fully inclusive from £8.85 per day.

DISABLED FACILITIES None.

DIRECTIONS B1021 to Bradwell Waterside. BR: Southminster.

VISITS OUT
EAST ANGLIA

Bradwell Power Station
- J Mogg
- Bradwell-on-Sea, Southminster, Essex. CM0 7HP
- 0621 776331

A working nuclear power station.

N C SUPPORT The Physics of Nuclear Power. Energy, Environmental issues, Geography and Chemistry.

OPENING Any time by arrangement.

CATERING Tea, coffee, hot chocolate and squash provided.

COST Free.

DISABLED FACILITIES Yes.

DIRECTIONS A12 to Chelmsford, then via Latchingdon and Steeple to Bradwell.

Bressingham Steam Museum
- Caroline Butler
- Bressingham, Diss, Norfolk. IP22 2AB
- 037 988 386 FAX 037 988 8085

Historic locomotives, three train rides. Victorian steam roundabout, fire engine, steam traction engines and wagons, gardens, play area, restaurant, shop and plant centre.

N C SUPPORT The Museum's exhibits are a source of information on the history of land transport, Victorian Britain, and for AT6, AT10 and AT13 of the Science Curriculum. Talks can be provided alongside educational packs.

ANNUAL OR ONE OFF EVENT Fire engine rally in August. Annual event with plenty of fire-fighting demonstrations.

OPENING Daily April–October 10.00am–5.30pm. Steam days every Thursday and Sunday.

CATERING Restaurant, coffee shop, picnic hut, picnic area.

COST Will always try to offer favourable admission prices, and have a wide range of ticket prices. Discount of 10% for parties of 12 or over. Please call for details.

DISABLED FACILITIES Toilets; access.

DIRECTIONS On A1066, Diss, Norfolk.

Bridewell Museum
- J R Renton
- Bridewell Alley, Norwich, Norfolk. NR2 1AQ
- 0603 667228 FAX 0603 765651

Trades and industries of the city of Norwich.

N C SUPPORT Key Stage 1: Living Memory; Key Stage 2: Victorian Britain, writing and printing. Education Department at Castle Museum, Norwich.

OPENING Monday to Saturday 10.00am–5.00pm.

CATERING None.

COST No charge for school parties.

DISABLED FACILITIES None.

DIRECTIONS City centre. Access from rail and bus stations in Norwich.

Charles Burrell Museum
- R Parrott
- Ministergate, Thetford, Norfolk
- 0842 751166

Museum with static displays of traction engine workshops and company and family history of the Burrell family.

ANNUAL OR ONE OFF EVENT Contact the Thetford Tourist Information Centre

(Tel: 0842 752599) for details of special events and steam days.

OPENING April to October: Saturday and Sunday 10.00am–5.00pm. Weekdays by appointment.

COST Children 75p, adults £1.25, Senior Citizens 75p.

DISABLED FACILITIES Access to ground floor only. Toilet.

DIRECTIONS Please contact the Museum for map.

Castle Acre Priory
- The Head Custodian
- Stocks Green, Castle Acre, Nr Swaffham, Kings Lynn, Norfolk. PE32 2AF
- 0760 755394

The great west front of the 12th-century church of this Clunaic priory still rises to its full height and is elaborately decorated. Other substantial remains include the splendid prior's lodgings and chapel, and the delightful walled herb garden should not be missed.

OPENING All year round. Good Friday or 1 April (whichever is earlier) to 30 September: daily 10.00am–6.00pm. 1 October to Maundy Thursday or 31 March (whichever is earlier): Tuesday to Sunday 10.00am–4.00pm. Closed 24–26 December and 1 January.

CATERING Picnic facilities.

DISABLED FACILITIES Wheelchair access to ground floor and grounds only.

DIRECTIONS Quarter of a mile west of village of Castle Acre, five miles north of Swaffham (OS Map 132; ref TF 814148).

Castle Rising Castle
- The Head Custodian
- Castle Rising, King's Lynn, Norfolk. NE1 3JF
- 0553 631330

A fine mid-12th-century domestic keep, set in the centre of massive defensive earthworks. The keep walls stand to their original height and many of the fortifications are still intact.

OPENING All year round. Good Friday or 1 April (whichever is earlier) to 30 September: daily 10.00am–6.00pm. 1 October to Maundy Thursday or 31 March (whichever is earlier): Tuesday to Sunday 10.00am–4.00pm. Closed 24–26 December and 1 January.

DISABLED FACILITIES Wheelchair access to the exterior only; toilets.

DIRECTIONS Four miles northeast of King's Lynn off A149 (OS Map 132; ref TF 666246). Bus: Eastern Counties 410/1 King's Lynn to Hunstanton (Tel: 0553 772343). Station: King's Lynn four and a half miles.

Colchester Zoo
- A K Tropeano, Director
- Maldon Road, Colchester, Essex. CO3 5SL
- 0206 331292 FAX 0206 331392

Set in 40 acres of beautiful gardens, with over 150 species, Colchester is one of England's finest zoos. The modern new enclosures not only provide a natural and stimulating environment for the animals, but also the best possible view for visitors.

N C SUPPORT Colchester Zoo can provide a variety of themes covering specific Attainment Targets in Science with plenty of opportunities for cross-curricular activities. To reduce the preparation required, a series of projects and accompanying worksheets have been developed based on the National Curriculum. These include: colour and the story of zoos, flight, animal senses, head and tails, living with animals in the Iron Age and Anglo-Saxon times.

OPENING July and August: daily 9.30am–6.00pm. Easter, June and September: daily 9.30am–5.00pm. October to March: daily 9.30am till one hour before dusk. Closed Christmas Day.

CATERING Licensed self-service restaurant for full or light meals. Takeaway and ice cream snack kiosks situated around the zoo.

COST Children £3.00, adults £5.50, Senior Citizens £3.50. Schools/people with disabilities £2.25 per adult and child. Groups of 20 or more: children (3–13 years) £2.25, adults £4.00.

DISABLED FACILITIES Toilets. The zoo is naturally hilly and can be hard going for wheelchairs. An easy route has been developed to give the easiest route possible. Wheelchair hire is available if booked in advance.

DIRECTIONS Along the A12, take the A604 Cambridge exit and follow the Elephant signs

Colne Valley Railway
- Dick Hymas
- Castle Hedingham, Halstead, Essex. CO9 3DZ
- 0787 461174

Victorian rural railway with large collection of operational vintage carriages and engines set up as an education centre. Talks, tours, rides, all ages, any topic, teaching staff available. Victorian specials (Ride on the Royal Pullman Train, Meet Queen Victoria and many characters from the period. Music Hall, Punch & Judy, School, Market Stalls, Victorian Classroom). The Rising Five Special (Steam Train Rides with Goldilocks and the Bears).

N C SUPPORT Schools Special 18-page Railway Topic Book available.

ANNUAL OR ONE OFF EVENT Numerous events throughout the year.

OPENING All year Monday to Friday. All visits must be booked in advance.

CATERING Picnic facilities.

COST £3.00 per person, one teacher admitted free with every ten paying children.

DISABLED FACILITIES Partly accessible.

DIRECTIONS On A604 between Castle Hedingham and Great Yeldham.

Dedham Rare Breeds Farm
- Peter Harris
- Shepherd's Lodge, Coles Oak Lane, Dedham, Colchester, Essex. CO7 6DR
- 0206 322176

16-acre farm stocked with rare British cattle, sheep, goats, pigs and poultry. Pets area, picnic area, play area, free bag of food for the children to feed the animals; lots of young animals.

N C SUPPORT All school parties have a free half-hour conducted tour. Teachers are asked if possible to

VISITS OUT
EAST ANGLIA

visit the site. Worksheets etc. provided.

ANNUAL OR ONE OFF EVENT Sheep shearing, dipping, lambing, etc.

OPENING 1 March to early January: 10.00am–5.30pm in summer, daylight hours in winter.

CATERING Light refreshment and picnic areas.

COST Children £1.00, adults £2.00, Senior Citizens £1.50. Groups of more than 12: 50p off (pre-booking essential).

DISABLED FACILITIES Limited.

DIRECTIONS A12 to Dedham Village. Follow sign for car and coach park entrance next to car park. Site: Mill Lane, Dedham, Colchester.

Denny Abbey
- The Head Custodian
- Ely Road, Chittering, Nr Waterbeach, Cambs. CB5 9TQ
- 0223 860489

What at first appears to be an attractive stone-built farmhouse is actually the remains of a 12th-century Benedictine abbey which, at different times, also housed the Knights Templar and Franciscan nuns.

OPENING Good Friday or 1 April (whichever is earlier) to 30 September: daily 10.00am to 6.00pm. Winter: Sunday only 10.00am–4.00pm.

DISABLED FACILITIES Wheelchair access to grounds and ground floor only.

DIRECTIONS Six miles north of Cambridge on A10 (OS Map 154; ref TL 495684). Bus: Cambus 109 Cambridge to Ely (passes close to BR Waterbeach) (Tel: 0223 423554). BR: Waterbeach three miles.

Dunwich Heath
- The Administrator
- Dunwich, Saxmundham, Suffolk. IP17 3DZ
- 0728 73505

Two hundred and fifteen acres of sandy cliffs and headland with one mile of beach; good walks and access to public hides at adjacent RSPB Minsmere; exhibition and lookout in the coastguard cottages.

N C SUPPORT Study centre; introductory talk by warden (must be pre-booked).

DISABLED FACILITIES Car park viewing point and some footpaths accessible. Please contact the warden for further information. Adapted WC at coastguard cottages; stairlift to viewing room. Self-drive powered car available. Holiday flat for disabled guests at the coastguard cottages.

DIRECTIONS One mile south of Dunwich, signposted off Dunwich to Westleton road. Bus: Eastern Counties 646 Ipswich to Lowestoft (summer Sundays only). BR: Darsham six miles.

ENGLISH HERITAGE

National Curriculum Support
Almost every aspect of the curriculum can be explored at English Heritage properties. They can be used not only for studying History but linked to other subjects as varied as English, Maths,

VISITS OUT
EAST ANGLIA

Science, Technology, Geography and Music. English Heritage has produced a wide range of National Curriculum teachers' guides and videos to give plenty of stimulating ideas. Write to English Heritage Education Service, Keysign House, 429 Oxford Street, London W1R 2HD, for a free copy of the resources catalogue.

Annual or one-off event At some sites each year there are special educational events, often with the involvement of experts such as musicians and storytellers, for visiting educational groups.

Cost Student groups and school parties are admitted free to English Heritage properties, but should book in advance through the relevant Regional Office.

See individual entries for all other information.

Audley End House and Park
Berney Arms Windmill
Castle Acre Priory
Castle Rising Castle
Denny Abbey
Framlingham Castle
Grime's Graves
Old Merchants House
Orford Castle
Saxtead Green Post
Tilbury Fort

East of England Bird of Prey & Conservation Centre
- Peter G Bridges
- St Jacobs Hall, Laxfield, Suffolk. IP13 8HY
- 0986 798844 FAX 0379 758180

Birds in aviaries and also three flying displays per day allowing everyone to realise the majesty and magic of these somewhat endangered birds. View a wide selection of birds of prey and be given guided tours and lectures by falconers. Seabirds fly free at the displays.

OPENING Daily 10.00am–5.30pm.

CATERING Tea room offering drinks, homemade snacks, lunches, savouries, cream teas, etc.

COST On application.

DISABLED FACILITIES Toilets, ramps and widened doors.

DIRECTIONS On B1117, one and a half miles south of the village of Laxfield.

Easton Farm Park
- Charlotte Barbour
- Easton, Nr Wickham Market, Suffolk. IP13 0EQ
- 0728 746475 FAX 0728 747736

Victorian model farm set in the picturesque Deben River Valley. Farm animals, food and farming exhibition, green trail, country bygones, dairy centre with viewing gallery, Victorian dairy, gift shop and tea room.

N C SUPPORT Key Stage 1 workbook and sheets for Key Stages 2 and 3 available.

OPENING Mid-March to end of September: daily 10.30am–6.00pm.

CATERING Tea room for light lunch, teas, coffees. Picnic area and inside picnic facilities in wet weather.

COST Rates for parties of 20 or more: children £1.60, adults £3.00, one adult free with every ten children.

DISABLED FACILITIES Level site with hard paths. Toilet.

VISITS OUT
EAST ANGLIA

DIRECTIONS Fifteen miles north of Ipswich, signposted off the A12 at Wickham Market.

Ely Cathedral
- Jan Pye, The Chapter Officer
- The College, Ely, Cambs. CB7 4DN
- 0353 667735 FAX 0353 665658

Begun by the Normans in 1083 and completed in 1189. Mainly Romanesque but with examples of later architecture. Octagon and lantern, Lady Chapel, Prior's Door and medieval domestic buildings are all outstanding.

N C SUPPORT Relevant to Religious Education, Science, Mathematics, History, Art, Music, Social Education, Personal Development. Resource and Study Centre with projector, video, computer, and sound equipment. Suitable for groups of up to 30. Experienced guides (ex-teachers). Worksheets.

OPENING Summer: daily 7.00am–7.00pm. Winter: Monday to Saturday 7.30am–6.00pm.

CATERING Refectory snack bar in Cathedral. Almonary tea rooms and restaurant in the College.

COST School groups within Diocese £5.00 per group; outside Diocese £10.00 per group.

DISABLED FACILITIES South door entry. Ramps to all ground floor of Cathedral.

DIRECTIONS M11 or A1 from London. A10 from Cambridge. A45/A142 from Ipswich. The Cathedral is in centre of Ely and can be easily found.

Epping Forest Field Centre
- The Warden
- High Beach, Loughton, Essex. IG10 4AF
- 081-508 7714 FAX 081-508 8429

This purpose-built Field Centre is managed by the FSC for the Corporation of London and provides high quality fieldwork day courses for all school groups on excellent sites.

N C SUPPORT Fieldwork courses are designed to meet the needs of individual schools and National Curriculum Attainment Targets, Statements of Attainment and Programmes of Study at all stages. Specialist providers of A-Level fieldwork courses (non-residential).

OPENING All year, including school holidays.

CATERING Snack bar facilities are available near to the Centre.

COST Fees range from £2.50 to £16.00 per student per day with various discounts available.

DISABLED FACILITIES The Centre has wheelchair access and a wheelchair path into the Forest.

DIRECTIONS The Centre is located in the heart of Epping Forest near to junction 26 of the M25 and to Loughton tube station.

Flag Fen Bronze Age
- Paul Mitchell
- Excavation, Fourth Drove, Fengate, Peterborough. PE1 5UR
- 0733 313414 FAX 0733 349957

Introductory video. Guided tour of site. Bronze Age wood handling.

VISITS OUT
EAST ANGLIA

Wide range of finds displayed. Reconstructed roundhouses and primitive breeds of sheep, Exmoor ponies and 'Iron Age' pigs.

N C SUPPORT Educational materials available. Education room. Activities such as spinning and pot making can be arranged.

OPENING Monday to Friday 9.30am–4.00pm for school parties.

CATERING Light refreshments.

COST School children/students £1.50, accompanying adults free.

DISABLED FACILITIES Toilet. Access for wheelchairs.

DIRECTIONS Signposted from Peterborough ring road.

Framlingham Castle
- ☛ The Head Custodian
- ✉ Framlingham, Woodbridge, Suffolk. 1P13 9BP

A superb 12th-century castle which, from the outside, looks almost the same as when it was built. From the continuous curtain wall, linking 13 towers, there are excellent views over Framlingham and the charming reed-fringed mere. At different times, the castle has been a fortress, an Elizabethan prison, a poorhouse and a school. The many alterations over the years have led to a pleasing mixture of historical styles. There is an Educational Centre at Framlingham Castle, equipped with audio-visual, printed and replica sources appropriate to the property, which teachers can use themselves. Education Centres can be booked in advance through English Heritage.

OPENING All year round. Good Friday or 1 April (whichever is earlier) to 30 September: daily 10.00am–6.00pm. 1 October to Maundy Thursday or 31 March (whichever is earlier): Tuesday to Sunday 10.00am–4.00pm. Closed 24–26 December and 1 January.

DISABLED FACILITIES Wheelchair access to grounds and ground floor.

DIRECTIONS In Framlingham on B1116 (OS Map 156; ref TM 287637). Bus: Eastern Counties 82/3, Suffolk Country Bus 651 from Ipswich (passes close to BR Woodbridge, except Sunday (Tel: 0473 265676). BR: Wickham Market six and a half miles; Saxmundham seven miles.

Gifford's Hall
- ☛ J M Kemp
- ✉ Hartest, Nr Bury St Edmunds, Suffolk. IP29 4EX
- ☎ 0284 830464

Vineyard with winery and horticultural enterprises, including flowers for cutting, free-range hens, tourist trails, organic vegetables, farm shop and tea rooms.

N C SUPPORT Science and Technology at Key Stages 2, 3 and 4. Much to offer A-level students of Biology and Chemistry and younger students on countryside and conservation awareness.

OPENING Easter to 31 October 12.00 noon–6.00pm (earlier or later by prior arrangement).

CATERING Tea rooms and light refreshments always available.

COST School children £1.50.

DISABLED FACILITIES Access for wheelchairs to all areas including lavatories.

VISITS OUT
EAST ANGLIA

DIRECTIONS Signposted from B1066, A134 and A1092.

Grime's Graves
- The Head Custodian
- Lynford, Thetford, Norfolk. IP26 5DE
- 0842 810656

Remarkable Neolithic flint mines, unique in England, which comprise over 300 pits and shafts. The visitor can descend some 30 feet by ladder into one excavated shaft, and look along the radiating galleries from where the flint, used to make axes and knives, was extracted.

OPENING All year round. Good Friday or 1 April (whichever is earlier) to 30 September: daily 10.00am–6.00pm. 1 October to Maundy Thursday or 31 March (whichever is earlier): Tuesday to Sunday 10.00am–4.00pm. Closed 24–26 December and 1 January.

DISABLED FACILITIES Wheelchair access to exhibition area only; access track rough.

DIRECTIONS Seven miles northwest of Thetford off A134 (OS Map 144; ref TL 818898). BR: Brandon three and a half miles.

Hamerton Wildlife Centre
- Mrs Swales
- Hamerton, Huntingdon, Cambs. PE17 5RE
- 0832 293362 FAX 0832 3677

Newly developed breeding centre, covering fifteen acres, for endangered and rarely seen animals: gibbons, lemurs, marmosets, sloths, meerkats, cats, birds; over 120 species.

N C SUPPORT School support continually updated. Please contact centre for details.

ANNUAL OR ONE OFF EVENT Falconry demonstrations, craft fairs, special event days. Details on application.

OPENING Summer: daily 10.30am–6.00pm. Winter: daily 10.30am–4.00pm.

CATERING Coffee shop selling drinks, snacks, ice cream.

COST Group discounts for pre-booked parties of 15 or more. Special rates for schools.

DISABLED FACILITIES Wheelchair access to all buildings. Toilet.

DIRECTIONS Follow brown and white tourist signs off A1 at Sawtry and A14 at B660 interchange.

Hedingham Castle
- Ian Harrington, Manager
- Castle Hedingham, Nr Halstead, Essex. CO9 3DJ
- 0787 60261 FAX 0787 61473

Famous Norman keep with beautiful grounds, lake and woods. Offer teachers a free preliminary visit to discuss school's requirements with the Manager and also supply teachers with information leaflets and notes.

N C SUPPORT Hedingham Castle provides an ideal environment to meet many of the Attainment Targets Key Stages 1–4. 'The Castle as a Home', 'Invaders and Settlers', 'Normans', 'Medieval Warfare', 'Tudors and Stuarts'. Links with other subjects: Environmental Education, Geography, Nature Study, Science, Mathematics, Art,

VISITS OUT
EAST ANGLIA

English Music and cross-Curriculum themes.

OPENING Easter Week to end October: daily 10.00am–5.00pm. All year by appointment.

CATERING Teas, coffee, home-made cakes and all light refreshments. Cream teas by arrangement.

COST Children £1.25, teachers or helpers free, people with disabilities free.

DISABLED FACILITIES There is a steep climb to the Castle.

DIRECTIONS One mile off A604 between Cambridge and Colchester. Easy reach of M11, A12, and M25. Sixty miles from London.

High Lodge Forest Centre
- Recreation Department
- Forest Enterprise, Santon Downham, Brandon, Suffolk. IP27 OTJ
- 0842 810271 FAX 0842 811309

Conducted visits to Thetford Forest with 'hands-on' activities designed to help pupils discover the importance of trees for timber, wildlife and people. Special practical sessions on request, e.g. paper-making.

N C SUPPORT Teachers' pack available including Curriculum Chart with links to Science, Geography, Maths, Art, History, English, CDT, Environmental Education. Themes include History, Forest Wildlife, focus on trees, plus project ideas sheet.

ANNUAL OR ONE OFF EVENT A team of qualified rangers is available to discuss and assist teachers and sixth-form pupils in formulating individual and group projects from conception through development stages. Study site available.

OPENING High Lodge: April to September: daily 10.00am–5.00pm. Education Department: all year.

COST Basic rate £25.00 per group (35 maximum) for 2 hours with a ranger (includes free teachers' pack).

DISABLED FACILITIES Toilets and easy access trail and access to Centre.

DIRECTIONS Signposted from B1107 off the A11.

Houghton Mill
- The Administrator
- Houghton, Huntingdon, Cambs. PE17 5AY
- 0480 301494

Large timber-built watermill on River Ouse; much of the 19th-century machinery is intact and still grinding wheat for demonstration and sale.

N C SUPPORT Sheets with ideas for teachers.

Imperial War Museum
- Sue Sharp, Education Officer
- Duxford Airfield, Duxford, Cambs. CB2 4QR
- 0223 835000 (252) FAX 0223 837267

Duxford houses large exhibits belonging to the Imperial War Museum. These include historic military aircraft, civil airliners (including Concorde 101), military vehicles, a V1 flying bomb and refurbished prefab. With accompanying exhibitions.

N C SUPPORT Ideas on how to link topics across the Curriculum with a visit. Teachers' information pack, support packs on 'Flight' and 'The Home Front WWII'. Talks and special studies and worksheets.

ANNUAL OR ONE OFF EVENT Special educational events for teachers and children throughout the year. Send for details.

OPENING Daily: Summer: 10.00am–6.00pm. Winter: 10.00am–4.00pm.

CATERING Restaurant on site. Schools' mess room for eating packed lunches under cover.

COST £1.85 for pre-booked educational groups (1993 prices).

DISABLED FACILITIES Access to most areas of the Museum. Toilets.

DIRECTIONS Duxford is next to junction 10 of the M11, eight miles from Cambridge.

Ingatestone Hall
- Lord Petre
- Hull Lane, Ingatestone, Essex. CM4 9NR
- 0277 353010 FAX 0245 248979

Tudor mansion and grounds built in 1540 by Sir William Petre, Secretary of State to four Tudor monarchs; containing furniture, portraits and memorabilia accumulated over the years.

N C SUPPORT Tudor History, also targets such as Heraldry, Tudor Costume, Stuart Kings and Queens, building. Key Stage 2 and observational tasks relevant to Attainment Targets 1 and 3; levels 1–5.

OPENING Easter to end September, Wednesday and Thursday during term time set aside for pre-arranged visits by school parties.

COST Children £2.00, adults £3.00, Senior Citizens £2.50. Reduction of 50p per head for parties of 20 or more.

DISABLED FACILITIES Limited. Many doors are too narrow for full-size wheelchairs and the only access to the upper floor is by a steep spiral staircase.

DIRECTIONS Ingatestone is between Brentwood and Chelmsford. At the London end of the village, take station lane, cross level crossing and continue, to reach gates after half a mile.

Ipswich Parachute Centre
- Sheila Cooper, Administrator
- 1 Ipswich Airport, Nacton Road, Ipswich, Suffolk. IP3 9QF
- 0473 710044

Parachute Centre (British Parachute Association approved) offering facilities for experienced parachutists and beginners. Minimum age 16 years. If under 18 years a parental consent form is required. The upper weight limit is 15 stone (210lbs or 95 kilos). If over 40 a medical certificate is required, signed by your doctor. The appropriate form will be sent if necessary.

OPENING Daily (except Tuesday) from 8.30am till dusk.

CATERING Cafeteria, bar and squash courts on the airfield and all the facilities of a large town nearby.

COST A deposit of £30 per person is payable upon booking. This deposit

VISITS OUT
EAST ANGLIA

is not refundable. The balance of the fee is payable on the day of the jump.

DIRECTIONS Airport is best reached by taking the exit signposted for Nacton Road Industrial Estate. Approaching from London or the south follow the A12 towards Ipswich and take a right turn at the roundabout signposted A45. First exit after crossing the Orwell Bridge.

Kingdom of the Sea
- J Sally Atkinson, Promotions Officer
- ✉ Marine Parade, Great Yarmouth, Norfolk. NR30 3AH
- ☎ 0493 330631 FAX 0493 330442

One of Britain's largest aquaria, Kingdom of the Sea provides the opportunity to observe a wide variety of native marine life, plus tropical sharks and smaller tropical fish. Regular talks by marine staff. Facilities: audio-visual room and gift shop.

N C SUPPORT Teachers' pack for 5–11 year olds, includes National Curriculum notes, photocopiable quizsheets, worksheets and practical information. Material for Key Stages 3 and 4 currently being developed.

OPENING All year (except 25 and 26 December): 10.00am till dusk.

CATERING Large restaurant with 200 seats and school menu: sausage and chips and fizzy drink £1.

COST School rate: children £2.20, one adult to every ten children free, extra adults £2.20.

DISABLED FACILITIES Flat access from pavement, marine displays, shop and restaurant all wheelchair accessible. Toilet.

DIRECTIONS From London, A12 to Colchester and Ipswich; from Midlands, A47.

Lee Valley Regional Park
- J Mansell
- ✉ Lee Valley Park Countryside Centre, Abbey Gardens, Waltham Abbey, Essex. EN9 1XQ
- ☎ 0992 713838 FAX 0992 893118

Twenty-three miles of countryside from London's East End to Hertfordshire. Half- and full-day programmes on environmental themes; classroom facilities; teacher activity packs; competitive rates. Good road and rail access.

N C SUPPORT All programmes related to National Curriculum, GCSE or A-Level. Assist in A-Level individual projects, self-led visits welcomed in Geography and Biology. Taught programmes on leisure and recreation in countryside.

OPENING Summer: daily 10.00am–5.00pm. Winter: daily (except Monday) 10.30am–4.00pm.

COST Primary school pupils £2.20 per half day, GCSE students £5.50 per day, A-Level students £8.00 per day.

DISABLED FACILITIES Fully accessible classrooms. Display area and shop. Toilets.

DIRECTIONS Junction 26 of the M25 (signposted). Also accessible from A406 North Circular and A10 Great Cambridge Road. BR: from Liverpool Street.

VISITS OUT
EAST ANGLIA

Living Ocean Aquarium
- Xanthe Eadie
- Clacton Pier, 1 North Sea, Clacton-on-Sea, Essex. CO15 1QX
- 0255 421115 FAX 0255 222163

Visit the fascinating world beneath our oceans. A unique experience in evolution and ecology, including the tunnel of life audio-visual history, aquarium displays and the successful Patagonian sea lion breeding programme and show.

N C SUPPORT Fish feeds and talks. 'Hands-on' touchpool. Fish fact sheets by tanks. Key Stages 1 and 2 worksheets. Teachers' pack and follow-up advisory service. RNLI talks for Key Stage 2.

OPENING Daily (except Christmas). October to end March: 12.00 noon–4.30pm. April: 12.00 noon–5.00pm. May to July: 10.30am–5.00pm. August: 10.30am–10.00pm. September: 10.30am–5.00pm.

CATERING Cafe available. Indoor picnic area. Outside seating through main pier.

COST Group discount for 15 or more: £2.00, one teacher free per ten children (special schools one per five children).

DISABLED FACILITIES Wheelchair access. Toilet, ramps.

DIRECTIONS From London: A12 to A120 then A133 to Clacton. BR: direct to Clacton from London, Liverpool Street.

Lynn Museum
- Kate Brown
- Market Street, King's Lynn, Norfolk. PE30 1NL
- 0553 775001

Local museum with displays reflecting archaeology, local history and natural history of King's Lynn and West Norfolk. Changing exhibitions and occasional special events.

N C SUPPORT Education Officer available to give handling lessons with museum objects.

OPENING Monday to Saturday 10.00am–5.00pm. Closed bank holidays.

CATERING Nearby in Town Centre.

COST Pre-booked school parties free.

DISABLED FACILITIES Good access.

DIRECTIONS Town Centre museum adjacent to bus station.

Museum of Palaeontology
- Stuart A Baldwin
- Fossil Hall, Boars Tye Road, Silver End, Witham, Essex. CM8 3QA
- 03765 83502 FAX 03765 84480

Fossil museum and falconry. Bookshop and gift shop. New dinosaur display for the opening of *Jurassic Park*: Allosaurus skull, T-rex, fossil mosquito in amber, dinosaur eggs, etc.

N C SUPPORT Manufacturer of over 2000 fossil replicas for schools: vertebrates, invertebrates, plants, trail posers, crystal models.

OPENING Most Saturdays 10.00am–4.00pm. Weekdays by appointment, closed Sunday.

COST A minimum charge of £25, excluding VAT, is made per visit. This covers class sizes up to 30. For over 30 and up to 45 children the charge is £35 plus VAT. These are nominal charges to cover the several hours' work involved. As this is a commercial organisation it relies on shop sales to make it viable.

DISABLED FACILITIES One wheelchair per group of 15. There are no toilet facilities at Fossil Hall, the nearest is a quarter of a mile away.

DIRECTIONS BR: one hour from London (Liverpool Street station to Witham). By road: 30 minutes off the M25 (exit 28 Chelmsford), or five minutes off the A12 or A120. A map is available on request.

NATIONAL TRUST

Opening Times Write or telephone the administrator of the house, give preferred day and time, the size and age of the group, and the main purpose of the visit. *The National Trust Handbook* contains further relevant information.

Cost Unless otherwise stated in the *Handbook*, there is a reduction of around 50% for children aged 16 and under, when accompanied by their teacher. Education Group Members are admitted free. However, please note that there may be a small charge for any additional educational facilities or activities.

See individual entries for all other information.

Anglesey Abbey
Blakeney Point
Dunwich Heath
Houghton Mill
Wicken Fen
Wimpole Hall
Wimpole Hall & Home Farm

National Horseracing Museum

- Graham Snelling
- 99 High Street, Newmarket, Suffolk. CB8 8JL
- 0638 667333

Four hundred years of horseracing history in fine paintings, bronzes, memorabilia. Home of the British Sporting Art Trust.

N C SUPPORT Social History, Art.

OPENING April to December: Monday to Saturday 10.00am–5.00pm, Sunday 2.00pm–5.00pm.

CATERING Licensed coffee shop. Marquee in garden for parties. Schools welcome to eat packed lunches.

COST Children 75p.

DISABLED FACILITIES Full access throughout Museum.

The National Stud

- Jonathan P Grimwade
- Newmarket, Suffolk. CB8 0XE
- 0638 663464 FAX 0638 665173

With 500 acres and 200 stables, the National Stud is one of the most prestigious breeding centres in Europe and offers guided tours lasting one and a quarter hours including viewing of young foals (seasonal) and stallions.

OPENING Tours operating from April to September: Monday to Friday 11.15am and 2.30pm, Saturday 11.15am only, Sunday 2.30pm only, bank holidays 11.15am and 2.30pm.

EAST ANGLIA

CATERING Light refreshments, e.g. tea and coffee.

COST Children, adults £2.70, Senior Citizens and students £1.80.

DISABLED FACILITIES Toilets and ramp.

DIRECTIONS Access to the Stud via the electric main gate is simple, lying beside Newmarket's July Racecourse, two miles southwest of the town at the junction of the A1303 (A45) Cambridge and the A1304 (A11) London.

The North End Trust
- Pat Midgley
- True's Yard, North Street, King's Lynn, Norfolk. PE30 1QW
- 0553 770479

Restored fishermen's cottages, museum, tearooms, gift shop and a large computerised archive of material relating to all aspects of the town of King's Lynn.

N C SUPPORT All material is sorted into the Key Stages and Attainment Targets of the Curriculum. Two retired teachers work with parties throughout the school visit. French, German and Spanish are spoken, also signing for those with special needs. Students are encouraged to come and work on individual or group projects and studies. Trained staff work with them.

OPENING Daily (except Christmas Day) 9.30am–4.30pm.

COST Students 75p, accompanying staff free. Free use of the archival material to those working on genuine research.

DISABLED FACILITIES Site ramped throughout. Special toilet for the disabled. Only difficult part is upstairs in the cottages.

DIRECTIONS Please send for leaflet showing the location.

Norwich Castle Museum
- Richard Wood
- Castle Meadow, Norwich, Norfolk. NR1 3JU
- 0603 630214 FAX 0603 765651

The region's premier Museum, housed in and around the Norman Castle keep. Displays on archaeology, art and natural history. Temporary exhibition programme.

N C SUPPORT Teachers' manual and sample worksheets available free.

OPENING Monday to Saturday 10.00am–5.00pm, Sunday 2.00pm–5.00pm.

CATERING Cafeteria.

COST No charge at present for pre-booked school groups.

DISABLED FACILITIES Wheelchair and lift.

DIRECTIONS On Castle Mound, City Centre.

Norwich Cathedral
- Lucy Paton, Visitors' Officer
- 62 The Close, Norwich, Norfolk. NR1 4EH
- 0603 764385 FAX 0603 766032

Norman cathedral of great beauty. Largest monastic cloisters in England. Unique roof bosses and Saxon bishop's throne amongst its treasures. Cathedral Close and extensive grounds leading to the river.

N C SUPPORT Teachers' pack in production. Also other material

VISITS OUT
EAST ANGLIA

particularly aimed at Key Stages 1 and 2.

OPENING Daily 7.30am–6.00pm. May to October: 7.30am–7.00pm.

CATERING Buffet selling light refreshments. Picnic lunches can be eaten in the cloisters.

COST Free. Contributions welcomed.

DISABLED FACILITIES Toilet; ramp access at south door; wheelchairs on request; audio loop; touch and hearing centre.

DIRECTIONS From London: M11, A11. From the West: A47 inner ring road then follow signs.

Old Merchants House
- The Head Custodian
- Row 117, South Quay, Great Yarmouth, Norfolk. NR30 2RQ
- 0493 857900

Two 17th-century Row Houses, a type of building unique to Great Yarmouth, containing original fixtures and displays of local architectural fittings salvaged from bombing in 1942–3. Nearby are the remains of a Franciscan friary, with a rare vaulted cloister, accidentally discovered during bomb damage repairs.

OPENING Summer season. Good Friday or 1 April (whichever is earlier) to 30 September: daily 10.00am–6.00pm. Entry by tour only.

DIRECTIONS Great Yarmouth on south quay half a mile inland from the beach. Follow signs to dock and south quay (OS Map 134; Houses ref TG 525072). BR: Great Yarmouth half a mile.

Orford Castle
- The Head Custodian
- Orford, Nr Woodbridge, Suffolk. IP12 2ND
- 03944 50472

A royal castle built for coastal defence in the 12th century. A magnificent keep survives almost intact with three immense towers reaching to 90 feet. Inside there are many rooms to explore.

OPENING All year round. Good Friday or 1 April (whichever is earlier) to 30 September: daily 10.00am–6.00pm. 1 October to Maundy Thursday or 31 March (whichever is earlier): Tuesday to Sunday 10.00am–4.00pm. Closed 24–26 December and 1 January.

DIRECTIONS One mile south of Felixstowe near docks (OS Map 169; ref TM 284318). Bus: Eastern Counties 75–9 Ipswich to Felixstowe Dock to within three-quarters of a mile (Tel: 0473 253734). BR: Felixstowe two and a half miles.

Park Farm
- Mrs M Stanton
- Snettisham, King's Lynn, Norfolk. PE31 7NQ
- 0485 542425

A genuine working farm where there's ample opportunity for 'hands-on' experience. Farm trails, sheep centre, gigantic adventure playground. Safari Ride to see red deer.

N C SUPPORT An information pack is available with details about all the animals and crops grown on the farm. Teachers are welcome to a free visit prior to booking.

VISITS OUT
EAST ANGLIA

ANNUAL OR ONE OFF EVENT Sheep shearing at the end of May.

OPENING Daily 10.30am–5.00pm.

CATERING A tea room serving light lunches, home-made cakes and refreshments. Indoor/outdoor picnic areas.

COST Children £2.00, adults £3.00. Approximately 25% discount for schools and groups.

DISABLED FACILITIES Toilet and paths through the farmyard.

DIRECTIONS Follow the brown signs off A149 in Snettisham.

Ripleys
- Christina Hannant
- The Windmill, 9 Marine Parade, Great Yarmouth, Norfolk. NR30 3AH
- 0493 332217 FAX 0493 332295

Museum with a difference. Full of unusual artefacts and oddities. Videos and illusions. Fun for all ages. A quiz for children is available.

OPENING April to November: daily 10.00am–8.00pm. November to April: Saturday and Sunday 10.00am–6.00pm.

CATERING None.

COST Children £1.50, adults £2.50.

DISABLED FACILITIES Disabled entrance (wheelchair: no charge as only three-quarters of the Museum can be seen).

DIRECTIONS On main road on Yarmouth sea front.

Rollerworld
- Andy Starr
- Eastgates, Colchester, Essex. CO1 2TJ
- 0206 868868 FAX 0206 870400

Great Britain's only world-class rollerskating rink: 25 x 50m, maple floor, rollerhire, roller cafe. Host venue for the National Championships. Roller bar plus new Quasar Centre. Designed and built by Andy Starr who is available to lecture to groups.

ANNUAL OR ONE OFF EVENT Has hosted the National Rollerskating Championships, since 1991.

OPENING Tuesday to Friday evening, Saturday and Sunday all day. School holidays extra sessions. Private hire available.

CATERING Rollercafe serving fast food and soft drinks. Rollerbar adults only.

COST £2.80–£5.20 per session. Discount of 10% for 15 or more in groups.

DISABLED FACILITIES Full access on ground floor. Toilet.

DIRECTIONS A12 to Colchester following brown tourist signs to Rollerworld, Eastgates.

Saxtead Green Post
- The Head Custodian
- The Mill House, Saxtead Green, Woodbridge, Suffolk. IP13 9QQ

The finest example of a Suffolk post mill. Still in working order. It is possible to climb the wooden stairs to the various floors, full of fascinating mill machinery.

VISITS OUT
EAST ANGLIA

OPENING Summer season. Good Friday or 1 April (whichever is earlier) to 30 September: Monday to Saturday 10.00am–6.00pm.

DIRECTIONS Two and a half miles northwest of Framlingham on A1120 (OS Map 156; ref TM 253645). Bus: Eastern Counties 82/3, Suffolk County Bus 651 from Ipswich (passes close to BR Woodbridge, except Sundays Tel: 0473 265676). Alight Framlingham, two miles. BR: Wickham Market nine miles.

Sizewell Visitor Centre
- Wendy Huggins
- Nuclear Electric plc, Sizewell B Power Station, Nr Leiston, Suffolk. IP16 4UR
- (0728) 642139 FAX (0728) 642146

Exhibition Centre covering all aspects of electricity generation, featuring nuclear power and the new Pressurised Water Reactor technology at Sizewell B. Environmental study facilitated by field study classroom and wildlife, beach and woodland areas.

N C SUPPORT Environmental workpack Key Stages 1–3 'Learning through the Environment'. Energy workpack Key Stage 3 'The Sizewell Workpack'. Relevance to Geography, History, Physics, Chemistry, Biology and cross-curricular studies.

ANNUAL OR ONE OFF EVENT Series of evening lectures for Environment Week 24–28 May.

OPENING October to March: Monday to Saturday 10.00am–4.00pm. April–September: Monday to Sunday 10.00am–4.00pm.

CATERING Snacks and drinks vending machines.

COST Free.

DISABLED FACILITIES Car parking, toilets.

DIRECTIONS A12, Yoxford B1122, Lovers Lane C228 to Sizewell.

Southend Sea Life Centre
- Rebecca Oakley
- Eastern Esplanade, Southend-on-Sea, Essex. SS1 2ER
- 0702 601834 FAX 0702 462444

Native marine aquarium with more than 30 high-tech displays providing incredibly close encounters with dozens of sea creatures from astonishing angles.

N C SUPPORT Talks and demonstrations available plus support teachers' notes and workbooks.

OPENING Daily (except Christmas Day) from 10.00am.

CATERING Self-service restaurant serving hot and cold food.

COST School groups: children £2.25, one adult free with every ten children, extra adults £2.25.

DISABLED FACILITIES Fully accessible to wheelchairs. Toilet.

DIRECTIONS From A127 or A13 follow signs to the sea front. The Centre is a large blue and white building.

Stitches & Lace
- Mrs L J Thomas
- Alby Craft Centre, Cromer Road, Alby, Norwich, Norfolk. NR11 7QE
- 0263 768002

VISITS OUT
EAST ANGLIA

300 years of bobbin and needlelace on display, easy to study with magnifying glasses provided. A lacemaker's cottage, bobbins, memorabilia and reference library. Lacemaking and embroidery supplies for sale.

OPENING 14 March to 19 December: Tuesday to Friday and Sunday 10.00am–1.00pm and 2.00pm–5.00pm, closed Saturday and Monday except bank holidays. 8 January to mid-March: Sunday only.

CATERING Tea room serving light lunches, home cooked fare.

COST Free.

DISABLED FACILITIES Ramps to all workshops and tea room. Toilet.

DIRECTIONS On A140 halfway between Aylsham and Cromer (signposted 'Craft Centre' with brown tourist information signs).

Stranger's Hall Museum
- Education Department, Castle Museum
- Charing Cross, Norwich, Norfolk. NR2 4AL
- 0603 667 229

A medieval merchant's house with period room displays from Tudor to Victorian times, and a changing programme of exhibitions on domestic life, costumes and textiles.

N C SUPPORT Especially History Key Stages 2 and 3; sixth form/college studies involving textiles, costume, fashion; teaching sessions bookable via Education Department, Castle Museum, Norwich.

OPENING Monday to Saturday 10.00am–5.00pm.

COST Booked school parties free, otherwise £1.00 (group discount 70p). The ticket admits the holder to three Norwich museums.

DISABLED FACILITIES Poor. The many steep flights of stairs make access difficult.

DIRECTIONS Two minutes from Norwich market place; follow signs.

Suffolk Forest District
- Richard Davis
- Tangham, Rendlesham Forest, Woodbridge, Suffolk. IP12 3NF
- 994 450164 FAX 994 450179

Heathland: predominantly coniferous forest in which a wide range of age groups are given study opportunities through a range of habitat types.

N C SUPPORT Educational support and teachers' pack available, teacher advice, link with various themes in the National Curriculum. Opportunities for more in-depth research or A-Level studies in Botany, Biology or Environmental/Recreational subjects.

OPENING Daily 8.30am–5.00pm.

COST £10.00 per hour for groups of up to 35.

DISABLED FACILITIES Toilet facilities and all-ability trail.

DIRECTIONS From Melton near Woodbridge follow A1152 and B1084 for approximately five miles, then signs to Forest office.

VISITS OUT
EAST ANGLIA

Suffolk Wildlife Park
- Richard Ross
- Kessingland, Suffolk. NR33 7TF
- 0502 740291 FAX 0502 741104

Come to 'The African Wildlife Experience' and follow one of the colour-coded trails in the footsteps of some of the great explorers, seeing lions, camels, zebras, chimpanzees, African parrots, plus other wildlife. Entertainment for children every afternoon (except Sunday) in the summer season.

OPENING Daily (except Christmas Day or Boxing Day) 10.00am–6.30pm (or dusk if earlier).

CATERING Explorers' cafeteria. Picnic area.

COST Children £3.00, adults £5.00, Senior Citizens £4.00. Organised parties of 15 or more: children £2.00, under fours free, adults £3.00, Senior Citizens £2.00.

DISABLED FACILITIES Easy access to all parts of the Park. Toilets. Free wheelchair loan.

DIRECTIONS On the A12 at Kessingland south of Lowestoft.

Tilbury Fort
- The Head Custodian
- No 2 Office Block, The Fort, Tilbury, Essex. RH18 7NR
- 0375 858489

The best and largest example of 17th-century military engineering in England, commanding the Thames and showing the development of fortifications over the following 200 years. Exhibitions, the powder magazine and the bunker-like 'casemates' demonstrate how the fort protected London from seaborne attack.

OPENING All year round: Good Friday or 1 April (whichever is earlier) to 30 September: daily 10.00am–6.00pm. 1 October to Maundy Thursday or 31 March (whichever is earlier): Tuesday to Sunday 10.00am–4.00pm. Closed 24–26 December and 1 January.

DISABLED FACILITIES Wheelchair access (exterior, fort square and magazines).

DIRECTIONS Half a mile east of Tilbury off A126 (OS Map 177; ref TQ 651754). Bus: Priory Minicoaches 380 BR: Standford-le-Hope to Tilbury Riverside (Tel: 0268 541062). BR: Standford-le-Hope; Tilbury Town one and a half miles.

University Botanic Garden
- Miss C Lawes
- Cory Lodge, Bateman Street, Cambridge. CB2 1JF
- 0223 336265

Rich variety of plants, glasshouse range features tropical rainforest plants. Other features include winter garden, scented garden and lake. Notification of all visits required.

N C SUPPORT Teachers' packs include tropical house and senses trail. Classroom available for hire. Tours of glasshouses available.

OPENING Winter: daily 8.00am–4.00pm. Summer: daily 8.00am–6.00pm. Glasshouses: 10.00am–12.30pm and 2.00pm–4.00pm.

CATERING Refreshments served: hot/cold drinks, snacks. Open Tuesday–Saturday.

COST Cost of room hire is £15.00 plus VAT per session.

DISABLED FACILITIES Toilets. Suitable for wheelchairs throughout.

DIRECTIONS From junction 11 of the M11, head into Cambridge on the A1309. Garden is on the left as enter the city.

West Stow Anglo-Saxon Village

- Alan Baxter
- The Visitor Centre, West Stow Country Park, Icklingham Road, Bury St Edmunds, Suffolk. IP28 6HG
- 0284 728718

Reconstruction of early Anglo-Saxon village on the site where it was excavated. Six buildings, farm project, visitor centre. Full education service. Large car park, 125 acre country park.

N C SUPPORT Education Officer provides service for schools on 'Invaders and Settlers' topic. Range of visit options available.

OPENING Daily (except Christmas) 10.00am–4.15pm.

CATERING Refreshment kiosk.

COST Standard entry £2.50. Group discounts: £1.50 per head (one adult free per ten). Free pre-visit with tape guide for teachers.

DISABLED FACILITIES Ramp access and toilets. Vehicle access to site available.

DIRECTIONS Off the A1101 (Bury St Edmunds to Mildenhall road). Six miles northwest of Bury St Edmunds.

Wherry Yacht Charter

- P J A Bower, Partner
- Barton House, Hartwell Road, Wrexham, Norfolk. NR12 8TL
- 0603 782470

Five glorious days afloat on the Norfolk Broads, messing about in dinghies, buying and cooking one's own food, bedding down in sleeping bags as the water laps the hull, and discovering nature's playground. The cruises follow a set route, from Wroxham to How Hill and back and include a choice of educational visits and activities at no extra cost.

N C SUPPORT Teachers' pack which gives full details of the cruise, books, material and suggestions for pupils' worksheets etc., and includes appropriate Broads Authority publications. Slide show on the history of Norfolk Wherries and the restoration of the wherries to the fleet can be viewed on board during the cruise.

OPENING Long week cruises: 6.00pm Friday to 6.00pm Sunday week. Two-week cruises: 11.00am Monday to 12.00 noon Friday at reduced rates. Short week cruises: 11.00am Monday to 12.00 noon Friday at favourable rates. Weekend cruises: 6.00pm Friday to 6.00pm Sunday.

CATERING A catering service to suit all pockets is usually available on day cruises. Can also provide four-course meals to be cooked and served aboard during the cruise. Full details on request. Vegetarians catered for.

VISITS OUT
EAST ANGLIA

COST Prices range from £200 per day to £500 per weekend to £1300 for two weeks. Please write for further details. N.B. During July and August advance bookings will normally be taken only for week cruises or longer.

DIRECTIONS In the Broads National Park.

Whipple Museum of the History of Science
- Jim Bennett
- Free School Lane, Cambridge. CB2 3RH
- 0223 334545 **FAX** 0223 334554

Collection of scientific instruments, special exhibitions. Special exhibition on 19th-century physics. Suitable for sixth-formers.

OPENING Telephone for details.

COST Free.

DISABLED FACILITIES By appointment.

DIRECTIONS Contact museum for directions.

Wicken Fen
- The Administrator
- Lode Lane, Wicken, Cambs. CB7 5XP
- 0353 723095

Six hundred acres of wetland reserve, undrained remnant of East Anglia's great fens; particularly rich in plant and insect life; wide variety of habitats for birds, including scrub, marsh, reeds and water; display of fen's evolution. Fen cottage illustrates how a family might have lived in the 1930s.

N C SUPPORT National Curriculum links with Science, Geography and History. Study centre; teaching materials; education officer.

DISABLED FACILITIES Raised boardwalk for disabled visitors; special parking by previous arrangement. Ramp into William Thorpe building. Limited access to fen cottage. Adapted toilet (closed December to end March, but alternative unadapted toilets available).

DIRECTIONS South of the A1123, three miles west of Soham (A142), nine miles south of Ely, 17 miles northeast of Cambridge via A10: Bus: Neals 13 Cambridge to Ely. BR: Ely.

Wildfowl & Wetlands Trust
- Tim Cox
- Welney, Hundred Foot Bank, Wilney, Wisbech, Cambs. PE14 9TN
- 0353 860711

One of Europe's most important nature reserves, with many thousands of wintering swans and ducks, wildflowers and other wetland wildlife throughout the summer.

N C SUPPORT Full range of educational support material available. Visits to the reserve have services of Education Officer. Educational programmes geared toward National Curriculum and pupil needs.

ANNUAL OR ONE OFF EVENT The Reserve varies throughout the seasons with winter being the best time for birdlife, spring and summer best for pond exploration.

VISITS OUT
EAST ANGLIA

OPENING Daily 10.00am–5.00pm. Closed Christmas Eve and Christmas Day.

CATERING Tea room, picnic site.

COST School children £1.10, one teacher free with every ten children, extra adults £2.40.

DISABLED FACILITIES Greatly improved in September 1993.

DIRECTIONS Located between Ely and Downham Market. Tourist signposted from A10.

Willers Mill Wildlife Park
- Mr Jake Willers
- Station Road, Shepreth, Nr Royston, Herts. SG8 6PZ
- 0673 262226

Set in over eight acres of natural grounds and lakes, Willers Mill provides an ideal day out for all the family. See many wild and domestic animals and fish in their natural surroundings.

N C SUPPORT None.

OPENING November to end of February 10.00am–5.00pm. February to October: 10.00am–6.00pm.

CATERING Cafeteria.

COST Monday to Saturday: children £1.50, adults £2.95, Senior Citizens £2.25. Sunday and bank holidays: children £1.75, adults £3.50, Senior Citizens £2.75.

DISABLED FACILITIES None as yet.

DIRECTIONS On A10 between Cambridge and Royston. In Shepreth by level crossing.

Wimpole Hall
- Helen Bradley
- National Trust, Arrington, Royston, Herts. SG8 0BW
- 0223 207257 FAX 0223 207838

Eighteenth-century mansion house with lavishly furnished rooms and servant basements. Eighteenth-century farm, working rare breeds farm. Dairy (Victorian) and Museum with farming implements.

N C SUPPORT Key Stages 1, 2 and 3 Resource books. Living History Programme. Talks and Farm workshops.

ANNUAL OR ONE OFF EVENT Lambing weeks.

CATERING Restaurant (Hall). Servery at Farm.

DISABLED FACILITIES Toilets, ramps at Farm.

DIRECTIONS Nine miles south west of Cambridge on the A603, signposted from junction 12 off the M11.

Wisbech & Fenland Museum
- D C Devenish
- Museum Square, Wisbech, Cambs. PE13 1ES
- 0945 583817

Founded 1835. Purpose-built Georgian building opened 1846. Collections cover local studies, art (especially ceramics and books with a library of old literary society and 17th-century town library), archives and manuscripts.

N C SUPPORT Geology: large modern display, local and general. Social history of The Fens. Local history. Note: Displays on 'Thomas Clarkson, Slavers & The Slave Trade'.

VISITS OUT
EAST ANGLIA

ANNUAL OR ONE OFF EVENT Please send for details of the various exhibitions and events.

OPENING Tuesday to Saturday 10.00am–5.00pm. (October to March closes 4.00pm).

CATERING None.

COST Free.

DISABLED FACILITIES None.

DIRECTIONS Near market place. Next to main car park, St Peter's Church and Wisbech Castle.

Woodgreen Animal Shelter
- Penny Grown
- London Road, Godmanchester, Huntingdon, Cambs. PE18 8LT
- 0480 830014 FAX 0480 830566

The charity provides a home for a large variety of animals, from hamsters to horses, on a 50-acre site. All are on view, also a large wind turbine: information pack can be provided.

N C SUPPORT Educational pack in production with activities geared to National Curriculum studies. Free guided tours of the shelter and pre-visit for teachers. Classroom and facilities available.

ANNUAL OR ONE OFF EVENT Events take place at the shelter most weekends. Leaflets on request. Careers Days twice a year for people interested in working with animals. Animal-related courses held throughout the year. Family fun days in August.

OPENING Daily: 9.30am–3.30pm.

CATERING Restaurant for snacks, or three-course meals. Picnic tables, drinks machines.

COST Free.

DISABLED FACILITIES All areas suitable for wheelchairs. Toilet.

DIRECTIONS Excellent road links for M11, A45, A604, A14 (A1–M1 link). Maps on request.

The Working Silk Museum
- R J Humphries/Frances Harper
- New Mills, South Street, Braintree, Essex. CM7 6GB
- 0376 553393

The country's last remaining handloom silk weavers. Using 150-year-old Jacquard card looms. Fabrics woven for stately homes, royal households, shop, factory and museum.

N C SUPPORT Key Stage 3 History, Design, Natural History.

OPENING Monday to Saturday 10.00am–12.30pm and 1.30pm–5.00pm. Saturday (shop only except tours) 2.00pm–3.00pm–4.00pm, closed Sunday and bank holidays. School parties are available for 7–11 year olds (mornings only). For teachers and students there are a series of educational aids available by mail order (Tel: 0375 553393).

CATERING For a light lunch, afternoon tea or evening meal drop into any of the three local restaurants less than two minutes from the Mill.

COST Non-guided tours and school parties (set group rate for up to 20 people): children £23.00, adults £46.00, Senior Citizens £23.00. Additional children £1.15, additional adults £2.30.

VISITS OUT
EAST ANGLIA

DISABLED FACILITIES New Mills is equipped with requirements for disabled people, and is therefore able to offer tour facilities. There are no steps. All surfaces are level from the coach and car park.

DIRECTIONS BR: direct line London Liverpool Street to Braintree, trains every hour; five-minute walk from Braintree station.

VISITS OUT
MIDLANDS

KINGSWOOD CENTRE

RESIDENTIAL TECHNOLOGY CENTRE
FOR PRIMARY, MIDDLE & SECONDARY SCHOOLS

- Apple Newsroom
- Archery
- Assault Course
- Canoeing
- Computing
- Climbing
- Drama
- Fencing
- Go-Karts
- Initiative Course

- Mini Motorbikes
- Molecular Lego
- Multi Media
- Orienteering
- Quads
- Rifle Shooting
- Robotics
- Swimming
- Scuba Diving
- Video Filming

Give Your Class A Brighter Future!

National Curriculum linked 2/3 & 5 day residential Computer & Activity Courses

FROM £35

The Kingswood Centre is ideally located for easy access. Lying peacefully in picturesque countryside on the Staffordshire / Shropshire border, the Kingswood Centre offers easy access from all areas in Britain. Excellent motorway links, means that the Kingswood Experience is never more than a few hours away.

- Free Teacher Inset Computer Courses
- 3 & 6 Day Technology Courses
- Exciting Range Of On Site Adventure Activities
- 1 to 1 Computer/Child Ratio

- Broad Range Of Curriculum Linked Courses From Only £35 Key Stage 1-7
- 9 Fully Equipped Computer Laboratories
- Central Location In The Heart Of Britain

PHONE FOR A FREE BROCHURE & VIDEO TEL (0902) 847000
Kingswood Centre Ltd, Barn Lane, Albrighton, Staffordshire WV7 3AW

VISITS OUT
MIDLANDS

Acorn Activities
- Charles Cordle
- 7 East Street, Hereford. HR1 4RY
- 0432 357335 **FAX** 0432 341871

Acorn Activities, the UK's leading activity provider, offers a choice of over 100 activities, with group accommodation. Brochure available.

OPENING All year.

CATERING Facilities available.

COST Guide price: £30.00 bed, breakfast and evening meal; £30.00 per day activities.

DISABLED FACILITIES Yes.

DIRECTIONS Given on receipt of booking.

The Aerospace Museum
- Mr D Prior
- Cosford, Shifnal, Shropshire. TF11 8UP
- 0902 374112/372 **FAX** 0902 374813

Museum covering many different aspects of aerospace. Seventy aircraft on display.

N C SUPPORT Subject areas include Science, Technology, English, History, Foreign Languages, etc. Studies at all Key Stages supported by planned activities e.g.: worksheets, interactive talks/demonstrations; guided tours, etc.

ANNUAL OR ONE OFF EVENT Flight Activities Week for families (October Half Term). RAF Cosford Open Day (Sunday mid-June). Open Air Concert (Summer/Autumn). Various special exhibitions.

OPENING Daily: 10.00am–5.00pm.

COST School Groups: £1.25 per pupil; one adult free per 10 pupils (extra adults £2.50).

DISABLED FACILITIES Access to all areas except one gallery. Access to view some aircraft interiors by steps only.

DIRECTIONS On A41 about one mile from M54 (Junction 3). Well signposted.

Alton Towers
- Marc Bell
- Staffs. ST10 4DB
- 0538 702200 **FAX** 0538 702724

The UK's premier theme park, with over 125 rides and attractions for all the family. A magical blend of live shows, theme areas and great rides, a place where wonders never cease.

N C SUPPORT Full education support packs for both primary and secondary schools, tailored to the needs of the National Curriculum.

ANNUAL OR ONE OFF EVENT The most popular event of the season is the fireworks display on 31 October.

OPENING March to November: rides and attractions from 9.30am.

CATERING Over 50 catering outlets from à la carte to fast food and picnics.

COST Group visits from schools: secondary £6.50 (one in ten free), £6.99 (one in ten free); primary £6.50 (one in five free), £6.99 (one in five free).

MIDLANDS

DISABLED FACILITIES All staff are trained to help visitors with disabilities. Many of the rides and attractions are accessible.

DIRECTIONS M6 junctions 15 and 16, M1 junctions 23A and 28; 14 miles from Stoke-on-Trent.

Ashby de la Zouch Castle
- The Head Custodian
- South Street, Ashby de la Zouch, Leics. LE6 5PR
- 0530 413343

The impressive ruins of this late medieval castle are dominated by a magnificent tower, over 80 feet high, which was split in two during the Civil War, when the castle defended the Royalist cause.

OPENING All year. Good Friday or 1 April (whichever is earlier) to 30 September: daily 10.00am–6.00pm. 1 October to Maundy Thursday or 31 March (whichever is earlier): Tuesday to Sunday 10.00am–4.00pm. Closed 24–26 December and 1 January.

DISABLED FACILITIES Wheelchair access to grounds only.

DIRECTIONS In Ashby de la Zouch, 12 miles south of Derby on A5 (OS Map 128; ref SK 363167). Bus: Stevensons 9, 27 Burton-on-Trent to Ashby de la Zouch; Midland Fox 118, 218 Leicester to Swadlincote (Tel: 0332 292200). BR: Burton-on-Trent nine miles.

Avoncraft Museum of Buildings
- Dr Simon Penn
- Stoke Heath, Bromsgrove, Worcs. B60 4JR
- 0527 31886

A collection of buildings covering seven centuries that have been rescued and re-erected on a 15-acre open-air site.

N C SUPPORT Award-winning programme of teaching, activity and demonstration sessions. Wide variety of educational literature.

ANNUAL OR ONE OFF EVENT Seventeenth-century Living History week for schools.

OPENING Early March to late November. June to August: daily 11.00am–5.30pm. April, May, September and October: Tuesday to Sunday 11.00am–5.00pm. March and November: Tuesday to Thursday and Saturday to Sunday 11.00am–4.30pm. Open bank holidays.

CATERING Tea room serving snacks, refreshments, ice cream, etc.

COST 1993 prices: £1.15 per head for school parties. All visits by schools and college groups must be booked in advance. Best to make a telephone booking.

DISABLED FACILITIES Ramps for wheelchair access to some buildings; braille and moon guides.

DIRECTIONS Two miles south of Bromsgrove off A38. Three miles north of M5 Junction five. Three and a half miles south of M42 junction one.

Baddesley Clinton
- The Administrator
- Knowle, Solihull. B93 0DQ
- 0564 783294

Romantic medieval moated manor house, little changed since the 17th century; tiny chapel and priest's hole show evidence of strong Catholic connections. Contact National Trust Regional Office, Mythe End House, Tewkesbury, Gloucestershire GL20 6EB (Tel: 0684 850051) for further details.

N C SUPPORT National Curriculum links with History. Teachers' resource book. Study centre.

DISABLED FACILITIES Access to ground floor and most of garden. Adapted toilet near shop.

DIRECTIONS Three-quarters of a mile west of A4141 Warwick to Birmingham road, at Chadwick End, seven miles northwest of Warwick 15 miles southeast of central Birmingham. BR: Lapworth (not Sunday), two miles; Dorridge (not Sundays except May to September), four miles; Birmingham International (BR & Airport) nine miles.

Belton House
- The Administrator
- Grantham, Lincs. NG32 2LS
- 0476 66116

The crowning achievement of Restoration country house architecture, built 1684–88 for Sir John Brownlow; alterations by James Wyatt in 1777; exhibition focusing on the abdication of Edward VIII; formal gardens; orangery; landscaped park with Bellmount Tower; children's TV series *Moondial* filmed here.

N C SUPPORT Study centre; teachers' pack; education officer.

DISABLED FACILITIES Access is difficult: contact the administrator. Adapted toilet. Park, garden and restaurant accessible.

DIRECTIONS Contact the administrator for details.

Berrington Hall
- The Administrator
- Nr Leominster, Hereford & Worcester. HR6 0DW
- 0568 5721

An elegant Neo-classical house of the late 18th century, designed by Henry Holland and set in a landscape by Capability Brown; the formal exterior belies the delicate interior, which has beautifully decorated ceilings and fine furniture; nursery, laundry and pretty tiled dairy; attractive garden with interesting plants.

N C SUPPORT National Curriculum links with History and Environmental Education.

ANNUAL OR ONE OFF EVENT Please contact the National Trust Regional Office, Mythe End House, Tewkesbury, Gloucestershire GL20 6EB (Tel: 0684 850051) for further details.

DISABLED FACILITIES Grounds only. Adapted toilet. Parking for disabled, please enquire at ticket office.

DIRECTIONS Three miles north of Leominster, seven miles south of Ludlow on west side of A49. Bus: Midland Red West 192, 292 Birmingham to Hereford (passing close BR Ludlow and Leominster), alight Luston two miles. BR: Leominster four miles.

VISITS OUT
MIDLANDS

Biddulph Grange Garden
- Bill Makecki or Chris Bedford
- The National Trust, Grange Road, Biddulph, Stoke-on-Trent. ST8 7SD
- 0782 517999

Recently restored High Victorian garden: a series of theme gardens within a garden, including 'China' and 'Egypt'. Interesting example of High Victorian taste. Extensive plant collection. Permanent exhibition.

N C SUPPORT Small geological fossil display.

DISABLED FACILITIES Access for disabled visitors is very difficult due to steep paths and steps. Adapted toilet.

DIRECTIONS Half a mile north of Biddulph, three and a half miles southeast of Congleton, seven miles north of Stoke-on-Trent; signposted off A527.

Birmingham Railway Museum
- Brian Wilkinson
- 670 Warwick Road, Tyseley, Birmingham. B11 2HL
- 021-707 4696

A working museum involved in restoration of locomotives. Driving courses available. Education services.

N C SUPPORT Offering guided 'hands-on' tours. Railway 'Show', worksheets, turntable ride, free coach at 'Headquarters'.

ANNUAL OR ONE OFF EVENT Gala days and Thomas Events. Check dates.

OPENING Daily (except 25–26 December and 1 January) 10.00am–5.00pm.

CATERING Full restaurant service.

COST Children £1.25, adults £2.50, family (two adults and two children) £6.50. Education tours: £1.25.

DISABLED FACILITIES Ramps in some parts at ground level. Gallery not accessible.

DIRECTIONS A41 road next to BR depot three and a half miles from city centre.

Bolsover Castle
- The Head Custodian
- Castle Street, Bolsover, Nr Chesterfield, Derbyshire. S44 6PR
- 0246 823349

An enchanting and romantic spectacle, situated high on a wooded hilltop dominating the surrounding landscape. Built on the site of a Norman castle, this is largely an early 17th-century mansion. Most delightful is the 'Little Castle', a bewitching folly with intricate carvings, frescoes and wall paintings. There is also an impressive 17th-century Indoor Riding School which is still used on occasions.

OPENING All year. Good Friday or 1 April (whichever is earlier) to 30 September: daily 10.00am–6.00pm. 1 October to Maundy Thursday or 31 March (whichever is earlier): Tuesday to Sunday 10.00am–4.00pm. Closed 24–26 December and 1 January.

CATERING Picnic facilities.

DISABLED FACILITIES Wheelchair access to grounds only.

DIRECTIONS In Bolsover, six miles east of Chesterfield on A632 (OS Map 120; ref SK 471707). Bus: East

Midland 81/A/B, Chesterfield Transport 81–3, 281/2 Chesterfield Bolsover (passes close to BR Chesterfield) (Tel: 0332 292200). BR: Chesterfield.

Boscobel House and the Royal Oak
- The Head Custodian
- Brewood, Staffs. ST19 9AR
- 0902 850244

Fully refurnished and restored, the panelled rooms, secret hiding places and pretty gardens lend this 17th-century timber-framed hunting lodge a truly romantic character. Its fame springs from the escapades of the fugitive King Charles II, who hid in the house and the nearby Royal Oak after the Battle of Worcester in 1651 to avoid detection by Cromwell's troops. There is an exhibition in the house.

OPENING All year round. Good Friday or 1 April (whichever is earlier) to 30 September: daily 10.00am–6.00pm. 1 October to Maundy Thursday or 31 March (whichever is earlier): Tuesday to Sunday 10.00am–4.00pm. Closed 24–26 December and 1 January.

CATERING Restaurant/cafe (normally open summer season only, Tuesday to Sunday). Picnic facilities in the gardens in summer.

DISABLED FACILITIES Wheelchair access to gardens only.

DIRECTIONS On unclassified road between A41 and A5, eight miles northwest of Wolverhampton (OS Map 127; ref SJ d837083). BR: Cosford three miles.

British Geological Survey
- Dr Brian J Taylor
- Keyworth, Nottingham. NG12 5GG
- 0602 363100 FAX 0602 363200

The British Geological Survey (BGS) is the UK's 'National Centre for earth science information and expertise'.

N C SUPPORT Provides talks/demonstrations that equate as closely as possible to the National Curriculum.

ANNUAL OR ONE OFF EVENT Contact administrator.

OPENING Office: daily 9.00am–5.30pm.

CATERING At Keyworth there is a cafeteria which can provide sandwiches, hot snacks, main meals, drinks, etc.

COST Free.

DISABLED FACILITIES Ramps and lifts are available so that access to most of the headquarters site is accessible. Other offices may have their own arrangements.

Brockhampton Hall
- The Administrator
- Nr Bromyard, Hereford &Worcester
- 0885 482077

Two thousand-acre traditional estate with superb woodlands, rich in wildlife; includes Lower Brockhampton, a 14th-century timber-framed moated manor house; waymarked walks through the park and woodlands.

N C SUPPORT National Curriculum links with Science, Geography and History. On-site warden. Fieldwork equipment, activity notes.

VISITS OUT
MIDLANDS

DISABLED FACILITIES Contact the administrator for access details.

DIRECTIONS Contact the administrator for details.

Buildwas Abbey
- The Head Custodian
- Nr Ironbridge, Telford, Shrops. TF8 7BW
- 0952 433274

Set beside the River Severn, against a backdrop of wooded grounds, are extensive remains of this Cistercian abbey built in 1135. The remains include the church, which is almost complete except for the roof.

OPENING All year round. Good Friday or 1 April (whichever is earlier) to 30 September: daily 10.00am–6.00pm. 1 October to Maundy Thursday or 31 March (whichever is earlier): Tuesday to Sunday 10.00am–4.00pm. Closed 24–26 December and 1 January.

DISABLED FACILITIES Wheelchair access.

DIRECTIONS On south bank of River Severn on B4378, two miles west of Ironbridge (OS Map 127d; ref SJ 642044). Bus: Williamsons X96 Birmingham to Shrewsbury (passes close to BR Telford Central) (Tel: 0345 056785). BR: Telford Central six miles.

Bushmead Priory
- The Head Custodian
- c/o Blaysworth Manor, Colmworth, Beds. MK44 2LD
- 023062 614

A rare surviving example of the medieval refectory of an Augustinian priory, with its original timber-framed roof almost intact and containing interesting wall paintings and stained glass.

OPENING Summer season: Saturday 10.00am–6.00pm, Sunday 2.00pm–6.00pm.

DIRECTIONS On unclassified road near Colmworth, two miles east of B660 (OS Map 153; ref TL 115607). BR: St Neots, six miles.

Butterfly & Falconry Park
- Peter Worth
- Long Sutton, Spalding, Lincs. PE12 9LE
- 0406 363833 FAX 0406 363182

Great Britain's longest indoor butterfly garden has over 500 butterflies flying freely. In the attractive surroundings of the Park, the falconer gives two displays every day at 12.00 noon and 3.00pm with his eagles, owls and falcons.

N C SUPPORT Free education pack which can be photocopied. Free Nature Trail leaflet.

OPENING Mid-March to end of October: daily 10.00am–6.00pm.

CATERING Indoor and outdoor picnic areas. Tea room seating 150 people.

COST Schools: £1.80 with guide, £1.50 without guide.

DISABLED FACILITIES Yes.

DIRECTIONS Follow signs off A17 at Long Sutton.

Cadbury World
- Margaret Lealan
- PO Box 1958, Linden Road, Bournville, Birmingham. B30 1UX
- 021-458 2000 FAX 021-451 1366

VISITS OUT
MIDLANDS

Cadbury World is a permanent exhibition devoted entirely to chocolate. Where it came from, who first drank this mysterious potion, when it became eating chocolate. The exhibition also includes a history of the Cadbury family.

N C SUPPORT Education packs available.

OPENING Please phone for details. All year.

CATERING Self-service restaurant.

COST 1993 prices: children £2.45, one teacher free with every 15 children, extra adults £3.95.

DISABLED FACILITIES All areas except packaging plant.

DIRECTIONS Close to A38 Bristol Road South, signposted from M5 junction two or four.

Canons Ashby House
- The Administrator
- Daventry, Northants. NN11 6SD
- 0327 860044

Home of the Dryden family since the 16th century; a manor house, c.1550, extended in the 1590s, and altered in the 1630s and c.1710; largely unaltered since. Elizabethan wall paintings and outstanding Jacobean plasterwork; formal garden with terraces, walls and gatepiers of 1710; medieval priory church; 70-acre park.

N C SUPPORT Teachers' pack available.

DISABLED FACILITIES Disabled access. House difficult but please contact Administrator for special arrangements. Adapted toilet.

Taped guide for visually impaired and guidebook for deaf visitors.

DIRECTIONS Easy access from either M40, junction 11, or M1, junction 16. From M1, signposted from A5 two miles south of Weedon crossroads, along unclassified road (three miles) to Banbury. From M40 at Banbury take A422 exit, then left along B4525 and after three miles turn left up unclassified road (signposted). Bus: Saunterbus from Northampton some Sundays (Tel: Northampton 0604 236712). BR: Banbury ten miles.

Charlecote Park
- The Administrator
- Wellesbourne, Warks. CV35 9ER
- 0789 470277

Home of the Lucy family since 1247; present house built in 1550s and visited by Queen Elizabeth I; park, landscaped by Capability Brown, supports herd of red and fallow deer, and a flock of Jacob sheep first introduced in 1756; principal rooms altered 1830s in Elizabethan Revival style.

N C SUPPORT National Curriculum links with History and Environmental Education. Study centre and teachers' pack.

DISABLED FACILITIES Contact the administrator for access details.

DIRECTIONS Contact the administrator for details.

Chatsworth
- S Seligman
- Bakewell, Derbyshire. DE45 1PP
- 0246 582204 FAX 0246 583536

Magnificent stately home with art collection, gardens, waterworks and park. Farmyard and adventure playground, shops and restaurant.

N C SUPPORT Packs, trails, a schools' room and a variety of tours are available to support work in many subjects.

ANNUAL OR ONE OFF EVENT Teachers' Day, angling and country fairs (dates to be confirmed).

OPENING April to October. House and Garden: 11.00am–4.30pm. Farmyard and playground: 10.30am–4.30pm.

CATERING Restaurant and other food outlets.

COST 1993 prices. House and Garden: £2.00–£3.00 per child. Farmyard: £1.60–£1.90.

DISABLED FACILITIES Toilets. Good access to garden. House has 160 steps.

DIRECTIONS Chatsworth is eight miles north of Matlock, off the B6012.

Chedworth Roman Villa
- The Administrator
- Yanworth, Nr Cheltenham, Gloucs. GL54 3LJ
- 024 289 256

The remains of a Romano-British villa; two bathhouses, two dining rooms; fine fourth-century mosaics; useful site museum.

N C SUPPORT National Curriculum links with History. All parties are met for an introduction and discussion. Audio-visual presentation. Teaching notes.

DISABLED FACILITIES All parts accessible but some with difficulty. Adapted toilet in reception building.

DIRECTIONS Three miles northwest of Fossebridge on Cirencester to Northleach road (A429), approach from A429 via Yanworth or from Withington (coaches must avoid Withington). BR: Cheltenham Spa nine miles.

Chestnut Centre
- Booking Office
- Castleton Road, Chapel-en-le-Frith, Derbyshire. SK12 6PE
- 0298 814099 FAX 0298 816213

Situated in the Peak National Park, the Chestnut Centre provides an itinerary for day educational visits which include conducted group tours of nature trails, aviaries and otter pens, etc., dividing into small groups for environmental study periods using the Centre's free brochures and equipment. Closing discussions and question time.

N C SUPPORT Environmental study packs available on request. Welcome teachers on preliminary visits.

OPENING March to December: 10.15am–3.00pm (or earlier to suit school arrangements).

CATERING Lunch: schools bring own packed lunch; Centre will provide free tea, coffee and drinks. There is a study room and picnic area.

COST Children £3.00, staff free.

DISABLED FACILITIES Write and ask for details.

DIRECTIONS Situated in the Peak National Park.

Cider Museum & King Offa Distillery

- Mrs Pauline Dabbs
- 21 Ryelands Street, Hereford, Hereford & Worcester. HR4 0LW
- 0432 354207

Fascinating story of cidermaking from the harvesting, milling and pressing of apples on the farm to hydraulic production in factories. Includes reconstructed farm cider house and original champagne cider cellars.

OPENING April to October: daily 10.00am–5.30pm. November to March: Monday to Saturday 1.00pm–5.00pm. Will open outside normal opening hours for pre-booked groups.

COST Children £1.40, adults £1.95, students £1.40, Senior Citizens £1.40. Group rate: Children 95p, adults £1.40, students 95p, Senior Citizens 95p.

Claydon House

- The Administrator
- Middle Claydon, Buckingham. MK18 2EY
- 0296 730349

Eighteenth-century house containing a series of magnificent and unique Rococo state rooms with carvings; museum with Florence Nightingale and Verney family mementoes.

N C SUPPORT National Curriculum links with Technology, Art, History and Science. Study centre and resource materials.

DISABLED FACILITIES Car park close to front door. Three steps to front door; ramps; then all ground floor rooms accessible. Access to garden via two steps; ramps. Half-price admission to ground floor only. Adapted WC. Guided tours for groups of visually handicapped people by arrangement; Braille guide.

DIRECTIONS In Middle Claydon 13 miles northwest of Aylesbury, three and a half miles southwest of Winslow; signposted from A413, A421 and A41; entrance by north drive only. Bus: Aylesbury Bus 15, 17 from Aylesbury (passing close BR Aylesbury).

Clumber Walk

- The Administrator
- Worksop, Notts. S80 3AZ
- 0909 476592

Three thousand eight hundred acres of parkland with double lime avenue; fine Gothic Revival chapel, built 1886–89 for seventh Duke of Newcastle; house demolished 1938; stable block with restaurant, shop, Information and Warden Centre; classical bridge, temples, lawned Lincoln terrace and pleasure grounds; Vineries and Garden Tools Exhibition: conservation centre.

N C SUPPORT Study centre; children's worksheet; nature trail.

DISABLED FACILITIES Thirteen miles of tarmac roads; most areas accessible; Vineries and Garden Tools Exhibition fully accessible. Restaurant and shop accessible. Wheelchairs (including child size) available to borrow (identification required) from NT shop. Adapted toilets. Visitors with special needs please contact Visitor Liaison Officer.

VISITS OUT
MIDLANDS

DIRECTIONS Four and a half miles southeast of Worksop, six miles southwest of Retford, one mile from A1/A57, 11 miles from M1 junction 30. Bus: Notts CC summer network services from Worksop and other towns to Park: East Midland 33 Worksop to Nottingham (passing close BR Worksop), alight Carburton, one and three-quarter miles (Tel: 0602 240000). BR: Worksop four and a half miles, Retford six and a half miles.

The Cotswold Teddy Bear Museum
- Des Carpenter
- 76 High Street, Broadway, Worcs. WR12 7AJ
- 0386 858 323 FAX 0386 858 112

Museum has a fine collection of teddy bears from 1902 and dolls and toys, many with interesting histories. Reference library of teddies.

OPENING Daily 10.00am–5.00pm.

COST Children (2–14 years) 75p, adults £1.50, Senior Citizens £1.00. Groups of 20 or more: children 50p, adults £1.00, Senior Citizens 75p.

DISABLED FACILITIES None. Small wheelchairs can enter the Museum.

DIRECTIONS A44 from Oxford to Tewkesbury.

Dean Heritage Centre
- Kate Baugh or David Evans
- Camp Mill, Soudley, Nr Cinderford, Gloucestershire. GL14 1BS
- 0594 822170

The story of the forest and its people with forester's cottage and pig, charcoal burners' camp, nature trails. Also craft shops and adventure play area set in the Forest of Dean.

N C SUPPORT Key Stage 2 Victorians and Key Stage 3 Industrial Expansion. Booklets and resource packs, charcoal burning, mining, human influences on forest, iron and coal, tourism and leisure pack.

ANNUAL OR ONE OFF EVENT Special events organised periodically.

OPENING November to March: 10.00am–5.00pm. April to October: 10.00am–6.00pm.

CATERING Picnic tables, barbecues outside. Room in which to eat packed lunches. Cafe for snacks, meals.

COST Children £1.50, adults £2.50, students £2.00. Group discount 10% but not from May to July.

DISABLED FACILITIES Toilet and ramps.

DIRECTIONS On B4227 between Cinderford and A48 at Blakeney.

Derby Industrial Museum
- Sue Christian
- Silk Mill Lane, Off Full Street, Derby. DE1 3AR
- 0332 255308

Standing on the site of the world's oldest factories, the silk mills of 1702 and 1717, the Museum introduces industry in Derbyshire: Rolls-Royce aero engines and railways.

N C SUPPORT Lessons on Industry, Technology and Science are carried out at the Industrial Museum by our education staff and are related to the National Curriculum.

ANNUAL OR ONE OFF EVENT Family Day in July. Demonstrations, working exhibits and 'hands-on' activities.

OPENING Monday 11.00am–5.00pm, Tuesday to Saturday 10.00am–5.00pm, Sunday and bank holiday Mondays 2.00pm–5.00pm.

CATERING None.

COST Children 10p, adults 30p, concessions 10p. Pre-booked educational parties free.

DISABLED FACILITIES Access to all areas open to public. Toilet.

DIRECTIONS Just off A6 in the centre of Derby.

Derby Museum Art Gallery
- Sue Christian
- The Strand, Derby. DE1 1BS
- 0332 255580

Internationally important Joseph Wright and Derby porcelain collections. New 'On the Rocks' gallery. Archaeology including the Roman Military gallery. Intensive temporary exhibition programme. Holiday activities and term-time teaching.

N C SUPPORT Varied programme of lessons for all ages geared to National Curriculum and the Museum's collections. Two education officers. Teachers' booklet and gallery worksheets available.

ANNUAL OR ONE OFF EVENT Family Day 24 July, Carnival Day 13 August, Christmas event 4 December.

OPENING Monday 11.00am–5.00pm, Tuesday to Saturday 10.00am–5.00pm, Sunday 2.00pm–5.00pm.

CATERING None.

COST Free.

DISABLED FACILITIES Lift. Chair lift for wheelchairs. Toilet.

DIRECTIONS Follow signs to city centre. Museum and Art Gallery on corner of the Strand and Cheapside. Nearest parking Bold Lane.

Didcot Railway Centre
- Charles Whetwath
- Didcot, Oxon OX11 7NJ
- 0235 817200 FAX 0235 510621

The Centre is based around the Great Western Railway Engine Shed with Great Western Steam locomotives and trains and many other relics and exhibits from the Steam Age.

N C SUPPORT Visits can be used to support History, Geography, Mathematics and Science topics.

OPENING All year round: weekends. Easter to September: daily. Open daily for pre-booked school parties.

CATERING Lunches and snacks.

COST School parties £3.00, teachers free.

DISABLED FACILITIES Steps at entrance, otherwise level paths around Centre.

DIRECTIONS At Didcot Parkway BR Station. Signposted from M4 (junction 13) 15 miles and A34.

Drayton Manor Theme Park & Zoo
- C E J Bryan, Managing Director
- Drayton Manor Park Limited, Tamworth, Staffs. B78 3TW
- 0827 287979 FAX 0827 288916

VISITS OUT
MIDLANDS

Family Theme Park and Zoo with over 40 major rides including new Splash Canyon rapidride. The Park offers an interesting day out. The Zoo has excellent facilities and education possibilities abound.

N C SUPPORT Education support can be supplied. Requested subjects can be documented ready for a visit. Some dinosaur project papers are available (7–13 yrs).

OPENING Easter to 2 October: daily 9.00am–6.00pm (park and grounds), rides 10.30am–5.00pm (some rides continue until 6.00pm or 7.00pm).

CATERING Full in-house catering from fast food to cafeteria and restaurant, plus parties up to 400.

COST Children £1.50, adults £2.50, Senior Citizens £1.50. Groups of 20 or more: children 75p, adults £1.50, Senior Citizens 75p. Discounts on Pay one Price (please ring).

DISABLED FACILITIES All rides and toilet facilities have access ramps etc.

DIRECTIONS On the A5/A4091 near Fazeley. M42 junctions 9 and 10.

ENGLISH HERITAGE

National Curriculum Support Almost every aspect of the curriculum can be explored at English Heritage properties. They can be used not only for studying History but linked to other subjects as varied as English, Maths, Science, Technology, Geography and Music. English Heritage has produced a wide range of National Curriculum teachers' guides and videos to give plenty of stimulating ideas. Write to English Heritage Education Service, Keysign House, 429 Oxford Street, London W1R 2HD, for a free copy of the resources catalogue.

Annual or one-off event At some sites each year there are special educational events, often with the involvement of experts such as musicians and storytellers, for visiting educational groups.

Cost Student groups and school parties are admitted free to English Heritage properties, but should book in advance through the relevant Regional Office.

See individual entries for all other information.

Ashby de la Zouch Castle
Bolsover Castle
Boscobel House and the Royal Oak
Buildwas Abbey
Bushmead Priory
Goodrich Castle
Hailes Abbey
Haughmond Abbey
Kenilworth Castle
Kirby Hall
Kirby Muxloe Castle
Lincoln Bishops Palace
Longthorpe Tower
Lyddington Bede House
Minster Lovell Hall & Dovecote
Peveril Castle
Rushton Triangular Lodge
Sibsey Trader Windmill
Stokesay Castle
Wall Roman Site (Letocetum)
Wenlock Priory
Witley Court
Wrest Park House & Gardens
Wroxeter Roman City

VISITS OUT
MIDLANDS

Federation of Workers, Writers & Community Publishers
- Tim Diggles
- Tunstall, 23 Victoria Park Road, Stoke-on-Trent. ST6 6DX
- 0782 822327

A federation of over 50 writing and publishing groups dedicated to the aim of making writing and publishing accessible to all.

N C SUPPORT Oral history, poetry, training, experience, publishing skills, almost anything. Writers available.

ANNUAL OR ONE OFF EVENT AGM/Festival of writing held week after Easter.

COST Affiliation is £30 for funded organisations, £15 unfunded (by vote at AGM).

DISABLED FACILITIES We have an Equal Opportunities policy; all events and training are fully accessible.

Forest Enterprise
- F Swain
- Sherwood Pines Forest Park, Sherwood & Lincs Forest District, Edwinstowe, Mansfield, Notts. NG21 9JL
- 0623 822447

Three and a half thousand acres of coniferous and broadleaf woodland; classroom, toilets, playground. Various full- and half-day programmes for schools; also events for the public.

N C SUPPORT School programmes are designed very much with the National Curriculum in mind though they steer clear of simply ticking off Attainment Targets. Support for fieldwork for GCSE/A-Level; also individual support/help for A-Level projects.

OPENING 8.00am to dusk (changes in year due to hours of daylight).

CATERING Cafe.

COST Schools: half day £20.00, full day £35.00, split day £40.00; free when no Ranger is involved.

DISABLED FACILITIES Paths and toilets.

DIRECTIONS The entrance to Sherwood Pines Forest Park is on the B6030 between Clipstone and Edwinstowe. Follow signs to Sherwood Pines. At car park follow the road through the signs which say 'No entry–service vehicles only'. This road leads down to the classroom where there is ample coach parking space.

Forest Enterprise
- Anne Delap, Ranger
- Chapel Hill Farm, Willingham Woods, Market Rasen, Lincs. LN8 3RQ
- 0673 844821

Ancient semi-natural limewoods. Facilities to study botany, birds, butterflies, trees, mammals etc. with schools trail, public trails, wood centre and education ranger services.

N C SUPPORT Cross-curricular.

OPENING All year round: flexible hours to suit visitors. By arrangement with ranger.

COST £10.00 per hour per group (max. group size 35 people).

DISABLED FACILITIES Toilet. Butterfly garden with easy access paths.

Metalled road (circular) through wood.

DIRECTIONS Will be sent on application.

Forest Enterprise
- Andrew Orland
- Forestry Commission, Top Lodge, Fineshade, Corby, Northants. NN17 3BB
- 078 083 394 FAX 078 083 561

Covers woodlands in Leicestershire, South Lincolnshire, North Bedfordshire, North Buckinghamshire and Cambridgeshire as well as Northamptonshire.

N C SUPPORT Led visits available. Regular events in What's On leaflet. Also teachers' pack available free. Send £1.50 in stamps to cover postage. Topic ideas in teachers' pack and suggested activities.

OPENING Woodlands open 24 hours all year round. Contact Education Ranger.

COST Led visits cost £25.00 per half day. Non-led visits free.

DISABLED FACILITIES Easy access trails in some woods. Toilets in some woods. Phone for details.

Forge Mill Needle Museum
- Sue Werner
- Bordesley Abbey Visitors Centre, Needle Mill Lane, Riverside, Redditch, Worcs. B97 6RR
- 0527 62509

Eighteenth-century mill with working waterwheel and machinery. Visitors' Centre uses archaeological evidence to tell the history of nearby Cistercian abbey ruins. Education Officer available. Textiles exhibition; medieval fair.

N C SUPPORT History, RE, Art, Design, Technology, Science, Geography. Teachers' packs available.

ANNUAL OR ONE OFF EVENT Apply for details.

OPENING Monday to Thursday 9.30am–4.30pm. February to November: Saturday and Sunday 2.00pm–5.00pm. 1 April to 30 September: Sunday 2.00pm–5.00pm.

COST 50p per pupil. Additional charges according to activity booked.

DISABLED FACILITIES Adapted toilet. Wheelchair access to basement and ground floor. No lift to first floor.

DIRECTIONS Redditch is signposted off M5 and M42 motorways. Museum off A441 Birmingham road. Please phone for details.

Goodrich Castle
- The Head Custodian
- Goodrich, Ross-on-Wye, Herefordshire. HR9 6HY
- 0600 890538

This magnificent red standstone castle is remarkably complete, with a 12th-century keep and extensive remains from the 13th and 14th centuries. From the battlements there are fine views of the Wye Valley.

OPENING All year round. Good Friday or 1 April (whichever is earlier) to 30

VISITS OUT
MIDLANDS

September: daily 10.00am–6.00pm. 1 October to Maundy Thursday or 31 March (whichever is earlier): Tuesday to Sunday 10.00am–4.00pm. Closed 24–26 December and 1 January.

DIRECTIONS Five miles south of Ross-on-Wye off A40 (OS Map 162; ref SO 579199). Bus: Red and White/Martin's 61 Monmouth to Ross-on-Wye to within half a mile (Ross-on-Wye is linked with Hereford and Gloucester) (Tel: 0905 766800).

Gorse Hill City Farm
- Jenny Rawes
- Anstey Lane, Leicester. LE4 0LF
- 0533 537582

A voluntary community project with small-scale humane farming and organic horticulture. Children are encouraged to touch the rare breeds of animals, see where they sleep and what they eat.

N C SUPPORT Aim to accommodate everyone's needs. Please phone to discuss particular requirements.

OPENING Winter: daily 10.00am–4.00pm. Summer: daily 10.00am–6.00pm.

CATERING Cafe serving teas, coffee, light snacks but flexible to schools' needs.

COST Guided tour: £10 (max 30 pupils). Donations kindly received (suggest 50p per child).

DISABLED FACILITIES Almost full access. Two toilets and parking.

DIRECTIONS The farm is situated on Anstey Lane (B5327) next door to English Martyrs' school lay-by.

Hailes Abbey
- The Head Custodian
- Nr Winchcombe, Cheltenham, Glos. GL54 5PB
- 0242 602398

Set in attractive wooded pastureland, the remains of the cloisters and foundations, with examples of high quality sculpture in the site museum, show visitors the extent of the wealth of this 13th-century Cistercian abbey.

OPENING All year round. Good Friday or 1 April (whichever is earlier) to 30 September: daily 10.00am–6.00pm. 1 October to Maundy Thursday or 31 March (whichever is earlier): Tuesday to Sunday 10.00am–4.00pm. Closed 24–26 December and 1 January.

DISABLED FACILITIES Personal stereo tours are available for those in wheelchairs. General access, one step to museum.

DIRECTIONS Two miles northeast of Winchcombe off B4632 (OS Map 150; ref SP 050300). Bus: Castleways from Cheltenham to within one and a half miles (Tel: 0242 602949). BR: Cheltenham ten miles.

Haughmond Abbey
- The Head Custodian
- Upton Magna, Uffington, Shrewsbury, Shrops. SY4 4RW
- 0743 77661

Set in pleasant wooded countryside, there are extensive remains of this 12th-century Augustinian abbey, including the chapter House which retains its late medieval timber ceiling, and some fine medieval sculpture.

OPENING All year round. Good Friday or 1 April (whichever is earlier) to 30 September: daily 10.00am–6.00pm. 1 October to Maundy Thursday or 31 March (whichever is earlier): Tuesday to Sunday 10.00am–4.00pm. Closed 24–26 December and 1 January.

DISABLED FACILITIES Wheelchair access.

DIRECTIONS Three miles northeast of Shrewsbury off B5062 (OS Map 126; ref SJ 542152). Bus: Shearings from Shrewsbury (Tel: 0345 056785). BR: Shrewsbury three and a half miles.

Eve: weekends and school holidays only. Closed January to Good Friday. Groups: other times by arrangement.

COST Children (5–16) 75p, adults £1.50, Senior Citizens £1.00. Schools: children 75p, accompanying adults free. Groups of ten or more 10% discount (not school parties).

DISABLED FACILITIES Access for wheelchairs. Assistance given if required.

DIRECTIONS A46, A15 or A158 to Lincoln. Trains to Lincoln. Uphill, near Cathedral, Castle opposite car park at foot of castle wall.

The Incredibly Fantastic Old Toy Show

- Hattie Hutchinson
- 26 Westgate, Lincoln. LN1 3BD
- 0522 520534

Entertaining and educational talk/display of moving toys for school parties. Includes tinplate, lead, balancing, clockwork, battery toys, illustrating cogs and centrifugal force. Qualified teacher encourages interactive response from children.

N C SUPPORT Talk and worksheets cover movement, forces, materials, History, play, Design, creative and oral work, observation.

ANNUAL OR ONE OFF EVENT The varied collection of toys dating from 1780s–1960s gives scope for research into Social History, Childhood, Design. The owner, Ross Hichinson, has expert knowledge of the collection.

OPENING Easter Saturday to end September: Tuesday to Saturday 11.00am–5.00pm, Sunday and bank holiday Monday 12.00 noon–4.00pm. 1 October to Christmas

To experience is to understand

Entrance gates produced by the Coalbrookdale Company for the Great Exhibition of 1851.

Technology, History, Science, Art... at Ironbridge.

- Guidelines by Key Stages
- Information packs
- Data bases
- Workshops
- Free planning visits
- Booking essential

THE IRONBRIDGE GORGE MUSEUM

Ironbridge Gorge Museum Trust, Education Dept., Ironbridge, Telford, Shropshire, TF8 7AW. Tel: 0952 433522

VISITS OUT
MIDLANDS

Ironbridge Gorge
- Diane Illingworth
- Museum Trust, Illingworth, The Wharfage, Telford, Shropshire. TF8 7AW
- 0952 433522 FAX 0952 432204

World Heritage site interpreting the Industrial Revolution and Victorian Britain across six main museums. Major opportunities to work across all Key Stages in History, Geography, Technology, Science and Art.

N C SUPPORT Guidelines for Teachers: under fives; Key Stages 1 and 2. Information files: Key Stages 1–3. Databases: Key Stages 2 and 3. Individual group support provided where necessary, appropriate and possible. Use of Library and archives.

OPENING Winter: daily 10.00am–5.00pm. Summer: daily 10.00am–6.00pm.

COST School trips: 35% discount in winter, 25% in spring and autumn, 5% in summer.

DISABLED FACILITIES Facilities, including wheelchairs, available at most sites.

DIRECTIONS M54 to Telford, then follow extensive signing to Museums.

Ironbridge Toy Museum
- Bernard Beech
- The Square, Ironbridge, Shropshire. TF8 7AQ
- 0952 433926

This bright and cheerful museum overlooks the famous Ironbridge, contains a large collection of toys from Victorian times to the present day and should appeal to all ages.

N C SUPPORT The topic of toys is extremely popular with infant and junior schools and the Museum welcomes school parties and provides facilities for 'hands-on' experience using old toys.

OPENING Daily (except Christmas Day) 10.00am–5.00pm.

COST Children 50p, adults £1.00, no group rates but teachers/helpers accompanying schools are free.

DISABLED FACILITIES Limited access.

DIRECTIONS In the centre of Ironbridge.

Jewellery Quarter
- Hamish Wood
- Discovery Centre, 77–79 Vyse Street, Birmingham. B18 6HA
- 021-554 3598 FAX 021-236 1766

An industrial Marie Celeste. Explore a jewellery factory frozen in time from the turn of the century and undisturbed after closure.

N C SUPPORT Excellent resource for studying the Victorians, Technology, Business and Geography. All visits receive a guided tour. Teachers' pack and study material available.

ANNUAL OR ONE OFF EVENT Jewellery Quarter Festival in June, workshops and exhibitions.

OPENING Monday to Friday 10.00am–4.00pm.

CATERING Tea and coffee available. Several cafes close to the museum.

COST Adults £2.00, students £1.50, 10% group discount. Special rates on request.

VISITS OUT
MIDLANDS

DISABLED FACILITIES Full access for disabled, lift, ramps, toilet, audio guides.

DIRECTIONS Close to Birmingham city centre. Follow signs for Jewellery Quarter and Hockley.

Kenilworth Castle
☛ The Head Custodian
✉ Kenilworth, Warwickshire. CV8 1NE
☎ 0926 52078

The dramatic red sandstone ruins of this great castle rise above rich green pastureland, with massive walls up to 20 feet thick and a 12th-century keep. There are impressive remains of the state rooms built and furnished by Elizabeth I's visits to Robert Dudley, Earl of Leicester, who was the Queen's favourite. There is a site exhibition.

OPENING All year round. Good Friday or 1 April (whichever is earlier) to 30 September: daily 10.00am–6.00pm. 1 October to Maundy Thursday or 31 March (whichever is earlier): Tuesday to Sunday 10.00am–4.00pm. Closed 24–26 December and 1 January.

DISABLED FACILITIES Personal stereo tour available for the partially sighted and those with learning difficulties.

DIRECTIONS In Kenilworth (OS Map 140; ref SP 278723). Bus: Midland Red X17/19, 18; Stratford Blue X16, G&G X12, 63B Coventry to Leamington Spa (Tel: 0788 535555). BR: Warwick five miles.

Kirby Hall
☛ The Head Custodian
✉ Deene, Nr Corby, Northants. NN17 3EN
☎ 0536 203230

Outstanding example of a large, stone-built Elizabethan mansion, begun in 1570 with 17th-century alterations. There are fine gardens, currently being restored.

OPENING All year. Good Friday or 1 April (whichever is earlier) to 30 September: daily 10.00am–6.00pm. 1 October to Maundy Thursday or 31 March (whichever is earlier): Tuesday to Sunday 10.00am–4.00pm. Closed 24–26 December and 1 January.

DISABLED FACILITIES Wheelchair access to grounds, gardens and ground floor only.

DIRECTIONS On unclassified road off A43 four miles northeast of Corby (OS Map 141; ref SP 926927).

Kirby Muxloe Castle
☛ The Head Custodian
✉ Oakcroft Avenue, Kirby Muxloe, Leics. LE9 9DM
☎ 0533 386886

Picturesque, moated, brick-built castle begun in 1480 by William Lord Hastings. Potentially a residence of grandeur and considerable strength, it was left unfinished after Hastings was executed in 1483.

OPENING All year. Good Friday or 1 April (whichever is earlier) to 30 September: daily 10.00am–6.00pm. 1 October to Maundy Thursday or 31 March (whichever is earlier): Tuesday to Sunday 10.00am–4.00pm. Closed 24–26 December and 1 January.

VISITS OUT
MIDLANDS

DIRECTIONS Four miles west of Leicester off B5380 (OS Map 140; ref SK 524046). Bus: Midland Fox 63, Citybus 152/3 from Leicester (Tel: 0533 313391). BR: Leicester five miles.

Leighton Lady Cruises
- Suzanne Thodey
- Brantoms Wharf, Canal Side, Leighton Buzzard, Beds. LU7 3BR
- 0525 384563

The 'Leighton Lady' is a 70-foot narrowboat and retains the canal tradition of polished brasses and bright paintwork. The Grand Union Canal is mellowed with occasional locks. Maximum 54 passengers.

N C SUPPORT A school canal trip is of geographical, historical and some scientific interest. Worksheets relate to the National Curriculum and pupils are welcome to ask questions. Map included in worksheet.

OPENING All year round.

CATERING Bar on board, tea, coffee, picnics aboard, pre-ordered buffets.

COST 1 hour £80, 2 hours £105, 3 hours £130.

DIRECTIONS Centre of Leighton Buzzard on A4146 below canal bridge.

Lincoln Bishops Palace
- The Head Custodian
- Minster Yard, Lincoln. LN2 1PU
- 0522 527468

In the shadow of Lincoln Cathedral are the remains of this medieval palace of the bishops of Lincoln.

OPENING Summer season. Good Friday or 1 April (whichever is earlier) to 30 September: daily 10.00am–6.00pm.

CATERING Picnic facilities.

DIRECTIONS South side of Lincoln Cathedral (OS MAP 121; ref SK 981717). Bus: from surrounding areas (Tel: 0522 553135).

Little Moreton Hall
- The Administrator
- Congleton, Cheshire. CW12 4SD
- 0260 272018

Begun in the 15th century, one of the most perfect examples of a timber-framed moated manor house in the country; remarkable carved gables; restored 16th-century wall paintings; long wainscoted gallery, chapel, great hall and knotgarden.

N C SUPPORT National Curriculum links with History, Technology and Art.

ANNUAL OR ONE OFF EVENT Study centre; teachers' resource book; children's guide.

DISABLED FACILITIES Contact the administrator for access details.

DIRECTIONS Contact the administrator for details.

Longshaw Estate
- The Administrator
- Sheffield. S11 7TZ
- 0433 31708

Sixteen hundred acres of open moorland, woodland and farms; dramatic views and varied walking. Stone for the Derwent and Howden Dams was quarried from Bolehill, and millstones may be seen in quarries on the estate; there is a quarry winding-house above Grindleford station.

DISABLED FACILITIES Carriage drives only suitable; disabled visitors may be driven to Visitor Centre and toilets. Drivers must, however, return and park in main car park, unless only visiting toilet.

DIRECTIONS Seven and a half miles from Sheffield, next to A625 Sheffield to Hathersage road; Woodcroft car park is off B6055, 200 yards south of junction with A625. Bus: Mainline 240 Sheffield to Bakewell (passing BR Grindleford), Mainline Hulley's 272 Sheffield to Castleton (passing BR Hathersage); all pass close BR Sheffield (Tel: 0298 23098).

Longthorpe Tower
- The Head Custodian
- Thorpe Road, Longthorpe, Peterborough. PE1 1HA
- 0733 268482

The finest example of 14th-century domestic wall paintings in northern Europe. The tower, with the Great Chamber that contains the paintings, is part of a fortified manor house. Special exhibitions are held in the upper floor.

OPENING Summer season: Good Friday or 1 April (whichever is earlier) to 30 September: daily 10.00am–6.00pm.

DIRECTIONS Two miles west of Peterborough on A47 (OS Map 142; ref TL 163983). Bus: Viscount 14/A 303 from Peterborough (Tel: 0733 545711). BR: Peterborough one and a half miles.

Lyddington Bede House
- The Head Custodian
- Blue Coat Lane, Uppingham, Lyddington, Leics. LE15 9LZ
- 057282 2438

Set among picturesque golden stone cottages, beside a handsome parish church of St Andrew, the Bede House was originally a medieval palace of the bishops of Lincoln. It was later converted into an almshouse.

OPENING Summer season. Good Friday or 1 April (whichever is earlier) to 30 September: daily 10.00am–6.00pm.

DISABLED FACILITIES Wheelchair access to ground floor rooms only.

DIRECTIONS In Lyddington, six miles north of Corby, one mile east of A6003 (OS Map 141; ref SP 875970). Bus: Fairfax 'Rutland Flyer' Corby Mowbray (Tel: 0533 313391).

Mappin Art Gallery
- Vivienne Sillar, Art Ed Officer
- Sheffield Arts Department, Weston Park, Sheffield. S10 2TP
- 0742 734789 FAX 0742 735994

The Mappin Art Gallery is set in Weston Park, next door to the Sheffield City Museum. The Gallery displays changing exhibitions/displays of contemporary art.

N C SUPPORT INSET training days for teachers. Materials trolley (paper, pencil, crayon, pastel, charcoal) available for pre-booked school/college groups, and INSET training days.

VISITS OUT

MIDLANDS

ANNUAL OR ONE OFF EVENT None.

OPENING Tuesday to Saturday 10.00am–5.00pm, Sunday 2.00pm–5.00pm, closed Monday except bank holidays.

CATERING If booked in advance to do practical work in the Galleries, schools/college groups can eat packed lunches in the Galleries in bad weather. Cafe for public.

COST Admission free to Galleries; occasionally an admission charge may be made for a special exhibition.

DISABLED FACILITIES Ramp and toilet near Museum entrance. Direct access (no steps) from Museum to Mappin Art Gallery.

DIRECTIONS One mile from city centre near Sheffield University.

Minster Lovell Hall & Dovecote

- The Head Custodian
- Minster Lovell, Nr Witney, Oxon. OX8 5RN
- 0993 775315

The handsome ruins of Lord Lovell's 15th-century manor house stand in a lovely setting on the banks of the River Windrush. A delightful medieval dovecote with nesting boxes is nearby.

OPENING Summer season. 1 April to 30 September: Thursday–Sunday and bank holidays 10.00am–6.00pm.

DIRECTIONS Adjacent to Minster Lovell church, three miles west of Witney off A40 (OS Map 164; ref SP 324114). Bus: Swanbrook Oxford to Tewkesbury (Tel: 0242 574444). BR: Charlbury seven miles.

Moseley Old Hall

- The Administrator
- Moseley Old Hall Lane, Fordhouses, Wolverhampton, Staffs. WV10 7HY
- 0902 782808

Brick-clad timber-framed house where Charles II hid after the Battle of Worcester; the bed in which he slept is on view, also the hiding place he used; small garden reconstructed in 17th-century style with knot garden and period plants.

N C SUPPORT National Curriculum links with History and English.

ANNUAL OR ONE OFF EVENT Teachers' resource book; education officer; living history days.

DISABLED FACILITIES Access to ground floor (three rooms) and garden only. Adapted toilet in garden. Braille and large print guides.

DIRECTIONS Four miles north of Wolverhampton; south of M54 between A449 and A460. Traffic from north on M6 leave motorway at Shareshill then A460; two and a half miles south of Shareshill island. Traffic from south on M6 and M54 take junction one to Wolverhampton. Coaches must approach via A460 to avoid low bridge. BR: Wolverhampton four miles.

Naseby Battle & Farm Museum

- E H Westaway
- Ivydene, High Street, Naseby, Northampton. NN6 7DD
- 0604 740241

Here the events of the great Battle of Naseby, which decided the fate of

England's Civil War in 1645, are recaptured and retold. And here, in a farm, in a village, the commonplace things of a few generations back recall a way of farming and a way of rural life now vanished.

N C SUPPORT None.

OPENING Easter to September: Sunday, Monday and bank holiday 2.00pm–5.00pm. Other times for parties by prior arrangement.

CATERING None.

COST Children 50p, adults £1.00.

DISABLED FACILITIES None.

DIRECTIONS At Purlieu Farm south of Naseby Village just off B4036 Daventry Market Harboro Road.

The National Snail Farming Centre

- Mr Tony Vaughan
- L'Escargot Anglais, Redewhill, Hereford. HR4 7DN
- 0432 760218 FAX 0432 760218

Exhibition of indoor and outdoor snail farming and guided tours of farm. Exhibition of wild British snails, both live and shells, and nature trail and guides of habitats containing wild snails.

Detailed research into a variety of British snails and their habitats and their place in nature. On Business Studies: setting up and running small business.

N C SUPPORT Science KS Attainment Target 1, levels 3 and 5. Attainment Target 2, levels 1–6.

OPENING October to April: Monday–Friday 11.00am–5.00pm. May to September: daily 11.00am–5.00pm.

COST Children (8–13 yrs) £1.00, adults £1.50, 20% discount for groups of 20 or more.

DISABLED FACILITIES None.

DIRECTIONS A480 roughly five miles from Hereford city centre in northwesterly direction. On left hand side.

National Tramway Museum

- D Lardge
- Crich, Matlock, Derbyshire. DE4 5DP
- 0773 852565 FAX 0773 852326

A unique open-air working Museum with 50 vintage horse, steam and electric tramcars. An electric tram service operates every few minutes, and all rides are free. Exhibition Hall, video theatre, depots, refreshments and shops available.

N C SUPPORT Information and activity pack covering appropriate core and foundation subjects up to Key Stage 2/3. Local schools may borrow artefacts on application. A resource pack containing documents and photographic material is available for £2.50. Local schools are able to borrow artefacts on application.

OPENING 10.00am–5.30pm.

CATERING Refreshments and shops.

COST About 15% discount off normal admission price. Car and coach parking free.

DISABLED FACILITIES Access ramps and toilets for disabled. Please note that all vintage trams have high steps for boarding and cannot carry wheelchairs.

DIRECTIONS Off M1 at junction 28 onto A38 to Ripley and follow tourist signs. Off A6 going north at Whatstandwell.

NATIONAL TRUST

Opening Times Write or telephone the administrator of the house, give preferred day and time, the size and age of the group, and the main purpose of the visit. *The National Trust Handbook* contains further relevant information.

Cost Unless otherwise stated in the *Handbook*, there is a reduction of around 50% for children aged 16 and under, when accompanied by their teacher. Education Group Members are admitted free. However, please note that there may be a small charge for any additional educational facilities or activities.

See individual entries for all other information.

Baddesley Clinton
Belton House
Berrington Hall
Biddulph Grange Garden
Brockhampton Hall
Canons Ashby House
Charlecote Park
Chedworth Roman Villa
Claydon House
Clumber Walk
Little Moreton Hall
Longshaw Estate
Moseley Old Hall
Sherbourne Park Estate
Shugborough
Snowshill Manor
South Peak Estate
Sudbury Hall & Museum of Childhood
Upton House
Wightwick Manor

The National Waterways Museum

- P M Williams
- Llanthony Warehouse, Gloucester Docks, Gloucester. GL1 2EN
- 0452 307009 FAX 0452 300072

The story of British canals illustrated by a wealth of original material. Interactive displays, archive film and working exhibits cover the history of 200 years of technological change.

N C SUPPORT The Museum covers a wide variety of National Curriculum areas. Special workshop sessions arranged for pupils with activities linked to National Curriculum requirements.

OPENING Summer: daily 10.00am–6.00pm. Winter: daily 10.00am–5.00pm.

CATERING The Waterside Cafe serves everything from a pot of tea to a full range of appetising snacks and meals.

COST Children £2.95, adults £3.95, Senior Citizens £2.95, family £9.50 (2 adults and 2 children), Saturday Shopper £8.00 (1 adult and 2 children). Group discount: school groups £1.70, children £1.75, adults £2.95, Senior Citizens £1.75.

DISABLED FACILITIES Full access.

DIRECTIONS From motorways follow brown 'Historical Docks' signs.

VISITS OUT
MIDLANDS

Nuclear Electric plc
- Delia Brotherton
- Barnett Way, Barnwood, Gloucester. GL4 7RS
- 0452 652618 FAX 0452 652674

Free talks service at school locations. Visits at any one of eight power station visitor centres around the country.

N C SUPPORT Educational material available.

OPENING Daily except Christmas Day, Boxing Day and New Year's Day.

CATERING Please bring refreshments.

COST Free.

DISABLED FACILITIES All visitor centres suitable for disabled visitors.

DIRECTIONS Please contact Delia Brotherton.

Oswestry Transport Museum
- David Higman
- Oswald Road, Oswestry, Shropshire. SY11 1RE
- 0691 671749

Over 100 bicycles on display: History and Development of the Bicycle. Twelve engines on site plus rolling stock. Cambrian Railways Museum: History of the Line. Rides available late 1994.

N C SUPPORT Suitable for 5–10-year-olds, History of Transport as the bicycle is one of the foundation stones.

ANNUAL OR ONE OFF EVENT Special Steam Days throughout the year.

OPENING Daily 10.00am–4.00pm.

COST Children 50p, adults £1.50, teachers/helpers free.

DISABLED FACILITIES No special facilities but people with disabilities welcome.

DIRECTIONS Oswestry town centre near bus station.

Peak District Mining Museum & Temple Mine
- Jo Anderson
- The Pavilion, Matlock Bath, Derbyshire. DE4 3PS
- 0629 583834

A museum where visitors can touch everything and handle the evidence left behind by miners and be drawn into a world now partly forgotten.

N C SUPPORT Under review.

OPENING Daily (except Christmas Day) 10.00am–4.00pm.

CATERING None.

COST Museum or Mine: children 80p, adults £1.20, groups 70p. Joint entry: children £1.80, adults £2.00, groups £1.20.

DISABLED FACILITIES Wheelchair access.

DIRECTIONS North on A6 from Derby towards Matlock.

Peak National Park
- Richard Campen, Educational Visits Manager
- Environmental Education Service, Losehill Hall, The Peak National Park Centre, Castleton, Derbyshire. S30 2WB
- 0433 620 373 FAX 0433 620 346

Day-long and residential programmes, including farm visits, role-play introducing National Park issues and conflicts, environmental activity and field study days for junior schools. GCSE and A-Level groups.

N C SUPPORT All activities are designed to meet National Curriculum Attainment Targets in a number of subjects.

OPENING All year; advanced booking for programmes essential.

CATERING None.

COST Prices vary according to type of visit. Please write for details.

DISABLED FACILITIES Limited access.

DIRECTIONS Eleven miles west of Sheffield on the A625.

Peveril Castle
- The Head Custodian
- Market Place, Castleton, Nr Sheffield. S30 2WX
- 0433 620613

There are breathtaking views of the Peak District from this castle, perched high above the pretty village of Castleton. The great square tower stands almost to its original height.

OPENING All year. Good Friday or 1 April (whichever is earlier) to 30 September: daily 10.00am–6.00pm. 1 October to Maundy Thursday or 31 March (whichever is earlier): Tuesday–Sunday 10.00am–4.00pm. Closed 24–26 December and 1 January.

COST Student groups and school parties are admitted free to English Heritage properties, but should book in advance through the relevant Regional Office.

DIRECTIONS On south side of Castleton 15 miles west of Sheffield on A625 (OS Map 110; ref SK 150827). Bus: Mainline/Hulleys/Chesterfield Transport 272/4. BR: Hope two and a half miles.

Pickford's House Museum
- Sue Christian
- 41 Friar Gate, Derby. DE1 1DA
- 0332 255363

Museum of social history and costume in Georgian townhouse. Period room including working kitchen. Changing costume displays. Toy theatres. Temporary exhibitions. Georgian garden. Special events and education programme.

N C SUPPORT Programme for History KS, 2 and 3, Science, Technology. Costume sessions for textile students to degree level. Education officers' worksheets.

OPENING Monday 11.00am–5.00pm, Tuesday to Saturday 10.00am–5.00pm, Sunday 2.00pm–5.00pm.

CATERING None.

COST Children (over 11) 10p, adults 30p. No charge if school party is booked in advance.

DISABLED FACILITIES Ramped access to ground floor and garden only. Taped commentary for visually impaired visitors.

DIRECTIONS Right hand side of Friar Gate A52 to Ashbourne. Parking at rear of houses.

Preston Montford Field Studies
- Adrian Bayley
- Council Centre, Montford Bridge, Shrewsbury, Shrops. SY4 1DX
- 0743 850380

A Field Centre, part of a network of Field Studies Council study centres, providing tailor-made courses in environmental topics to suit schools' curriculum needs.

N C SUPPORT Courses can be designed to suit all Key Stages on a day or residential basis. There is a long tradition of A-Level provision with specialist courses in Geography and Biology. INSET provision and student courses available.

OPENING End January to beginning of December.

CATERING Fully catered courses are offered as part of the package.

COST Full costs available on application.

DISABLED FACILITIES Limited special facilities are available.

DIRECTIONS The Centre is 12 miles from the end of the M54. BR: from London, Cardiff and Manchester.

Rockingham Castle
- Kay Barton
- Market Harborough, Leics. LE16 5TH
- 0536 7702040 FAX 0536 771692

Rockingham, on its hilltop site, encapsulates 900 years of history. Holder of the Sandford Awards for Heritage Education; special education pack of 287 booklets available, £7.50.

N C SUPPORT Rockingham combines the magic of a castle with a living interpretation of the National Curriculum History course. The Norman, Tudor, Civil War and Victorian periods are particularly well evidenced. Rockingham is an excellent resource for History, Art, Drama and Literary studies and can provide a stimulating background for creative work in these fields.

ANNUAL OR ONE OFF EVENT A Civil War Siege Re-enactment weekend and a 15th-century Living History weekend are held annually in July.

OPENING Daily by appointment for parties.

COST Students £1.45. Minimum school group 25.

DISABLED FACILITIES Adapted toilets. Ramps provided. Please contact for further details.

DIRECTIONS Two miles north of Corby, eight miles from Kettering on A6003.

Rover Group Ltd
- Mrs S Shattock
- Education Partnership Centre, Cowley, Oxford. OX4 5NL
- 0865 746479

N C SUPPORT A centre dedicated to supporting curriculum studies, at all Key Stages in any subject. Students can, as part of a planned module, visit design, tooling production and commercial functions, according to subject matter. Support for students' individual projects.

OPENING Monday to Thursday 9.00am–4.00pm.

COST Free.

DISABLED FACILITIES Access OK. Toilets five minutes away.

DIRECTIONS Gate 5; access off Horspath Road roundabout, eastern bypass.

Royal Show
- Press Officer
- National Agricultural Centre, Stoneleigh Park, Warwickshire. CV8 2LZ
- 0203 696969 FAX 0203 696900

The country's largest agricultural exhibition, covering all aspects of food, farming and the countryside.

N C SUPPORT Information available from the Royal Agricultural Society of England. Also schools may participate in the Schools Challenge Scheme which encompasses the Royal Show.

OPENING Daily from 8.00am. No admittance after 6.00pm.

CATERING Various outlets around the showground.

COST Children (under 16) £5, adults £10, Senior Citizens £5. School party discounts available.

DISABLED FACILITIES Disabled transport service available.

DIRECTIONS Five entrances to car parks, signposted off the A46, A45 and the B4113.

Rugby School
- Graham Hedges
- Rugby, Warwickshire. CV22 5EH
- 0788 565871 FAX 0788 565871

Guided tour of the older buildings including two chapels and Old Big School. Enthralling school museum includes football memorabilia and reminders of Rupert Brooke.

OPENING 1 April to 30 September: Tuesday to Saturday 1.30pm–5.00pm. 1 October to 31 March: Saturday 10.00am–4.00pm.

COST Museum plus tour: adults £2.50, concessions £1.50, 50p discount for groups of 20 or more.

DIRECTIONS Rugby town centre.

Rushton Triangular Lodge
- The Head Custodian
- Desborough Road, Rushton, Nr Kettering, Northants. NN14 1RP
- 0536 710761

This extraordinary building was built by the Roman Catholic Sir Thomas Tresham on his return in 1593 from imprisonment for his religious beliefs. It symbolises the Holy Trinity: it has three sides, three floors, trefoil windows and three triangular gables on each side.

OPENING Summer season. Good Friday or 1 April (whichever is earlier) to 30 September: daily 10.00am–6.00pm.

DIRECTIONS One mile west of Rushton, on an unclassified road three miles from Desborough on A6 (OS Map 141; ref SP 830831). Bus: UC Kettering to Market Harborough, alight Desborough, then two miles (Tel: 0536 512411). BR: Kettering five miles.

Ruskin Gallery & Craft Gallery
- Vivienne Sillar, Art Education Officer
- Sheffield Arts Department, 101 Norfolk Street, Sheffield. S1 2JE
- 0742 734789 FAX 0742 735994

In the City Centre, the Ruskin Gallery houses the collection of the Guild of St George, created by John Ruskin. Changing displays and exhibitions.

OPENING Monday to Saturday 10.00am–5.00pm (including bank

VISITS OUT
MIDLANDS

holidays, excluding Christmas), closed Sunday.

CATERING None. Packed lunches cannot be eaten in the Ruskin Gallery or Ruskin Craft Gallery.

COST Admission free to Galleries; occasionally an admission charge may be made for a special exhibition.

DISABLED FACILITIES Ramp at Tudor Square entrance. Toilet.

DIRECTIONS In city centre, near Crucible and Lyceum Theatres. Limited on-street 'Pay and Display' (one-hour) parking in nearby streets.

Ryton Organic Gardens
- Peter Clark
- Ryton-on-Dunsmore, Coventry. CV8 3LG
- 0203 303517 FAX 0203 639229

Ten acres of gardens and demonstrations showing all aspects of organic gardening. Learn how to make compost from garden and kitchen waste and how to control plant problems without harmful sprays.

N C SUPPORT Information pamphlets (50p each) on wide range of organic topics. Worksheets (£1 each, photocopyable).

ANNUAL OR ONE OFF EVENT Annual: Organic Gardening Weekends, Apple Day, Wine Fair. Various one-off events.

OPENING Daily 10.00am–5.30pm (last admission to gardens is 5.00pm or dusk if earlier).

CATERING Restaurant (80 seats). Picnic area.

COST School visits free. Guided tour: £1.00 per person. Prior booking essential.

DISABLED FACILITIES Easy access. Toilet.

DIRECTIONS Take the B4029 road to Wolston, off the A45, five miles southeast of Coventry. Look for the brown 'Ryton Gardens' signs.

Sheffield Industrial Museum at Kelham Island
- Robin Fielder
- Off Alma Street, Sheffield. S3 8RY
- 0742 722106

Growth of the city of steel and cutlery in the age of steam power. The largest working steam engine in Britain; working knife and surgical instrument makers; Bessemer convertor and crucibles. Victorian street and workshops.

N C SUPPORT Teachers' guide notes. Object handling sessions or talks can be arranged. History: Victorians and Expansion; Trade and Industry; Science: Forces and Materials; Technology projects.

OPENING Monday to Thursday 10.00am–4.00pm, Sunday 11.00am–4.00pm, closed Friday and Saturday.

CATERING Lunch room for sandwiches (must be booked). Cafe for adults and small groups.

COST School groups and full-time students 85p. Free pre-visits to leaders of booked groups (enquire for individual rates).

DISABLED FACILITIES Most of the Museum is accessible to wheelchairs. Toilet. A good venue

VISITS OUT
MIDLANDS

for visually impaired: plenty of sounds, smells and things to touch.

DIRECTIONS Half a mile northwest of Sheffield city centre.

Sheffield Ski Village
- J Fleetham or T Richardson
- Vale Road, Parkwood Springs, Sheffield. S11 9SE
- 0742 769459 FAX 0742 760413

The UK's only artificial ski resort comprising six individual ski runs of varying difficulty. Alpine lodge provides bars, cafe, diner, saunas, shops and gym. Sledging and artificial snowballs available.

N C SUPPORT Over 600 children on curricular ski programmes and 300 non-curricular. Duke of Edinburgh's Award Scheme.

ANNUAL OR ONE OFF EVENT British Snowboard Championships, National University Championships, Freestyle Championships, National Mogul Competition, Festival of Disabled Skiing.

OPENING Daily 9.00am–10.30pm.

CATERING Cafe, diner, bars, vending machines, barbecue gazebo and snackshack.

COST £3.30 including instruction, £5.50 for 2 hours, teachers/organisers ski for free.

DISABLED FACILITIES Total wheelchair access to all areas. Ski club for people with disabilities and specialist equipment including sit-ski sledges.

DIRECTIONS Located one mile north of Sheffield city centre just off the A61. Ten minutes drive from M1 junction 33.

Sherbourne Park Estate
- The Administrator
- Sherbourne, Cheltenham, Gloucs
- 0451 844257

Four thousand-acre working Cotswold estate, including the village of Sherbourne. The River Windrush and Sherbourne Brook flow through the estate, which has areas of parkland and woodland as well as waymarked walks; information leaflets available.

N C SUPPORT National Curriculum links with Geography, Science, History and Environmental Education. Study centre. On-site warden, fieldwork equipment, activity notes.

DISABLED FACILITIES Contact the administrator for access details.

DIRECTIONS Contact the administrator for details.

Sherwood Forest Farm Park
- Felicity Shaw Browne
- Lamb Pens Farm, Edwinstowe, Mansfield, Notts. NG21 9HL
- 0623 823558

Collection of many different rare and interesting breeds of farm animals in secluded lakeside setting. Facilities for all ages of children.

N C SUPPORT National Curriculum-related school packs available free of charge. Contain detailed information about animals on display. Complimentary tickets for preliminary visit, word searches, quizzes, etc.

OPENING April to mid-October: daily from 9.30am by arrangement.

VISITS OUT
MIDLANDS

CATERING Cafeteria serving hot and cold drinks, home-made cakes, sandwiches and light snacks.

COST 1993 prices: £1.25 per head for groups of 20 and over (including accompanying adults).

DISABLED FACILITIES Fully fitted toilet.

DIRECTIONS Just off A6075 between Edwinstowe and Mansfield-Woodhouse.

Shugborough
- The Administrator
- Milford, Nr Stafford. ST17 0XB
- 0889 881388

Eighteenth-century home of the Earls of Lichfield; enlarged c.1750, altered by Samuel Wyatt 1790–1806. Staffordshire County Museum with re-creations of 19th-century life; original kitchens, laundry and brewhouse; Georgian farmstead with rare breeds of livestock and working flourmill.

N C SUPPORT National Curriculum links with Art and History. Study centre; teachers' pack; education officer.

DISABLED FACILITIES Servants' quarters and farm accessible (reduced admission charge); access can be arranged to the ground floor of the house for wheelchairs by way of a step-climber. Adapted WC. Braille, taped and large-print guides.

DIRECTIONS Signed from M6; six miles east of Stafford on A513; entrance at Milford. Bus: Chaserider 5, 822/3/5 Stafford to Lichfield (passing close BR Lichfield City) (Tel: 0785 58388). BR: Stafford six miles.

Sibsey Trader Windmill
- The Head Custodian
- Sibsey, Nr Boston, Lincs. PE22 0SY

An impressive old mill built in 1877, with its machinery and six sails still intact. It can still be seen in action on occasions.

OPENING Write for details.

DISABLED FACILITIES Wheelchair access.

DIRECTIONS Half a mile west of the village of Sibsey, off A16 five miles north of Boston (OS Map 122; ref TF 345511). Bus: various services and operators from Boston to Sibsey, from there half a mile (Tel: 0522 553135). BR: Boston five miles.

Snibston Discovery Park
- Dorothy Wood
- Ashby Road, Coalville, Leics. LE67 3LN
- 0530 510851 FAX 0530 813301

The 100-acre site includes Museum of Science and Industry. Indoor galleries: Science Alive, Leicestershire history, transport, engineering. Extraction industries and fashion and textiles. Out of doors there is a science play area, grange and sculpture trail.

N C SUPPORT Free education pack which includes National Curriculum Attainment Targets on Science, Geography, History, Technology and English. Advice from education staff available by telephone, written request or by personal appointment.

ANNUAL OR ONE OFF EVENT Schools' Dance and Drama Festival, access days for under fives, in-service

VISITS OUT
MIDLANDS

arranged. Please telephone for further information.

OPENING Summer: daily 10.00am–6.00pm. Winter: daily 10.00am–5.00pm.

CATERING Cafe and schools lunch room available (pre-booking required).

COST Children £2.00, adults £3.00. School parties: students/pupils £1.25, adults £1.50.

DISABLED FACILITIES Site fully accessible. Braille labels, tape guides and wheelchairs available.

DIRECTIONS Four miles from junction 22 of M1; clearly signposted on the A50 towards Ashby.

Snowshill Manor
- The Administrator
- Nr Broadway, Gloucs. WR12 7LU
- 0386 852410

A Tudor house with façade c.1700; 21 rooms containing Charles Paget Wade's collection of craftsmanship, including musical instruments, clocks, toys, bicycles, weavers' and spinners' tools, Japanese armour; small formal garden and Charles Wade's cottage.

N C SUPPORT National Curriculum links with History and Technology. Teachers' pack. Children's guide.

DISABLED FACILITIES Contact the administrator for access details.

DIRECTIONS Three miles southwest of Broadway, turning off the A44. Bus: Castleways BR Evesham to Broadway, thence three miles. BR: Moreton-in-Marsh seven miles.

South Peak Estate
- The Administrator
- Ilam Country Park, Nr Ashbourne, Derbyshire. DE6 2AZ
- 033529 245/503

Day-visit room for school groups visiting Ilam/Maniford/Dovedale areas; also available by arrangement are field trips, pond dipping, farm trails, walks with a National Trust warden; operated jointly with Youth and Schools Service of Peak National Park. To book with Losehill National Park Study Centre call 0433 20373.

N C SUPPORT National Curriculum links with History, Environmental Education.

DISABLED FACILITIES Access to Information Centre; adapted toilet.

DIRECTIONS Four and a half miles northwest of Ashbourne. Bus: Warrington 443 from Ashbourne, Thursday, Saturday only, with connections from Derby; also various services from BR Buxton and Derby, summer Sundays only; otherwise GM 210 Derby to Manchester (passing close BR Derby & Macclesfield), alight Ilam Cross Roads, two miles (Tel: 0332 292200).

Stokes Bunkhouse
- Mrs S M Hill
- Newtown House Farm, Much Wenlock, Shropshire. TF13 6DB
- 0952 727293 FAX 0952 727293

Stokes Bunkhouse has group, school and family accommodation set in spacious grounds away from roads on beautiful Wenlock Edge. Close to Ironbridge and motorway network. Camping also available.

MIDLANDS

N C SUPPORT Featured in Shropshire location for learning. Near historic working farm, aerospace museum, Ironbridge Gorge, English Heritage sites, National Trust houses, Wroxeter Roman City.

ANNUAL OR ONE OFF EVENT Festival of the Edge. Story-telling festival July each year.

OPENING February to end of November or by arrangement.

CATERING Self-catering with all facilities or evening meals/breakfast/packed lunches at group rates.

COST Discount on groups of ten or more, one teacher free. Telephone for details.

DISABLED FACILITIES Downstairs toilets and sleeping area.

DIRECTIONS Much Wenlock situated half a mile along A458 towards Shrewsbury, just past thirty MPH signs on right.

Stokesay Castle
- The Head Custodian
- Craven Arms, Shropshire. SY7 9AH
- 0588 672544

A rare and wonderfully preserved example of a 13th-century fortified manor house situated in peaceful countryside. The castle now stands in a picturesque group with its own splendid timber-framed Jacobean gatehouse and parish church.

OPENING All year round. Good Friday or 1 April (whichever is earlier) to 30 September: daily 10.00am–6.00pm. 1 October to Maundy Thursday or 31 March (whichever is earlier): Tuesday to Sunday 10.00am–4.00pm. Closed 24–26 December and 1 January.

DISABLED FACILITIES Wheelchair access to gardens and Great Hall only.

DIRECTIONS One mile south of Craven Arms off A49 (OS Map 137; ref SO 4364817). Bus: Midland Red West 435 Shrewsbury to Ludlow (Tel: 0345 212555). BR: Craven Arms one mile.

Stratford Brass Rubbing Centre
- Manager
- Summerhouse of Royal Shakespeare Company, Avonbank Gardens, Stratford-upon-Avon, Warwickshire
- 0789 297671

Merchants and courtiers of the time and town of Shakespeare make rubbings for useful study in Medieval Realms. Materials and instruction supplied. History, Social Studies and Craft links.

N C SUPPORT Teachers' notes. Historical data in guide book. All free. Perfect adjunct to Medieval Realms, Key Stage 3.

OPENING April to September: daily 10.00am–6.00pm. October: daily 11.00am–4.00pm.

CATERING Adjacent park could be used for picnics.

COST £1.50–£10.50. Pre-booked groups £1.50 each.

DISABLED FACILITIES All on level from road.

DIRECTIONS Past theatre along Southern Lane. Avonbank Gardens is on left hand side.

VISITS OUT

MIDLANDS

Sudbury Hall & Museum of Childhood
- The Administrator
- Sudbury, Derbyshire. DE6 5HT
- 0283 585305

Richly decorated Charles II house, former seat of the Vernon family; woodcarvings by Gibbons and Pierce, plasterwork by Bradbury and Pettifer, ceiling paintings by Laguerre. Museum of Childhood in servants' wing contains Cadbury Collection of playthings past, Sudbury Hall Pots, incorporating the Ballantyne Collection. Pots Study Centre; garden.

N C SUPPORT Study centre; teachers' resource book; education officer; special tours for schools by arrangement.

DISABLED FACILITIES Hall difficult, but arrangements can be made for group access to the ground floor with prior notice. Grounds and tea room accessible; for special arrangements and for parties, please contact the administrator. Adapted toilet in Museum.

DIRECTIONS Six miles east of Uttoxeter at the crossing point of A50 Derby to Stoke and A515 Lichfield to Ashbourne roads (128: SK 160323). Bus: Stevensons 401 Burton-on-Trent to Uttoxeter (passing BR Tutbury & Hatton and close BR Burton-on-Trent) (Tel: 0332 292200) BR: Tutbury & Hatton five miles.

Sundown Kiddies
- Mrs A B Rhodes
- Adventureland, Rampton, Retford, Notts. DN22 0HX
- 0777 248 274 **FAX** 0777 248 967

Theme park for tiny children, animated nursery rhymes, fantasy castle, under fives Noah's Ark, play area, Western Street, boozey barrell boat ride, indoor jungle, Rocky Mountain railroad, mini farm, sand pits, etc.

N C SUPPORT None.

OPENING Daily (except 25, 26 December): 10.00am–6.00pm (earlier closing out of season).

CATERING Two fast-food cafes, tea room, jacket potato bar, ice cream kiosks, etc.

COST 1993 prices: two years and over £3.00, parties of 20 or more (pre-booked) £2.50 each. No reductions Sunday or bank holiday.

DISABLED FACILITIES Toilets.

DIRECTIONS Three miles from Dunham-on-Trent crossroads A57.

Tattershall Castle
- Colin Watson
- Tattershall, Lincoln. LN4 4LR
- 0526 342543

Unique 15th-century brick-built tower, 100 feet high, one floor partly furnished with tapestries and oak furniture; double moat, small museum with model of castle as it was in the 17th century.

OPENING April to October: Saturday to Wednesday 10.30am–5.30pm. November to December: Saturday and Sunday 12.00 noon–4.00pm.

COST Pre-booked groups of 15 or more: children 90p, adults £1.80.

DISABLED FACILITIES Toilet. Grounds and shop accessible for wheelchairs. Three steps up into ground floor of castle, spiral staircase to upper floors.

DIRECTIONS On south side of A153 in Tattershall village, 15 miles northeast of Sleaford, ten miles southwest of Horncastle.

The Tales of Robin Hood
- Ann Coyne
- 30–38 Maid Marian Way, Nottingham. NG1 6GF
- 0602 483284 **FAX** 0602 501536

Travel back in time to medieval Nottingham. Ride through the sights, sounds and smells of Robin Hood's world and join the search for the real Robin Hood.

N C SUPPORT Key Stage 2 storytelling (autumn & spring terms only). Key Stage 3 study days. Free INSET for groups of eight or more teachers tailored to specific needs.

OPENING Winter: daily 10.00am–3.30pm. Summer: daily 10.00am–4.30pm

CATERING Cafe. Group menus available.

COST A special admission rate is available for school groups (5–16 yrs), one adult free with every ten pupils.

DISABLED FACILITIES Access for disabled throughout the centre. Any special arrangements should be discussed when booking.

DIRECTIONS Situated in Nottingham city centre.

Trek Cliff Cavern
- Peter Harrison
- Castleton, Sheffield. S30 2WP
- 0433 620571

Natural caverns with stalactites, stalagmites, rich visible veins of Blue John Stone; 330 million-years-old marine life fossils; large water-formed caverns with beautiful flowstone formations.

N C SUPPORT Free work pack available on request. Full guided tour. Geological information to suit all school age ranges.

OPENING Summer: daily 9.30am–5.30pm. Winter: daily (except 25 December) 9.30am–4.00pm.

CATERING Hot and cold drinks, light refreshments, ice cream, etc.

COST 1993 prices: primary and junior pupils £1.00, secondary pupils £1.03. For a more detailed price list please contact the offices.

DISABLED FACILITIES Not suitable for wheelchairs.

DIRECTIONS Sixteen miles west of Sheffield, 29 miles east of Manchester, three-quarters of a mile west of Castleton on A625. In the Peak District National Park.

Upton House
- The Administrator
- Banbury, Oxon. OX15 6HT
- 029 587 266

The house dates from 1695, but the collections are the chief attraction; assembled this century by the second Lord Bearsted, they include paintings by English and continental Old Masters, Brussels tapestries, Sèvres porcelain, Chelsea figures and 18th-century furniture.

N C SUPPORT National Curriculum links with History and Art.

MIDLANDS

DISABLED FACILITIES Ground floor rooms and part of garden. Adapted toilet. Special parking near house for disabled drivers. Motorised buggy with driver available for access to/from lower garden, manned by volunteers from Banbury NT Association.

DIRECTIONS On A422 seven miles northwest of Banbury, 12 miles southeast of Stratford-upon-Avon. BR: Banbury seven miles.

Wall Roman Site (Letocetum)
- The Head Custodian
- Watling Street, Wall, Nr Lichfield, Staffs. WS14 0AW
- 0543 480768

The remarkable achievements of the Romans are demonstrated by these remains of a staging post, alongside Watling Street. Foundations of an inn and bath house can be seen, and there is a display of finds in the site museum.

OPENING All year. Good Friday or 1 April (whichever is earlier) to 30 September: daily 10.00am–6.00pm. 1 October to Maundy Thursday or 31 March (whichever is earlier): Tuesday to Sunday 10.00am–4.00pm. Closed 24–26 December and 1 January.

DISABLED FACILITIES Personal stereo tour.

DIRECTIONS Off A5 at Wall near Lichfield (OS Map 139; ref SK 099067). BR: Shenstone one and a half miles.

Warwick Castle
- Sales Office
- Warwick. CV34 4QV
- 0926 408000 FAX 0926 401692

Warwick Castle stands on the banks of the River Avon, just a few miles from Shakespeare's Stratford, on the site first fortified by William the Conqueror in 1068. Many of England's most celebrated figures are enwrapped in its full and colourful history. For centuries Warwick Castle was home to the mighty Earls of Warwick, including Richard Neville, 'The Kingmaker'. In beautiful grounds, Warwick Castle remains to this day the most noble and picturesque of England's ancient fortresses.

N C SUPPORT Schools' pack available.

ANNUAL OR ONE OFF EVENT A number of special events are prepared every year, e.g. Medieval Wedding in October: a colourful pageant celebrating the medieval wedding between the Black Prince and Joan of Kent; Christmas at the Castle from 4 December: enjoy the magic of the festive season at Warwick Castle with a massive Yule Log in the hearth of the Great Hall fireplace and traditional laurel, holly, mistletoe and decorations.

OPENING Daily (except Christmas Day) 10.00am–5.30pm (closes 4.30pm October to February).

CATERING Meals and light refreshments available daily; evening banquets and dinner parties can be pre-booked; Christmas lunches served throughout December.

COST Children (4–16) £3.50, adults £5.50, students £4.80, Senior Citizens £4.25 (1993 prices).

DISABLED FACILITIES Toilets. Access to grounds and gardens only.

VISITS OUT
MIDLANDS

DIRECTIONS M40 junction 15; part of Warwick town.

Warwickshire Fly Boat Co.
- Tim or Jenny Higton
- Shop Lock Cottage, Stockton, Nr Rugby. CR23 8LD
- 0926 812093

Traditional 70-foot narrowboats, 12 berth with resident skipper, travelling along canals and rivers for periods of weekend, five-day or seven-day cruises. Boats are fully equipped, self-contained, heated, etc.

N C SUPPORT Environmental Studies, canal-side museum visits, e.g. Stoke Bruerne Waterways Museum, Black Country Museum, Warwick Castle, Stratford-upon-Avon, Black Country, etc.

OPENING March to November.

CATERING Full-size cookers, fridges and all catering equipment provided. Food planned and provided at £4.75 per head.

COST 1993 prices for party of 12: weekend £366, Monday to Friday £552–£624, seven days £636–£684, according to season.

DISABLED FACILITIES Boats do not have wheelchair access although we have carried groups of people with disabilities.

DIRECTIONS Just off A423, 11 miles south of Coventry on the Grand Union Canal.

Wenlock Priory
- The Head Custodian
- Much Wenlock, Shropshire. TF13 6HS
- 0952 727466

The ruins of a large Cluniac priory in an attractive garden setting featuring delightful topiary. There are substantial remains of the early 13th-century church and Norman chapter house.

OPENING All year. Good Friday or 1 April (whichever is earlier) to 30 September: daily 10.00am–6.00pm. 1 October to Maundy Thursday or 31 March (whichever is earlier): Tuesday to Sunday 10.00am–4.00pm. Closed 24–26 December and 1 January.

DISABLED FACILITIES Personal stereo tour available for the partially sighted and those with learning difficulties.

DIRECTIONS In Much Wenlock (OS Map 127; ref SJ 625001). Bus: Midland Red West 436/7 Shrewsbury to Bridgnorth (passes close to BR Shrewsbury) (Tel: 0345 056 785). BR: Telford Central nine miles.

Wightwick Manor
- The Administrator
- Wightwick Bank, Wolverhampton, Staffs. WV6 8EE
- 0902 761108

Built in 1887, the house is a notable example of the influence of William Morris, with many original Morris wallpapers and fabrics; Kempe glass, de Morgan ware and other Pre-Raphaelite objets d'art and paintings; Victorian and Edwardian gardens with yew hedges and topiary, terraces and two pools. Study centre; teachers' pack.

N C SUPPORT National Curriculum links with History, Art and Technology.

VISITS OUT
MIDLANDS

DISABLED FACILITIES Access to five rooms and garden (but site slopes). Braille guides.

DIRECTIONS Three miles west of Wolverhampton, up Wightwick Bank (A454), beside the Mermaid Inn. Bus: Tellus/Midland Red West 890 Wolverhampton to Bridgnorth; 516 Wolverhampton to Pattingham (both pass close BR Wolverhampton). BR: Wolverhampton three miles.

Witley Court
- The Head Custodian
- Great Witley, Hereford & Worcester
- 0299 896636

Spectacular ruins of a once great house. This vast mansion, in the Victorian Italian style, incorporates porticoes by John Nash and the nearby church, which has a remarkable 18th-century baroque interior.

OPENING All year. Good Friday or 1 April (whichever is earlier) to 30 September: daily 10.00am–6.00pm. 1 October to Maundy Thursday or 31 March (whichever is earlier): Tuesday to Sunday 10.00am–4.00pm. Closed 24–26 December and 1 January.

CATERING Refreshments (not managed by English Heritage).

DISABLED FACILITIES Wheelchair access to exterior and grounds only.

DIRECTIONS Ten miles northwest of Worcester on A443 (OS Map 150; ref 769649). BR: Droitwich Spa eight and a half miles.

Wrest Park House & Gardens
- The Head Custodian
- Silsoe, Beds. MK45 4HS

Acres of wonderful gardens originally laid out in the early 18th century, including the Great Garden, with charming buildings and ornaments, and the delightfully intricate French Garden, with statues and fountain. The house, once the home of the de Grey family, whose Mausoleum at Flitton is nearby, was inspired by 18th-century French chateaux.

OPENING Summer season: Good Friday or 1 April (whichever is earlier) to 30 September: Saturday, Sunday and bank holidays only 10.00am–6.00pm.

CATERING Refreshments available.

DIRECTIONS Three-quarters of a mile east of Silsoe off A6, ten miles south of Bedford. (OS Map 153; ref TL 093356). Bus: United Counties X1, X2, X52 (pass within half a mile of BR Luton to Bedford) (Tel: 0234 262151). BR: Flitwick four miles.

Wroxeter Roman City
- The Head Custodian
- Wroxeter, Nr Shrewsbury, Shropshire. SV5 6PH
- 0743 761330

The excavated centre of the fourth largest city in Roman Britain, with impressive remains of the second-century municipal baths. The Museum has finds from the town and the earlier legionary fortress.

OPENING All year round. Good Friday or 1 April (whichever is earlier) to 30 September: daily 10.00am–6.00pm. 1 October to Maundy Thursday or 31 March (whichever is earlier): Tuesday to Sunday 10.00am–4.00pm. Closed 24–26 December and 1 January.

MIDLANDS

DISABLED FACILITIES Wheelchair access.

DIRECTIONS At Wroxeter, five miles east of Shrewsbury, one mile south of A5 (OS Map 126; ref SJ 568088). Bus: Williamson X96 Birmingham to Shrewsbury (passes close to BR Telford Central) (Tel: 0345 056785). BR: Shrewsbury five and a half miles; Wellington Telford West six miles.

Wyedean Canoe & Adventure Centre

- Paul & Jane Howells
- Holly Barn, Symonds Yat, Coleford, Gloucs. GL16 7NZ
- 0594 833238 FAX 0594 833238

Come to Wyedean Canoe and Adventure Centre in the beautiful Symonds Yat Gorge and experience a 'quest' for adventure, surrounded by the placid white waters of the river Wye and forest.

N C SUPPORT Tailor-made programmes to suit school itinerary, Field Studies, History, Culture, etc.

OPENING All year round.
CATERING Self catering.

COST £4.00 per person per night indoors. Camping from £1.25 per person. Activities £13.50 per person.

DIRECTIONS Turn off at Hereford Garages; after two and a half miles turn right; take right for A40 exit and Little Chef to Forest of Dean, Symonds Yat East.

NORTH EAST

Abbey House Museum
- June Bridgewater
- Kirkstall Road, Kirkstall, Leeds. LS5 3EH
- 0532 755821

The entire family can marvel at Castelow's the chemists, the ironworks and the pipemakers in the streets of Victorian Leeds, all recreated in this delightful museum.

N C SUPPORT Teachers' pack currently in preparation.

OPENING Monday to Friday 9.30am–5.30pm, Sunday 2.00pm–5.00pm.

CATERING By arrangement only.

COST Children 60p.

DISABLED FACILITIES Access to ground floor only. Access is possible leading directly onto Victorian streets.

DIRECTIONS Three miles west of Leeds city centre on A65 Kirkstall road; situated opposite Kirkstall Abbey.

Aldborough Roman Town
- The Head Custodian
- Main Street, Nr Boroughbridge, North Yorks. YO5 9EF
- 0423 322768

Once the principal town of the Brigantes, the largest tribe in Roman Britain. The remains include parts of the Roman defences and two mosaic pavements from a large townhouse. A museum displays finds from the site.

OPENING Summer season. Good Friday or 1 April (whichever is earlier) to 30 September: daily 10.00am–6.00pm. Winter: grounds only.

CATERING Picnic facilities in summer.

DIRECTIONS Three-quarters of a mile southeast of Boroughbridge, on minor road off B6265 (OS map 99; ref SE 405667). Bus: United 142 BR York to Ripon (Tel: 0325 468771).

Archaeological Resource Centre
- Dr Andrew K G Jones
- St Saviourgate, York. YO1 2NN
- 0904 054324 FAX 0902 640029

A 'hands-on' exploration of archaeology for pupils of all ages. Sort real archaeological finds, learn ancient skills: spinning and weaving. Have fun with computers.

N C SUPPORT Key Stage 1 History and Science; Key Stage 2 Invaders and Settlers; Key Stage 3 Roman Empire, Medieval Knaves.

ANNUAL OR ONE OFF EVENT Temporary demonstrations and exhibitions throughout the year.

OPENING Monday to Friday 10.00am–5.00pm. Saturday and Sunday 1.00pm–5.00pm. Evenings by prior arrangement.

CATERING None. Picnics can be eaten in the garden.

COST Children £2.20, adults £3.20.

DISABLED FACILITIES Toilets. No steps to ground floor.

DIRECTIONS Close to Shambles in central York.

Armley Mills
- Peter Kelley
- Canal Road, Leeds. LS12 2QF
- 0532 637861

Explore the history of 'Working Leeds' at Armley Mills, once the

VISITS OUT
NORTH EAST

world's largest woollen mill. Expect a warm welcome whatever the weather.

N C SUPPORT Displays, activities and evidence linked to all Key Stages, relating to Industrial Expansion, Science and Technology. World Wars I and II, the Victorians, Transport and Communications, Economic Awareness and Environmental issues.

OPENING Tuesday to Saturday 9.00am–5.00pm, Sunday 2.00pm–5.00pm.

CATERING Vending machine, indoor and outdoor picnic facilities.

COST Children 60p, teachers free.

DISABLED FACILITIES Museum fully accessible: lifts and toilet, one steep ramp.

DIRECTIONS Two miles west of Leeds city centre off the A65 on Canal Road, Armley.

The Arts Centre
- Sarah Richards, General Manager
- Vane Terrace, Darlington, Co Durham. DL3 7AX
- 0325 483271

Mid-19th-century building offering a wide variety of artistic experiences. Programme includes theatre, dance, film, children's events, exhibitions, classes, workshops. Myles Meehan Gallery is a well-appointed gallery showing national and international contemporary artists.

N C SUPPORT Contact Gaye Sutherland, Outreach Officer, for specific projects.

ANNUAL OR ONE OFF EVENT 'Spring-Thing' Festival of Folk: music, song and dance. A four-day event, colourful and action packed. Based on core of free workshops and skill sessions. Plus dances and concerts.

OPENING Monday to Saturday 9.00am–11.00pm.

CATERING Bistro: Monday to Friday 10.00am–3.30pm and 5.30pm–9.00pm, Saturday 10.00am–3.30pm. Bar: Monday to Friday 12.00 noon–2.00pm and 6.00pm–11.00pm, Saturday 11.30am–3.00pm and 6.00pm–11.00pm.

COST Varies.

DISABLED FACILITIES Parking for disabled drivers at front of building with ramped access. Ramped access to art studios and media workshops. All ground-floor rooms accessible for wheelchair users. Induction loop in theatre and public telephone.

Aydon Castle
- The Head Custodian
- Corbridge, Northumberland. NE45 5PJ
- 0434 632450

One of the finest fortified manor houses in England, dating from the late 13th century and situated in a position of great natural beauty. Its survival, remarkably intact, can be attributed to its conversion to a farmhouse in the 17th century.

OPENING Summer season. Good Friday or 1 April (whichever is earlier) to 30 September: daily 10.00am–6.00pm.

CATERING Picnic facilities.

DISABLED FACILITIES Wheelchair access to ground floor.

VISITS OUT
NORTH EAST

DIRECTIONS One mile northeast of Corbridge, on minor road off B6321 or A68 (OS Map 87; ref NZ OO2663). BR: Corbridge four miles, approach by bridlepath from west side of Aydon Road, immediately north of Corbridge bypass.

Bagpipe Museum
- Anne Moore
- The Chantry, Bridge Street, Morpeth, Northumberland. NE24 4BW
- 0670 519466

This unusual Museum specialises in the History and Development of Northumbrian smallpipes and their music. They are set in the context of bagpipes around the world, from India to Inverness.

N C SUPPORT In preparation.

ANNUAL OR ONE OFF EVENT Monthly concerts. Occasional music and dance workshops.

OPENING Monday to Saturday 9.30am–5.30pm, closed bank holidays.

CATERING Light refreshments for party groups by prior arrangement.

COST Party rate £3.00.

DISABLED FACILITIES No wheelchair access.

DIRECTIONS Off A1.

Bagshaw Museum
- Brian Haigh
- Wilton Park, Batley, West Yorks. WF17 0AJ
- 0924 472514

A delightful Victorian mansion with local history and social history displays, and galleries featuring natural history. Mythical beasts, oriental ceramics and ancient Egypt. Butterfly conservation centre, woodland walks, orienteering course.

N C SUPPORT Key Stages CSU3 Victorian Britain; Key Stages 35U Ancient Egypt; Key Stage SSUB Local History: and cross-curricular opportunities. Teachers' packs, educational materials, videos, workbase, etc.

ANNUAL OR ONE OFF EVENT Teachers' study days; adult workshops; children's holiday activities; programme of events supporting temporary exhibition.

OPENING Monday to Friday 11.00am–5.00pm, Saturday and Sunday 12.00 noon–5.00pm. Groups at other times by arrangement.

CATERING By arrangement. Room may be available for packed lunches.

COST Free.

DISABLED FACILITIES Ramped access available. Assistance available. Access to upper floor may be difficult for severely disabled.

DIRECTIONS Near junction 27 of the M62 between A652 Dewsbury to Bradford and A62 Leeds to Huddersfield roads, from which it is signposted.

Barnard Castle
- The Head Custodian
- Castle House, Durham, Co Durham. DL12 9AT
- 0833 38212

The substantial remains of this large castle stand on a rugged escarpment overlooking the River Tees. Visitors can still see parts of the 14th-century Great Hall and the cylindrical 12th-century tower, built by the Baliol family.

OPENING All year. Good Friday or 1 April (whichever is earlier) to 30 September: daily 10.00am–6.00pm. 1 October to Maundy Thursday or 31 March (whichever is earlier): Tuesday to Sunday 10.00am–4.00pm. Closed 24–26 December and 1 January.

CATERING Picnic facilities.

DISABLED FACILITIES Wheelchair access.

DIRECTIONS In Barnard Castle (OS Map 92; ref NZ 049165). Bus: United 75/A, X75. BR Darlington–Barnard Castle (Tel: 0325 468771).

Batley Art Gallery
- Jane Speller
- Market Place, Batley, West Yorks. WF17 5DA
- 0924 435521

Recently refurbished Batley Art Gallery offers an exciting continuous programme of exhibitions throughout the year, featuring a diverse range of painting, photography, crafts, graphics and sculpture, with an accent on local and regional artists and craftspeople.

N C SUPPORT Artist-led educational activities on a broad range of topics organised in conjunction with exhibitions programme.

ANNUAL OR ONE OFF EVENT Winter Open, an annual open submission exhibition for local and regional artists and craftspeople.

OPENING Monday and Wednesday to Friday 10.00am–5.00pm. Tuesday 10.00am–1.00pm, Saturday 10.00am–4.00pm, closed Sunday.

CATERING None on site. Cafes nearby.

COST Free.

DISABLED FACILITIES None.

DIRECTIONS Situated in Batley town centre, above library. Town situated between Leeds and Huddersfield.

Bayle Museum
- J S Walker
- 58 Viking Road, Bridlington, Yorks. YO16 5TW
- 0262 603170

The Museum, in the Augustinian monastic gatehouse, displays local history collections covering all aspects of Bridlington's history, from the dissolution of the monasteries (1537) through to the end of the Victorian period.

OPENING June to September: Tuesday to Thursday 2.00pm–4.00pm and 7.00pm–9.00pm, Wednesday 2.00pm–4.00pm. Parties by arrangement throughout the year.

CATERING None.

COST Children 20p, adults £1.00.

DISABLED FACILITIES None.

DIRECTIONS Old Town near Priory Church. Ample on-road parking close by.

Baysgarth House Museum
- Miss J M Bunclark
- Baysgarth Leisure Park, Caistor Road, Barton-on-Humber, South Humberside. DN18 6AH
- 0652 632318

VISITS OUT
NORTH EAST

Georgian house, stable block, cottage. Displays on rural crafts, industry, archaeology, geology and social history of Glanford area. Also changing temporary exhibition programme. No teacher on site.

N C SUPPORT Key Stage 2 core study unit (1) Anglo Saxons, (2) supplementary study unit A: Domestic Life, Unit B: Local History, (3) Unit 3, Unit 4, Agriculture.

OPENING Thursday and Friday 10.00am–4.00pm, Saturday and Sunday 10.00am–5.00pm. Other times by arrangement.

CATERING None.

COST Free.

DISABLED FACILITIES Toilets in park. Access to stable block, ground-floor cottage and main building.

DIRECTIONS Situated in Baysgarth Park off Caistor Road. Signposted off A15 and in town.

Beamish Hall
- T M McKeon
- Beamish Hall, Co Durham. DH9 0RG
- 0207 233147 FAX 0207 281723

Beamish Hall is a residential educational establishment based in a Georgian mansion adjacent to Beamish Open-Air Museum. The Hall can cater for groups of up to 42.

N C SUPPORT Cross-curriculum and Environmental Education support via Deputy Warden.

OPENING All year.

CATERING Full catering included.

COST Children approximately £10.26 per day, teachers £19.06 per day (including VAT).

DISABLED FACILITIES None.

DIRECTIONS Signposted from A1(M), nine miles south of Newcastle-upon-Tyne.

Beamish North of England Open Air Museum
- Keeper of Education
- Beamish, Co. Durham. DH9 0RG
- 0207 231811 FAX 0207 290933

Travel by tram to the Town, Colliery Village, Working Farm and Railway Station, which have been vividly recreated to show how the people of the North of England lived and worked early this century. A winter visit is centred on the Town.

N C SUPPORT An ideal resource for all National Curriculum subjects. Interactive study areas are available. Information and teacher training sessions are provided by the Education Department.

ANNUAL OR ONE OFF EVENT Full programme of special events in summer. Events list available.

OPENING April to end October: daily 10.00am–5.00pm. mid-July to early September daily 10.00am–6.00pm (last admission 4.00pm). November to mid-March 10.00am–4.00pm (last admission 3.00pm). Closed Monday, Friday, 20–25 December and New Year's Day.

CATERING Tea room (summer only). Snack bars, coffee shop.

VISITS OUT

NORTH EAST

COST 1993 prices. Summer: £2.99 per pupil. Winter: £1.50 per pupil.

DISABLED FACILITIES Toilets. Beamish is not ideal for wheelchairs.

DIRECTIONS Chester-le-Street exit, A1(M) County Durham. Follow signs along A693 towards Stanley (four miles).

Stephen G Beaumont Museum

- A L Ashworth
- Stanley Royd Hospital, Aberford Road, Wakefield. WF1 4DQ
- 0924 201688

Museum of Psychiatry, depicting the history of what was the West Riding Pauper Lunatic Asylum, founded in 1818. Contains instruments of restraint, padded cell, original documents, model of original building.

OPENING Wednesday 10.30am–1.00pm and 1.30pm–4.00pm. As the museum is operated single-handed, prior notice of visits is essential.

CATERING Limited facilities for small parties (a dozen or so) can be arranged, but again prior notice is a necessity.

COST Free.

DISABLED FACILITIES No particular facilities, but there are no steps or stairs.

DIRECTIONS Within the grounds of Stanley Royd Hospital, Aberford Road, Wakefield (one mile from city centre).

Beck Isle Museum

- Mrs Janette Leigh
- Bridge Street, Pickering, North Yorks. YO18 8DU
- 0751 73753

Regency house containing 30 period room settings including shops, pub and costume display. Outdoor agricultural exhibition.

N C SUPPORT History Key Stages 1–3.

OPENING 26 March to 31 October: daily 10.00am–5.00pm.

COST Children 75p, adults £1.75, Senior Citizens £1.50. Parties of ten or more: children/students 65p.

DISABLED FACILITIES Limited to ground floor and outdoor exhibitions.

DIRECTIONS Centre of town, 200 yards from North Yorkshire Moors railway station.

Bede Gallery

- Vincent Rea
- Springwell Park, Butchers Bridge Road, Jarrow. NE32 5QA
- 091-489 1809 FAX 091-489 1807

Varied programme of contemporary art exhibitions and events featuring local, national and international artists. Small museum of local history including the Jarrow March, Palmers Shipyard and the gibbeting of William Jobling. Comprehensive film library of art videos available for viewing in the Gallery.

OPENING Tuesday to Friday 10.00am–5.00pm, Sunday 2.00pm–5.00pm, closed Saturday and Monday.

CATERING Coffee or tea only.

COST Free.

DISABLED FACILITIES None at present. Plans in hand to build toilets.

VISITS OUT
NORTH EAST

DIRECTIONS A194 to South Shields. Follow brown Bede Gallery signs from turn-off for Jarrow.

Bede's World
- Graeme K Talboys
- The Museum, Church Bank, Jarrow, Tyne & Wear. NE32 3DY
- 091-489 2106 FAX 091-428 2361

Museum of early medieval Northumbria focusing on the monastic life of the Venerable Bede and secular life of the same period.

N C SUPPORT Full-scale education programme run by Museum Education Department. Contact Museum for details.

OPENING April to October: Tuesday to Saturday 10.00am–5.30pm. Sunday 2.30pm–5.30pm. November to March: Tuesday to Saturday 11.00am–4.30pm, Sunday 2.30pm–5.30pm.

CATERING Dining area for eating packed lunches.

COST South Tyneside and Sunderland LEA schools free; all others £2.00 per pupil for full day (all staff and adults free).

DISABLED FACILITIES Toilet. Ground floor access only for wheelchairs.

DIRECTIONS Signposted from roundabout at south end of Tyne Tunnel (A19).

Belsay Hall Castle & Gardens
- The Head Custodian
- Belsay, Nr Ponteland, Northumberland. NE20 0DX
- 0661 881636

One of the most important Neo-classical houses in Britain, completed in 1815, together with a well-preserved 14th-century castle and ruined 17th-century mansion. It has 30 acres of magnificent landscaped parkland and gardens, including the famous quarry gardens.

OPENING All year. Good Friday or 1 April (whichever is earlier) to 30 September: daily 10.00am–6.00pm. 1 October to Maundy Thursday or 31 March (whichever is earlier): Tuesday to Sunday 10.00am–4.00pm. Closed 24–26 December and 1 January.

CATERING Restaurant/cafe (normally open summer season only).

DIRECTIONS Fourteen miles northwest of Newcastle on A696 (OS Map 88; ref NZ 088785). Bus: Vasey's/Snaith's 808 from Newcastle (Tel: 0830 20202/20609); otherwise National Express 370-2 Newcastle to Edinburgh to within one mile. (Tel: any National Express agent). BR: Morpeth ten miles.

Beningbrough Hall
- The Administrator
- Shipton-by-Beningbrough, North Yorks. YO6 1DD
- 0904 470666

A Georgian mansion built by John Bourchier in 1716 and set in 365 acres. Excellent carving; over 100 pictures on loan from the National Portrait Gallery; cantilevered staircase, furniture and porcelain; servants exhibition; well-equipped Victorian laundry; seven-acre garden; Pike Ponds walk; potting shed; wilderness play area for young children.

NORTH EAST

N C SUPPORT National Curriculum links with History, Science and Art. Study centre, teachers' pack, children's guide, living history days, touch and go fabric/costume projects.

DISABLED FACILITIES Ground floor only, by ramp; level garden paths (embedded gravel); special parking spaces. Adapted toilet in stable block. Motorised scooter available.

DIRECTIONS Eight miles northwest of York, two miles west of Shipton, two miles southeast of Linton-on-Ouse. Bus: Rider York 31. BR York to Newton-on-Ouse, thence one mile. BR: York eight miles.

Berwick-upon-Tweed Barracks

- The Head Custodian
- The Parade, Berwick-upon-Tweed, Northumberland. TD15 1DF
- 0289 304493

Among the earliest purpose-built barracks, these have changed very little since 1717. They house an exhibition 'By Beat of Drum', which recreates scenes such as a barrack room from the life of the British infantryman, the Museum of the King's Own Scottish Borderers and the Borough Museum with fine art, local history exhibition, and other collections.

N C SUPPORT An Education Centre has been provided for study use by school parties. These are equipped with audio-visual, printed and replica sources appropriate to the property, which teachers can use themselves. Education Centres can be booked in advance. For more information, please contact the English Heritage Education Service, Keysign House, 429 Oxford Street, London W1R 2HD.

ANNUAL OR ONE OFF EVENT At some sites each year we arrange special educational events, often with the involvement of experts such as musicians and storytellers, for visiting educational groups.

OPENING All year. Good Friday or 1 April (whichever is earlier) to 30 September: daily 10.00am–6.00pm. 1 October to Maundy Thursday or 31 March (whichever is earlier): Tuesday to Sunday 10.00am–4.00pm. Closed 24–26 December and 1 January. Museum of the King's Own Scottish Borderers: Monday to Friday 10.00am–4.00pm, Saturday 10.00am–11.00pm.

COST Student groups and school parties are admitted free to English Heritage properties, but should book in advance through the relevant Regional Office.

DIRECTIONS On the Parade, off Church Street, Berwick town centre (OS Map 75; ref NT 994535). Bus: from surrounding areas (Tel: 0289 307283/307461). BR: Berwick-upon-Tweed quarter of a mile.

Binchester Roman Fort

- John Pickin
- Binchester Roman Fort, Binchester, Bishop Auckland, Co. Durham

Excavated remains of part of Roman fort of Vinovia. Includes a stretch of Roman Dere Street and best presented military bath house in Britain.

N C SUPPORT Key Stage 2 Unit 1, Key Stage 3 Unit 1.

VISITS OUT
NORTH EAST

OPENING April to September: Saturday to Wednesday 10.30am–6.00pm, closed Thursday and Friday.

CATERING None.

COST 1993 prices: children 40p, adults 80p.

DISABLED FACILITIES None.

DIRECTIONS One and a half miles north of Bishop Auckland. Signposted from town centre, A690 and A688.

The Botanic Centre
- Jan McDonald
- Ladgate Lane, Acklam, Middlesbrough, Cleveland. TS5 7YN
- 0642 594895

The Botanic Centre is an innovative environmental centre. Features include organic demonstration, gardens, exhibition hall with working models, beehive and videos, wildlife areas and ponds, gift shop and tea room.

N C SUPPORT A full-time Education Manager and support staff deliver a National Curriculum-linked programme. Special studies, problem-solving projects by arrangement. Experimental learning through senses encouraged.

ANNUAL OR ONE OFF EVENT Year-round events; ask for details.

OPENING 1 April to 30 September:daily 10.00am–5.00pm.

CATERING Excellent award-winning tea rooms selling a range of wholefood and vegetarian meals and snacks.

COST Children 50p, adults £1.50. Educational visit: £1.00 per pupil.

DISABLED FACILITIES Tea rooms have toilets. Garden sales area, terraces and some of garden accessible but some parts of garden have soft substrate paths.

DIRECTIONS Take the Whitby turning on the A19 and follow A174. At Acklam turning take A1044 past Bluebell Hotel and turn left at the next mini-roundabout. Follow signs to car park.

The Bowes Museum
- Margaret Eaglestone
- Barnard Castle, Co. Durham. DL12 8NP
- 0833 690606 FAX 0833 37163

Comprehensive European and decorative arts c.1400–1900. South Durham prehistory to 19th century.

N C SUPPORT Education room; advice to teachers; publications, video, music tape; two pupil workbooks on 18th-century France. Work suitable for Art, Craft, Textiles, Design, History, European and French Studies, Religious Education and early keyboards.

OPENING Monday to Saturday 10.00am–5.30pm (5.00pm October, March, April; 4.00pm November to February), Sunday 2.00pm–5.00pm. Closed 20–25 December and 1 January.

COST Children £1.30, adults £2.30, Senior Citizens/disabled/unemployed, 10% discount for groups of 10 or more. Student cards free. Enquire about schools' subscription scheme.

VISITS OUT
NORTH EAST

DISABLED FACILITIES Parking, easy entrance, flat surfaces, lift, toilets, access to all but four rooms; access to cafe and shop.

DIRECTIONS A67 or A688 to Barnard Castle, signposted in town. A66 four miles; A1 12 miles.

Bridestones Moor
- c/o The Warden
- Low Staindale Cottage, Dalby, Pickering, North Yorks. YO18 7LR
- 0751 60396

Nature reserve owned by the National Trust. The Bridestones themselves are impressive and oddly shaped Jurassic sandstone outcrops resulting from erosion; the reserve contains wooded slopes and deep, narrow ravines as well as open flat-topped moorland.

N C SUPPORT National Curriculum links with Science, Geography and Environmental Education.

DISABLED FACILITIES Contact the warden for access details.

DIRECTIONS Contact the warden for details.

Brimham Moor & Rocks
- c/o The Warden
- Summerbridge, Harrogate, North Yorks. HG3 4DW
- 0423 780688

The rocks are spectacular stacks of millstone grit set in open moorland overlooking Nidderdale. Excellent examples of glacial erosion and weathering; moorland flora and fauna.

N C SUPPORT National Curriculum links with Science and Geography. There is a study centre; information room with video; education officer available for talks on request; teachers' pack.

DISABLED FACILITIES Driven by car to house. No access to information room upstairs. Access to refreshment area. Adapted toilet. Paths too narrow and uneven for wheelchair access.

DIRECTIONS Six miles from Harrogate on road to Pately Bridge; towards Burnt Yates turn right; signposted Brimham Moor.

Brinkburn Priory
- The Head Custodian
- Long Framlington, Morpeth, Northumberland. NE65 8AS
- 0665 570628

This late 12th-century church is a fine example of early Gothic architecture, almost perfectly preserved, and is set in a lovely spot beside the River Coquet.

OPENING Summer season. Good Friday or 1 April (whichever is earlier) to 30 September: daily 10.00am–6.00pm.

CATERING Picnic facilities.

DIRECTIONS Four and a half miles southeast of Rothbury off B6334 (OS Map 81; ref NZ 116984). Bus: Northumbria 514/6 Morpeth to Rothbury to within half a mile (Tel: 091-232 4211). Station: Acklington ten miles.

NORTH EAST

John Bull School of Adventure
- John Bull
- 12 Littlethorpe Park, Ripon, North Yorks. HG4 1UQ
- 0765 604071

Accommodation is in a converted water mill or a farm complex in the Dales. Groups of up to 20 can be accommodated either full board or self-catering. Smaller groups in local hostelries in the area. The School provides expert instruction in mountain biking, abseiling, canoeing, rock climbing, mountain walking, caving, cross-country skiing and windsurfing; survival/courses for families, small groups and individuals, novice or expert in a friendly small group situation. Day courses and adventure holidays have been carefully designed to be suitable for those with little or no experience, yet still provide enough challenge to keep even the most ardent enthusiast happy. VHS video is available lasting 30 mins. Made by Yorkshire Television with Liz Hobbs and the John Bull School of Adventure, it shows what takes place on a multi-activity course.

ANNUAL OR ONE OFF EVENT One-day, weekend or one-week courses.

OPENING Please write for details of the various options. It is necessary to book well in advance.

CATERING Full board or self-catering.

COST One-day course: under 16s £15.00, adults £35.00. Weekend course: under 16s £28.00, adults full board and instruction £90.00, instruction only £68.00. One-week course: under 16s £70.00, adults full board and instruction £210.00, instruction only £150.00. One leader free with group booking (minimum of 4 children).

DIRECTIONS Children's weeks can take place in the Dales, Wales or the Lake District. Apply for details and instructions.

D G Burleigh
- Rothbury Road, Longframlington, Morpeth, Northumberland. NE65 8HL
- 0665 570635

Maker of Northumbrian smallpipes. Short talks on the instrument: history, manufacture, etc.

N C SUPPORT None.

OPENING Monday to Thursday 8.00am–4.00pm, closed for lunch 12.00 noon–1.30pm.

CATERING None.

COST Free.

DISABLED FACILITIES None.

DIRECTIONS Centre of village, next to Mace store.

Byland Abbey
- The Head Custodian
- Nr Coxwold, North Yorks. YO6 4BD
- 0347 6614

A hauntingly beautiful ruin, set in peaceful meadows in the shadow of the Hambleton Hills. It illustrates later developments of Cistercian churches, including a beautiful floor of mosaic tiles.

OPENING All year. Good Friday or 1 April (whichever is earlier) to 30 September: daily 10.00am–6.00pm. 1 October to Maundy Thursday or 31 March (whichever is earlier): Tuesday to Sunday 10.00am–4.00pm. Closed 24–26 December and 1 January

CATERING Picnic facilities.

DISABLED FACILITIES Wheelchair access and toilets.

DIRECTIONS Two miles south of A170 between Thirsk and Hemsley, near Coxwold village (OS Map 100; ref SE 549789).

Captain Cook Memorial Museum
- A Milson
- John Walker's House, Grape Lane, Whitby, North Yorks. YO22 4BE
- 0947 601900

Home of the Walker family of shipowners for whom Cook worked and with whom he lodged. Rooms furnished as in his time. Models, original letters, drawings and paintings of his voyages.

N C SUPPORT Contact the Museum direct for details of National Curriculum support.

OPENING April to October: daily 9.45am–4.30pm. March and November: Saturday and Sunday 11.00am–3.00pm.

CATERING None.

COST Children £1.00. adults £1.50, Senior Citizens £1.00, family ticket £4.00. Pre-booked school parties 80p.

DISABLED FACILITIES None as this is an old house.

DIRECTIONS Centre of Whitby. Harbourside near to Swing Bridge.

Castle Eden Walkway
- Marian Clough
- Country Park, Station House Visitor Centre, Thorpe Thewles, Stockton-on-Tees, Cleveland. TS21 3JG
- 0740 30011

Visitor Centre based in old railway station with wildlife displays and souvenir shop. Three and a half miles of linear walkway and approximately 45 acres of ancient woodland on Thorpe Wood Local Nature Reserve.

N C SUPPORT Two educational programmes geared to Science Curriculum Key Stages 1 and 2 look particularly at energy flow, interrelationships, change and cycles in the natural environment and relating lifestyles to environmental problems.

OPENING Monday to Friday 8.30am–4.30pm, Saturday and Sunday 9.00am–5.00pm, closed Saturday during winter.

CATERING Ice cream van in the car park during summer months.

COST School visits free.

DISABLED FACILITIES Access to all facilities for disabled, e.g. visitor centre, toilets, etc. No access to Thorpe Wood due to steep banks.

DIRECTIONS Main access point can be reached by following the brown highway signs located at the Thorpe Thewles junction of the A177 (Stockton to Durham road).

VISITS OUT
NORTH EAST

Cathedral Church of St Nicholas
- D C Govier
- St Nicholas Churchyard, Newcastle-upon-Tyne. NE1 1PF
- 091-232 1939 FAX 091-230 0735

Mainly 14th–15th-century building with monuments to many local and national figures, including Admiral Lord Collingwood.

N C SUPPORT New fact sheets and worksheets underway in conjunction with Church Schools Officer to comply with National Curriculum requirements.

OPENING Open for school project visits or guided tours Monday to Friday 9.00am–4.30pm. Also (with at least 4 weeks notice) Saturday 10.00am–3.00pm.

CATERING Monday to Friday only. Room available for packed lunches. Tea, coffee or soft drinks on sale.

COST Free.

DISABLED FACILITIES Toilets (male and female) and ramps throughout.

DIRECTIONS Five minutes walk from BR station; 300 yards from Castle keep.

Chesters Roman Fort & Museum
- The Head Custodian
- Cilurnum, Chollerford, Humshaugh, Hexham, Northumberland. NE46 4EP
- 0434 681379

The best-preserved example of a Roman cavalry fort in Britain, including remains of the bath house on the banks of the River North Tyne. The museum houses a fascinating collection of Roman sculpture and inscriptions.

OPENING All year. Good Friday or 1 April (whichever is earlier) to 30 September: daily 10.00am–6.00pm. 1 October to Maundy Thursday or 31 March (whichever is earlier): Tuesday to Sunday 10.00am to 4.00pm. Closed 24-26 December and 1 January.

CATERING Refreshments (not managed by English Heritage).

DIRECTIONS Half a mile west of Chollerford on B6318 (OS Map 87; ref NY 913701). Bus: Rochester & Marshall 890; Tyne Valley 880/2 from BR Hexham to within half a mile (Tel: 0434 602217). BR: Hexham five and a half miles.

Cleveland Crafts Centre
- Barry Hempton
- 57 Gilkes Street, Middlesbrough, Cleveland. TS1 5EL
- 0642 226351 FAX 0642 226351

Crafts resource centre with fine collections of studio pottery and contemporary jewellery. Exhibition programme, retail shop, studio workshops.

N C SUPPORT Can offer workshops and lectures.

OPENING Tuesday to Saturday 10.00am–5.00pm.

CATERING None.

COST Free.

DISABLED FACILITIES Ground-floor public area.

DIRECTIONS Centre of Middlesbrough.

VISITS OUT
NORTH EAST

Clifford's Tower
- The Head Custodian
- Tower Street, York. YO1 1SA
- 0904 646940

A 13th-century tower on one of two mottes thrown up by William the Conqueror to hold York. There are panoramic views of the city from the top of the tower.

OPENING All year. Good Friday or 1 April (whichever is earlier) to 30 September: daily 10.00am–6.00pm. 1 October to Maundy Thursday or 31 March (whichever is earlier): Monday to Sunday 10.00am–4.00pm; Closed 24–26 December and 1 January.

DIRECTIONS In Tower Street (OS Map 105; ref SE 605515). Bus: from surrounding areas (Tel: 0904 624161). BR: York one mile.

Cober Hill
- Colin Wigglesworth
- Cloughton, Scarborough, Yorks. YO13 0AR
- 0723 870310 FAX 0723 870271

Education and Conference Centre offering quality residential accommodation at modest cost to educational groups of all ages. Owned by the Rowntree charitable trusts, it is a non-profit-making venture.

N C SUPPORT The area is rich in educational opportunity. A comprehensive information guide suggesting National Curriculum links is provided. A resource bank is being assembled and educational advice is available.

OPENING All year.

CATERING Breakfast, packed lunches, dinner and drinks (waitress service) included in full-board charges.

COST Children £13.60, adults £21.00 (15% reduction for low season).

DISABLED FACILITIES Two bedrooms en suite (Cober could, however, prove difficult for people with mobility problems).

DIRECTIONS Five miles north of Scarborough on the A171; on the edge of Cloughton Village.

Conisbrough Castle
- The Head Custodian
- Castle Hill, Conisbrough, Doncaster. DN12 3BU
- 0709 863329

The spectacular white circular keep of this 12th-century castle rises majestically above the River Don. It is the oldest circular keep in England and one of the finest medieval buildings. There is a visitor centre and exhibition.

OPENING All year. Good Friday or 1 April (whichever is earlier) to 30 September: daily 10.00am–6.00pm. 1 October to Maundy Thursday or 31 March (whichever is earlier): Tuesday to Sunday 10.00am–4.00pm. Closed 24–26 December and 1 January.

DISABLED FACILITIES Limited wheelchair access.

DIRECTIONS Northeast of Conisbrough town centre off A630 four and a half miles southwest of Doncaster (OS Map 111; ref SK 515989). Bus: from surrounding areas (Tel: 0742 768688). BR: Conisbrough half a mile.

VISITS OUT
NORTH EAST

Corbridge Roman Site
- The Head Custodian
- Corbridge-on-Tyne, Northumberland. NE45 5NT
- 0434 632349

A fascinating series of excavated remains, including foundations of granaries with a grain ventilation system. From artefacts found, which can be seen in the site museum, it is clear a large settlement developed around this supply depot.

OPENING All year. Good Friday or 1 April to 30 September (whichever is earlier): daily 10.00am–6.00pm. 1 October to Maundy Thursday or 31 March (whichever is earlier): Tuesday to Sunday 10.00am–4.00pm. Closed 24–26 December and 1 January.

DISABLED FACILITIES Wheelchair access. Personal stereo tour available at extra cost.

DIRECTIONS Half a mile northwest of Corbridge on minor road signposted for Corstopitum, Hexham and Beaufront (OS Map 87; ref NY 983649). Bus: Northumbria 602, 685 Newcastle-upon-Tyne to Hexham to within half mile (Tel: 091 232 4211). BR: Corbridge one and a half miles.

Cragside House, Gardens and Grounds
- The Administrator
- Rothbury, Morpeth, Northumberland. NE65 7PX
- 0669 20333

A Victorian mansion, designed by Richard Norman Shaw, in a 900-acre park created by Lord Armstrong. Thirty rooms open. The first house in the world lit by hydro-electricity; the system was developed with man-made lakes and underground piping. 'The Power Circuit', a three-mile circular walk, includes the restored ram and power houses with their hydraulic and hydro-electric machinery. Visitor Centre in which is located the Armstrong Energy Centre. Teachers' resource book; contact the National Trust Regional Office, Scot's Gap, Morpeth, Northumberland NE61 4EG (Tel: 067 074 691).

N C SUPPORT National Curriculum links with Science, Technology and History.

DISABLED FACILITIES Contact the administrator for access details.

DIRECTIONS Contact the administrator for details.

Cragside Pony Trekking Centre
- Pauline Greener
- Langley Road, Haydon Bridge, Northumberland. NE47 6RT
- 0434 684761

Small friendly yard with emphasis on enjoyment in safety. Kind ponies who are patient with non-riders yet respond to experienced riders. Variety of treks with magnificent views in Hadrian's Wall country.

N C SUPPORT Joint owner is a practising primary teacher of 26 years' experience. 'Own a Pony for a Day' covers Science AT3 levels 2 and 3, plus English AT1 Speaking and Listening.

VISITS OUT

NORTH EAST

ANNUAL OR ONE OFF EVENT 'Own a Pony for a Day' weekdays throughout children's school holidays (or school term-time by arrangement).

OPENING All year: Tuesday to Sunday, closed Monday.

CATERING None. Indoor and outdoor facilities for eating packed lunches. Excellent facilities in village.

COST One-hour trek £7.50, two-hour trek £12.50, three-hour trek £15.00, 'Own a Pony' £19.00, BBQ trek £18.00, centre for the day £20.00. Groups of 10 or more 10% discount: all day £22.00.

DISABLED FACILITIES Full access for wheelchairs (except toilet). No specific facilities such as adapted saddles but plenty of willing hands.

DIRECTIONS Haydon Bridge six miles west of Hexham, on A69. Trekking Centre is half a mile south of village on A686 towards Langley Castle.

Grace Darling Museum

- D W N Calderwood, Hon. Curator
- Radcliffe Road, Bamburgh, Northumberland.

In the museum are pictures, books, etc., and the original coble in which Grace Darling and her father rescued nine survivors from the SS Forfarshire, wrecked on the Farne Islands on 7 September 1838.

N C SUPPORT None specifically; brochure, cards, etc., on sale in Museum. For further information contact the Curator, 109 Main Street, Seahouses, Northumberland NE68 7TS. Tel: 0665 720037 (Museum not on phone).

OPENING Easter to 30 September: daily 11.00am–6.00pm.

CATERING None.

COST Free. Donations to Royal National Lifeboat Institution (RNLI) appreciated.

DISABLED FACILITIES Museum on one floor only. Ramp for wheelchairs available.

DIRECTIONS In village opposite St Aidan's Church, Bamburgh.

Darlington Museum

- Alan Suddes, Curator
- Tubwell Row, Darlington, Co Durham. DL1 1PD
- 0325 463795

A small local museum with displays relating to the history and natural history of Darlington and surrounding areas. Talks to local schools by arrangement.

N C SUPPORT Primary sources for local history. The museum sells a good range of local publications. Loans to local schools. Regional Natural Sciences (geology, flora, fauna).

OPENING All year: Monday to Wednesday and Friday 10.00am–1.00pm and 2.00pm–6.00pm, Thursday 10.00am–1.00pm, Saturday 10.00am–1.00pm and 2.00pm–5.30pm.

CATERING None.

COST Free.

DISABLED FACILITIES Ground floor only access for wheelchairs.

DIRECTIONS One hundred yards east of Darlington Town Clock on Tubwell Row. Adjacent to parish church (St Cuthbert's).

VISITS OUT
NORTH EAST

Darlington Railway Centre & Museum
- Steven Dyke
- North Road Station, Darlington, Co. Durham. DL3 6ST
- ☎ 0325 460532

Restored Victorian station on the original route of the Stockton and Darlington Railway, the first steam-worked public railway. Exhibits include Stephenson's Locomotion, built in 1825.

N C SUPPORT Particular relevance to Technology, Geography and History. Short introductory talk may be arranged for group visits. Meeting/lunch room available.

ANNUAL OR ONE OFF EVENT Darlington Railway Carnival annually. Various attractions and entertainment.

OPENING Daily 9.30am–5.00pm. Last admission 4.30pm.

CATERING Drinks and confectionery on sale.

COST Children 80p, adults £1.60. Pre-booked school groups free.

DISABLED FACILITIES Wheelchair access to most areas. Toilet guide tape for visually impaired.

DIRECTIONS Off A2167 approximately three-quarters of a mile north of Darlington town centre. Free parking.

Derwentcote Steel Furnace
- The Head Custodian
- Forge Lane, Hamsterley Colliery, Newcastle, Tyne & Wear. NE39 1QA
- ☎ 0207 562573

The Derwent Valley steel works were once the centre of the British steel industry, and Derwentcote, built in the 18th century, is the earliest and most complete authentic steel-making furnace to have survived. Closed during the 1870s and allowed to fall into disrepair, the furnace has now been restored and opened to the public by English Heritage and includes a small exhibition.

OPENING Summer season. Good Friday or 1 April (whichever is earlier) to 30 September: daily 10.00am–6.00pm.

DIRECTIONS Ten miles southwest of Newcastle on A694 between Rowland's Gill and Hamsterley (OS Map 88; ref NZ 131566). Bus: Go-Ahead Northern 745 Newcastle-upon-Tyne to Consett (Tel: 091 386 4411). BR: Blaydon seven miles.

Dewsbury Museum
- Richard Butterfield
- Crow Nest Park, Heckmondwike Road, Dewsbury, West Yorks. WF13 0SJ
- ☎ 0924 468171

Historic mansion set in parkland with displays on the theme of childhood: Children at Work, Children at Play, Children at School 1940s classroom. Urban wildlife centre; conservatory with world economic plants. Orienteering course.

N C SUPPORT Key Stage 1, Key Stage 2 CSU 4 Britain Since 1930; Key Stage 2 SUA Families & Childhood. Cross-curricular opportunities. Teachers' study days and packs; provision of workbase for groups etc.

ANNUAL OR ONE OFF EVENT Historic vehicle rally; children's holiday activities; teachers' study days and full programme of events to support exhibition programme.

OPENING Monday to Friday 11.00am–5.00pm, Saturday and Sunday 12.00 noon–5.00pm. Groups at other times by arrangement.

CATERING By arrangement. Space may be available for packed lunches.

COST Free.

DISABLED FACILITIES Limited access to upper floors for severely disabled; ramped entrance; assistance available.

DIRECTIONS Near junction 40 of the M1 and junction 28 of the M62, signposted from A644 Huddersfield to Dewsbury road.

Dorman Museum
- Education Officer
- Linthorpe Road, Middlesbrough, Cleveland. TS5 6LA

Collections on local history, social history, natural history, archaeology, and the locally made Linthorpe and Middlesbrough pottery.

N C SUPPORT Workshops, worksheets, trails and competitions are organised by the Education Officer in conjunction with local schools and National Curriculum guidelines.

OPENING Tuesday to Saturday 10.00am–5.30pm.

CATERING None.

COST Free.

DISABLED FACILITIES Wheelchair ramp at rear door. Toilets.

DIRECTIONS Follow Linthorpe Road away from the town centre; on the left hand side of the road, past Albert Park main gates.

Durham Heritage Centre
- Miss D Meade
- St Mary-le-Bow, North Bailey, Durham. DH1 3ET
- 091-384 0406

Medieval church with 17th–18th-century furnishings and exhibits on history, architecture, art, entertainments, industries of city and county. Colour slide shows commentated by D Bellamy and C W Gibby.

N C SUPPORT Pictorial boards on local historical themes can be produced for groups, with questionnaires, in addition to leaflet on relevance of standing displays.

OPENING April to June and September: 2.00pm–4.30pm. July to August: 11.00am–4.30pm. Group visits possible in mornings by arrangement.

CATERING None; garden/churchyard available for picnics.

COST Group visits £6.00 per hour for a party of ten or more children at 20p per head, one adult free for every ten (maximum 20).

DISABLED FACILITIES Ground floor accessible; gallery with tape slide show not accessible to wheelchairs.

DIRECTIONS Immediately to east of Durham Cathedral. Ten-minute walk uphill from coach park; three minutes from car park.

VISITS OUT
NORTH EAST

Durham Light Infantry Museum & Art Gallery
- Terry Deary
- Aykley Heads, Durham. DH1 5TU
- 091-384 2214 FAX 091-386 1770

A regimental museum of the Durham Light Infantry, tracing its history through Victorian times to its disbandment in 1968. Also an art gallery with a changing programme of exhibitions.

N C SUPPORT Teachers' courses and pupil workshops in History (Victorian and Britain Since the 1930s) and Art (practical and observation).

ANNUAL OR ONE OFF EVENT Military Vehicle Rally every August Bank Holiday.

OPENING Tuesday to Saturday 10.00am–5.00pm, Sunday 2.00pm–5.00pm, closed Monday.

CATERING Cafe with drinks, confectionery, sandwiches, snacks and light cooked meals (salads etc.).

COST No group discounts. Free admission every Friday.

DISABLED FACILITIES Full access.

DIRECTIONS Walking distance from Durham station. By road take the A691 to Consett from Durham city centre. Signposted right after half a mile.

Durham Wildlife Trust
- Richard Wood
- Low Barns Nature Reserve, Witton-le-Wear, Bishop Auckland, Co Durham. DL14 0AG
- 0388 88728 FAX 0388 88529

Taking action to protect the wildlife of county Durham.

N C SUPPORT Thirty nature reserves. Active WATCH groups (junior wing of the Trust). Talks, guided walks. Teachers' resource pack.

ANNUAL OR ONE OFF EVENT National WATCH day and annual Open Day.

OPENING Daily (except Christmas Day) 9.00am–5.00pm.

CATERING Tea, coffee, juice, ice cream, biscuits, crisps, chocolate.

COST Free. Donations welcome

DISABLED FACILITIES Toilet, nature trail, access to observation hides, access to Visitor Centre.

Dunstanburgh Castle
- The Head Custodian
- Craster, Alnwick, Northumberland
- 0665 576231

An easy, but bracing, coastal walk leads to the eerie skeleton of this wonderful 14th-century castle sited on a basalt crag, rearing up more than 100 feet from the waves crashing on the rocks below. The surviving ruins include the large gatehouse, which later became the keep, and curtain walls.

OPENING All year. Good Friday or 1 April (whichever is earlier) to 30 September: daily 10.00am–6.00pm. 1 October to Maundy Thursday or 31 March (whichever is earlier): Tuesday to Sunday 10.00am–4.00pm; Closed 24–26 December and 1 January.

CATERING Picnic facilities.

DIRECTIONS Eight miles northeast of Alnwick, on footpaths from Craster or Embleton (OS Map 75; ref NU 258220). Bus: Northumbria 501

VISITS OUT

NORTH EAST

Alnwick to Berwick-upon-Tweed (passes close to BR Berwick-upon-Tweed) with connections from Newcastle (passing Tyne and Wear Metro Haymarket), alight Craster, one and a half miles (Tel: 091-232 4211).

Eden Camp Modern History Theme Museum
- S A Jaques
- Malton, North Yorks. YO17 0SD
- 0653 697777 FAX 0653 698243

This unique museum will transport visitors back to civilian life in wartime Britain. Experience the Home Front. Vehicle and Humberside visitor attraction of the year 1992.

N C SUPPORT Fully cross-referenced resource packs available at Key Stages 2 and 3. They claim 'a visit to Eden camp is worth a thousand hours in the classroom'.

OPENING 14 February to 23 December: daily 10.00am–5.00pm. Allow three hours for a visit.

CATERING Full catering facilities. Junior mess huts for own packed lunches.

COST Children £1.50, one teacher free per ten children for supervision purposes.

DISABLED FACILITIES Fully accessible. Braille sheets and Walkman tapes. England for Excellence, tours for all available.

DIRECTIONS Junction of A64 York to Scarborough road. A169 Malton to Pickering road.

Elsecar at Barnsley
- Sarah Twentyman
- Elsecar Workshops, Wath Road, Barnsley. S74 8HJ
- 0226 740203 FAX 0226 350239

Victorian industrial workshops which are currently being restored to create an industrial heritage attraction incorporating craft workshops, exhibitions, historical walks and the only Newcomen beam engine in its original location (1795).

N C SUPPORT At present under development. Classroom available for school parties. Teacher resource packs.

ANNUAL OR ONE OFF EVENT A steam railway and 'The Powerhouse', a 'hands-on' educational exhibition of power and energy.

OPENING Daily 10.30am–5.00pm.

CATERING Light refreshments available.

COST Free.

DISABLED FACILITIES Toilets, level site, car parking.

DIRECTIONS Leave M1 junction 36 and follow brown Elsecar heritage signs taking A6135 for two miles. Turn left onto Boardcar Road and right onto Armroyd Lane.

ENGLISH HERITAGE

National Curriculum Support Almost every aspect of the curriculum can be explored at English Heritage properties. They can be used not only for studying History but linked to other subjects as varied as English, Maths, Science, Technology, Geography and Music.

VISITS OUT
NORTH EAST

English Heritage has produced a wide range of National Curriculum teachers' guides and videos to give plenty of stimulating ideas. Write to English Heritage Education Service, Keysign House, 429 Oxford Street, London W1R 2HD, for a free copy of the resources catalogue.

Annual or one-off event At some sites each year there are special educational events, often with the involvement of experts such as musicians and storytellers, for visiting educational groups.

Cost Student groups and school parties are admitted free to English Heritage properties, but should book in advance through the relevant Regional Office.

See individual entries for all other information.

Aldborough Roman Town
Aydon Castle
Barnard Castle
Belsay Hall Castle & Gardens
Brinkburn Priory
Byland Abbey
Chesters Roman Fort & Museum
Clifford's Tower
Conisbrough Castle
Corbridge Roman Site
Derwentcote Steel Furnace
Dunstanburgh Castle
Finchale Priory
Guisborough Priory
Hadrian's Wall
Helmsley Castle
Housesteads Roman Fort
Kirkham Priory
Lindisfarne Priory
Middleham Castle
Monk Bretton Priory
Mount Grace Priory
Pickering Castle
Prudhoe Castle
Richmond Castle
Rievaulx Abbey
Roche Abbey
Scarborough Castle
Bessie Surtees House
Thornton Abbey
Tynemouth Castle & Priory
Vindolanda Trust
Warkworth Castle & Hermitage
Whitby Abbey

The Farne Islands

- John Walton
- c/o 8 The Shieling, St Aidans, Seahouses, Northumberland
- 0665 720651

National nature reserve with 17 species of seabirds and colony of grey seals. Chapel on inner Farne in memory of St Cuthbert.

N C SUPPORT Teachers' resource book on islands and Northumberland coast. Links with Science, Geography and History.

OPENING 1 April to 30 April and 1 August to 31 September: daily 10.30am–6.00pm. 1 May to 31 July: Staple Island: daily 10.30am–1.30pm, Inner Farne: daily 1.30pm–5.00pm.

CATERING None on islands.

COST Boat crossings costs not included. Schools' Corporate Members free.

DISABLED FACILITIES Limited access, partly due to boat crossing.

DIRECTIONS By boat crossing from Seahouses (no landings in bad weather).

VISITS OUT
NORTH EAST

Finchale Priory
- The Head Custodian
- Brasside, Newton Hall, Co. Durham. DH1 5SH

These beautiful 13th-century priory remains are located beside the curving River Wear.

OPENING Any reasonable time.

DIRECTIONS Three miles northeast of Durham, on minor road off A167 (OS Map 88; ref NZ 297471). Bus: Gardiners 737 Durham to Chester-le-Street (passes close to BR Durham) (Tel: 0388 814417). BR: Durham five miles.

Flamingo Land
- Isobel Taylor
- Kirby Misperton, Malton, North Yorks. YO17 0UX
- 065 386 287 FAX 065 386 280

Over 100 rides: slides, shows and attractions featuring the Bullet, Waikiki Wave, Sky Flyer, Ten Great Shows and Europe's largest privately owned zoo.

N C SUPPORT Full educational pack available on request.

OPENING April to end October.

CATERING Yes.

COST £7.00 per person, under fours free. Group discounts available.

DISABLED FACILITIES Yes.

DIRECTIONS Situated off the A169 Malton to Pickering Road.

Ford Castle
- David Etheridge
- Ford, Nr Berwick-upon-Tweed, Northumberland. TD15 2PX
- 0890 820257 FAX 0890 820413

Eighty-bed residential Field Study Centre in 14th-century castle. Ideal location for freshwater/coast moorland field studies and outdoor pursuits.

N C SUPPORT Three qualified and experienced teaching staff to assist with programme planning and in teaching courses up to A-Level.

OPENING All year.

CATERING Full catering in main building. Full or self-catering in annexe.

COST On application.

DISABLED FACILITIES None.

DIRECTIONS Eight miles north of Wooler on B 63553 Wooler to Berwick road.

Forest Enterprise
- Pippa Kirkham, Education Ranger
- Dalby Forest District Office, 42 Eastgate, Pickering, North Yorks. YO1 7DU
- 0751 72771 FAX 0751 74503

Dalby Forest at the centre of the North Riding Forest Park offers a nine-mile forest drive, plenty of parking and picnic places, waymarked walks, a forest shop and visitor centre.

N C SUPPORT The resident Education Ranger at Dalby Forest can cater for school visits through guided walks or offering advice on curriculum-related activities. Geography projects, visitor surveys.

OPENING Dalby Forest: all year. Shop and Visitor Centre: Easter to October 10.00am–5.00pm.

CATERING Picnic facilities.

COST School visits free. Booking necessary. Education Ranger £10.00 plus VAT per hour.

DISABLED FACILITIES Toilets.

DIRECTIONS Turn off the A170 Pickering to Scarborough Road in Thornton Dale towards Whitby. Follow brown forest drive signs to Dalby Forest.

Forest Enterprise
- Brian Walker
- Hamsterley Forest, Redford, Hamsterley, Bishop Auckland, Co Durham. DL13 3NL
- 0388 88312 FAX 0388 88762

Varied forest environment, high degree of multi-use, forest walks, orienteering course, cycle trails, visitor centre. Broadleaf and coniferous woodland.

N C SUPPORT Teachers' pack geared to National Curriculum written by teachers and FE staff. Experienced ranger staff on hand. Guided walks available.

OPENING Forest: all year 7.30am–9.00pm. Visitor centre open any time for organised groups. Tel: 0751 73810/72771 for bookings.

COST Admission for educational visits is free. Guided walks are currently £13.22 per hour including VAT.

DISABLED FACILITIES Access to Visitor Centre. Toilet (unisex). Tracks and paths.

DIRECTIONS Access from A68 at Witton-le-Wear five miles north of West Auckland.

Forest Enterprise
- Fiona Simpson
- North & East England Regional Office, 1A Grosvenor Terrace, York. YO3 7BD
- 0904 620221 FAX 0904 010664

A range of educational services and facilities over north and east England from Northumberland and the lakes to Suffolk. Forest classrooms, educational material and guidance for specialist staff in many districts.

N C SUPPORT Specialist recreation/education staff will advise on National Curriculum subjects linking into the forest environment. A regional pack linking themes to areas of the curriculum is available. Programmes to fit individual schools' needs on a day visit. Talks, slide shows and interactive projects also available.

OPENING All year round.

COST Costs vary in the region of £20.00–£50.00 per day per group.

DISABLED FACILITIES In many areas.

Fountains Abbey & Studley Royal Fountains
- The Administrator
- Ripon, North Yorks. HG4 3DZ
- 0765 620333

Cistercian abbey on the banks of the River Skell, founded in 1132 and the largest monastic ruin in Britain. The ruins provide the dramatic focal point of the 18th-century landscape garden at Studley Royal: water garden temples, follies, vistas, deer park; small museum; St Mary's Church, built by William Burges 1871–78

N C SUPPORT National Curriculum links with History and English. Education officer; teachers' resource book; primary source materials available; children's guide; BTEC Leisure and Tourism Seminar available.

DISABLED FACILITIES Access to Abbey grounds, Studley Royal Garden and Visitor Centre. Powered 'runarounds' and wheelchairs available by prior booking only; adapted toilet in Studley car park. Studley tea room and Visitor Centre. Minibus available from Visitor Centre.

DIRECTIONS Four miles west of Ripon off B6265 to Pateley Bridge, eight miles west of A1, ten miles north of Harrogate (A61). Bus: United 145 from Ripon (with connections from BR Harrogate).

Green Dragon Museum
- Mark Rowland-Jones
- Theatre Yard, Stockton-on-Tees. TS18 1AT
- 0642 674308 FAX 0642 602474

Displays about the Stockton area, its people and personalities, including the audio-visual exhibition '1825 – The Birth of Railways', local ceramics, school room, historic films and community-led temporary exhibitions.

N C SUPPORT Victorian activity sessions for primary schools, comprising school lesson, object handling, wash-day and others, by prior arrangement. Teachers' resource packs on local themes. Displays in schools. INSET sessions.

ANNUAL OR ONE OFF EVENT Art and Creative Writing competitions.

OPENING Monday to Saturday 9.00am–5.00pm, closed bank holidays.

CATERING School room for use by groups with packed lunches; otherwise town centre location.

COST Free.

DISABLED FACILITIES Linked access for wheelchair users and other people with disabilities. Staff very willing to assist where possible, please contact.

DIRECTIONS The museum is in central Stockton between the High Street and River Tees, and off Silver Street. In middle of Stockton. Drop off young people in Stockton High Street, go down Finkel Street and turn right into Green Dragon yard. Coaches park in Riverside Car Park.

Guisborough Priory
- The Head Custodian
- Guisborough, Cleveland. TS14 6HL
- 0287 638301

The impressive east end of this Augustinian priory stands like a triumphal arch in the landscape. The remains also include the gate house and east end of an early 14th-century church.

OPENING All year. Good Friday or 1 April (whichever is earlier) to 30 September: daily 10.00am–6.00pm. 1 October to Maundy Thursday or 31 March (whichever is earlier): Tuesday–Sunday 10.00am–4.00pm. Closed 24–26 December and 1 January.

VISITS OUT
NORTH EAST

CATERING Picnic facilities.

DISABLED FACILITIES Wheelchair access.

DIRECTIONS In Guisborough town, next to parish church (OS map 94; ref NZ 618163). Bus: Tees and District X56, 93, 256/8 from Middlesbrough (passing close to BR Middlesbrough) (Tel: 0642 210131). BR: Marske four and a half miles.

The Green Howards Museum
- Lt Col. N D McIntosh
- Trinity Church Square, Richmond, North Yorks. DL10 4QN
- 0748 822133 FAX 0748 826561

Over 300 years of regimental history from the regiment's formation in 1688, is related by means of weapons, pictures, memorabilia, uniforms, musical instruments and a superb medal collection featuring twelve Victoria Crosses.

OPENING February to November: Monday to Friday 9.00am–4.30pm. Closed December and January.

CATERING None.

COST Pre-booked school visits free. Minimum five days' notice.

DISABLED FACILITIES None.

DIRECTIONS Situated in the converted church in the centre of Richmond market place.

Grindon Museum
- Helen Sinclair
- Grindon Lane, Sunderland, Tyne and Wear
- 091-514 1235 FAX 091-510 0675

Once an Edwardian shipbuilder's house. Room interior displays include kitchen, sitting room, child's nursery and bedroom. There is also a chemist's shop, post office, shoemaker and dentist.

N C SUPPORT Teachers' notes and quiz sheets are available free. Loan packs of domestic items and costumes may be borrowed through Sunderland Museum. Staff can advise on planning a visit.

OPENING Monday, Tuesday, Wednesday and Friday 9.30am–12.30pm and 1.30pm–5.00pm, Saturday 9.30am–12.00 noon and 1.15pm–4.00pm. June to September: also Sunday 2.00pm–5.00pm.

CATERING None.

COST Free.

DISABLED FACILITIES Guide dogs allowed.

DIRECTIONS Grindon Museum is a few minutes out of Sunderland off the A183 Chester Road. Bus services from Sunderland town centre (15, 16, 126).

Hadrian's Wall
- Housesteads Fort
- Bardon Mill, Hexham, Northumberland. NE47 6NN
- 0434 344363

National Trust owns four and a half miles of wall including steel rigg to Housesteads. Roman wall display in Housesteads Information Centre. Perched high on a ridge overlooking open moorland, this is the best-known part of the Wall. The fort covers five acres and the remains of many buildings, such as granaries, barrack blocks and gateways, can be seen.

VISITS OUT

NORTH EAST

OPENING All year. Good Friday or 1 April (whichever is earlier) to 30 September: daily 10.00am–6.00pm. 1 October to Maundy Thursday or 31 March (whichever is earlier): Monday to Sunday 10.00am–4.00pm. Closed 24–26 December and 1 January.

CATERING Limited refreshments available.

DISABLED FACILITIES Fort not suitable for wheelchairs. Access to Information Centre only.

DIRECTIONS Six miles northeast of Haltwhistle, four miles north of Bardon Hill. Signposted from A1 and A69.

Helmsley Castle
- The Head Custodian
- Helmsley, North Yorks. YO6 5AB
- 0439 70442

Close to the market square, with a view of the town, is this 12th-century castle. Spectacular earthworks surround a great ruined keep dating from the Norman Conquest. There is an exhibition and tableau on the history of the castle.

OPENING All year. Good Friday or 1 April (whichever is earlier) to 30 September: daily 10.00am–6.00pm. 1 October to Maundy Thursday or 31 March (whichever is earlier): Tuesday to Sunday 10.00am–4.00pm. Closed 24–26 December and 1 January.

DIRECTIONS Near town centre (OS Map 100; ref SE 611836). Bus: Scarborough and District 128 from BR Scarborough (Tel: 0723 375463); Yorkshire Coastliner 94 from BR Malton (Tel: 0653 692556).

Herb & Heather Centre
- C A Atkinson
- West Haddlesey, Nr Selby, North Yorks. YO8 8QA
- 0757 228279

A working plant nursery which includes fragrant medicinal, culinary and dye herbs, lotions and potions, knotgardens, winter gardens, etc., animals. Information Centre for herbs.

N C SUPPORT Can provide nature trail, advise on herb gardens, bee and butterfly gardens, growing wild flowers, 17th-century use of herbs and herbs through the ages.

ANNUAL OR ONE OFF EVENT Christmas demonstration days.

OPENING Daily 9.30am–5.30pm.

CATERING Tea room and pergola, picnic facilities. Juice/lemonade and biscuits 50p per child.

COST Children £1.00, staff free.

DISABLED FACILITIES Everything ramped, no steps.

DIRECTIONS Six miles south of Selby, A19 Selby to Doncaster road, junction 34 off M62.

Hornsea Museum
- C Walker, Curator
- Burns Farm, 11 Newbegin, Hornsea, North Humberside. HU18 1AB
- 0964 533443

Victorian home and village life housed in charming Georgian farmhouse and associated buildings. Large garden, small shop, winner of numerous national awards, featured on TV.

VISITS OUT
NORTH EAST

N C SUPPORT Victorian activity sessions for school parties by request: schoolroom, laundry, dairy, etc. Teachers' pack available, also sets of fact sheets on 14 different subjects relating to 19th-century life.

OPENING Easter to October: Monday to Saturday 10.00am–5.00pm, Sunday 2.00pm–5.00pm. By appointment all year, day or evening.

CATERING Picnic area.

COST Ordinary visit: 90p. Two Victorian activities and tours: £1.50. Four Victorian activities: £2.00.

DISABLED FACILITIES Wheelchair access to about two thirds of the site. Toilet.

DIRECTIONS On East Yorkshire coast, approximately 20 miles northeast of Hull.

Hornsea Pottery
- Jane McDonnell
- Hornsea, Yorks. HU18 IUT
- 0964 532161 FAX 0964 536363

Leisure and educational facilities include the Birds of Prey Conservation Centre, the Yorkshire Car Collection, Butterfly World, Minidale Model Village, Minidale Farmyard, the adventure playground and Neptune's Kingdom.

N C SUPPORT Teachers' guidance notes and video.

OPENING Daily (except 24–26 December) from 10.00am.

CATERING Ridings Restaurant with schools menu. Picnic areas. Barbecue, pizza and snack cabins.

COST Groups of over 20: children £1.99, one adult free with every ten children, additional adults £1.99.

DISABLED FACILITIES Parking and toilets.

DIRECTIONS Nearest motorway: M62. Nearest A road: A165.

Horsforth Village Museum
- Mrs N De Dombal
- The Green, Horsforth, Leeds, West Yorks. LS18 SJB

A small museum opened in 1988 and run by volunteer members of Horsforth Historical Society. The Museum aims to depict aspects of life in Horsforth from Domesday to the present day.

N C SUPPORT Good liaison exists between the museum and local schools. Walks, slide talks and guided tours of the museum are arranged by appointment. A teachers' resource pack is in preparation.

OPENING Saturday 10.00am–4.00pm, Sunday 2.00pm–5.00pm. School visits by arrangement.

CATERING None.

COST Free.

DISABLED FACILITIES None.

DIRECTIONS Horsforth is about five miles northwest of Leeds centre. Follow ring road A6120. Turn right at Hall Park.

House of Hardy Ltd
- Michael Lamcock
- Willowborn, Alnwick, Northumberland. NE66 2PG
- 0665 602771 FAX 0665 602389

Manufacturer of the world's finest fishing tackle. Museum gives insight

NORTH EAST

into the history of the company and its wide variety of products. Factory tour shows manufacture of products.

OPENING March to October. Museum and countryside: Monday to Friday 9.00am–5.00pm, Saturday and Sunday 10.00am–5.00pm. Guided factory tours: Monday to Thursday 10.00am and 2.00pm, Friday 10.00am (under 16s must be accompanied by an adult on factory tours).

CATERING None.

COST Free.

DISABLED FACILITIES Suitable for people with disabilities.

DIRECTIONS Signposted on brown information signs on Alnwick route off A1.

Housesteads Roman Fort

- The Head Custodian
- Haydon Bridge, Hexham, Northumberland. NE47 6NN
- 0434 344363

Perched high on a ridge overlooking open moorland, this is the best-known part of Hadrian's Wall. The fort covers five acres and the remains of many buildings, such as granaries, barrack blocks and gateways, can be seen. A museum displays altars, inscriptions and models.

OPENING All year. Good Friday or 1 April (whichever is earlier) to 30 September: daily 10.00am–6.00pm. 1 October to Maundy Thursday or 31 March (whichever is earlier): daily 10.00am–4.00pm. Closed 24–26 December and 1 January.

DISABLED FACILITIES Wheelchair access. Car park on site; enquire at NT/National Park information centre on main road.

DIRECTIONS Two and three-quarter miles northeast of Bardon Mill on B6318 (OS Map 87; ref NY 790687). Bus/Rail: West of Hexham the Wall roughly parallels the A69 Carlisle to Newcastle-upon-Tyne road, lying between one and four miles north of it; an hourly bus service takes this road; Northumbria/CMS 685 Newcastle to Carlisle (Tel: 091-232 4211).

Impressions Gallery

- Stefan Sadofski
- 29 Castlegate, York. YO1 1RN
- 0904 654724 FAX 0904 651509

Photographic gallery with changing contemporary exhibitions.

OPENING Monday to Saturday 9.30am–5.30pm, Sunday 10.00am–5.00pm.

CATERING Cafe.

COST Free.

DIRECTIONS Gallery situated in the centre of York. Near the Jorvik Viking Centre, Castle Museum and Clifford's Tower.

Jorvik Viking Centre

- Liz Stanners, Head of Marketing
- Coppergate, York. YO1 1NT
- 0904 611944 FAX 0904 613215

The Jorvik Viking Centre conveys its visitors by 'Time Car' to the sights, sounds and smells of the Viking-age city of Jorvik, uncovered by archaeologists beneath Coppergate, York.

OPENING All year: daily (except Christmas Day). 1 April to 31 October: 9.00am–7.00pm. November to 31 March: 9.00pm–5.30pm.

COST Children £2.00, adults £3.95, one teacher free with every ten children.

DISABLED FACILITIES Good provision for the disabled: adapted toilet, lift and adapted car for wheelchair users.

DIRECTIONS Located in central York. Coach parking available at Clarence Street and Kent Street; well signposted in city.

Kielder Forest Visitor Centre
- Simon Blenkinsop
- Forestry Commission, Kielder Castle, Hexham, Northumberland. NE48 1ES
- 0434 250209 FAX 0434 220756

Ranger service offering guided walks into the forest, a Forestry Visitor Centre equipped with modern audio-visual interpretive facilities and clubroom. Events include open days, walks, talks and visits to see modern timber production.

N C SUPPORT Fulfils Attainment Target 2 in Science: study of animals and their habitats. Suitable for study of cross-curricular themes on the environment.

ANNUAL OR ONE OFF EVENT Study of forestry, landscape design, conflicting land use, ecological studies of flora and fauna and conservation issues.

OPENING Easter to end October: daily 10.00am–5.00pm.

COST £15 per session (morning or afternoon).

DISABLED FACILITIES Centre is fully accessible to people with disabilities.

DIRECTIONS Thirty-five miles northwest of Hexham off A69; 40 miles east of Carlisle.

Kielder Water
- Patricia Murray
- Tower Knowe Visitor Centre, Kielder Water, Falstone, Hexham, Northumberland. NE48 1BX
- 0434 240398 FAX 0434 240060

Europe's largest man-made lake. Exhibition: 'The First 500 Million Years'. Dam and hydro-electric tours. Round-lake cruises with commentary. Free itinerary planning service.

N C SUPPORT Unit of work for Key Stage 4 Class (YR 10). An Environmental Issue: Kielder Water Scheme, Physical, Human, Environmental Geography.

OPENING April to October: 10.00am–6.00pm. November to March: 10.00am–4.00pm.

CATERING Yes.

COST Free.

DISABLED FACILITIES Yes.

DIRECTIONS Please apply for details.

King's Own Scottish Borderers
- Lt Col. C G O Hogg
- Regimental Museum, The Barracks, Berwick-on-Tweed, Northumberland. TD15 1DG
- 0289 307426 FAX 0289 331928

Military museum of the King's Own Scottish Borderers containing medals, weapons, silver and a variety of items telling their history from 1889 until the present day.

N C SUPPORT No specific support but guide available if requested before visit to explain display and answer questions.

OPENING Monday to Friday 9.00am–4.00pm, Saturday 9.00am–11.00am, closed Sunday. Closed Easter and Christmas and certain other public holidays.

CATERING Soft drinks and sweets available at entrance to the Barracks.

COST Children £1.00, adults £2.00. concessions £1.50. Entrance fee includes Koss Museum, English Heritage 'By Beat of Drum' and Berwick Town Museum. All three Museums are within the Barracks.

DISABLED FACILITIES Toilets within Barracks complex. No facilities within Regimental Museum.

DIRECTIONS Barracks to be found on the Parade.

Kirkham Priory
- The Head Custodian
- Whitwell-on-the-Hill, York. YO6 7JS
- 0653 81768

The ruins of this Augustinian priory, including a magnificent carved gate house, are set in a peaceful and secluded valley by the River Derwent.

OPENING All year: Good Friday or 1 April (whichever is earlier) to 30 September: daily 10.00am–6.00pm. 1 October to Maundy Thursday or 31 March (whichever is earlier): Tuesday to Sunday 10.00am–4.00pm. Closed 24–26 December and 1 January.

CATERING Picnic facilities.

DISABLED FACILITIES Wheelchair access.

DIRECTIONS Five miles southwest of Malton on minor road off A64 (OS Map 100; Ref SE 735657). Bus: Yorkshire Coastliner 840/2/3 Leeds to Scarborough (passes BR York and Malton) to within three-quarters of a mile (Tel: 0653 692556). BR: Malton six miles.

Kirkleatham Old Hall Museum
- Miss L Lampard
- Kirkleatham Village, Redcar, Cleveland. TS10 5NW
- 0642 479500

Local history museum with permanent displays of local life and industry, ironstone mining, shipping, fishing, sea rescue, natural history, seaside rock making. Also varied temporary exhibitions.

N C SUPPORT Worksheets available for several of the galleries. School information sheets circulated for new exhibitions.

ANNUAL OR ONE OFF EVENT Charity fair in June, Christmas fair in December.

OPENING Thursday to Monday 10.00am–5.00pm, closed Tuesday and Wednesday, Good Friday, 25 December to 1 January.

CATERING Cafe open daily 10.30am–4.00pm (closes earlier in winter).

COST Free.

DISABLED FACILITIES Access to all ground floor areas: shop, cafe, toilets, gardens.

VISITS OUT
NORTH EAST

DIRECTIONS Signposted from the A19 and A174; in Kirkleatham Village just off the A1042.

Knaresborough Castle
- Ros Watson or Barbara Blakeson
- c/o Harrogate Museums Service, Royal Pump Room Museum, Crown Place, Harrogate, North Yorks. HG1 2RY
- 0423 503340

Castle site including keep, Sallyport and Courthouse Museum, a local history museum which includes an original Tudor court and a Civil War gallery.

OPENING May to September: daily 10.30am–5.00pm.

CATERING None.

COST Children 60p, adults £1.00, Group rate 80p. Local Authority schools free.

DISABLED FACILITIES Access difficult. No specific facilities.

Laing Art Gallery
- Ewen Carr
- Higham Place, Newcastle-upon-Tyne. NE1 8AG
- 091-232 7734 FAX 091-222 0952

Largest gallery in the northeast. Collection of paintings, sculptures, applied art, 18th century to present day. Education Officer and education suite. Talks, activities. Necessary to book.

N C SUPPORT Regular workshops, quiz sheets, videos based on current exhibitions. Cross-curricular art and design, living history. 'Art on Tyneside' permanent interpretive exhibition with inter-activities.

OPENING Tuesday to Friday 10.00am–5.30pm, Saturday 10.00am–4.30pm, Sunday 2.30am–5.30pm.

CATERING Cafe in Gallery. Use of education room for packed lunch. Must book.

COST Free.

DISABLED FACILITIES See leaflet (free on application to Gallery).

DIRECTIONS Free leaflet with map on application to Gallery.

Leeds City Art Gallery
- Amanda Phillips, Education Officer
- The Headrow, Leeds. LS1 2AA
- 0532 748254

Permanent collection of 19th-century to contemporary practice. Specialism in 1930s with Henry Moore, Stanley Spencer, Barbara Hepworth, Eileen Agar. Temporary exhibition programme.

N C SUPPORT Education service provides workshops and support system for groups wishing to explore temporary and permanent exhibitions. Promotes Equal Opportunity to the Arts, innovation and links between art and society.

ANNUAL OR ONE OFF EVENT Activities and events, e.g. music, performance, poetry, organised to coincide with exhibitions.

OPENING Monday to Friday 10.00am–5.30pm, Saturday 10.00am–4.00pm.

CATERING Cafe; education room for picnics.

COST Donations welcome.

DISABLED FACILITIES Ramp, toilets.

DIRECTIONS Centre of Leeds, next to the Town Hall.

VISITS OUT
NORTH EAST

Leeds City Council
- K T Roberts
- Tropical World, Canal Gardens, Roundhay Park, Leeds. LS8 2ER
- 0532 661850 FAX 0532 370077

Tropical paradise where butterflies flutter amongst exotic blooms. Underwater world of the North Sea. Amazon river and tropical seas. Snakes, ants, spiders. All safely tucked away behind glass.

N C SUPPORT Yes.

OPENING Daily (except Christmas Day) 10.00am till dusk.

CATERING Gardens. Tea rooms on site.

COST Free.

DISABLED FACILITIES Yes.

DIRECTIONS Three miles north of Leeds city centre, off the A58 Wetherby Road at Oakwood.

Leeds City Museum
- Jim Nunney
- Municipal Buildings, Calveley Street, Leeds. LS1 3AA
- 0532 478275 FAX 0532 426761

Explore the temples and jungles of Leeds City Museum and watch out for the bogeyman! Wander through the world of costume and crafts from five continents, ranging from the frozen wastes to the tropical equator.

N C SUPPORT Contact museum direct.

OPENING Tuesday to Friday 9.30am–5.30pm, closed Sunday, Monday, bank holiday Mondays and Tuesday following bank holiday.

CATERING In adjacent Art Gallery.

COST Free.

DISABLED FACILITIES Steps to lift at entrance give access to people with disabilities but ramps and assistance available if requested in advance.

DIRECTIONS In Leeds city centre on the Headrow adjacent to Leeds Town Hall.

Lightwater Valley
- Phil Reed
- North Stainley, Ripon, North Yorks. HG4 3HT
- 0765 635321 FAX 0765 635359

One hundred and twenty-five acres of the most beautiful country park and lakeland. An even wider range of exciting rides, attractions and live entertainment than ever before. Home of the world's biggest rollercoaster.

N C SUPPORT To help schools make the most of a visit to Lightwater Valley, a series of free worksheets is available, geared to specific age groups and the requirements of the National Curriculum.

OPENING Until 5 September: daily 10.00am–5.30pm.

CATERING Numerous catering outlets, including self-service restaurant, Amanda's coffee shop and Victorian-style conservatory.

COST Group rates (parties of 12 or more in minibus): Tuesday to Thursday, Sunday and bank holidays £6.75 per person with one free ticket for every 20 purchased, Monday, Friday and Saturday (except bank holidays) £6.26 per person with one free ticket for every 20 purchased.

DISABLED FACILITIES Wheelchair accessible. Toilets, easy access, changing facilities.

DIRECTIONS Lightwater Valley is easily accessible by road and is well signposted; just off the A1 north of Ripon on the A6108.

Lindisfarne Priory
- The Head Custodian
- Holy Island, Berwick-upon-Tweed, Northumberland. TD15 2RX
- 0289 89200

The site of one of the most important early centres of Christianity in Anglo-Saxon England. St Cuthbert converted pagan Northumbria, and miracles occurring at his shrine established this 11th-century priory as a major pilgrimage centre. The evocative ruins, with the decorated 'rainbow' arch curving dramatically across the nave of the church, are still the destination of pilgrims today. The story of Lindisfarne is told in an exhibition which gives an impression of life of the monks.

OPENING All year. Good Friday or 1 April (whichever is earlier) to 30 September: daily 10.00am–6.00pm. 1 October to Maundy Thursday or 31 March (whichever is earlier): Tuesday to Sunday 10.00am–4.00pm. Closed 24–26 December and 1 January.

DIRECTIONS On Holy Island, which can be reached at low tide across a causeway. Tide tables are posted at each end of the causeway. (OS Map 75; ref NU 126418). Bus: Northumbria 477 from Berwick-upon-Tweed. Times vary with tides (Tel: 0289 307283). BR: Berwick-upon-Tweed 14 miles via causeway.

Lotherton Hall
- D Rooke
- Aberford, Leeds. LS25 3EB
- 0532 813259

The Gascoigne family created a charming home in the halcyon days before World War I. Edwardian country house and gardens. Explore the wilder side of the estate too.

N C SUPPORT Worksheets available. Contact the curator.

OPENING Tuesday to Sunday 10.30am–5.30pm.

CATERING Stable courtyard cafe.

COST Children 60p.

DISABLED FACILITIES Two steps to front door. Multi-level building. Estate and bird garden accessible.

DIRECTIONS Off the A1, three-quarters of a mile east of the junction with B1217 Towton road.

Manor House Art Gallery & Museum
- Mary Bentham
- Ilkley, North Yorks. LS29 9DT
- 0943 600066 FAX 0943 817079

Picturesque Elizabethan building on the site of a Roman fort; local history material, mainly Roman and Victorian on ground floor. Upper galleries: temporary shows.

N C SUPPORT Displays useful for Roman archaeology Key Stages 2 and 3. Information pack and Victorian Key Stage 2 teachers' pack £5.50. Study sessions and

VISITS OUT
NORTH EAST

workshops on Wednesdays and Fridays.

OPENING April to September: daily Tuesday–Sunday 10.00am–6.00pm. October to March: daily 10.00am–5.00pm, closed Monday (except bank holidays).

CATERING Small kitchen for making and serving drinks in Activity Centre immediately adjacent to cafes.

COST Free.

DISABLED FACILITIES Ground floor of museum and Activity Centre suitable for wheelchair users.

DIRECTIONS Behind Ilkley Parish Church through the archway on Church Street (the Skipton A65), five minutes' walk from station.

Marine Life Centre
- J S Allan
- 8–10 Main Street, Seahouses, Northumberland. NE68 5RG
- 0665 721257

The Centre provides a unique opportunity to examine local fish in seven tanks. There is a touch pool for the children. The museum is set on three levels above aquarium.

N C SUPPORT The Centre is ideal for studying marine life and fishing history, ideal for Marine Biology Sciences for 7–18-year-olds.

OPENING April to end of May: daily 10.00am–5.00pm. June to end of August: daily 10.00am–6.00pm. September to end of October: daily 10.00am–4.00pm.

CATERING Four cafes and restaurants within 30 yards of museum.

COST Children £1, adults £1.50, Senior Citizens £1.00. Group rates (schools): children 80p, teachers free.

DISABLED FACILITIES Ramp to seawater and freshwater aquarium.

DIRECTIONS Centre of Seahouses Village, 100 yards from main car park.

Mel House Bird Garden
- Caroline Rudland
- Newton-on-Rawcliffe, Pickering, North Yorks. YO18 8QA
- 0751 76538

Owl and animal sanctuary. Animals to feed and handle. Daily owl flying display at 2.00pm.

OPENING Easter through to first week in September: Sunday to Friday 1.00pm–5.00pm.

COST Threes and under free; 3–14 £1.00; 14 and older £1.50. No concessions.

DISABLED FACILITIES Flat site with wide doorways.

DIRECTIONS From Pickering, past station and trout farm, over level crossing, continue for four miles. Mel House is in centre of Newton-on-Rawcliffe, opposite pond, next door to pub.

Mercer Art Gallery
- Barbara Blakeson or Ros Watson
- 31 Swan Road, Harrogate, North Yorks. HG1 2SA
- 0423 503340

Municipal art gallery with changing exhibitions. Also permanent displays of Greek ceramics and Egyptian and Roman artefacts.

VISITS OUT
NORTH EAST

N C SUPPORT Activities room where items from the reserve collection can be seen. Collection development officer and visual arts officer can give talks.

OPENING Tuesday to Saturday 10.00am–5.00pm, Sunday 2.00pm–5.00pm.

CATERING None.

COST Free.

DISABLED FACILITIES Full access.

DIRECTIONS Contact the gallery for directions.

Merchant Adventurers' Hall
- I S Wheatley
- Fossgate, York. YO1 2XD
- 0904 654818

Finest medieval guildhall in Europe. Still owned by the company which built it over 600 years ago. Furniture, paintings, displays about life and work of merchant adventurers.

N C SUPPORT Free teachers' notes and pupils' activity sheets covering cross-curricular subjects aimed mainly at ages 8–12.

OPENING Mid-March to early November: daily 9.00am–5.00pm. Early November to mid-March: Monday–Saturday 9.00am–3.00pm.

CATERING Picnic lunches may be eaten in the Hall or surrounding garden.

COST 50p per child and accompanying adult.

DISABLED FACILITIES Toilet.

DIRECTIONS In middle of York in Piccadilly.

Metroland
- Veronica Connell
- 39 Garden Walk, Metrocentre, Gateshead. NE11 9YZ
- 091-493 2048 FAX 091-493 2904

All-weather theme park. There's so much scope using either the rides or the live entertainment provided daily or just the fantastic backdrop. Workpacks available for some age groups – or schools can bring their own.

OPENING Summer: Monday to Wednesday 10.00am–8.00pm, Thursday to Saturday 10.00am–10.00pm, Sunday 12 noon–6.00pm. Winter: Monday to Wednesday 12.00 noon–8.00pm, otherwise as for summer.

CATERING Restaurant, packed lunch facilities, snack bars.

COST 1993 special group rates schools £2.00 per person.

DISABLED FACILITIES Toilets, lifts and walkways.

DIRECTIONS Any direction via A1(M). Minutes from Newcastle-upon-Tyne.

Middleham Castle
- The Head Custodian
- Middleham, Leyburn, North Yorks. DL8 4QR
- 0969 23899

This childhood home of Richard III stands controlling the river that winds through Wensleydale. There is a massive 12th-century keep standing within later fortifications.

OPENING All year. Good Friday or 1 April (whichever is earlier) to 30 September: daily 10.00am–6.00pm. 1 October to Maundy Thursday or 31 March (whichever is earlier):

Tuesday to Sunday 10.00am–4.00pm. Closed 24–26 December and 1 January.

CATERING Picnic facilities.

DISABLED FACILITIES Wheelchair access (except to tower).

DIRECTIONS At Middleham, two miles south of Leyburn on A6108 (OS Map 99; ref SE 128875).

Middlesbrough Art Gallery
- Education Officer
- 320 Linthorpe Road, Middlesbrough, Cleveland. TS1 4AW
- 0642 211347

Collections of British 20th-century and contemporary art, and a smaller collection of Old Masters. Temporary exhibitions programme with regular changes. Outdoor sculpture court.

N C SUPPORT Education Officer in regular contact with schools. School programmes run in conjunction with each exhibition and follow National Curriculum guidelines.

ANNUAL OR ONE OFF EVENT Saturday Art Club.

OPENING Tuesday to Saturday 10.00am–5.30pm.

CATERING None.

COST Free.

DISABLED FACILITIES Easy access; no steps. Toilet on ground floor.

DIRECTIONS From the town centre, move down Linthorpe Road away from the centre for approximately five minutes on foot; Gallery is on the left hand side, on the corner of Linthorpe Road and Park Road North.

Milebush Open Farm
- L and S Rickatson
- Milebush Farm, Nettledale Lane, Snainton, Scarborough, North Yorks. YO13 9PR
- 0723 859203

Farm tour including a supervised tractor/trailer ride. Allowed to touch the animals. Coffee/gift shop/farm shop to visit. Small 'By-gones' museum.

OPENING April to end October: 10.00am–5.00pm. Every Sunday throughout the year.

CATERING Picnics allowed in a field or in a covered barn if wet.

COST No discounts.

DISABLED FACILITIES Level. Toilets for the disabled including pull-up rail. No steps.

DIRECTIONS Scarborough to Pickering road (A170). Turn right middle of Snainton (by Peacock Pub) and follow sign to Troutsdale. One mile Nettledale Lane on the right.

Military Vehicle Museum
- Walter Tearse
- Exhibition Park Pavilion, Newcastle-upon-Tyne. NE2 4PZ
- 091-281 7222

A museum of World War II vehicles plus 60 cabinets of military memorabilia; last remaining pavilion of the 1929 northeast coast exhibition.

ANNUAL OR ONE OFF EVENT A military spectacular depicting the Soldier throughout History plus military wagons and guns.

OPENING Summer: daily 10.00am–4.00pm. Winter: daily 10.00am–

3.30pm. Closed Christmas Day, Boxing Day and New Year's Day.

CATERING Cold drinks machine in the Museum.

COST Children 75p, adults £1.50, Senior Citizens 75p, concessions 75p. Discounts negotiable

DISABLED FACILITIES Ramp for wheelchairs. There is only one level.

DIRECTIONS Metro at Jesmond just outside the park.

Monk Bretton Priory
- The Head Custodian
- c/o 17 Abbey Lane, Barnsley, South Yorks. S71 5QD
- 0226 204089

Partial sweeps of broken arches and grime-stained blocks of red sandstone mark the peaceful ruin of this Cluniac monastery founded in 1153. There are extensive remains of the fully restored 14th-century gate house.

OPENING All year. Good Friday or 1 April (whichever is earlier) to 30 September: daily 10.00am–6.00pm. 1 October to Maundy Thursday or 31 March (whichever is earlier): Tuesday to Sunday 10.00am–4.00pm. Closed 24–26 December and 1 January.

CATERING Picnic facilities.

DISABLED FACILITIES Wheelchair access.

DIRECTIONS One mile east of Barnsley town centre off A633 (OS Map 111; ref SE 373065). Bus: from surrounding areas (Tel: 0742 768688). BR: Barnsley two and a half miles.

Monkwearmouth Station
- Jo Cunningham
- Station Museum, North Bridge Street, Sunderland, Tyne and Wear
- 091-567 7075 FAX 091-510 0675

A converted station where trains still pass through. This museum houses a display of local transport since 1900, an Edwardian booking office and interactive bicycle and bus exhibits.

N C SUPPORT Teachers' notes and quiz sheets are available free. Loan packs are available via Sunderland Museum. Staff can advise on planning a visit.

ANNUAL OR ONE OFF EVENT There are activities for children during each school holiday.

OPENING Tuesday to Friday 10.00am–5.30pm, Saturday 10.00am–4.30pm, Sunday 2.00pm–5.00pm.

CATERING None.

COST Free.

DISABLED FACILITIES Adapted toilet, ramped access, level access. Guide dogs allowed.

DIRECTIONS Across the A1018 to Newcastle.

The Moors Centre
- Education Officer
- North York Moors National Park, Danby, Nr Whitby, North Yorks. YO21 2NB
- 0287 660 540 FAX 0287 660 308

The Moors Centre is set in pleasant surroundings alongside the River Esk, near Danby. A wide range of activities have been specially designed to interest and involve students of all ages. Bookshop, exhibition, lecture room, study base, nature and activity trails, toilets, free coach parking.

N C SUPPORT Topics covered at the Moors Centre relate to Attainment Targets in Science, Geography, Mathematics and English and are also strongly relevant to cross-curricular dimensions, skills and themes.

ANNUAL OR ONE OFF EVENT Year-round National Park Study and Activity Centre for educational groups.

OPENING April to October: daily 10.00am–5.00pm. November to March: Saturday and Sunday 11.00am–4.00pm. Open to pre-booked educational groups all year.

CATERING Tea rooms, picnic area.

COST Please contact the Education Officer. Approximate costs are: half-day per student £1.50; full-day per student £3.00. Booking for groups is essential.

DISABLED FACILITIES Toilets and ramps.

DIRECTIONS Please write or call for Educational Visits leaflet for details.

Mother Shipton's Cave
- Robert McBrakney
- Prophesy House, The High Bridge, Knaresborough, North Yorks. HG5 8DD
- 0423 864600 FAX 0423 868888

Mother Shipton's Cave and the Petrifying Well. Birthplace of Mother Shipton in 1488 and one of England's oldest attractions. It is set in a 12-acre woodland/riverside park originally laid out by Sir Henry Slingsby in the mid-17th century. Fabulous features, such as a guided tour of the cave and the historic Knaresborough Museum, children's adventure play area, etc. It makes a superb day out for all the family.

N C SUPPORT Mother Shipton's Cave has its own Primary Science Teaching Aid which is fully cross-referenced to the Science National Curriculum. It can be used complete or teachers may 'cut and paste'. (Received many commendations for both the Primary Science Teaching Aid and the 'Back at School Experiment Pack'.)

OPENING Daily 9.30am–5.45pm (last admission 5.00pm).

CATERING Mother Shipton's Kitchen.

COST Children £1.65, adults £2.95, Senior Citizens £2.65.

DISABLED FACILITIES None.

DIRECTIONS Situated on the A59, 18 miles from York and 4 miles from Harrogate.

Mount Grace Priory
- The Head Custodian
- Saddle Bridge, Northallerton, North Yorks. DL6 3JG

The only well-preserved Carthusian monastery in England, founded in 1398 and beautifully situated in attractive woodland. Each of the monks had his own two-storey cell, one of which has been fully restored and now contains hand-carved replica cabinets, beds and chests. There are also extensive remains of the cloister, church and outer court.

OPENING Good Friday or 1 April (whichever is earlier) to 30 September: daily 10.00am–6.00pm.

CATERING Picnic facilities.

DISABLED FACILITIES Wheelchair access.

DIRECTIONS Seven miles northeast of Northallerton on A19 near Ingleby Arncliffe (OS Map 99; ref SE 453982). Bus: United/Tees & District 90/A Northallerton to Middlesbrough (passes close to BR Northallerton) to within half a mile (Tel: 0642 210131). BR: Northallerton six miles.

Museum of Army Transport
- The Curator
- Flemingate, Beverley, North Humberside
- 0482 860445 FAX 0482 866459

Explore the fascinating story of Army Transport, on land, sea and in the air. There's a wide variety of vehicles and methods of transport, set in themes which recreate the atmosphere of bygone days.

N C SUPPORT School pack available, including Visitors Guide, Activity Guide and school teachers' notes. Twenty-minute video about the museum. Educational talks and demonstrations. Guided tours.

OPENING Daily (except 24–26 December) 10.00am–5.00pm.

CATERING The Cookhouse serves snacks and full meals.

COST Groups of over 15: children £1.50, adults £1.99, one adult free with every ten children.

DISABLED FACILITIES Toilets and parking.

DIRECTIONS Follow signs to Beverley from M62, Hull, Bridlington, Scarborough, York, etc.

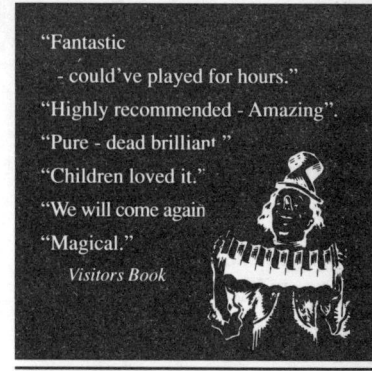

"Fantastic - could've played for hours."
"Highly recommended - Amazing".
"Pure - dead brilliant."
"Children loved it."
"We will come again"
"Magical."
Visitors Book

MUSEUM of AUTOMATA
A magical outing for all the family.
Open daily, all year round.

TOWER STREET YORK
OPPOSITE CLIFFORDS TOWER
Telephone 0904 655550

Museum of Automata
- Jim Butler
- 9 Tower Street, York. YO1 1SA
- 0904 655550 FAX 0904 620390

Mechanical marvels past and present – displayed using the latest computer sound and lighting techniques. Many 'hands-on' operated pieces. Regular schools' workshop.

N C SUPPORT Project pack available. Initially allied to Key Stage 2 National Curriculum Technology. Now has additional work cards. Although Museum is relevant to Sixth Form Studies, no specific material is available. More advanced workshops planned.

VISITS OUT
NORTH EAST

OPENING January 10.00am–4.00pm. 9.30am–5.30pm.

COST School children £1.95, older students £2.80, one adult free per ten children.

DISABLED FACILITIES Complete access for wheelchairs. Toilets, etc. No steps.

DIRECTIONS Museum is directly opposite Cliffords Tower in the Eyre York.

Museum of Mechanical Music
☞ Mrs Sheila Harrison
✉ Bradley Grange, Bradley Lane, Rufforth, York. YO2 3QW
☎ 0904 83773 FAX 0904 83659

Musical tour of Europe: large dance, fair and street organs, restored and beautifully presented in working order. Also British Compton Cinema organ butt from the Astoria Cinema Hall in 1934.

N C SUPPORT Suitable subjects: Music, Geography, History (building, working, restoration), Art and Design, Woodwork, Carving. Specialist music making (cardboard book music). Can be worked to any theme.

OPENING Any morning by arrangement for 40 or more.

CATERING Drinks available.

COST Groups: £2.20 per person.

DISABLED FACILITIES Full facilities.

DIRECTIONS One mile south of Rufforth between Rufforth and Askham Richard. Five miles west of York.

National Fishing Heritage Centre
☞ Ms C Parker
✉ Alexandra Dock, Great Grimsby, South Humberside. DN31 1UF

Experience the sights, sounds and smells of a 1950s trawler and Grimsby Docks. Visit the Ross Tiger trawler. Plus a programme of exciting temporary exhibitions.

N C SUPPORT Talks and guidance from Schools' Liaison Officer and team. Free education resource pack, activity sheets for Key Stage 2, resource materials for temporary exhibitions.

OPENING All year: daily 10.00am–6.00pm.

CATERING Small cafe. At present education room available for packed lunches (under review).

COST Party rates: children £1.65 (£2.10 with Ross Tiger), adults £3.00, one adult free per ten pupils.

DISABLED FACILITIES Lift, disabled route, toilets.

DIRECTIONS Well signposted on all routes into Grimsby.

NATIONAL TRUST

Opening Times Write or telephone the administrator of the house, give preferred day and time, the size and age of the group, and the main purpose of the visit. *The National Trust Handbook* contains further relevant information.

Cost Unless otherwise stated in the *Handbook*, there is a reduction of around 50% for children aged 16 and under, when accompanied by their

VISITS OUT
NORTH EAST

teacher. Education Group Members are admitted free. However, please note that there may be a small charge for any additional educational facilities or activities.

See individual entries for all other information.

Beningbrough Hall
Bridestones Moor
Brimham Moor & Rocks
Cragside House
Fountains Abbey & Studley Royal Fountains
Ormesby Hall
Ravenscar
Souter Lighthouse and The Leas
Treasurers House

Newcastle Airport
- Bob Harrison
- Tourist Information Centre, Newcastle Airport, Woolsington, Newcastle-upon-Tyne. NE13 8B2
- 091-271 1929 **FAX** 091-271 6080

Guided tours of the airport for school parties, maximum number 20 children, aged 7–16 years. Requests for visits must be made in writing.

OPENING Guided tour available November to March: Tuesday–Thursday 10.30am–12.00 noon.

CATERING Yes.

COST Free.

DISABLED FACILITIES Yes.

DIRECTIONS Newcastle Airport is located six miles from Newcastle city centre; accessible by metro rail link with a journey time of 20 minutes, as well as by excellent road network.

Nidderdale Museum
- Mrs E Burgess
- Council Offices, King Street, Pateley Bridge, Harrogate, North Yorks. HG3 5LE
- 0423 711225

Folk museum with Victorian kitchen, sitting room, cobbler's shop, 1930s general store. Other displays include costume, agriculture, transport, industry. 1990 National Heritage Museum of the Year Award.

N C SUPPORT Victorian and 1930s life, all aspects.

OPENING Easter to end September: daily 2.00pm–5.00pm. Winter: Sundays only. Parties at any time by special appointment.

CATERING None.

COST 1993 prices. Children 40p, adults 80p.

DISABLED FACILITIES Stairlift currently on order.

DIRECTIONS Opposite St Cuthbert's church.

North Yorkshire Moors Railway
- Moira Russell
- Pickering Station, Pickering, North Yorks. YO18 7AS
- 0751 72508 **FAX** 0751 76970

Eighteen-mile steam railway in the heart of National Park. Built originally by George Stephenson in the 1830s.

N C SUPPORT Excellent background notes for Victorian Britain.

OPENING Easter to end October: daily. Other services December to March: 10.00am–6.00pm.

CATERING Tea rooms at Grosmont and Pickering. Picnic at sites or on train.

COST Apply for details. One adult or teacher free with every ten children.

DISABLED FACILITIES Very limited. Toilets at Grosmont. Helpful staff on the trains.

DIRECTIONS Pickering A169/170 intersection.

Oakwell Hall Museum and Country Park
- Wendy Wilshaw
- Nutter Lane, Birstall, Batley, West Yorks. WF1 9LG
- 0924 474926

Oakwell Hall is a 16th-century manor house displayed as the Batt family home in the 1690s and set in over 100 acres of country park.

N C SUPPORT The site can provide activities in support of almost all National Curriculum areas, in particular those of History, Science and Geography. Pre-booking is essential.

OPENING Monday to Friday 11.00am–5.00pm, Saturday and Sunday 12.00 noon–5.00pm. To pre-booked schools site opens at 10.00am.

CATERING Lunch may be eaten in classroom or picnic areas in park.

COST £60.00 per visit for non-Kirklees schools. LEA schools subject to revision.

DISABLED FACILITIES Adapted toilet. Access to shop, wildlife garden and ground floor of Hall. Children with disabilities and special needs can be catered for providing staff are informed in advance.

DIRECTIONS Close to junctions 26 and 27 of the M62. Situated off the A652.

Once Brewed Youth Hostel
- The Warden
- Military Road, Bardon Mill, Hexham, Northumberland. NE46 7AN
- 0434 344360 FAX 0434 344045

Youth hostel on Hadrian's Wall: 75 beds, central heating; coach guide available.

N C SUPPORT Area for study on Invaders (Romans). Blue badge guides available.

ANNUAL OR ONE OFF EVENT Can organise to suit school/group.

CATERING Full meal service. Packed lunches arranged if required.

COST 1993 prices: Under 18s £13.10, adults £15.60, one for every ten free. Seasonal discounts.

DISABLED FACILITIES Limited.

DIRECTIONS On B6318 above Bardon Hill. Approximately midway between Carlisle and Newcastle.

Ormesby Hall
- The Administrator
- Middlesbrough, Cleveland. TS7 9AS
- 0642 324188

Mid-18th-century house with opulent decoration including fine plasterwork by contemporary craftsmen; a Jacobean doorway with a carved family crest which survives from an earlier house on the site; the stable block, attributed to Carr of York, is a particularly fine mid-18th-century building with an

VISITS OUT
NORTH EAST

attractive courtyard leased to the Mounted Police; garden.

N C SUPPORT National Curriculum links with History. Teachers' resource book available. Visits can include church, stables and estate.

DISABLED FACILITIES Ground floor of house, shop, tea room and garden. Cars may bring disabled visitors to front door; please notify Administrator in advance of visit. Adapted toilet opposite car park.

DIRECTIONS Three miles southeast of Middlesbrough west of A171. Bus: from Middlesbrough (passing close BR Middlesbrough). BR: Marton, Middlesbrough.

Osmotherley Youth Hostel
- Helen Ward
- Cote Ghyll, Osmotherley, Northallerton, North Yorks. DL6 3AH
- 0609 883575

Converted mill in beautiful countryside, on edge of North Yorkshire Moors. Ideally based for visiting York, East Coast, Moors, Dales. Fully modernised, excellent facilities including classroom and full catering service.

N C SUPPORT Teachers' pack available with details of all local attractions, etc.

ANNUAL OR ONE OFF EVENT Introductory leader days/weekend arranged a couple of times a year. Approach hostel for details.

OPENING Daily 7.00am–10.00am, 5.00pm–11.00pm. Full daytime access can be arranged.

CATERING Great value home-cooked meals, three-course evening meals (always vegetarian option). Breakfast and standard and large lunch packs.

COST 1993 prices: under 18 £12.70, over 18s £15.00, full board, one leader free for every ten paying guests, plus special winter discounts. Self-catering: under 18s £4.60, over 18s £6.90.

DISABLED FACILITIES None.

DIRECTIONS One and a half miles off A19. Take Osmotherley turn-off into village and follow signs to Youth Hostel.

Park Rose Pottery
- David Hindle
- Carnaby Court Lane, Carnaby, Bridlington, Yorks. YO15 3QF
- 0262 602823 FAX 0262 400202

Pottery and leisure park. Factory tour, owl sanctuary and conservation area with flying display and lecture on birds of prey. Children's play areas, gift shops. Ideal school visit venue.

N C SUPPORT Comprehensive schools' pack produced by teachers and pupils of local school, covering Science, Maths, Geography, History, Art and Technology.

OPENING Daily 10.00am–5.00pm. Other times by arrangement.

CATERING On-site cafeteria and picnic areas.

COST Pottery tour: 30p per person. Owl sanctuary and flying display: £1.50. Combined: £1.20.

DISABLED FACILITIES Toilets. Level or ramped access to all areas.

VISITS OUT
NORTH EAST

DIRECTIONS Two miles south of Bridlington between the A166 and A165 at Carnaby.

Penny Arcadia
- Jon or Pat Gresham
- Market Place, Pocklington, Yorks. YO4 2AR
- 0579 303420 FAX 0482 226863

Award-winning collection of coin-operated amusement machines; these are demonstrated and their history explained in a multi-media presentation followed by a guided tour. A unique and exciting entertainment.

N C SUPPORT Visits may be tailored to suit requirements: History of Mechanical Development, Industrial Design, Popular Art and Entertainment, Movement and Probability are all covered.

OPENING May and September: 12.30pm–5.00pm. June to August 10.00am–5.00pm. Groups any time by appointment.

CATERING Place available to eat packed lunch.

COST Children £2.00, adults £3.00, Senior Citizens £2.00. Groups: children £1.50, adults £2.00, Senior Citizens £1.50.

DISABLED FACILITIES Access to 95% of attractions; coaches stop right outside.

DIRECTIONS Pocklington is off main York to Hull road, A1079, 12 miles from York. Penny Acardia is signposted.

Phoenix Hot Glass
- Anne Tye
- 10a Denshaw Way, Sedeletch Industrial Estate, Houghton-le-Spring. DH4 6JN
- 091-385 7204 FAX 091-385 7204

Traditional glass-blowing techniques, unchanged since Roman times, are used to make glassware in contemporary designs. Work involves the use of colours and precious metals from all over the world.

OPENING Daily: 10.00am–1.00pm and 2.00pm–4.00pm.

COST Free.

DISABLED FACILITIES No special facilities but accessible for wheelchairs.

DIRECTIONS Telephone for map.

Pickering Castle
- The Head Custodian
- Pickering, North Yorks. YO18 7AX

A splendid motte and bailey castle, once a royal ranch. It is well preserved, with much of the original walls, towers and keep, and there are spectacular views over the surrounding countryside. There is an exhibition on the castle's history.

OPENING All year. Good Friday or 1 April (whichever is earlier) to 30 September: daily 10.00am–6.00pm. 1 October to Maundy Thursday or 31 March (whichever is earlier): Tuesday to Sunday 10.00am–4.00pm. Closed 24–26 December and 1 January.

CATERING Picnic facilities.

DISABLED FACILITIES Wheelchair access (except motte).

VISITS OUT
NORTH EAST

DIRECTIONS In Pickering, 15 miles southwest of Scarborough (OS Map 100; ref SE800845). Bus: Yorkshire Coastliner 840/2 from BR Malton (Tel: 0653 692556); Scarborough and District 128 from BR Scarborough (Tel: 0723 37563). BR: Malton nine miles; Pickering (North Yorkshire Moors Raillway) quarter of a mile.

The Planetarium
- E M Hans
- South Tyneside College, St George's Avenue, South Shields, Tyne & Wear. NE34 6ET
- 091-456 0403 FAX 091-427 0267

Planetarium, Observatory and Astronomy resource centre. Maximum group size 75. Suitable for age six upwards. Visiting time one to two hours depending on age group.

N C SUPPORT Planetarium shop with wide range of educational materials, including Association for Astronomy Education teachers' packs. Qualified astronomer on staff to answer queries. Teachers' in-service courses. Telescope hire service.

ANNUAL OR ONE OFF EVENT Association for Astronomy Education Regional Meeting.

OPENING 9.00am–9.00pm during school terms. Exhibition open from 6.00pm. (School parties must book in advance.)

CATERING College refectory open until 6.00pm; thereafter vending machines.

COST Children £1.00, adults £2.00. School parties 50p per head.

DISABLED FACILITIES Steps to both Planetarium and Observatory.

DIRECTIONS Good access by local bus services and metro (nearest station: Chichester).

Predator Indoor Paintball Arena
- Les Fry
- 4 Forth Banks, The Quayside, Newcastle-upon-Tyne. NE1 3PA
- 091-222 0981

Europe's most original paintball arena. Fast action, multi-level energy games. The perfect vehicle for team building plus feature-length paintball adventures and live role-play game worlds.

N C SUPPORT Supply specialist games to schools' requirements. Massive and adaptable space to suit different needs.

ANNUAL OR ONE OFF EVENT Special live-action role-play events set throughout the year, including: Cyber Punk, Gothic Horror, Murder Mystery, Fighting Fantasy, Vampires and many more.

OPENING Ring to book.

CATERING Light buffets can be booked in advance.

COST £15.00 though several discounts are available and some events may vary in price.

DISABLED FACILITIES In preparation.

DIRECTIONS Right in the centre of Newcastle, just behind the Newcastle Central station.

NORTH EAST

Prudhoe Castle
- The Head Custodian
- Prudhoe, Northumberland. NE42 6NA
- 0661 833459

The extensive remains of this 12th-century castle include a gate house, curtain wall and keep. There is much to see, including a video about the castles of Northumbria.

OPENING All year. Good Friday or 1 April (whichever is earlier) to 30 September: daily 10.00am–6.00pm. 1 October to Maundy Thursday or 31 March (whichever is earlier): Tuesday to Sunday 10.00am–4.00pm. Closed 24–26 December and 1 January.

DIRECTIONS In Prudhoe, on minor road off A695 (OS Map 88; ref NZ 092634). Bus: from surrounding areas (Tel: 091-232 4211). BR: Prudhoe quarter of a mile.

Ravenscar
- c/o The Warden
- Peakside, Ravenscar, North Yorks. YO13 0NE
- 0723 870138

An open site, part of the extensive National Trust land on the Yorkshire coast; the High Peak stands 600 feet above sea level at the eastern end of the peak fault. Jurassic rocks covered with boulder clay. The bay contains an extensive wave-cut platform; habitats for both seashore and moorland flora and fauna. Historically important since Roman times. Visits can include church, stables and estate.

N C SUPPORT National Curriculum links with History, Science and Geography. Teachers' resource book available.

DISABLED FACILITIES Contact the warden for access details.

DIRECTIONS Contact the warden for details.

Reivers of Tarset
- Paul Hodgson
- Leaplish Waterside Park, Kielder Water, Falstone, Hexham, Northumberland
- 0434 250203 FAX 0434 240050

Watersports centre. Hire of equipment and tuition for windsurfing, canoeing and sailing. RYA recognised. BCU approved centre. Features a shop, changing, hire facilities and a lounge area.

OPENING Easter to October: 9.00am–6.00pm.

COST Group rates (minimum 12 people). Two and a half hours £10.00, one day £20.00. Please write and ask for further details. Contact Paul for individual costs for windsurfing, canoeing, sailing, hire of boats, etc.

DIRECTIONS Contact above for directions.

Richmond Castle
- The Head Custodian
- Richmond, North Yorks. DL10 4QW
- 0748 822493

A splendid medieval fortress, with a fine 12th-century keep and 11th-century remains of the curtain wall and domestic buildings. From the battlements you can see nearby Easby Abbey.

OPENING All year. Good Friday or 1 April (whichever is earlier) to 30 September: daily 10.00am–6.00pm. 1 October to Maundy Thursday or 31 March (whichever is earlier): Tuesday to Sunday 10.00am–4.00pm. Closed 24–26 December and 1 January.

CATERING Picnic facilities.

DISABLED FACILITIES Wheelchair access.

DIRECTIONS In Richmond (OS Map 92; ref NZ 174006). Bus: United 27/A/B, 28/A. BR: Darlington to Richmond (Tel: 0325 468771).

Rievaulx Abbey
- The Head Custodian
- Rievaulx, Helmsley, North Yorks. YO6 5LB
- 0439 6228

In a deeply wooded valley by the River Rye you can see some of the most spectacular monastic ruins in England, dating from the 12th century. The church has the earliest large Cistercian nave in Britain. A fascinating exhibition shows how successfully the Cistercians at Rievaulx ran their many businesses and explains the part played by the Abbot Ailred, who ruled for 20 years.

OPENING All year. Good Friday or 1 April (whichever is earlier) to 30 September: daily 10.00am–6.00pm. 1 October to Maundy Thursday or 31 March (whichever is earlier): Monday to Sunday 10.00am–4.00pm. Closed 24–26 December and 1 January.

CATERING Picnic facilities.

DISABLED FACILITIES Personal stereo tours available for the partially sighted and those with learning difficulties. Wheelchair access.

DIRECTIONS Two and a quarter miles west of Helmsley on minor road off B1257 (OS Map 100; ref SE 577849). Bus: Tees and District 294 from Stokesley with connections from Middlesbrough (passes close to BR Middlesbrough), Friday only (Tel: 0642 21013).

Roche Abbey
- The Head Custodian
- Maltby, Rotherham, South Yorks. S66 8NW

This Cistercian monastery, founded in 1147, lies in a secluded grassy valley sheltered by limestone cliffs and trees. Some of the walls still stand to their full height and excavation has revealed the complete layout.

OPENING Summer season. Good Friday or 1 April (whichever is earlier) to 30 September: daily 10.00am–6.00pm.

CATERING Picnic facilities.

DISABLED FACILITIES Wheelchair access.

DIRECTIONS One and a half miles south of Maltby off A634 (OS Map 111; ref SK 544898). Bus: Main Line 100–2, 122 Rotherham to Maltby, thence one and a half miles (Tel: 0742 768688). BR: Conisbrough seven miles.

Roman Army Museum
- Mrs P Birley
- Carvoran, Greenhead, Northumberland. CA6 7JB
- 0697 747485

VISITS OUT
NORTH EAST

A spacious museum situated next to an outstanding section of Hadrian's Wall. Life-sized figures, models, sound presentations and displays of Roman objects bring the Roman frontier to life.

N C SUPPORT Schools and groups who book in advance receive pre-visit information, a preliminary staff visit voucher and can request a museum talk and demonstration.

OPENING Mid-February to end October: daily from 10.00am (closing time seasonally).

CATERING Cafe for sandwiches and drinks; picnic tables in grounds.

COST Children £1.50, adults £2.20, Senior Citizens £2.00. 10% group discounts, one teacher free per 20 children, all other staff at child rate and included for discount.

DISABLED FACILITIES Whole museum ramped. Easy access from car park. No toilets.

DIRECTIONS Via Greenhead from the A69 or follow brown and white signs on B6318.

Rothbury District Forest Enterprise

- Blair Wilkie
- Forestry Commission, 1 Walby Hill, Rothbury, Morpeth, Northumberland. NE65 7NT
- 0669 20569/20062 FAX 0669 21454

Chopwell Woodland Park, 960 acres of conifer and deciduous woodland. Recreation/education ranger available on request for educational visits. Rangers also available for visits to other forest enterprise woodland in Rothbury district.

N C SUPPORT Details on request.

ANNUAL OR ONE OFF EVENT Details on request.

OPENING Monday to Friday 8.30am–5.00pm, weekends on request.

COST No cost at present but will be reviewed.

DISABLED FACILITIES No public conveniences at all at present but will be reviewed. Some walks will be wheelchair accessible.

DIRECTIONS From the A1 at Newcastle-upon-Tyne, take the A694 Consett Road to Roland's Gill, take the B6315 through to High Spen and turn first left after Lintzford Lane. Follow road; main car park on left.

RNLI Zetland

- George Levett
- 5 Kings Street, Redcar, Cleveland. TS10 3PF
- 0642 471813

Museum containing the oldest existing lifeboat in the world. Also local history photographs, models, fisherman's cottage, breeches buoy, history of lifeboat/sea rescue.

N C SUPPORT Guided tours for school children any time by appointment during the year.

ANNUAL OR ONE OFF EVENT Open Day; guided tours.

OPENING May to September: daily 11.00am–4.00pm.

CATERING None.

COST Free.

DISABLED FACILITIES Access to boat house only.

VISITS OUT
NORTH EAST

DIRECTIONS From A19, take A174 to Redcar then A1042 to sea front. Follow Amajuna Road, left turn onto Esplanade. Follow for about a quarter of a mile. Museum on right.

Royal Pump Room Museum
- Barbara Blakeson or Ros Watson
- Crown Place, Harrogate, North Yorks. HG1 2RY
- 0423 503340

Local history museum showing development of Harrogate as a spa. Original sulphur well; water can still be tasted. Other displays of toys, bicycles, ceramics, jewellery.

N C SUPPORT Activities room where reserve collection can be handled. Collection development officer will talk to groups.

OPENING Monday to Saturday 10.00am–5.00pm, Sunday 2.00pm–5.00pm. October to March closing time 4.00pm.

CATERING None.

COST Children 60p, adults £1.00, group rate 80p. Local Authority schools free.

DISABLED FACILITIES Access to 90% of building. Toilets.

DIRECTIONS In centre of Harrogate close to Crown Hotel off roundabout. Near the entrance to Valley Gardens. Follow road signs.

Ryedale Folk Museum
- Helen Mason
- Hutton le Hole, York. YO6 6UA
- 0751 5367

Open-air museum. Rescued buildings, covering 2000 years of history. Events include: crafts, rare breeds, machines, living history.

N C SUPPORT Free pre-visit. Subjects covered are Key Stage 1 CSU1, Key Stage 2 CSU2/3, SSU(a), SSU(b), Key Stage 3 CSU4, SSU(a). 'Hands-on' sessions, object handling work sessions.

ANNUAL OR ONE OFF EVENT Student work experience, combined work projects. Special visits.

OPENING March to October: daily 10.00am–5.30pm (last admission 4.30pm).

COST Children £1.25, adults £2.50, Senior Citizens £2.00. Group rates: children £1.00, adults £2.00, Senior Citizens £1.60.

DISABLED FACILITIES Ramps, toilet; 70% site access.

DIRECTIONS Leave Kirkbymoorside on A170 eastbound, turn right and follow brown and white signs.

St Coombes Open Farm
- Alison Brigham
- Holy Island, Berwick-on-Tweed, Northumberland. TD15 2SE
- 0289 89294 evenings

A farm park with a variety of farm animals, many of which are rare breeds. Children are allowed to walk around, touch and feed the animals whilst learning about them.

N C SUPPORT General education, Agriculture or any other Nature or Biology classes.

ANNUAL OR ONE OFF EVENT No one-off events as yet but children can watch seasonal events, i.e. lambing and sheep clipping.

VISITS OUT
NORTH EAST

OPENING 1 April–31 October: daily 10.00am–6.00pm. Any other time can be arranged with prior notice.

CATERING None.

COST Children 60p, under fives free, adults £1.20, Senior Citizens 60p. Schools receive 20% discount, teachers free. Free pre-school visit. Free for people with disabilities as well as for whole groups of helpers.

DISABLED FACILITIES Accessible for wheelchairs.

DIRECTIONS Five miles from A1 at Beal. Signposted on reaching island.

St Peter's Church
- Rev Gareth Lloyd
- St Peter's Way, Sunderland. SR6 0DY
- 091-567 3726

Saxon church with substantial original remains, including carved porchway and west wall.

N C SUPPORT In preparation; collaborating with local schools.

OPENING Daily 2.00pm–5.00pm.

CATERING Tea and coffee (limited).

COST Free.

DISABLED FACILITIES Entry ramp.

DIRECTIONS Follow tourist signs from Wearmouth Bridge.

The Saxon Escomb
- Nicholas Beddow
- Escomb, The Vicarage, Bishop Auckland, Co Durham. DL1 47S
- 0388 602861

Saxon church dating from the seventh century. Roman chancel arch, inscriptions and stonework.

N C SUPPORT Saxon history, Roman history. Village development for Geography studies.

OPENING Daylight hours. Evening visits by arrangement.

CATERING The Saxon Inn, next to the church. The post office sells sweets and ice creams.

COST Donations welcome.

DISABLED FACILITIES None.

DIRECTIONS Signposted from A68 and Bishop Auckland.

Scarborough Castle
- The Head Custodian
- Castle Road, Scarborough, North Yorks. YO1 1HY
- 0723 372451

An enormous 12th-century castle with spectacular coastal views. The buttressed castle walls stretch out along the cliff edge and the remains of the great rectangular stone keep still stand to over three storeys high. There is also the site of a 4th-century Roman signal station.

OPENING All year. Good Friday or 1 April (whichever is earlier) to 30 September: daily 10.00am–6.00pm. 1 October to Maundy Thursday or 31 March (whichever is earlier): Tuesday to Sunday 10.00am–4.00pm. Closed 24–26 December and 1 January.

DISABLED FACILITIES Wheelchair access (except to keep).

DIRECTIONS Castle Road, east of town centre (OS Map 101; ref TA 050893). Bus: from surrounding areas (Tel: 0723 375463). BR: Scarborough one mile.

VISITS OUT
NORTH EAST

Seaham Harbour Coastal Centre
- D Miller
- Seaham House, Seaham, Co Durham. SR7 7EU
- 091-581 9848 FAX 091-513 0700

A base for students of coastal activities (natural and industrial), run by a teacher. Building within private port, overlooking habour. Well-equipped for field work.

N C SUPPORT Contrasting habitats and localities; Environmental Awareness; Economic and Industrial Understanding. Group leadership by experienced teacher.

OPENING School hours; other times by arrangement.

CATERING Hot drinks. Facilities to warm own food. Soup during winter months, by arrangement.

COST Free. By arrangement.

DISABLED FACILITIES Unsuitable due to stairs.

DIRECTIONS From A19, follow signs for Seaham. From A690 at Houghton-le-Spring, signs for Seaham. Then Port or Docks or Harbour.

Seaton Delaval Hall
- The Curator
- Seaton Sluice, Whitley Bay, Northumberland. NE26 HQ12
- 091-237 1493/3040

A splendid house, regarded by many as Sir John Vanbrugh's masterpiece. Comprises centre block with underground passages between two arcaded and pedimented wings. Centre gutted by fire and partially restored. Gardens.

OPENING 1 May to 30 September: Wednesday, Sunday and bank holidays. 2.00pm–6.00pm.

CATERING Tea room.

COST Children 50p, adults £2.00.

DISABLED FACILITIES None.

DIRECTIONS Half a mile from coast at Seaton Sluice between Blyth and Whitby Bay. Ten miles from Newcastle.

Silkworth Sports Complex
- Mrs R Edwards
- Silkworth Lane, Silkworth, Sunderland. SR3 2AN
- 091-522 9119

A large premiere outdoor complex, Silkworth offers a wealth of high-class facilities including ski slopes (main slope 165 metres, nursery slope 55 metres), artificial surface, athletics arena, watersports lake, orienteering, heritage/wildlife train.

N C SUPPORT Heritage/wildlife trail.

OPENING Monday, Tuesday, Thursday, Friday 11.00am–9.30pm (last admission 8.15pm), Wednesday 11.00am–7.00pm (last admission 5.45pm), Saturday and Sunday 10.00am–5.00pm (last admission 3.45pm).

CATERING Vending machines.

COST Special rates for schools using skiing facilities with or without instruction. Write for price list.

DISABLED FACILITIES Access to building and toilets.

DIRECTIONS Five miles from Sunderland city centre.

VISITS OUT
NORTH EAST

Souter Lighthouse and the Leas
- The Administrator
- Coast Road, Whitburn, Sunderland, Tyne and Wear. SR6 7NH
- 091-529 3161

Souter Lighthouse, situated on the Durham coast halfway between the rivers Tyne and Wear, was built in 1870 by Trinity House, the body responsible for commissioning Britain's coastal lights. The world's first reliable electrically powered lighthouse; a perfect working example of Victorian technology. Contact the National Trust Regional Office, Scot's Gap, Morpeth, Northumberland NE61 4EG (Tel: 067 074 691) for further information.

N C SUPPORT National Curriculum links with Science, Technology, History (Victorian) and Geography. INSET day.

DISABLED FACILITIES Contact the Administrator for access details.

DIRECTIONS Contact the Administrator for details.

Station House, Norham
- Mrs K M Short
- Berwick-on-Tweed, Northumberland. TD15 2LW
- 0289 382217

Original country station. Signal box, signals, model railway, porter's room, station master's office, booking office. Local history items.

OPENING Monday and Thursday, 1.30pm–5.00pm. Other times and days by appointment.

CATERING None.

COST Free. Donations welcome.

DISABLED FACILITIES All buildings accessible except top of signal box.

DIRECTIONS Berwick-on-Tweed, seven miles west on Coldstream to Kelso Road, A698. Turn right at Salutation Inn then first left; station 150 yards.

Stump Cross Caverns
- Gordon Hanley
- Greenhow, Pateley Bridge, Harrogate, North Yorks. HG3 5JL
- 0756 75280

Five hundred thousand years ago the Stump Cross area was a wilderness over which bison, reindeer, fox, wolf, wolverine and other animals roamed. At this time the caves were forming their intricate system, typical of water-worn limestone caverns, of fantastic shapes and sizes. Discovered in the mid-19th century, exploration has yielded a richness of animal remains, the untold wonders of stalactite and stalagmite, and fossil bones between 30,000 and 200,000 years old.

OPENING Mid-March to mid-November: daily from 10.00am. By appointment during winter months, weather permitting, 11.00am until dusk. Last party in caves 5.00pm.

CATERING Enjoy a meal or snack in the cafe which seats up to 60.

COST Children £1.35, adults £2.70. Group rates: children 4–13 yrs £1.20, 14–15 yrs £1.50, 16 yrs £1.70, adults £2.40, one adult free with every 20 children.

DIRECTIONS Situated between Pateley Bridge and Grassington on B6265.

VISITS OUT
NORTH EAST

Sunderland Museum & Art Gallery
- Helen Sinclair
- Borough Road, Sunderland, Tyne & Wear. SR1 1PP
- 091-514 1234 FAX 091-510 0675

Displays include: local wildlife, geology, with 'hands-on' exhibits; the story of Sunderland from prehistoric times; art, pottery and glass collections; shipbuilding history and an exciting programme of temporary exhibitions.

N C SUPPORT Quiz sheets and the museum loans service are free. An education area is available for activities or to have lunch. Staff can support visits and help with National Curriculum planning.

ANNUAL OR ONE OFF EVENT Activities for children during each school holiday. Events are organised to coincide with temporary exhibitions.

OPENING Tuesday to Friday 10.00am–5.30pm, Saturday 10.00am–4.00pm, Sunday 2.00pm–5.00pm.

CATERING Cafe on premises.

COST Free.

DISABLED FACILITIES Adapted toilet, ramped access, lift. Guide dogs allowed.

DIRECTIONS Sunderland Museum is in the town centre in the same building as the Central Library.

Bessie Surtees House
- The Head Custodian
- 41-44 Sandhill, Newcastle, Tyne & Wear. NE1 3JF
- 091-261 1585

Two 16th- and 17th-century merchant's houses stand on the quayside near the Tyne Bridge. One is a remarkable and rare example of Jacobean domestic architecture. The principal rooms are on view.

OPENING All year. Good Friday or 1 April (whichever is earlier) to 30 September: daily 10.00am–6.00pm. 1 October to Maundy Thursday or 31 March (whichever is earlier): Tuesday to Sunday 10.00am–4.00pm. Winter: also Monday. Closed 24–26 December and 1 January.

DIRECTIONS OS Map 88; ref NZ 252639. Bus: from surrounding areas (Tel: 091-232 5325). BR: Newcastle half a mile. Metro: Central station half a mile.

Temple Newsam House
- Adam White
- Leeds, West Yorks. LS15 0AE
- 0532 647321 FAX 0532 602285

Tudor–Jacobean mansion set in 1000-acre estate with outstanding collections of furniture, silver, pottery, porcelain, paintings and sculpture.

N C SUPPORT Guided tours, interpretive visits and historic role-play events available by arrangement with Education Officer. Visits to the farm on the estate must be separately booked (Tel: 0532 645535). All visits can be tailored to National Curriculum requirements.

OPENING Tuesday to Sunday 10.30am–6.15pm (or dusk if earlier), closed Monday.

VISITS OUT
NORTH EAST

CATERING Cafe in stable block open for coffee and light lunches and teas (Tel: 0532 602435).

COST Adults £1.20, concessions 60p. Leeds schools free; other schools at concessionary rate. No group discounts.

DISABLED FACILITIES Ground floor only of house viewable in wheelchairs (six out of 33 rooms). No lift.

DIRECTIONS About five miles east of Leeds, off A63 Selby Road.

Thornton Abbey
- The Head Custodian
- Ulceby, Nr Grimsby, South Humberside. DN39 6TU
- 0469 40357

The magnificent brick gate house of this ruined Augustinian priory stands three storeys high, with a facade ornamented with finely carved details, including some surviving 14th-century statues.

OPENING Summer season: daily 10.00am–6.00pm. Winter: Saturday and Sunday 10.00am–4.00pm. Gate house and sales office may be closed some days; telephone before visiting to avoid disappointment.

CATERING Picnic facilities.

DISABLED FACILITIES Wheelchair access (except interior of gatehouse and part of chapter house ruins).

DIRECTIONS Ten miles northeast of Scunthorpe on minor road north of A160 (OS Map 113; ref TA 115190). BR: Thornton Abbey quarter of a mile.

Thwaite Mills
- Derek Davies
- Thwaite Lane, Stourton, Leeds. LS10 1RP
- 0532 498453 FAX 0532 776737

This unique water-powered mill, once the hub of a tiny island community, with cottages, crops and gardens, drives the wheels which crushed stone for putty and paint throughout the 19th century.

N C SUPPORT Key Stages 1 and 2: Movement, Change and Continuity, and Waterpower. Key Stage 4. Change and Decline, War on the Home Front, the Labour Force.

OPENING All year: Tuesday to Sunday 10.00am–5.00pm, Closed Monday (except bank holiday Mondays).

CATERING Vending machine. Indoor and outdoor picnic areas.

COST Children 60p.

DISABLED FACILITIES Access to all areas.

DIRECTIONS Two miles south of Leeds city centre off the A61; easily accessible from M1 (junction 43).

Treasurers House
- Norma Sutherland
- The National Trust, Minster Yard, York. YO1 2SH
- 0904 624247 FAX 0904 624247

The house, dating from the 17th century, houses a collection of furniture and pictures which offer an insight into the ways of life, decoration and style of both Victorian and Tudor and Stuart times.

VISITS OUT
NORTH EAST

N C SUPPORT Children's guide available and 12-minute introductory video.

CATERING Tea room serving morning coffee, light lunches and afternoon teas.

DISABLED FACILITIES Difficult for wheelchairs. Fully adapted toilet facilities at nearby NT tea room.

DIRECTIONS Behind York Minster; entrance in Chapter House Street.

Tropical World
- K Roberts
- Canal Gardens, Roundbay Park, Leeds. LS8 1DF
- 0532 661850

Waterfalls tumble into crystal pools amidst luxuriant jungle, butterflies flutter through the air and fish dart amongst coral reefs. New desert, orchid and nocturnal house open in 1995.

N C SUPPORT Worksheets (over fives, over sevens and over 12s) available from gift shop.

OPENING Daily (except Christmas Day) 10.00am till dusk.

CATERING Cafe in adjacent Canal Gardens.

COST Free.

DISABLED FACILITIES Access for people with disabilities: ramp.

DIRECTIONS Three miles north of Leeds city centre off the A58 Wetherby Road at Oakwood or from Moortown ring road onto Park Lane.

Tynemouth Castle & Priory
- The Head Custodian
- East Street, Tynemouth, North Shields, Tyne & Wear. NE30 4BZ
- 091-257 1090

The castle walls and gate house enclose the substantial remains of a Benedictine priory founded c.1090 on a Saxon monastic site. Their strategic importance has made the castle and priory the target of attack for many centuries. In World War I, coastal batteries in the castle defended the mouth of the Tyne.

OPENING All year. Good Friday or 1 April (whichever is earlier) to 30 September: daily 10.00am–6.00pm. 1 October to Maundy Thursday or 31 March (whichever is earlier): Tuesday to Sunday 10.00am–4.00pm. Closed 24–26 December and 1 January.

CATERING Picnic facilities.

DISABLED FACILITIES Wheelchair access to castle.

DIRECTIONS In Tynemouth, near North Pier (OS Map 88; ref NZ 374695). Bus: from surrounding areas (Tel: 091-232 5325). Metro: Tynemouth half a mile.

University of Hull Art Collection
- John G Bernasconi
- University of Hull, Cottingham Road, Hull. HU6 7RX
- 0482 465035 FAX 0482 465192

British paintings, drawings and sculpture 1890–1940. Works by Sickert, Steer, Peploe, Lucien Pissarro, Augustus John, Stanley Spencer, Epstein and Moore. Also the Thompson collection of Chinese

Transitional Period porcelain (c.1620–1680).

ANNUAL OR ONE OFF EVENT Regular loan exhibitions and annual public lecture series.

OPENING Monday to Friday 2.00pm–4.00pm, Wednesday 12.30pm–4.00pm, closed public holidays.

CATERING Available on campus or for groups by prior arrangement.

COST Free.

DISABLED FACILITIES Access (ask at University Reception on arrival) and toilets on same level as gallery.

DIRECTIONS On approaches to the city, follow signposts to the University if travelling by car. Frequent buses from the city centre pass the gates.

Vindolanda Trust Chesterholm Museum

- Mrs L Thompson
- Bardon Mill, Hexham, Northumberland. NE47 7JN
- 0434 344277 FAX 0434 344060

A fascinating Roman excavation of a fort and town in the Hadrian's Wall area with a superb site museum set in charming gardens. Finds include rare ink writing tablets.

OPENING February to November: daily from 10.00am (closing time seasonal). November and early February only: Saturday and Sunday. Museum closed December and January.

CATERING Cafe for sandwiches and drinks; picnic tables in gardens and grounds.

DISABLED FACILITIES Toilets at site car park. Museum accessible. Site difficult.

DIRECTIONS Follow signs from A69 at Bardon Mill or from the B6318.

Wakefield Museums, Galleries & Castles

- Don Henson
- Wakefield Art Gallery, Wentworth Terrace, Wakefield. WF1 3QW
- 0924 375402

Wakefield Museum: Social History, Archaeology and Natural History (Charles Waterton). Wakefield Art Gallery: 20th-century British Art. Pontefract Museum: Local History and Pontefract Castles. Elizabethan Gallery: temporary exhibitions.

N C SUPPORT One Education Officer with activity rooms and teaching packs. Artefact handling sessions and artist-led workshops can be arranged.

OPENING Monday to Saturday 10.30am–5.00pm, Sunday 2.30pm–5.00pm.

CATERING None.

COST Free.

DISABLED FACILITIES None.

DIRECTIONS From city centre follow signs to Clayton Hospital; Art Gallery is on Bond Street.

Walk Whitby Way

- Harry Collett
- Ashford Guest House, 8 Royal Crescent, Whitby, North Yorks. YO21 3EJ
- 0947 602138

Join 'The Baron' to explore the folklore myths and legends of historical Whitby in a one and a half hour guided walk, designed to inform, amuse and entertain. Ghost walks. An invitation to discover the strange and supernatural tales of ancient Whitby.

N C SUPPORT Will adapt to suit your needs with Geography, History, Botany on guided town walks or country walks.

OPENING All year.

COST £1.50 per head. Groups (more than 15): £30.

DIRECTIONS Contact H Collett. Can meet groups anywhere in Whitby by prior arrangement.

Warkworth Castle & Hermitage
- The Head Custodian
- Warkworth, Nr Amble, Morpeth, Northumberland. NE65 0UJ
- 0665 711423

The great towering keep of this 15th-century castle dominates the town and River Coquet. Just upstream by boat is a curious hermitage cut from the rock.

OPENING Castle: all year. Good Friday or 1 April (whichever is earlier) to 30 September: daily 10.00am–6.00pm. 1 October to Maundy Thursday or 31 March (whichever is earlier): Tuesday to Sunday 10.00am–4.00pm. Closed 24–26 December and 1 January. Hermitage: access by boat; ring for details of opening hours.

CATERING Picnic facilities.

DISABLED FACILITIES Wheelchair access to castle (except keep).

DIRECTIONS Seven and a half miles south of Alnwick on A1068 (OS Map 81; Castle ref NU 247057, Hermitage ref NU 242060). Bus: Northumbria X18 Newcastle to Alnwick (Tel: 091-232 4211). BR: Alnmouth three and a half miles.

Washington 'F' Pit
- Helen Sinclair
- Albany Way, Washington, Tyne & Wear
- 091-416 7640 FAX 091-510 0675

A relic of the great days of the Durham and Northumberland coalfields. Preserved winding house where the 1888 winding engine is demonstrated on request, driven by an electric motor.

N C SUPPORT Local maps, mining artefacts and coal measure fossils may be borrowed through Sunderland Museum.

OPENING April to October: Tuesday to Friday 10.00am–1.00pm and 1.30pm–5.30pm, Saturday 10.00am–1.00pm and 1.30pm–4.30pm, Sunday 2.00pm–5.00pm.

CATERING None.

COST Free.

DISABLED FACILITIES None.

DIRECTIONS The Pit is situated in District 12 of Washington Town and easily reached from the A1290, A1231, A182 and A1(M).

Whitby Abbey
- The Head Custodian
- Whitby, North Yorks. YO22 4JT
- 0947 603568

Ancient holy place. A religious community was first established at

VISITS OUT

NORTH EAST

Whitby in 657 by Abbess Hilda and was the home of Caedmon, the first English poet. The remains we can see today are of a Benedictine church built in the 13th and 14th centuries and include a magnificent three-tiered choir

OPENING All year. Good Friday or 1 April (whichever is earlier) to 30 September: daily 10.00am–6.00pm. 1 October to Maundy Thursday or 31 March (whichever is earlier): Monday to Sunday 10.00am–4.00pm. Closed 24–26 December and 1 January.

CATERING Picnic facilities.

DISABLED FACILITIES Access is unsuitable for wheelchairs.

DIRECTIONS On cliff top east of Whitby town centre (OS Map 94; ref NZ 904115). Bus: from surrounding areas (Tel: 0947 602146). BR: Whitby half a mile.

Whitby Museum
- David White
- Pannett Park, Whitby, North Yorks. YO21 1RE
- 0947 602908

A treasure-trove of Whitby's past. Sections on shipping, whaling and jet industries, Captain Cook, pioneering Arctic scientist and whaling captain William Scoresby Jr, Social History, fossils and more.

N C SUPPORT Work sheets available.

OPENING May to September: Monday–Friday 9.30am–5.30pm, Sunday 2.00pm–5.00pm. October to April: Monday and Tuesday 10.30am–1.00pm, Wednesday and Saturday 10.30am–4.00pm, Sunday 2.00pm–4.00pm, Easter Monday 10.30am–4.00pm, closed Christmas and New Year holidays.

CATERING Picnic lunches can be eaten in Pannett Park.

COST Children 50p, adults £1.00. School parties: children and first four adults 25p.

DISABLED FACILITIES Level access can be arranged. The museum is all on one level. However, manoeuvring between cases can be difficult. No toilet.

DIRECTIONS There is no parking available at the museum. Coaches must park in designated parking areas, which are well signposted.

Wigfield Farm
- Debra Bushby
- Haverlands Lane, Worsbrough Bridge, Barnsley, South Yorks. S70 5NQ
- 0226 204828

Open interpretative farm with rare and commercial breeds of pigs, sheep, cattle, goats, ponies and poultry.

N C SUPPORT Full guided tour given to school groups; tour varies according to age and National Curriculum interest.

ANNUAL OR ONE OFF EVENT Events every bank holiday, Sunday and Monday; Country Fair August bank holiday.

OPENING Summer: Monday to Sunday 10.00am–5.00pm. Winter: Monday to Sunday 10.00am–4.00pm. Open bank holiday Mondays, closed Christmas period.

CATERING Weekend tea room.

COST General admission by donation. £10.00 charge for group visits.

DISABLED FACILITIES Accessible.

DIRECTIONS Off A61, two miles north of M1 junction 36. Follow brown and white signs.

Wildfowl & Wetland Trust
- Niki Warner
- District 15, Washington, Tyne & Wear. NE38 8LE
- 091-416 5454 FAX 091-416 5801

Ten acres of wetlands and woodland, home to many of the world's wildfowl, and other wildlife. Visitor Centre provides tea room, giftshop and information with special adventure play area.

N C SUPPORT Variety of outdoor, activity-based programmes designed in line with National Curriculum. These are supported by free teachers' packs, educational publications and worksheets.

ANNUAL OR ONE OFF EVENT Seasonal activities, but predominantly 'out of school'.

OPENING Summer: 9.30am–5.00pm. Winter: 9.30am–4.00pm.

CATERING Tea room offers light meals and snacks. Picnic sites available in grounds.

COST Children £2.60. Group rates for schools: children £1.20, one adult free with every ten children; special schools free.

DISABLED FACILITIES Hard paths, wheelchairs available, toilet. Static playground for handicapped children.

DIRECTIONS Off A1231 Sunderland road, follow brown signs (close to A1 and A19).

Withernsea Lighthouse Museum
- Mrs J Standley
- Hull Road, Withernsea, East Yorks. HU19 2DY
- 0964 614834

Withernsea Lighthouse uniquely towers 127 feet over the town. Climb 144 steps. See breathtaking views. Open 1989 memorium, exhibits, RNLI, HM Coastguard, local history.

N C SUPPORT Local history, including Victorian and Edwardian. Geographical coastlines, erosion, collection of fossils. History of lighting system and structure. RNLI coastguard lifesaving and maritime articles.

ANNUAL OR ONE OFF EVENT Spring celebration of abseil event on spring Bank Holiday. Centenary 1894–1994. Garden party August.

OPENING March to October: Saturday, Sunday and bank holidays 1.00pm–5.00pm. Mid-June to mid-September: Monday–Friday 11.00am–5.00pm.

CATERING Cafe serving light refreshments (seating 30). Also large garden picnic area.

COST Children 50p, one adult free per ten.

DISABLED FACILITIES Toilet. Entrance ramp to ground floor only, museum and lighthouse base.

DIRECTIONS From M180 over Humber Bridge to Hull from M62, A63 to Hull, then A1033 to Withernsea.

VISITS OUT
NORTH EAST

Worsbrough Mill Museum
- Debra Bushby
- Worsbrough Bridge, Barnsley, South Yorks. S70 5LJ
- 0226 774527

A working industrial museum comprising a 17th-century watermill and a 19th-century former steam-driven mill. A range of stoneground flours are produced for sale on the restored machinery.

N C SUPPORT Full guided tour given to school groups; tour varies due to age and National Curriculum interests.

ANNUAL OR ONE OFF EVENT Events every bank holiday, Sunday and Monday. Country Fair August bank holiday.

OPENING Summer: Wednesday to Sunday 10.00am–5.00pm. Winter: Wednesday to Sunday 10.00am–4.00pm. Open bank holiday Mondays.

CATERING Mobile caravan.

COST General admission by donation. £10 charge for group visits.

DISABLED FACILITIES Accessible. Toilets.

DIRECTIONS Off A61, two miles north of M1 junction 36. Follow brown and white signs.

Wylam Railway Museum
- P R B Brooks
- Falcon Centre, Falcon Terrace, Wylam, Northumberland. NE41 8EE
- 0661 852174

George Stephenson was born in Wylam and the world's oldest locomotive 'Puffing Billy' was built at Wylam. This attractive small museum illustrates Wylam's unique place in railway history with interesting exhibits. For further information contact P R B Brooks at 20 Bluebell Close, Wylam, NE41 8EU, Tel: 0661 853520.

N C SUPPORT Informative descriptive panels tell of the importance of Wylam and famous local pioneers George Stephenson, William Hedley and Timothy Hackworth and the early development of waggonways and local railways.

OPENING Tuesday and Thursday 2.00pm–5.00pm and 5.30pm–7.30pm, Saturday 9.00am–12.00 noon.

CATERING Pubs within a quarter of a mile.

COST Free. Donations welcome. Charge for special opening outside normal hours.

DISABLED FACILITIES Wheelchair access into museum.

DIRECTIONS Wylam is on banks of the River Tyne one mile south of A69 and one mile north of A695. The Museum is in centre of the village off main street by Fox & Hounds Inn.

York Minster
- Mrs A Willey
- 6 College Street, York. YO1 2JF
- 0904 611124

York Minster is the largest Gothic cathedral in Northern Europe. The Centre for School Visits uses slides, models and activities for a child-centred preparation for any visit.

N C SUPPORT As well as general visits, many topics relating to the National Curriculum are covered. Topics in

Religious Education, History, Science and Technology are specifically catered for.

OPENING Daily 10.00am–2.00pm (last entry).

CATERING None.

COST 80p per pupil and £3.00 booking fee.

DISABLED FACILITIES Ramped access. Toilet in the Minster.

DIRECTIONS Well signposted in York.

Yorkshire Air Museum
- David Lamb
- Halifax Way, Elvington, York. YO4 5AU
- 0904 608306 FAX 0904 608846

World War II bomber base, with control tower and other buildings. Aircraft collection. Aviation displays and the Barnes Wallis Collection.

OPENING Monday to Friday 10.30am–4.00pm, Saturday, Sunday and bank holidays 10.30am–5.00pm.

CATERING NAAFI restaurant.

COST Children £1.50, adults £2.50, Senior Citizens £1.50, one adult free with every ten children.

DISABLED FACILITIES Yes.

DIRECTIONS Contact the Administrator.

The Yorkshire Mining Museum
- Tina Lewis
- Caphouse Colliery, New Road, Overton, Wakefield. WF4 4RH
- 0924 848806

Fascinating, award-winning museum of the Yorkshire coalfield, including guided tour 450 feet underground with experienced local miners. Many varied indoor and outdoor surface displays. An authentic mining experience.

N C SUPPORT A cross-curricular resource: Science, Technology, Maths, English, Art. Free schools' pack, leader preview visit, use of school room, handling collection, mining reference files. Also extensive range of teachers' resource material available.

ANNUAL OR ONE OFF EVENT Free teacher familiarisation visits in February half-term.

OPENING Daily 10.00am–5.00pm, closed 25, 26 December and 1 January.

CATERING Snacks/meals available in cafeteria. School packed lunches can be ordered.

COST Children £3.65, adults £4.40, one teacher free per 15 pupils.

DISABLED FACILITIES Five awards for provision. Please telephone (minicom also) to discuss details.

DIRECTIONS On A642 halfway between Wakefield and Huddersfield.

Yorkshire Museum
- Sian Lewis
- Museum Gardens, York. YO1 2DR
- 0904 629745 FAX 0904 651221

Set in ten acres of botanical gardens, the Yorkshire Museum houses some of the finest Roman, Viking and Anglo-Saxon treasures ever discovered in Britain. There are also exciting temporary exhibitions.

N C SUPPORT Roman, Anglo-Saxon and Viking displays are of direct relevance to Key Stages 2 and 3 in the National Curriculum. Education pack and worksheets available.

OPENING 1 April to 31 October: daily 10.00am–5.00pm (last admission 4.30pm). 1 November to 31 March: Monday to Saturday 10.00am–5.00pm, Sunday 1.00pm–5.00pm (last admission 4.30pm).

CATERING None.

COST Children £1.75, adults £3.00, concessions £1.75. Groups (more than ten): children £1.15, adults £2.25, concessions £1.15.

DISABLED FACILITIES Access to all areas. Toilet.

DIRECTIONS Central York between Lendal Bridge and the Minster. Easy access from all major routes.

Yorkshire Sculpture Park

- Anna Bowman or Rory Francis
- West Bretton, Wakefield, West Yorks. WF4 4LG
- 0924 830642 FAX 0924 830044

Yorkshire Sculpture Park is an open air gallery situated in beautiful 18th-century landscaped parkland. There is a changing exhibition programme, a permanent collection of 20th-century sculpture and Access Sculpture Trail.

N C SUPPORT Visits are arranged to cater for individual needs, specific interests and the National Curriculum. Activities include talks, guided tours and practical workshops. INSET and weekend courses for students are available.

ANNUAL OR ONE OFF EVENT Educational programmes and activities related to current exhibitions and the permanent collection all year round.

OPENING Spring and Summer: daily 10.00am–6.00pm. Autumn and Winter: daily 10.00am–5.00pm.

CATERING Picnic area, drinks and snacks at shop and Information Centre. Hot meals, sandwiches, etc. at Bothy Cafe.

COST Yorkshire schools free. Donations of £2.00 per head for workshop days.

DISABLED FACILITIES Cafe and indoor gallery areas wheelchair accessible. Toilets. Two Booster Electric Vehicles available free. Acidis tape-guides available for Access Sculpture Trail and current exhibitions.

DIRECTIONS M1 junction 38 signed YSP. BR: Wakefield Westgate. Bus: 484 from Wakefield. Coach parties by prior arrangement only.

Yorkshire Water Museum

- D W Atkinson
- Springhead Avenue, Willerby Road, Hull. HU5 5HZ
- 0482 652283

Housed in an operational pumping station; developments in water supplies are traced to the present day. Special features include the well, medieval water pipes and a huge Victorian beam engine.

N C SUPPORT Teachers' pack available. Also slide shows. Teachers are encouraged to visit early and prepare their own materials suitably slanted to History, Art or Technology.

OPENING Tuesday to Sunday 2.00pm–4.00pm, closed December.

VISITS OUT
NORTH EAST

CATERING **None.**

COST **Free.**

DISABLED FACILITIES **Toilets.**

DIRECTIONS **Follow the signposts from the Humber Bridge roundabout at the junctions of the A63 and A164.**

VISITS OUT
NORTH WEST

Abbothall Art Gallery
- Mrs June Hall
- Kirkland, Kendal, Cumbria. LA9 5AL
- 0539 722464

Georgian house of c.1760. Ground-floor display of period rooms with paintings (including Ruskin, Turner). Gillow and other furniture. First-floor art gallery: Lake District landscape gallery. Twentieth-century fine decorative art.

N C SUPPORT History, Art, English, Local Studies, Design, Art curriculum pack with examples for almost every aspect of AT1. Education Officer. Information pack. Study sessions in school or art gallery. School picture loans.

ANNUAL OR ONE OFF EVENT Major temporary exhibitions. Request current programme.

OPENING April to end October: Monday to Saturday 10.30am–5.00pm. Sunday 2.00pm–5.00pm. 1 November to 31 March: reduced hours; telephone for details.

CATERING None.

COST Cumbria schools: children 50p, supervising adults 50p. Schools outside Cumbria: children £1.00, supervising adults £1.00.

DISABLED FACILITIES Lifts and stairlifts suitable for wheelchairs.

DIRECTIONS South end of Kendal. Right hand lane of one-way system. Take first right after parish church. Peppercorn car park to art gallery car park.

America Adventure
- Marinia Efstatiou
- c/o Granada Theme Parks & Hotels, Water Street, Manchester. M60 9EA
- 061-832 9090 FAX 061-834 3684

American adventure theme park, Ilkeston, Derby, open throughout the summer; 100 attractions.

N C SUPPORT Education packs provided relevant to Key Stages 1–2.

OPENING 10.00am until early evening depending on weather and time of year. Please telephone 0773 531521 for details.

COST Under fours free, adults £10.00. Pre-booked groups £4.50 (minimum 12). School parties £4.25.

DISABLED FACILITIES Toilets, ramps. Certain rides and attractions accommodate people with disabilities depending on disability.

DIRECTIONS Signposted from junction 26 of the M1. Junction 15 of the M6.

Animation World
- Miss Jane Clarke
- Britannia Pavilion, Albert Dock, Liverpool. L3 4AA
- 051-707 1828 FAX 051-707 1575

An exhibition showing the complete process of Cosgrove Hall's productions. Presenting 'hands-on' exhibits. Life size rooms such as Castle Duckula, including the original models and sets from 'The Wind in the Willows'.

N C SUPPORT Group tours on any day of the week and at any time include a free tour guide and a free guest appearance by Count Duckula or Dangermouse.

VISITS OUT
NORTH WEST

OPENING Daily 10.00am–6.00pm.

CATERING None.

COST Children £2.50, adults £3.00. Groups: children £2.25. adults £2.70, one adult free with every ten children.

DISABLED FACILITIES Lift at entrance which can also be used to exit; one level. Plenty of wheelchair space throughout. Toilet.

DIRECTIONS Follow signs for Liverpool, then signs for Albert Dock. Park in free car park, cross wooden bridge; directly in front on the right.

Apollo Canal Cruises Ltd
- David Lowe
- Wharf Street, Shipley, West Yorks. BD17 7DW
- 0274 595914

Educational cruises of one to three hours on Leeds and Liverpool Canal. Three traditional canal boats, capacity 48, 72 or 78 passengers. Locks, aqueducts, running commentary. Department of Transport certified.

N C SUPPORT Teachers' pack available.

OPENING All year daily: any time (must book in advance). Also waterbus service (school holidays).

CATERING Snacks, drinks, light meals.

COST Charter rates from £30–£145.00.

DISABLED FACILITIES Adequate access onto boats.

DIRECTIONS Off A657/A6038, near Shipley BR station. Three miles from Bradford city centre.

Beatrix Potter Gallery
- Fiona Clark
- National Trust, Main Street, Hawkshead, Ambleside, Cumbria. LA22 0NS
- 05394 36355

An exhibition (changed annually) of Beatrix Potter's original artwork. The building once housed the offices of her husband, solicitor William Heelis.

DISABLED FACILITIES None.

DIRECTIONS Off M6 at junction for Kendal, then follow signs to Windermere, Ambleside and Hawkshead, then it is signposted.

Beeston Castle
- The Head Custodian
- Beeston, Nr Tarporley, Ches. CW6 9TX
- 0829 260464

Standing majestically on sheer, rocky crags which fall sharply away from the castle walls, Beeston has possibly the best views of the surrounding countryside of any castle in England and the rock has a history stretching back over 2,500 years.

OPENING All year round. Good Friday or 1 April (whichever is earlier) to 30 September: daily 10.00am–6.00pm. 1 October to Maundy Thursday or 31 March (whichever is earlier): Tuesday to Sunday 10.00am–4.00pm. Closed 24–26 December and 1 January.

CATERING Picnic facilities.

DIRECTIONS Eleven miles southeast of Chester on minor road off A49 (OS Map 117; ref SJ 537593). Bus:

VISITS OUT
NORTH WEST

Cheshire Bus 64, C83, L2 from Chester (Tel: 0244 602666). BR: Chester ten miles.

Blackburn Museum & Art Gallery
- M Millward
- Museum Street, Blackburn, Lancs. BB1 7AJ
- 0254 667130

Superb collections of paintings, ceramics, Japanese prints, icons, illuminated manuscripts, printed books, Classical and British coins, social and local history, South Asian Gallery.

N C SUPPORT Writing and Printing, Egyptians, local projects, Middle Ages, Classical Civilisation. Study centre; teachers' pack. Tailor-made support for teachers.

OPENING Tuesday to Saturday 9.45am–4.45pm. Party visits welcome by appointment on Monday.

COST Free.

DISABLED FACILITIES Access to ground floor, including toilets. Lift elsewhere.

DIRECTIONS In town centre, very close to Town Hall.

Blackpool Sea Life Centre
- Emma Haddock
- The Promenade, Blackpool, Lancs. FY1 5AA
- 0253 22445 FAX 0253 751647

At Sea Life Centres people of all ages can discover the amazing life that lives from the surface of our seas down to the ocean depths.

N C SUPPORT Teachers' packs with information and workbooks in a choice of three subject areas are available for each of three age ranges: 5–7 years, 8–11 years and 12 years and over.

OPENING Daily 10.00am–6.00pm.

CATERING Restaurant facilities; packed lunches by arrangement.

COST Children £2.25.

DISABLED FACILITIES Full access and facilities available.

DIRECTIONS Located midway between Towerworld and central pier on Promenade.

The National Curriculum comes alive at Blackpool Tower

ATTENTION

That's what you'll get when you take your class to Blackpool Tower. We reach Key Stage 1 and 2 topics including History, Science, Technology and Human Geography in ways that'll keep your pupils fascinated.

With different activities to watch and participate in such as Bug World, The Dawn of Time and Undersea World, learning has never been so exciting. Also on offer are activity sessions, guided tours, detailed itineraries, lunches and lots more - for a very reasonable all-inclusive price.

To book or receive our Educational Brochure ring our Co-ordinator on **0253 22242**. for a great day's entertainment and learning.

Worlds Of Entertainment

Blackpool Tower: Promenade. Blackpool FY1 4BJ.
Tel: 0253 22242

VISITS OUT
NORTH WEST

Blackpool Tower
- Julie Park
- The Promenade, Blackpool, Lancs. FY1 4BY
- 0253 22242 FAX 0253 25194

Blackpool Tower offers a variety of attractions and entertainment for the whole family plus special events on its Centenary Year. It has eleven superb attractions that will enthral and educate children of all ages.

N C SUPPORT Topics covered: Life under the Sea, Contrasting Locations, Shape and Structure, Human Geography, Minibeasts, The Victorian Experience.

COST Education package: £2.95 per child, accompanying teachers free. Duration: three hours. Educational fee: £4.45 per child, accompanying teachers free. Duration: full day. Pre-booking required.

Blackpool Transport
- David Eaves
- Rigby Road, Blackpool, Lancs. FY1 5DD
- 0253 23931 FAX 0253 752604

Public transport operator; includes Blackpool's famous coastal tramway.

N C SUPPORT Occasional site visits are available. Will provide speaker on Environmental, Public Transport issues.

COST Contact the office to discuss.

DISABLED FACILITIES None.

Blencathra
- Rob Lucas
- Field Studies Council Centre, Threlkeld, Keswick, Cumbria. CA12 4SG
- 0768 779601 FAX 0768 779264

A Field Centre, part of a network of Field Studies Council study centres, providing tailor-made courses in environmental topics to suit schools' curriculum needs.

N C SUPPORT Courses can be designed to suit all Key Stages on a day or residential basis. There is a long tradition of A-Level provision with specialist courses in Geography and Biology.

ANNUAL OR ONE OFF EVENT A range of courses designed to suit customers. INSET provision and student courses available.

OPENING End of January to beginning of December.

CATERING Fully catered courses are offered as part of the package. Self-catering options are provided.

COST Full costs available on application.

DISABLED FACILITIES Limited special facilities are available.

DIRECTIONS The Centre is approximately 20 miles from junction 40 of the M6. BR: Penrith.

Bolton Museum & Art Gallery
- David Edwards
- Le Mans Crescent, Bolton, Lancs. BL1 1SE
- 0204 22311 ext 2193 FAX 0204 391352

Regular art exhibitions.

N C SUPPORT Ancient Egypt, Romans and Saxons, Natural History, Art. Teaching service and loan service to schools. Art gallery teachers' guides, Geology handling sessions.

OPENING Monday to Tuesday and Thursday to Friday 9.30am–5.30pm,

VISITS OUT
NORTH WEST

Saturday 10.00am–5.00pm, closed Wednesday and Sunday.

COST **Free.**

DISABLED FACILITIES **Lift to all floors.**

DIRECTIONS **Behind Bolton Town Hall and opposite Octagon Theatre.**

Bracken Hall
- C Rosenbloom
- Countryside Centre, Glen Road, Baildon, Bradford, West Yorks. BD17 5EA
- 0274 584140

Bracken Hall is a countryside museum with a variety of habitats within easy walking distance. Displays tell the story of the local countryside. There is a shop, wildlife gardens, toilets.

N C SUPPORT **Education staff available to work with groups on Natural History, Geology, Geography topics. Fully equipped classroom. Worksheets and teaching materials. Advanced booking essential.**

OPENING **April to October: Wednesday to Sunday 11.00am–5.00pm. November to March: Wednesday and Sunday only 11.00am–5.00pm. For booked groups all year: Tuesday to Sunday 11.00am–5.00pm.**

CATERING **Small shop selling ice cream. Cafe and pub 200 yards down the road.**

COST **Free. Donations welcome.**

DISABLED FACILITIES **Wheelchair access. Interactive units. Toilet.**

DIRECTIONS **From Bradford take A6038 then B6151 to Baildon, second left at roundabout and continue for one mile. Right at end; the Hall is 200 yards on right.**

Bradford Design Exchange
- Neil Hereweds
- 34 Peckover Street, Little Germany, Bradford, West Yorks. BD1 5BD
- 0274 729707 FAX 0204 729680

A design centre with studios and 6000 square feet of exhibition space, offering an ongoing Design-based exhibition programme as well as conference facilities. Check what's on before visiting.

N C SUPPORT **Key shows/events to support Design and Technology, in conjunction with the Design Council, including teacher/pupil seminars etc.**

OPENING **Monday to Friday 9.00am–5.30pm, Saturday 12.00 noon–4.00pm, Sunday 12.00 noon–4.00pm; depending on show.**

CATERING **Full range available.**

COST **Free.**

DISABLED FACILITIES **Full access.**

DIRECTIONS **Five minutes walk from Bradford city centre.**

Bradford Industrial Museum
- Lyn Killick
- Moorside Mills, Moorside Road, Eccleshill, Bradford. BD2 3HP
- 0274 621756 FAX 0274 636362

Original spinning mill complex, complete with mill-owner's house, back-to-back cottages, mill stables with shire horses. Demonstrations and horse-drawn rides daily.

N C SUPPORT **Museum education service provides a full back-up** support to teachers plus a Victorian schoolroom and wash-days.

ANNUAL OR ONE OFF EVENT 'Christmas at t'Mill' with carol singers, lantern-lit carriage rides, entertainment.

OPENING Tuesday to Sunday and bank holiday Mondays 10.00am–5.00pm. Closed Christmas Day, Boxing Day.

CATERING Bobbins Bistro serves light meals, home-made cakes and children's menus.

COST Free.

DISABLED FACILITIES Toilets. Ramped access. Lifts to all floors.

DIRECTIONS Signposted from Bradford ring road and Harrogate Road.

The British Commercial Vehicle Museum
- P Dawson, Manager
- King Street, Leyland, Preston, Lancs. PR5 1LE
- 0772 451011

Museum devoted to the history of British commercial vehicles from 1896 to the present day, including steam wagons, lorries, buses, fire engines, vans.

N C SUPPORT Museum exhibits can be used for History, Technology, Art, Geography, and Maths examples.

ANNUAL OR ONE OFF EVENT Spring Rally in May; Autumn Rally in September.

OPENING April to September: Tuesday to Sunday 10.00am–5.00pm. October and November: Saturday and Sunday 10.00am–5.00pm. Open bank holidays.

COST Children £1.50, adults £3.00, Senior Citizens £1.50, 10% discount for pre-booked groups of 15 or more.

DISABLED FACILITIES Toilets; ramps and seats in Museum.

DIRECTIONS Three-quarters of a mile from junction 28 of M6 in Leyland town centre.

Brontë Parsonage Museum
- Pat Goff
- Church Street, Haworth, Keighley, West Yorks. BD22 8DR
- 0535 642323 FAX 0535 647131

Former home of the Brontë family from 1820 to 1861 and now a museum with collections of Brontë manuscripts, drawings, furnishings, costume and personal belongings.

N C SUPPORT A range of services are available to schools and other educational groups. Please write for details.

OPENING April to September: daily 10.00am–5.00pm. October to March: daily 11.00am–4.30pm.

CATERING None.

COST School groups: 16 years and under 50p. 17–18 years £1.00. Students over 18 (individually) £2.50.

DISABLED FACILITIES Very limited.

DIRECTIONS The Parsonage is above the parish church at the top of Main Street.

The Brontë Weaving Shed
- Mrs Ellen Akeroyd
- Townend Mill, North Street, Haworth, Nr Keighley, West Yorks. BD22 8EP
- 0535 646217

VISITS OUT
NORTH WEST

Half-hour talk and demonstrations of spinning and weaving: 'From Fleece to Fabric'. Combined with the Timmy Feather exhibition highlighting the life of the last handloom weaver in Yorkshire.

OPENING Daily 11.00am–4.00pm. Times may vary according to the availability of part-time handloom weaver.

COST Free.

DIRECTIONS At the top of the village opposite large coach/car park.

Brough Castle
- The Head Custodian
- High Street, Brough, Kirby Stephen, Cumbria. CA17 4EJ

Perched on a superb vantage point overlooking an old trade route, now the A66, this ancient site dates back to Roman times. The 12th-century keep replaced an earlier stronghold destroyed by the Scots in 1174. The castle was restored by Lady Anne Clifford in the 17th century.

OPENING All year. Good Friday or 1 April (whichever is earlier) to 30 September: daily 10.00am–6.00pm. 1 October to Maundy Thursday or 31 March (whichever is earlier): Tuesday to Sunday 10.00am–4.00pm. Winter: closed Tuesday. Closed 24–26 December and 1 January.

DIRECTIONS Eight miles southeast of Appleby, south of A66 (OS Map 91; ref NY 791141). Bus: various services from BR Kirkby Stephen to Brough (Tel: 0228 812812). BR: Kirkby Stephen six miles.

Brougham Castle
- The Head Custodian
- Brougham, Nr Penrith, Cumbria. CA10 2AA
- 0768 62488

These impressive ruins on the banks of the River Eamont include an early 13th-century keep and later buildings. You can climb to the top of the keep and survey the domain of its eccentric one-time owner Lady Anne Clifford, who restored the castle in the 17th century. there is a small exhibition of Roman tombstones from the nearby fort.

OPENING All year. Good Friday or 1 April (whichever is earlier) to 30 September: daily 10.00am–6.00pm. 1 October to Maundy Thursday or 31 March (whichever is earlier): Tuesday to Sunday 10.00am–4.00pm. Closed 24–26 December and 1 January

CATERING Picnic facilities.

DIRECTIONS One and a half miles southeast of Penrith (OS Map 90; ref NY 537290). BR: Penrith two miles.

Calderdale Industrial Museum
- Jennie Forrester
- Winding Road, Halifax. HX1 1RE
- 0422 3588087 FAX 0422 349310

The museum reflects the working lives of local people over 150 years. Over 20 industries represented, from textiles to engineering to sweet-making. Evocative sounds, smells and working machinery.

N C SUPPORT Hand textile demonstrations with opportunities for role play (Key Stage 1 and Key Stage 3). Activity guide and 'Daily

Grind' publication with site-related news stories from 1857, 1875 and 1912. Projects for schools.

ANNUAL OR ONE OFF EVENT Sculpture and history workshops supporting History and Art National Curriculum requirements, an opportunity to work with artist Chris Coe and to discover Home Front artefacts (September).

OPENING Tuesday to Saturday 10.00am–5.00pm, Sunday 2.00pm–5.00pm, closed Mondays (except bank holidays).

CATERING None.

COST Educational group rate: LEA schools 50p, private and opted out 60p.

DISABLED FACILITIES Toilet, lift, ramp from Winding Road.

DIRECTIONS BR: Halifax. Museum adjoins the Halifax Piece Hall, which is signposted.

Calderdale Museums & Arts
- Debbie Newell
- The Piece Hall, Halifax. HX1 1RE
- 0422 358087

The Museums and Arts service includes the Piece Hall Art Gallery, Brighouse Art Gallery and Bankfield Museum. Each site provides a changing exhibition programme of art, crafts and other media.

N C SUPPORT Practical art activities, workshops, talks and demonstrations. All are linked to the National Curriculum and are available to school groups of all ages.

OPENING Tuesday to Sunday 10.00am–5.00pm. Closed Monday.

CATERING None.

COST Varies from free to a nominal charge.

DISABLED FACILITIES Access via lift. Assistance can be given.

DIRECTIONS Piece Hall is five minutes walk from BR station in Halifax town centre.

Calvert Trust
- John Crosbie
- Little Crosthwaite, Keswick, Cumbria. CA12 4QD
- 0768 772254 FAX 0768 772254

Provision of outdoor education, field study, outdoor pursuits or courses which are fully accessible for pupils with special needs.

COST Dependent on season, group numbers and course.

DISABLED FACILITIES Full wheelchair access.

DIRECTIONS Three miles north of Keswick on A591.

Camelot Theme Park
- Sandra Dempsey
- Charnock Richard, Chorley, Nr Preston, Lancs. PQ7 5LP
- 061-833 0880 FAX 061-834 3684

Theme of King Arthur and medieval times. There are over 100 exciting rides and show attractions, including spectacular live jousting.

N C SUPPORT Two free education packs available, newly written in 1993 based on the National Curriculum core subjects: Key Stage 2 pack (7–10 years) and Key Stage 3 pack (11–14 years).

VISITS OUT
NORTH WEST

OPENING April to October. Please telephone 0257 452100 to check opening times.

CATERING Various outlets and picnic areas.

COST 1993 prices: children £4.25, one teacher free for every eight paying pupils. Telephone for 1994 prices.

DISABLED FACILITIES Yes.

DIRECTIONS Short drive from M6 (junction 27 northbound, junction 28 southbound) or M61 (junction 8); well signposted.

Carlisle Castle
- The Head Custodian
- Carlisle, Cumbria. CA3 8UR

This impressive medieval castle, where Queen Mary of Scots was once imprisoned, has a long and tortuous history of warfare and family feuds. A portcullis hangs menacingly over the gate house passage, there is a maze of passages and chambers, endless staircases to lofty towers and visitors can walk the high ramparts for stunning views. There is also a medieval manor house in miniature with a suite of medieval rooms furnished as they might have been when used by the castle's former constable. The castle is also the home of the Museum of the King's Own Border Regiment.

OPENING All year. Good Friday or 1 April (whichever is earlier) to 30 September: daily from 9.30am. 1 October to Maundy Thursday or 31 March (whichever is earlier): Tuesday to Sunday 10.00am–4.00pm. Closed 24–26 December and 1 January.

DISABLED FACILITIES Parking for people with disabilities only. Wheelchair access except to interiors of buildings.

DIRECTIONS North of Carlisle town centre (OS Map 85; ref NY 397563). Bus: from surrounding areas (Tel: 0228 48484). BR: Carlisle half a mile.

Cartwright Hall Art Gallery
- Vicky Mitchell
- Lister Park, Bradford. BD9 4NS
- 0274 493313 FAX 0274 481045

Talks about exhibitions, workshops related to temporary exhibitions, trolley of materials available for school visits if not attending for a workshop.

N C SUPPORT Gallery teacher and two gallery Education Officers. Special project about a permanent collection painting called 'The Emigrant Ship'. Key Stages 2 and 3: History, Geography, Art and English.

ANNUAL OR ONE OFF EVENT Regular special teachers' private views.

OPENING Tuesday to Sunday 10.00am–6.00pm, open bank holidays.

CATERING Cafe in gallery.

COST At the moment free to schools, except independent schools.

DISABLED FACILITIES Lift, toilets, wheelchair, changing facilities.

DIRECTIONS Two miles north of city centre, in Lister Park on the A650 Keighley Road.

VISITS OUT
NORTH WEST

The Castle Dairy
- E Wright
- 26 Wildman Street, Kendal, Cumbria. LA9 6EN
- 0539 721170

Twelfth-century building, first built as fortified food store to service 12th-century Norman castle. Open courtyards covered in 1560 to convert into Elizabethan residence. Roman Road is incorporated into building.

OPENING Easter to end of September: Wednesdays only 2.00pm–4.00pm.

CATERING None.

COST 5p per person.

DISABLED FACILITIES None.

DIRECTIONS On main A6 from the north. Railway station 200 yards.

The Colour Museum
- S L Burge
- Perkin House, 82 Grattan Road, Bradford, West Yorks. BD1 2JB
- 0274 390955 FAX 0274 392888

The Colour Museum is Britain's only museum of colour. It consists of two galleries which examine light, colour, dyeing and printing. Both galleries are packed with visitor-operated exhibits.

N C SUPPORT Worksheets for 7–9, 9–13 and 13–16-year-olds. All recently updated to fit in with the National Curriculum.

OPENING Tuesday to Friday 2.00pm–5.00pm, Saturday 10.00am–4.00pm. Pre-booked parties: Tuesday to Friday 9.30am–12.30pm.

CATERING None.

COST 1993 prices: pre-booked parties in full-time education 35p each.

DISABLED FACILITIES Lift access to all floors.

DIRECTIONS Located in the centre of Bradford just off the B6144.

Commonwealth Institute
- N Brown
- Salts Mill, Victoria Road, Saltaire, Shipley, Bradford, West Yorks. BD18 3LB
- 0274 530231 FAX 0274 530253

The Regional Centre of the Commonwealth Institute provides resources, workshops and exhibitions based on the Commonwealth and designed to support the National Curriculum.

N C SUPPORT The education resources and workshop programmes are all geared to the National Curriculum.

ANNUAL OR ONE OFF EVENT The Regional Centre produces a programme of exhibitions and workshops each term.

OPENING Monday to Friday 10.00am–5.00pm, Sunday 11.00am–4.00pm.

CATERING None.

COST Admission free to exhibitions. Fees payable for workshop programmes.

DISABLED FACILITIES Toilet.

DIRECTIONS Salts Mill is directly opposite Saltaire train station. The Regional Centre is situated down the inner courtyard next to the 1853 David Hockney Gallery.

VISITS OUT
NORTH WEST

Craven Museum
- Ms S Kirrane
- Town Hall, High Street, Skipton, Bradford, North Yorks. BD23 1AN
- 0756 794079

Museum with collections of archaeology, social history and geology, mainly relating to the Craven Dales of northwest Yorkshire: a small and easily assimilated museum.

N C SUPPORT Pleased to discuss requirements.

OPENING April to September: Monday and Wednesday to Friday 11.00am–5.00pm, Saturday 10.00am–12.00 noon and 1.00pm–5.00pm. Sunday 2.00pm–5.00pm, closed Tuesday. October to March: Monday and Wednesday to Friday 2.00pm–5.00pm, Saturday 10.00am–12.00 noon and 1.30pm–4.30pm, closed Tuesday and Sunday.

CATERING None.

COST Free.

DISABLED FACILITIES Not accessible to severely disabled. No special facilities.

DIRECTIONS In the Town Hall, near parish church and War Memorial at the top of the High Street.

The Cumberland Toy & Model Museum
- Rod Moore
- Banks Court, Market Place, Cockermouth, Cumbria. CA13 9NG
- 0900 827606

Mainly British toys from the 1920s. Working tinplate Hornby trains, Lego models and other toys. Large Scalextric layout. Free quiz and 'Find the Little Teddies'.

N C SUPPORT Teachers' packs should be available. At present the museum offers guided tours on specific topics, e.g. mechanisms, and an objects loan pack.

ANNUAL OR ONE OFF EVENT A special exhibition is normally arranged each year.

OPENING 1 February–30 November: daily 10.00am–5.00pm. December and January and evening visits by appointment.

CATERING None.

COST Children 70p, adults £1.40. School groups: children 50p, teachers free.

DISABLED FACILITIES Help is given but the buildings are very old with several staircases. Objects available for touching for partially sighted people.

Dove Cottage
- Claire Benbow
- The Wordsworth Trust, Dove Cottage, Townend, Grasmere, Cumbria. LA22 9PS
- 0539 435544 FAX 0539 435748

William Wordsworth's home (1799–1808). Education team provides tours of house and museum for all age groups. Options for school groups: video presentation, Wordsworth walk and artefacts workshops.

N C SUPPORT Resource material relating to English and History National Curriculum.

ANNUAL OR ONE OFF EVENT Poetry competition.

OPENING Mid-February to mid-January: daily 9.30am–5.00pm.

Closed mid-January to mid-February.

CATERING Tea shop on site.

COST Children £2.00, accompanying adults/teachers free.

DISABLED FACILITIES None.

DIRECTIONS On A591 between Keswick and Windermere. Four miles from Ambleside.

Dunham Massey
- The Administrator
- Altrincham, Cheshire. WA14 4SJ
- 061-941 1025

Eighteenth-century house in 250-acre wooded deer park. Georgian and Edwardian interiors; collections of furniture, paintings and silver; library, kitchen, laundry and stables; on the site of a Tudor building whose moat provides power for a working mill, 1616. Park with fallow deer.

Study centre; teachers' pack, education officer; role-play activities; problem-solving in Design Technology; nature trail; archive material.

N C SUPPORT National Curriculum links with Environmental Education and History.

DISABLED FACILITIES Some steps to ground floor of house; garden, park, outbuildings and shop via cobbled area; car parking by prior arrangement; electric wheelchair and scooter; wheelchair path to canal. Adapted toilet. Braille guide; large print guide.

DIRECTIONS Three miles southwest of Altrincham off A56; junction 19 of M6; junction 7/8 of M56. Bus: North Western/GM Buses 38. BR: Altrincham three miles; Hale three miles.

East Riddlesden Hall
- The Administrator
- Bradford Road, Keighley, West Yorks. BD20 5EL
- 0535 607075

A traditional 17th-century West Yorkshire manor house with panelled rooms and fine plasterwork, providing an ideal setting for pewter, domestic utensils and Yorkshire oak furniture; formal walled garden, monastic fishpond and grounds running down to River Aire; 120-feet-long great barn, with collection of traditional agricultural machinery.

N C SUPPORT National Curriculum links with History, Technology and Science. Children's guide; living history days.

DISABLED FACILITIES Contact the administrator for access details.

DIRECTIONS One mile northeast of Keighley. Fully accessible by public transport.

Embsay Steam Railway
- Stephen Walker
- The Station, Embsay, Skipton, North Yorks. BD23 6AK
- 0756 794727 FAX 0756 795189

Steam railway running two and a half miles in Yorkshire Dales. Station built in 1888. Fine collection of locomotives.

N C SUPPORT Trained teachers available to advise.

VISITS OUT
NORTH WEST

ANNUAL OR ONE OFF EVENT Special steaming days in June for school visits.

OPENING Steam trains run every Sunday throughout the year. Also on Tuesdays and Saturdays in July. Then daily (except for Monday and Friday from 27 July until the end of August. Also bank holidays (except Christmas Day and Boxing Day). A diesel train service runs on Saturdays in June and September.

CATERING Cafe and buffet cars.

COST Group rates: children £1.10, adults £2.40.

DISABLED FACILITIES Accommodation on most trains. Please book in advance.

DIRECTIONS Signposted from A59 Skipton by-pass.

ENGLISH HERITAGE

National Curriculum Support Almost every aspect of the curriculum can be explored at English Heritage properties. They can be used not only for studying History but linked to other subjects as varied as English, Maths, Science, Technology, Geography and Music. English Heritage has produced a wide range of National Curriculum teachers' guides and videos to give plenty of stimulating ideas. Write to English Heritage Education Service, Keysign House, 429 Oxford Street, London W1R 2HD, for a free copy of the resources catalogue.

Annual or one-off event At some sites each year there are special educational events, often with the involvement of experts such as musicians and storytellers, for visiting educational groups.

Cost Student groups and school parties are admitted free to English Heritage properties, but should book in advance through the relevant Regional Office.

See individual entries for all other information.

Beeston Castle
Brough Castle
Brougham Castle
Carlisle Castle
Lanercost Priory
Stott Park Bobbin Mill

Eureka! The Museum for Children

☞ Tim Carlton
✉ Discovery Road, Halifax. HX1 2NE
☎ 0422 330069 FAX 0422 330275

Eureka! is an interactive museum for children under 12 and their adult helpers. Exhibition themes: 'Me and My Body', 'Living and Working Together', 'Inventing and Creating'.

N C SUPPORT Education resource pack available. INSET and school workshop programme. Please phone for details.

OPENING Monday 10.00am–2.00pm in term time, 10.00am–5.00pm during holidays, Tuesday to Sunday 10.00am–5.00pm, Wednesday 10.00am–7.00pm, closed Christmas Day.

CATERING Cafeteria. Limited packed lunch facilities (must be pre-booked).

COST Children under 12 £3.50, under threes free, adults £4.50. Group rate

£2.50, one adult free for every ten children over seven years old or for every seven children under seven years old.

DISABLED FACILITIES All the exhibitions are accessible for visitors in wheelchairs. Lift to first floor. Toilets for disabled on both floors.

DIRECTIONS Eureka! is situated next to Halifax BR. It is well signposted in Halifax town centre. Nearest exit from M62 is junction 24.

The Gallery of English Costume
- Mrs A M Jarvis
- Platt Hall, Rusholme, Manchester. M14 5LL

Extensive collections of men's, women's and children's clothes, 1700–1990s. Small percentage on display. Also collections of embroideries and ethnic textiles, not normally on view, available by prior request.

N C SUPPORT 'Home and Dry': display, interactives and school loan collection available (protective clothing). Linked to junior Science and Technology curriculum. Displays of 18th-century and Victorian clothes.

ANNUAL OR ONE OFF EVENT Study facilities available by appointment for individual students doing personal projects in Fashion, History, Costume and Textiles.

OPENING November to February: Monday and Wednesday to Saturday 10.00am–5.45pm, Sunday 2.00pm–5.45pm, closed Tuesdays. Gallery closes 4.00pm.

COST Free.

DISABLED FACILITIES Access to ground floor only for wheelchairs (three steps at entrance). Special sessions can be arranged for small groups of people with visual impairment or learning difficulties.

DIRECTIONS Located in Platt Fields Park, Wilmslow Road, two miles south of city centre.

Gatehouse Gallery
- Stephen Morton
- The Square, Cartmel, Grange-over-Sands, Cumbria. LA11 6QB
- 05395 36602

14th-century gatehouse.

ANNUAL OR ONE OFF EVENT Exhibition of Helen Bradley prints on permanent display.

OPENING 11.00am–5.00pm.

COST Free.

DISABLED FACILITIES 14th-century spiral staircase impossible to climb.

DIRECTIONS Situated in the village square.

Gawthorpe Hall
- The Administrator
- Padiham, Nr Burnley, Lancs. BB12 8UA
- 0282 78511

House built in 1600, restored by Sir Charles Barry in the 1850s, is the home of the Shuttleworth family. Display of Rachel Kay-Shuttleworth textile collections; National Portrait Gallery portraits. Study centre. 'All Change', an issue-based teachers' pack on the National Trust's work in the Lake District, is available from

NORTH WEST

the National Trust Regional Office, The Hollens, Grasmere, Ambleside, Cumbria LA22 9QZ (Tel: 05394 33883).

N C SUPPORT Courses in Art, Craft and Management.

DISABLED FACILITIES Bumpy access across cobbled yard to shop. Unisex adapted toilet in same area. Limited access to ground floor of hall via ramps (prior warning of visit is essential). Some steps inside ground floor. Access to grounds and garden include rose garden and top terrace; some steps and gradients.

DIRECTIONS On eastern outskirts of Padiham; three-quarters of a mile drive to house on north of A671. Bus: frequent services from Burnley; all pass close to BR Burnley Barracks and Burnley Manchester Road. BR: Rose Grove two miles.

Granada Studios Tour

- Sandra Dempsey
- Water Street, Manchester. M60 9EA
- 061-833 0880 FAX 061-834 3684

Europe's only television theme attraction. A chance to enjoy a mixture of entertainment and education together with television fact-finding and fun.

N C SUPPORT Two education packs, a primary school pack and a separate secondary school pack, newly written in 1993 based on the National Curriculum.

OPENING April to September: Tuesday to Sunday. October to March: Wednesday to Sunday. January: Saturday and Sunday.

CATERING Various outlets.

COST 1993/94 prices: children £5.00, one teacher free for every eight paying pupils.

DISABLED FACILITIES Lifts, ramps and toilet facilities.

DIRECTIONS City centre Manchester, one mile from end of M602 motorway; well signposted.

Great Explorations

- Barbara Dunn
- Pleasure Island, International Festival Park, Riverside Drive, Otterspool, Liverpool. L17 7HJ
- 051-728 8686 FAX 051-727 5031

Features simple, exciting state-of-the-art interactive exhibits, educational resources of the highest quality, serving schools, families and children of all ages.

N C SUPPORT Seventy exhibits covering ten subjects. Primary Science and Technology. Key Stages 1 and 2 National Curriculum. 'Nature in the City'. International Festival Gardens also a wonderful resource.

ANNUAL OR ONE OFF EVENT Theme/topic weeks. Please phone for details.

OPENING 9.30am–5.30pm.

CATERING Packed lunch areas. Megabites fast-food restaurant. Picnic areas outdoors.

COST Children £1.95, adults £2.50, one free place for every 15 children.

DISABLED FACILITIES Easy access entrance. Toilet facilities. Car parking spaces.

DIRECTIONS Contact above for directions.

VISITS OUT
NORTH WEST

Greater Manchester Police Museum
- Duncan Broady, Curator
- Newton Street, Manchester. M1 1ES
- 061-856 3287

Situated in a Victorian police station and featuring a turn-of-the-century charge officer and cell block. Displays of police equipment and forgery exhibits.

N C SUPPORT Police from Victorian period through war years to present. Loan packs: Victorian Police and World War II leaflets; curator will give talks. Archive.

ANNUAL OR ONE OFF EVENT Participating in Open Days held in police stations in Greater Manchester area.

OPENING By appointment only.

CATERING None.

COST Free.

DISABLED FACILITIES Access to ground floor, no lift to first floor.

DIRECTIONS Situated on the corner of Newton Street and Faraday Street close to Piccadilly Station.

Grosvenor Museum
- Pauline Sharp
- 27 Grosvenor Street, Chester. CH1 2DD
- 0244 321616

Internationally famous Roman galleries plus period house with rooms from Stuart times to the 1920s. Also silver gallery, art gallery and exhibition programme.

N C SUPPORT Key Stage 2: Settlers and Invaders – The Romans in Britain. Resource packs and teaching sessions.

ANNUAL OR ONE OFF EVENT Contact the Museum for details.

OPENING Monday to Saturday 10.30am–5.00pm, Sunday 2.00pm–5.00pm.

CATERING Cafe scheduled.

COST Free.

DISABLED FACILITIES None.

DIRECTIONS The Museum is in the centre of Chester.

Haigh Country Park
- T G Sharratt or C Ingram
- Haigh, Wigan. WN2 1PE
- 0942 832895 FAX 0942 8311081

Country park with zoo, children's playground, miniature train, model village and 250 acres of woodland. Ranger service for education etc. Classroom.

N C SUPPORT Many ranger activities relate to the National Curriculum; full details from the Head Ranger, C Ingham.

ANNUAL OR ONE OFF EVENT All events by rangers repeated throughout the year.

OPENING All year: all day.

CATERING Cafeteria, wet-weather picnic area.

COST Discount dependent on group size. All ranger activities are low cost.

DISABLED FACILITIES Toilets and access to cafe, zoo and woodland trail.

DIRECTIONS M6 junction 27; M61 Junction 6 and follow signs.

VISITS OUT
NORTH WEST

Hardcastle Crags
- c/o The Warden
- Hollin Hall Farm, Hebden Bridge, West Yorks.
- 0422 844518

Mixed woodland on the steep sides of Hebden Water and Crimsworth Dean Beck; the landscape, typical of this Pennine area, consists of clough woodland, steep valleys, small walled fields, and then open, dissected moorland plateau rising to 1500 feet; the main stream has been used for water power and there is evidence of this in mill ponds and a disused early 19th-century cotton mill; the area is rich in flora and fauna.

N C SUPPORT National Curriculum links with History, Science, Geography and Technology.

DISABLED FACILITIES Contact the warden for access details.

DIRECTIONS Contact the warden for details.

Heaton Park Farm Centre
- Jean Dowler
- Prestwich, Manchester. M25 5SW
- 061-773 1085

A 40-acre municipal park. Two classrooms (with toilet facilities) located within the Farm Centre, which houses pigs, goats, sheep, hatchery, horses.

N C SUPPORT Life Sciences, Environmental Education, Park and Farm, great potential, Attainment Target headed under Variety of Life, Properties of Life, even Genetics and Education. A wealth of living materials and opportunities.

OPENING All year: Monday–Friday 9.00am–4.00pm.

COST Large room £30.00, small room £25.00. Discount for Manchester Authority establishments: large room £25.00, small room £20.00.

DISABLED FACILITIES Full access for people with disabilities. Classrooms on ground floor, toilets on ground floor.

DIRECTIONS Exit 18 off M66 then turn right on to Middleton Road. Park on right hand side.

Heysham Power Station
Nuclear Electric plc
- Information Officer
- Visitor Centre, PO Box 17, Morecambe, Lancs. LA3 2YB
- 0524 855624 FAX 0524 855883

Power station tours and information centre with interactive videos, computers and exhibits on the subjects of power generation and nature reserve.

N C SUPPORT Projects in line with National Curriculum: Generating Electricity, Soil, Energy in Nature, Pond Dipping, etc. as well as Physics, Chemistry, Radioactivity.

Physics/chemistry laboratory with project sheets, computers; station tours; nature reserve with field study centre; project on radioactivity. All linked to National Curriculum.

OPENING November to end March: Monday to Friday 10.00am–4.00pm. April to end October: Monday to Friday 10.00am–5.00pm, Saturday and Sunday 1.00pm–5.00pm. Times to accommodate school (pre-booking necessary).

VISITS OUT
NORTH WEST

COST Free.

DISABLED FACILITIES Yes.

DIRECTIONS M6 to Lancaster, A589 to Morecambe; signposted from Morecambe (follow Heysham) then HPS signs.

Holker Hall & Gardens
- Mrs C Johnson
- Cark-in-Cartmel, Grange-over-Sands, Cumbria. LA11 7PL
- 0539 558328 FAX 0539 558776

Historic house. Award-winning gardens, ice house, deer park, interest room, Victorian/Edwardian kitchen exhibition, patchwork and quilting. Holder of two Sandford Awards for Heritage Education.

N C SUPPORT Fully qualified Education Officer liaises with schools prior to visit. Areas such as Victorians; Houses and Homes; Mapping Topics; Technology and Design; Structures. With two weeks notice tours can be specifically worked out for a school's curricular needs.

ANNUAL OR ONE OFF EVENT The Great Garden and Countryside Festival 3-5 June 1994.

OPENING 1 April to 31 October: Sunday to Friday 10.00am–4.30pm.

CATERING Picnic areas, covered area; self-service cafeteria.

COST £2.00–£2.75 depending on tours booked.

DISABLED FACILITIES Toilets; two wheelchairs; ramps.

DIRECTIONS Junction 36 off M6 and follow signs on A590.

Huddersfield Art Gallery
- Robert Hall
- Princess Alexandra Walk, Huddersfield, West Yorks. HD1 2SU
- 0484 513808 FAX 0484 531983

The gallery presents an exciting Visual Arts programme featuring exhibitions by artists working in all media, from Britain and abroad. In addition the gallery houses an excellent permanent collection of British Art of the last 100 years.

N C SUPPORT In conjunction with this broad cultural programme the gallery organises a diverse range of artist-led educational activities.

OPENING Monday to Friday 10.00am–5.00pm, Saturday 10.00am–4.00pm.

CATERING None on site, cafes nearby.

COST Free.

DISABLED FACILITIES Good access to building and galleries. Toilet.

DIRECTIONS Situated in Huddersfield town centre above Central Library. Town situated between Leeds and Manchester.

Huddersfield Canal Society
- Frank Smith
- 239 Mossley Road, Ashton-under-Lyne, Lancs. OL6 6LN
- 061-339 1332 FAX 061-343 2262

Huddersfield Canal Society Limited is a registered charity restoring the Huddersfield Narrow Canal. It operates two boat trips on the canal: Portland Basin to Ashton-under-Lyne; and Tunnel End, Marsden. Public trips at weekend, charter weekdays.

NORTH WEST

N C SUPPORT Speakers are available to talk to schools with audio-visual presentations on canals in general and in particular the Huddersfield Narrow Canal's Restoration.

ANNUAL OR ONE OFF EVENT Thameside Canals Festival at Ashton 9, 10, 11 July and Huddersfield Canals Festival 3–4 September 1994.

OPENING Daily (for both trips) 11.00am–5.00pm.

CATERING Hot and cold meals available.

COST Ashton: adults £1.00, accompanying children free. Huddersfield: 50p. No discounts.

DISABLED FACILITIES Toilets available on both festivals but not easy to get to.

DIRECTIONS Ashton: A635 signposted Portland Basin Heritage Centre. Huddersfield: inner ring road, Queensgate to Wakefield road.

Kendal Museum of Natural History & Archaeology
- Mrs June Hall
- Station Road, Kendal, Cumbria. LA9 5AL
- 0539 721374

Fine collections of the flora, fauna and geology of the Lake District. World wildlife gallery. Prehistory, Roman and later displays. Kendal town history. Small wildlife garden, changing exhibitions.

N C SUPPORT Study pack available on request. Tudors, Vikings, Romans. Study boxes and small school loans service.

ANNUAL OR ONE OFF EVENT Request current programme.

OPENING April to end October: Monday to Saturday 10.30am–5.00pm, Sunday 2.00pm–5.00pm. 1 November to 31 March: reduced hours; telephone for details.

CATERING None.

COST Cumbria schools: children 50p, supervising adults 50p. Schools outside Cumbria: children £1.00, supervising adults £1.00.

DISABLED FACILITIES Stairlift.

DIRECTIONS Opposite Kendal railway station.

Lakeland Motor Museum
- E L Maher
- Holker Hall, Cark-in-Cartmel, Grange-over-Sands, South Lakeland, Cumbria. LA11 7PL
- 0539 558309 FAX 0539 558309

Over 100 cars, motorcycles, cycles and tractors, plus numerous items of rare motoring automobilia. Esso historical exhibition; Shorrock Super Charger Exhibition; 1920s Garage Re-creation; Classic Motorboat Collection.

OPENING 1 April to end October: Sunday to Friday 10.30am–5.00pm (last admission 4.30pm), closed Saturday.

COST Bookings should be made through Holker Hall Administration Office (Tel: 0539 558328).

DISABLED FACILITIES Adapted toilet.

DIRECTIONS Located at Holker Hall on the B5278; ten minutes drive south of Newby Bridge and signposted from junction 36 of the M6 via the A590.

NORTH WEST

Lanercost Priory
- ☛ The Head Custodian
- ✉ Lanercost, Nr Brampton, Cumbria. CA8 2HQ
- ☎ 06977 3030

This Augustinian priory was founded c.1166. The nave of the church, which is intact and in use as the local parish church, contrasts with the ruined chancel, transepts and priory buildings.

OPENING Summer season. Good Friday or 1 April (whichever is earlier) to 30 September: daily 10.00am–6.00pm.

CATERING Picnic facilities.

DIRECTIONS Off minor road south of Lanercost, two miles northeast of Brampton (OS Map 86; ref NY 556637). Bus: CMS/Northumbria 685 Carlisle to Newcastle-upon-Tyne to within one and a half miles (Tel: 0228 48484). BR: Brampton three miles.

Laurel & Hardy Museum
- ☛ Bill Cubin
- ✉ 4c Upper Brook Street, Ulverston, Cumbria. LA12 7BQ
- ☎ 0229 861614 FAX 0229 580870

World's only Laurel and Hardy Museum. A wonderful collection of rare memorabilia. Archive films shown in video cinema continually.

ANNUAL OR ONE OFF EVENT Ulverston Carnival Parade (Laurel and Hardy lookalikes).

OPENING All year: daily 10.00am–4.30pm.

CATERING Vending machine for drinks.

COST Children and students £1.00, adults £2.00.

DISABLED FACILITIES Full access. Ground floor and toilet suitable for wheelchairs.

DIRECTIONS Off M6, junction 36. The A590 Barrow Road to Ulverston. BR: Ulverston.

Library Theatre Company
- ☛ Hazel Ray
- ✉ St Peter's Square, Manchester. M2 5PD
- ☎ 061-236 1915 FAX 061-228 6481

The Library Theatre Company is a producing theatre company based in the basement of the Central Library. Its mixed programme September to June includes plays for children, students and family audiences.

N C SUPPORT Regular productions of plays suited to schools and 'play days' where children or students can meet the directors and cast.

ANNUAL OR ONE OFF EVENT Open Days at the Forum Theatre, Wythenshawe, to see production departments (by arrangement).

OPENING 10.00am–6.00pm; 10.00am–8.00pm on performance days. Contact Box Office on 061-236 7110 Monday to Saturday.

CATERING By arrangement.

COST Contact group booking organiser on 061-234 3156.

DISABLED FACILITIES Ramp to front door, lift to basement. Two wheelchair spaces. Guide dogs accommodated. Adapted toilets (male and female). Parking opposite front door.

DIRECTIONS By Metrolink to front door, by train to Piccadilly/Oxford Street. Buses pass the door.

VISITS OUT
NORTH WEST

Lyme Hall & Park
- The Administrator
- Disley, Stockport, Cheshire. SK12 2NX
- 0663 62023

Home of the Legh family for 600 years; part of the Elizabethan house survives, but altered in the 18th century by Giacomo Leoni and later by Lewis Wyatt; 18th- and 19th-century interiors. Visitors are welcomed by staff who reconstruct the life of Edwardian servants at Lyme.

N C SUPPORT National Curriculum links with Environmental Education and History. Living languages (French & German days for Key Stage 4); Talking and Touching (The Tudors Key Stage 2); Validating the Victorians (Key Stage 2). Each visit is tailored to the teachers' and pupils' specific requirements. Publications available for preparation and follow-up work.

ANNUAL OR ONE OFF EVENT Illustrated talks on management, conservation, etc. Contact the Administrator.

DISABLED FACILITIES Access to some parts of the Hall, garden and park. Special arrangements; please telephone in advance. Adapted toilet by lakeside; parking at Hall on request.

DIRECTIONS On south side of A6, six and a half miles southeast of Stockport; entrance on western outskirts of Disley. Bus: limited service from surrounding areas (Tel: 061-228 7811). BR: Disley half a mile from Park entrance.

Malham Tarn
- Kingsley Iball
- Malham Tarn Field Studies, Council Centre, Settle, North Yorks. BD24 9PU
- 0792 830331 FAX 0792 830584

A Field Centre, part of a network of Field Studies Council study centres, providing tailor-made courses in environmental topics to suit schools' curriculum needs.

N C SUPPORT Courses can be designed to suit all Key Stages on a day or residential basis. There is a long tradition of A-Level provision with specialist courses in Geography and Biology.

ANNUAL OR ONE OFF EVENT A range of courses designed to suit customers. INSET provision and student courses available.

OPENING End of January to beginning of December.

CATERING Fully catered courses are offered as part of the package.

COST Full costs available on application.

DISABLED FACILITIES Limited special facilities are available.

DIRECTIONS The Centre is an hour from the M6 and 30 minutes off the A65 Trunk Road. BR: from Settle or Giggleswick.

Malham Youth Hostel
- Martin or Christine Peryer
- John Dower Memorial Hostel, Malham, Skipton, North Yorks. BD23 4DE
- 0729 830321

Superbly located purpose built hostel close to the centre of the picturesque village of Malham. An excellent base for individuals, families and groups keen on walking, mountain biking, geology or just relaxing.

N C SUPPORT Resource pack for National Curriculum studies available on request. Malham is an ideal base for Geography and Geology studies for all age groups.

ANNUAL OR ONE OFF EVENT Activity breaks available at weekends and other times for groups of six or more. Contact the warden for details.

OPENING Late February to early November: 7.00am–10.00am and 5.00pm–11.00pm. Day use available at a small charge. Will open for groups during the winter months on request.

CATERING Breakfast £2.40, lunch pack £2.80, evening meal £3.70. Small self-catering kitchen also available.

COST Under 18s £5.00, adults £7.50, 10% discount if full board taken by groups of ten or more.

DISABLED FACILITIES All facilities on the ground floor are accessible for wheelchair users, including washrooms, showers and toilets.

DIRECTIONS Eight miles north of Gargrave and 13 miles east of Skipton, in the Yorkshire Dales National Park.

Manchester City Art Galleries

- Catherine Braithwaite
- Mosley Street & Princess Street, Manchester. M2 3JL
- 061-236 5244 FAX 061-236 7369

Magnificent collection of paintings, sculptures, ceramics, silver, glass and furniture, including works by continental Old Masters, Stubbs, Gainsborough and a famous collection of Pre-Raphaelites.

N C SUPPORT Please telephone for further details.

OPENING All year (except Good Friday, Christmas Day and Boxing Day): Monday to Saturday 10.00am–5.45pm, Sunday 2.00pm–5.45pm.

CATERING Cafe/restaurant.

COST Free.

DISABLED FACILITIES Limited.

DIRECTIONS On corner of Mosley Street and Princess Street. Twenty minutes walk from BR Manchester Piccadilly.

Merseyside Tourism & Conference Bureau

- Jackie Wilson
- Atlantic Pavilion, Albert Dock, Liverpool. L3 4AE
- 051-709 2444 FAX 051-709 8129

Specialised tours, talks, walks by Blue Badge Guides tailored for individual student groups, eg Tourism, Business Studies, Regeneration. Further details on request.

COST Guide fees: coach tour £28.75 (two hours) 1.5 walk or talk £29.10.

Mirehouse

- Clare Spedding
- Keswick, Cumbria. CA12 4QE
- 0768 772287

Historic family house held under the same ownership since 1688. Literary connections. Playgrounds,

VISITS OUT
NORTH WEST

natural meadows. Tenth-century church. Access to mountain lakeshore and forest.

N C SUPPORT Notes have been prepared to assist school staff by indicating what is on offer and resources can be matched with the skills of the teachers to produce a visit which is educative, interesting and enjoyable. Of interest to the National Curriculum in the areas of Science, Mathematics, English, Technology, Health Education, History, Music, Art.

OPENING 1 April to 31 October. Grounds and tea room: daily 10.30am–5.30pm. House: Sunday, Wednesday (and Friday in August) 2.00pm–5.00pm and by appointment.

CATERING Tea room, home cooking.

COST Grounds: children 70p, adults 90p. House and grounds: children £1.40, adults £2.80, 10% discount for groups of 20 or more booked in advance.

DISABLED FACILITIES Access for wheelchairs everywhere but limited in toilets.

DIRECTIONS A591 three miles north of Keswick.

Muncaster Castle Gardens & Owl Centre
- Peter Frost-Pennington
- Ravenglass, Cumbria. CA18 1RQ
- 0229 717614 FAX 0229 717101

Historic castle and gardens commanding superb views of the Lakeland Fells. Owl Centre with daily talk and display at 2.30pm (April to October). Facilities include cafe, shops, nature trail and playground.

N C SUPPORT Most periods of history from Romans to World War II can be covered at Muncaster. Conservation, Nature Study, Horticulture, Art and Antiques are some of the many other subjects available (including worksheets).

OPENING Gardens and Owl Centre open all year daily: 11.00am–5.00pm. Castle open April to end October: Tuesday to Sunday 1.00pm–4.00pm and at any time for school groups.

CATERING Stable buttery can provide everything from light snacks to full meals. Indoor seating capacity 60. Covered area outside. Parties can picnic in the gardens.

COST Group discounts available. For further information please request an information pack.

DISABLED FACILITIES Two toilets. Wheelchair available on loan. Access possible to all buildings except first floor of castle. Tapes for Walkman tour for partially sighted or those with learning difficulties and induction book for hard of hearing.

DIRECTIONS On the A505 one mile south of Ravenglass on the west coast of Cumbria.

Museum of Childhood
- Mrs David Wild
- Church Street, Ribchester, Lancs. PR3 3YE
- 0254 878520 FAX 0254 823977

An independent museum with eight exhibition rooms and 250,000 items on show covering childhood over the last 200 years.

N C SUPPORT Children's toys and games. Talks given by arrangement.

ANNUAL OR ONE OFF EVENT Changing special exhibitions throughout the year.

OPENING All year: Tuesday to Sunday 10.30am–5.00pm.

CATERING Self-service, tea and biscuits.

COST Children £1.50, adults £2.25.

DISABLED FACILITIES None.

DIRECTIONS Take exit 31 on M6 then A59 to Ribchester then follow brown signposts.

Museum of Lakeland Life and Industry
- Mrs June Hall
- Abbot Hall Art Gallery, Kirkland, Kendal, Cumbria. LA9 5AL
- 0539 722464

Regional folk-life collections reflecting traditional lives of working people from the 17th century into living memory. Homes, farming, wool, woodland crafts, mining, leisure, shops, Arthur Ransome.

N C SUPPORT Education service, information pack on request. All areas of National Curriculum. Study sessions available in museum or in school. Loans collection.

ANNUAL OR ONE OFF EVENT Enquire for current programme.

OPENING April to end October: Monday to Saturday 10.30am–5.00pm, Sunday 2.00pm–5.00pm: 1 November to 31 March: reduced hours; telephone for details.

CATERING None.

COST Cumbria schools: children 50p, supervising adults 50p. Schools outside Cumbria: children £1.00, supervising adults £1.00.

DISABLED FACILITIES Ground floor only suitable for wheelchairs.

DIRECTIONS South end of Kendal. Right hand lane of one-way system. Take first right after parish church through Peppercorn cark park to Art Gallery car park.

National Museum of Photography
- Education Unit
- Pictureville, Bradford. BD1 1NG
- 0274 725347 FAX 0274 723155

National Museum exploring the worlds of photography, film and television. Education Unit offers pre-booked workshops. Home of Imax, Britain's biggest cinema screen.

N C SUPPORT Support provided through information, advice on visits, workshops, in-service courses. Please send for Group Visit Organiser's pack. Most curriculum areas relevant.

OPENING Tuesday to Sunday 10.30am–6.00pm. Special exhibitions open until 8.00pm.

CATERING Small restaurant. Facilities for eating packed lunches.

COST Free. Check for film prices.

DISABLED FACILITIES Ramp access, wheelchair lift, adapted toilet.

DIRECTIONS Centre of Bradford off M62, then M606.

NORTH WEST

NATIONAL TRUST

Opening Times Write or telephone the administrator of the house, give preferred day and time, the size and age of the group, and the main purpose of the visit. *The National Trust Handbook* contains further relevant information.

Cost Unless otherwise stated in the *Handbook*, there is a reduction of around 50% for children aged 16 and under, when accompanied by their teacher. Education Group Members are admitted free. However, please note that there may be a small charge for any additional educational facilities or activities.

See individual entries for all other information.

Beatrix Potter Gallery
Dunham Massey
East Riddlesden Hall
Gawthorpe Hall
Hardcastle Crags
Lyme Hall & Park
Quarry Bank Mill
Rufford Old Hall
Sizergh Castle
Speke Hall
Tatton Park
Townend
Wordsworth House

Pankhurst Centre

- Sarah Vince
- 60–62 Nelson Street, Manchester. M13 9WP
- 061-273 5673

Emmeline Pankhurst's home and birthplace of the suffragettes. Exhibitions on the Suffragettes and Women's History. The Pankhurst parlour, furnished in Edwardian style, evokes Mrs Pankhurst's era. Shop stocks suffrage information.

N C SUPPORT Talk and slide show on suffragette history. Questions/worksheets can be arranged.

OPENING Monday to Friday 9.30am–4.30pm.

CATERING Annie Kenney's vegetarian cafe (Tel: 061-274 3525).

COST Free.

DISABLED FACILITIES Fully accessible.

DIRECTIONS Two miles outside city centre. Oxford Road (south of the city) past University of Manchester opposite MRI entrance.

Pennine Boat Trips

- Alan or Judith Hughes
- The Wharf Office, Waterside Court, Coach Street, Skipton, North Yorks. BD23 1LM
- 0756 790829 FAX 0756 796342

The Leeds and Liverpool Canal from the 200-year-old canal wharf in Skipton through the Yorkshire Dales.

N C SUPPORT Canal transport worksheets for two different trips lasting one and a quarter hours each.

OPENING April to October.

CATERING Tea and coffee, soft drinks, snacks, etc.

COST 1993 prices: £65 for up to 50 passengers (mornings only).

DISABLED FACILITIES None.

DIRECTIONS Contact the office for directions.

NORTH WEST

Pilkington Glass Museum
- I M Burgoyne
- Prescot Road, St Helens, Lancs. WA10 3TT
- 0744 692499 FAX 0744 30569

Four thousand years of glassmaking. Very rare collection of vessel glass. The many applications of glass in building, science, technology, transport and optics.

N C SUPPORT Please write for leaflets, brochure, quiz and workbook linked to the National Curriculum.

OPENING Monday to Friday 10.00am–5.00pm, Saturday, Sunday and bank holidays 2.00pm–4.30pm.

COST Free.

DISABLED FACILITIES Toilets, Ride-a-stair, lift.

DIRECTIONS A58, one and a half miles from St Helens town centre at the Pilkington Head Office. (Further details on map of the Pilkington Glass Museum Workbook.)

Port Sunlight Heritage Centre
- Karen Duncan
- 95 Greendale Road, Port Sunlight, Wirral, Merseyside. L62 4XE
- 051-644 6466 FAX 051-645 8973

Port Sunlight is the garden village founded in 1888 by William Hesketh Lever for his soap factory workers and named after his famous Sunlight soap. It is now a conservation area.

N C SUPPORT Not directly: loan boxes for local schools, containing photographs, reference books, soap and fact sheets for teachers' use. Reference facilities for teachers.

OPENING Summer (1 April to 31 October): daily 10.00am–4.00pm. Winter (1 November to 31 March): Monday to Friday 12.00 noon–4.00pm.

COST Adults 20p. Free to educational parties.

DISABLED FACILITIES None, but Centre is on the ground floor.

DIRECTIONS Junctions four and five of the M53 or A41 from Chester.

The PumpHouse People's History Museum
Bridge St, Manchester M3
Tel: 061 228 7212

Opening May 1994

Exhibitions and displays on the Victorians, life in the 1930s, cotton workers, suffragettes, dockers etc. unique collection of trade union banners on display. Suitable for Key Stages 2, 3 and 4 National Curriculum History, Art and other subjects.

Education room.

Taught sessions bookable including handling sessions using museum objects.

Resource packs available.

Cafe and bookshop

The PumpHouse People's History Museum
- The Administrator
- Bridge Street, Manchester. M3
- 061-228 7212

The PumpHouse People's History Museum is a new museum with exhibitions on the Victorians, life in the 1930s, dockers.

N C SUPPORT Suitable for KS2, 3 and 4 History, Art and other NC subjects.

OPENING May 1994. Contact administrator.

VISITS OUT
NORTH WEST

Quarry Bank Mill
- The Administrator
- Styal, Nr Wilmslow, Cheshire. SK9 4LA
- 0625 527468/523012

Restored Georgian cotton mill at working museum of the cotton industry with giant iron waterwheel. Demonstrations of weaving and spinning; galleries illustrating the millworker's world, textile finishing processes and the Gregs as pioneers of the factory system; restored Apprentice House with handling collection.

N C SUPPORT National Curriculum links with History, Geography, Art, Technology, Science, Maths, English.

ANNUAL OR ONE OFF EVENT Study centre; teachers' pack; INSET provision; role-play activities; arts and crafts skills development.

DISABLED FACILITIES Access to exterior and special route through part of interior, using step lift; wheelchair available on request; cars may set down passengers in Mill yard. Please telephone for special access leaflet. Adapted toilets. Mill unsuitable for guide dogs. Braille guide and large print guides.

DIRECTIONS One and a half miles north of Wilmslow off B5166; one mile from M56 junction 5. Ten miles south of Manchester. BR: Styal half a mile.

Ribchester Roman Museum
- Patrick Tostevin
- Riverside, Preston, Lancs. PR3 3XS
- 0254 878261

Lancashire's only specialist, and recently refurbished, Roman Museum containing many Roman objects and complementary models, including the Tombstone of the Asturian Cavalryman and a replica of the famous Ribchester Helmet.

N C SUPPORT The Museum caters for educational visits from all age groups and specifically those studying Key Stage 2, 'Invaders and Settlers', adopting a practical approach to learning about Roman life in Ribchester.

ANNUAL OR ONE OFF EVENT Sixth formers are welcome in groups for educational visits or as individuals carrying out research. Applications for work experience and holiday placements also considered.

OPENING Telephone for details.

COST Telephone for details.

DISABLED FACILITIES Entrance to ground floor and toilet.

DIRECTIONS Leave M6 at junction 31, follow A59 for Clitheroe, left at lights for Museum (brown sign). Leaflet with map on request.

Rufford Old Hall
- The Administrator
- Rufford, Nr Ormskirk, Lancs. LA40 1SG
- 0704 821254

One of the finest 15th-century buildings in Lancashire; the late medieval half-timbered hall is remarkable for its ornate hammer-beam roof and screen; here, and in the Carolean Wing (altered in 1821) there are fine collections of 17th-century oak furniture, 16th-century arms, armour and tapestries. Study centre; teachers' resource book; children's guide. 'All Change', an issue-based teachers' pack on the National Trust's work in the Lake District, is available from the National Trust Regional Office, Grasmere, Ambleside, Cumbria LA22 9QZ (Tel: 05394 33883).

N C SUPPORT National Curriculum links with History.

DISABLED FACILITIES Entrance hall and garden only. House and garden suitable if escorted. Braille guide.

DIRECTIONS Seven miles north of Ormskirk, in village of Rufford on eastern side of A59. Bus: Ribble/North Western 101 Ormskirk to Preston; ABC 758 Liverpool to Preston. BR: Rufford (not Sunday) half a mile.

Ruskin Museum
- Mrs E Marsh
- Yewdale Road, Coniston, Cumbria. LA21 8DU
- 0539 41164

Material associated with John Ruskin and his circle; also relating to Coniston and District.

N C SUPPORT Suitable for specialist Art A-level students.

OPENING Easter to end of October: Sunday to Friday 11.00am–1.00pm and 2.00pm–5.00pm.

COST Schoolchildren 50p.

DISABLED FACILITIES Clear access for wheelchairs.

DIRECTIONS Opposite the fire station in Yewdale Road.

St Helens Museum
- Roger Hart
- College Street, St Helens, Merseyside. WA10 1TW
- 0744 26429

Permanent exhibitions of social history, industry, wildlife.

OPENING Tuesday to Friday 10.00am to 5.00pm.

COST Free.

Senhouse Roman Museum
- Lindsay Williamson
- The Battery, Sea Brows, Maryport, Cumbria. CA15 6JD
- 0900 816168

Oldest antiquarian collection in the country; most complete collection of Roman altar stones and inscriptions, deriving from Hadrianic Fort adjacent to the museum; property of the Senhouse family since c.1570. Also stunning Celtic artefacts (serpent stone, warrior gods). Drawing site of Roman town (Alauna) attached to the fort.

N C SUPPORT Demands of National Curriculum understood. Imminent appointment by Allerdale Borough Council of schools/museums specialist.

OPENING April to June, and October: Tuesday and Thursday 10.00am–5.00pm, Friday to Sunday 10.30am–4.00pm. July to September: daily 10.00am–5.00pm. Open bank holidays.

CATERING Ice cream, soft drinks, confectionery.

COST Children 75p, adults £1.50. Groups: children 60p, adults £1.30.

DISABLED FACILITIES Yes.

VISITS OUT

NORTH WEST

DIRECTIONS To Maryport then ask for 'Sea Brows' museum on cliff to north of town. Walking distance from centre.

Sizergh Castle
- The Administrator
- Nr Kendal, Cumbria. LA8 8AE
- 0539 560070

The Strickland family home for over 700 years, it has an impressive 14th-century pele tower which was extended in Tudor time, with some of the finest Elizabethan carved overmantels in the country. It also has good English and French furniture, family portraits and Stuart relics. Children's guide. 'All Change', an issue-based teachers' pack on the National Trust's work in the Lake District, is available from the National Trust Regional Office, The Hollens, Grasmere, Ambleside, Cumbria LA22 9QZ (Tel: 05394 33883).

N C SUPPORT National Curriculum links with History and Environmental Education.

DISABLED FACILITIES Most of the garden, mainly via gravel paths. Lower Hall and tea room accessible. Adpated toilet at Peppercorn Lane car park, near Abbot Hall, Kendal three miles. Garden and first floor suitable for accompanied visually impaired visitors; Braille guide.

DIRECTIONS Three and a half miles south of Kendal northwest of A590/A591 interchange. Bus: CMS 555 Keswick to Lancaster (passing close BR Lancaster and Kendal). BR: Oxenholme three miles; Kendal three and a half miles.

Smithills Hall and Hall i' th' Wood
- D Edwards
- Smithills Dean Road, Green Way (Off Cromton Way), Bolton. BC1 8UA
- 0204 841265

Period houses 1485–1648. Victorian wing of Smithills is being redeveloped.

N C SUPPORT Tudors and Stuarts, Victorian Britain, etc.

OPENING April to September: 11.00am–5.00pm. School visits by arrangement at other times.

COST Free to Bolton schools. Small charge for others.

DIRECTIONS Please write for leaflet showing location on map.

Sooty's World
- Pat Redmonds
- Windhill Manor, Leeds Road, Shipley, Bradford, West Yorks. BD18 1BP
- 0274 531122 FAX 0274 531359

Animatronically operated characters portray the history of Britain's premier glove puppet. Original photos and television series bring the past to life.

N C SUPPORT The change and progress in television and marketing in forty years.

OPENING Term-time: Monday to Friday 10.30am–4.30pm. School holidays: Friday only.

CATERING Coffee shop for drinks, sandwiches, biscuits and cake (seats 45).

VISITS OUT

NORTH WEST

COST Ring for details.

DISABLED FACILITIES Full access. Toilet.

DIRECTIONS Two hundred and fifty yards out of Shipley town on the A657.

South Tynedale Railway
- Dr Tom Bell
- The Railway Station, Alston, Cumbria. CA9 3JB
- 0434 381696

Narrow-gauge railway built on trackbed of former standard-gauge Alston branch. Preserved steam and diesel locomotives haul trains along beautiful south Tyne Valley from restored Victorian station.

N C SUPPORT Information sheets for teachers available. Tours of signal box and workshops. Worksheets for children in preparation.

ANNUAL OR ONE OFF EVENT Open Day second Sunday in October. Steam train service. Guided tours of workshops etc.

OPENING Easter to December: Saturday and Sunday. July to August: daily. June, September and October: daily (except Monday and Friday). Usually available for groups on non-operating days.

CATERING Cafe at station (not owned by railway).

COST Children 90p, adults £1.80. Pre-booked groups of 10 or more: children 70p, adults £1.40.

DISABLED FACILITIES Wheelchair access to train, shop and toilet facilities.

DIRECTIONS On A686 Hexham road, quarter of a mile north of Alston town centre.

Southport Zoo & Conservation Trust
- Mr or Mrs Petrie
- Princes Park, Southport, Merseyside. PR8 1RX
- 0704 538102

Lions, snow leopards, lynx, chimpanzees and monkeys are included in the varied collection of animals; mostly in family groups, in landscaped gardens.

N C SUPPORT Education talks for groups of any size with 'hands-on' experience of certain animals.

OPENING Winter: 10.00am–4.00pm. Summer: 10.00am–6.00pm.

CATERING Tea bar, picnic areas, gift shop.

COST Groups of 25 or more: children £1.20, adults £2.00.

DISABLED FACILITIES Wide concrete pathways. Access to cafe and giftshop. Toilet.

DIRECTIONS Town centre next to Pleasureland. Brown signs from all roads leading into Southport.

Speke Hall
- The Administrator
- The Walk, Liverpool. L24 1XD
- 051-427 7231

A remarkable Tudor manor house, one of the most famous half-timbered houses in the country; the Great Hall evokes the communal living of Tudor times; smaller panelled rooms reflect the Victorian preference for privacy and comfort; kitchen and servants' hall; Jacobean plasterwork; Morris wallpaper; priest's holes.

VISITS OUT
NORTH WEST

N C SUPPORT National Curriculum links with History, Technology, Environmental Education, Geography and English; Key Stages 2, 3; Attainment Targets: Scientific Investigation, Life and Living Processes, Materials and their Properties: Physical Processes. Teachers' resource book; children's guide; living history activities.

CATERING A tea room and a shop are open from April to October: daily 12.00 noon–5.30pm.

DISABLED FACILITIES The garden, woodland and all principal rooms on the ground floor of the house are suitable for wheelchairs. There is a toilet with wheelchair access. Special car parking can be made available by arrangement.

DIRECTIONS On the north bank of the River Mersey, six miles southeast of Liverpool city centre; one mile south of the A561, on the west side of Liverpool Airport (follow signs for Liverpool Airport).

Stott Park Bobbin Mill
- The Head Custodian
- Finsthwaite, Nr Ulverston, Cumbria. LA12 8AX
- 0539 531087

When this working mill was built in 1835 it was typical of the many mills in the Lake District which sprang up to supply the spinning and weaving industry in Lancashire but have since disappeared. A remarkable opportunity to see a demonstration of the machinery and techniques of the Industrial Revolution.

OPENING Summer season. Good Friday or 1 April (whichever is earlier) to 30 September: daily 10.00am–6.00pm. October: 10.00am–6.00pm or till dusk if earlier.

CATERING Picnic facilities.

DIRECTIONS Half a mile north of Finsthwaite near Newby Bridge (OS Map 96; ref SD 373883). Bus: CMS 518 Ulverston to Ambleside to within one and a half miles (Tel: 0539 733221). BR: Grange-over-Sands eight miles.

Tatton Park
- The Administrator
- Knutsford, Cheshire. WA16 6QN
- 0565 750790

Over 1000 acres of deer park and woodland; Georgian house containing collections of pictures, furniture, china, glass and silver. Sixty-acre grounds with Japanese garden, orangery, fernery, rose garden and arboretum; Old Hall, Middle Ages to 1950s; 1930s farm with rare breeds; adventure playground.

N C SUPPORT National Curriculum links with all subjects. Education officer; ranger service.

DISABLED FACILITIES Parking in the stableyard, at Old Hall and at Home Farm. Easy access to Mansion and ground floor, garden, park, farm tea room and shop. Adapted toilet.

DIRECTIONS Three and a half miles north of Knutsford, four miles south of Altrincham, five miles from M6, junction 19; three miles from M56, junction 7, well signposted on A556; entrance on Ashley Road, one and a half miles northeast of junction of

VISITS OUT
NORTH WEST

A5034 and A50. Bus: Cheshire Bus X2; BR Altrincham Interchange to Chester. BR: Knutsford two miles.

Tobilane Designs
- Paul Commander
- Newton Holme Farm, Whittington, Nr Carnforth, Lancs. LA6 2NZ
- 0524 2726625

Traditional toymaker's workshop and showroom. Pupils shown how wooden toys are designed and made, their history and play value. Large range for both students and pupils to play with.

N C SUPPORT Helpful for Craft, Design and Technology students.

OPENING All year. Parties by prior arrangement.

CATERING None.

COST Free.

DISABLED FACILITIES Wheelchair access to workshop only.

DIRECTIONS Between Arkholme and Whittington on B6254, three miles south of Kirkby Lonsdale.

Townend
- The Administrator
- Troubeck, Windermere, Cumbria. LA23 1LB
- 0539 432628

An exceptional relic of Lake District life of past centuries, a 'statesman' (wealthy yeoman) farmer's house, built about 1629, containing carved woodwork, books, papers, furniture and fascinating domestic implements of the past, collected by the Browne family who lived here from the 17th century until 1944. 'All Change', an issue-based teachers' pack on the National Trust's work in the Lake District, is available from the National Trust Regional Office, The Hollens, Grasmere, Ambleside, Cumbria LA22 9QZ (Tel: 05394 33883).

DISABLED FACILITIES Restricted coach access. Unsuitable for wheelchairs.

DIRECTIONS Three miles southeast of Ambleside at south end of village. Bus: from surrounding areas (many passing BR Windermere) to within one mile. BR: Windermere three miles.

Tullie House
- Grant Ogilvie
- Castle Street, Carlisle. CA3 8TP
- 0228 34781 FAX 0228 810249

New, five and a half million pound refurbishment consisting of the 'Border Galleries' and Museum catering for the family, with interactive displays and audio-visual presentations. Facilities include restaurant/cafe; lecture theatre, education base, shop, facilities for people with disabilities, modern art gallery.

N C SUPPORT Education officer can help plan visits; the emphasis on the displays is interpretation and is therefore accessible to schools, with most texts at a reading age of 12. Themes relevant to National Curriculum.

ANNUAL OR ONE OFF EVENT An Educational Newsletter giving details of current programmes is available each term.

OPENING All year round: 10.00am–5.00pm.

VISITS OUT
NORTH WEST

CATERING Cafe, restaurant, special school lunch available by booking.

COST User Group Scheme available for Cumbrian schools; booked parties outside area £1.20 per child.

DISABLED FACILITIES Toilets, lift, ramps. All areas of the Museum are accessible by wheelchair, except Hadrian's Wall recreation.

DIRECTIONS Leave M6 at junction 43 and follow signs for Tullie House. Park at Devonshire Walk car park.

The Undercliffe Cemetery Charity
- Mr Colin Clark
- Undercliffe Lane, Bradford, West Yorks. BD3 0QB
- 0274 631445

Opened 1854. Fine examples of Victorian cemetery design and funerary art. Panoramic views of the Bradford countryside and 24,000 graves, including those of wool barons, mayors, artisans and paupers. A conservation area.

N C SUPPORT Schools' educational pack, price £10.00 including postage. Cheques payable to: the Undercliffe Cemetery Charity.

ANNUAL OR ONE OFF EVENT None.

OPENING Open at all times.

CATERING None.

COST Free.

DISABLED FACILITIES Smooth level drives to most parts from car park.

DIRECTIONS From town centre take Harrogate to Otley Road signposted for Leeds Bradford Airport; one mile from city centre on right.

University of Liverpool
- Jamie Carpenter
- Art Gallery, 3 Abercromby Square, Liverpool. L69 3BX
- 051-794 2347 FAX 051-708 6502

A selection from the University's collection of fine and decorative arts displayed in a late Neoclassical terraced house.

OPENING Monday, Tuesday, Thursday 12.00 noon–2.00pm; Wednesday, Friday 12.00 noon–4.00pm. Other times by appointment. Closed August and bank holidays.

COST Negotiable–can be free.

DISABLED FACILITIES None.

DIRECTIONS On the precinct of the University of Liverpool.

Victorian Reed Organ and Harmonium Museum
- Phil and Pam Fluke
- Victoria Hall, Victoria Road, Shipley, West Yorks
- 0274 585601 after 6pm

Guided tours. Visitors can attend in Victorian dress, which creates atmosphere. Examples of most types of reed organs, some arranged in setting. Young people encouraged to have guided 'hands-on' experience.

N C SUPPORT Victorians.

OPENING Sunday to Thursday 11.00am–4.00pm. Contact Phil and Pam Fluke at 6 Albert Terrace, Saltaire, Shipley, Bradford BD18 4PS for further details.

CATERING None.

COST Small admission charge. Reductions for groups of more than 15.

VISITS OUT
NORTH WEST

DISABLED FACILITIES None.

DIRECTIONS Follow signs for Saltaire Village. The Museum is in the front part of Victoria Hall.

Vintage Railway Carriage
☛ J Cope
✉ Museum, Ingrow, Keighley, West Yorks. BD22 8NJ
☎ 0535 646472 **FAX** 0535 646472

A unique collection of vintage railway carriages and small steam locomotives. Climb into compartments and enjoy 'Travellers Tales', a fascinating sound presentation of travellers from the past.

N C SUPPORT History: using carriages to illustrate land transport rail and steam, the Victorians (the class system), war-time travel in London. Mathematics: measurement, timetables. Science: force and energy.

OPENING Saturday, Sunday and bank holidays 11.30am–5.00pm. Easter spring bank holiday and mid-June to early September: mid-week, any time by prior arrangement.

CATERING None.

COST Children 50p, adults 80p. Group rates: children 40p, adults 50p, adults with school parties free.

DISABLED FACILITIES Braille guide and taped guide.

DIRECTIONS By road one mile from Keighley on A629 Halifax Road. By rail (when Worth Valley Railway is running) Keighley to Inglow.

The Weaver's Triangle
☛ Brian Hall
✉ Visitor Centre, 85 Manchester Road, Burnley, Lancs. BB11 1JZ
☎ 0282 452403

Displays on Burnley's textile industry and its workers: weaver's dwelling, Burnley Fair room with working model fairground, toll office with exhibits on Leeds/Liverpool Canal, Wharfronter's parlour, school room.

N C SUPPORT Displays relate to History Key Stage 2 Unit 3: Victorian Britain; supplementary unit on Local History; Key Stage 3 Unit 4: Expansion, Trade and Industry. Four worksheets available.

OPENING Easter to September: Saturday and Monday to Wednesday 2.00pm–4.00pm, Sunday 2.00pm–5.00pm. October: Sunday 2.00pm–5.00pm. Other times by appointment.

COST Free. Donations appreciated. Special opening at other times with guides: £15.00 per class (1993 price).

DISABLED FACILITIES Access difficult because of numerous steps.

DIRECTIONS One mile from M65 junction 10, on Manchester Road in Burnley Centre 200 yards from Town Hall.

West Lancashire Light Railway
☛ The Track Manager
✉ Station Road, Hesketh Bank, Nr Preston, Lancs. PR4 6SP
☎ 0772 815881 **FAX** 0772 627815

Two-feet-gauge railway, featuring industrial steam, diesel and petrol

VISITS OUT
NORTH WEST

locomotives and rolling stock. Short demonstration line open Sundays or mid-week by appointment.

N C SUPPORT Ideal site to show Industrial use of Railways and Locomotive Development.

OPENING Sunday 11.30pm–5.30pm. Other days by appointment to suit group.

COST Children 60p, adults £1.00. Special mid-week terms to groups. Contact Track Manager.

DISABLED FACILITIES None.

DIRECTIONS Approximately two miles from intersection of A565/A59. Take unclassified road from Tarleton signposted Hesketh Bank.

Whinlatter Forest Park

- Alison Butcher, Education Ranger
- Forest Enterprise, Whinlatter Forest Park, Braithwaite, Keswick, Cumbria. CA12 5TW
- 0768 778469 FAX 0768 778469

Forest Park with unique high-tech exhibition telling the story of the Forest; orienteering, special junior trails, giant badger sett, forest tea room, shop/information centre, mountain bikes, Forest study centre.

N C SUPPORT Full-time Education Ranger with programmes designed to link with the National Curriculum. Well-equipped Forest classroom; free teachers' resource pack. Facilities for GCSE and A-Level project work. Education Ranger support (will visit local schools).

OPENING All year (except January): 10.00am–5.30pm.

COST Car park: cars £1.00, minibuses £2.00, coaches, £3.00. Visitor Centre and Exhibition free. Ranger-assisted activities £20.00 plus VAT per half day.

DISABLED FACILITIES Trail orienteering course for the less able; parking free; toilets.

DIRECTIONS Situated at the summit of Whinlatter Pass between Braithwaite and Lorton on the B5292.

Whitehaven Museum

- Harry Fancy, Curator
- Civic Hall, Lowther Street, Whitehaven, Cumbria. CA28 7SU
- 0946 592302

Local mining, maritime, industrial and social history; archaeology, geology, marine paintings, Whitehaven pottery, American connections; temporary exhibitions, programme of monthly evening lectures.

N C SUPPORT Wide range of original publications; local photographic collection of 5000 negatives. Extensive dossiers of local newspaper cuttings, reference library, video showings, guided tours on request. Brief lectures by arrangement.

OPENING Monday to Tuesday and Thursday to Friday, Saturday 10.00am–4.30pm, closed Wednesday, Sunday and bank holidays.

CATERING In Civic Hall

COST Free.

DISABLED FACILITIES Accessible by wheelchair. Toilet.

VISITS OUT
NORTH WEST

DIRECTIONS Ten minutes' walk from Whitehaven bus and railway stations.

Williamson Park, Lancaster
- Elaine Chatton
- The Ashton Memorial, Williamson Park, Lancaster, Lancs. LA11 1VX
- 0524 33318 FAX 0524 33318

Tropical butterfly house, foreign birds, mini beasts, 40 acres of parkland with historic folly and art gallery. Education room.

N C SUPPORT Trained entomologists on hand to assist teachers. Maths trail and education resource pack available.

OPENING All year. Summer: daily 10.00am–5.00pm. October to end March: daily 11.00am–4.00pm.

COST £1.50; 10% discount for groups of more than ten, one teacher free per ten pupils.

DISABLED FACILITIES Access to most areas.

DIRECTIONS Well signposted from Lancaster; follow Ashton Memorial.

Windermere Steamboat Museum
- Mrs Lee Clarke
- Rayrigg Road, Windermere, Cumbria. LA23 1BN
- 0539 445565 FAX 0539 445847

The Museum houses the world's finest collection of steamboats moored in lakeside wet dock. Also classic motorboats, record-breaking speedboats, Beatrix Potter's rowing boat, Amazon of *Swallows and Amazons* and many more.

N C SUPPORT In a unique lakeside setting, original boats dating from 1870 to 1962 cover design and technology through this long period, with particular strength on Victorian and Edwardian family leisure, and lakeside commerce. Education packs.

ANNUAL OR ONE OFF EVENT Model Boat Rally in June; sailings of Amazon of *Swallows and Amazons* fame in May and June; Historic car rallies; British Classic Motorboat Rally; Annual Steamboat Rally.

OPENING Easter to end of October: daily 10.00am–5.00pm.

CATERING Light refreshments, chocolates, sweets, ice cream.

COST Group rates (12 or more): children £1.40, adults £2.40, Senior Citizens/students £2.10. Education rate when pre-booked: £1.00 (including adults).

DISABLED FACILITIES Graded A1 site.

DIRECTIONS Quarter of a mile from centre of Bowness-on-Windermere on the A592 from Newby Bridge.

Wittan Country Park & Visitor Centre
- Robert Wilson
- Preston Old Road, Blackburn, Lancs. BB2 2TP
- 0254 55423

Facilities in the Country Park include orienteering course, tree trail and nature trails. Facilities at the Visitor Centre include restored stable, carriages and carts, children's corner and British small mammal centre.

N C SUPPORT Geared mostly towards primary schools. Also Local History and Transport.

VISITS OUT
NORTH WEST

OPENING Thursday to Saturday 1.00pm–5.00pm, Sunday and bank holidays 11.00am–5.00pm. Other times by arrangement.

COST Conducted full-day tours: £1.00.

DISABLED FACILITIES Most of the Centre is accessible. Toilets.

DIRECTIONS Off the A674 road from Blackburn to Chorley (and Preston).

Wordsworth House
- The Administrator
- Main Street, Cockermouth, Cumbria. CA13 9RX
- 0900 824805

North Country Georgian townhouse, built in 1745, birthplace of William Wordsworth (1770); furnished in 18th-century style, with some personal effects of the poet; also his childhood garden with terraced walk. Video display in old stables. 'All Change', an issue-based teachers' pack on the National Trust's work in the Lake District, is available from the National Trust Regional Office, The Hollens, Grasmere, Ambleside, Cumbria LA22 9QZ (Tel: 05394 33883).

DISABLED FACILITIES Unsuitable for severely disabled people, but suitable for escorted visually impaired visitors; Braille guide.

The World of Beatrix Potter
- Hilary Pezet
- Crag Brow, Bowness-on-Windermere. LA23 3BX
- 0539 488444 FAX 0539 488444

Nine-screen video-wall tells the story of Beatrix Potter; countryside walk inside to meet all the characters in their story settings, walk under giant trees, sit with J Fisher on his pond; final film tells of Potter's conservationist work.

N C SUPPORT We supply a teachers' resource pack which interprets the exhibition according to National Curriculum aims.

ANNUAL OR ONE OFF EVENT Special exhibition for 1994 on Jemima Puddleduck.

OPENING Easter to 31 September: 10.00am–6.00pm. 30 September to Easter: 10.00am–4.00pm. Closed Christmas Day.

CATERING Tea room and courtyard area for schools to have packed lunches.

COST Group rate: children £1.35, adults £2.45. School groups of 40 plus: £1.20).

DISABLED FACILITIES Access to all of the exhibition. Toilet.

DIRECTIONS Elevated up from Rayrigg Road two minutes walk from Windermere Lake.

Yorkshire Dales National Park
- Kate Jonas, Education Officer
- Grassington, Hebden Road, Skipton, North Yorks. BD23 5LB
- 0756 752748

Helps group leaders at the planning and preparation stages of their visit. Can provide resources and advice including fieldwork, talks, guided walks, slide sets, aerial photographs and resource sheets.

N C SUPPORT Currently developing factsheets for GCSE, A-Level and

BTEC; resource packs or geographical enquiry-based fieldwork at Key Stages 2–4; fieldwork packages, including tuition for GCSE and BTEC groups.

Yorkshire Dales Falconry & Conservation Centre
- Mrs S T O'Donnell
- Crows Nest, Nr Giggleswick, Settle. LA2 8AS
- 0729 822832 FAX 0729 825163

All-weather attraction. Fully equipped lecture room. Private tours/guides. Largest bird of prey in the world, the Andean Condor with 10 feet six wing span, flies free at the Centre.

N C SUPPORT Worksheets for all ages. Educational videos and educational officers fully trained in conservation and birds of prey.

OPENING Daily 10.00am–5.30pm.

CATERING Tea rooms, picnic areas and stable block catering.

COST Children under 14 £2.00, teachers free.

DISABLED FACILITIES Toilet, ramps, drive-in for coaches/buses to arena edge.

DIRECTIONS A65 from Settle to Kendal. Tourist Board signposted.

Youth Hostels Association Arnside
- John Gibbs
- Oakfield Lodge, Redhills Road, Arnside, Carnforth, Lancs. LA5 0AT
- 0524 761781

A mellow, comfortable, Edwardian house enjoying views towards the Lake District and renowned for its home-baked wholefood cuisine. Weekend courses, leader rooms, field study rooms, games room and laundry.

N C SUPPORT Resource packs are available and cover itineraries ranging in suitability from years 4–11 and provide opportunities for cross-curricular study. A library provides additional support.

ANNUAL OR ONE OFF EVENT A tutor is available for sixth-form and tertiary education groups. The hostel library has unpublished studies on the local area.

OPENING All year except for short maintenance breaks.

COST Full board: £14.80. Group discount: one free place for every ten paid.

DISABLED FACILITIES None.

DIRECTIONS Off M6, junction 35 Milnthorpe, then B5282 Arnside. Turn right after around 2 miles, turn right down Redhills Road (YHA sign) then 400m on right. BR: Arnside.

VISITS OUT
SOUTH WEST

Alice in Wonderland Maze and Family Park
- Russell Lucas-Rowe
- Merritown Farm, Hurn, Christchurch, Dorset. BH23 6BA
- 0202 483444

Alice and her Wonderland friends welcome children to the south's largest hedge maze, adventure playground, caterpillar train, crazy croquet, etc. Lively performance readings and quiz from Lewis Carroll's story daily at 12.00 noon and 3.00pm.

N C SUPPORT Primary school children witness animals and birds with their young; watch the different seasons and effect on all growing things; the maze in bud and in leaf, a wild flower bank. Full teachers' notes available.

OPENING 26 March to 30 October: 10.00am–5.00pm.

COST Children (under 16s) £1.50, adults £2.50. Discount of 10% for groups of 15 or more, one teacher free for every 15 pupils.

DISABLED FACILITIES None.

DIRECTIONS Opposite Bournemouth International Airport.

The Ammerdown Centre
- Sr Carolyn Wicks
- Radstock, Bath. BA3 5SW
- 0761 433709

Eucumenical Conference and Retreat Centre with youth programme especially aimed at sixth formers.

N C SUPPORT Religious Education courses offered. Taste of Judaism, Buddhism, etc. Facilities for schools to arrange their own events for teachers (INSET) or pupils. Ecological field courses also possible.

ANNUAL OR ONE OFF EVENT Usually an event for Religious Education teachers.

OPENING All year round.

CATERING Full-board or self-catering.

COST Student rates (subsidised) £13.50 per day. Special weekends £30.00 per head. Other rates on enquiry.

DISABLED FACILITIES Two bedrooms with wheelchair access. Bathrooms etc.

DIRECTIONS Twelve miles south of Bath.

Arlington Court
- The Administrator
- Arlington, Nr Barnstaple, Devon. EX31 4LP
- 0271 82296

Set in beautiful steep wooded country west of Exmoor; the park is grazed by Shetland ponies and Jacob sheep; the house, built in 1822, contains fascinating collections and examples of Victorian handicrafts, such as paintings, photographs, papier-maché, scrapbooks, shells and pewter; stables with a large collection of horse-drawn vehicles; carriage rides.

N C SUPPORT National Curriculum links with English, Maths, Technology, History, Geography and Environmental Education. Study centre; teachers' resource book.

DISABLED FACILITIES Contact the National Trust Regional Office,

VISITS OUT
SOUTH WEST

Killerton, Broadclyst, Exeter EX5 3LE (Tel: 0392 881691).

DIRECTIONS Contact the Regional Office.

Avebury Museum
- The Head Custodian
- Avebury, Nr Marlborough, Wilts. SN8 1RF
- 06723 250

The investigation of Avebury Stone Circle was largely the work of Alexander Keiller in the 1930s. He put together one of the most important prehistoric archaeological collections in Britain, and this can be seen in the Avebury Museum.

OPENING All year round. Good Friday or 1 April (whichever is earlier) to 30 September: daily 10.00am–6.00pm. 1 October to Maundy Thursday or 31 March (whichever is earlier): Tuesday to Sunday 10.00am–4.00pm. Closed 24–26 December and 1 January.

DISABLED FACILITIES Wheelchair access.

DIRECTIONS In Avebury seven miles west of Marlborough (OS Map 173; ref SU 100700). Bus: Thamesdown 49 Swindon to Devizes/Marlborough; Wilts and Dorset 5/6 Salisbury to Swindon (Tel: 0345 090899). Both pass close to BR Swindon. BR: Pewsey ten miles, Swindon 11 miles.

Bedruthan Steps/Beach Head
- The Administrator
- Nr Newquay, Cornwall
- 0208 74281

Fascinating property on the rugged north Cornish coast with sheer cliffs and impressive stone outcrops; an ideal site for geographical, scientific and environmental fieldwork.

N C SUPPORT National Curriculum links with English, Science, Geography and Environmental Education.

DISABLED FACILITIES Steps to beach currently closed for safety reasons. Contact the Administrator for access details.

DIRECTIONS Contact the administrator for details.

Berry Pomeroy Castle
- The Head Custodian
- Berry Pomeroy, Nr Totnes, Devon. TQ9 6NJ
- 0803 866618

A romantic late medieval castle, dramatically sited halfway up a wooded hillside, looking out over a deep ravine and stream. It is unusual in combining the remains of a large castle with a flamboyant courtier's mansion.

OPENING Summer season: Good Friday or 1 April (whichever is earlier) to 30 September: daily 10.00am–6.00pm.

CATERING Refreshments (not managed by EH).

DISABLED FACILITIES Wheelchair access to grounds and ground floor only.

DIRECTIONS Two and a half miles east of Totnes off A385 (OS Map 202; ref SX 839623). Bus: Devonbus 149 BR Torquay to Berry Pomeroy (Tel: 0392 382800). BR: Totnes three and a half miles.

Bickleigh Castle

- O N Boxall
- Bickleigh, Nr Tiverton, Devon. EX16 8RP
- 0884 855363

Royalist Stronghold: 900 years of history and architecture and still lived in. Armoury, Guard Room, Great Hall, 17th-century farmhouse: museum. Maritime exhibition: 'Mary Rose', 'Titanic', model ships; World War II spy and escape gadgets; 'spooky' tower; shop; moated garden.

N C SUPPORT Specialises in schools, having twice received the Heritage Education Trust Award. 'Spotter' guides available. Tours are conducted by experienced qualified guides, one a recently retired headmistress. Children are encouraged to participate and handle armour etc.

ANNUAL OR ONE OFF EVENT Civil War display of authentic Cromwellian arms and armour: portraits and pictures; tableau of documents.

OPENING Easter week (Good Friday to Friday), then Wednesday, Sunday and bank holidays to late May bank holiday and then to early October: daily (except Saturday) 2.00pm–5.30pm. Schools, by prior arrangement only, at any time.

CATERING Cafeteria: cake, coffee, ice cream, etc. Picnic area in 11th-century Chapel orchard. Tea room if wet.

COST Groups of 25–30: children £1.40 and one teacher free. Groups of 31–40: children £1.30 and two adults free. Groups of 41–50: children £1.20 and three adults free. Groups of 50 or more: children £1.10 and four adults free.

DISABLED FACILITIES Easy staircase to Great Hall and 'Tudor' bedroom. Short but steep staircase to Museum/Exhibition area.

DIRECTIONS Off the A396 Exeter to Tiverton road. Follow the signs from Bickleigh Bridge. From the east, leave M5 at junction 27, take A361 to Tiverton, then A396 to Bickleigh.

'The Big Sheep'

- Rick Turner
- Bideford, North Devon. EX39 5AP
- 0237 472366 FAX 0237 478800

Educational fun for all ages. From Sheep to Jumper, sheep milking: try the milk, ice cream, yogurt and cheeses, sheepdog trials, sheep racing, newborn lambs to bottle feed, extensive playgrounds, 'hands-on', all under cover.

N C SUPPORT Teachers' packs, expert supervision. A most constructive day out in the countryside.

ANNUAL OR ONE OFF EVENT Royal Ascot Sheep Racing Week in mid-June. National Sheepdog Trialing first Sunday in August.

OPENING All year round: daily 10.00am–6.00pm.

COST Children (4–16 years) £2.25, adults £3.25, family £11.00. School rates: children £2.00, teachers free.

DIRECTIONS On A39 North Devon Link Road. Two miles west of Bideford.

VISITS OUT
SOUTH WEST

Blackdown Goat & Donkey Centre
- W L or Mrs J M Martin
- Rings Lane, Loddiswell, Kingsbridge, Devon.
- 0548 821387

Working specialist goat farm making 'Loddiswell cheese', yoghurt and other goats' and cows' milk products on farm.

N C SUPPORT National Curriculum needs are understood and implemented by prior arrangement with the teacher in charge of the party. Support is given for advanced agricultural, environmental and food production requirements. Covered facilities.

OPENING Normally Easter to November: 11.00am–6.00pm. Other times by arrangement.

COST Varies according to requirements, numbers and length of visit. Arranged with organisers prior to visit.

DISABLED FACILITIES Wheelchairs catered for. Toilet facilities.

DIRECTIONS From A38 to California Cross. Follow the signs for Blackdown Rings.

Brean Leisure Park
- A Ferguson
- Brean Leisure Park, Coast Road, Brean, Somerset. TA8 2RF
- 0278 751595 FAX 0278 751595

Fun park with 30 rides; fun pool with four water slides; cabaret nights and family entertainment; all adjoining seven miles of beach at Brean Sands.

OPENING Easter to September.

CATERING Three bars, two restaurants and two cafeterias.

COST Pay as you go. £1.00 all day car parking. Discount for groups booked in advance.

DISABLED FACILITIES Toilets. All facilities at ground level.

DIRECTIONS Junction 22 of M5 south.

Brewers' Quay
- David Allen
- Hope Square, Weymouth, Dorset. DT4 8TR
- 0305 777622 FAX 0305 761680

Visitors follow the historical themes of the Museum before entering the Time Walk journey with tales of the Great Plague, looting of a Spanish Galleon and of Royalty.

N C SUPPORT Worksheets produced aimed at Key Stages 2 and 3, possibly useful for Key Stage 4. Museum Curator may be available for talks if requested beforehand.

ANNUAL OR ONE OFF EVENT Three one-off events: 50 years of Weymouth Civic Society, D-Day exhibition – A Face of War, Tall Ships exhibition.

OPENING Daily (except third week of January) 9.30am–5.30pm. Late nights in summer school holidays.

CATERING Cafe facilities available if pre-booked. Lunch room available.

COST Group rates of 20 plus: children (5–16 years) £1.50, one adult free for every ten children, extra adults £2.50.

DISABLED FACILITIES Toilets. Timewalk unsuitable for those with walking difficulties.

DIRECTIONS By foot: across Town Bridge from town centre and turn left. Follow signs for Brewers' Quay.

Bristol Museums & Art Gallery

- Museum Education Service
- City Museum, Queens Road, Bristol. BS8 1RL
- 0272 223623 FAX 0272 222047

The Museum Education Service supports teachers' use of six museums, four heritage sites, the City Docks and Bristol Record Office.

N C SUPPORT A range of support is available for schools at all Key Stages, GCSE and A level for various curriculum subjects.

OPENING Vary from site to site. On application.

CATERING Cafe at City Museum, none at other museums.

COST No charge for school groups of under 16s.

DISABLED FACILITIES Industrial Museum has toilet and wheelchair stair lift.

DIRECTIONS Available on request.

Bristol Zoo Gardens

- Stephen Woollard, Education Officer
- Guthrie Road, Clifton, Bristol. BS8 3HA
- 0272 706176 FAX 0272 736814

Set amongst twelve acres of beautiful gardens and rare trees, Bristol Zoo is an important haven for some three hundred species of wildlife, many of which are endangered in the wild.

N C SUPPORT Full-time education officers, two classrooms and a lecture theatre. Interactive learning, 'hands-on' with live animals, special effects and drama. Wide range of teachers' packs and resources available.

ANNUAL OR ONE OFF EVENT Special events throughout the year. Animal encounters, touch-tables during holidays. Easter egg hunt, Christmas festival, etc.

OPENING Daily (except Christmas Day). Winter: 9.00am–5.00pm. Summer: 9.00am–6.00pm.

CATERING Picnic areas under cover. Restaurant and snack kiosks. Group meal bookings available.

COST Children (3–13 years) £2.50, under three free, adults £5.00, Senior Citizens £4.00. Groups of 20 or more: children £2.25, adults £4.50, Senior Citizens £3.50.

DISABLED FACILITIES Access for all throughout the Zoo.

DIRECTIONS From the M5 take A4018 from junction 17, A4 from junction 18, then follow signs. From City follow signs to Zoo or Clifton.

Brownsea Island

- The Administrator
- Poole Harbour, Dorset. BH15 1EE
- 0202 707744

A 500-acre island of heath and woodland; nature reserve run by the Dorset Trust for Nature Conservation; wide views of Dorset coast.

N C SUPPORT National Curriculum links with Science and Geography. Study centre, teachers' resource book and nature trail.

SOUTH WEST

DISABLED FACILITIES Island paths are hilly and rough, but the area around the Quay is accessible; powered chair available; mainland car parking near Poole Quay; all boats will accept and help wheelchair users. Adapted toilet near Island Quay. Braille guide.

DIRECTIONS Bus: from surrounding area to Poole Quay; to Sandbanks: Wilts and Dorset 150 Bournemouth to Swanage (passing BR Branksome); 152 from Poole (passing close BR Parkstone). BR: Poole half a mile to Quay; Branksome or Parkstone three and a half miles to Sandbanks.

Buckland Abbey
- The Administrator
- Yelverton, Devon. PL20 6EY
- 0392 881691

Originally a 13th-century monastery, the Abbey was ingeniously transformed into a family residence by Sir Richard Grenville of *Revenge* fame before being bought by Sir Francis Drake in 1581; an excellent example of change and continuity; includes exhibitions on Drake's life and achievements and on Buckland's Four Lives; additional monastic and farm buildings are open; rural working craftsmen can be seen in the ox shed.

N C SUPPORT National Curriculum links with Geography, History, Science and Technology. A Study Centre with handling collection, maps and charts on Elizabethan seafarers, books, projector, archive and reference materials, models, audio-visual presentation; 'hands-on' collection of kitchen equipment, special winter opening for pre-arranged parties including schools; teachers' packs; children's guide.

ANNUAL OR ONE OFF EVENT Special activities for schools including Theatre-in-Education, themed activity days and Tudor dance workshops.

DISABLED FACILITIES Contact the Administrator for access details.

DIRECTIONS Contact the administrator.

Canute House Study Centres
- Mrs M Cooper, Director
- Hennings Wharf, The Quay, Poole, Dorset. DT2 9SD
- 0305 260731

Two Study Centres in Dorset: Canute House on Poole Quayside, New Barn in a rural location outside Dorchester. Both Centres offer accommodation and varied programmes for schools.

N C SUPPORT A variety of programmes to support the National Curriculum Key Stages 2 and 3 are available, particularly Science, Technology, History and Geography.

OPENING All year round.

CATERING Full catering provided.

COST Depends upon length of stay.

DIRECTIONS Canute House on Poole Quay. New Barn approached through village of Bradford Peverell.

Castle Drogo
- The Administrator
- Nr Drewsteignton, Devon. EX6 6PB
- 0647 433306

Designed by Sir Edwin Lutyens as a unique mixture of family home and

VISITS OUT
SOUTH WEST

20th-century baronial castle; comfortable rooms and labour-saving devices (such as telephone system and lift) are combined with medieval touches: portcullis, turrets with arrow slits; fascinating kitchen; variety of walks leading from the castle to the Teign Gorge, a Site of Special Scientific Interest.

N C SUPPORT National Curriculum links with History, Geography, Environmental Education, English, Science and Technology. Children's guide; leaflet on Teign Valley Gorge.

DISABLED FACILITIES Contact the administrator for access details.

DIRECTIONS Contact the administrator.

Chysauster Ancient Village
- The Head Custodian
- c/o Jenny Tort, Bone Valley Caravan Park, Heamore, Penzance. TR20 8UJ
- 0736 61889

On a windy hillside, overlooking the wild and spectacular coast, is this deserted Romano-Cornish village with a 'street' of eight well-preserved houses, each comprising a number of rooms around an open court.

OPENING Summer season. Good Friday or 1 April (whichever is earlier) to 30 September: daily 10.00am–6.00pm.

DIRECTIONS Two and a half miles northwest of Gulval off B3311 (OS Map 203; ref SW 473350). Bus: Western National 16 BR Penzance to St Ives to within one and a half miles (Tel: 0736 69469). BR: Penzance three and a half miles.

Cleeve Abbey
- The Head Custodian
- Washford, Somerset
- 0984 40377

There are few monastic sites where visitors will see such a complete set of cloister buildings, including the refectory with its magnificent timber roof. Built in the 13th century, this Cistercian abbey was saved from destruction at the Dissolution by being turned into a house and then a farm. There is an exhibition which explains the way of life of the Cistercian monks and provides a fascinating insight into the history of the Abbey.

OPENING 1 April to 30 September: daily 10.00am–6.00pm. Winter: Tuesday to Sunday 10.00am–4.00pm.

DISABLED FACILITIES Access for visitors in wheelchairs to grounds and ground floor; toilets; parking.

DIRECTIONS By road: in Washford, quarter of a mile south of A39. Bus: 28, 28C (Taunton station to Minehead) and 38 (from Minehead). BR: Washford station half a mile.

Clevedon Court
- The Administrator
- Clevedon, Dorset. BS21 6QU
- 0272 872257

Home of the Elton family; 14th-century manor house, once partly fortified; 12th-century tower and 13th-century hall; collection of Nailsea glass and Eltonware; beautiful terraced garden.

N C SUPPORT National Curriculum links with History and English.

VISITS OUT
SOUTH WEST

DISABLED FACILITIES Contact the administrator for access details.

DIRECTIONS One and a half miles east of Clevedon, on Bristol road (B3130) signposted from exit 20 M5. Bus: Badgerline X7, 36–3, 661–4 Bristol to Clevedon; X23/4, 823 from Weston-super-Mare, alight Triangle. BR: Yatton three miles.

Cornish Engines
- The Administrator
- Pool, Nr Redruth, Cornwall
- 0209 216657

Impressive relics of the tin-mining industry, these great beam engines were used for pumping water and winding men and ore from great depths; the engines exemplify the use of high-pressure steam engines patented by the Cornish engineer Richard Trevithick in 1802.

N C SUPPORT National Curriculum links with English, Maths, Science, Technology, History and Economic and Industrial Understanding. Teachers' pack suitable for Humanities at Key Stages 2 and 3.

DISABLED FACILITIES Unsuitable for disabled visitors, many flights of stairs. Braille guide. No WCs.

DIRECTIONS Contact the administrator for details.

Cotehele
- The Administrator
- St Dominick, Nr Saltash, Cornwall. PL12 6TA
- 0579 50434

Cotehele was built in 1485–1627 and contains original furniture, armour and needlework; medieval dovecote; Cotehele Mill has been restored to working condition along with adjoining cider press; Cotehele Quay on the Tamar with 18th- and 19th-century buildings; outstation of National Maritime Museum; restored Tamar sailing barge 'Shamrock', the only one of its kind left.

N C SUPPORT National Curriculum links with English, Maths, Science, Technology, Geography, History, Economic and Industrial Understanding and Environmental Education. Teachers' resource book.

DISABLED FACILITIES Hall and kitchen only: most of the garden is unsuitable as it is very steep; special parking and entrance arrangements; some loose gravel; ramps available at the house and restaurant. Adapted toilet. Braille guides for the house, garden and mill.

DIRECTIONS On the west bank of the Tamar, one mile west of Calstock by footpath (six miles by road), eight miles southwest of Tavistock. BR: Calstock, not Sunday (except July to August) one and a quarter miles; Cotehele is signposted from the station.

Dartmoor National Park
- Willem Montague, Education Officer
- Dartmoor National Park Authority, Duchy Hotel, Princetown, Yelverton, Devon. PL20 6QF
- 0822 899565 FAX 0822 899566

The Education Officer is available to assist youth and school groups wishing to use Dartmoor: advice and information for teachers and

VISITS OUT
SOUTH WEST

individual students with regard to the Dartmoor environment, the work of the Authority, organising fieldwork as well as outdoor activities.

N C SUPPORT The Education Service supplies a range of free literature and publications for sale for all levels of education. There is also a Guide Hire Service for youth and school groups.

Dartmouth Castle
- The Head Custodian
- Castle Road, Dartmouth, Devon. TQ6 0JN
- 0803 833588

This brilliantly positioned defensive castle juts out into the narrow entrance to the Dart estuary, with the sea lapping at its foot. It was one of the first castles constructed with artillery in mind and has seen 450 years of fortification and preparation for war.

OPENING All year round: Good Friday or 1 April (whichever is earlier) to 30 September: daily 10.00am–6.00pm. 1 October to Maundy Thursday or 31 March (whichever is earlier): Tuesday to Sunday 10.00am–4.00pm. Closed 24–26 December and 1 January.

DIRECTIONS One mile southeast of Dartmouth off B3205, narrow approach road (OS Map 202; ref SX 887503). Bus: Devon General 22 Brixham to Kingswear (with connections from BR Paignton), thence car ferry to Dartmouth and local ferry to Castle (Tel: 0803 613226). BR: Paignton eight miles via car ferry.

Devon & Dorset Adventure Holidays
- Chris McCarthy
- 6 Kew Green, Richmond, Surrey. TW9 3BH
- 081-940 7782/3/4 FAX 081-948 4999

Multi-activity residential centres for schools specialising in outdoor adventure activities, personal development and training, cross-curricular weeks, field studies and educational visits. Three centres in Devon and Dorset.

N C SUPPORT Offer activities opportunities and facilities to meet many Attainment Targets for Key Stages 2, 3 and 4, covering Physical and Outdoor Education, Personal and Social, Geography, Science and History.

OPENING All year round.

CATERING Full board with packed lunches.

COST Weekend: from £54.00 plus VAT. Week: from £98.00 plus VAT. One free place for every eight guests.

DISABLED FACILITIES One centre suitable.

DIRECTIONS Hyde House near Wareham, Dorset, Buckland Manor near Shebbear, Devon, and Woodside in Bideford, North Devon.

Devon Rural Skills
- The Administrator
- Cockington Court, Cockington, Torquay, Devon.
- 0803 605377

Rural skills workshops. Demonstrations and displays include blacksmithing, wood turning, wheelwright, thatching, wattle hurdle making, drystone walling, patchwork quilting, stained glasswork, chair caning, basketry.

N C SUPPORT None as yet, studies being carried out. Joint liaison with Torbay's Cockington Country Park Ranger. Service can extend facilities available to include nature studies etc.

OPENING Daily 10.00am–5.00pm.

COST Children 50p, adults £1.50.

DISABLED FACILITIES Yes.

DIRECTIONS Follow Cockington signs from Torquay sea front (one mile).

The Dinosaur Museum
☛ Tim Batty
✉ Icen Way, Dorchester, Dorset. DT1 1EW
☎ 0305 269880 FAX 0305 268885

Actual fossils, skeletons and life-size dinosaur reconstructions combine with audio-visual, 'hands-on' and computerised displays to bring the fascinating world of dinosaurs alive. Learning is fun at the Dinosaur Museum.

N C SUPPORT Science AT2–4: the variety and processes of life, genetics, evolution and extinction. Key Stage 1. Available to visiting schools: free reconnaissance visit for one teacher, teachers' notes, worksheets, introductory video and talk.

OPENING All year: daily 9.30am–5.30pm.

CATERING None. School groups may eat outside at Salisbury Fields, only 200 yards away.

COST Children £1.50, one adult free with every ten children, extra adults £2.50. Concessionary rate for disabled visitors.

DISABLED FACILITIES Access to ground floor only for wheelchairs.

DIRECTIONS In the centre of Dorchester, just off High Street East.

Dinosaur Safari
☛ Tim Batty
✉ Level 3, Expocentre, Old Christchurch Lane, Bournemouth. BH1 1NE
☎ 0305 269741 FAX 0305 268885

An indoor adventure through time. See dinosaurs compared to animals that are alive today. Dinosaur reconstructions and fossils, both real and rare casts, plus many computerised and 'hands-on' displays.

N C SUPPORT Science AT 2–4, the variety and processes of life, genetics, evolution and extinction. Key Stage 1. Available to visiting schools: teachers' notes, free worksheets and teacher reconnaissance visit, introductory talk and video.

OPENING All year: daily 9.30am–5.30pm.

CATERING None. Packed lunches can be eaten on Horseshoe Common only 150 yards away.

COST Children £1.50, one adult free with every ten children, extra adults £2.50.

DISABLED FACILITIES Not suitable for wheelchairs.

DIRECTIONS In the heart of Bournemouth, just off Old

VISITS OUT
SOUTH WEST

Christchurch Road at its junction with Dean Park Crescent.

Dinosaurland
- Cindy Longland
- Coombe Street, Lyme Regis, Dorset
- 0297 442844

Meet Peter Langham, featured in 'Lost Worlds—Vanished Lives'. See exhibits discovered during filming with David Attenborough. Dinosaurland is devoted mainly to the Jurassic period of 195 million years ago for which Lyme Regis is famous. The ever crumbling cliffs are constantly yielding new materials enabling this exhibition to be frequently changing and adding new exhibits.

ANNUAL OR ONE OFF EVENT Fossil exhibition. Giant 'Sea Dragons', an amazing collection of marine fossils: Ammonites, Ichthyosaur, Plesiosaur and much, much more. See The Fossil Woman of Lyme Mary Anning (1799-1847). Live Birds and Reptiles. Guided fossil beach walks. Discover fossils with one of the experienced Dinosaurland team and learn how to fossil hunt safely and correctly. Safe walks on level beach.

OPENING Telephone for details.

CATERING Refreshments available.

COST Children 4–16 years £1.75, adults £2.50, Senior Citizens £2.10. Group rates for exhibition entrance.

DISABLED FACILITIES Limited to ground floor only for wheelchairs as there are entrance steps.

DIRECTIONS Ring for more detailed information.

Dorset County Museum
- Linda Poulsen
- High West Street, Dorchester, Dorset. DT1 1XA
- 0305 262735

The museum is housed in a historic building with displays reflecting the rich diversity of Dorset's archaeology, natural history, geology and social history, as well as information on local celebrities such as Thomas Hardy.

N C SUPPORT Practical activities geared to the National Curriculum can be provided for pre-booked school parties on any aspect of the museum's collections. Please contact the Education Officer for further details.

OPENING Monday to Saturday 10.00am–5.00pm.

COST Children (up to 16 years) £1, adults £2.00. Free to pre-booked Dorset schools.

DISABLED FACILITIES Very restricted. Please contact museum for advice/assistance.

DIRECTIONS Between St Peter's Church and National Trust shop.

Dunster Castle
- The Administrator
- Dunster, Nr Minehead, Somerset. TA24 6SW
- 0643 821314

Fortified home of the Luttrell family for 600 years; castle dating from the 13th century, remodelled by Anthony Salvin in the 19th century; fine 17th-century staircase and plaster ceilings; terraced garden of rare shrubs; 28-acre park.

N C SUPPORT National Curriculum links with History, English, Art and Science.

DISABLED FACILITIES The Castle is situated on a steep hill and access is difficult, but not impossible with a willing helper. Volunteer-driven multi-seater and self-drive Batricar available from car park; special parking available by arrangement. Areas of the house can be visited and assistance given if needed. Adapted toilet. Braille guide available.

DIRECTIONS In Dunster, three miles southeast of Minehead. NT car park approached direct from A39. Bus: Southern National 28 Taunton to Minehead (passing BR Taunton); 38/9 from Minehead. On all, alight Dunster Steep, half a mile. BR: Dunster one mile.

Dyrham Park

- The Administrator
- Dyrham, Nr Chippenham, Wilts. SN14 8ER
- 0275 822501

Mansion built 1691–1702 for William Blathwayt, Secretary of State to William III; rooms little changed since Blathwayt furnished them; 263 acres of parkland with fallow deer.

N C SUPPORT National Curriculum links with Art, History, English and Environmental Education. Study centre.

DISABLED FACILITIES Access to ground floor and terrace only; parking by house. Adapted toilet. Taped guide to house. Braille guide.

DIRECTIONS Eight miles north of Bath, 12 miles east of Bristol; approached from Bath to Stroud road (A46), two miles south of Tormarton interchange with M4, exit 18. BR: Bath Spa eight miles.

ENGLISH HERITAGE

National Curriculum Support Almost every aspect of the curriculum can be explored at English Heritage properties. They can be used not only for studying History but linked to other subjects as varied as English, Maths, Science, Technology, Geography and Music. English Heritage has produced a wide range of National Curriculum teachers' guides and videos to give plenty of stimulating ideas. Write to English Heritage Education Service, Keysign House, 429 Oxford Street, London W1R 2HD, for a free copy of the resources catalogue.

Annual or one-off event At some sites each year there are special educational events, often with the involvement of experts such as musicians and storytellers, for visiting educational groups.

Cost Student groups and school parties are admitted free to English Heritage properties, but should book in advance through the relevant Regional Office.

See individual entries for all other information.

Avebury Museum
Berry Pomeroy Castle
Chysauster Ancient Village
Cleeve Abbey
Dartmouth Castle
Farleigh Hungerford Castle
Glastonbury Abbey
Glastonbury Tribunal

SOUTH WEST

Launceston Castle
Muchelney Abbey
Okehampton Castle
Old Sarum Castle
Old Wardour Castle
Pendennis Castle
Portland Castle
Restormel Castle
St Mawes Castle
Sherborne Old Castle
Stonehenge
Tintagel Castle
Totnes Castle

Exmoor Bird Gardens
- Danny or Lynn Reynolds
- South Stowford, Bratton Fleming, Nr Barnstaple, North Devon. EX31 4SG
- 05983 352 FAX 05983 352

Beautiful setting with scattered animal and bird enclosures, many at liberty within grounds. Playground with emphasis on children and animal interaction.

N C SUPPORT Close animal interaction, questionnaires adaptable to requirements.

OPENING Daily (except Christmas Day) 10.00am–6.00pm.

CATERING Cafeteria (seats 35) for light refreshments only. Good picnic facilities.

COST Children £2.50, adults £3.50. Parties of 20 or over 20% discount.

DISABLED FACILITIES Wheelchair access, separate toilets. The site is on an incline.

DIRECTIONS Situated on the A399 (B32256) between Blackmoor Gate and Bratton Fleming.

Exmoor National Park
- David Gurnett, Education Ranger
- Exmoor House, Dulverton. TA22 9HL
- 0348 23665 FAX 0398 23150

The role of each National Park authority is to preserve and enhance the natural beauty of outstanding areas, whilst promoting their quiet enjoyment by the public.

N C SUPPORT Staff expertise to cope with most levels of enquiry and Exmoor experience. New 'Filexmoor' material for teachers and students available.

ANNUAL OR ONE OFF EVENT Woodland Craft Week, an interactive display of old and new techniques of working wood.

OPENING All year round.

COST Full-time state education groups free, but small voluntary donation is welcome.

DISABLED FACILITIES Lecture room at Dunster.

DIRECTIONS Motorway to Taunton junction 25 (A358) to Minehead and East. North Devon link road to West and South.

THE EXPLORATORY
Hands-on Science Centre, Bristol

The Exploratory Hands-on Science Centre
- Kevin Downes, Education Officer
- Bristol Old Station, Temple Meads, Bristol. BS1 6QU
- 0272 225944 FAX 0272 257342

SOUTH WEST

A huge exciting space, filled with eye-catching exhibits through which everyone from 5–85 years can explore natural phenomena and scientific wonders at their own pace.

N C SUPPORT Chemistry programme (workshops/shows) for all Key Stages, a 'Pathways' scheme which focuses visits onto one topic, general interest talks, teachers' evenings and theme weeks.

OPENING Daily (except Christmas week) 10.00am–5.00pm.

CATERING Cafe serving snacks, drinks (hot and cold) and light meals.

COST Children £2.50, adults £3.75, Senior Citizens £2.50, family ticket (two adults and four children) £11.50. Groups (ten minimum): children £2.00, adults £2.50. Up to ten years: one adult free per seven children. Ten years and over: one adult free per ten children.

DISABLED FACILITIES Lift to all floors.

DIRECTIONS Next door to BR Temple Meads Station. Many buses go to Temple Meads. Park at NCP car park or multistorey in Templegate.

Farleigh Hungerford Castle

- The Head Custodian
- Farleigh Hungerford, Nr Bath, Somerset. BA3 6RS
- 0225 754026

Extensive ruins of a 14th-century castle with a splendid chapel containing wall paintings, stained glass and the fine tomb of Sir Thomas Hungerford, builder of the castle.

OPENING All year round. Good Friday or 1 April (whichever is earlier) to 30 September: daily 10.00am–6.00pm. 1 October to Maundy Thursday or 31 March (whichever is earlier): Tuesday to Sunday 10.00am–4.00pm. Closed 24–26 December and 1 January.

DISABLED FACILITIES Wheelchair access to exterior only.

DIRECTIONS In Farleigh Hungerford three and a half miles west of Trowbridge on A366 (OS Map 173; ref ST 801577). Bus: Badgerline X3 Bristol to Frome (passes BR Bath Spa and close to BR Frome) to within one mile (Tel: 0272 553231). BR: Avoncliff two miles; Trowbridge three and a half miles.

Farmer Giles Farmstead

- John Vining
- Teffont, Salisbury, Wilts. SP3 5QY
- 0722 716338

A working dairy farm where children can milk a cow, bottle-feed lambs and touch many other farm animals and pets. Farmer Giles is on hand to answer questions.

N C SUPPORT Ideal for Science AT2 ('Life and Living Processes') plus some relevance to AT4 ('Physical Processes'). Most teachers regard the 'real experience' opportunity as especially beneficial.

ANNUAL OR ONE OFF EVENT Military Vehicle Weekend in May. Vintage Farm Working in June. Classic Veteran Car Show in July. Country Craft Festival in September.

OPENING March to November: daily 10.30am–6.00pm. November to Christmas: weekends 10.30am–6.00pm. Booked parties all year round.

SOUTH WEST

CATERING Licensed restaurant (seats 140) with home-cooked food.

COST Children £2.00, adults £3.00, Senior Citizens £2.50. Discount of 20% booked parties.

DISABLED FACILITIES Specially laid out for people with disabilities. No steps or stairs. Extensive paved paths and toilet.

DIRECTIONS Just off A303 at Teffont, 11 miles west of Salisbury and 15 miles from Stonehenge.

The First Emperor of China
- Tim Batty
- Level 1, Expocentre, Old Christchurch Lane, Bournemouth. BH1 1NE
- 0305 269741 FAX 0305 268885

He conquered and unified China and built the Great Wall. 70,000 workers built his tomb, which is filled with legendary treasures. This thrilling exhibition brings to Britain the wonder of the discovery.

N C SUPPORT History Key Stage 3: supplementary study unit, China. 'Imperial China from the First Emperor to Kublai Khan'. Available to visiting schools. Free teacher reconnaissance visit, teachers' notes, worksheets.

OPENING All year: daily 9.30am–5.30pm.

CATERING None. Packed lunches may be eaten on Horseshoe Common only 150 yards away.

COST Children £1.50, one adult allowed free with every ten children, extra adults £2.50.

DISABLED FACILITIES Not suitable for wheelchairs.

DIRECTIONS In the heart of Bournemouth, just off Old Christchurch Road at the junction with Fir Vale Road.

Fleet Air Arm Museum
- Mrs Sue Morse
- Box D6, RNAS, Yeovilton, Somerset. BA22 8HT
- 0935 840565 FAX 0935 840181

Museum of Naval Aviation suitable for all age ranges and abilities. Over 40 aircraft on show, dating from 1912 to the present. Aircraft can also been seen flying on the airbase.

N C SUPPORT Schools' room for 'hands-on' experience; can assist with a wide variety of topics. Please contact for Education Pack.

OPENING April to November: 10.00am–5.30pm. November to March: 10.00am–4.30pm.

CATERING Swordfish Restaurant with full menu and light refreshments.

COST Group/party rates (15 or more): schools, colleges, cubs and scouts £1.90, one teacher or leader free for every ten children, extra adults £3.00. Simulator: children £1.00, pre-booked school children 80p, adults £1.50.

DISABLED FACILITIES Access to most exhibits.

DIRECTIONS Located just off the A303/A37 on the B3151 near Ilchester.

Lacock Fox Talbot Museum
- The Administrator
- Lacock, Nr Chippenham, Wilts. SN15 2LG
- 0249 730459

A museum of photography commemorating the achievements of pioneer photographer William Henry Fox Talbot.

N C SUPPORT National Curriculum links with Science and Technology.

DISABLED FACILITIES Access to ground floor only. Adapted toilet at Abbey and in Red Lion car park.

DIRECTIONS At entrance gates to Lacock Abbey. Bus and BR: Chippenham three and a half miles.

Glastonbury Abbey
- M Scadding
- Abbey Gatehouse, Glastonbury, Somerset. BA6 9EL

Ruins in spacious grounds. New display area: History of Abbey and Monastic life. Site of early Christian settlements in Britain. Legends of Joseph of Arimathea and King Arthur.

OPENING Daily (except Christmas Day) 9.30am–6.00pm (or dusk if earlier); 9.00am June to August.

CATERING Nearby in town. Picnic area.

DISABLED FACILITIES Toilet.

DIRECTIONS Entrance adjacent to Town Hall, Glastonbury.

Glastonbury Tribunal
- The Head Custodian
- Glastonbury High Street, Somerset BA6 9DP
- 0458 32949

Long associated with the myth of King Arthur, Glastonbury is a fascinating town with many medieval remains. Two doors up the High Street from the George and Pilgrim Inn is Glastonbury Tribunal, a remarkably well-preserved medieval town house.

OPENING April to end September: daily 10.00am–6.00pm. October to end February: Tuesday to Sunday 10.00am–4.00pm.

DISABLED FACILITIES Access for visitors in wheelchairs to ground floor (two steps); toilets; car parking nearby.

DIRECTIONS Bus: 376, 677, 29, 29A (Bristol Temple Meads station street).

Golden Cap Estate
- Regional Education Officer
- c/o National Trust Regional Office, Estleigh Court, Bishopstrow, Warminster, Wilts. BA12 9AW
- 0985 847777

The Trust owns about 2000 acres of hill, farmland, cliff, undercliff and beach (five miles of coast) between Charmouth and Eypemouth; this includes Golden Cap, the highest cliff in southern England, so named because of the yellow limestone and clumps of golden gorse near its summit.

N C SUPPORT National Curriculum links with Science and Geography.

DISABLED FACILITIES Contact the Education Officer for access details.

DIRECTIONS Contact the Education Officer.

Hemyock Castle
- Mrs P M Sheppard
- Hemyock, Cullompton, Devon. EX15 3RJ
- 0823 680745

Medieval moated castle site. Displays illustrate 700 years of

VISITS OUT
SOUTH WEST

castle history as a 12th-century fortified manor house, 14th–17th-century castle (Civil War siege), 17th–20th-century farm.

N C SUPPORT History. Site and displays illustrate Key Stage 2: Tudor and Stuart Times, Victorian Britain, local history; Key Stage 3: Medieval Realms, Making of UK, Era of World War II. Book available (£2.00). Worksheets in preparation.

OPENING Easter to end September: Sunday and Bank Holidays 2.00pm–5.00pm; also Tuesday and Thursday in July and August. All year to groups by arrangement.

CATERING Tea, coffee, soft drinks by arrangement.

COST Children 50p, adults £1.00. Group rates: children 50p, adults 75p, helpers free.

DISABLED FACILITIES Toilet in village (200 yards). Level site; most areas accessible for wheelchairs.

DIRECTIONS Approximately five miles from junction 26 of the M5, also route from A303.

Hinkley Point Power Station
- George Burch
- Bridgwater, Somerset. TA5 1UD
- 0278 652845 FAX 0278 654225

The Hinkley Point Visitor Centre tells the story of the energy source of the 21st century. Learn how electricity is made and about the new reactor planned for the site. Displays and touch-screen interactive videos cover a wide range of subjects; from the science and technology of electricity generation to local areas of natural beauty and ecological interest.

N C SUPPORT Educational resource material is available and includes energy workpacks, tailor-made for the National Curriculum. The workpacks involve both computer-based project work on-site and technical talks on specific aspects of electricity generation. Cross-curricular themes on Energy and Industry. Key Stages 1, 2, 3, 4 and A-Levels.

OPENING 10.00am–4.00pm.

CATERING Pupils should bring their own packed lunches. Picnic area available.

DISABLED FACILITIES Yes.

DIRECTIONS Contact the Education Liaison Engineer for a leaflet with a map giving directions.

Holnicote Estate
- The Administrator
- Selworth, Somerset TA24 8TS
- 0643 862452

Six thousand-acre estate of hill, moorland, woodland and farmland.

N C SUPPORT National Curriculum links with Geography, Science and History. Study centre and teachers' pack.

DISABLED FACILITIES Contact the administrator for access details.

DIRECTIONS Contact the administrator for details.

International Helicopter Museum
- Wendy Cowlin
- The Airport, Locking Moor Road, Weston-super-Mare, Avon. BS22 8PP
- 0934 635227 FAX 0934 822400

Britain's only Helicopter and Autogyro Museum, indoor/outdoor displays, rides, simulator, souvenir shop, etc. More than 50 exhibits showing UK, French, American and Russian technology and models, components, etc.

N C SUPPORT Teachers' pack available on request showing how to orientate subject matter in terms of classroom teaching. Guide available by prior request, plus 30-seat 'classroom' in passenger transport helicopter.

OPENING March to October: 10.00am–6.00pm. November to March: 10.00am–4.00pm.

COST Children £1.50, adults £2.50. Group discount of 15%: children £1.30, adults £2.15, one adult free with every ten children.

DISABLED FACILITIES Ramps. Toilet.

DIRECTIONS Junction 21 of M5 and follow brown tourist signs to A371, Weston-super-Mare Airport.

ISCA Residential Centre
- Paddy or Margaret Shephard
- Centre Bonnaford, Brentor, Tavistock, Devon. PL19 0LX
- 0822 810514

Schools' Residential Centre on Dartmoor ideally suited for primary/middle school groups. Heated indoor swimming pool and excellent facilities.

OPENING March to November.

CATERING Accommodation and full board provided.

COST Please write for details.

DISABLED FACILITIES Please write for details.

DIRECTIONS On application.

Killerton
- The Administrator
- Broadclyst, Exeter, Devon. EX5 3LE
- 0392 881345

Seven thousand-acre working estate of farm, wood and parkland, including a village and two hamlets; at its heart is Killerton house, home of the Aclands, which was rebuilt in 1778 and houses costume displays dating from the 18th century. Park with Iron Age hillfort and other archaeological remains; medieval cottage on the estate open by appointment.

N C SUPPORT National Curriculum links with History, Science, Technology, Geography and cross-curricular themes. Study centre with handling collection, maps, microscopes, replica costumes; environmental education workshops, river dipping site; teachers' resource book; children's guide; education officer.

DISABLED FACILITIES Contact the administrator for access details.

DIRECTIONS Contact the administrator.

Kingston Lacy
- The Administrator
- Wimborne Minster, Dorset. BH21 4EA
- 0202 883402

Seventeenth-century house designed for Sir Ralph Bankes by Sir

VISITS OUT
SOUTH WEST

Roger Pratt; altered by Sir Charles Barry in the 19th century; outstanding collection of paintings; set in 250 acres of wooded park.

N C SUPPORT National Curriculum links with History, Art and English. Teachers' resource book.

DISABLED FACILITIES Garden only; some thick gravel; self-drive buggy. Adapted toilet; special parking by arrangement with Administrator. Visitors with guide dogs please contact Administrator in advance. Braille guide.

DIRECTIONS On B3082 Blandford to Wimborne road, one and a half miles west of Wimborne. Bus: Wilts & Dorset X13, 132/3/9 from Bournemouth, Poole, Shaftesbury (passing close BR Bournemouth and Poole). On all alight Wimborne Square one and a half miles. BR: Poole eight and a half miles.

Lackham College
- O N Menhinick
- Wacock, Chippenham, Wilts. SN15 2NY
- 0249 443111 FAX 0249 444474

Large teaching gardens with vegetables, fruit, flowers, glasshouses, plant propagation, plus woodland trail, rare breeds of farm animals, large museum collection of agricultural artefacts and tools.

ANNUAL OR ONE OFF EVENT Annual Country Day in late May.

OPENING Easter to end October: daily 11.00am–4.00pm.

CATERING Coffee shop: eight days notice required for meals. Please enquire about menu (Mr P Jennings).

COST Weekday group rates: children £1.00, adults £1.85 (1993 prices).

DISABLED FACILITIES Quite good.

DIRECTIONS Three miles south of Chippenham on A350. Come off the M4 at junction 17.

Lacock Abbey
- The Administrator
- Nr Chippenham, Wilts. SN15 2LG
- 0249 730227

Abbey founded in 1232 and converted into a country house after 1539; medieval cloisters, sacristy and chapter house; 16th-century stable court, tower and chimneys; Gothick hall built in 1754; home of the Talbot family who gave the Abbey and village to the Trust.

N C SUPPORT National Curriculum links with Science and Technology.

DISABLED FACILITIES Grounds and cloisters; house is less easy; special car parking arrangements; wheelchairs available at Museum. Adapted WC at house. Pre-booked guide parties for visually handicapped visitors. Braille guide and taped guides.

DIRECTIONS Three miles south of Chippenham, just east of A350. Bus: Badgerline 234/7 Chippenham to Trowbridge (passing close BR Chippenham & Trowbridge). BR: Chippenham three and a half miles.

SOUTH WEST

Land's End
- Mr J C Boston
- Custom House, Land's End, Sennen, Penzance, Cornwall. TR19 7AA
- 0736 871501 FAX 0736 6871812

The Legendary Last Labyrinth, a breathtaking journey down through the tunnels of Land's End to a mystical cavern. A sensational and enchanting experience visitors will never forget. Stunning electronic wizardry animates the exciting history of Land's End in a dazzling theatrical spectacle. Tales of shipwrecks, smugglers, pirates; of legends, magic, sorcery; of danger, destruction and heroism are conjured as if by mysterious forces. A fascinating combination of sound, vision and sensational special effects.

ANNUAL OR ONE OFF EVENT RNLI Air Day in August.

OPENING Daily (except Christmas Day) 10.00am to dusk.

CATERING Cafeteria, burger bar, coffee shop, restaurant and bar.

COST Children (up to 15 years) free, supervisors free.

DISABLED FACILITIES Two toilets, one nursing mother/disabled. Level ground, wide doorway, land train.

DIRECTIONS End of A30, 11 miles from Penzance.

Lanhydrock
- The Administrator
- Bodmin, Cornwall. PL30 5AD
- 0208 73320

A 17th-century house, largely rebuilt after a fire in 1881 (the original 1641 gatehouse and north wing, including 116-foot gallery with fine plasterwork, remain); 42 rooms are open; beautiful formal gardens of interest in all seasons; large park on the River Fowey; walks and woodland.

N C SUPPORT National Curriculum links with English, Maths, Science, Technology, Geography, History and Environmental Education. Study centre; teachers' resource book; children's guide; handling collection.

DISABLED FACILITIES Disabled visitors may be driven to the house; special parking, for assistance please consult car park attendant; access to house via loose gravel and shallow steps, or via ramp to the restaurant, then most ground floor rooms easily accessible; small lift to first floor. Adapted toilet. Steps to shop and gardens. Braille guides for house and gardens.

DIRECTIONS Two and a half miles southeast of Bodmin, overlooking the valley of the river Fowey; follow signposts from either A38, Bodmin to Liskeard, or B3268, Bodmin to Lostwithiel roads. BR: Bodmin Parkway by original carriage-drive to house. Signposted in station car park. Three miles by road.

Launceston Castle
- The Head Custodian
- Castle Lodge, Launceston, Cornwall. PL15 7DR
- 0566 772365

Set on the motte of the original Norman castle and commanding the town and surrounding countryside, the shell keep and tower survive of this medieval castle which controlled the main route into Cornwall.

OPENING All year round. Good Friday or 1 April (whichever is earlier) to 30 September: daily 10.00am–6.00pm. 1 October to Maundy Thursday or 31 March (whichever is earlier): Tuesday to Sunday 10.00am–4.00pm. Closed 24–26 December and 1 January.

CATERING Picnic facilities.

DISABLED FACILITIES Wheelchair access to outer bailey.

DIRECTIONS In Launceston (OS Map 201; ref SX 330846). Bus: Western National 76 Plymouth to Launceston (Tel: 0752 664011); Tilleys from Exeter (Tel: 0840 3244).

Longleat House & Safari

- The Estate Office
- Warminster, Wilts. BA12 7NW
- 0985 844400 FAX 0985 844885

Sixteenth-century stately home containing items of historical interest. The surrounding safari park contains a vast collection of wild animals, including many endangered species. Other attractions include exhibitions of educational value.

N C SUPPORT The house and certain exhibitions depict varying lifestyles over 400 years. The safari park outlines the importance of conservation of endangered species. Guided tours, worksheets and teachers' notes available on request.

ANNUAL OR ONE OFF EVENT Special events programme available on request.

OPENING House: Easter to end September: daily 10.00am–6.00pm; 10.00am–4.00pm at other times. Safari: end March to end October: daily 10.00am–6.00pm.

CATERING Cafe providing light lunches. Children's menu available.

COST House £3.00 per child, safari £4.50 per child, one adult free for every ten children. Concessionary party rates for special needs available on request.

DISABLED FACILITIES Access possible to most attractions. Toilet facilities.

DIRECTIONS Situated on A362 Warminster to Frome half a mile off the A36 Warminster by-pass, Bath to Salisbury trunk road.

Lydford Gorge

- The Administrator
- Lydford, Nr Okehampton, Devon. EX20 4BH
- 0822 82441

Formed around 450,000 years ago when the River Lyd was 'captured' by a smaller neighbouring stream, wearing away the rocks to make a deep ravine scooped into a succession of potholes; 90 feet White Lady Waterfall; habitat for a variety of wildlife.

N C SUPPORT National Curriculum links with Geography, English and Environmental Education. Leaflet for schools: geological field guide.

DISABLED FACILITIES Contact the administrator for details. This particular site can be very slippery.

DIRECTIONS Contact the administrator for details.

SOUTH WEST

The Milky Way
- Jacqui Stanbury
- Downland Farm, Clovelly, Bideford, Devon. EX39 5RY
- 0237 431255 **FAX** 0237 431255

One of the South West's largest undercover attractions. Fantastic North Devon Bird of Prey Centre. Laser shooting, bottle feeding, hand milking, modern milking, face painting, pottery, cafe, shop.

OPENING 1 April to end October: daily 6.30am–6.00pm.

CATERING Cafe serving hot and cold snacks.

COST Children £2.50, adults £4.00. School groups: children £2.00 plus VAT, teachers £1.00 plus VAT.

DISABLED FACILITIES Toilets. Level throughout, wide doors, easy access.

DIRECTIONS On main A39, two miles Bideford side of Clovelly.

Mill on the Brue
- Tricia Rawlingson-Plant
- Trendle Farm, Tower Hill, Bruton, Somerset. BA10 0BA
- 0749 812307 **FAX** 0749 812706

Emphasis throughout courses on building individual self-confidence/achievement through group problem-solving tasks. Also climbing, canoeing, ropes courses, etc. Permanent trained, experienced staff. First UK centre to win IIP award.

N C SUPPORT River, conservation and town study projects. Programme covers all aspects of the National Curriculum.

OPENING End of January to beginning of December.

CATERING Full board; breakfast, two-course lunch, supper, tea with cake, bedtime hot drink. Packed lunches can be provided.

COST Midweek (Monday to Friday): from £69.50 plus VAT per person; weekends: from £45 plus VAT per person. One free place per ten. No extra costs.

DISABLED FACILITIES Not for wheelchairs.

DIRECTIONS From London: M3, A303 to Somerset, B3091 to Bruton. From Bristol: A37 to Shepton Mallett, Castle Cary.

Montacute House
- The Administrator
- Montacute, Somerset. TA15 6XP
- 0935 823289

Late 16th-century house; H-shaped ground plan and many Renaissance features, including contemporary plasterwork, chimneypieces and heraldic glass; fine 17th- and 18th-century furniture; exhibition of samplers dating from the 17th century; Elizabethan and Jacobean portraits from the National Portrait Gallery displayed in the Long Gallery and adjoining rooms; formal garden; landscaped park.

N C SUPPORT National Curriculum links with History, Art, English and Technology. Teachers' resource pack and children's guide.

DISABLED FACILITIES Access to garden, restaurant and shop only; self-drive buggy. Adapted toilet. Braille guide.

DIRECTIONS In Montacute village, four miles west of Yeovil, on south side of

A3088, three miles east of A303 near Ilchester. Bus: Safeway/Stennings Yeovil to South Petherton (passing close to BR Yeovil Pen Mill). BR: Yeovil Pen Mill five and a half miles; Yeovil Junction seven miles; Crewkerne seven miles.

Muchelney Abbey
- The Head Custodian
- Muchelney, Langport, Somerset. TA10 0DQ
- 0458 250664

There may have been an abbey on this site as early as the seventh century, but most of what visitors can see today dates from after the Norman Conquest. The church has gone, but many of the other abbey buildings remain to be explored, including the fine 16th-century abbot's lodging with its splendid fireplace carved with lions' heads.

OPENING Summer season. Good Friday or 1 April (whichever is earlier) to 30 September: daily 10.00am–6.00pm.

DISABLED FACILITIES Wheelchair access to grounds and part of ground floor only.

DIRECTIONS In Muchelney two miles south of Langport (OS Map 193; ref ST 428248). Bus: Southern National 54 Taunton to Yeovil (passes close to BR Taunton) to within one mile (Tel: 0823 272033).

Mummies & Magic
- Tim Batty
- Level 2, Expocentre, Old Christchurch Lane, Bournemouth. BH1 1NE
- 0305 269741 FAX 0305 268885

Explore the ultimate mystery, the ancient Egyptians' quest for immortality, and wonder at the amazing royal mummies of some of the most famous pharaohs recreated in one amazing exhibition.

N C SUPPORT History Key Stage 2: supplementary unit – the study of a past non-European society: Ancient Egypt. Available to visiting schools: free teacher reconnaissance visit, teachers' notes, worksheets.

OPENING All year: daily 9.30am–5.30pm.

CATERING None. Packed lunches can be eaten on Horseshoe Common 150 yards away.

COST Children £1.50, one adult free with every ten children, extra adults £2.50.

DISABLED FACILITIES Five steps down into exhibition.

DIRECTIONS In the heart of Bournemouth just off Old Christchurch Road at junction with Fir Vale Road.

Museum of Costume
- Essex Havard, Education Officer
- Assembly Rooms, Bennett Street, Bath. BA1 2QH
- 0225 461111 x2752

One of the finest collections in the world, embracing many aspects of fashionable dress from the 16th century to the present day.

N C SUPPORT Key Stages 1 and 2 education pack available containing activity ideas and teacher support materials for before, during and after the visit. Fashion Research Centre, 4 Circus, Bath BA1 2EW. Ideal for GCSE level and upwards.

ANNUAL OR ONE OFF EVENT Special exhibition for 1994: 30 Years of the Dress of the Year 1963–1993.

OPENING March to October: Monday to Saturday 9.30am–6.00pm, Sunday 10.00am–6.00pm. November to February: Monday to Saturday 10.00am–5.00pm, Sunday 11.00am–5.00pm.

COST Children £1.40, adults £2.50. Group rates (20 or more): children £1.30, adults £2.00.

DISABLED FACILITIES Level access, ramped floors, lift, emergency exit ramp, two adapted lavatories.

DIRECTIONS City centre. Bath is 100 miles west of London, exit 18 of M4 motorway.

The Museum of Historic Cycling
- Sue & John Middleton
- The Old Station, Camelford, Cornwall. PL32 9TZ
- 0840 212811

The nation's foremost museum of cycling history.

N C SUPPORT Guided tour to groups (10–35 people) showing all aspects of the history of cycling.

OPENING Sunday to Thursday 10.00am–5.00pm. Evenings and other times for parties by arrangement.

COST Normal rate: children £1.50, adults £2.00. Groups of ten or more £1.25, two helpers free; groups of 25 or more £1.00, three helpers free; extra adults £1.50.

DISABLED FACILITIES All on the ground floor and level.

DIRECTIONS One mile north Camelford on the Boscastle Road B3266.

NATIONAL TRUST

Opening Times Write or telephone the administrator of the house, give preferred day and time, the size and age of the group, and the main purpose of the visit. *The National Trust Handbook* contains further relevant information.

Cost Unless otherwise stated in the *Handbook*, there is a reduction of around 50% for children aged 16 and under, when accompanied by their teacher. Education Group Members are admitted free. However, please note that there may be a small charge for any additional educational facilities or activities.

See individual entries for all other information.

Arlington Court
Bedruthan Steps/Beach Head
Brownsea Island
Buckland Abbey
Castle Drogo
Clevedon Court
Cornish Engines
Cotehele
Dunster Castle
Dyrham Park
Lacock Fox Talbot Museum
Golden Cap Estate
Holnicote Estate
Killerton
Kingston Lacy
Lacock Abbey
Lanhydrock
Lydford Gorge
Montacute House
The North Devon Basecamp

VISITS OUT
SOUTH WEST

Poltesco
St Michael's Mount
Saltram Park
Stourhead
Studland Peninsula
Tintagel Old Post Office
Trelissick Garden
Trerice

Nettlecombe Court
- John Crothers
- ✉ The Leonard Wills Field Centre, Williton, Taunton, Somerset. TA4 4HT
- ☎ 0984 40320

A Field Centre, part of a network of Field Studies Council study centres, providing tailor-made courses in environmental topics to suit schools' curriculum needs.

N C SUPPORT Courses can be designed to suit all Key Stages on a day or residential basis. There is a long tradition of A-Level provision with specialist courses in Geography and Biology. A range of courses designed to suit customers. INSET provision and student courses available.

OPENING End January to beginning of December.

CATERING Fully catered courses are offered as part of the package.

COST Full costs available on application.

DISABLED FACILITIES Limited special facilities are available.

DIRECTIONS About 45 minutes from the M5. BR: half an hour from Taunton station, which has regular services from London, the North and South West.

The North Devon Basecamp
- The Warden
- ✉ Exmoor Basecamp, 1 Town Farm Cottages, Conitsbury, Lynton, Devon. EX35 6NE
- ☎ 0598 7297

The National Trust owns eighty miles of coastline and 30,000 acres of countryside in Devon which are used by schools for a variety of project work. Trust wardens welcome practical help from schools.

N C SUPPORT A National Curriculum-related teachers' pack on the North Devon coastal properties, with projects, maps, etc., is available from the Regional Office, priced £3.00 + 50p p&p. The North Devon basecamp offers opportunities for schools to work with Trust wardens on conservation projects; it can also be used for field studies. Booking forms and information from the Warden.

DISABLED FACILITIES Contact the Warden for access details.

DIRECTIONS Contact the Warden for details.

Okehampton Castle
- The Head Custodian
- ✉ Castle Lodge, Okehampton, Devon. EX20 1JB
- ☎ 0837 52844

The ruins of the largest castle in Devon stand above a river surrounded by splendid woodland. There is still plenty to see, including the Norman motte and the jagged remains of the keep. There is a picnic area and lovely walks.

OPENING All year round. Good Friday or 1 April (whichever is earlier) to 30

September: daily 10.00am–6.00pm. 1 October to Maundy Thursday or 31 March (whichever is earlier): Tuesday to Sunday 10.00am–4.00pm. Closed 24–26 December and 1 January.

CATERING Picnic tables available.

DIRECTIONS One mile southwest of Okehampton town centre (OS Map 191; ref SX 584942). Bus: Devon General 51, Bow Belle 628, Jennings 629, Tilleys from Exeter (some pass BR Exeter St David's) to within one mile (Tel: 0392 382800).

Old Sarum Castle
- The Head Custodian
- Castle Road, Salisbury, Wilts. SP1 3SD
- 0722 335398

First an Iron Age fort, later inhabited by Romans, Saxons, Danes and Normans, there is much to disentangle from the 56 acres of ruins on this fascinating site. The Normans created a castle, the first Salisbury Cathedral and the Bishop's Palace. From the castle ramparts there are fine views of the surrounding countryside.

OPENING All year round. Good Friday or 1 April (whichever is earlier) to 30 September: daily 10.00am–6.00pm. 1 October to Maundy Thursday or 31 March (whichever is earlier): Monday to Sunday 10.00am–4.00pm. Closed 24–26 December and 1 January.

CATERING Picnic facilities.

DIRECTIONS Two miles north of Salisbury off A345 (OS Map 184; ref SU 138327). Bus: Wilts and Dorset/Hampshire Bus 3, 5–9, X96 from Salisbury (Tel: 0722 336855). BR: Salisbury two miles.

Old Wardour Castle
- The Head Custodian
- Tisbury, Salisbury, Wilts. EX20 1JB
- 0747 870487

In a picture-book setting, the unusual hexagonal ruins of this 14th-century castle stand on the edge of a beautiful lake, surrounded by landscaped grounds which include an elaborate rockwork grotto.

OPENING Good Friday or 1 April (whichever is earlier) to 30 September: daily 10.00am–6.00pm. Winter: weekends only 10.00am–4.00pm.

DISABLED FACILITIES Wheelchair access to grounds only.

DIRECTIONS Off A30 two miles southwest of Tisbury (OS Map 184; ref ST 939263). BR: Tisbury two and a half miles.

Paradise Park
- Alison Reynolds
- Hayle, Nr St Ives, Cornwall. TR27 4HY
- 0736 753365 FAX 0736 756438

Cornwall's outstanding wildlife park. Home of the Cornish otter sanctuary, the World Parrot Trust and the Eagle of Paradise. Miniature train and play area. A memorable and worthwhile visit for all ages.

N C SUPPORT Basic pack and three topics offered (flight, colour and jungles). Also 'Owl Prowl' for children to follow at the park.

ANNUAL OR ONE OFF EVENT 'Families Day' on the last Sunday in July.

VISITS OUT

SOUTH WEST

OPENING All year round: daily 10.00am.

CATERING Cafe (seasonal, pre-Easter to October).

COST Children £2.50, adults £4.50, Senior Citizens £3.75. Schools rates: £2.00.

DISABLED FACILITIES Yes.

DIRECTIONS A30 to Hayle, then clearly signposted.

Pendennis Castle
- The Head Custodian
- Falmouth, Cornwall. TR11 4LP

This castle is a testament to the quality of the coastal defenses erected by Henry VIII. The well-preserved granite gun fort and outer ramparts with great angled bastions defended against invasion from the sea, but it was captured from the land after a long siege during the Civil War.

OPENING All year. Good Friday or 1 April (whichever is earlier) to 30 September: daily 10.00am–6.00pm. 1 October to Maundy Thursday or 31 March (whichever is earlier): Tuesday to Sunday 10.00am–4.00pm. Closed 24–26 December and 1 January.

CATERING Restaurant/cafe (normally open summer season only). Picnic facilities.

DISABLED FACILITIES Wheelchair access to grounds and parts of the keep.

DIRECTIONS On Pendennis Head one mile southeast of Falmouth (OS Map 204; ref SW 824318). BR: Falmouth Docks half a mile.

PGL Adventure Holidays
- School Adventure Reservations
- Alton Court, Penyard Lane, Ross-on-Wye, Herefordshire. HR9 5NR
- 0989 764211 FAX 0989 768769

PGL is the most experienced adventure course operator in Britain. Formed in 1957, the company now operates 16 UK centres, two in the north of France and nine in the south of France.

N C SUPPORT Our courses meet the requirements of Key Stages 2 and 3 of the PE National Curriculum. Our IT Advantage course fulfils requirements for Information Technology.

OPENING April to October.

CATERING Full board.

COST Apply for details.

Poltesco
- The Administrator
- The Lizard, Cornwall
- 0326 290865

A rich countryside site of physical and geographical diversity in an Area of Outstanding Natural Beauty; ideal for geographical and scientific investigation; includes a variety of ruins and relics; unusual range of flora and fauna.

N C SUPPORT National Curriculum links with English, Maths, Science, Technology, Geography, History and Environmental Education. Study centre; teachers' pack.

DISABLED FACILITIES No access for people with disabilities.

DIRECTIONS Reached from Helston, past Goonhill Earth station to St Kevin, Kemrack Sands. Follow signs to Poltesco.

VISITS OUT
SOUTH WEST

Portland Castle
- The Head Custodian
- Castleton, Portland, Dorset. DT5 1BD
- 0305 820539

One of the best preserved of Henry VIII's coastal forts, built of white Portland stone. Now standing quietly overlooking the harbour, it was originally intended to thwart attack by the Spanish and French, and changed hands several times during the Civil War.

OPENING Summer season. Good Friday or 1 April (whichever is earlier) to 30 September: daily 10.00am–6.00pm.

DISABLED FACILITIES Wheelchair access to exterior and ground floor only (one deep step).

DIRECTIONS Overlooking Portland harbour adjacent to RN helicopter base (OS Map 194; ref SY 684743). Bus: Southern National 1/A, 10, 501, Smith's Coaches Weymouth to Portland (Tel: 0305 783645). BR: Weymouth four and a half miles.

Portland Museum
- Dr Aldridge-Goult
- 217 Wakeham, Portland, Dorset. DT5 1HS
- 0305 821804

Community museum of the island. Displays of social and natural history and temporary exhibitions.

N C SUPPORT Key Stages 2–3 in History, Science, Technology and cross-curricular subjects. Outreach to local schools with talks, demonstrations and temporary exhibitions on loan.

OPENING Summer: daily 10.30am–5.45pm. Winter: daily except Monday 10.30am–4.30pm.

CATERING No catering, but there is a picnic area in the gardens.

COST School children free, accompanying teachers free.

DISABLED FACILITIES Limited access for wheelchairs. 'Talking Museum' for visually impaired.

DIRECTIONS To top hill of island. Follow Museum signs to bottom of Wakeham. Street parking only.

Potter's Museum of Curiosity
- Mrs R Mullins, Curator
- Jamaica Inn Courtyard, Bolventor, Launceston, Cornwall. PL15 7TS
- 0566 86836

Museum of curiosities from all over the world, and Victorian taxidermy. Set out as a typical Victorian museum, this wonderful collection has been put together over a period of 130 years.

OPENING April, May and October: 9.30am–4.00pm. June to September: 9.30am–6.00pm (or later).

CATERING Snack bar at Inn open all day.

COST Children £1.50, adults £2.25. Groups of ten or more: £1.25 per person.

DISABLED FACILITIES Easy access to both Inn, toilets, etc., but Museum on two floors.

DIRECTIONS A30 halfway between Launceston and Bodmin. Now bypassed so look for signs one or two miles ahead of turn off.

VISITS OUT
SOUTH WEST

Restormel Castle
- The Head Custodian
- Lostwithiel, Cornwall. PL22 0HN
- 0208 872687

Perched on a high mound, surrounded by a deep moat, the huge circular keep of this splendid Norman castle survives in remarkably good condition.

OPENING Summer season. Good Friday or 1 April (whichever is earlier) to 30 September: daily 10.00am–6.00pm.

CATERING Picnic facilities.

DIRECTIONS One and a half miles north of Lostwithiel off A390 (OS Map 200; ref SX 104614). BR: Lostwithiel one and a half miles.

Roman Baths Museum
- Essex Havard
- Pump Room, Stall Street, Bath. BA1 1LZ
- 0225 461111 x2774 **FAX** 0225 448521

Extensive remains of Roman Baths and Temple, including a wide variety of artefacts and displays illustrating everyday life and religious practices in the Roman town of Aquaesulis.

N C SUPPORT Key Stages 1 and 2 education pack available containing activity ideas and teacher support material for before, during and after the visit. Teaching sessions are available in autumn and spring terms. Suitable for seven years and upwards. (Write to The Education Officer, 4 Circus, Bath, BA1 2EW.)

OPENING On application.

CATERING The Pump Room restaurant provides morning coffee, lunch and afternoon tea.

COST On application.

DISABLED FACILITIES Wheelchair access to baths is not possible. Access to ground floor only. Usual toilet facilities for disabled visitors.

DIRECTIONS In the centre of Bath. Coach parking at Riverside Coach Park a few minutes walk away.

St Mawes Castle
- The Head Custodian
- St Mawes, Nr Truro, Cornwall. TR2 3AA
- 0326 270526

St Mawes Castle was built by Henry VIII to guard the entrance to safe anchorage in the Carrick Roads. Its three huge circular bastions with gun ports were formidable defences indeed but today stand in delightful subtropical gardens.

OPENING All year round. Good Friday or 1 April (whichever is earlier) to 30 September: daily 10.00am–6.00pm. 1 October to Maundy Thursday or 31 March (whichever is earlier): Tuesday to Sunday 10.00am–4.00pm. Closed 24–26 December and 1 January.

CATERING Picnic facilities.

DIRECTIONS In St Mawes on A3078 (OS Map 204; ref SW 842328). Ferry: St Mawes Ferry Co from Falmouth, Prince of Wales Pier (Tel: 0209 861020). BR: Penmere, via Prince of Wales Pier, four and a half miles by sea.

VISITS OUT
SOUTH WEST

St Michael's Mount
- The Administrator
- Marazion, Nr Penzance, Cornwall. TR17 0HT
- 0736 710507

Originally the site of a Benedictine chapel established by Edward the Confessor; the spectacular castle on its rock dates from the 14th century; fine views towards Land's End and the Lizard.

N C SUPPORT Teachers' pack; National Curriculum links with English, Maths, Technology, Geography, History and Environmental Education.

DISABLED FACILITIES The causeway and paths are cobbled and are therefore unsuitable for wheelchairs.

DIRECTIONS Half a mile south of A394 at Marazion, whence there is access on foot over the causeway at low tide or, during summer months only, by ferry at high tide (return ferry tickets should not be taken). For tide and ferry information only phone: 0736 710265.

Saltram Park
- The Administrator
- Plympton, Devon. PL7 3UH
- 0752 336546

Although better known for its magnificent 18th-century house, the 470-acre estate, one of Plymouth's 'green lungs', is an excellent site for cross-curricular studies and is open throughout the year; habitats include ponds, old meadows, estuary and woodland.

N C SUPPORT National Curriculum links with Science, Geography and Environmental Education. Pond dipping site and equipment; study centre; walks and workshops with the warden.

DISABLED FACILITIES Contact the administrator for access details.

DIRECTIONS Contact the administrator for details.

Sheppy's Cider & Rural Life Museum
- Mr R J Sheppy
- Three Bridges, Bradford-on-Tone, Taunton, Somerset. TA4 1ER
- 0823 461 233

Farm and cider museum. See the video showing the cider-making year and the modern press room where the apple crop is processed each autumn. Follow the orchard and farm trails.

N C SUPPORT Information sheets and questionnaires.

ANNUAL OR ONE OFF EVENT Craft & Cider Country Fayre with demonstrations and entertainment last weekend in July.

OPENING May to end September: Monday to Saturday 8.30am–6.30pm. October to end April: Monday to Saturday 8.30am–6.00pm. Easter to Christmas: Sunday 12.00 noon–2.00pm only.

CATERING Tea room open in season or by special arrangement and sells morning coffee, snacks and light lunches, home-made cakes and cream teas.

COST Unescorted tours: children £1.00, adults £1.50, Senior Citizens £1.25. Guided tours: Children under 14 £2.00, adults £3.00, Senior Citizens £2.75, staff free.

VISITS OUT

SOUTH WEST

DISABLED FACILITIES Yes.

DIRECTIONS Junction 26 of the M5. On A38 between Taunton and Wellington.

Sherborne Old Castle
- The Head Custodian
- Castleton, Sherborne, Dorset. D19 5NR
- 0935 812730

The ruins of this early 12th-century castle are a testament to the 16 days it took Cromwell to capture it during the Civil War, after which it was abandoned.

OPENING All year round. Good Friday or 1 April (whichever is earlier) to 30 September: daily 10.00am–6.00pm. 1 October to Maundy Thursday or 31 March (whichever is earlier): Tuesday to Sunday 10.00am–4.00pm. Closed 24–26 December and 1 January.

DISABLED FACILITIES Wheelchair access.

DIRECTIONS Half a mile east of Sherborne off B3145 (OS Map 183; ref ST 647167). BR: Sherborne three-quarters of a mile.

Slapton Ley Field Studies
- Keith Chell
- Council Centre, Kingsbridge, Devon. TQ7 2QP
- 0548 580466 FAX 0548 580123

A Field Centre, part of a network of Field Studies Council study centres, providing tailor-made courses in environmental topics to suit schools' curriculum needs.

N C SUPPORT Courses can be designed to suit all Key Stages on a day or residential basis. There is a long tradition of A-Level provision with specialist courses in Geography and Biology. A range of courses designed to suit customers. INSET provision and student courses available.

OPENING End January to beginning of December.

CATERING Fully catered courses are offered as part of the package.

COST Full costs available on application.

DISABLED FACILITIES Limited special facilities are available.

DIRECTIONS The Centre is only 40 minutes from the A38. BR: Totnes.

Southcliffe Hotel
- Roy and Margaret Anderson
- Torrs Park, Ilfracombe, North Devon. EX34 8AZ
- 0271 862958

Detached Victorian mansion which has been hosting school parties for over 15 years. Mostly en-suite. Half an acre of grounds. Skittles, disco, etc. available. Sense of humour. Capacity 50 plus.

ANNUAL OR ONE OFF EVENT Ilfracombe Victorian Week in June.

OPENING September to mid-June.

CATERING Usual hotel facilities.

COST Dinner, bed, breakfast and packed lunch; £11.50 plus £2.01 VAT per person per night, including adults. (June £1 supplement.)

DISABLED FACILITIES None.

SOUTH WEST

DIRECTIONS From A361 Barnstaple turn left at first lights, left second lights and immediately left Torrs Park. Continue 450 metres.

Southern Electric Museum
- John Newton, Administrator
- The Old Power Station, Bargates, Christchurch, Dorset. BH23 1QE
- 0202 480467 FAX 0202 480468

The Southern Electric Museum offers a step back into a time when electricity was a luxury, not an everyday convenience. It houses one of the most extensive collections of historic electrical equipment in Great Britain. There are more than 700 exhibits in the Museum, tracing the development of the electricity supply industry in all its aspects, from electricity generation to distribution, as well as the many uses of electricity which have developed over the years. Working models and other working displays.

N C SUPPORT The Museum has become a popular venue for school parties. Qualified staff give guided tours to demonstrate the exhibits, adding a personal touch which helps ensure an enjoyable and worthwhile visit.

OPENING March to end September: Monday and Wednesday 10.00am–4.00pm. Guided tours for schools and organised groups can be arranged from Monday to Friday throughout the year.

CATERING None.

COST Free.

DISABLED FACILITIES None.

DIRECTIONS Off A35 Fairmile Road, Bargates.

Stonehenge
- The Head Custodian
- Stone Circle, Nr Amesbury, Wilts. SP4 7DE
- 0272 750700

A famous prehistoric monument started 5000 years ago and remodelled several times in the centuries that followed, Stonehenge represents one of the most remarkable achievements of prehistoric engineering. Yet why it was built remains a mystery.

OPENING All year round. Good Friday or 1 April (whichever is earlier) to 30 September: daily 10.00am–6.00pm. 1 October to Maundy Thursday or 31 March (whichever is earlier): Monday to Sunday 10.00am–4.00pm. Closed 24–26 December and 1 January.

DISABLED FACILITIES Wheelchair access.

DIRECTIONS Two miles west of Amesbury on the junction of the A303 and A344/A360 (OS Map 184; ref SU 123422). Bus: Wilts & Dorset 3 BR Salisbury to Stonehenge (Tel: 0722 336855). BR: Salisbury nine and a half miles.

Stourhead
- The Administrator
- Stourton, Warminster, Wilts. BA12 6QH
- 0747 840348

Landscape garden laid out in 1741–80, with lakes and temples, rare trees and plants; the house was begun in 1721 by Colen Campbell; furniture by the younger Chippendale; fine paintings; King Alfred's Tower, a red-brick folly built

SOUTH WEST

in 1772 on the edge of the estate, is 160 feet high, giving fine views.

N C SUPPORT National Curriculum links with Geography, Science, History and Art.

DISABLED FACILITIES Garden accessible, but there are 13 steps up to the house then ground floor rooms are on one level. The path around the lake is accessible to wheelchair users, but very steep in places; level walk to Tower. Battery-powered self-drive buggy. Please avoid congested times at weekends and in May and June. Adapted toilet in Spread Eagle courtyard.

DIRECTIONS At Stourton, off B3092, three miles northwest of Mere (A303). Bus: Leathers 20 BR Gillingham to Stourton. BR: Gillingham and Bruton.

Studland Peninsula
- The Regional Education Officer
- c/o National Trust Regional Office, Eastleigh Court, Bishopstrow, Warminster, Wilts. BA12 9AW
- 0985 847777

Part of the 7000-acre Corfe Castle estate; includes the whole of Studland Bay with Old Harry Rocks and Shell Bay; the heathland behind Studland beach is recommended to naturalists in winter because of its variety of overwintering birds; several public paths and two nature trails; one of the classic field studies regions of Great Britain.

N C SUPPORT National Curriculum links with Science and Geography. Teachers' pack.

DISABLED FACILITIES Contact the administrator for access details.

DIRECTIONS Contact the administrator for details.

Surfrider Activity Holidays
- Steve Rosenbaum
- Waters Fall Hotel, Beach Road, Woolacombe, North Devon. EX34 7AD
- 0271 870365

Half-day and day courses in surfing, waveskiing, climbing, abseiling, mountain biking, canoeing. All coaching and equipment included. Several years' experience teaching school groups. Tailor-made courses for groups.

OPENING All year round.

CATERING Can include a packed lunch for an additional £1.50 per person.

COST £12 per person per activity, including coaching and all specialist equipment.

DIRECTIONS From junction 27 on M5, take A361 to Mullacoff Cross and B3343 to Woolacombe, which passes the Waters Fall Hotel.

Tintagel Castle
- The Head Custodian
- Tintagel, Cornwall. PL34 0AA
- 0840 770328

The spectacular setting for the legendary castle of King Arthur is the wild and windswept Cornish coast. Clinging precariously to the edge of the cliff face are the extensive ruins of a medieval royal castle built by Richard, Earl of Cornwall, younger brother of Henry III.

OPENING All year. Good Friday or 1 April (whichever is earlier) to 30 September: daily 10.00am–6.00pm. 1 October to Maundy Thursday or 31

March (whichever is earlier): Monday to Sunday 10.00am–4.00pm. Closed 24–26 December and 1 January.

DISABLED FACILITIES There is a steep climb up steps to reach the Castle.

DIRECTIONS On Tintagel Head, half a mile along uneven track from Tintagel; no vehicles (OS Map 200, ref SX 048891). Bus: Western National 52B from BR Bodmin Parkway (Tel: 0872 40404).

Tintagel Old Post Office
- The Administrator
- Tintagel, Cornwall. PL34 0DB
- 0840 770024

One of Cornwall's most interesting buildings, this small 14th-century manor house, with its crumpled roof, is full of charm and character and is now restored in the fashion of the post office that it was for nearly 50 years during the 19th century.

N C SUPPORT National Curriculum links with English and History.

DISABLED FACILITIES Braille guide.

DIRECTIONS In the centre of the village. Bus: Fry's service from Bodmin, Bude and Wadebridge.

Totnes Castle
- The Head Custodian
- Castle Street, Totnes, Devon. TQ9 8NU
- 0803 864406

By the North Gate of the hill town of Totnes visitors will find a superb motte-and-bailey castle, with splendid views across the roof tops and down to the river Dart. It is a symbol of lordly feudal life and a fine example of Norman fortification.

OPENING All year round. Good Friday or 1 April (whichever is earlier) to 30 September: daily 10.00am–6.00pm. 1 October to Maundy Thursday or 31 March (whichever is earlier): Tuesday to Sunday 10.00am–4.00pm. Closed 24–26 December and 1 January.

CATERING Picnic facilities.

DIRECTIONS In Totnes, on a hill overlooking the town (OS Map 202; ref SX 800605). BR: Totnes.

Trelissick Garden
- The Administrator
- Feock, Nr Truro, Cornwall. TR3 6QL
- 0872 862090

Large garden, lovely in all seasons; rare shrubs and plants; extensive park and woods; beautiful views over Fal estuary; woodland walk beside the river Fal; arts and crafts gallery.

N C SUPPORT National Curriculum links with English, Maths, Science, Geography and Environmental Education. Study centre; teachers' pack.

DISABLED FACILITIES Upper parts of the garden are accessible, but there are loose gravel paths; special parking; powered self-drive buggy. Adapted toilet near shop and car park. Small walled garden, specially planted with aromatic plants. Braille guide.

DIRECTIONS Four miles south of Truro, on both sides of B3289 above King Harry Ferry. Bus: Truronian 311 from Truro (passing close BR Truro). BR: Truro five miles; Perranwell (not Sunday, except July and August) four miles.

SOUTH WEST

Trerice
- The Administrator
- Nr Newquay, Cornwall. TR8 4PG
- ☎ 0637 875404

A small Elizabethan manor house built in 1572; a simple yet elegant property; summer-flowering garden and an orchard of Cornish fruit trees.

N C SUPPORT National Curriculum links with English, Maths, Technology, History and Environmental Education.

CATERING Restaurant.

DISABLED FACILITIES Ground and upper floors of house, restaurant and shop accessible, upper floors via grass slope; some loose gravel and cobbles; garden more difficult; special parking by prior arrangement with the administrator. Adapted toilet. Braille guide.

DIRECTIONS Three miles southeast of Newquay via A392 and A3058 (turn right at Kestle Mill). Bus: Western National 90 Newquay to Truro, alight Kestle Mill. BR: Quintrell Downs, (not Sunday, except July and August).

Tuckes Maltings
- Joanna Webber
- Teign Road, Osborne Park, Newton Abbot, South Devon. TQ12 4AA
- ☎ 0626 334734 FAX 0626 334734

Making malt from barley for beer, a working malthouse built in 1900, with working Victorian machinery, exhibits, audio and visual effects, guided tour lasting over one hour, and 'hands-on' fun. 'New Big Upstairs' with many more things to see and do. Unique and highly educational.

N C SUPPORT History, Victorians, Science and Technology. A chance for children to see a working Victorian industry, including temperature control, health and safety, transportation, energy. How do complicated modern and traditional mechanics work? Energy, Environmental Industry.

OPENING Easter to 31 October: 10.00am–4.00pm. Winter by arrangement.

COST Children of 7–14 years £1.75, children of 14–18 years £2.20.

DISABLED FACILITIES Due to the many stairs people with certain disabilities may not be able to take the full tour. Guide dogs welcome.

DIRECTIONS Follow brown and white signs from Newton Abbot railway station.

The Tutankhamun Exhibition
- Daphne Main
- High West Street, Dorchester, Dorset. DT1 1VW
- ☎ 0305 269571 FAX 0305 268885

Experience the wonder and mystery of the world's greatest discovery of ancient treasure. Tutankhamun's tomb, treasures and mummy are superbly recreated in this internationally acclaimed exhibition, frequently featured on television.

N C SUPPORT History Key Stage 2: supplementary unit – the study of a non-European society: Ancient Egypt. Available to visiting schools: free teacher reconnaissance visit, teachers' notes and worksheets, introductory talk, book list.

OPENING All year: daily 9.30am–5.30pm.

CATERING None. Schools can eat packed lunches in the Borough Gardens only 200 yards away.

COST Children £1.50, one adult free with every ten children, extra adults £2.50.

DISABLED FACILITIES Wheelchair access to whole of exhibition.

Victoria Art Gallery
- Essex Havard, Education Officer
- Poulteney Bridge, Bath, Avon. BA2 4AT
- 0225 461111 x2772 FAX 0225 469982

Extensive permanent collection and a new purpose-built temporary exhibition gallery providing one of the best exhibition programmes in the region.

N C SUPPORT Workshops associated with selected temporary exhibitions. Activity sheets for the permanent collection. Study room available, suitable for individuals and small groups from GCSE-level upwards.

ANNUAL OR ONE OFF EVENT Varied programme of temporary exhibitions which change every 4–6 weeks.

OPENING Monday to Friday 10.00am–5.30pm, Saturday 10.00am–5.00pm, closed Sunday and bank holidays.

CATERING None.

COST Free.

DISABLED FACILITIES Access to ground floor (wide entrance on Bridge Street). Toilet (ground floor).

DIRECTIONS Situated close to the junction of Walcott Street and Bridge Street. Visitors are advised to use public car parks. A Park-and-Ride service is also available.

West Somerset Railway
- H Burgess, Commercial Manager
- The Railway Station, Minehead, Somerset. TA24 5BG
- 0643 704996 FAX 0643 706349

West Somerset railway is Britain's longest preserved railway, running trains over the twenty miles from Minehead to Bishops Lydeard with bus connections to Taunton. Visitors' Centre and model railways at Bishops Lydeard, GW Museum at Blue Anchor, S&D Museum at Washford.

ANNUAL OR ONE OFF EVENT Special events throughout the year.

OPENING Telephone for details.

CATERING Buffet on train.

COST Return Bishops Lydeard to Minehead: children £3.65, adults £7.30, Senior Citizens £5.85, family (two adults and two children) £18.50. Single: children £2.45, adults £4.90, Senior Citizens £3.95.

DISABLED FACILITIES Special saloon for wheelchair passengers with wheelchair lifts.

DIRECTIONS Contact above for directions.

Weymouth Sealife Park
- Penny Corp-Palmer
- Lodmoor Country Park, Weymouth, Dorset. DT4 7SZ

Makes learning fun, brings the fascinating underwater world to life with its amazing variety of creatures; our recreated rainforest allows

VISITS OUT
SOUTH WEST

pupils to learn about both the beauty and importance of rainforests.

N C SUPPORT A range of teachers' notes and workbooks for both senior and junior levels. Also a talk is arranged for each group and can be developed to meet specific requirements.

OPENING Daily from 10.00am.

CATERING Restaurant serving snacks and meals. Also large picnic areas outside.

COST School groups: £2.45 per child, one adult free with every ten children, additional adults £2.45.

DISABLED FACILITIES Most displays accessible by wheelchair. Toilet.

DIRECTIONS At Lodmoor Country Park on the A353 towards Wareham.

Wheal Martyn Museum
- Myra Hutton
- Carthew, St Austell, Cornwall. PL25 8XG
- 0726 850362

Open-air Museum of the china clay industry, incorporating 19th-century clay works, working waterwheels, nature trail and working pit views.

N C SUPPORT Guides to the Museum and to the history of the industry available. National Curriculum guide under preparation.

OPENING Easter to October: daily 10.00am–6.00pm.

CATERING Coffee shop.

COST Children £1.40, adults £3.15, one adult free with every ten pupils.

DISABLED FACILITIES Access limited for wheelchairs.

DIRECTIONS On the B3274, two miles north of St Austell.

Wheelwright & Gypsy Museum
- Pat or Katrina Atkinson
- Webbington Loxton, Nr Axbridge, Somerset. BS26 2HX
- 0934 750841

A craft workshop showing the wheelwright at work, an exhibition of wheelwrights tools (approximately 100 years old). A large collection of gypsy caravans, the Romany museum showing the history, traditions and life of the true Romany gypsy.

N C SUPPORT Suitable for National Curriculum in Woodwork, Transport, History, Art, Ethnic Studies.

OPENING Summer: Wednesday to Sunday 10.00am–6.00pm. Winter: Wednesday to Sunday 11.00am–4.00pm. Also bank holidays and every day in July and August.

CATERING Tea rooms indoors seating 35; tea gardens.

COST Children £1.50, adults £2.00, Senior Citizens £1.50, family (two adults and up to three children). Groups: children £1.00, adults £1.50, Senior Citizens £1.00.

DISABLED FACILITIES Paths, ramps, doors; museum was built on flat surface with wheelchairs in mind.

DIRECTIONS West two and a half miles from A38 (18 miles south of Bristol) at Axbridge. East three miles A370 Weston to Bridgwater road from Bleadon. Signposted.

Wookey Hole Caves & Papermill

- Paquita Webb
- Wookey Hole, Wells, Somerset. BA5 1BB
- 0749 672243 **FAX** 0749 677749

Britain's most spectacular caves. The papermill houses a fascinating variety of exhibitions including papermaking by hand, fairground memories, the popular Old Penny Arcade and the latest addition, the Magical Mirror Maze.

N C SUPPORT Free 24-page teachers' guide with 12 activity sheets suitable for lower junior, upper junior and lower secondary pupils. Geography AT1, AT2, AT3, AT4; History (Key Stage 2) HSU4, HSU11; Science AT3; English AT1, AT3; Technology T4. Schoolroom.

OPENING Summer: 9.30am–5.30pm (last tour). Winter: 10.30am–4.30pm (last tour). Closed 17–25 December inclusive.

CATERING Self-service restaurant (seats 250). Discounts available for pre-booked parties.

COST Children £2.25, adults £4.25, Senior Citizens £3.35. Group rates for parties of ten or more, one adult free with every ten children.

DISABLED FACILITIES The cave tour is not suitable for wheelchairs and the severely disabled, but all other attractions and facilities are accessible.

DIRECTIONS From M5, junction 22, follow brown and white signs via A38 and A371. From Bath, A376 to Wells, only two miles from Wookey Hole.

World of Country Life

- C J Lee
- Sandy Bay, Exmouth, Devon. EX8 5BU
- 0392 873230 **FAX** 0392 873533

Exhibition with Victorian Keeper's cottage, shops, village inn. Also working models, vintage and steam vehicles, nature gallery, puzzle corner, craft demonstrations, deer parks, adventure playgrounds, pets' corner, skidcars, bouncy castles.

N C SUPPORT Worksheets for National Curriculum in Science, Key Stage 2 (7–11 years) and also for 5–7 years.

ANNUAL OR ONE OFF EVENT Events happen at intervals throughout the season and range from Silver Band concert to Morris dancing and vintage car rallies.

OPENING Good Friday to end October: daily 10.00am–6.00pm (last admission 5.00pm).

CATERING Restaurant serving hot and cold meals, cream teas, etc. Kiosk serving hot and cold drinks and ices. Picnic areas.

COST Group rates (10 and over): children £2.25, adults £3.25, Senior Citizens £2.50, school children £2.00, one adult free for every ten children, wheelchair occupants free.

DISABLED FACILITIES Toilets. Access to whole exhibition except safari train.

DIRECTIONS Follow Tourist Board signs from traffic lights on A376 Exeter to Exmouth road on the outskirts of Exmouth (approximately two miles).

VISITS OUT
SOUTH WEST

YMCA

- T J Durbridge, Chief Executive
- International House, Broad Street Place, Bath, Avon. BA1 5LN
- 0225 460471

City centre-based residential hostel/community centre with provision for individual or group accommodation. Also sports hall, restaurant, health suite, classroom, meeting rooms, etc. Open to all.

N C SUPPORT On demand.

OPENING All year round except Christmas period.

CATERING Restaurant service.

COST £12 single room, £11 shared room, £9.50 dormitories. All B&B (Continental).

DISABLED FACILITIES Possible but difficult.

DIRECTIONS Approach from Walcot Street or Broad Street in the city centre.

VISITS OUT
NORTHERN IRELAND

Annaghmore

- U Farrington, Administrator
- Portadown, Co Armagh. BT62 1SQ
- 0762 851236

Seventeenth-century farm house with 18th-century additions and embellishments. Farmyard with outbuildings furnished with farm tool collection and animals. Picnic area and playground; garden and woodland walk.

N C SUPPORT School tours. Educational pack. Teachers' preliminary visits. Annual historical competition. Activity leaflets.

ANNUAL OR ONE OFF EVENT Apple Blossom Day in May. Music in the garden in June.

OPENING Morning openings arranged for schools except Tuesday.

CATERING Picnic area.

COST House and farm: children £1.00. Farm only: children 75p. Accompanying adults free.

DISABLED FACILITIES Toilets. Acess to most of farmyard and some of house.

DIRECTIONS Seven miles from Portadown on the Moy Road.

Ardress

- Mary Salter, Regional Education Officer
- National Trust, Annaghmore, Co Armagh. BT62 1SQ
- 0238 510721

Seventeenth-century farm house, main front and garden façades added in 18th century by owner–architect George Ensor; Neo-classical plasterwork in drawing room; good furniture and pictures; display of farm implements and livestock in farmyard; garden; woodland walks.

N C SUPPORT Information and resource materials to enable further research and study by teachers and pupils are available at Ardress House and displayed at local Teachers' Centres. The Teacher's Resource Pack contains the building history of Ardress House, the Ensor family history, a booklet on the Arable Farming Year and nature trail activities and notes. Various project leaflets to occupy the children on their visits are also available.

CATERING No facilities. Pupils should provide their own food and they can eat indoors in bad weather.

DISABLED FACILITIES Contact Ardress House for details.

DIRECTIONS Seven miles from Portadown on the Moy Road B28. Five miles from Moy. Three miles from the Loughall intersection. Junction 13 on the M1.

The Argory

- Mary Salter, Regional Education Officer
- Moy, Dungannon, Co Tyrone. BT71 6NA
- 0868 784753

Set in 300 acres of woodland overlooking the Blackwater river, the house dates from 1820 and was substantially changed in the 19th century; fascinating furniture and contents including an 1824 Bishop's barrel organ; imposing stable yard with coach house, harness room, laundry and acetylene gas plant; sundial garden; extensive walks and adventure playground; special Meet the Servants tours.

N C SUPPORT The education programme for Key Stage 1 is based on Tommy N MacGeough Bond's early childhood at the Argory, where he grew up under the care of Mama and Nanny. This story is interpreted by special guides dressed in period costumes and is relevant to the various themes within AT 1–3. The programme is suitable for aspects of Cultural Heritage and EMU studies.

DISABLED FACILITIES Limited wheelchair access; induction loop; adapted toilet.

DIRECTIONS Off B28, seven miles west of Portadown.

Armagh County Museum

- Catherine Kelly
- The Mall East, Armagh, Northern Ireland. BT61 9BE
- 0861 523070 FAX 0861 522631

Community museum with fine collections of art, archaeology, local and natural history, textile, militaria and railway collections. Eight to ten temporary exhibitions annually complete the programme.

N C SUPPORT Especially relevant to History Key Stages 1–2: 'Life in Early Times', 'Introduction to History' and 'Life in Victorian Times'.

ANNUAL OR ONE OFF EVENT Sixth forms find the temporary exhibitions of great use, especially the art shows.

OPENING Monday to Friday 10.00am–5.00pm, Saturday 10.00am–1.00pm and 2.00pm–5.00pm.

COST Free.

DISABLED FACILITIES As the museum galleries are on the first floor visitors with walking difficulties will find access difficult.

Armagh Planetarium

- College Hill, Armagh. BT61 9DB
- 0861 523689 FAX 0861 524725

Explore the universe with 'hands-on' computers. Telescopes and other astronomical instruments are on display. Theatre shows.

ANNUAL OR ONE OFF EVENT Shows every Saturday 2.00pm and 3.00pm, booking strongly advised. Extra shows at Easter, Christmas, bank holidays. Daily shows July to August excluding 12 July and Sunday.

OPENING Hall of Astronomy: Monday to Saturday 2.00pm–4.45pm.

COST Children under 16 £1.50, adults £2.50, Senior Citizens £1.50.

DISABLED FACILITIES Ground floor wheelchair access only, adapted toilet.

Belfast City Council Parks & Amenities Services

- R Scott
- Malone House, Malone Road, Barnett Demesne, Belfast. BT9 5PB
- 0232 681246 FAX 0232 682197

Education service includes Nature Study Centre, annual 'Tree Teach-in', birdwatching sites, tropical rainforest experience in Botanic Gardens.

N C SUPPORT Relevant to several areas in Science and Geography curriculum.

NORTHERN IRELAND

OPENING Monday to Friday (except bank/public holidays).

COST Nature Study Centre: children 30p.

DISABLED FACILITIES Access to all facilities.

DIRECTIONS On application.

Belfast Zoo
- Robert Osborne
- Belfast BT36 7PM
- 0232 776277 FAX 0232 370 578

In a picturesque mountain park above the city. Underwater viewing of sea lions and penguins. Look out for gorillas, red pandas, spectacled bears, rare tamarins and marmosets.

N C SUPPORT Teachers' packs and worksheets with contents related to the curriculum available free of charge. Visits to schools by staff members and talks at the Zoo on various topics.

ANNUAL OR ONE OFF EVENT A guidebook is available with details of events etc. (not free).

OPENING April to September: daily 10.00am–5.00pm; October to March: daily 10.00am–3.30pm, Friday 10.00am–2.30pm. Closed Christmas Day.

CATERING Restaurant, tea house.

COST Summer: children £1.80, adults £3.90. Winter: children £1.40, adults £2.90. Under fours and Senior Citizens free. Group rate: children £1.30, one adult free with every ten children (1993 prices).

DISABLED FACILITIES Wheelchair access adapted toilets.

DIRECTIONS Antrim Road, four miles north of city, close to Glengormley village.

Belleek Pottery Visitor Centre
- Patricia McCauley
- Belleek, Co Fermanagh. BT93 3FY
- 0365 658501 FAX 0365 658625

This magnificent pottery building was erected over 100 years ago. Winner of 1990 British Airways Tourism Award. The Centre offers a fascinating insight into the life and times of a company that has come to represent the highest standard of Irish craftsmanship. The methods and techniques developed by the very first Belleek craftsmen are still followed today.

OPENING Daily. Times vary according to season.

COST £1.00 per person. 50p for groups.

DISABLED FACILITIES Factory tour. All areas accessible. Toilets.

DIRECTIONS Contact the Centre for a copy of map giving directions.

Brontë Interpretive Centre
- The Administrator
- Drumballyroney, Co Down
- 0820 631152

The life and times of Patrick Brontë, father of the novelist sisters. He was parish schoolmaster at Drumballyroney school and preached his first sermon in the church next door to the Centre. The Brontë Homeland trail starts here. Place of interest on the drive is Patrick's birthplace (1777) at Emdale where there is a memorial.

VISITS OUT
NORTHERN IRELAND

N C SUPPORT Curriculum links with English and History.

OPENING March to September: daily (except Monday) 10.00am–6.00pm.

COST Telephone for details.

DISABLED FACILITIES Wheelchair access.

DIRECTIONS Nine miles southeast of Banbridge, off A1 and A50.

Carrickfergus Castle
- David Steele
- Marine Highway, Carrickfergus, Co Antrim. BT38 7BG
- 0960 365190 FAX 0960 365190

Most complete medieval castle in Northern Ireland, c.1180 John De Courcey. Keep, gate house with chapel and portcullis. New exhibits throughout castle: life-size models, audio-visual theatre; theme displays; visitors' centre.

N C SUPPORT 'Day in the Life of a Medieval Castle' package suitable for projects on Defences through the Ages; historic development explained through reconstruction drawings; new medieval style furniture and fittings which can be discussed and handled.

ANNUAL OR ONE OFF EVENT Details available on request.

OPENING 1 October to 31 March: Monday to Saturday 10.00am–4.00pm, Sunday 2.00pm–4.00pm. 1 April to 30 September: Monday to Saturday 10.00am–6.00pm, Sunday 2.00pm–6.00pm. Last admission 30 minutes before closing.

COST Educational permits provide entry for school groups free of charge (must be pre-booked).

DISABLED FACILITIES Toilets. Chair-lift allows wheelchair entry to first floor of keep; flat paths throughout the castle.

DIRECTIONS Travelling from Belfast take M5. Carrickfergus signposted throughout; 11 miles from Belfast.

Castle Coole
- The Curator
- Enniskillen, Co Fermanagh
- 0365 322690

Superb late 18th-century Neo-classical house designed by James Wyatt, family home of the Earls of Belmore. Very fine interior furnishings and plasterwork. Landscaped parkland with mature oak woodland and lough. Grounds open all year round for walks. Recently restored Grand Yard.

N C SUPPORT Curriculum links with History.

OPENING Grounds: all year. Castle: April to May and September: Saturday, Sunday and bank holidays: daily 2.00pm–6.00pm. June to August: daily (except Thursdays) 2.00pm–6.00pm. Closed during winter.

COST Children £1.15, adults £2.30. Group reduction.

DISABLED FACILITIES Access always to grounds for walks. Wheelchair access to house. Adapted toilet. Sympathetic hearing scheme.

DIRECTIONS On A4 one mile southeast of Enniskillen.

Castle Ward
- The Administrator
- Strangford, Downpatrick, Co Down. BT30 7LS
- 039 686 204

VISITS OUT
NORTHERN IRELAND

Seven hundred-acre country estate with woodlands, lake and seashore: unique 18th-century mansion with opposing façades in different styles (west front Classical, east front Gothic); Victorian laundry; formal and landscape gardens with specimen shrubs and trees; fortified towers; cornmill and sawmill; wildfowl collection; information centre, shop, theatre in stable yard; caravan site; holiday cottages; base camp for young people; exhibition and audio-visual shows on wildlife of Strangford Lough.

N C SUPPORT National Curriculum links with History, Environmental Education, Geography, Art and English. Guided schools talks, Victorian Past-time Centre. Victorian Laundry. Summer Craft School–Key Stages 1 and 2.

DISABLED FACILITIES Contact the administrator for access details.

Crom
- Ian Herbert
- Crom Estate, Newtownbutler, Co Fermanagh
- 0365 738174

The exceptional harmony of woodland, water, parkland and old buildings gives Crom its very special quality. One of the most important nature conservation sites owned by the National Trust, the estate woodlands consist of fine stands of ancient oak, providing a rich and diverse habitat, while the shorelines of Crom support many very rare plants. The fine old buildings which enhance the landscape include Crom Old Castle, Crichton Tower and Crom Church.

N C SUPPORT Key Stages 1 and 2 Science and Geography.

DISABLED FACILITIES Property partially accessible to disabled visitors.

DIRECTIONS On the Newtownbutler to Crom Road, 3 miles west of Newtownbutler.

Down County Museum
- Gerard Lennon
- The Mall, Downpatrick, Co Down. BT30 6AH
- 0396 615218 FAX 0396 615590

Down County Museum occupies the old Down County gaol, built between 1789 and 1796. It is the most complete surviving Irish gaol of its type and period. Within the high walls are the gate houses, now the Saint Patrick Heritage Centre which tells the story of Ireland's patron saint through large-scale illustrations and other objects.

N C SUPPORT Many relevant displays. Education Officer offers assistance on National Curriculum and planning visits. Reference library available. Guided tours by arrangement.

OPENING Tuesday to Friday 11.00am–5.00pm, Saturday 2.00pm–5.00pm, closed Mondays. July–mid-September: Sunday afternoon and Monday.

COST Admission free. Guided tours and 'hands-on' activities by arrangement (approximately 50p–£1.00 per pupil).

DISABLED FACILITIES Contact the curator for details.

DIRECTIONS Close to the cathedral in Down.

VISITS OUT
NORTHERN IRELAND

Enniskillen Castle
- Helen Lanigan Wood
- Castle Barracks, Enniskillen, Co Fermanagh. BT74 7HL
- 0365 325000 FAX 0365 327342

Fermanagh County Museum (Fermanagh District Council). Local archaeology, natural history, rural life and crafts, audio-visual programmes and special exhibitions. Royal Inniskilling Fusiliers Museum housed in 15th-century castle.

N C SUPPORT Guided tours for special projects (all Key Stages). 'Fermanagh Folk' study pack (Key Stage 1 History, Cultural Heritage and Education for Mutual Understanding).

OPENING Tuesday to Friday 10.00am–1.00pm and 2.00pm–5.00pm, Monday 2.00pm–5.00pm. May to September only: Saturday 2.00pm–5.00pm. July to August only: Sunday 2.00pm–5.00pm. Open most bank holidays, closed Christmas and New Year.

COST Children 50p, adults £1.00, students and Senior Citizens 75p. Groups of ten or more: children 30p, adults 75p, students and Senior Citizens 50p.

DISABLED FACILITIES Lift and toilets.

DIRECTIONS From Sligo to Donegal, turn right at traffic lights, go along Wellington Road, signposted County Museum. From Belfast, first left off the roundabout, along Wellington Road, signposted County Museum.

Exploris CNI Aquarium
- Dee Davison, Education Officer
- The Ropewalk, Castle Street, Portaferry, Co Down. BT22 1NZ
- 0247 728062 FAX 0247 728296

Exploris is an innovative new aquarium that has developed from the success of the NI Aquarium. It takes visitors on a stimulating journey through live and multi-media displays. Starting in Strangford Lough visitors travel through a variety of Irish seashore and seabed habitats out into the open Irish Sea.

N C SUPPORT The guided aquarium tours, resource room, workshop and shorework activities fulfil a number of Attainment Targets for Science and Geography, Key Stages 1–4. The accompanying education packs develop cross-curricular links. Specific resource room and shorework investigative activities fulfil Field Study, Habitat, Ecosystems and Environmental Education objectives for Biology and Geography A-Level, as well as form and function topics, Behaviour and Classification for Biology.

OPENING Telephone for details.

COST Varies according to activity.

DISABLED FACILITIES Whole building and grounds wheelchair accessible. Two touch tanks are especially popular.

DIRECTIONS From Belfast: either Newtownards A20; or A7, Saintfield, A25 and Strangford Ferry. Allow one to one and a half hours for travelling from Belfast.

VISITS OUT
NORTHERN IRELAND

Florence Court
- Mrs Vicky Gilfillan, Education Officer
- Nr Enniskillen, Co Fermanagh. BT92 1DB
- 0365 348249

One of the most important houses in Ulster, built in the mid-18th century by John Cole, father of the First Earl of Enniskillen: fine Rococo plasterwork; pleasure grounds with ice house, eel house, water-powered sawmill and hydraulic ram; walled garden with fine views over surrounding mountains; picnic sites; four miles from Marble Arch Caves.

N C SUPPORT A visit to Florence Court can be used to provide Key Stage 1 pupils with 'An Introduction to History'. The sawmills and the harnessing of water power provide examples of Technology and Change in Victorian Times. Science, Key Stage 2 highlights science within a historical context. Also, the beautiful interior of Florence Court provides pupils with first-hand experience of the work of designers and craftworkers in the past (Art and Design, Key Stage 2).

CATERING Apply for details.

DISABLED FACILITIES Partially accessible to disabled visitors. Adapted toilets.

DIRECTIONS A4 from Belfast, A509 Cavan, A46 Bundoran. Eight miles southwest of Enniskillen, via A4 and A32 Swanlinbar Road.

Ford Farm Park & Museum
- The Curator
- 8 Low Road, Islandmagee, Co Antrim BT40 3RD
- 0960 353264

Small country museum in former farm outhouse with folk collection, fishing nets, lobster pots, farming implements, butter-making demonstrations. Sheep from the Hall family's farm provide wool for spinning demonstrations.

OPENING Daily (except Christmas Day) 2.00pm–6.00pm.

COST Children £1.00, adults £1.25, under threes free.

DISABLED FACILITIES Ground floor is wheelchair accessible.

DIRECTIONS Islandmagee on B90.

The Giant's Causeway
- Mr Dick Hill
- Causeway Centre, 42 Causeway Road, Bushmills, Co Antrim. BT57 8SU
- 0265 731582

A World Heritage site: coast and cliff paths, unusual basalt and volcanic rock formations and a wealth of local and natural history; the wreck site of the Armada treasure ship Girona is found at Port-na-Spaniagh; visitors' centre, providing interpretive displays, audio-visual theatre, tourist information and guided walks.

N C SUPPORT As an educational resource the Giant's Causeway is relevant to Geography AT1, AT2 and AT5; Geology A-Level Science; AT1, AT2 and AT5; History Key Stage 2 and HSU2; Biology A-Level. School-based lectures Key Stages 1–4.

CATERING Apply for details.

DISABLED FACILITIES Partially accessible to disabled visitors with suitable toilets.

VISITS OUT
NORTHERN IRELAND

DIRECTIONS On B146 Causeway to Dunseverick Road.

Gray's Printing Press
- M Salter
- 49 Main Street, Strabane, Co Tyrone. BT28 8AU
- 0504 884094

One of the most attractive façades on Main Street, Strabane is that with 'Gray, Printer' above the bow windows. The shop front, restored by the National Trust in 1992, has remained unchanged since the 18th century. Through the shop you will find the press room in which a fascinating collection of 19th-century hand-operated printing presses are displayed together with an array of wooden and metal type and other tools of the printer's trade. There is also an impressive new audio-visual show.

N C SUPPORT Key Stage 2 History and Key Stage 2 Technology.

DISABLED FACILITIES For further information contact the National Trust, The Public Affairs Manager, Rowallane, Saintfield, Co Down BT24 7LH.

DIRECTIONS Write for leaflet showing map.

Hezlett House
- The Curator
- Liffock, Castlerock, Co Londonderry
- 0265 848567

Seventeenth-century thatched cottage, important because of the cruck truss construction of the roof. Now furnished in late Victorian style. Small museum of farm implements.

OPENING April to June and September: Saturday, Sunday and bank holidays 1.00pm–5.00pm. July to August: daily (except Tuesdays) 1.00pm–5.00pm.

COST Children 65p, adults £1.30. Group rate.

DISABLED FACILITIES One-storey cottage.

DIRECTIONS At Liffock, five miles west of Coleraine on the Coleraine to Downhill coast road (A2).

Irish Linen Centre/Lisburn Museum
- Education Officer
- Market Square, Lisburn, Co Antrim. BT28 1AG
- 0846 663377 FAX 0846 672624

The history of the Irish linen industry and its role in economic and social development. A series of audio-visual presentations and interactive displays bring the past very much to life.

OPENING Daily.

COST Please contact the Education Officer to discuss concessionary rates for educational groups.

DISABLED FACILITIES Toilet; lifts.

Knight Ride
- The Administrator
- Antrim Street, Carrickfergus, Co Antrim
- 0960 366455

Knight Ride is the only monorail theme ride in Ireland, north or south. Present-day 'time travellers' step into a specially designed car and are taken on an exciting trip through more than 800 years of Carrickfergus history. Walk-through exhibition, including a huge model of the town, photographs, illustrations and information on emigration and the local traditional industries of Carrickfergus.

N C SUPPORT National Curriculum links with History. Ride high above the new Mall, weaving through sailing ships and shoals of fish and hearing about Carrickfergus's maritime past. Next is the 'Dark Ride', where history comes to life in a series of expositions of the past: a lively market scene, a haunted house, the landing of William of Orange. Light, movement and sound come together to give a realistic living picture of the town and its history.

OPENING Monday to Saturday 10.00am–8.00pm, Sunday 12.00 noon–8.00pm (last admission 7.30pm).

COST Children £1.00, adults £2.00, family ticket £5.40. Group rates available.

DISABLED FACILITIES Contact the administrator for details of access.

DIRECTIONS Contact the administrator for details.

Leslie Hill Heritage Farm Park

- John Leslie
- Leslie Hill, Antrim, Co Antrim. BT53 6QL
- 02056 63109

Open farm based around 500-acre 18th-century estate with museum of horse-drawn machinery, carriages, rare breeds, adventure playground, walled garden and lakes. The museum depicts an exhibition of social history; farm buildings open for exploration; the forge, working and still used, with a blacksmith working on arranged days. A comprehensive collection of farm machinery and implements.

N C SUPPORT Pets Corner: rabbits and guinea pigs, a favourite with children; working horses and a display of falconry; deer; extensive walks; nature trail; wild flowers; butterflies; badger setts, animal tracks. A 12-page information booklet is available for teachers.

OPENING Easter to end May: Sunday and bank holidays 2.00pm–6.00pm. May to June: Saturday and bank holidays 11.00am–6.00pm, Sunday 2.00pm–6.00pm. July and August: Monday to Saturday 11.00am–6.00pm, Sunday 2.00pm–6.00pm. September: Sunday 2.00pm–6.00pm.

CATERING Picnic facilities.

COST Children £1.40, adults £2.10, Senior Citizens £1.40. Groups of 15 or more: children £1.10, adults £1.50.

DISABLED FACILITIES None, but access is good anyway and a number of groups of people with disabilities have visited.

DIRECTIONS Half a mile out of Ballymoney on Malfin Road or follow brown Tourist Board signs.

Marble Arch Caves

- A Gallagher
- Marlbank Scenic Loop, Florencecourt, Co Fermanagh. BT92 1EW
- 0365 348855 FAX 0365 348928

Showcave with guided tours lasting one and a quarter hours. Explore a fascinating underworld and rivers, winding passages, lofty caverns, nature trail through national nature reserve. Site offers Interpretive Centre with exhibitions, lecture theatre, education service.

N C SUPPORT Education officer available for school visits; education packs on sale at centre. Assistance with Geography, fieldwork and projects.

OPENING Late March to late September: 11.00am–4.00pm.

CATERING Cafeteria.

COST Children 5–16 years admitted half price; parties of 10 or more qualify for group rate (teacher and bus driver free).

DISABLED FACILITIES Toilets and car parking.

DIRECTIONS Twelve miles from Enniskillen following the A4 (Sligo road) for three miles and branching off on the A32 (Swanlinbar road). The caves are well signposted.

Monuments & Buildings Record
- Clare Johnson
- Environment Service, Historic Monuments & Buildings, 5–33 Hill Street, Belfast. BT1 2LA
- 0232 235000 FAX 0232 310288

Publicly accessible database of Northern Ireland historic monuments, buildings, industrial archaeology, historic gardens, photographs and drawings.

N C SUPPORT No Education Officer. Much material suitable for Northern Ireland National Curriculum, especially History and Cultural Heritage.

OPENING Monday to Friday 9.00am–1.00pm and 2.00pm–4.30pm.

COST Free. Charges for reproduction, copyright, etc.

DISABLED FACILITIES Access. Toilet.

Mount Stewart House & Gardens
- Harry Hutchman
- The National Trust, Newtownards, Co Down. BT22 2AD
- 0247 788387 FAX 0247 788569

Fascinating 18th-century house with 19th-century additions. Home of Lord Castlereagh. Unrivalled collection of rare and unusual plants in the gardens. Temple of the Winds overlooks Strangford Lough.

N C SUPPORT Support for Key Stages 1 and 2 History. Life in 'The big House' which is relevant to 'Life in Victorian Times'.

ANNUAL OR ONE OFF EVENT Craft fairs and band concerts.

DISABLED FACILITIES Access to most of gardens and house. Toilets.

DIRECTIONS On the east shore of Strangford Lough, five miles southeast of Newtownards; 15 miles east of Belfast on north side of Belfast Portaferry Road (A20).

Murlough National Nature Reserve
- Sarah Anderson, Head Warden
- Dundrum, Co Down
- 039675 467

Murlough National Nature Reserve has a beautiful setting on the coast

VISITS OUT
NORTHERN IRELAND

below the Mourne Mountains. It is a fragile 5000-year-old sand dune system with heathland and woodland surrounded by estuary and sea. The different habitats within the reserve are rich in insects and other animals, and it also has a wide variety of plants including delicate flowers such as the pyramidal orchid and dune burnet rose, and rare and colourful butterflies.

N C SUPPORT Key Stages 1 and 2 Geography and Science.

CATERING Picnics welcome.

DISABLED FACILITIES Contact the Head Warden, Sarah Anderson on 039675 467.

DIRECTIONS South of Dundrum, on the Belfast to Newcastle road (A2).

NATIONAL TRUST

Opening Times Write or telephone the administrator of the house, give preferred day and time, the size and age of the group, and the main purpose of the visit. *The National Trust Handbook* contains further relevant information.

Cost Unless otherwise stated in the *Handbook*, there is a reduction of around 50% for children aged 16 and under, when accompanied by their teacher. Education Group Members are admitted free. However, please note that there may be a small charge for any additional educational facilities or activities.

See individual entries for all other information.

Ardress
The Argory
Castle Ward
Crom
Florence Court
The Giant's Causeway
Gray's Printing Press
Mount Stewart House & Gardens
Murlough National Nature Reserve
Springhill
Strangford Lough Wildlife Centre

The Navan Centre

☛ The Administrator
✉ Navan at Armagh, Killylea Road, Armagh. BT60 4LD
☎ 0861 525550 FAX 0861 522323

Housed within a building specially designed to become an integral part of the landscape, the Navan offers the visitor a rich, multi-layered understanding of Navan, the ancient seat of Ulster's kings. The visitor will first be introduced to the world of pre-Christian Ireland and the wonders of Celtic culture before embarking upon a journey into 'The Realworld'. This central feature will explain how archaeology has uncovered some of Navan's secrets. The final segment of the experience allows the visitor to pass on to 'The Otherworld', where the mysteries of Celtic rituals and beliefs will be explored and tales told of the times when Navan was the central location of The Ulster Cycle.

N C SUPPORT National Curriculum links with History and Archaeology. A wide variety of audio-visual techniques, narration, interactive devices and the design of the Centre itself are employed to bring to life the area's history, archaeology and mystery.

OPENING 1 April to 30 September: Monday to Saturday 10.00am–7.00pm, Sunday 11.00am–7.00pm. 1 October to 31 March: Monday to Saturday 10.00am–5.00pm. Sunday 10.00am–5.00pm.

CATERING Cafe capable of catering for a large number of people.

COST For further information and group bookings contact the Centre.

DISABLED FACILITIES Car park for people with disabilities near entrance; automatic doors; wheelchair available. Adapted toilet.

DIRECTIONS Two miles from Armagh on the A28.

Palace Stables Heritage Centre

- The Curator
- The Palace Demesne, Armagh. BT60 4EL
- 0861 522722

Set in the magnificent parkland of the Palace Demesne, the Palace Stables is a picturesque Georgian building enclosing a cobbled courtyard. The building has been expertly restored and brought back to life as a heritage interpretive centre. Features include: live stables area; 18th-century exhibitions of 'A Day in the Life' of Archbishop Robinson with life-like models, props, audio tracks and colourful murals.

N C SUPPORT National Curriculum links with History, Art, Crafts (craftsmen and women can be found demonstrating their individual expertise). Children's play/activity room.

ANNUAL OR ONE OFF EVENT In the Hayloft Gallery, complete with original beams, a variety of temporary exhibitions are displayed throughout the year. The Tack Room and Coachman's House: period room sets portraying living and working conditions of the coachman, with life-like model and murals.

OPENING April to August: Monday to Saturday 10.00am–7.00pm, Sunday 1.00pm–7.00pm. September to March: Monday to Saturday 10.00am to 5.00pm, Sunday 2.00pm–5.00pm. Closed bank/public holidays.

CATERING Stables restaurant looking onto the courtyard.

COST Free.

DISABLED FACILITIES Access and facilities including lift.

St Patrick's Train

- The Curator
- English Street, Armagh BT61 7BA
- 0861 527808

The history of Armagh is told at the interpretive centre and the imaginative 'Land of Lilliput' interprets Jonathan Swift's association with Armagh and his writing of *Gulliver's Travels*. Temporary exhibitions include St Patrick's Confessions and historic Armagh battles.

N C SUPPORT Curriculum links with History and English.

VISITS OUT
NORTHERN IRELAND

OPENING Daily 10.00am–7.00pm.

COST Children £2.50, adults £3.50.

DISABLED FACILITIES Wheelchair access, adapted toilet.

Seaforde Butterfly House
- Lady Anthea Forde
- Seaforde, Downpatrick, Co Down. BT30 8PG
- 0396 811 225 FAX 0396 811 370

A large greenhouse with hundreds of free-flying exotic tropical butterflies. Also reptiles, insects, birds and other creatures in a beautiful fantasy setting.

N C SUPPORT We can demonstrate all parts of the life cycle of butterflies and other insects, including bees.

OPENING Easter to end of September: Monday–Saturday 10.00am–5.00pm, Sunday 2.00pm–6.00pm.

COST Student groups £1.00 each.

DISABLED FACILITIES Yes.

DIRECTIONS On main Belfast to Newcastle road, 20 miles south of Belfast.

Sperrin Heritage Centre
- J L McGinley
- 274 Glenelly Road, Cranagh, Nr Plumbridge, Co Tyrone. BT79 8LS
- 0662 648142 FAX 0504 382264

Hi-tech audio-visual presentation in English, French and German explaining the area's glacial past, its folklore. View the region in 3D and 'pan' for gold.

N C SUPPORT Explains history of glaciation of the region from Ice Age to 3000 years ago and Man's Settlement here.

OPENING April to November: Monday to Friday 11.00am–6.00pm, Saturday 11.30am–6.00pm, Sunday 2.00pm–7.00pm.

COST Children 80p, adults £1.80, Senior Citizens/disabled 80p. Groups: 10–20 people £1.50, 20–40 people £1.40, 40 or more people £1.30.

DISABLED FACILITIES Ramps, toilets.

DIRECTIONS Midway between Draperstown and Plumbridge on B47.

Springhill
- Mrs Libby Keys
- Moneymore, Co Londonderry. BT45 7NQ
- 0648 748210

Springhill is a 17th-century Plantation house built and lived in by the Conynghams (later Lenox-Conynghams) until the National Trust acquired it in 1959. It was the home of ten generations of the family, who came from Ayrshire, and still has the feel of a home, with many portraits, furniture and memorabilia filling the rooms. The house is surrounded by a beautiful estate which is said to contain trees that are remnants of the ancient Forest of Ulster. A perfect setting which conveys the wonder of a bygone era.

N C SUPPORT General Visit provides lots of examples and information which is of value to pupils undertaking studies in the Key Stage 1 and 2 areas. Victorian Day is linked to Key Stage 2. Local Study, a series of four visits over 12 months, provides tours, involvement in nine conservation activities, lunch. In groups, the children prepare a children's guide book for younger pupils.

ANNUAL OR ONE OFF EVENT Special events include Schools Sunday in June: an extravaganza of music, drama and dance as over 100 school children bring the property to life for the general public.

CATERING Refreshments; picnic area.

DISABLED FACILITIES Access to ground floor rooms; special car parking at rear of house and adjacent to costume museum; light refreshments; access to small sales point by arrangement with guiding staff; picnic area accessible. Adapted toilet.

DIRECTIONS From Cookstown on the A29. One mile from Moneymore on Moneymore to Coagh road (B18).

Strangford Lough Wildlife Centre

- David Thompson
- Castle Ward Estate, Strangford, Co Down. BT30 7LS
- 0396 881411

Wildlife centre with audio-visual presentation, touch tables and interpretation panels.

N C SUPPORT Key Stages 1 and 2 Science–AT2 'Living Things'.

DISABLED FACILITIES Contact David Thompson for details.

DIRECTIONS 1 km west of Strangford village on A25 on southern shore of Strangford Lough.

Streamvale Farm

- Judith Morrow
- 38 Ballyhanwood Road, Belfast. BT5 7SN
- 0232 483244

Privately run dairy farm with educational tours covering milking process, nature study, farm animals. Tours last two hours.

N C SUPPORT Individually geared tours cover Key Stages 1–4. Special History tours during harvest time.

OPENING February to June and September to October: Monday to Friday for guided tours.

CATERING Facilities available for lunches.

COST Children £1.75 (includes guided tour and break), teachers free.

DISABLED FACILITIES Tours for people with disabilities by arrangement. Individual children with disabilities welcome.

DIRECTIONS Take main Newtownards road from Belfast. Signposted from Ulster Hospital.

The Tower Museum

- The Curator
- Union Hall Place, Derry, Co Londonderry. BT48 6LU
- 0504 372411

The Story of Derry: the exhibition recounts the history of the area from its original geological formation to the development of today's modern, vibrant and forward-looking European city. Of particular interest are the sections which illustrate the spread of Irish monasticism, the famous Siege of Derry and the road to the partition of Ireland.

N C SUPPORT National Curriculum links with History and Geology.

ANNUAL OR ONE OFF EVENT Contact the Heritage and Museum Service of Derry City for details of current and planned events.

OPENING Tuesday to Saturday 10.00am–1.00pm (last admission 12.30pm) and 2.00pm–5.00pm (last admission 4.30pm). Seasonal adjustments to be announced.

COST Please telephone for further information and group bookings.

DISABLED FACILITIES Please telephone for details.

DIRECTIONS Send for a copy of our leaflet showing map.

Ulster-American Folk Park
- The Curator
- Camphill, Omagh, Co Tyrone
- 0662 243292

Established showpieces include ancestral homestead of the Mellons of Pittsburgh, boyhood home of John Hughes, Archbishop of New York, and the 18th-century Plumbridge family home of Robert Campbell, the Rocky Mountain pioneer. Ulster emigrations are brought to life at the ship and dockside gallery. Victorian chemist's, craftshop, cafe.

N C SUPPORT National Curriculum links with History.

OPENING 10 April to 3 October: Monday to Saturday 10.30am–6.00pm, Sundays/bank holidays 11.30am–7.00pm. 4 October–

THE ULSTER AMERICAN FOLK PARK
- THE LIVING MUSEUM

Visit the Ulster American Folk Park and experience a real sense of history.
Our comprehensive schools programme offers:-

* Drama and Role Play
* Seasonal Customs
* Craft Demonstrations
* Guided Tours and Much, Much, More.

A new 37 bed Residential Block is available from April 1994.
For further information contact
The Ulster American Folk Park, Omagh
Co Tyrone, BT78 5QY.
Tel: (0662) 243292   Fax: (0662) 242241

VISITS OUT
NORTHERN IRELAND

Easter: Monday to Friday 10.30am–5.00pm. Last admission one and a half hours before closing. Closed 24–26 December, 1 January and 17 March.

CATERING Cafe.

COST Apply for current rates.

DISABLED FACILITIES Wheelchairs available. Adapted toilets.

DIRECTIONS Camphill, 3 miles north of Omagh on A5.

Ulster Folk & Transport Museum
- Mrs Deirdre Brown
- Cultra, Holywood, Co Down. BT18 0EU
- 0232 428428 FAX 0232 428728

National museum illustrating the social history of the north of Ireland. Over 20 farm houses, mills, schools, churches and urban houses moved from all over Ulster. Also history of transport in Ireland from earliest times to present.

N C SUPPORT Educational publications suitable to meet need of Northern Ireland National Curriculum (contact Publications Department for list). Work programmes. Museum Residential Centre available to schools, youth groups, etc.

ANNUAL OR ONE OFF EVENT Theme days, seasonal customs. Details on request.

OPENING September to June: Monday to Friday 9.30am–4.00pm, Sunday 12.30pm–6.00pm (closes 4.30pm October to March). July to August: Monday to Friday 10.30am–6.00pm, Saturday 10.30am–6.00pm, Sunday 12.30pm–6.00pm.

CATERING Yes.

COST Telephone for prices.

DISABLED FACILITIES Yes.

DIRECTIONS Contact the Museum for a map showing directions.

The Ulster History Park
- Mrs Elizabeth Harkin
- Cullion, Omagh, Co Tyrone. BT79 7SU
- 0662 648188 FAX 0662 648011

Full-scale models of homes and monuments, artefacts and illustrations. Explore the history of settlement in Ireland from the Stone Age to the Plantations. Activity workshops, theme visits and special events.

N C SUPPORT Primarily supports Key Stage 2 History. Also Key Stage 2 Home Economics, Art and Design, Technology and Key Stage 3 History.

OPENING April to September: Monday to Saturday 10.30am–6.30pm, Sunday 11.30am–7.00pm, public holidays 10.30am–7.00pm. October to March: Monday to Friday 10.30am–5.00pm.

COST Children £1.50, adults £2.50, students/Senior Citizens £1.50. Group of 15 or more: children £1.20, adults £2.00, students/Senior Citizens £1.20.

DISABLED FACILITIES Park and building are accessible for the disabled. Toilet facilities.

DIRECTIONS On B48 seven miles from Omagh on the Gortin road.

VISITS OUT
NORTHERN IRELAND

Watertop Open Farm
- Patsy or Terry McBride
- 188 Cushendall Road, Ballycastle, Co Antrim. BT54 6RL
- 0265 762576

Family activities include pony trekking, fishing, boating, farm tours, walks, etc. Sheep shearing demonstrations every day.

N C SUPPORT Used by Geography Departments for Study of the Land; 'Watertop Farm' case study; 'Farming as a Business' in National Curriculum Business Studies course.

OPENING July and August: daily for casual visits. Schools and groups by arrangement all year.

COST July and August: children 50p, adults £1.00. Guided farmyard tours: 80p–£1.20.

DISABLED FACILITIES Yes.

DIRECTIONS From Ballycastle take A2 to Cushendall six miles. Forty miles from Larne; 58 miles from Belfast; 30 miles from Coleraine.

Wellbrook Beetling Mill
- Mrs Beth Black
- Cookstown, Co Tyrone BT80 9RY
- 0648 751715

Wellbrook is a beetling mill in which the last process of linen manufacture was completed. Beetling is the hammering of linen after weaving so that the fibres flatten and spread to give a smooth glowing finish. Built in the middle of the 18th century, the mill was in commercial operation until the 1960s. Wellbrook is one of the last surviving examples of that era.

N C SUPPORT History: Key Stage 2 Life in Victorian Times, especially Industrial Development, Technological Change and Social History. Technology and Design: Energy and Control, the actual workings of the mill will be of interest and relevance to all age groups dealing with mechanisms or hydraulics. Science AT4 Key Stage 1: Forces and Energy, water-powered wheels, levers, gears and the forces involved in movement. Science AT1 Key Stage 2: Exploring and Investigating.

OPENING Please ring well in advance for details.

COST School visit: children 60p, teachers free.

DISABLED FACILITIES Please contact Wellbrook direct for details.

DIRECTIONS Off the A505 from Cookstown to Omagh.

The Wildfowl & Wetlands Centre
- The Curator
- Castle Espie, Ballydrain Road, Comber, Co Down. BT23 6EA
- 0247 874146

Castle Espie is one of eight national centres encouraging visitors to develop close personal contact with a total of 7000 wetland birds of 200 different types, some species owing their very existence to the Wildfowl & Wetlands Trust. The Trust offers an educational programme that has benefited a total of one million children. Many birds only put in an appearance at certain times of the year due to migratory cycles or a

VISITS OUT
NORTHERN IRELAND

natural diffidence, so schools may prefer to time their visits to coincide with those of their particular favourites. The Trust puts emphasis on fun, with friendly staff and guided tours.

ANNUAL OR ONE OFF EVENT Regular special events like 'Downy Duckling Days'.

OPENING Monday to Saturday from 10.30am, Sunday from 2.00pm. Closed Christmas Eve and Christmas Day.

CATERING Scenic restaurant offering home-cooked food.

COST Trust members and children under four free (membership available at the Centre). Special rates for Senior Citizens, students, claimants and parties booked in advance.

DISABLED FACILITIES Contact the Centre for access details.

DIRECTIONS Located on Strangford Lough, three miles south of Comber and 13 miles southeast of Belfast. Signposted from the A22 Comber to Killyleagh to Downpatrick road.

SCOTLAND

Aberdeen Art Gallery
- David Atherton
- School Hill, Aberdeen. AB9 1FQ
- 0224 646333

The gallery runs an extensive programme of arts events; these include permanent and temporary displays of art and crafts, plus workshops, music, dance, etc.

N C SUPPORT Since the gallery is District Council and the Education Department Regional, there is no official Curriculum link-up, however the Information Officer endeavours to be as helpful as possible, co-ordinating and guiding tours and making as much information as possible available to pupils.

OPENING Monday to Saturday 10.00am–5.00pm (8.00pm on Thursday), Sunday 2.00pm–5.00pm.

COST Free.

DISABLED FACILITIES Fully accessible.

DIRECTIONS Contact the gallery for directions.

Aberdour Castle
- The Head Custodian
- High Street, Aberdour, Fife
- 0383 860519

A 14th-century tower, extended in the 16th and 17th centuries, with splendid residential accommodation and a terraced garden and bowling green. There is a fine circular dovecot.

OPENING Summer (1 April to 30 September): Monday to Saturday 9.30am–6.00pm, Sunday 2.00pm–6.00pm. Winter: Monday to Wednesday and Saturday 9.30am–4.00pm, Sunday 2.00pm–4.00pm.

DISABLED FACILITIES Contact the site for details.

Arbroath Abbey
- The Head Custodian
- Arbroath
- 0241 78756

The substantial ruins of a Tironensian monastery, founded by William the Lion in 1178. Parts of the abbey church and domestic buildings remain. This was the scene of the Declaration of Arbroath of 1320, which asserted Scotland's independence from England.

OPENING 1 April to 30 September: Monday to Saturday 9.30am–6.00pm (last admission), Sunday 2.00pm–6.00pm (last admission). Monuments close at 6.30pm. Winter: Monday to Saturday 9.30am–4.00pm, Sunday 2.00pm–4.00pm.

COST Children 60p; adults £1.20.

DISABLED FACILITIES Yes, but display upstairs. Public/adapted toilets are 80 metres from Abbey.

Ardeonaig Outdoor Centre
- Mrs Rachel MacDonald
- By Killin, Perthshire. FK21 8SY
- 0567 820523 FAX 0567 820523

A residential outdoor centre providing high-quality and safe outdoor adventurous activities. Fully equipped and staffed to ensure a fun and varied learning experience for a wide range of pupils.

N C SUPPORT Outdoor adventurous activities are included in the PE guidelines. Personal and social education is inherent through the residential experience and small group work used for pupils of all ages and abilities.

VISITS OUT
SCOTLAND

OPENING January to November.

CATERING Fully catered.

COST Phone administrator for details.

DISABLED FACILITIES None.

DIRECTIONS Forty-five miles north of Stirling on the south side of Loch Tay.

Ardfern Riding Centre
- Nigel Boase
- Craobh Haven, By Lochgilphead, Argyll. PA31 8QR
- 08525 270

Stables and 3,000-acre West Highland coastal estate. Appaloosa horses a speciality, western riding, long distance and national methods of learning.

Belongs to British Horse Society (BHS), Riding for the Disabled Association (RDA), Western Equestrian Society (WES). Takes a few working pupils at any time.

ANNUAL OR ONE OFF EVENT Western riding clinic and show in June.

OPENING All year: 9.00am–5.00pm. Summer: closed Saturday.

CATERING The Centre staff can give advice on accommodation and help with bookings.

COST Group discount of 10%. Brochure available.

DISABLED FACILITIES None. But riding is provided for disabled groups.

DIRECTIONS Turn off A816 at Craobh Haven sign 16 miles north of Lochgilphead, 22 miles south of Oban.

Ayrshire Equitation Centre
- Kevin Galbraith
- Hillfoot Road, Ayr. KA7 3LW
- 0292 266267 FAX 0292 610323

A large riding centre with a great variety of horses and ponies to suit the needs of the beginner or experienced rider. Excellent places to ride ranging from a beach to the country park.

OPENING All year round.

COST £7.00 per person per hour, plus 50p hat hire. Group reduction: less 50p hat hire per person.

DIRECTIONS One and a half miles from the town centre, in the Castlehill Gait/Hillfoot area.

Barcaple Christian Outdoor Pursuits Centre
- David Grout
- Ringford, Castle Douglas, Kirkcudbrightshire. DG7 2AP
- 0557 22261

Residential outdoor centre catering for all types of groups including the disabled. Qualified staff. BCV-approved centre.

N C SUPPORT Physical education. Environmental awareness.

OPENING All year round.

CATERING All food provided.

COST School groups start at £45 per person.

DISABLED FACILITIES Yes. RNIB-approved centre.

DIRECTIONS Half a mile from A75 Euroroute.

Barrie's Birthplace

- Mrs Karen Gilmour
- 9 Brechin Road, Kirriemuir, Angus. DD8 4BX
- 0575 72646

Two-storey house where J M Barrie was born. Contains important documents and artefacts belonging to the author. The adjacent house contains an exhibition on literary and theatrical works. The outside washhouse was his first theatre.

OPENING 1 May to 30 September: Monday to Saturday 11.00am–5.30pm, Sunday 1.30pm–5.30pm (last admission 5.00pm). Also Easter weekend and weekends in early October.

COST Children 90p, adults £1.80, Senior Citizens 90p. Party rates (20 or more paying visitors): children 70p, adults £1.40, Senior Citizens 70p (parties must book in advance).

DISABLED FACILITIES Chair-lift to upper floor.

DIRECTIONS Six miles northwest of Forfar.

Bibleworld

- David Cochrane
- 7 Hampton Terrace, Nr Haymarket, Edinburgh. EH12 5XU
- 031-337 9701 FAX 031-337 0641

Two-hour 'hands-on' experience for P4–S2. Spaceship, computers, printing, dressing up and lots more. Booking essential. Free follow-up pack with photocopiable worksheets.

N C SUPPORT 5–14 Curriculum: Religions and Moral Education; sacred writings (Christianity) can also be used within projects on language development, communications and computers.

OPENING By prior arrangement; for groups only (no public access).

CATERING None.

COST £3.00 basic plus 75p per person.

DISABLED FACILITIES None.

DIRECTIONS On main road to Glasgow from city centre, half a mile west of Haymarket; Church building.

Biggar Little Theatre *see* Purves Puppets

Blackness Castle

- The Head Custodian
- Blackness, Nr Linlithgow, Fife
- 0506 834807

Built in the 1440s, and massively strengthened in the 16th century as an artillery fortress, Blackness became an ammunition depot in the 1870s. It was restored by the Office of Works in the 1920s.

OPENING Summer (1 April to 30 September): Monday to Saturday 9.30am–6.00pm, Sunday 2.00pm–6.00pm. Winter: Monday to Wednesday and Saturday 9.30am–4.00pm, Sunday 2.00pm–4.00pm, closed Thursday pm and Friday.

DISABLED FACILITIES None: stairs to climb.

DIRECTIONS Four miles north of Linlithgow, on a promontory in the Forth estuary.

VISITS OUT
SCOTLAND

Blair Castle
- Brian H Nodes
- Blair Atholl, Pitlochry, Perthshire. PH18 5TL
- 0796 481207 FAX 0796 481487

Home of the Duke of Atholl. Visitors can see 32 rooms displaying beautiful collections of furniture, paintings, arms and armour, china, lace and embroidery, children's games and other unique treasures.

N C SUPPORT None.

OPENING 31 March 1994 to 28 October: daily 10.00am–6.00pm (last admission 5.00pm).

COST Students/children £3.50. Group rate: £3.10 per person, including accompanying teacher.

DISABLED FACILITIES Toilets. Twelve rooms on ground floor accessible to wheelchairs.

DIRECTIONS Well-signposted off A9 trunk road, seven miles northwest of Pitlochry, in the village of Blair Atholl.

Bonawe Iron Works
- The Head Custodian
- c/o Area Office, Stirling Castle, Stirling. FK8 1EJ
- 031-244 3101

Founded in 1753 by a Lake District partnership, this is the most complete charcoal-fuelled ironworks in Britain. Displays illustrate how iron was made here.

OPENING 1 April–30 September: Monday to Saturday 9.30am–6.30pm, Sunday 2.00pm–6.30pm. Closed all winter.

DISABLED FACILITIES None: fairly steep climb, although negotiable with assistance.

DIRECTIONS Close to the village of Taynuilt.

Bo'ness & Kinneil Railway
- David Morrison
- 99 Greenbank Road, Union Street, Edinburgh. EH10 5RT
- 031-447 1433

Working steam railway with relocated railway buildings and Scotland's largest collection of locomotives, carriages and wagons. Steam service to Birkhill for a guided tour of a Fireclay Mine.

N C SUPPORT Schools' pack available, covering Scottish railway history, technology; worksheets.

OPENING On application.

CATERING Facilities for packed lunches.

COST Discount of 10% for groups, special rate for schools includes education pack. Ring to request price list.

DISABLED FACILITIES Limited, mine not suitable for disabled.

DIRECTIONS Off the M9, junction 3 northbound, junction 5 southbound.

Boreland Riding Centre
- Miss Fiona Menzies
- Fearnan, Aberfeldy, Perthshire. PH15 2PG
- 0887 830212 FAX 0887 830606

Riding and trekking centre. Instruction to advanced level.

OPENING Daily 10.00am–5.30pm.

CATERING None.

COST Groups: one-hour ride: £7.00 per person. Two-hour ride: £11.00 per person.

DISABLED FACILITIES No special facilities, but horses are available for riders with disabilities.

DIRECTIONS Nine miles west of Aberfeldy on A827 Killin Road, in village of Fearnan.

Bothwell Castle
- The Chief Custodian
- Bothwell, G71 6HD
- 0698 816894

The largest and finest 13th-century stone castle in Scotland, much fought over during the Wars of Independence. Part of the original circular keep survives, but most of the castle dates from the 14th and 15th centuries.

OPENING Summer: daily 9.30am–5.15pm (last admission). Winter: Monday to Thursday and Saturday 9.30am–4.00pm, Sunday 2.00pm–4.00pm, closed Thursday pm.

COST Children 80p; adults £1.50.

DISABLED FACILITIES Apply to the Custodian for access details.

DIRECTIONS In Bothwell, but approached from Uddingston.

Brass Rubbing Centre
- Sandra Marwick
- Chalmers Close, High Street, Edinburgh. EH1 1SS
- 031-556 4364

The building is a remnant of a medieval church. It houses a collection of replicas moulded from ancient Pictish stones and Scottish and medieval church brasses from which rubbings can be made.

N C SUPPORT Brass rubbing kits, booklets, postcards.

OPENING Monday to Saturday 10.00am–6.00pm (closes 5.00pm October to May).

COST Admission free, small charge per rubbing.

DIRECTIONS Chalmers Close is off the Royal Mile, in the centre of Edinburgh.

Robert Burns Centre
- Susan Kee
- Mill Road, Dumfries. DG2 7BE
- 0357 64808

A newly developed Visitors' Centre focusing on Robert Burns and his life in Dumfries. Exhibitions and models, audio-visual presentations, bookshop and cafe.

OPENING April to September: Monday to Saturday 10.00am–8.00pm, Sunday 2.00pm–5.00pm. October to March: Tuesday to Saturday 10.00am–1.00pm and 2.00pm–5.00pm.

COST Admission free. Charge for audio-visual presentations 35p (20% discount on parties of 15 or more).

DISABLED FACILITIES Chair-lift to exhibitions, induction loop in auditorium, adapted toilets.

DIRECTIONS In the town of Dumfries, on the west of River Nith.

Burns Cottage
- J Manson, Curator
- Alloway, Ayrshire. KA7 4PY
- 0292 441215

SCOTLAND

Birthplace of Robert Burns (1759–96), Scotland's national poet. The adjacent Museum contains many relics and manuscripts of the poet.

N C SUPPORT Worksheets available for primary schools. Talks given.

OPENING All year round. Summer and spring: daily 9.00am–6.00pm. Winter and autumn: daily 10.00am–4.00pm.

COST Children and accompanying teachers £1.20.

DISABLED FACILITIES Yes.

DIRECTIONS Two miles south of Ayr (off A77).

The Burrell Collection
- Linda Simi
- Pollok Country Park, 2060 Pollokshaws Road, Glasgow. G43 1AT
- 041-649 7151

The Burrell Collection was amassed by Sir William Burrell and presented to the City of Glasgow in 1944.

N C SUPPORT Through the Museum Education Service, opportunities for investigation and creative activity within Strathclyde Region Museums can be arranged. The 5–14 guidelines recommend the use of museums as a primary source. Development plans for secondary projects using local studies, gallery and archive resources can be networked by the MES to areas of specific needs for both gifted and less able students.

ANNUAL OR ONE OFF EVENT Events include concerts, lectures, touring exhibitions and workshops.

OPENING Monday to Saturday 10.00am–5.00pm, Sunday 11.00am–5.00pm.

COST Free; parking fee £7.50 per coach and 80p per car (Parks Dept).

DISABLED FACILITIES Access; toilets; lifts to all floors.

DIRECTIONS Bus: for city centre to Pollokshaws Road entrance of the park about 25 minutes' walk from the Gallery. Public transport in the Park to the collection and Pollok House. BR: regular service from Glasgow Central to Pollokshaws West or Shawlands station.

Butlins Wonderwest World
- Mary Martin, Training Manager
- Dunure Road, Ayr. KA7 4LB
- 0292 265141 FAX 0292 445206

Seasonal holiday business offering a wide range of leisure activities, including wondersplash, musical arts, amusement park with over 20 mechanical rides, sporting facilities, etc.

OPENING March to October: daily.

COST £2.50 per person, one teacher free for every ten pupils.

DISABLED FACILITIES Toilets. Ramp access to some venues. Special accommodation units.

DIRECTIONS From Ayr, follow A77 south towards Maybole, then follow signs to Wonderwest World.

Caerlaverock Castle
- The Head Custodian
- Glencaple Road, Dumfries. DG1 4RU
- 0387 77244

One of the finest castles in Scotland, on a triangular site surrounded by moats. Its most remarkable features are the twin-towered gatehouse and the Nithsdale Lodging, a splendid Renaissance range dating from 1638.

OPENING Summer hours (1 April to 30 September): Monday to Saturday 9.30am–6.00pm (last admission), Sunday 2.00pm–6.00pm (last admission). Monuments close at 6.30pm. Winter hours (1 October to 31 March): Monday to Saturday 9.30am–4.00pm (last admission), Sunday 2.00pm–4.00pm (last admission). For further information ring 031-244 3101.

DISABLED FACILITIES Yes. Toilets, but not adapted.

DIRECTIONS Eight miles southeast of Dumfries.

Camera Obscura
- Andrew Johnson
- Castlehill, Royal Mile, Edinburgh. EH1 2LZ
- 031-226 3709 FAX 031-225 4239

Step inside a giant 140-year-old camera for a unique live, moving panorama of Edinburgh. The guide reveals all with humour and enthusiasm. Also fascinating exhibitions on pinhole photography, old Edinburgh and international holography.

N C SUPPORT Open to suggestions.

OPENING All year round. April to October: daily 9.30am–6.00pm. November to March: daily 10.00am–5.00pm.

COST Children of 5–15 years £1.50, children of 16–18 years £2.30.

Group rates: children of 5–15 years £1.15, children of 16–18 years £1.85.

DISABLED FACILITIES None.

DIRECTIONS At the top of the Royal Mile, next to Edinburgh Castle.

CARBERRY TOWER
031 665 3488

Nine miles from Edinburgh, just off the motorway. Easy access to the city, to Glasgow, Stirling, fife and Borders. Castle and conference centre with lovely and safe grounds.

Widely used and commended by schools & churches

Carberry Tower
- Jock Stein
- Musselburgh. EH21 8PY
- 031-665 3135 FAX 031-653 2930

Historic castle and conference centre in lovely grounds near Edinburgh. Ideal base for school educational holidays.

ANNUAL OR ONE OFF EVENT Residential Duke of Edinburgh award course in June.

VISITS OUT
SCOTLAND

OPENING All year.

COST Secondary pupils £15.10 per day mid-week full board, adults £19.20.

DISABLED FACILITIES Limited facilities.

DIRECTIONS On A6124 two miles south of Musselburgh, just off A1.

Andrew Carnegie Birthplace Museum
- Derrick Barclay
- Moodie Street, Dunfermline, Fife. KY12 7PL
- 0383 724302

The Museum tells the story of Andrew Carnegie, the weaver's son who became 'King Steel' in America and gave away his huge fortune.

N C SUPPORT Guided tours and worksheets available for class visits. Enquiries from secondary school pupils are dealt with individually by the Custodian. Classroom available.

ANNUAL OR ONE OFF EVENT Weaving Days demonstrating Jacquard handloom held first Friday of every month from May to October.

OPENING November to March: daily 2.00pm–4.00pm. April to October: Monday to Saturday 11.00am–5.00pm, Sunday 2.00pm–5.00pm. Visits can be arranged outside of these hours.

CATERING No, but a classroom can be made available for groups wishing to eat packed lunches.

COST Free.

DISABLED FACILITIES Toilet. Ramp to entrance and Memorial Hall, cottage inaccessible.

DIRECTIONS Two hundred metres south of Dunfermline Abbey. The Museum is on the corner of Priory Lane and Moodie Street.

Castle Campbell
- The Head Custodian
- Dollar, Clackmannanshire. FK14 7PP
- 0259 7424408

Traditionally known as the 'Castle of Gloom'. The oldest part is a well-preserved 15th-century tower, around which other buildings were constructed, including an unusual loggia.

OPENING Summer (1 April–30 September): Monday to Saturday 9.30am–6.30pm, Sunday 2.00pm–6.30pm. Winter (1 October–31 March): Monday to Thursday and Saturday 9.30am–4.30pm, Sunday 2.00pm–4.30pm (closed Thursday pm).

DISABLED FACILITIES None: steep hill, cobbles and stairs.

DIRECTIONS At the head of Dollar Glen.

Castle Jail and Museum
- Rosi Capper
- The Castlegate, Jedburgh, Roxburghshire. TD8 6QD
- 0835 863254 FAX 0450 78526

Standing on the original site of the medieval castle, the Castle Jail, built in 1820, reflects prison life in the 19th century and the history of the Royal Burgh of Jedburgh.

N C SUPPORT Part-time education officer offers school workshops, loan kits, handling sessions, etc. Archives open for investigative learning visits.

VISITS OUT
SCOTLAND

OPENING Easter to end October: Monday to Saturday 10.00am–5.00pm, Sunday 1.00pm–5.00pm.

COST Free to schools in the Borders region. Otherwise: children 40p, adults 80p, concessions 40p, 5% discount for parties of 20 or more.

DISABLED FACILITIES Difficult for wheelchairs, although grounds and ground floor have ramps.

DIRECTIONS Quarter of a mile from the Town Square, going south out of the town.

Craigmillar Castle
- The Head Custodian
- Castle Cottage, Castle Road, Edinburgh
- 031-661 4445

Built round an L-plan tower house of the early 15th century, Craigmillar was much expanded in the 15th and 16th centuries. It is a handsome ruin, and includes a range of private rooms.

OPENING Summer (1 April to 30 September): Monday to Saturday 9.30am–6.00pm, Sunday 2.00pm–6.00pm. Winter: Monday to Thursday and Saturday 9.30am–4.00pm, Sunday 2.00pm–4.00pm, closed Thursday pm.

COST Children 60p; adults £1.20.

DISABLED FACILITIES Grounds accessible, but not interior of castle. Adapted toilets.

DIRECTIONS Two and a half miles southeast of central Edinburgh, to east of Edinburgh to Dalkeith road.

Culzean Castle & Country Park
- Gordon Riddle
- Visitor Centre, Maybole, Ayrshire. KA19 8LE
- 0655 6269 FAX 0655 6615

Heritage site: 30 programmes offered to both primary and secondary schools. Teaching staff: rangers, castle guides, education supervisor.

N C SUPPORT Programmes campatible with standard grade and higher courses. Schools' information sheets. Assistance given to SYS students in project work.

OPENING All year round. Pre-booking essential. Facilities close between November and March but can be opened on request.

COST Booking form with current prices available from the Reservations Secretary.

DISABLED FACILITIES Ramps. Unisex toilets. Tapes and disability sheet available. Wheelchairs available.

DIRECTIONS Culzean is off the A719, four miles west of Maybole and 12 miles south of Ayr.

Dean Castle Country Park
- Mr J Hunter
- Dean Road, Kilmarnock. KA3 1XB
- 0563 22702 FAX 0563 29661

Ancient home of the Boyd family with splendid collections of arms and armour and early musical instruments. Displays also show everyday life, family history and life and works. Guided tours.

OPENING Grounds: dawn to dusk. Castle 12.00 noon–5.00pm. School

VISITS OUT
SCOTLAND

groups must book and are generally put through in the morning.

CATERING Tea room.

COST Children £1.00, two adults free for every 30 children, other adults on school visits £1.00.

DISABLED FACILITIES Toilets. Access to tea room. Limited access to shop and castle.

DIRECTIONS The Castle is entered from Dean Road, one mile north of Kilmarnock town centre, off Glasgow Road. It is signposted from the north side of Kilmarnock for both north- and southbound traffic on the A77 (Glasgow to Ayr road).

Dick Institute
- Mr J Hunter
- Elmbank Avenue, Kilmarnock. KA1 3BU
- 0563 26401 FAX 0563 29661

The Art Gallery contains an important collection of paintings and hosts a wide variety of touring exhibitions. The Museum has collections on geology, natural history, engineering, archaeology and local history.

OPENING Monday, Tuesday, Thursday and Friday 10.00am–8.00pm, Wednesday and Saturday 10.00am–5.00pm.

COST Free. There may be charges for special exhibitions.

DISABLED FACILITIES Access for disabled people. Lift to upper floor.

DIRECTIONS Off London Road. Near town centre.

Dirleton Castle
- The Head Custodian
- Dirleton, East Lothian
- 0620 85330

The oldest part of this romantic castle dates from the 13th century. It was rebuilt in the 14th century and extended in the 16th century. Beside the castle lie the gardens, first established in the late 16th century.

OPENING Summer (1 April to 30 September): Monday to Saturday 9.30am–6.30pm, Sunday 2.00pm–6.30pm. Winter (1 October to 31 March): Monday to Saturday 9.30am–4.30pm, Sunday 2.00pm–4.30pm.

DISABLED FACILITIES Access to grounds only.

Dryburgh Abbey
- The Head Custodian
- Dryburgh, St Boswells, Roxburghshire. TD6 0RQ
- 0835 22381

Both beautifully situated and of intrinsic quality, the ruins of Dryburgh Abbey are remarkably complete. Much of the work is of the 12th and 13th centuries. Sir Walter Scott and Field Marshal Earl Haig are buried in the Abbey.

OPENING Summer (1 April to 30 September): Monday to Saturday 9.30am–6.00pm, Sunday 2.00pm–6.00pm. Winter: Monday to Saturday 9.30am–4.00pm, Sunday 2.00pm–4.00pm.

DISABLED FACILITIES Stairs; facilities are limited in the Abbey.

DIRECTIONS Five miles southeast of Melrose, near St Boswells.

SCOTLAND

Dumfries Archive Centre
- Miss M M Stewart, Archivist
- 33 Burns Street, Dumfries. DG1 2PS
- 0387 69254

Holds records of Dumfries and area of 16th–20th century, including those regarding crime, poverty and local affairs of every kind. Small visiting parties only. Talks given if possible.

N C SUPPORT Records made available to pupils and/or teachers for study in archive centre. Help with reading and interpreting material given by archivist.

OPENING Tuesday, Wednesday and Friday 11.00am–1.00pm and 2.00pm–5.00pm, Thursday 6.00pm–9.00pm only. Booking essential.

COST Free. Any xeroxes required normally charged at 25p per sheet.

DISABLED FACILITIES Entry at ground level with one small doorstep.

DIRECTIONS In Dumfries, opposite poet Robert Burns' house. Archive centre is well signposted.

Dumfries Museum
- Siobhan Ratchford
- The Observatory, Dumfries. DG2 7SW
- 0387 53374 FAX 0387 65081

Museum collections covering the natural and human history of southwest Scotland; camera obscura.

N C SUPPORT No education officer at present, but teachers are offered familiarisation visits and use of schools' loan material. One-to-one support for research projects from relevant museum staff.

ANNUAL OR ONE OFF EVENT Lively programme of temporary exhibitions.

OPENING Monday to Saturday 10.00am–1.00pm and 2.00pm–5.00pm, Sunday 2.00pm–5.00pm. October to March: closed Sunday and Monday.

COST Museum: free. Camera obscura: 35p (free to schools from Dumfries and Galloway region).

DISABLED FACILITIES Lift to exhibition galleries. Toilets.

DIRECTIONS In the town of Dumfries, on the west of River Nith.

Dunbar Underground
- Rachel Woods
- Old Town House, High Street, Dunbar.

'Hands-on' introduction to archaeology and changing local history exhibitions.

N C SUPPORT Welcomes groups by prior arrangement. Material can be shown on request. Research work can be done by students.

OPENING Monday to Sunday 2.00pm–4.30pm.

COST Free.

DISABLED FACILITIES Limited access to part of the Museum (local history).

Dundee Art Galleries & Museums
- Mrs Nancy Davey
- McManus Galleries, Albert Square, Dundee. DD1 1DA
- 0382 23141 Ext(133)(65) FAX 0382 27621

Regular introductory talks, handling sessions especially on local and natural history. Planned activity time for teachers can be arranged. Loans.

N C SUPPORT Help with 5–14 guidelines and standard grade for pupils and teachers. Individual help with relevant topics.

OPENING Monday to Saturday 10.00am–5.00pm at McManus and Barrack Street Museum. Broughty Castle is closed on Friday.

COST Free. Out-of-town schools pay for teachers' packs.

DISABLED FACILITIES Only at McManus Galleries.

DIRECTIONS Can be given when booking.

Dunfermline Abbey & Palace
- The Head Custodian
- Dunfermline
- 0383 739026

The remains of a great Benedictine abbey founded by Queen Margaret in the 11th century. The foundations of her church are under the superb nave, built in the 12th century in the romanesque style. Robert the Bruce was buried in the choir, now the site of the present parish church.

OPENING Summer (1 April to 30 September): Monday to Saturday 9.30am–6.00pm, Sunday 2.00pm–6.00pm. Winter (1 October to 31 March): Monday to Thursday and Saturday 9.30am–4.00pm, Sunday 2.00pm–4.00pm, closed Thursday pm.

DISABLED FACILITIES Steep stairs restrict viewing. Access to Abbey nave and church.

Edinburgh Butterfly & Insect World
- Gordon Spiers
- Melville Nursery, Lasswade, Midlothian. EH18 1AZ
- 031-663 4932 FAX 031-654 2548

Children can walk through the wonderful world of a tropical rainforest and enjoy the unique pleasure of watching hundreds of the world's most spectacular and colourful butterflies.

N C SUPPORT The educational programme is closely tied in to the school curriculum and covers such topics as minibeasts, rainforests, colour and camouflage. Several projects have been devised for sixth-form studies.

OPENING On application.

COST £1.65.

DISABLED FACILITIES Wheelchair access to all areas.

DIRECTIONS South of Edinburgh on A7 main road to Galashiels, 300m south of the city by-pass. In Dobbies Gardening World.

Edinburgh Castle
- Visitor Services Supervisor
- Crown Square, Edinburgh. EH21 2NG
- 031-225 9846

This most famous of Scottish castles has a complex history. The oldest part dates from the Norman period; there is a Great Hall built by James IV; the Half Moon Battery was built by the Regent Morton in the late 16th century; the Scottish National War Memorial was formed after World War I. The castle houses the crown jewels (Honours) of

Scotland and the famous 15th-century gun Mons Meg.

OPENING Summer: daily 9.30am–5.15pm (last admission). Winter: daily 9.30am–4.15pm (last admission).

COST Children £1.00; adults £4.

DISABLED FACILITIES Yes, with limitation on access to apartments. Disabled vehicle access permitted. Toilets, but only one adapted.

Fort George
- The Head Custodian
- Ardersier, Inverness. JV1 2TP
- 0667 62777

A vast site and one of the most outstanding artillery fortifications in Europe. It was planned in 1747 as a base for George II's army, and was completed in 1769. Since then it has served as a barracks. There are reconstructions of barrack rooms in different periods and a display of muskets and pikes.

OPENING Summer (1 April to 30 September): Monday to Saturday 9.30am–6.00pm, Sunday 2.00pm–6.00pm. Winter (1 October to 31 March): Monday to Saturday 9.30am–4.00pm, Sunday 2.00pm–4.00pm.

COST Children £1.20; adults £2.30.

DISABLED FACILITIES Yes, but not on ramparts. Adapted toilet.

DIRECTIONS Eleven miles northeast of Inverness, by the village of Ardersier.

FRIENDS OF HISTORIC SCOTLAND

National Curriculum Support
Teaching Notes are available, giving details of the site and how to get there, and the history of the building, facilities for school parties, bibliography, plans and drawings, information panels on the site and additional source material.

Cost For further details regarding eligibility and booking of free educational visits to monuments, telephone 031-244 3087.

See individual entries for all other information.

Aberdour Castle
Arbroath Abbey
Blackness Castle
Bonawe Iron Works
Bothwell Castle
Caerlaverock Castle
Castle Campbell
Craigmillar Castle
Dirleton Castle
Dryburgh Abbey
Dunfermline Abbey & Palace
Edinburgh Castle
Fort George
Historic Scotland
Jedburgh Abbey Visitor Centre
Linlithgow Palace
Melrose Abbey Visitor Centre
New Abbey Cornmill
St Andrews Castle and Visitor Centre
Skara Brae
Smailholm Tower
Stirling Castle
Sweetheart Abbey
Tantallon Castle
Urquhart Castle

Galloway Sailing Centre
- Roddy Hermon
- Loch Ken, Castle Douglas, Kirkcudbrightshire. DG7 3NQ
- 06442 626 FAX 06442 626

SCOTLAND

Beautifully situated sailing centre, recognised by the Royal Yachting Association for dinghy sailing and windsurfing. Special adventure courses for school groups, boats for hire, launching for visitors' boats.

N C SUPPORT RYA recognised for dinghy levels 1–4. RYA-recognised for windsurfing levels 1 and 2. May be linked with Duke of Edinburgh Awards.

ANNUAL OR ONE OFF EVENT Junior race training week (camping with full evening programme).

OPENING Easter to end October: daily 10.00am–5.00pm (except adventure and training camps).

CATERING Normal cafe service daily. Full catering for groups if required. Meals in clubhouse.

COST Individual from £15.00–£115.00. Group discounts vary (up to 35%).

DISABLED FACILITIES For people who are partially disabled, e.g. toilets, ramp for wheelchairs. No special facility on the water.

DIRECTIONS Follow A75 from Dumfries/Stranraer. Turn off Castle Douglas by-pass on to A713, Ayr road. Two miles through Parton on left.

Glasgow Zoo

- Dr Stephen Bostock, Education Officer
- Uddingston, Glasgow. G71 7RZ
- 041-771 1185 FAX 041-771 2615

Wildlife garden, including facilities for pond dipping.

N C SUPPORT Talks available at Zoo. Range of worksheets and information sheets.

OPENING Daily 10.00am–5.00pm

COST Free entry to Zoo for Strathclyde region schools (phone Zoo for permit arrangements). Party rate for other schools: 25% discount on normal entry.

DISABLED FACILITIES Suitable for wheelchairs. Toilet.

DIRECTIONS M8 from Glasgow or Edinburgh. M74 from Hamilton and South. Follow motorway signs for 'Zoo Park'.

Gorgie City Farm

- Malcolm Bruce
- 51 Gorgie Road, Edinburgh. EH11 2LA
- 031-337 4202

One-hectare site with wide range of farm life and domestic animals; large organic garden; wildlife and herb gardens; cafe; education centre.

N C SUPPORT Learning materials based on 5–14 Curriculum, particularly Environmental Studies.

ANNUAL OR ONE OFF EVENT Regular open days.

OPENING Monday to Sunday 9.30am–4.30pm.

COST Admission free. Tours 50p per person. Other support negotiable.

DISABLED FACILITIES Toilets. Access to all parts including cafe.

DIRECTIONS A71 to Kilmarnock. One and a half miles from city centre.

VISITS OUT
SCOTLAND

Craig Gowar Riding Centre
- Robert Duncan
- Main Street, Fettercairs, Kincardineshire. AB30 1XX
- 0561 340498

Riding centre in the heart of Mearns countryside and providing riding and tuition for all ages and standards, children's fun weeks, youth holidays and courses. Most other sports and activities available locally; indoor school.

Field trips (day basis) of riding and stable management, horse-shoeing demonstrations: weekly riding courses. Accommodation: camping/caravan, bed and breakfast and hotel.

OPENING All year round.

CATERING Full packages in local hotel and local restaurants.

COST Riding tuition: £10-£15.00 per hour. Six nights' accommodation and five days riding including meals (up to 20 years): £285.00. Group discounts available.

DISABLED FACILITIES People with disabilities catered for.

DIRECTIONS A94 Dundee to Aberdeen, branch left above Brechin on to B966, signposted Edsell/Fettercairs Riding Centre, through arch in Fettercairs, first lane on left.

Hamilton District Museum
- Joyce J R Brown
- 129 Muir Street, Hamilton, Lanarkshire. ML3 6BJ
- 0698 233981 FAX 0698 283479

Local history museum housed in a 17th-century coaching inn with restored stable and assembly room with Musicians' Gallery. Displays include reconstructed Victorian kitchen; transport, costume, local industries, etc.

N C SUPPORT Worksheets, factsheets and resource packs available to assist with projects, investigations, etc.

ANNUAL OR ONE OFF EVENT Regular temporary exhibition programme.

OPENING Monday to Saturday 10.00am-5.00pm (closed 12.00 noon-1.00pm Wednesday and Saturday).

COST Free.

DISABLED FACILITIES None.

Hawick Museum & Art Gallery
- Rosi Capper
- Wilton Lodge Park, Hawick, Roxburghshire. TD9 7JL
- 0450 73457 FAX 0450 78526

A local history museum reflecting life in this Borders town. Home of the internationally renowned knitwear industry; displays include textile manufacture and domestic life. The Art Gallery has 19th- and 20th-century Scottish paintings and temporary exhibitions.

N C SUPPORT Part-time education officer offers school workshops, loan kits, handling sessions, etc. Archives open for investigative learning visits.

OPENING Summer: Monday to Saturday 10.00am-12.00 noon and 1.00pm-5.00pm, Sunday 2.00pm-5.00pm. Winter: Monday to Friday 1.00pm-4.00pm, Sunday 2.00pm-4.00pm.

SCOTLAND

COST Free to schools in the Borders region. Otherwise: children 40p, adults 80p concessions 40p, 5% discount to parties of 20 or more.

DISABLED FACILITIES Access to ground floor only for wheelchairs. Garden for the blind next door to the museum.

DIRECTIONS Three-quarters of a mile from the High Street heading southwest.

Highland Riding Centre
- A D MacDonald-Haig
- Borlum Farm Country Holidays, Drumnadrochit, Inverness-shire. IV3 6XN
- 0456 850358

Borlum is a historic farm dating back to its service to Urquhart Castle in the 16th century, providing castle inmates and retainers with the necessary sustaining provisions. Visitors can take part in some of the aspects of farming life: caring for lambs, bringing in ponies, helping the farrier, dipping the sheep, haymaking, or searching for eggs laid by the unruly hens.

N C SUPPORT Borlum Bay woods are a Nature Conservancy Site for rare woodland, bog plants and wildlife.

OPENING All year round.

CATERING Ranges from self-catering cottages to farmhouse accommodation with full Scottish breakfast.

COST Prices vary according to the type of accommodation and the seasons. Details on request.

DISABLED FACILITIES Centre for the Riding for the Disabled Association (Highland Group). The indoor school has ramps and mounting facilities for wheelchairs. The toilet facilities are suitable for disabled people with wheelchairs.

DIRECTIONS Half a mile from Castle Urquhart on the A82 by the shores of Loch Ness.

Historic Scotland
- Mrs M Fry, Education Officer
- 20 Brandon Street, Edinburgh. EH3 5RA
- 031-244 5996 FAX 031-244 3030

Historic Scotland is an executive agency of the Secretary of State for Scotland responsible for safeguarding Scotland's built heritage for future generations and presenting it to the public. Properties in care include Edinburgh Castle, Fort George, Stirling Castle and Jedburgh Abbey.

OPENING In summer (1 April to 30 September): 9.30am–6.30pm. Many monuments are closed in winter. For details telephone 031-244 3101.

CATERING Depends on site.

DISABLED FACILITIES Contact the Education Officer for access details.

DIRECTIONS Contact the Education Officer.

Hunterston Power Station and Tornes Power Station
see Scottish Nuclear

SCOTLAND

Inveralligin Field Centre
- Jeremy Robertson
- Inveralligin, Loch Torridon, Wester Ross. IV22 2HB
- 0445 791247

Small centre on the seashore in magnificent mountains, specialising in wildlife and environmental studies. Fully equipped with sampling equipment, microscopes, library, seagoing boat, etc. Highly qualified staff, friendly atmosphere.

N C SUPPORT Can design courses in Biology and Environmental Studies.

OPENING All year: usually run one-week holidays (Saturday to Saturday).

CATERING Fully catered with excellent home cooking, using local produce such as venison and salmon. Vegetarians catered for.

COST £265 per person per week. Group discount: 10% for groups of 4–7 people, 15% for groups 8–12 people (max.).

DISABLED FACILITIES None, due to extreme rugged terrain.

DIRECTIONS BR and airport: Inverness. By car: from Inverness via Achnasheen, Kinlochewe and Torridon.

Inveraray Jail
- Jim Linley
- Inverary, Argyll. PA32 8TX
- 0499 2195 FAX 0499 2381

Scotland's living 19th-century prison. Costumed prisoners and warders, life-like figures, imaginative exhibitions, sounds, smells and trials in progress all bring the former county prison of Argyll back to life.

OPENING All year round. April to October: daily 9.30am–6.00pm (last admission 5.00pm). November to March: daily 10.00am–5.00pm (last admission 4.00pm).

COST Pupils £1.60, supervisors £2.85. One supervisor/teacher free for every ten children.

DISABLED FACILITIES Not all areas are suitable for wheelchair access, only the ground floor of the courthouse and prisons. Toilet: cubicle door width 63cm, door closes with wheelchair inside; cubicle with grab rails, door width 92cm; female, level access entrance door, width 80cm, door does not close with chair in.

DIRECTIONS Situated on A83, Glasgow to Cambeltown road.

Jedburgh Abbey Visitor Centre
- The Head Custodian
- 4–5 Abbey Bridge Road, Jedburgh. TD8 6JQ
- 0835 63925

One of the border abbeys founded for Augustinian canons by David I and the Bishop of Glasgow in around 1138. The church is mostly in the Romanesque and early Gothic styles, and is remarkably complete.

OPENING Summer (1 April to 30 September): Monday to Saturday 9.30am–6.00pm, Sunday 2.00pm–6.00pm. Winter (1 October to 31 March): Monday to Saturday 9.30am–4.00pm, Sunday 2.00pm–4.00pm.

Jonah's Journey
- Rev. David Graham
- Rosemount Celebration Centre, 120 Rosemount Place, Aberdeen. AB2 4YW
- 0224 647614

Activity-based learning centre: experience life in biblical times or Third World today. Choice of 30 topics, e.g. houses, clothes, water.

N C SUPPORT Includes elements specified in the SED National Guidelines 5–14 in Religious and Moral Education and Environmental Studies.

ANNUAL OR ONE OFF EVENT Christmas/Easter dramatisations throughout December and March.

OPENING Monday to Friday 10.00am–4.00pm. Phone for reservation and to give details of the topic required.

COST School groups: children £1.00, includes worksheets for follow-up lessons.

DISABLED FACILITIES Unfortunately no wheelchair access as the Centre is in an upstairs gallery with no lift.

DIRECTIONS Within one mile of the city centre on bus routes 13 and 22.

Kelso Museum & Turret Gallery
- Rosi Capper
- Turret House, Abbey Court, Kelso, Roxburghshire. TD5 7JA
- 0573 225470

Housed in one of Kelso's oldest buildings is the Museum and Art & Craft Gallery; reflecting life in a thriving market town and 19th-century school room, which is used for lessons.

N C SUPPORT Part-time education officer offers school workshops, loan kits, handling sessions, etc. Archives open for investigative learning visits. 'Hands-on' displays.

OPENING Easter to end October: Monday to Saturday 10.00am–12.00 noon and 1.00pm–5.00pm, Sundays 2.00pm–5.00pm.

COST Free to Borders regional schools. Otherwise: children 40p, adults 80p, concessions 40p, 5% discount for parties of 20 or more.

DISABLED FACILITIES Ramp to entrance but otherwise difficult due to spiral stair.

DIRECTIONS Situated just off Bridge Street, opposite Kelso Abbey.

Landmark Highland Heritage & Adventure Park
- Danny Fullerton
- Carrbridge, Inverness-shire. PH23 3AJ
- 0479 84613 FAX 0479 84384

Many unique and exciting things to see and do. Set in an ancient pinewood are 'The Highlander' multivision show, nature trail and centre, treetop trail, working steam-powered sawmill, heavy horse demonstrations, giant forestry machines, adventure playground and trail, woodland fun maze, shop.

N C SUPPORT Not provided, but the park covers a wide range of subjects including Environmental Studies, Scottish History, Tourism and Leisure.

VISITS OUT
SCOTLAND

OPENING January to March and November to December: daily 9.30am–5.00pm. April to June: daily 9.30am–6.00pm July to August: daily 9.30am–8.00pm. September to October: daily 9.30am–5.30pm.

COST Group rates: children £2.85, one supervising adult free with every ten children.

DISABLED FACILITIES All accessible except Tower and Treetop Trail. Toilets.

DIRECTIONS Just off the A9, 23 miles south of Inverness, seven miles north of Aviemore.

Linlithgow Palace
- The Head Custodian
- Linlithgow, West Lothian. EH49 7AL
- 0506 842896

The magnificent ruin of a great Royal Palace, set in its own park or 'peel'. All the Stewart Kings lived here, and work commissioned by James I, II, IV, V and VI can be seen. The great hall and the chapel are particularly fine. Mary, Queen of Scots, was born here in 1542.

OPENING Summer (1 April to 30 September): Monday to Saturday 9.30am–6.00pm, Sunday 2.00pm–6.00pm. Winter (1 October to 31 March): Monday to Saturday 9.30am–4.00pm, Sunday 2.00pm–4.00pm.

DISABLED FACILITIES Grounds accessible, but the rest is not suitable for wheelchairs as there are too many steps.

Loch Ness Riding Centre
- Candy Cameron
- Drummond, Dores, Inverness-shire. IV1 2TX
- 0463 75251 FAX 0463 75240

Hacking, trekking and tuition for all standards. Superb riding country overlooking Loch Ness. Qualified instruction in indoor/outdoor arenas on well-schooled mounts.

N C SUPPORT Career student training for British Horse Society (BHS) examinations to Stage III/IV.

OPENING All year round: daily except Christmas Day.

CATERING None: self-catering accommodation on site. Bar meals in Dores, all types in Inverness.

COST Group discounts of 10%: one hour £10.00, one and a half hours £13.00, two hours £16.00, three hours £20.00.

DISABLED FACILITIES Toilets and access to gallery in indoor school suitable for wheelchairs.

DIRECTIONS B862 Inverness to Dores. Fork left uphill in Dores and go two miles. Sign on right.

Marischal Museum
- Neil Curtis
- Marischal College, University of Aberdeen, Aberdeen. AB9 1AS
- 0224 273131 FAX 0224 645519

Permanent displays explore the character of the North East and of humanity throughout the world. A series of object-handling workshops is available throughout the year for school groups.

N C SUPPORT The workshops have been designed to relate to the 5–14

National Guidelines and encourage skills in Maths, Language, Environmental Studies, Expressive Arts and other curricular areas.

OPENING Monday to Friday 10.00am–5.00pm, Sunday 2.00pm–5.00pm.

COST Free.

DISABLED FACILITIES None.

Mary Queen of Scots House
- Rosi Capper
- Scots House, Queen Street, Jedburgh, Roxburghshire. TD8 6EN
- 0835 863331 FAX 0450 78526

The house tells the story of the life of Mary Stewart, in particular her visit to Jedburgh in 1566, in a thought-provoking contemporary display.

N C SUPPORT Part-time education officer offers school workshops, loan kits, handling sessions, etc. Archives open for investigative learning visit.

OPENING Easter to mid-November: daily 10.00am–5.00pm.

COST Free to Borders regional schools. Otherwise: children 60p, adults £1.20, concessions 60p, 5% discount for parties of 20 or more.

DISABLED FACILITIES Very difficult for wheelchairs and partially sighted because of spiral staircases.

DIRECTIONS In the centre of town, easily seen from A68.

McLean Museum & Art Gallery
- Judith Rankin
- 15 Kelly Street, Greenock. PA16 8JX
- 0475 23741

Displays on local and industrial history, maritime exhibits, technological models, ethnography displays, big game mounts and Clyde Steamer photographs.

N C SUPPORT Free quiz sheets, colouring sheets; talks/demonstrations provided on request; children's activities during school holidays.

OPENING Monday to Saturday 10.00am–12.00 noon and 1.00pm–5.00pm. Closed local and national public holidays.

CATERING None.

COST Free.

DISABLED FACILITIES Ramped access to ground floor displays.

DIRECTIONS BR: Greenock West, Greenock bus station close by.

Mellerstain Trust
- Mrs F Turnbull
- Mellerstain House, Gordon, Berwickshire. TD3 6LG
- 0573 410225

Scotland's finest Adam mansion with beautiful decorated ceilings in all the main rooms; period furniture and fine art collection.

OPENING Easter weekend four days. 1 May to 30 September: daily (except Saturdays) 12.30pm–5.00pm.

COST Children £1.50, adults £3.50, Senior Citizens £3.00. Groups (minimum 20 persons): children £1.50, adults £3.00.

DISABLED FACILITIES Main floor only.

VISITS OUT
SCOTLAND

DIRECTIONS Seven miles northwest of Kelso on the A6089. From Edinburgh, A68 to Earlston (five miles).

Melrose Abbey Visitor Centre
- The Head Custodian
- Abbey Street, Melrose, Roxburghshire. TD6 9LG
- 0896 822562

Probably the most famous ruin in Scotland, founded around 1136 as a Cistercian abbey by David I, and repeatedly wrecked in the Wars of Independence. The surviving remains of the church date from the 15th century, and are of an elegance unique in Scotland. The Commendator's house contains displays relating to the abbey's history and to the Roman fort at Newstead.

OPENING Summer (1 April to 30 September): Monday to Saturday 9.30am–6.00pm, Sunday 2.00pm–6.00pm. Winter (1 October to 31 March): Monday to Saturday 9.30am–4.00pm, Sunday 2.00pm–4.00pm.

DISABLED FACILITIES Yes. Toilets, but not adapted.

Mills Observatory
- Dr F Vincent
- Balgay Park, Dundee. DD2 2UB
- 0382 67138

Public astronomical observatory. Viewing through large telescope on clear winter evenings. Small planetarium (group visits only). Exhibition area, audio-visual show, etc.

N C SUPPORT Group visits welcome (limit 30; must be pre-booked). Sky viewing if conditions permit. Guided tour; talk with slides or models (topic negotiable); planetarium show, about one and a half hours.

ANNUAL OR ONE OFF EVENT Public talks and planetarium shows approximately once a month.

OPENING Winter (October to March): Monday to Friday 3.00pm–5.00pm, Saturday 2.00pm–5.00pm. Summer (April to September): Monday to Friday 10.00am–5.00pm, Saturday 2.00pm–5.00pm.

COST Free.

DISABLED FACILITIES None.

DIRECTIONS Centre of Dundee along Perth Road and Blackness Avenue and Balgay Road; enter Balgay Park.

Museum of Childhood
- Sandra Marwick
- 42 High Street (Royal Mile), Edinburgh. EH1 1TG
- 031-529 4142 FAX 031-558 3103

Displays on the history of childhood: toys, games, costume, school items, health and welfare, etc.

N C SUPPORT Resource packs published on aspects of the collection (health and hygiene/schooldays, etc.) and available by mail order. Mail-order sales list with other resources/publications available on request.

ANNUAL OR ONE OFF EVENT Regular temporary exhibitions throughout the year.

VISITS OUT
SCOTLAND

OPENING Monday to Saturday 10.00am–5.00pm. Also Sunday 2.00pm–5.00pm during the Edinburgh Festival.

COST Free.

DISABLED FACILITIES Three of the five galleries are accessible by lift. Toilet adapted for visitors with disabilities.

DIRECTIONS Located in the Royal Mile in the centre of Edinburgh.

Museum of Education
- Dorothy Stewart
- Scotland Street School, 225 Scotland Street, Glasgow. G5 8QB
- 041-429 1202 FAX 041-420 3292

Victorian, World War II, 1950s and 1960s classrooms and Edwardian cookery room. Designed by Charles Rennie Mackintosh. Permanent exhibition on history of education in Scotland. Temporary exhibition gallery. Old-fashioned games in the playground.

N C SUPPORT Teaching materials and lesson plans on Victorian and World War II classes. Activity sheets are available from the shop or by mail order, priced £1.00–£8.00.

ANNUAL OR ONE OFF EVENT Frequent weekend and holiday activities for children linked to temporary exhibitions.

OPENING Monday to Saturday 10.00am–5.00pm, Sunday 2.00pm–5.00pm. Closed public holidays.

CATERING Cafe serving coffee, tea, home baking, lunches; catering for seminars and functions.

COST Free.

DISABLED FACILITIES Access currently limited for wheelchairs to ground floor (exhibition gallery, audio-visual cafe). Toilet.

DIRECTIONS The Museum is opposite Shields Road Underground Station. M8 take East Kilbride/Rutherglen turn-off. Follow signposts for Museum.

Museum of Flight
- R J Major
- East Fortune Airfield, North Berwick, East Lothian. EH39 5LF
- 0620 88308 FAX 0620 88355

A fascinating collection of aircraft, rockets, engines and aeronautical memorabilia housed in hangars of a World War II airfield.

N C SUPPORT Worksheets available; project support.

ANNUAL OR ONE OFF EVENT Rallies and demonstrations during the season.

OPENING April to September: 10.30am–4.30pm.

CATERING Shop/cafe.

COST Children £1.00, adults £2.00, Senior Citizens £1.00, family £5.00, schools £5.00.

DISABLED FACILITIES Level site and toilets.

DIRECTIONS Off A4, 1.7 miles on B1347 to North Berwick, signs on A1 and B1347.

Museum of Leadmining
- Mrs J Orr
- Visitor Centre, Wanlockhead, Lanarkshire. ML12 6UT
- 0659 74387

Indoor and open-air museum with mineral displays, working models, audio-visuals and guided tours into lead mine and period cottage. Also outdoor trail with beam engine, historic sites and picnic areas.

N C SUPPORT Ten-page work pack covering historical and geological investigations in conjunction with special pre-booked tours, involving role-playing interaction, group tasks and quizzes. Information sheets, booklets and slide packs aimed at teachers for historical, geological and industrial architecture talks.

OPENING 1 April to 31 October: 11.00am–4.30pm (last guided tour leaves 4.00pm). Winter booking taken November to March.

CATERING Picnic areas.

COST Children £1.25, Adults £2.99, concessions £2.50, family £8.00. Discount of 10% for groups of ten or more.

DISABLED FACILITIES All sites (including the mine) are accessible by wheelchair and ramps. Purpose-built adapted toilet (Radar scheme).

DIRECTIONS Thirty miles north of Dumfries, signposted from the A76 at Mennock and junction 14 of the M74.

National Galleries of Scotland

- Education Department
- The Mound, Edinburgh. EH2 2EL
- 031-556 8921 FAX 031-220 0917

The Gallery houses an outstanding collection of paintings, drawings and prints dating from the early Renaissance to the late 19th century. These include works by Raphael, Titian, Velazquez, Poussin, Rembrandt, Rubens, Raeburn Wilkie, Turner, Constable and the Impressionists. The Gallery also holds the Scottish Photography Archive with collections of work by Hill and Adamson and a wide range of recent Scottish photography.

N C SUPPORT The Education Department organises a varied programme of activities including lectures, teachers' courses, study days and exhibitions and other special events. In particular, welcome requests for gallery talks and lectures from schools and other groups. Each talk is prepared according to the age and interests of the particular group. For example, teachers may ask for talks on Colour, Composition or the Human Figure, or they may request more specific subjects such as the Renaissance, the Stewarts, etc.

ANNUAL OR ONE OFF EVENT The National Galleries Bulletin gives details of all exhibitions and events which take place at the Galleries. Teachers wishing to add their school to the mailing list should write to the Information Department.

OPENING Monday to Saturday 10.00am–5.00pm, Sunday 2.00pm–5.00pm. At least two weeks' notice is required. Teachers should have a first and second preference for visiting dates. Group bookings: min. 10, max. 30.

CATERING Cafes in the Gallery of Modern Art and the Portrait Gallery, though space is very limited indeed. Prior notice of group visits to either cafe should be given to the Manageress (tel: 031-556 8921;

Gallery of Modern Art ext. 309, Portrait Gallery ext. 421).

COST Free.

DISABLED FACILITIES Wheelchair access is possible in almost all Gallery rooms.

DIRECTIONS Car parking is available in the St James Centre, which is near the National Gallery and the Portrait Gallery. The Gallery of Modern Art has a free car park, though space is limited, particularly for coaches. A leaflet for teachers is available showing the various gallery locations.

New Abbey Cornmill
- The Head Custodian
- Old Mill House, New Abbey, Dumfries. DG2 8BU
- 0387 85260

A carefully renovated water-powered oatmeal mill, in working order, and demonstrated regularly to visitors.

OPENING Summer (1 April to 30 September): Monday to Saturday 9.30am–6.00pm, Sunday 2.00pm–6.00pm. Winter (1 October to 31 March): Monday to Thursday and Saturday 9.30am–4.00pm, closed Thursday pm, Sunday 2.00pm–4.00pm.

DISABLED FACILITIES No wheelchairs: stairs. Adapted toilet in the car park.

North Berwick Museum
- Rachel Woods
- School Road, North Berwick, East Lothian. EH39 4TU
- 0620 5457

Local history and wildlife, with changing exhibitions each year. 'Hands-on' exhibits.

N C SUPPORT Welcomes school groups by prior arrangement. Material can be shown on request. Educational material in preparation. Welcomes students doing research projects. Material and space can be made available for research to be carried out within the Museum.

ANNUAL OR ONE OFF EVENT Various temporary exhibitions.

OPENING 1 April to 30 September: Monday to Saturday 11.00am–5.00pm, Sunday 1.00pm–5.00pm.

COST Free. Small charge for special exhibitions.

DISABLED FACILITIES Limited, but material can be specially located, if requested, to allow for disabled access.

DIRECTIONS East side of North Berwick.

Oban Sea Life Centre
- Margaret Wills
- Barcaldine, Connel, Argyll. PA37 1SE
- 0631 72386 FAX 0631 72529

A sea life centre where people of all ages can discover the amazing life that lives from the surface of our seas down to the ocean depths. There is also a seal nursery and open seal display.

N C SUPPORT Teachers' packs with information and workshops for each of three age ranges are available (choice of three subject areas).

OPENING February to November: daily 10.00am–5.00pm.

VISITS OUT
SCOTLAND

CATERING Yes.

COST Children £2.25.

DISABLED FACILITIES Some displays are accessible by steps. Restaurant and shop fully accessible.

DIRECTIONS Situated on the shores of beautiful Loch Greran.

The Open Museum
- Nat Edwards
- Hagg's Castle, 100 St Andrew's Drive, Glasgow. G41 4RB
- 041-427 2725

Glasgow Museums' outreach service offers exhibitions and handling kits to be loaned free of charge for use in schools and community venues.

N C SUPPORT 'Elephants and Peacocks' exhibition on South Asian decorative arts. Social history object handling kits. Fossil handling kits etc.

OPENING 9.00am–5.00pm. Teachers may borrow exhibitions etc. for their own use and therefore access is variable.

COST Free to all Glasgow galleries.

DIRECTIONS BR: Maxwell Park. Off motorway exit 22 follow signs for Kilmarnock junction of M8 to Titwood Road, Hagg's Road and St Andrew's Road.

The People's Story
- Sandra Marwick
- 163 Canongate, Edinburgh. EH8 8BN

Tells the story of the ordinary people of Edinburgh from the late 18th century to the present through reconstructions, displays, video, oral history.

N C SUPPORT Series of themed resource packs. Educational resource list available on request.

OPENING Monday to Saturday 10.00am–6.00pm (closes 5.00pm October to May).

COST Free.

DISABLED FACILITIES Wheelchair access to first floor. Toilet.

DIRECTIONS Located in the Royal Mile, in the centre of Edinburgh.

Prestongrange Industrial Heritage Museum
- Rachel Woods or Sue Jenkinson
- Preston Road, Prestonpans, East Lothian. EH32 9RW
- 031-653 2904

Guided tours of historic site; with Cornish beam engine; changing display of local social and industrial history. East Lothian Artspace shows display of local art and craftwork.

N C SUPPORT School parties welcome by prior arrangement. Guided tours can focus on particular areas of site interest. If pre-warned, educational projects etc. can be planned. Welcomes research students. Material can be made available for study on request.

ANNUAL OR ONE OFF EVENT Steam engines are working on first Sunday of the month from April to September.

OPENING 1 April to 30 September: daily 11.00am–4.00pm.

CATERING Hot and cold drinks and snacks.

SCOTLAND

COST Free.

DISABLED FACILITIES Ramp access to most of the site, toilets.

DIRECTIONS North of the A1 between Musselburgh and Prestonpans, about six miles from Edinburgh.

Purves Puppets
- Jill or Ian Purves
- Biggar Little Theatre, Broughton Road, Biggar, Lanarkshire. ML12 6HA
- 0899 20631 FAX 0899 20521

Complete miniature Victorian theatre, seating 100. Beautiful grounds, tea room, shop, picnic and games areas. Car park. Plays, guided tours, in-service courses, workshops, museum displays, talks. Touring company.

N C SUPPORT Special shows and workshops for all ages, in-service courses and placements linked with National Curriculum and individual needs. Teachers' resource packs. Shows and workshops for special needs.

OPENING All year round: Monday to Saturday 10.00am–5.00pm, Sunday 2.00pm–5.00pm. Show times vary. Advance booking essential

CATERING Tea room serves light refreshments; wine licence; meals by prior arrangement.

COST Public prices for plays: children £3.00, adults £4.00. Schools: all seats £2.50, one adult free for every ten children.

DISABLED FACILITIES Full wheelchair access and toilet. Please notify in advance.

DIRECTIONS Forty-five minutes by car from Edinburgh, one hour from Glasgow, one and a half hours from Carlisle.

Raasay Outdoor Centre
- Lyn Rowe
- Isle of Raasay by Kyle, Ross-shire. IV40 8PB
- 0478 660266

Multi-activity centre, based in Georgian mansion on beautiful Hebridean island. Offers educational outdoor courses, including sailing, windsurfing, climbing, abseiling, canoeing, gorge-walking, orienteering. Courses tailor-made for group requirements.

OPENING March to October.

CATERING Excellent food and accommodation. Self-catering available on request.

COST Activities: full day £25.00, half day £12.50. Full board: adults £24.00. Half board: adults £20.00.

DISABLED FACILITIES None.

DIRECTIONS Fifteen minutes by ferry from Skye. Bus: to Sconser (Skye). BR: to Kyle of Lochalsh.

Royal Observatory
- Mark McAuley
- Visitor Centre, Blackford Hill, Edinburgh. EH9 3HJ
- 031-668 8405 FAX 031-668 8264

Two large exhibition telescopes; 'The Universe' exhibition; throughout the year another exhibition area varies from history to art to interactive science exhibits; winter lectures.

N C SUPPORT Worksheets provided for school groups; workpacks and books on sale suitable for both primary and secondary level 'Earth and Space'. Specific talks can be arranged for older pupils given by research astronomers at the Observatory or at local schools.

ANNUAL OR ONE OFF EVENT Various temporary exhibitions.

OPENING School groups welcome at any time, but suggest mornings to avoid clashing with tourists.

COST School group rates: children £1.00, one adult free with every ten pupils.

DISABLED FACILITIES Toilet. Lift to main exhibition area.

DIRECTIONS Bus: 40 or 41 from city centre, alight at Blackford station.

St Andrews Castle and Visitor Centre

- The Head Custodian
- St Andrews, Fife
- 0334 77196

The ruins of the castle of the Archbishops of St Andrews, dating in part from the 13th century. Notable features include a 'bottle dungeon' and mine and countermine tunnelled during the siege that followed the murder of Cardinal Beaton in 1546.

OPENING Summer: Monday to Saturday 9.30am–6.00pm, Sunday 2.00pm–6.00pm. Winter: Monday to Saturday 9.30am–4.00pm, Sunday 2.00pm–4.00pm.

DISABLED FACILITIES Grounds only.

St Andrews Sea Life Centre

- Gordon S Croft
- The Scores, St Andrews, Fife. KY16 9AS
- 0334 74786 FAX 0334 72950

The Sea Life Centre exhibits native British marine life. Species at St Andrews include seals, octopus and conger eels. Regular events include daily display talks and feeding demonstrations.

N C SUPPORT General workbooks on Life in Our Seas for age groups 5–7 and 8–12, along with a selection of Teachers' Notes. Please apply for details.

OPENING All year round: daily 10.00am–6.00pm. Summer holidays: 9.00am–9.00pm.

COST School children £2.25, one teacher free for every 10 pupils (1993 prices).

DISABLED FACILITIES Exterior ramp allows access to 70% of displays, including new seal-viewing gallery.

DIRECTIONS Adjacent to British Golf Museum, West Sands, St Andrews.

St Nicholas House

- David Atherton
- Arts & Recreation Division, Broad Street, Aberdeen. AB9 1XJ

Gallery and three museums with a unique and rich collection of material and international artefacts. Featuring displays of a varied nature, both temporary and permanent, from extensive collections.

N C SUPPORT None, although the interpretation officer runs a wide-ranging programme for children and young people, including informative tours. There is a comprehensive library.

ANNUAL OR ONE OFF EVENT Various temporary exhibitions.

OPENING All year round (except Christmas Day): Monday to Saturday 10.00am–5.00pm (8.00pm on Thursday), Sunday 1.00pm–5.00pm.

COST Free.

DISABLED FACILITIES Access, toilets, etc.

DIRECTIONS Aberdeen Art Gallery, Schoolhill, Aberdeen: from Union Street, down Belmont Street; the facilities are opposite.

Scotch Whisky Heritage Centre
- George Melville
- 354 Castlehill, The Royal Mile, Edinburgh. EH1 2NE
- 031-220 0441 FAX 031-220 6288

The story of Scotch Whisky brought to life. Tour of whisky-making processes. Audio-visual show. A journey in a whisky barrel traces the history of Scotland's national drink. Gift shop.

N C SUPPORT Guided tours in a choice of languages for group bookings. Educational folders available on request.

OPENING Daily (except Christmas Day and New Year's Day) 10.00am–5.00pm. Extended hours in summer.

CATERING Private reception room.

COST Children (5–17 years) £1.75, one adult free for every ten children.

DISABLED FACILITIES Wheelchair access, lift and toilet for people with disabilities (Tourism for All Award 1990).

DIRECTIONS Beside Edinburgh Castle. Seven minutes' walk from car park in Castle Terrace, ten minutes from the railway station and fifteen from the bus station.

Scottish Cycling Holidays
- The Manager
- Ballintuim, Nr Blairgowrie, Perthshire. PH10 7NJ
- 0250 886201 FAX 0250 886327

Gentle self-led holidays throughout Scotland and the Western Isles and East Anglia, England. Also tailor-made/short-break holidays. Large or small groups. Established 1979.

COST From £155 for seven nights B&B (including cycle).

DIRECTIONS Contact the Manager for directions.

Scottish Field Studies Association
- A Laver
- Kindrogan Field Centre, Enochdhu, Blairgowrie, Perthshire. PH10 7PG
- 0250 881286 FAX 0250 881433

Residential Field Centre with courses covering all aspects of environmental education and training.

N C SUPPORT Course based on Scotland 5–14 programme available.

OPENING All year round.

CATERING Full board.

COST Varies: write for details.

DISABLED FACILITIES Fully accessible.

DIRECTIONS Contact the Association for directions.

Scottish Nuclear Limited
- Mrs Jill Kent
- 3 Redwood Crescent, Peel Park, East Kilbride. G74 5PR
- 0355 262000 FAX 0355 262626

Scottish Nuclear Limited is owned by the Secretary of State for Scotland. It is Scotland's nuclear power-generating company and produces 50% of the country's electricity requirements from Torness and Hunterston Power Stations.

N C SUPPORT Publication: *Nuclear Rectors Section R*. SCE Higher Course. Free coach facility for visits to power stations. Speakers available to give presentations. Contact 0800 204420 for further information.

OPENING Daily: 9.30am–4.30pm.

CATERING Vending machines for tea, coffee, soft drinks and snacks.

COST Free.

DISABLED FACILITIES Easy access to Visitors Centres. Wheelchairs available for tours of power stations.

DIRECTIONS Hunterston: on A75, south of Largs on the west coast. Torness: on A1, south of Dunbar on the east coast.

Scottish Ski Tours
- Keith
- Nethy Bridge, Inverness-shire. PH25 3ED
- 0479 821333 FAX 0479 821418

High quality ski activity holidays with highly qualified staff. Tailored to individual requirements.

OPENING December to April.

CATERING Fully catered.

COST Approximately £200.00 plus VAT per person, all inclusive.

DISABLED FACILITIES Special needs by arrangement.

DIRECTIONS Between Aviemore and Grantown-on-Spey, on the B970.

Shaws Sweet Factory
- Mr or Mrs Shaw
- Fulton Road, Wester Gourdie, Dundee. DD2 4SW
- 0382 610369 FAX 0382 610488

Come and see the sweetmakers at work, see the age old art of sugar pulling and striping the sweeties the traditional way. The factory is based on a 1950s-style workshop with machinery dating from 1936 through to 1956, all restored to original condition, using recipes dating back to 1879 and producing by hand traditional confectionery, such as fudges, toffees, boiled sweets, etc.

N C SUPPORT By arrangement with the teacher.

OPENING Summer (1 May to 30 September): Monday to Friday 11.30am–4.00pm, closed last week of July and first week of August. Winter (1 October to 30 April): Wednesday 1.30pm–5.00pm, closed two weeks Christmas and New Year.

COST Free.

VISITS OUT
SCOTLAND

Our power stations are also generating a lot of interest.

Apart from helping to supply around half of Scotland's electricity needs, our nuclear power stations at Hunterston and Torness also provide an interesting and informative day out for families, groups or individuals.

If you'd like to find out more about nuclear power or you'd be interested to see state of the art technology in action, call free on 0800 250255 for Torness and 0800 838557 for Hunterston to arrange a guided tour.

Torness is just off the A1, East of Dunbar and Hunterston is off the A78, South of Largs.

A free luxury coach is available to provide transport for organised parties of 15 people or more. For coach bookings call free on 0800 204420.

SCOTTISH NUCLEAR
come see
PROGRAMME

Scottish Nuclear Limited, 3 Redwood Crescent, Peel Park, East Kilbride G74 5PR

VISITS OUT
SCOTLAND

DISABLED FACILITIES All facilities, including special arrangements for blind people.

DIRECTIONS West of Dundee; signposted 'Sweet Factory'.

Skara Brae
- The Head Custodian
- Prehistoric Village, Orkney. KW15 3LR
- 0856 84815

The best-preserved group of Stone-Age houses in Western Europe. The houses contain stone furniture, hearths and drains and give a remarkable picture of life in Neolithic times.

OPENING Summer hours (1 April to 30 September): Monday to Saturday 9.30am–6.00pm, Sunday 2.00pm–6.00pm. Monuments close at 6.30pm. Winter hours (1 October to 31 March): Monday to Saturday 9.30am–4.00pm, Sunday 2.00pm–4.00pm. Monuments close at 4.30pm. Please telephone visitor services on 031-244 3101 in case of changes.

DISABLED FACILITIES Not suitable, due to the distance and the state of the path.

DIRECTIONS About nine miles west of Kirkwall.

Smailholm Tower
- The Head Custodian
- c/o Area Office, 28–31 Fleming House, Kinnaird Park, Edinburgh. EH15 3RD
- 031-244 3101

Smailholm is a simple rectangular tower in a good state of preservation. Since 1983 it has housed a collection of costume figures and tapestries relating to Sir Walter Scott's 'Minstrelsy of the Scottish Borders'.

OPENING 1 April to 30 September: Monday to Saturday 9.30am–6.30pm, Sunday 2.00pm–6.30pm. Closed throughout the winter.

DISABLED FACILITIES None. Uneven, the stairs are narrow and steep.

DIRECTIONS Near Smailholm village, six miles northwest of Kelso.

Stirling Castle
- The Head Custodian
- Stirling. FK8 1EJ
- 7864 50000

Without doubt the grandest of all Scottish castles. The Great Hall and the Gatehouse of James IV, the marvellous Palace of James V, the Chapel Royal remodelled by James VI, and the artillery fortifications of the 16th and 18th centuries, are all of outstanding interest.

OPENING Summer (1 April to 30 September): daily 9.30am–5.15pm (last admission). Winter (1 October to 31 March): daily 9.30am–4.15pm (last admission). The Castle closes 45 minutes after the above times. The services of official guides cannot be reserved in advance.

DISABLED FACILITIES Unsuitable, although negotiable with care. Cobbled roadway and steep climb.

Strathspey Railway Co Ltd
- Laurence Grant
- Aviemore Speyside Station, Dalfaber Road, Aviemore. PH22 1PY
- 0479 810725

VISITS OUT
SCOTLAND

Scotland's steam railway in the Highlands. Trains run between Aviemore and Boat of Garten from April to October. Small relics display and living steam. Smell the atmosphere; enjoy the ride.

N C SUPPORT Children's guide to the railway.

OPENING 9.30am–5.00pm on operating days.

CATERING On-train buffet car.

COST Third class return: children £1.90, adults £3.80. Party rate (min. ten adult fares): children £1.50, adults £3.00.

DISABLED FACILITIES Limited on the equipment, which dates back to the 1950s or before. Many wheelchair parties have been carried without major problems.

DIRECTIONS A9 to Aviemore, then B970 and follow the signs.

The exhibition centre is available for project work. Telephone to check that the relevant exhibits are available.

OPENING Monday to Friday (closed Tuesday) 10.00am–5.00pm, Saturday 10.00am–5.00pm, Sunday 1.30pm–5.00pm. Holiday opening times: Monday to Saturday 10.00am–5.00pm; Sunday 1.30pm–5.00pm.

COST Children £1.50, adults £3.00. Group discounts: children £1.50, teachers free.

DISABLED FACILITIES All on one level. Access for wheelchairs. Toilets.

DIRECTIONS West end of Union Street off Holborn Junction, along from Odeon Cinema and Bon Accord Baths.

Stratosphere
- Jackie Traynor
- 19 Justice Mill Lane, Aberdeen. AB1 2EQ
- 0224 213232

'Hands-on' interactive science centre. Over 70 exhibits to try out scientific experiments. The themes of the exhibition change every two months to highlight the different aspects of science as they relate to the exhibits.

N C SUPPORT Themes relate to the schools curriculum as closely as possible. There are discussions with teachers prior to deciding themes.

Struan House Hotel
- Heather Davidson
- Carrbridge, Inverness-shire. PH23 3AS
- 0479 84242

A very good area for outdoor activities. Hill walking, sightseeing, skiing, golfing. Private tennis court.

N C SUPPORT Many primary schools from Ireland use the Struan as a base for an adventure week.

ANNUAL OR ONE OFF EVENT Various events and activities in the area throughout the year.

OPENING All year round.

CATERING Bar, dining room, packed lunches, etc.

VISITS OUT

SCOTLAND

COST B&B: adults normally £25.00. Price negotiable, according to age, numbers.

DISABLED FACILITIES Three bedrooms on the ground floor; no steps.

DIRECTIONS A9 north turn right; signposted just north of Aviemore, eight miles.

Summerlee Heritage Trust
- Carol Haddow
- West Canal Street, Coatbridge. ML5 1QD
- 0236 431261 FAX 0236 440429

Summerlee Museum of industrial and social history; with electric tramway; large exhibition hall with working machinery; reconstructed miners' cottages 1840–1970; underground coal mine experience.

N C SUPPORT Schools' packs are provided on a number of topics for individual pupils; worksheets and activities are provided for visiting schools. Classroom facility available. Information pack, reference facilities and access to photographic collections for individual students or small groups.

ANNUAL OR ONE OFF EVENT Events days through the year.

OPENING Daily 10.00am–5.00pm. Closed Christmas Day, Boxing Day, 1–2 January.

COST Free.

DISABLED FACILITIES All parts of the museum are accessible and toilets are provided. Wheelchairs available.

DIRECTIONS Eastbound M8; exit junction 8 and follow signs to Coatbridge and Summerlee.

Sweetheart Abbey
- The Head Custodian
- New Abbey Village, Dumfries
- 0387 53862

The splendid ruin of a late 13th- and early 14th-century Cistercian abbey founded by Dervorgilla, Lady of Galloway, in memory of her husband John Balliol. Apart from the abbey church, the principal feature is the well-preserved precinct wall, enclosing 30 acres.

OPENING Summer (1 April to 30 September): Monday to Saturday 9.30am–6.30pm, Sunday 2.00pm–6.30pm. Winter (1 October–31 March): closed Thursday pm and Friday. Joint entry ticket with New Abbey Corn Mill.

DISABLED FACILITIES Suitable for elderly people but those less able would require help for steps. Public toilets/adapted toilets at the car park opposite the Abbey.

DIRECTIONS In New Abbey village, seven miles south of Dumfries.

Tantallon Castle
- The Head Custodian
- Nr North Berwick, East Lothian. DG2 0SA
- 0620 2727

A remarkable fortification, on a promontory, with earthwork defences, and a massive 14th-century curtain wall with towers. The castle had a stormy history owing to its strategic position. Interpretative displays include replica guns.

OPENING Summer (1 April to 30 September): Monday to Saturday 9.30am–6.30pm, Sunday 2.00pm–6.30pm. Winter (1 October to 31 March): Monday to Thursday and

VISITS OUT
SCOTLAND

Saturday 9.30am–4.30pm, closed Thursday pm, Sunday 2.00pm–4.30pm.

DISABLED FACILITIES Access to grounds and ground floor only.

DIRECTIONS Three miles east of North Berwick.

Traquair House
- Ms C Maxwell Stuart
- Innerleithen, Peeblesshire. EH44 6PW
- 0396 830323 FAX 0896 830639

Traquair is the oldest continually inhabited house in Scotland. Visited by 27 Scottish monarchs and has strong associations with Mary Queen of Scots and the Jacobite Risings.

N C SUPPORT Children's questionnaires; special school visits catered for.

ANNUAL OR ONE OFF EVENT Traquair Fair on first weekend in August, two days of superb family entertainment.

OPENING Easter week 1 May to 30 September: 1.30pm–5.30pm. July and August: 10.30pm–5.30pm.

CATERING Cottage restaurant (built 1745) serving light lunches and teas.

COST Group rates: children £1.30, adults £2.75. Children £1.50, adults £3.50.

DISABLED FACILITIES Grounds and ground floor of house accessible.

DIRECTIONS Peebles six miles, Galashiels 12 miles, St Mary's Loch 12 miles, Moffat 32 miles, Selkirk ten miles, Dumfries 48 miles, Carlisle 75 miles, Edinburgh 29 miles (50 minutes), Glasgow 60 miles (one and a half hours), Newcastle 96 miles, Berwick-upon-Tweed 60 miles, Edinburgh Airport 40 miles.

The Trekking & Riding Society of Scotland
- Mrs Liz Menzies
- Horse Trials Office, Blair Atholl, Perthshire. PH18 5TH
- 0796 481543 FAX 0796 481455

The Society deals with equestrian tourism in Scotland, promoting and marketing holiday riding centres. It also trains staff and inspects centres to ensure a high level of safety and the welfare of both horse and rider.

OPENING Office open: Monday to Friday 9.00am–5.00pm.

Urquhart Castle
- The Head Custodian
- Drumnadrochit, Inverness-shire
- 0456 2551

Standing above Loch Ness, this was one of the largest castles in Scotland before it fell into decay after 1689. Most of the existing buildings date from after the 16th century, and include a tower, which is the best-preserved part of the complex.

OPENING Summer hours (1 April to 30 September): Monday to Saturday 9.30am–6.00pm, Sunday 2.00pm–6.00pm. Monuments close at 6.30pm. Winter hours (1 October to 31 March): Monday to Saturday 9.30am–4.00pm, Sunday 2.00pm–4.00pm. Monuments close at 4.30pm. Please telephone visitor services on 031-244 3101 in case of changes.

DISABLED FACILITIES Not suitable for people with disabilities: downhill and steps. No adapted toilet.

DIRECTIONS On Loch Ness, near Drumnadrochit.

VISITS OUT
WALES

NATIONAL MUSEUM OF WALES

A wide selection of National Curriculum topics from KS 1-4 can be followed at the 10 branches of the Museum located throughout Wales:

> Art, Craft and Design
> Archaeology and History
> Geography and Earth Sciences
> Industrial and Social History
> Technology and Science

Facilities include:
- ~ Hands-on activities for school groups
- ~ Talks, lectures and study facilities for Further and Higher Education schools/ colleges
- ~ INSETs
- ~ Special admission rates for groups
- ~ Shops, eating/ picnic facilities

Education Service, National Museum of Wales, Cathays Park, Cardiff, CF1 3NP.
Tel No: 0222 - 397951 Fax: 0222 - 373219

THE NATWEST STUDENT BOOK 1995

The applicant's guide to UK colleges and universities

Editors: Klaus Boehm and Jenny Lees-Spalding

Fully revised and updated, *The Student Book* is essential reading for all prospective students. It contains:

How To Go About It Your survival guide to application procedures, grants, loans, accommodation, welfare and lots more.

Where To Study Profiles of over 280 colleges and universities, including vital 'what it's *really* like' student views.

What To Study 70 university teachers describe their subject and outline what's taught at degree level.

'Indispensable for sixth-formers'
Sunday Times

Published by Macmillan, priced £12.99 paperback

VISITS OUT

WALES

Aberdulais Falls
- The Administrator
- Aberdulais, Nr Neath, West Glamorgan. SA10 8EU
- 0639 636674

A site which combines natural beauty and fascinating industrial history; Aberdulais has one of the most famous waterfalls in South Wales, harnessed for centuries to power a variety of early industries; a favourite visiting place for artists and writers including Turner, Richard Colt Hoare and Thomas Horner; a unique hydro-electric scheme has involved the installation of a turbine and waterwheel to generate power.

N C SUPPORT National Curriculum links with Art, Science and Technology.

DISABLED FACILITIES Most of the property is accessible; special lift in Turbine House provides access to the top of the falls. Adapted toilet at Tourist Information Centre; wheelchairs available. Limited car parking on site. Taped guide.

DIRECTIONS Contact the administrator for details.

Alice in Wonderland
- M Ratcliffe
- Visitor Centre, The Rabbit Hole (Llandudno) Ltd, 3/4 Trinity Square, Llandudno. LL30 2PY
- 0492 860082 FAX 0492 860082

See and hear Alice's Wonderland story come to life in an enchanting rabbit hole. Life-size characters provide a fascinating experience for all ages.

N C SUPPORT Alice in Wonderland has recently been returned to the National Curriculum. The centre provides worksheets free and staff also talk to the pupils giving them further information.

OPENING Daily 10.00am–5.00pm. Will open at any time by appointment to suit the party.

CATERING None.

COST Children £1.75, teachers, drivers, etc. free for parties over 25 in number.

DISABLED FACILITIES The whole place was built with accompanied wheelchair users in mind.

DIRECTIONS In the centre of Llandudno town just off the main shopping street. Apply for leaflet showing map.

Amgueddfa Diwydiant Museum of the Welsh Woollen Industry
- John S Jones, Museum Officer
- Dre-Fach Felindre, Llandysul, Dyfed. SA44 5UR
- 0339 370929

Demonstrations of the fleece-to-fabric process by hand and on 19th-century machines, together with an exhibition tracing the evolution of the industry from its beginnings to the present.

N C SUPPORT Teachers' pack based on the Museum and the Woollen Industry, produced by the Education Department of Dyfed County Council, Carmarthen, Dyfed. Resource centre for textile studies for Dyfed and all visiting schools. Portfolio preparation for textile studies colleges.

ANNUAL OR ONE OFF EVENT Welsh cloth from the woollen mills of Wales,

WALES

from January 1994; hand-woven textiles, June to September 1994; Tom Mathias, folk-life photographer.

OPENING October to March: Monday to Friday 10.00am–5.00pm. April to September: Monday to Saturday 10.00am–5.00pm.

CATERING Cafe.

COST Children 50p, adults £1.00, Senior Citizens 75p. Group discount over 20 people by arrangement; school group 33p per child.

DISABLED FACILITIES Ground floor access. One adapted toilet. Access to cafe and workshops.

DIRECTIONS Signed from the A484; six miles from Newcastle Emlyn and 12 miles from Carmarthen.

Amgueddfa'r Gogledd

- The Education Officer
- Llanberis, Gwynedd. LL55 4UR
- 0286 870636 FAX 0286 871331

Power of Wales is a high-technology, multi-media presentation describing the generation and transmission of electricity at the Dinorwig pumped storage station.

N C SUPPORT We can support Science, Technology, Environmental Studies and Welsh history. Worksheets are available for primary and secondary pupils. Assistance can be given on individual projects.

ANNUAL OR ONE OFF EVENT Various temporary exhibitions supplement the main presentation.

OPENING Contact the Education Officer.

COST School children £1.70, teachers £1.70. One teacher free for every 15 pupils.

DISABLED FACILITIES Toilets, lift; pre-book for special adapted bus to Power Station.

DIRECTIONS On the A4086 at the foot of Snowdon alongside the Lake of Llanberis.

Anglesey Sea Zoo

- Dr Amanda Young
- Brynsiencyn, Anglesey, Gwynedd. LL61 6TQ
- 0248 430411 FAX 0248 430213

As Wales' largest aquarium, accent is placed on the variety and beauty of the local marine life around Anglesey. Conservation counts: there is an ongoing lobster breeding/restocking programme. Five-acre site.

N C SUPPORT The 14-page curriculum-based teachers' pack (Welsh/English) includes all the relevant information for educational visits. Worksheets for Key Stages 1–4 are included. A-Level sheets are available on request.

OPENING Summer: 10.00am–6.00pm (last admission 5.00pm). Winter (November to February): 11.00am–4.00pm (last admission 3.00pm).

CATERING Restaurant/tea room for 100, fast-food outlet for 50 and 50 picnic tables.

COST Group rate for parties of 12 or more: children/students £2.50, one teacher free for every ten children/students.

DISABLED FACILITIES One toilet. Wheelchair access throughout.

VISITS OUT
WALES

Bala Lake Railway
- Roy Hardiman
- The Station, Llanuwchllyn, Bala, Gwynedd. LL23 7DD
- 0675 84666

A delightful four and a half mile ride by narrow-gauge steam train through the beautiful scenery of the Snowdonia National Park.

OPENING Easter to October: times vary according to season.

CATERING Light refreshments at Llanuwchllyn.

COST Standard fares for 1993. Return: children £2.50, adults £4.50, Senior Citizens £4.00. Single: children £1.50, adults £3.00. Family Saver tickets: one adult and one child £6.00, two adults and one child £10.00, each additional child £1.00.

DISABLED FACILITIES Three wheelchairs can be carried on the train.

DIRECTIONS Off the A494 Bala to Dolgellau road, easily accessible from the A5 or via the motorway network.

Beaumaris Castle
- The Custodian
- Beaumaris, Gwynedd. LL58 8AP
- 0248 810361

Beaumaris was the last and largest of the castles built by Edward I to contain the Welsh. Begun in 1295 on a virgin site overlooking the Menai Straits, the new castle was given the French name of Beau Mareys (Beautiful Marsh). The flat site enabled the King's mason-architect, Master James of St George, to build a castle of geometric symmetry. Although never completed, Beaumaris is the most perfect example of the concentrically planned castle in Britain. Castles of Edward I Exhibition in the Chapel Tower.

OPENING Summer (end March to end October): daily 9.30am–6.30pm. Winter (end October to end March): Monday to Friday 9.30am–4.00pm, Sunday 2.00pm–4.00pm. Closed Christmas Eve, Christmas Day, Boxing Day and New Year's Day.

DISABLED FACILITIES Accessible (one of the best): Ramps, adapted toilet 50–70 yds away.

DIRECTIONS Access: via B5109 and A545. BR: Bangor ten miles.

Big Pit Mining Museum
- Mrs Pat Edwards or Mrs Viv Heward
- Blaenafon, Gwent. NP4 9XP
- 0495 790311 FAX 0495 792618

Underground tours led by experienced miners down the 90m shaft and through roadways, underground stables, engine houses and the wall face of a former working colliery. Exhibitions, catering and picnic areas, giftshop.

N C SUPPORT Suitable for a range of curricular and cross-curricular activities. Study pack/worksheets available. The Blaenafon area offers unrivalled opportunities to study the impact of the Industrial Revolution and its aftermath. History, Economic Geography, Geology and Tourism.

VISITS OUT

WALES

OPENING March to November: daily 9.30am–5.00pm (first tour 10.00am, last tour starts 3.30pm). Telephone for details of winter opening.

CATERING The miners' canteen, offers a range of hot and cold snacks and meals, confectionery and ice cream.

COST Prices vary according to the season. Prior booking is essential for groups of 31 or more in order to attract discounts. One teacher/supervisor is admitted free for every ten children. For school groups the lower age limit is seven years.

DISABLED FACILITIES Toilets and ramps, but the site is not easy for severely handicapped and prior notice is required for wheelchairs on underground tours.

DIRECTIONS Signposted from M4 (junction 26), A456 at Brynmawr and Llanfoist, A4042/3 at Pontypool.

Boderwyddan Castle
- Clare Cookson
- Boderwyddan, Clwyd. LL18 5YA

Magnificent Victorian house containing collections from the National Portrait Gallery, the Victoria and Albert Museum and the Royal Academy of Art.

N C SUPPORT The house and portraits provide a source of evidence for National Curriculum work (particularly Art and History) and worksheets are available to guide pupils around the collections. Victorian-based 'hands-on' exhibits. Ring for details.

OPENING April to October: daily (except Friday) 10.30am–5.00pm.

November to March: please ring for details.

CATERING Yes.

COST School children £1.50, teachers free.

DISABLED FACILITIES Yes.

DIRECTIONS Off the A55 near St Asaph.

Bod Petrual Visitor Centre
- Mr J Ferguson, Forest Officer
- Forest Enterprise, Clawdd Newydd, Ruthin, Clwyd. LL15 2NL
- 08245 208 FAX 08245 482

An old gamekeeper's cottage by a pool is the centre for Clocaenog Forest. The forest's story, past and present, is told.

N C SUPPORT Educational visits: contact Forest District Manager.

OPENING Easter to October.

DISABLED FACILITIES Yes.

DIRECTIONS Contact the office for directions.

Brecon Beacons
- Peter Williams
- The National Park Visitor Centre, Libanus, Brecon, Powys. LD3 8ER
- 0874 623366

Visitor Centre and Education Day Centre for Brecon Beacons National Park: spectacular views, picnics and catering; educational trails and guided walks; lectures and slide talks; services primary to undergraduates.

N C SUPPORT Fact sheets and publications to support Key Stage 2 investigating 'Mountain and Moorland Environments' and

'Peoples of the Past'. Also to support Key Stages 3 and 4: Geography investigations of rural land-use management problems.

ANNUAL OR ONE OFF EVENT Special programme of events for families during the summer vacation.

OPENING All year round: daily (except Christmas Day). School parties must book in advance for staff assistance.

CATERING Full self-service cafe/tea room. Welsh recipes baked daily on the premises.

COST No general admission fee. For educational help: half day £17.50, full day £35 (per group).

DISABLED FACILITIES Wheelchair access to all parts of the building (limited for trails and walks). Special toilets.

DIRECTIONS Signed as 'The National Park Visitor Centre' from the A470 at Libanus, five miles west of Brecon.

Brecon Mountain Railway

- K L Lewis
- Pant Station, Dowlass, Merthyr Tydfil, Mid-Glamorgan. CF48 2UP
- 0685 722988

The Brecon Mountain Railway runs through magnificent scenery into the Brecon Beacons National Park. The four-mile return trip behind a vintage steam locomotive takes 50 minutes, including a stop for a picnic, forest walk or visit to the lakeside snackbar at the Taf Fechan Reservoir. If they wish visitors may stay longer here and return by a later train. On their return they can see old steam locomotives being restored.

ANNUAL OR ONE OFF EVENT A special service operates in December. Father Christmas meets the train and distributes presents to the children. Advance booking essential. Special leaflet and booking form available on request.

OPENING The timetable will be sent along with booking form upon enquiry.

CATERING Licensed restaurant serving morning coffee, light lunch or afternoon tea.

COST Special fares for parties of 10 or more. School parties (min. 30 people): children £1.50, adults £1.50, coach drivers and couriers travel free; a deposit of £10.00 must be paid and the balance paid on arrival at the station in one payment.

DISABLED FACILITIES There are excellent facilities for disabled people, including ramps, toilets and a carriage specially designed to carry wheelchairs.

DIRECTIONS Coach parking is free, with plenty of spaces (15 coaches). The station is only one mile off the A465 Heads of the Valleys Trunk Road. Follow the 'Mountain Railway' signs from this road.

Bryn Bach Park

Bryn Bach Park
- Colin Cheesman
- Visitor Centre, Merthyr Road, Gwent. NP2 3AY
- 0495 711816

Six hundred-acre Country Park with 36-acre lake, picnic areas, children's adventure playground, Visitor

Centre with self-catering accommodation, souvenir shop, catering facilities, fishing; and windsurfing and waterskiing by Club arrangement.

N C SUPPORT Resource pack showing how the Park has been developed from reclaimed land.

ANNUAL OR ONE OFF EVENT Country Fair, Raft Race, Waterski competitions.

OPENING All year round: daily (except Christmas Day).

CATERING Cafe.

COST Free entry, charge for fishing, waterskiing, windsurfing.

DISABLED FACILITIES Fishing stations, toilets.

Butterfly and Bird Palace *see* Pili Palace

Caerleon Isca
- The Custodian
- Fortress Baths, High Street, Caerleon, Gwent. NP6 1AE
- 0633 422518

Caerleon has the only remains of Roman legionary barracks on view anywhere in Europe. Each of these buildings once housed a century of eighty men and its centurion. Visitors can walk along a Roman street and discover the remains of turrets, cookhouses, bread-ovens and a latrine. The Roman Amphitheatre stands just outside the fortress walls; Isca, the legendary fortress, was one of the three principal military bases in Roman Britain, and the architectural showpiece of the fortress is the baths.

OPENING Fortress, baths and amphitheatre: end March to end October: daily 9.30am–6.30pm; end October to end March: Monday to Friday 9.30am–4.00pm. Baths: Sunday 2.00pm–4.00pm. Amphitheatre: open site. Contact the Custodian for information on booking visits and opening times for the Museum.

DISABLED FACILITIES There is access to the museum, fortress, amphitheatre. Barracks rather difficult. Adapted toilet in the Museum.

DIRECTIONS The M4 to junction 25; Caerleon lies two miles north and is well signposted from the motorway. Cardiff 16 miles; Bristol 30 miles; Severn Bridge 14 miles. Bus: from Newport on a very regular basis. BR: Newport; only 90 minutes from London and on direct routes from Birmingham and many other cities.

Caernarfon Castle
- The Custodian
- Caernarfon, Gwynedd. LL58 2HY
- 0286 677617

Caernarfon Castle was the setting for the Investiture of HRH Prince Charles in July 1969. Begun in 1283 by Edward I, it is one of Europe's great medieval fortresses whose walls, with their varying bands of stone, were modelled on the walls of Constantinople. In the Eagle Tower, 'The Eagle and the Dragon' exhibition combines multi-slide images with commentary and music.

VISITS OUT

WALES

In the Chamberlain Tower can be seen 'Castles of Edward I in Wales'. There is a Regimental Museum of the Royal Welch Fusiliers and situated on the ground floor room of the North-East Tower is 'The Prince of Wales Exhibition' whose centrepiece combines the throne and stool made for the Investiture of Prince Charles at the castle in 1969.

OPENING Summer (end March to end October): daily 9.30am–6.30pm. Winter (end October to end March): Monday to Friday 9.30am–4.00pm, Sunday 2.00pm–4.00pm. Closed Christmas Eve, Christmas Day and New Year's Day.

DISABLED FACILITIES None.

DIRECTIONS Access via A4085, A487(T) A4086, B4366. BR: Bangor nine miles.

CADW: WELSH HISTORIC MONUMENTS

NC Support For details of educational material and guidebooks available please contact the Education Officer, CADW, Welsh Historic Monuments, Brunel House, 2 Fitzlan Road, Cardiff CF2 1UY (Tel 0222 465511).

Cost Free entry to the sites will be granted to educational parties subject to a number of conditions (details on the back of the Educational Visit Application Form).

See individual entries for all other information.

Beaumaris Castle
Caerleon Isca
Caernarfon Castle
Caerphilly Castle
Castell Coch
Chepstow Castle
Conwy Castle
Criccieth Castle
Kidwelly Castle
Raglan Castle
St David's Bishops' Palace
Tintern Abbey
Tretower Court & Castle
Valle Crucis Abbey

Caerphilly Castle

- The Custodian
- Caerphilly, Mid-Glamorgan. CF8 1JL
- 0222 883143

This vast fortress is one of the greatest surviving castles of the medieval western world. Caerphilly's huge 30-acre site is equalled in size among British castles only at Windsor and perhaps Dover. With its massive gatehouses, water defences and concentric lines of defence the castle was virtually impregnable against contemporary siege methods. There is a 'Castles of Wales' exhibition in the northwest tower, while in the outer gate, there is an exhibition describing Caerphilly's many stages of development. Look out also for siege engines: four full-size working replicas of medieval artillery pieces are positioned on the south platform and ready to fire across the lake. Visitors can also discover more about the castle with the popular cassette tour.

OPENING Summer (end March to end October): daily 9.30am–6.30pm. Winter (end October to end March): Monday to Friday 9.30am–4.00pm,

VISITS OUT
WALES

Sunday 2.00pm–4.00pm. Closed Christmas Eve, Christmas Day, Boxing Day and New Year's Day.

DISABLED FACILITIES None. Steep paths and steps.

DIRECTIONS Access via the A468 and the A4263. BR: Caerphilly quarter of a mile.

Cambrian Woollen Mill
- Sue Beetlestone, Visitor Manager
- Llanwrtyd Wells, Powys. LD5 4SD
- 05913 211 **FAX** 05913 399

A working woollen mill. The tour includes video and museum and covers the history of the Welsh woollen industry as well as wool processing.

N C SUPPORT Activity packs for children. Worksheets and seminar days in preparation. Happy to supply information to teachers.

OPENING All year round: daily 9.30am–4.30pm.

CATERING Drinks, snacks, ice cream, light meals.

COST Children £1.50, teachers free.

DISABLED FACILITIES All facilities accessible but it is best to check in advance.

DIRECTIONS On the A483 half a mile from Llanwrtyd Wells.

Castell Coch
- The Custodian
- Tongwynlais, Cardiff. CF4 7JS
- 0222 810101

The castle was the creation of two men hopelessly in love with the Middle Ages, the fabulously wealthy Lord Bute and his architect, the 'eccentric genius' William Burges. Work began in 1875 on a site intended as a country retreat and companion piece to Lord Bute's opulent castle in the centre of Cardiff.

ANNUAL OR ONE OFF EVENT December: a Victorian Household prepares for Christmas, portrayed by the Heritage Theatre Company and local players.

OPENING Summer (end March to end October): daily 9.30am–6.30pm. Winter (end October to end March): Monday to Friday 9.30am–4.00pm, Sunday 2.00pm–4.00pm. Closed Christmas Eve, Christmas Day, Boxing Day and New Year's Day.

DISABLED FACILITIES Contact the administrator for access details.

DIRECTIONS By road: M4 (junction 32) onto A470, then signposted. BR: Taffs Well three-quarters of a mile. Bus: 136 (Cardiff Bus/Countryside Service).

Centre for Alternative Technology
- Ann MacGarry
- Machynlleth, Powys. SY20 9AZ
- 0654 703743 **FAX** 0654 702782

An Exhibition Centre with displays of energy conservation, wind, water and solar power, organic growing, CAT runs adult courses and school residentials, produces publications and does consultancy.

N C SUPPORT The displays are relevant to National Curriculum Science, Technology and Geography. Residential courses specifically cover Technology at any Key Stage and aspects of Key

VISITS OUT
WALES

Stages 3 and 4 Science. Worksheets/study guides are available at all levels, including sixth form. Residential courses geared specifically to sixth form for A-Level Physics, Technology, Biology. Teachers' leaflet available concerning guided tours etc.

OPENING March to end October: daily 10.00am–5.00pm. Limited opening November to February.

COST School children £2.00, staff free.

DISABLED FACILITIES Access via Cliff Railway. Paths, restaurant and shop are wheelchair accessible.

DIRECTIONS Three miles north of Machynlleth on the A487. Parking for cars and coaches. BR: from Birmingham to Machynlleth.

Ceredigion Museum
- Michael Freeman
- Coliseum, Terrace Road, Aberystwyth, Dyfed. SY23 2AQ
- 0970 634212

Museum with collections on local folk life, geology and archaeology and local art exhibitions.

N C SUPPORT Relevant to Geology and Art.

OPENING Monday to Saturday 10.00am–5.00pm.

COST Free.

DISABLED FACILITIES Lift, toilets.

DIRECTIONS One hundred yards from the beach.

Chepstow Castle
- The Custodian
- Chepstow, Gwent. NP6 5EZ
- 0291 624065

Set in a beautiful landscape, Chepstow has been a strategic fortress for hundreds of years. The Castle, high up on its river cliff above the Wye, guards one of the main crossings between England and Wales. Visitors can trace the history of medieval fortification from a stone hall-keep built within a decade of the Battle of Hastings in 1066 by one of William the Conqueror's principal lieutenants, through to the 17th century. An exhibition on 'Chepstow and the Civil War' contains displays of original and replica armour, together with military uniforms and hand weapons of the time. Another exhibition, 'Chepstow: The Development of a Medieval Castle', illustrates the story of the castle and the powerful men who built it.

OPENING Summer (end March to end October): daily 9.30am–6.30pm. Winter (end October to end March): Monday to Friday 9.30am–4.00pm, Sunday 2.00pm–4.00pm. Closed Christmas Eve, Christmas Day, Boxing Day and New Year's Day.

DISABLED FACILITIES None.

DIRECTIONS Follow Chepstow Town Trail and take Wyndcliff Nature Trail. Car and coach parking nearby. Access: Chepstow via A465, B4235, A48 or M4 (junction 22). BR: Chepstow half a mile.

Chirk Castle
- The Administrator
- Chirk, Clwyd. LL14 5AF
- 0691 777701

Marcher fortress, completed in 1310, commanding fine views over the surrounding countryside; elegant state rooms with elaborate

WALES

plasterwork, superb neo-Classical furniture, tapestries and portraits; formal gardens with clipped yews.

N C SUPPORT A teachers' resource book is available, along with a children's guide. Study centre and Education Officer.

DISABLED FACILITIES Parts of castle and garden only (very limited access). Special parking arrangements. Braille guide.

DIRECTIONS Half a mile west of Chirk village off the A5; additional one and a half miles of private driveway to Castle. Bus: Crosville Wales 2/X Wrexham to Oswestry. BR: Chirk one and a half miles.

The Christian Mountain Centre
- Leo Crossling
- Gorffwysfa, Tremadog, Gwynedd. LL49 9PS
- 0766 512616

Fully equipped residential centre running outdoor activities and environmental studies for schools, youth clubs and church weekends.

N C SUPPORT Educational courses can be tailored to meet the needs of the National Curriculum in outdoor and adventurous activities, Geography, History and Science.

OPENING All year round.

CATERING Full board, breakfast, packed lunch, evening meal, supper, drinks and biscuits.

COST Environmental Studies: seven days £122, five days £87. Adventure Course: seven days £156, five days £112 (up to 14 years). Multi-Activity Course: seven days £163, five days £117 (14 years and over). Low season October to February discounts, up to £20 per person for seven-day Multi-Activity course. Free leader's place with every 12 children.

DIRECTIONS A487 from Caernarfon to Porthmadog, just out of Tremadog village square towards Porthmadog. Last house on the left hand side.

Clan-y-Borth Holiday Village
- W R Sudbury
- Betws Road, Llanrwst, Gwynedd. LL26 0HB
- 0492 641543

Twenty-one self-catering chalets/bungalows on a small site on the banks of River Conwy and within easy travelling distance from most sites and attractions.

N C SUPPORT Not applicable to the site but there are many attractions, such as the slate mines, power station and woollen mills, which do special rates for parties.

OPENING 1 January to 31 December.

CATERING Self-catering barbecue area provided for general use.

COST Discounts depend on the size of party and time of booking. Prices vary per different type of unit.

DISABLED FACILITIES Six units built for people who use wheelchairs.

DIRECTIONS In Llanrwst (by Inigo Jones Bridge) on the A470, four miles from Betws-y-Coed.

Colby Woodland Garden
- Philip James
- Nr Stepaside, Dyfed
- 0834 811885

WALES

A secluded woodland garden of beauty and tranquillity.

OPENING April to October: daily 10.00am–5.00pm.

COST School groups (min. 15 people): 80p (1993 prices).

DISABLED FACILITIES Limited facilities, parts of garden accessible; disabled visitors may park closer to the garden on request.

DIRECTIONS Signposted from the A477.

Conwy Castle

- The Custodian
- Conwy, Gwynedd. LL32 8AY
- 0492 592358

One of the most picturesque of Welsh castles, and a masterpiece of medieval architecture. Built by Edward I as part of his master plan to subdue the Welsh, Conwy was both fortress and garrison town. Outside the castle gates visitors will find one of the finest and most complete circuits of town walls anywhere in Europe, over three-quarters of a mile in length with 22 towers and three original gateways. Built between 1283 and 1289, the castle's shape is dictated by the very rock on which it stands. The Chapel Tower contains a colourful and informative exhibition about Castle Chapels, and includes a life-size tableau. The top floor of the same tower houses a scale model of Conwy Castle and town as it may have appeared around 1312. Regular guided tours are available.

OPENING Summer (end March to end October): daily 9.30am–6.30pm. Winter (end October to end March): Monday to Friday 9.30am–4.00pm, Sunday 2.00pm–4.00pm. Closed Christmas Eve, Christmas Day, Boxing Day and New Year's Day.

DISABLED FACILITIES Very restricted as there are 12 steps up.

DIRECTIONS Conwy by A55 or B5106. BR: Conwy adjacent.

Corris Craft Centre

- Richard Withers
- Corris, Machynlleth, Powys. SY20 9SP
- 0654 761249

This is a genuine working craft centre, where visitors can see the production process and speak to the craftworkers about their work.

OPENING Winter: Monday to Friday 10.00am–4.00pm. Summer: daily 10.00am–6.00pm.

CATERING Large restaurant.

COST Free.

DISABLED FACILITIES Toilets and access.

DIRECTIONS A487 between Dolgellau to the north and Machynlleth to the south.

Criccieth Castle

- The Custodian
- Criccieth, Gwynedd. LL52 0DP
- 0766 522227

Perched in an imposing position, the castle is still dominated by the twin-towered gatehouse built by Prince Llywellyn ab Iorwerth ('The Great'). Later remodelled by Edward I and Edward II. Criccieth houses two exhibitions, one on the castles of Native Welsh princes and another on

VISITS OUT
WALES

Gerald of Wales and the Welsh Princes, both recipients of Britain's top heritage interpretation award.

OPENING All educational visits must take place on weekdays during normal school hours.

COST Free entry to the sites will be granted to educational parties provided a number of conditions are satisfied. These are listed on the Educational Visits application form. No free passes will be granted for Saturday, Sunday, bank holidays and bank holiday weekends.

DISABLED FACILITIES Access to Visitors Centre. Help is needed for the remainder. Adapted toilet.

DIRECTIONS On the coastal bluff, near Criccieth town centre.

Dale Fort Field Studies
- David Emerson
- Council Centre, Haverfordwest, Dyfed. SA62 3RD
- 0646 636205 FAX 0646 636205

A Field Centre, part of a network of Field Studies Council study centres, providing tailor-made courses in environmental topics to suit schools' curriculum needs.

N C SUPPORT Courses can be designed to suit all Key Stages on a day or residential basis. There is a long tradition of A-Level provision with specialist courses in Geography and Biology. INSET provision and student courses available.

OPENING End January to beginning December.

CATERING Fully catered courses are offered as part of the package.

COST Full costs available on application.

DISABLED FACILITIES Limited special facilities are available.

DIRECTIONS The Centre is about one and a half hours from the end of the M4 at Cross Hands. BR: Milford Haven.

Dan-yr-Ogof Caves
- Ian Gwilym
- Glintawe, Abercraf, Upper Swansea Valley, Powys. SA9 1GJ
- 0639 730284 FAX 0639 730293

The largest show-cave complex in Western Europe, including the new Morgan Bros Shire Horse Centre.

N C SUPPORT Range of teaching packs covering caves, dinosaur park, Iron-Age village and woodlands.

OPENING 1 April to 31 October: daily 10.00am. All year round for pre-booked schools.

CATERING Coffee shop (seats 100).

COST Educational rate (groups of 15 or more): children £2.50, adults £4.00, teachers free.

DISABLED FACILITIES Unsuitable for wheelchairs.

DIRECTIONS Midway between Swansea and Brecon on the A4067.

Dinefwr Park
- Gavin Hogg
- Llandeilo, Dyfed. SA19 6RT
- 0558 823902

A landscaped park of beauty and tranquillity, at the heart of Welsh history for a thousand years.

VISITS OUT
WALES

N C SUPPORT Guided tours available by arrangement with the warden.

OPENING April to October: daily 10.00am–5.00pm.

COST School groups (min. 15 people): 60p (1993 prices).

DISABLED FACILITIES Toilet.

Dolaucothi Gold Mines
- The Administrator
- Pumsaint, Llanwrda. SA19 8RR
- 055 85 359

Gold mines on the Dolaucothi Estate set amid wooded hillsides overlooking the beautiful Cothi valley, first exploited by the Romans, last worked in 1938; the Visitor Centre and Miners' Way provide information on the history and geology of the mine; underground tours are available mid-summer; displays of 1930s mining machinery.

N C SUPPORT There is a study centre; teachers' pack; audio-visual presentations.

DISABLED FACILITIES The tour is unsuitable for disabled or infirm visitors.

DIRECTIONS Between Lampeter and Llanwrda on the A482. Bus: Bws Dyfed 234 from Llandeilo, Tuesday only. BR: Llanwrda (not Sunday, except May–September) eight miles.

Dyfed Wildlife Trust
- June Glennerster
- 7 Market Street, Haverfordwest, Dyfed. SA61 1HF
- 0437 765462 FAX 0437 767163

School visits to Skomer Island National Nature Reserve. School pack and video provided. Reduced boat fares, free landing on the reserve. Aimed at 9–14-year-olds.

OPENING 10.00am–3.00pm

CATERING None.

COST On the island is free, one member of staff for every ten students advised.

DISABLED FACILITIES None.

DIRECTIONS Boats leave Martins Haven, one mile west of Marloes, daily except Monday.

East Nolton Riding Stables
- John Owen
- East Nolton, Nolton, Haverfordwest, Dyfed. SA62 3NW
- 0437 710360

Riding holidays (weekly or mini-breaks); half-day, one-and-a-half- or one-hour hacks; beach riding, wooded valley with optional jumps and riding over fields overlooking St Bride's Bay; indoor BHS instruction, fun gymkhana. Holidays tailored to meet groups' requirements.

OPENING All year round.

CATERING Self-catering accommodation or full board. Groups of up to 45 catered for.

COST Two-and-a-half-hour, one-and-a-half hour and one-hour rides: available to groups of more than ten with a 10% discount. Weekly and mini-break prices: contact John Owen.

DISABLED FACILITIES None.

DIRECTIONS M4 to end, then Carmarthen A40 to Haverfordwest; take St David's road from

VISITS OUT

WALES

Haverfordwest A487 to Simpson Cross, turn left for Nolton and follow stable signs.

Felin Crewi Water Mill
- Patti Partridge
- Felin Crewi, Penegoes, Machynlleth, Powys. SY20 8NH
- 0654 703113 FAX 0653 703113

Beautifully restored 16th-century watermill operating commercially as a flour mill and educational centre. Busy, exciting environment using principles of mechanics, hydraulics and renewable energy. Nature trail (commended by David Bellamy). Bird hide, animals, water birds.

N C SUPPORT The facilities offered cover specific subject areas within the National Curriculum: mainly Technology, History and Science, Key Stages 1–3. Teachers' pack available on receipt of two first class stamps. Guided walks available.

OPENING Easter to October: daily 10.30am–5.30pm. Winter: Wednesday 9.30am–3.30pm. Other times by arrangement.

CATERING Cafe serves drinks, ice creams, hot and cold snacks and meals.

COST Children 75p, teachers and helpers free. Informative guided tour £5.00 per group.

DISABLED FACILITIES Two floors of mill, the whole of the nature trail, bird hide and cafe are all wheelchair accessible.

DIRECTIONS Fifty yards off the A489, two miles east of Machynlleth.

Ffestiniog Railway
- Hywel William
- Harbour Station, Porthmadog, Gwynedd. LL49 9NF
- 0766 512340 FAX 0766 514576

A narrow-gauge railway, steam-hauled with a 13-mile-long track running through Snowdonia National Park from Porthmadog to Blaenau Ffestiniog.

N C SUPPORT Education pack available. Currently attempting to set up National Curriculum-recognised pack in conjunction with local TEC.

OPENING March to November: daily. Limited winter service.

CATERING Full buffet service on trains. Restaurant at Harbourt Station, cafe midway along line.

COST Full round trip £11.40, family (two adults and two children) £22.80, shuttle (shorthaul) £2.50.

DISABLED FACILITIES Adapted doors on carriages for wheelchairs. Toilets available.

DIRECTIONS Follow signs.

Forest Enterprise
- D Case
- Government Buildings, Aran Road, Dolgellau, Gwynedd. LL40 1LW
- 0341 422289 FAX 0341 423893

Forest park, nature reserve, Information Centre, exhibition, forest waymarked walks, mountain bike routes/hire, slide show, children's play area, forest shop.

N C SUPPORT Conducted parties from Information Centre.

OPENING Information Centre 10.00am–5.00pm.

WALES

CATERING Cafe at Information Centre.

COST Conducted parties by appointment. Free at present, but under review.

DISABLED FACILITIES All toilets. Access to Information Centre, exhibition and forest shop.

DIRECTIONS The Information Centre is two and a half miles north of Ganllwyd on the A470 (well signposted).

Gigrin Farm
- E P Powell
- South Street, Rhayader, Powys. LD6 5BL
- 0597 810243

A working hill farm offering a varied and exciting environment for exploration from deciduous woodland to upland vegetation. A safe, though challenging trail incorporates trout pool, badger sett, adventurous play, etc.

N C SUPPORT Would support any outdoor pursuits or Environmental Studies programme and National Curriculum, particularly in Geography (all ATs), Science (AT2), Art (AT1). All English ATs covered in follow-up. Adaptable to all Key Stages.

ANNUAL OR ONE OFF EVENT Open Days in August.

OPENING March to November: daily 10.00am–6.00pm.

CATERING By arrangement.

COST Children 50p, adults £1.50.

DIRECTIONS Signposted 200 yards off the A470, the main north–south Wales road. Half a mile south of Rhayader, Powys, mid-Wales.

Harlech Castle
- The Custodian
- Harlech, Gwynedd. LL46 2YM
- 0766 780552

Harlech formed part of a bold military strategy; its power and might are unquestioned even today, 700 years after the castle was built. Its soaring walls and towers are challenged for supremacy only by the purple mass of distant Snowdonia. These rugged peaks played a large part in determining Harlech's siting as one of the so-called 'iron-ring' of fortresses, built to contain the Welsh in their mountain fastness. Castle Gatehouse Exhibition: 'A Castle and its People'.

N C SUPPORT For details of educational material and guidebooks available please contact the Education Officer, CADW, Welsh Historic Monuments, Brunel House, 2 Fitzalan Road, Cardiff CF2 1UY (Tel: 0222 465511).

OPENING Summer (end March to end October): daily 9.30am–6.30pm. Winter (end October to end March): Monday to Friday 9.30am–4.00pm, Sunday 2.00pm–4.00pm. Closed Christmas Eve, Christmas Day, Boxing Day and New Year's Eve.

COST Free entry to the sites will be granted to educational parties subject to a number of conditions (details on the back of the Educational Visit Application Form).

DISABLED FACILITIES None.

DIRECTIONS Access via the A496. BR: Harlech quarter of a mile.

VISITS OUT
WALES

Inigo Jones Slateworks
- R E Davis
- Tudor Slateworks, 4 Groeslon, Caernarfon. LL54 7ST
- 0286 830242 FAX 0286 831247

Inigo Jones Slateworks was established in 1861 to prefabricate school writing slates. Today, the company produces architectural, monumental and craft items from the same raw material, natural slate.

N C SUPPORT The self-guided tour comprises a video presentation followed by a Walkman audio guide around the workshops. There is a historical letter-cutting and calligraphy exhibition.

OPENING Easter to September: Monday to Friday 9.00am–5.00pm, weekends and bank holidays 10.00am–5.00pm. October to Easter: Monday to Friday 9.00am–5.00pm, Saturday 9.00am–12.00 noon.

CATERING Cafe from Easter to September.

COST Children £1.50, adults £2.50. Discount of 20% for groups of ten or more.

DISABLED FACILITIES Toilet.

DIRECTIONS On main A487, six miles from Caernarfon in the direction of Porthmadog, between Groeslon and Penygroes.

Kidwelly Castle
- The Custodian
- Kidwelly, Dyfed. SA17 5BG
- 0554 890104

Impressive remains of a castle established as a huge earthwork in the early 12th century. The stone castle was first raised by the de Chaworths, and was much modified later by the Earls of Lancaster.

OPENING Free entry to sites will be granted to educational parties provided a number of conditions are satisfied. These are listed on the Educational Visits application forms. All educational visits must take place on weekdays during normal school hours.

DISABLED FACILITIES Contact the Custodian for access details.

KNIGHTS CAVERNS

A fantastic multi-media look at the legends, castles and rebellions of Ancient North Wales.
- Right on the seafront in Rhyl
- Perfect for all ages.
- The Magnificent Castles of North Wales - an "in-the-round" film show.
- The Path of the Spirits - a walk through the myths of the region.
- The Tales of the Mabinogion - some of Wales' greatest stories brought to life in an atmospheric Celtic chamber.

38/41 West Parade, Rhyl, Clwyd, LL18 1HJ. Tel: 0745 338562
Please contact us for group details

Knights' Caverns
- Megan Chambers
- 38–41 West Parade, Rhyl, Clwyd. LL18 1HG
- 0745 338562 FAX 0745 336502

The Knights' Caverns bring to life the excitement of North Wales' legends and history with fascinating tales from the Mabinogion, the

VISITS OUT

WALES

building of Wales' great castles and much more.

N C SUPPORT Information/education pack is available on request and is provided on any enquiry.

OPENING End October to Easter: 10.00am–6.00pm. Easter to end October: 10.00am–10.00pm.

CATERING Cafe (seats 80).

COST Children 75p; adults £2.00; Senior Citizens £1.75. Groups of ten or more: under 14s £1.25, under 12s 75p, two adults free for every ten pupils.

DISABLED FACILITIES Able to cater for small parties.

DIRECTIONS A55 Expressway, then signs to Rhyl. Situated on Rhyl Promenade, close to the rotating tower.

Lampeter Greek & Latin

- K R Hopwood
- Summer Workshop, Department of Classics, St David's University College, Lampeter, Dyfed. SA48 7ED
- 0570 422351

Beginners and advanced courses in Greek and/or Latin, taught in two one-week modules. Students may take one or two modules.

N C SUPPORT This is the official summer school of the Joint Association of Classical Teachers and The Classical Association. We also receive support from the Hellenic Society and The Roman Society.

OPENING 24 July–6 August 1994

CATERING All tastes catered for.

COST £100 per week for residence. £40.00 for tuition.

DISABLED FACILITIES Yes.

Llanberis Lake Railway

- B Yarborough
- Gilfach Ddu, Llanberis, Gwynedd. LL55 4TY
- 0286 870549

A 40-minute ride through spectacular lakeside scenery on a quaint historic narrow-gauge steam train. Set within the Padarn Country Park.

N C SUPPORT Worksheets available for the railway, also nearby Slate Museum and nature and industrial trails.

OPENING Times vary from season to season. Write for leaflet.

CATERING Cafe.

COST Party rate: under 15s £1.25, adults £2.50, one adult free with every ten children.

DISABLED FACILITIES Full access to cafeteria and shop. Restricted access on train, but no steps.

DIRECTIONS Just off A4086 at Llanberis; follow the Padarn Country Park signs.

Llandow Motor Leisure Centre

- D Evans or T Cole
- Llandow Race Circuit, Llandow, Nr Cowbridge, South Glamorgan
- 0656 862437

The largest outdoor go-kart circuit in Wales, catering for private parties and individuals. Action packed fun one inch off the ground. Off-road buggies and rally cars also available. Individual training available for go-karts, buggies and rally cars.

ANNUAL OR ONE OFF EVENT Banger race meetings every bank holiday, custom car show throughout the year.

OPENING Daily. Floodlight evenings on request.

CATERING On request.

COST On application.

DISABLED FACILITIES None.

DIRECTIONS Junction 33 of the M4, then A4232 and A48 Cowbridge to Llandow Industrial Estate B4268; B4270 (not Llandow village).

Llanfair Slate Caverns
- Robert Owen
- Llanfair, Harlech, Gwynedd. LL46 2SA
- 0766 780247

Slate mine tourist attraction: see how the miners worked 200ft below ground. Chambers of up to 70ft high. Guided tours and slate splitting for all school groups.

N C SUPPORT Visit to mine goes hand in hand with Geology for younger children with 'hands on' experience. Also mineral section with stones and minerals from all over the world.

OPENING Easter to October 10.00am–5.00pm. Open all year for school and educational groups.

CATERING Cafe and picnic area.

COST Children £1.30, adults £2.30. Group discount of 10%.

DISABLED FACILITIES Half of the mine can be visited by people with disabilities.

DIRECTIONS One mile south of Harlech, eight miles north of Barmouth on the A496.

Llangollen YHA Centre
- Mr Bev Bamber
- Tyndwr Hall, Tyndwr Road, Llangollen, Clwyd. LL20 8AR
- 0978 860330 FAX 0978 861709

Llangollen YHA Centre is a residential centre offering accommodation to groups. Classroom facilities are available, together with a wide range of activity packages led by experienced staff.

N C SUPPORT Resource pack available for educational visits. Activities offered may be tailored to fit in with National Curriculum requirements. Staff will be pleased to discuss exact requirements.

ANNUAL OR ONE OFF EVENT Teachers' Educational Introductory weekends: send for details.

OPENING All year round.

CATERING Full cafeteria/meals service.

COST According to package required. One leader free for every ten paying participants. Free YHA membership for activity groups.

DISABLED FACILITIES None.

DIRECTIONS One mile from Llangollen in Shrewsbury direction. Easy access from London, West Midlands and North West.

Llywernog Mine Caverns
- Peter Lloyd Harvey
- Llywernog Silver Lead Mine, Ponterwyd, Aberystwyth, Dyfed. SY23 3AB
- 0970 85620

VISITS OUT

WALES

Cap Lamp Tours into 18th-century silver mine caverns. Award-winning Mining Museum, Miner's Trail, rock and mineral shop, tea room. Panning demonstrations in high season. Working waterwheels and old mining machinery.

N C SUPPORT Teaching support packages in preparation. Worksheets are available for Miner's Trail. Relevant to History, Geography, Geology and Technology.

ANNUAL OR ONE OFF EVENT Traditional Miners' 'Gala Day' with contests of 'mining skills' as traditionally used in the 19th century.

OPENING Easter to September: daily 10.00am–6.00pm (last admission 5.00pm). October: daily 10.00am–5.00pm (last admission 4.00pm). Winter opening by appointment.

CATERING Tea rooms, light lunches. Picnic area.

COST Option A, Museums and Surface Trail (including one underground tunnel): children (5–16 years) £1.60, adults £2.95, Senior Citizens/students £2.50, family ticket £8.50. Option B, the above plus guided underground Cap Lamp Tour: children £2.50, adults £3.95.

DISABLED FACILITIES Part access to the surface trail. No underground access.

DIRECTIONS Alongside the A44, one mile west of Ponterwyd, 11 miles inland from Aberystwyth and some three and a half miles from Devil's Bridge.

Maes Artro Village
- Carolyn Valizadeh
- Llanbedr, Barmouth, Gwynedd. LL45 2PZ
- 0341 23467

RAF Museum: 'Spitfire', military tanks and original air-raid shelter; re-created old Welsh street and rural exhibition; large sea-life aquarium and nature walk; adventure playground and picnic areas.

N C SUPPORT Worksheets available.

OPENING Easter to end September: daily 10.00am–5.30pm.

CATERING Picnic areas, counter service, coffee house.

COST School rates: children £1.80, adults £2.45, one adult free with every ten children.

DISABLED FACILITIES Wheelchair access throughout.

DIRECTIONS On the A496, between Barmouth and Harlech.

Manor House Wildlife Park
- C Williams
- St Florence, Tenby, Dyfed. SA70 8RJ
- 0646 651201

Set in 25 acres of wooded grounds and floral gardens with exotic birds, mammals, reptiles and fish. Large children's play area with go-karts, roundabouts, remote-control models. Model railway exhibition. Daily falconry displays (except Saturday).

N C SUPPORT Worksheets. Bird of prey displays with talks. Educational name plates on all the animals etc.

OPENING Daily 10.00am–6.00pm.

CATERING Self-service cafeteria.

COST Children £1.50, adults £3.50. Group rates: children £1.00, adults £3.00, one teacher free with every ten paying children (1993 prices).

DISABLED FACILITIES Toilets. Wheelchair accessibility throughout the Park

VISITS OUT
WALES

DIRECTIONS Situated on the B4318, two and a half miles outside Tenby on the Pembroke Road.

Marine Life Centre
- Mrs N Copley
- Feidr Pant-y-Bryn, St David's, Haverfordwest, Dyfed. SA62 6QS
- 0437 721665 FAX 0437 721665

Aquarium of marine fish native to Pembrokeshire, including touch tank, wave tank and shipwreck tank; 'Use of Sea' displays, video presentation and ex-RNLI lifeboat within the grounds.

N C SUPPORT Relevant to: Science in the National Curriculum (Variety of Life; Processes of Life and Human Influence on the Earth); Geography in the National Curriculum (Physical Geography, Environmental Geography).

OPENING March to end October: daily 10.00am–5.00pm.

COST Children £1.50, one adult free for every ten children, additional adults £2.70.

DISABLED FACILITIES All facilities accessible to people in wheelchairs.

DIRECTIONS Take the A487 from Haverfordwest to St David's. The Centre is situated on the left-hand side just before St David's.

Minerva Training
- Sarah Derry
- Plas Glansevin, Llangadog, Dyfed. SA19 9HY
- 0550 777121 FAX 0550 777890

Situated close to the Brecon Beacons National Park, with over 19 years' experience: exciting activities and personal development courses are run by qualified staff with an excellent safety record.

N C SUPPORT Personal development programmes which can link with National Curriculum requirements for Key Stages 2–4. Activities include abseiling, caving, gorge walking, initiative exercises and many more.

OPENING All year round.

CATERING Fully catered.

COST On application.

DISABLED FACILITIES None.

DIRECTIONS Thirty minutes from junction 49 of the M4. Llangadog is midway between Llandovery and Llandeilo, just off the A40.

Museum of Childhood
- Robert Brown
- 1 Castle Street, Beaumaris, Anglesey, Gwynedd. LL58 8AP
- 0248 712498

The Museum is in a Georgian building. Nine rooms packed with nostalgic items illustrating the more pleasurable side of family life.

N C SUPPORT Many aspects of the National Curriculum can be explored in a visit to the Museum. There are working models of music boxes, polyphons, phonographs, gramophones and organettes, displays which can enrich any topic of Sound and Music. Any class studying Victorian Britain would find a visit to the Museum informative and instructive since the Museum reflects many aspects of this period. There is plenty of scope for observational drawing. The Museum's collection is a source of inspiration for art work, e.g. beadwork, shellwork, Victorian samplers. There is a four-fold screen six feet high, decorated in collage: perhaps the children could create a modern equivalent back in the classroom.

OPENING Monday to Saturday 10.00am–5.30pm (last admission 4.30pm), Sunday 12.00 noon–5.00pm (last admission 4.00pm).

COST Children £1.25, adults £2.50. Discount of 15% for more than 25 people, discount of 10% for more than 12 people.

DISABLED FACILITIES Access to ground floor only.

DIRECTIONS Opposite the castle in Beaumaris town.

Museum of Welsh Woollen Industry *see* Amgueddfa Diwydiant

The National Coracle Centre
- Martin Fowler
- Cenarth, Newcastle Emlyn, Dyfed. GA38 9JL
- 0239 710980

A unique display of coracles from Wales and many parts of the world, a full guided tour of the Centre and the 17th-century flour mill.

N C SUPPORT An ancient form of transport used worldwide, method of fishing still used today, made from many different natural materials. Great History subject.

ANNUAL OR ONE OFF EVENT Coracle fishing still carried out. Coracle races in August.

OPENING Easter to end October: Sunday to Friday 10.30am–5.30pm. Saturday and evenings and winter months by appointment.

CATERING Picnic sites in the village.

COST Children 50p, three teachers free.

DISABLED FACILITIES Easy access.

DIRECTIONS A484 between Carmarthen and Cardigan beside the River Teify in Cenarth village.

National Museum of Wales
- Ms R M Jones
- Main Building, Cathays Park, Cardiff. CF1 3NP
- 0222 397951 FAX 0222 373219

Comprehensive art galleries (Medieval and Renaissance art up to the present day and including an extensive Impressionists collection). Ceramics and sculpture. New Natural History in Wales and Evolution of Wales galleries plus a Man and the Environment gallery. Archaeology galleries: Early Peoples temporary exhibition also.

N C SUPPORT Support for studies at Key Stages 1 to 4 in Art, Craft and Design; Earth Sciences; Geography; Archaeology and History; Natural and Physical Sciences and Technology through numerous work packs. INSET courses introduce workshops, activity sessions, handling sessions plus other activities as the basis of cross-curricular work, including language work and information technology. Education Officers assist in study and research in Art, Archaeology, Geology, History, Geography, the

Sciences. Access to library facilities through the Education Department.

OPENING Tuesday to Saturday 10.00am–5.00pm, Sunday 2.30pm–5.00pm.

COST Children (5–16 years) £1.00, adults 2.00, Senior Citizens £1.50. Group bookings: 10% discount for groups of 20 or more. Please book group in by phoning the above number. Further information from the Marketing Assistant.

DISABLED FACILITIES Wheelchair access to all galleries. Adapted toilets.

DIRECTIONS Situated in Cardiff's beautiful Civic Centre.

NATIONAL TRUST

Opening Times Write or telephone the administrator of the house, give preferred day and time, the size and age of the group, and the main purpose of the visit. *The National Trust Handbook* contains further relevant information.

Cost Unless otherwise stated in the *Handbook*, there is a reduction of around 50% for children aged 16 and under, when accompanied by their teacher. Education Group Members are admitted free. However, please note that there may be a small charge for any additional educational facilities or activities.

See individual entries for all other information.

Aberdulais Falls
Chirk Castle
Dolaucothi Gold Mines
Penrhyn Castle

Plas Newydd
Plas-yn-Rhiw
Snowdonia

Nuclear Electric

- G Thomas
- Transfynydd Power Station, Transfynydd, Blaenau Ffestiniog, Gwynedd. LL41 4DT
- 0766 87622 FAX 0766 87619

Tours of nuclear and hydro-electric power stations. Nature trails with environmental projects. Exhibitions using interactive laser-disc computers.

N C SUPPORT 'Learning through the Environment' projects. Schools' packs for primary schools.

OPENING Daily 9.00am–5.00pm. Closed Christmas Day, Boxing Day and New Year's Day.

CATERING Cafe.

COST Free.

DISABLED FACILITIES Yes.

DIRECTIONS From Harlech on the A496; from Dolgellau on the A470; from Porthmadog on the A487.

Oakwood Park Theme Park

- Mrs Daily
- Canaston Bridge, Narberth, Dyfed. SA67 8DE
- 0834 891373 FAX 0834 891380

Theme park set in 80 acres. One of Wales' top tourist attractions. A

VISITS OUT

WALES

whole day of fun for all ages. All-inclusive entrance price.

OPENING Easter to end September: daily 10.00am. Restricted opening in October.

CATERING Large 140-seat restaurant, many fast-food outlets, ice cream parlour, candy store.

COST Special rates for schools and groups.

DISABLED FACILITIES Toilets. Staff always on hand.

DIRECTIONS Signposted off the A40 between Carmarthen and Haverfordwest.

Orielton Field Studies Council Centre

- Robin Crump
- Pembroke, Dyfed. SA71 5EZ
- 0646 661225

A Field Centre, part of a network of Field Studies Council study centres, providing tailor-made courses in environmental topics to suit schools' curriculum.

N C SUPPORT Courses can be designed to suit all Key Stages on a day or residential basis. There is a long tradition of A-Level provision with specialist courses in Geography and Biology. INSET provision and student courses available.

OPENING End January to beginning December.

CATERING Fully catered courses are offered as part of the package.

COST Full costs available on application.

DISABLED FACILITIES Limited special facilities are available.

DIRECTIONS The Centre is about one hour from the M4. BR: Pembroke.

Oriel Ynys Mon

- Dr Kath Davies
- Rhosmeirch, Llangefni, Anglesey. LL77 7TQ
- 0248 724444 FAX 0248 750282

A Museum and art gallery with a permanent exhibition on the history of Anglesey, natural history and archaeology. It also holds a large collection of wildlife paintings by C F Tunnicliffe.

N C SUPPORT Worksheets on History and ornithology. Small handling collections for History and archaeology. Curriculum-related workshops and special art workshops can be arranged on request

ANNUAL OR ONE OFF EVENT Wide range of temporary art exhibitions.

OPENING Tuesday to Sunday 10.30am–5.00pm.

CATERING Cafe.

COST Free admission for any pre-booked educational groups.

DISABLED FACILITIES Full access. Adapted toilet. Car park for use by people with disabilities.

DIRECTIONS The Museum is on the B5111, half a mile north of Llangefni on the Amlwch Road.

Robert Owen Museum

- John Hatton Davidson
- The Cross, Broad Street, Newtown, Powys. SY16 2BB
- 0686 626345

VISITS OUT
WALES

An intimate museum, intriguingly laid out, telling the remarkable life of Robert Owen from shop-boy to model employer, social reformer, socialist and cooperator, with fascinating pictures and Owen memorabilia.

N C SUPPORT Publications include a Resource Pack on Robert Owen: 52 pages A4 with 27 black and white illustrations (£1.80 plus p&p); and a children's activity sheet (p&p only).

OPENING Monday to Friday 9.45am–11.45am and 2.00pm–3.30pm, Saturday 10.00am–11.30am. Groups much larger than 30 are advised to split and visit in shifts.

COST Free.

DISABLED FACILITIES Ramp available if given prior notice.

DIRECTIONS In the centre of Newtown opposite the town clock.

Padarn Country Park *see* Llanberis Lake Railway

Parc Padarn
- The Promotions Officer
- Llanberis, Gwynedd
- 0286 870892

Padarn Park is established in land once part of the former Dinorwic Slate Quarries in Llanberis. In its heyday Dinorwic was one of the two largest quarries in Wales. There are many acres of woodland criss-crossed with footpaths created by the quarrymen. The old buildings where the men used to work and live lie silent and empty, waiting to be explored.

N C SUPPORT There are various interests which can be linked to the National Curriculum: the Lake Railway; the Slate Museum; the Quarry Hospital (a restored Victorian quarrymen's hospital ward, operating theatre and sister's room); craftspeople at work; walks and trails.

ANNUAL OR ONE OFF EVENT Contact the Promotions Officer for further details.

OPENING Easter to October or by arrangement. Grounds open all year round.

CATERING Picnic tables beside the lake and on the Quarry Hospital terrace overlooking the lake.

COST Contact the Promotions Officer.

DISABLED FACILITIES Wheelchair access to most areas (except woodland paths).

DIRECTIONS A leaflet is available giving details and a map with directions.

Penmachno Woollen Mill
- Kathy Senior
- Betws-y-Coed, Gwynedd. LL41 0VL
- 0690 710545 FAX 0690 710100

Eighteenth-century working woollen mill, situated on River Machno. Still produces tweed and rugs on 1940s dobcross looms.

N C SUPPORT Industrial Heritage, Industrial Revolution.

OPENING Daily 9.00am–5.30pm.

CATERING Cafe (seats 55). Home-made cakes, soup, salads, etc.

COST Free.

DIRECTIONS One and a half miles from Betws-y-Coed on the A5 towards Llangollen.

VISITS OUT
WALES

Penrhyn Castle
- A Laing or Marion Evans
- Bangor. LL57 4HN
- 0248 353084 **FAX** 0248 371281

A neo-Norman castle built 1820–40 by architect Thomas Hopper on the site of a medieval building; housing fine classical art; original furniture and soft furnishings. A unique collection of quarry locomotives, rolling stock and track.

N C SUPPORT A Schools' Educational qualified teacher coordinates 'hands-on' activities of hand painting; strict schoolroom lesson; laundry. A children's audio tour of the Castle guides children through the interior of the Castle.

ANNUAL OR ONE OFF EVENT Country Fayre end of July with rare breeds; spinning and weaving competition; mobile engines; archery, etc.

CATERING Tea rooms, picnic tables and seats in grounds. Railway Museum foyer can be used if wet.

DISABLED FACILITIES Two wheelchairs available, ramps to ground floor rooms; toilets for disabled at front and rear; audio tour loop, braille guided.

DIRECTIONS On the A5122, one mile east of Bangor (OS Map 115: ref SH 603720); signposted from junction of A5 and A55 trunk routes.

Penscynor Wildlife Park
- Howie Watkins
- Cilfrew, Neath, West Glamorgan. SA10 8LF
- 0639 642189 **FAX** 0639 635152

Sixteen-acre site, captive breeding centre for parrots, penguins, primates (monkeys and apes) and others. Public feeding times, full-time education staff.

N C SUPPORT Talks, tours, animal handling, drama/art workshops, lecture theatre, over 35 teachers' packs. Resource library and lots more. Key areas Biology (Environmental Education), all Key Stage levels supported.

OPENING 10.00am–6.00pm or dusk.

CATERING Coffee shop; burger bar (summer only).

COST Group rates (discount of over £1.00 per head) for parties of 20: children (3–14 years) £2.00, adults and over 14s £3.00, one adult free for every ten children, under 3s free.

DISABLED FACILITIES 80% access.

DIRECTIONS Two miles north of Neath, just off the A465 at Aberdulais.

Perth-y-Pia Outdoor Centre
- Jane Peacegood
- Craig Llwydd, Llanbedr, Crickhowell, Powys. NP8 1SR
- 0873 810050

Renovated farmhouse and barn situated in the heart of the Black Mountains. Accommodates 34. Superb area for field studies and outdoor activities. The exceptional food and friendly atmosphere has resulted in many repeat bookings.

N C SUPPORT The Centre Manager is a graduate in Geography and can advise on fieldwork locations.

OPENING All year round.

CATERING Fully catered or self-catering available.

COST £17.00 plus VAT per person for bed, breakfast, packed lunch and evening meal.

DISABLED FACILITIES None, though some bedrooms and the dining room, toilet, kitchen, lounge are on the ground floor.

DIRECTIONS Take the A40 to Crickhowell, turn up Llanbedr road by Action Garage and continue two miles Perth-y-Pia. Drive is on right hand side.

Pili Palace
- Mrs G Evans
- Butterfly & Bird Palace, Ffordd Penmynydd, Menai Bridge, Anglesey, Gwynedd. LL59 5RP
- 0248 712474

Experience a tropical environment with hundreds of free-flying butterflies; tropical birds in a walk-through aviary, tarantulas, scorpions and leaf-cutting ants in the creepy crawly cavern.

N C SUPPORT Talk and video and guided tour. All aspects based on the National Curriculum. Special education packs and worksheets.

OPENING Mid-March to 31 December.

CATERING Hungry Caterpillar cafe and picnic areas.

COST £1.65, one teacher free for every 12 children.

DISABLED FACILITIES Disabled access; toilets.

DIRECTIONS Follow brown-and-white signs from Britannia and Menai Bridges. Manchester two hours. Liverpool one and a half hours.

Pinewood Stables
- Miss Pat Oldfield
- Sychnant Pass Road, Conwy, Gwynedd. LL32 8BZ
- 0492 592256

All accompanied rides are taken on nearby mountains within Snowdonia National Park.

OPENING All year round: daily; times vary. Please ring for details.

CATERING Small shop supplying sweets, crisps and cold drinks.

COST One hour £8.50, one and a half hours £12.50, two hours £16.50. Groups: one hour £8.00, one and a half years £12, two hours £15.50.

DISABLED FACILITIES None.

DIRECTIONS One mile off the A55 Expressway. Take A547 for Conwy straight through town, drive through archway going out of town walls; turn left then right at junction. The stables are half a mile on the right.

Plas Newydd
- Mr J L Evans, Administrator
- Llanfairpwll, Anglesey, Gwynedd. LL61 6EQ
- 0248 714 795

Late 18th-century house situated on the banks of the Menai Straits. Rex Whistler's largest wall painting and an exhibition devoted to his life and works. A military museum with relics from the battle of Waterloo.

N C SUPPORT Military museum/Battle of Waterloo. Famous artificial leg. Paintings. School teachers' pack £4.00. Eighteenth-century house (Contents Georgian/Victorian).

OPENING March 30 to October: daily 12–4.30pm, except Saturday. October: Friday and Sunday 12–4.30pm.

WALES

CATERING Tea room.

DISABLED FACILITIES Toilet at reception. Ramps at the house.

DIRECTIONS Two miles from the village of Llanfairpwll on the A4080 to Brynsiencyn.

Plas Teg
- Mrs C G N Bayley
- Pontblyddyn, Mold, Clwyd. CH7 4HN
- 0352 771335

The most important Jacobean house in Wales, built in 1610. Ideal for outings as people can walk around approximately 25 rooms, each with furniture and fabrics.

OPENING Saturday and Sunday 11.00am–5.00pm. Other times by appointment, including evenings.

COST Children £1.25, adults £2.50.

DISABLED FACILITIES None.

Plas-yn-Rhiw
- Mrs M M Dick
- Rhiw, Pwllheli, Gwynedd

Small manor house (17th–19th century) overlooking Port Neigwl on the Lleyn Peninsula. It is an enchanting place with spectacular views.

DISABLED FACILITIES Limited.

DIRECTIONS From Pwllheli follow the south coast road to Aberdaron.

Powysland Museum
- Eva Bredsdorff
- The Canal Wharf, Welshpool, Powys. SY21 7AQ
- 0938 554656

Local museum housed in a restored and renovated warehouse by the Montgomery Canal. The collection consists of archaeology and social history of Welshpool and Montgomeryshire.

N C SUPPORT Quiz sheets (price £3.00) on several subjects within the National Curriculum, e.g. Transport, Agriculture, Crafts.

ANNUAL OR ONE OFF EVENT A programme of temporary exhibitions each lasting two to three months.

OPENING Monday, Tuesday, Thursday and Friday 11.00am–1.00pm and 2.00pm–5.00pm, Saturday 2.00pm–5.00pm. 1 May to 1 October: Saturday and Sunday 10.00am–1.00pm and 2.00pm–5.00pm

CATERING None.

COST Free.

DISABLED FACILITIES Parking for people with disabilities. Lift to first floor.

DIRECTIONS In the centre of Welshpool en route to the BR station.

Quasar Barry Island
- Demetria Panayides
- 5 Roman Well Road, Barry Island, South Glamorgan. 0446 421611

A high-tech laser game for adults and children. Armed with a space pack and laser gun, two teams battle it out in a space-age game-zone for points. Individual score sheets at the end of the game.

N C SUPPORT Schools and colleges also use the centre as a recreational facility for sponsored events.

OPENING April to September: daily 11.00am–10.00pm. October to

VISITS OUT
WALES

March: daily 5.00pm–10.00pm. Any time available if pre-booked.

CATERING Food available if requested on booking.

COST Children under 15 years £3.00, 15 and over £3.50. Groups of 20 or more: £2.75.

DISABLED FACILITIES Not suitable for disabled visitors.

DIRECTIONS When coming onto the 'Island' the centre is on the left hand side opposite the fairground.

Raglan Castle
- The Custodian
- Raglan, Gwent. NP5 2BT
- 0291 690228

Raglan Castle belongs mainly to the 15th century and was as much a product of social grandeur as it was a military necessity. It was begun, probably on the site of a small Norman Castle, in the 1430s by Sir William ap Thomas. His great tower or 'Yellow Tower' of Gwent is strikingly positioned outside the castle walls and its strength was almost sufficient to defy Cromwell's demolition engineers. An exhibition on the history of Raglan is situated in the Closet Tower and two rooms of the Gate Passage.

OPENING Summer (end March to end October): daily 9.30am–6.30pm. Winter (end October to end March): Monday to Friday 9.30am–4.00pm, Sunday 2.00pm–4.00pm. Closed Christmas Eve, Christmas Day, Boxing Day and New Year's Eve.

DISABLED FACILITIES Not really suitable as there are many steps.

DIRECTIONS Access via A40 and signposted. BR: Abergavenny ten miles.

Rheidol Study Centre
- Simon Hulme
- Penrhyncoch, Aberystwyth, Dyfed. SY23 3EX
- 0970 828322

Purpose-built outdoor education and field study centre for 60 people, with three teaching rooms, seven single rooms, five dormitories, shop, lounge, refectory, bar, kit hire, drying room.

N C SUPPORT Two resident qualified teachers, three purpose-built and fitted teaching rooms, resource packs. Full programmes at centre for Geography, Geology and Ecology and Fieldwork. Outdoor pursuits also.

OPENING All year round.

CATERING Fully equipped kitchen, bar, drinks machine.

COST £22.00 plus VAT per person per night, one free place for every ten.

DISABLED FACILITIES Toilet and shower.

DIRECTIONS Seven miles east of Aberystwyth.

Rhondda Heritage Park
- Sarah Wheatley
- Lewis Merthyr, Coed Cae Road, Trehafod, Mid-Glamorgan. CF37 7NP
- 0443 682036 FAX 0443 687420

The only colliery buildings remaining in the Rhondda. Combining 'Black Gold', a unique audio-visual presentation which portrays the social history of the Rhondda, with

VISITS OUT

WALES

'The Energy Zone', an educational play area based on the energy cycle.

N C SUPPORT Black gold education pack for Key Stages 1 and 2. Study notes and worksheets. The Energy Zone worksheets for Key Stages 1–4. All materials are bilingual and may be photocopied.

OPENING Daily (except Christmas Day and Boxing Day) 10.00am–6.00pm. (last admission 4.30pm).

CATERING Gallery restaurant or Energy Zone cafe.

COST Adults £3.50, school parties £2.50, discount of 10% for groups of ten or more.

DISABLED FACILITIES Toilet, ramp access, lift access.

DIRECTIONS Twenty minutes' drive from junction 32 of the M4, just off the A470 between Pontypridd and Porth.

Rhyd-y-Creuau

- Julian Ellis
- The Drapers Field Centre, Betws-y-Coed, Gwynedd. LL24 0HB
- 0690 710494

A residential and day centre specialising in fieldwork. Accommodation for 70 people, five laboratories, scientific library, Met station and five tutors with detailed knowledge of valley, mountain, forest and coast sites in Snowdonia.

N C SUPPORT Courses for students (Key Stages 1–4, and A-level) and INSET for teachers, in Science (ATs 1–5), Geography, and cross-curricular themes in outdoor education: one day, weekend or up to a week.

OPENING All year round: daily, residential. Office: Monday to Saturday 9.00am–5.00pm.

CATERING Breakfast, packed lunches and evening meal provided in the dining hall. Meat and vegetarian dishes.

COST Examples: GCSE one-day £12 per pupil; A-level one-week £188. Group and seasonal reductions available.

DISABLED FACILITIES Fieldwork sites used have difficult access for disabled people.

DIRECTIONS One mile north of Betws-y-Coed on the A470. Manchester/Liverpool 90 minutes, Birmingham three hours.

Rhyl Sea Life Centre

- Nigel Davies
- East Parade, Rhyl, Clwyd. LL18 3AF
- 0745 344660 FAX 0745 332991

The Sea Life experience is a delight for all ages. Children and adults alike love the special Quiz Trails, cuddly mascots Sammy Seal and Shakey Shark, the thrilling 'hands-on' experience of a touch pool and the surprises and wonders that are to be found in the unique Sea Labs. Some centres even have adventure playgrounds where the children can let off steam.

N C SUPPORT Teachers' packs with information and workshops for each of three age ranges are available (choice of three subject areas). Material can be formulated on request.

OPENING February to November: daily 10.00am–5.00pm. Closed December to January.

WALES

CATERING Restaurant available.

COST Children £2.25, one teacher free with every ten pupils, extra teachers £2.25.

DISABLED FACILITIES Some displays are accessible by steps. Restaurant and shop are fully accessible.

DIRECTIONS Head for Promenade and then the clock-tower roundabout next to the Sea Life Centre.

Rock Park Centre
- Mrs Liz Higginson
- Llandrindod Wells, Powys. LD1 6AE
- 0597 822021 FAX 0597 825199

Family centre in magnificent mid-Wales: accommodation comprises dormitories, single and en-suite rooms for up to 160. Indoor heated pool, multi-activity holidays: canoeing, abseiling, assault course, archery, etc.

N C SUPPORT Geography/river studies; environmental field trips; visits to places of interest (e.g. Big Pit, Dan yr Ogof show caves). Outdoor education includes team-building and overnight camping experience.

ANNUAL OR ONE OFF EVENT Royal Welsh Show in July. Victorian Festival in August.

OPENING All year round.

CATERING Fully catered.

COST Charges range from £14.00 per night to £90.00 per week depending on the season. Please apply for details.

DISABLED FACILITIES No ground-floor bedrooms.

DIRECTIONS Llandrindod Wells lies on A483 crossing A44 three miles away. The centre is adjacent to the Rock Park Spa on the edge of this small town.

Roman Legionary Museum
- David Zionkiewicz
- High Street, Caerleon, Gwent. NP6 1AE
- 0633 423134

Museum displays finds from the Roman Legionary fortress at Isca. Life-size models of three Roman soldiers.

N C SUPPORT An educational resource pack is available and includes activity sheets and all information to support a Key Stage 2 visit.

ANNUAL OR ONE OFF EVENT Regular half-term activities and a schools' week (usually in June, phone for details).

OPENING 15 March to 15 October: Monday to Friday 10.00am–6.00pm, Sunday 2.00pm–6.00pm. 16 October to 14 March: Wednesday 10.00am–4.30pm, Sunday 2.00pm–4.30pm.

CATERING None.

COST Admission free to school parties (if pre-booked).

DISABLED FACILITIES Wheelchair access. Many objects can be touched by visually impaired visitors.

DIRECTIONS About one mile from the M4 (junction 25) near Newport.

St David's Bishops' Palace
- The Custodian
- St David's, Dyfed. SA62 6PE
- 0437 720517

VISITS OUT
WALES

St David's is Britain's smallest city and is set in the Pembrokeshire Coast National Park. As it stands, the richly decorative Bishops' Palace was built largely by Henry de Gower (1328–47). It is situated within the Cathedral Close, and is among a group of medieval buildings unique in Wales. The battlements, curtain walls and gatehouse speak eloquently of great men, rich in experience of church and state. 'Life in the Palace of a Prince of the Church' and 'Lords of the Palace' Exhibitions.

OPENING Summer (end March to end October): daily 9.30am–6.30pm. Winter (end October to end March): Monday to Friday 9.30am–4.00pm, Sunday 2.00pm–4.00pm. Closed 24–26 December and New Year's Day.

DISABLED FACILITIES Contact the administrator for access details.

DIRECTIONS Access via A487 to St David's, minor road past Cathedral.

St Donats Arts Centre
- Angela Rogers
- St Donats Castle, Nr Llantwit Major, South Glamorgan. CE61 1LF
- 0446 794848 FAX 0446 794163

Professionally run centre for the arts involved in a wide variety of public performances and children's events, including theatre, jazz, storytelling, folk music and the visual arts.

N C SUPPORT Annual residency by professional crafts artists covers Design and Technology. Other projects stimulate interest in Communication Skills, History, Geography, Physical Education and Science.

ANNUAL OR ONE OFF EVENT Crafts in Action Festival in late May. Storytelling Festival in early July.

OPENING Monday to Friday 10.00am–6.00pm, plus all performance evenings January to December.

CATERING By arrangement.

COST All children and students half price, plus 10% discount on group bookings. Some events free.

DISABLED FACILITIES Not good, but friendly staff always on hand to help.

DIRECTIONS Thirty minutes from Cardiff along the A48, 40 minutes from Swansea. The Centre is set in the grounds of a cliff-top castle by the sea.

Sealyham Activity Centre
- Mrs Valerie Richards
- Wolfscastle, Haverfordwest, Dyfed. SA62 5NF
- 0348 840763 FAX 0348 840763

Outdoor pursuits, surfing, orienteering, coasteering, archery, shooting, pony trekking; residential courses for schools and colleges. BAHA approved. Wales Tourist Board accredited.

N C SUPPORT Courses compatible with National Curriculum: Environmental Studies etc.

OPENING March to October.

CATERING Full residential and some self-catering.

COST Write for details. One place free for every ten full paying guests.

VISITS OUT
WALES

DISABLED FACILITIES Cater for special needs but there are no facilities for wheelchairs.

DIRECTIONS Turning for Sealyham on A40 between Fishguard and Haverfordwest. Centre is three-quarters of a mile down the lane on the right.

Segontium Roman Fort Museum
- Officer in Charge
- Beddgelert Road, Caernarfon, Gwynedd. LL55 2LN
- 0286 675625

A small museum, a branch of the National Museum of Wales, on the site of the Roman fort at Caernarfon. The displays set the fort in its historic context and give a vivid impression through artefacts, reconstructions and models of the life of the soldiers there.

N C SUPPORT A handling collection of artefacts from the site is available, together with a range of activity sheets. Teachers' courses and events are also held at the site. Specialised support is available from the staff of the Archaeology and Education Departments, National Museum of Wales.

OPENING March to October: Monday to Saturday 9.30am–5.30pm; November to February: Monday to Saturday 9.30am–4.00pm; Sundays 2.00pm–5.00pm, all year.

COST Free.

DISABLED FACILITIES Contact the Officer in Charge.

DIRECTIONS In Caernarfon town.

Senedd-Dy Owain Glyndwr
- Tegwyn Griffiths
- Parliament House, Maengwyn Street, Machynlleth, Powys. SY20 8EE
- 0654 702827

Interpretive and brass-rubbing centre. Visit for souvenirs and see a display of photographs, notes, models and books.

N C SUPPORT Owain Glyndwr's Parliament House of the 15th century depicts Welsh history in the Middle Ages, and the story of Owain Glyndwr's rebellion.

OPENING Easter to 1 October: 10.00am–5.00pm. Winter by arrangement.

CATERING None.

COST Free admission, but donations gratefully received.

DISABLED FACILITIES On ground floor: easy access.

DIRECTIONS On Main Street within Machynlleth.

Snowdonia
- The Administrator
- Llewelyn Cottage, Beddgelert, Gwynedd. LL55 4YA
- 0766 86293

The National Trust owns more than 40,000 acres of Snowdonia and nine of the fourteen highest peaks, as well as 32 miles of coastline in North Wales.

N C SUPPORT A countryside education officer is now based at Beddgelert, working with schools and undertaking project work on the coast and in the countryside on a cross-curricular basis and in the

Trust's coastal and hill-farming properties, and can provide information at all educational levels.

DISABLED FACILITIES Contact the Administrator for access details.

DIRECTIONS Contact the Administrator.

Graham Sutherland Gallery
- Mrs Sally Moss
- Picton Castle, The Rhos, Haverfordwest, Dyfed. SA62 4AS
- 0437 751296 FAX 0437 751322

The Graham Sutherland Gallery is a unique educational resource. Watch 'Sutherland in Wales' (video), look at the paintings he has just explained and then within minutes be walking in his footsteps at the Cleddau Estuary.

N C SUPPORT Workbooks and teachers' notes: junior/primary information pack, secondary. Workshops/lectures can be tailor-made to suit requirements.

ANNUAL OR ONE OFF EVENT Annual programme of temporary exhibitions and events and permanent collection of work by Graham Sutherland.

OPENING End March to end September: Tuesday to Sunday 10.30am–12.00pm and 1.30pm–5.00pm, closed Monday but open bank holiday Mondays. Open by appointment October to February.

CATERING Cafe in the courtyard and picnic areas in the grounds of Picton Castle (no wet-weather facilities in the gallery for packed lunches).

COST Children 50p, adults £1.00. Most schools in Wales free, other schools 33p each child.

DISABLED FACILITIES Access to all of gallery (one floor, no steps) and toilet.

DIRECTIONS The Gallery is situated in the courtyard of Picton Castle to the south of the A40; five miles east of Haverfordwest and 25 miles west of Carmarthen. Follow the signs from the A40 southwards to The Rhos.

Swansea Museum and Swansea Maritime Industrial Museum
- Gerald Gabb
- Victoria Road, Swansea. SA1 1SN
- 0792 653763

Swansea Maritime Museum: real vessels afloat, working woollen mill, tram shed, etc. Swansea Museum: Early Peoples, Romans, Victorians, Egyptology, etc.

N C SUPPORT Key Stage 1: sessions on Transport, Houses and Homes, etc. Key Stage 2: Land Transport, Ships and areas listed above.

OPENING Every day except Saturday 10.30am–5.20pm.

CATERING Coffee machine.

COST Free.

DISABLED FACILITIES Maritime Museum fully accessible. Swansea Museum has limited access (staircases etc.).

DIRECTIONS Both institutions are in Swansea's maritime quarter, near the Leisure Centre and Marina.

Sygun Copper Mine
- Mrs S Amies
- Beddgelert, Gwynedd. LL55 4NE
- 0766 86595 FAX 0766 86564

Sygun tells the story of copper mining. Not only that, but it also takes a look at minerals in general and the geological forces that formed Snowdonia, and gives a vivid insight into working conditions endured by the Victorian miner. On the surface there is also a great deal to see and do. An audio-visual film tells the story of Sygun's renovation and the copper-production process is shown at the Visitor Centre. Displays of old machinery, including waterwheels and crushers.

N C SUPPORT Educationally, the levels of experience include National Curriculum subjects such as Social history, Geology, Industrial Heritage, Earth Sciences and Geography, imparted in various ways with relevance to primary and secondary schoolchildren. Write for a copy of the Sygun Copper Mine report.

OPENING 10.00am–5.00pm. All year round groups of 20 leave on the underground tour every eight minutes. The tour takes 40 minutes but visitors should allow two hours at the very least for their visit.

CATERING Light refreshments (sandwiches, snacks and drinks) are served in the Visitor Centre which has a small eating area. Picnic lunches can be taken outside.

COST Pupils £1.80, students £2.95.

DIRECTIONS One mile from the village of Beddgelert on the A498 road to Capel Curig.

Talyllyn Railway Company
- M J Wilson
- Wharf Station, Tywyn, Gwynedd. LL36 9EY
- 0654 710472 FAX 0654 711755

Narrow-gauge steam trains through seven and a quarter miles of National Park, forest walks and waterfalls.

N C SUPPORT Narrow-Gauge Railway Museum exhibits a wide range of locomotives, wagons and items from various narrow-gauge railways originally operating in Wales, England and Ireland.

OPENING Normally 9.00am–5.30pm. Train services Easter to October: daily.

CATERING Light refreshments in cafes at Tywyn Wharf and Abergynolwyn.

COST Group rates (min. 15 passengers): children (5–15 years) £2.70, adults £5.40 (return fares), up to two teachers free.

DISABLED FACILITIES Special coach for invalids and wheelchairs can be arranged (previous notice preferred). Toilet facilities at Wharf and Abergynolwyn.

DIRECTIONS Tywyn lies on the A493 coast road between Aberdovey and Dolgellau.

Techniquest
- Dr Brian Delf
- 72 Bute Street, Pierhead, Cardiff. CF1 6AA
- 0222 460211 FAX 0222 482517

An interactive Science Centre, with a well-developed educational programme. A new and bigger Centre will open in the autumn of 1994.

N C SUPPORT Theme Week programme for primary schools; developing secondary schools' equivalent; equipment loan service; INSET.

VISITS OUT
WALES

ANNUAL OR ONE OFF EVENT Each year's programme is different. Contact Techniquest for current list of events.

OPENING Tuesdays to Fridays 9.30am–4.30pm, Saturday, Sunday and bank holidays 10.30am–5.00pm.

CATERING A small cafe offering snacks and drinks.

COST Children £1.60, adults £3.00, concessions £1.60, family ticket £7.60, school pupils £1.50, one adult free for every eight pupils.

DISABLED FACILITIES Wheelchair access to all areas. Disabled toilets.

DIRECTIONS From junction 33 of the M4: proceed to the very end of the link road and take the first exit at mini roundabout, then first exit at following mini roundabout (by Windsor Quay Housing); along Ferry Road, right under bridge, straight on at traffic lights; second exit at mini roundabout over Clarence Road Bridge, then left at T-junction. Techniquest is 100 yds on the left.

Tintern Abbey
- The Custodian
- Tintern, Gwent. NP6 6SE
- 0291 689251

Tintern Abbey was a Cistercian house, founded in 1131 by Walter de Clare, and survived until the Dissolution of the Monasteries under Henry VIII in the 1530s. The building reveals very clearly the daily life of the monks. The centre of their life was the abbey church, which still survives almost intact.

OPENING Summer (end March to end October): daily 9.30am–6.30pm. Winter (end October to end March): Monday to Friday 9.30am–4.00pm. Sunday 2.00pm–4.00pm. Closed 24–26 December and New Year's Day.

DISABLED FACILITIES The site is suitable for disabled visitors.

DIRECTIONS Tintern via the A466, from the M4 (junction 22). BR: Chepstow six miles.

The Towers Centre
- L C Goodey
- Promenade, Llanfairfechan, Gwynedd. LL33 0DA
- 0248 680012

Beautiful old manor house standing in own private lawned grounds on Lavan Sands, Anglesey, and with a backdrop of the Snowdonia Mountains.

N C SUPPORT National Curriculum relevance to outdoor education/adventure training; Field Studies (Town Studies; River; Coast and Glacial); Art and History.

OPENING Easter to September.

CATERING Self-contained rooms only. B&B or full board.

COST All negotiable, according to group size.

DISABLED FACILITIES Some. For small groups on ground floor.

DIRECTIONS Midway between Conway and Bangor just one minute off the main A55.

VISITS OUT
WALES

Transfynydd Power Station
see **Nuclear Electric**

Tredegar House & Park
- Marion Tregenza
- Newport, Gwent. NP1 9YW
- 0633 815880 FAX 0633 815895

Seventeenth-century stately home. School parties tour below stairs; country park trail; home farm trail; play farm; craft workshops. All school visits must be booked in advance.

N C SUPPORT Tredegar House Guide Book. Slide/tape packs available. Country park trail/home farm trail (self-guide walks). Tree trail: ten-page leaflet for children with project work.

ANNUAL OR ONE OFF EVENT Open-air Shakespeare and other events during the summer months. Phone for details.

OPENING October to December: Monday to Friday 10.00am–12.30pm. Good Friday to end September: Wednesday to Friday 10.00am–12.30pm.

CATERING Parties may picnic in the park. Covered area available during wet weather. Refreshments available near play farm.

COST £1.00 each.

DISABLED FACILITIES Limited; please phone in advance and staff will be happy to assist. Wheelchairs available.

DIRECTIONS Tredegar House is two miles west of Newport town centre. By road: follow signs from the A48 or M4 (junction 28).

Tretower Court & Castle
- The Custodian
- Crickhowell, Powys. NP8 2RF
- 0874 730279

Motte-and-bailey castle established during the Norman conquest of Brycheiniog. The shell-keep was raised on the mount about 1150, and a round tower added in the early 13th century.

OPENING All educational visits must take place on weekdays during normal school hours.

DISABLED FACILITIES Access to gardens and lower levels. Remainder restricted. Adapted toilets.

DIRECTIONS In Tretower, off the A40, three miles northwest of Crickhowell.

Tudor Merchant's House
- W Hardy
- Quay Hill, Tenby, Dyfed. SA70 7BX
- 0834 842279

A late 15th-century townhouse, in which a successful Tudor merchant would have lived.

N C SUPPORT Support material for teachers. Guided tours for school parties. National Curriculum links with History.

OPENING April to October: Monday to Friday 11.00am–6.00pm, Sunday 2.00pm–6.00pm, closed Saturday.

COST 60p minimum for groups of 15 (1993 prices).

DIRECTIONS Overlooking the harbour, Tenby.

VISITS OUT
WALES

Turner House
- Officer in Charge
- Plymouth Road, Penarth, South Glamorgan. CF6 2TH
- 0222 708870

A gallery with a changing programme of pictures and objets d'art from the National Museum's own art collection and for travelling exhibitions and displays of work by local artists.

N C SUPPORT Educational resources only when appropriate for a long-term exhibition.

ANNUAL OR ONE OFF EVENT Various exhibitions; apply to National Museum of Wales, main branch, in Cardiff for details.

OPENING Tuesday to Saturday 11.00am–12.45pm, 2.00pm–5.00pm, Sunday 2.00pm–5.00pm.

COST Pre-booked school groups 17p each child.

DISABLED FACILITIES Contact the Officer in Charge.

DIRECTIONS Penarth lies five miles south of Cardiff.

Twr-y-Felin Outdoor Centre
- Matthew Exley
- Twr-y-Felin, St David's, Dyfed. SA62 6QL
- 0437 720391 FAX 0437 721838

Small high-quality outdoor centre providing residential action holiday for children aged eight and upwards. Professionally qualified staff lead small groups in coasteering, surfing, kayaking, abseiling, rock climbing, canoeing.

N C SUPPORT A 19th-century windmill as a setting for school visits: Geography, History, Geology, Environmental Studies, Biology; study sites on the doorstep.

OPENING All year round.

CATERING All food cooked by the Centre's excellent staff.

COST £195 per week including VAT and insurance.

DISABLED FACILITIES None.

DIRECTIONS On the southeast side of Britain's smallest city, St David's.

Vale of Rheidol Railway
- N Thompson
- Park Avenue, Aberystwyth, Dyfed. SY23 1PG
- 0970 615993

The Vale of Rheidol Railway runs through magnificent scenery between Aberystwyth and Devil's Bridge. The 24-mile return trip behind a vintage steam locomotive takes three hours, including a stop to visit the Mynach Falls, climb Jacob's Ladder or marvel at the Devil's Punchbowl. If they wish visitors may stay longer at Devil's Bridge and return by a later train. Most carriages are enclosed so there is no need to worry about the weather.

OPENING Please write for timetable.

CATERING Cafe at Devil's Bridge terminus.

COST There are special fares for parties of 10 or more persons. School parties (min. 30 people): return: children £3.50, adults £3.50, single: children £2.60, adults £2.60; a deposit of £10.00 is required in advance and the balance paid on arrival at the station in one payment.

WALES

DISABLED FACILITIES Enquire at booking office.

DIRECTIONS In the centre of Aberystwyth, adjacent to the British Rail station. Coach parking is available.

Valle Crucis Abbey
- The Custodian
- Llangollen, Clwyd. LL20 8DD
- 0978 860326

There are extensive remains of this Cistercian abbey founded in 1201. The church dates from the 13th century, and the east range of the cloister was remodelled around 1400. Visitors can see the sculptured memorial slabs in the monks' dormitory and a small exhibition of the Cistercian monks and the abbey. The Eisteddfod town of Llangollen is only a short distance away.

OPENING All educational visits must take place on weekdays during normal school hours.

DISABLED FACILITIES The new Visitors Centre is wheelchair accessible. No adapted toilet.

DIRECTIONS One and a half miles northwest of Llangollen on the A542.

Welsh Folk Museum
- Walter Jones, Education Officer
- St Fagans, Cardiff, South Glamorgan. CF5 6XB
- 0222 569441 FAX 0222 578413

An open-air museum with buildings mostly collected from all over Wales, demonstrating craftsmen; a Victorian schoolroom; a Celtic village; a toll house; a late 19th-century general store; a terrace of houses.

N C SUPPORT Worksheets linked to the National Curriculum, in particular History; INSET for teachers; free preview visit to meet education staff. Talks by arrangement on specific themes linked to the history of Wales.

OPENING April to October: daily 10.00am–5.00pm. November to March: Monday to Saturday 10.00am–5.00pm.

COST Pre-booked parties: school children £1.20 (a third of the adult rate).

DISABLED FACILITIES Toilets, changing area; some wheelchairs if booked in advance; ramps through galleries.

DIRECTIONS Four miles west of Cardiff and three miles from junction 33 of the M4 along the A4232.

Welsh Industrial & Maritime Museum
- Rhian Thomas, Education Officer
- Bute Street, Cardiff, South Glamorgan. CF1 6AN
- 0222 481919 FAX 0222 487252

The Museum deals with the industrial, land transport and maritime history of Wales. There are galleries dealing with various aspects of this history and an outside exhibits area with large-scale items. The site is encompassed by a miniature passenger-carrying railway which normally operates during opening hours.

N C SUPPORT The Museum exhibits, displays and educational support material are particularly relevant to

VISITS OUT

WALES

the History, Science and Technology National Curricula but enquiries are invited on any subject with which schools may be dealing.

ANNUAL OR ONE OFF EVENT Various educational themes run at different times and further information may be obtained on request.

OPENING Tuesday to Saturday 10.00am–5.00pm, Sunday 2.30pm–5.00pm, closed Monday.

CATERING Vending machine.

COST Children 50p, adults £1.00, Senior Citizens 75p. Admission is free to schools in Gwent, Mid-Glamorgan and South Glamorgan only. Teachers/supervisors accompanying school parties are admitted free of charge within the following ratios: 1:5 for pupils aged five and under, 1:10 pupils aged six to eight and 1:15 for pupils aged over eight.

DISABLED FACILITIES Total and easy access to all parts of the site.

DIRECTIONS Located at the bottom of Bute Street, on the waterfront in the heart of Cardiff.

The Welsh Institute of Sport

- Pauline Ferns
- Sophia Gardens, Cardiff. CF1 9SW
- 0222 397571 FAX 0222 222431

A centre for sporting excellence, with an extensive range of quality facilities. The WIS offers classroom and teaching support materials and use of staff room. En-suite accommodation for 60.

N C SUPPORT Tailor-made study packages for A-Level PE and sports studies. Key Study notes as support for practical experience. An excellent urban base for Geography field trips. A comprehensive resource base is available.

OPENING All year round.

CATERING Residents' dining room. Cafe open 8.00am–9.00pm.

COST By negotiation. Quality residential packages for school groups at realistic prices are available throughout the year.

DISABLED FACILITIES Lift access, ramps; toilet; adapted bedroom.

DIRECTIONS Contact the office for directions.

Welsh Mountain Zoo

- Kim Taylor, Education Officer
- Colwyn Bay, Clwyd. LL28 5UY
- 0492 532938 FAX 0492 530498

Part of the Zoological Society of Wales, a registered charity which seeks to inform and educate about wildlife and conservation. Over 100 species to be seen. The Education Department has a full-time Education Officer, a school room which can seat up to 40 people and full audio-visual facilities are available.

N C SUPPORT A full range of printed resources is available, including zoo trails, as well as a range of 'Learning Sessions' for all levels. All materials are designed using the National Curriculum.

ANNUAL OR ONE OFF EVENT Various themed days throughout the year. Telephone for details.

OPENING Winter: 9.30am–4.00pm. Summer: 9.30am–5.00pm. Bird of prey feeding, followed by sea lion feeding and penguin feeding.

VISITS OUT

WALES

CATERING Safari restaurant open all year. Flagstaff cafe, sweet shop, kiosks open during the summer.

COST Groups of 15 or more: children £1.80, adults £3.60, students and Senior Citizens £1.80, under 3s free.

DISABLED FACILITIES Toilets. Wheelchairs available. Wheelchair users admitted free. The Zoo is very steep in places but there are many disabled visitors.

DIRECTIONS Signposted from the A55 at the Rhos-on-Sea interchange. Free transport from Colwyn Bay train station in summer.

Welsh Royal Crystal
- Sue Beetlestone, Visitor Manager
- 5 Brynberth, Rhayader, Powys
- 0597 811005 FAX 0597 811129

A working crystal factory. There is usually glass blowing and cutting in progress but it is best to check before visiting.

N C SUPPORT Worksheets in preparation. Happy to supply information to teachers.

OPENING All year round: daily 9.30am–4.30pm.

CATERING Coffee bar serving drinks and snacks.

COST Children £1.00, teachers free.

DISABLED FACILITIES Access to all areas.

DIRECTIONS On the edge of Rhayader off the A44 to Leominster.

Welsh Slate Museum
- The Promotions Officer
- Padarn Country Park, Llanberis, Gwynedd. LL55 4TY
- 0286 870630 FAX 0286 871906

This is a living working museum where much of the machinery and equipment of the former quarry workshops is still in regular use. There are regular demonstrations of traditional slate crafts and engineering skills. Audio-visual demonstrations.

N C SUPPORT National Curriculum links with History: 'y Caban', the Mess Room, where the heated discussions and banter on political, cultural and trade union matters of yesterday still echo; the loco shed houses UNA, a carefully restored steam locomotive; workshop where the blacksmith still produces specialised tools and machinery for today's working quarries; one of the largest waterwheels in the world and skilled craftsmen, slate splitting and dressing.

OPENING Contact the Promotions Officer. The Welsh Slate Mines are now managed by the National Museum of Wales.

CATERING Cafeteria.

COST Contact the Promotions Officer.

DISABLED FACILITIES Most of the site is accessible.

DIRECTIONS Nine miles from Caernarfon, 12 miles from Bangor and 17 miles from Betws-y-Coed. Follow signs for Llanberis from the A55 Expressway and the A5.

Welshpool and Llanfair Light Railway
- Andy Carey
- The Station, Llanfair Caereinion, Powys. SY21 0SF
- 0938 810441

VISITS OUT
WALES

A turn-of-the-century narrow-gauge railway built to serve a farming community. Now the home of a collection of trains from local railways all around the world. Steam operated.

N C SUPPORT Teachers' pack available; primary school teacher can give an introductory lesson. Resources on site for aspects of Geography, History and Maths.

OPENING Trains run Easter to October: weekends and bank holidays; mid-June to mid-September: daily.

CATERING Picnic area at both terminals, small tea room at Llanfair Caereinion.

COST Return: pupils £2.30, adults £4.60; single: pupils £1.50, adults £3.00; one teacher free for every ten pupils (1993 prices).

DISABLED FACILITIES Two coaches for wheelchairs. Toilets.

DIRECTIONS Both terminal stations are alongside the A458 Shrewsbury to Dolgellau road.

Wildfowl & Wetlands Trust
- Alyson Jenkins
- Penclacwydd, Llwynhendy, Llanelli, Dyfed. SA14 9SH
- 0554 741087

Forty acres of parkland with over 90 species of wildfowl from all over the world. A thousand birds to see from (tarmacked) paths, wild birds seen from hides. Spacious Visitor Centre.

N C SUPPORT Participatory and active programmes for infants and juniors on a variety of themes, designed with the National Curriculum in mind. Tailor-made programmes for older children and students. Teachers' pack available.

ANNUAL OR ONE OFF EVENT During the holidays there are special events such as 'Downy Duckling Days' at Whitsun; Holiday Club during the summer.

OPENING Winter: daily 9.30am–4.00pm. Summer: daily 9.30am–5.00pm.

CATERING Coffee shop serving light meals and snacks.

COST Group rates (school group): pupils under 16 years £1.20, over 16s £1.90, one adult free with every ten pupils, other adults £2.60.

DISABLED FACILITIES Throughout grounds and buildings.

DIRECTIONS From the M4 westbound take junction 47 towards Llanelli; M4 eastbound take junction 48 towards Llanelli. Follow signs, a white duck on brown background.

Wrexham Library Arts Centre
- Martin Barlow or Dawn Parry
- Rhosddu Road, Wrexham, Clwyd. LL11 1AU
- 0978 261932 FAX 0978 361876

The main gallery runs a continuous changing exhibition programme of contemporary and historical interest, featuring work of local, national and international artists. The gallery operates as a smaller community exhibition space.

N C SUPPORT Schools workshops are held on Monday and Tuesday in relation to the current exhibition and National Curriculum specifications. Children's art and drama workshops

WALES

on Saturday. Adult life-drawing classes on Tuesday and Thursday evenings.

ANNUAL OR ONE OFF EVENT Annual Clwyd Children's Art competition, sponsored by Lego UK; Open Art Exhibition; Urban Art-funded children's summer project.

OPENING Monday to Friday 9.30am–6.45pm, Saturday 9.30am–4.45pm, closed Sunday and bank holidays.

CATERING Coffee shop on premises: Monday to Friday 9.30am–9.00pm.

COST Free admission to gallery. Schools workshops £35.00 for two-hour session (max. 35 children).

DISABLED FACILITIES Access to all areas.

DIRECTIONS Centre of town, adjacent to Llwyn Isaf Green and the Guildhall. Car park opposite swimming baths on Chester Road.

PART THREE

EVENTS

EVENTS

APRIL – 1994

1994 has been declared the United Nations International Year of the Family

Key

EA	East Anglia	**N**	Nationwide	**S**	Scotland
L	London and the South East	**NE**	North East	**SW**	South West
M	Midlands		**NW**	North West	**W**	Wales

* Provisional dates only. Check with organiser.

R	DURATION	EVENTS

APRIL

S — **Edinburgh Butterfly and Insect World**
Melville Nursery, Lasswade, Midlothian, EH18 1AZ
☎ 031 663 4932
Organise projects for Sixth Form studies. Ring for details.

N — **Charter 88**
Exmouth House, 3–11 Pine Street, London EC1
☎ 071-833 5813
Charter 88 holds conferences on constitutional issues such as The Monarchy, Women in Democracy which are open to all age groups. Contact for details.

L — Apr* **Exhibition to Mark the 65th Anniversary of the Hendon Synagogue**
Church Farmhouse Museum, Greyhound Hill, Hendon, London NE4 4JR
☎ 081-203 0130

NE — **Made in Gateshead**
Shipley Art Gallery, Prince Consort Road, Gateshead
☎ 091-477 1495

L — to 1 May **Partners by Design**
The Design Council, 28 Haymarket, London SW1Y 4SU
☎ 071-839 8000
This exhibition demonstrates the many ways in which secondary schools and sixth form colleges can work with professional designers, across a wide range of disciplines, and the educational benefits that can be gained from the experience. Work on display comes from schools and colleges in England, Northern Ireland, Scotland and Wales. Projects on show will include chairs, silver, jewellery, footwear and telephones.

EVENTS

APRIL – 1994

R	DURATION	EVENTS

L   April*

Bank of England Tercentenary
Exhibition to mark the issue of the new £50 note
Bank of England Museum, Bartholomew Lane, London EC2
☎ 071-601 5545

EA   to 1 May*

Hiroshige: Snow, Moon and Flowers
Fitzwilliam Museum, Cambridge
☎ 0223 332900
Hiroshige's prints and late landscape triptychs from the museum's collection.

SW   to 1 May

The Body Trail
The Exploratory Hands-on Science Centre, Bristol Old Station, Temple Meads, Bristol
☎ 0272 252008
Exhibition aims to encourage pupils to know more about their body using special equipment to measure heart rate, take blood pressure, and take fingerprints.

L   to 2 May

Demand for the Exotic
V & A, Cromwell Road, London SW7
Education Dept: ☎ 071-938 8638
One-room display of 18th- and 19th-century English woodblock-printed textiles from the Museum's collections.

L   to 8 May

Picasso: Sculptor/Painter
Tate Gallery, Millbank, London SW1P 4RG
☎ 071-887 8000

L   to 7 May

Spanish Contemporary Photography
Photographer's Gallery, 5 Great Newport Street, London WC2
☎ 071-831 1772
With over 300 works by over 40 photographers, the exhibition explores trends in Spanish photography over the last twenty years.

L   to May

Wartime Kitchen and Garden Exhibition
Imperial War Museum, Lambeth Road, London SE1
☎ 071-416 5000
Exhibition covers rationing, cookery during the war, the allotment movement and the Land Army.

EVENTS
APRIL – 1994

R	DURATION	EVENTS

Gravure and Grace – Engravings
National Museum of Wales, Cathways Park, Cardiff
☎ 0222 397951

S — to 15 May — **Photographer's Choice: David Williams**
Scottish National Portrait Gallery, 1 Queen Street, Edinburgh
☎ 031-556 8921

W — to 15 May — **Francis Bacon: Study for a Portrait of Van Gogh**
Graham Sutherland Gallery, Picton Castle, Rhos, Haverfordwest, Dyfed
☎ 0437 751296

W — to 15 May — **Landscapes**
Graham Sutherland Gallery, Picton Castle, Rhos Haverfordwest, Dyfed
☎ 0437 751296

L — to 15 May — **The Peopling of London**
Museum of London, London Wall, London EC2Y 5HN
☎ 071-600 1058
15,000 years of settlement from overseas.

L — to 15 May — **Venice Preserved: The Greenall Gift of Venetian Coins**
Room 69a, British Museum, Great Russell Street, London WC1
☎ 071-636 1555

L — to 30 Jul — **Use Your Loaf**
Livesey Museum, 682 Old Kent Road, London
☎ 071-639 5604
Interactive exhibition with educational theme. Will cover themes such as health, hygiene and distribution of food including historical background.

NE — to end Aug* — **Science Exploration Exhibition**
Sheffield Industrial Museum, off Alma Street, Sheffield S3 8RY
☎ 0742 722106
Exhibition will feature structures, buildings and interactive displays.

L — to Dec* — **From D-Day to Victory**
Imperial War Museum, Lambeth Road, London SE1
☎ 071-416 5000
Story of the landings in Normandy, liberation of Paris and VE Day. Material includes films, photographs, uniforms, equipment and personal memorabilia.

EVENTS

APRIL – 1994

R	DURATION	EVENTS

L — to Dec

Paradise – Change and Continuity in the New Guinea Highlands
Museum of Mankind, 6 Burlington Gardens, London W1X 2EX
☎ 071-636 1555

L — to Jul 94

Talking Pictures: Van Dyck
Dulwich Picture Gallery, London SE21
☎ 081-693 5254
An actor dressed as Van Dyck gives entertaining information about his style and technique and provides social and historical background of the artist's life. All ages.

EA — to 27 May*

Awards of Merit: School Medals of the 18th and 19th Centuries
Fitzwilliam Museum, Cambridge
☎ 0223 332900
Collection of medals awarded to school pupils during the last two centuries.

SW — to 16 Oct

D-Day Exhibition and Trail
Shanklin, Isle of Wight
☎ 0983 866432
Traces the role of the Isle of Wight in the build-up to D-Day.

NW — to early 95

Art from Post-War Europe
Tate Gallery, Liverpool
☎ 051-709 3223
Survey of Western European art 1945–68 from the gallery collection including Picasso and Miro.

L — to 29 May

Salvador Dali Exhibition
Hayward Gallery, London
☎ 071-921 0888
Exhibition of works by the Surrealist painter as part of the Spanish Festival in London.

L — to 29 May

Photographs by Annie Leibobitz
National Portrait Gallery, London
☎ 071-306 0055

NW — to early 95

Matisse, Maillol and Rodin Exhibition from the Tate Collection
Tate Gallery, Liverpool
☎ 051-709 3223

EVENTS

APRIL – 1994

R	DURATION	EVENTS

NW to early 95   **Moral Tales**
Tate Gallery, Liverpool
☎ 051-709 3223
Eight artists who dealt with social issues in the 1980s.

L   to 12 Jun   **Goya: Truth and Fantasy**
Royal Academy of Arts, Piccadilly, London W1
☎ 071-439 7438
Cabinet pictures, sketches and miniatures.

L   to 30 May   **Eighteenth-century Mezzotints of the Theatre**
Courtauld Institute Galleries, Somerset House, London WC2
☎ 071-873 2526

L   spring/summer term   **Art/Science Alliance**
Dulwich Picture Gallery, London SE21
☎ 081-693 6911
Demonstration of how chemistry and art are combined in works of art. Suitable for all ages.

EA   Apr–Nov*   **1900: The New Age**
Whipple Museum of the History of Science, Free School Lane, Cambridge CB2 3RH
☎ 0223 334545
The International Exhibition staged in Paris in 1900 looked forward to the 20th century. This exhibition examines how they contemplated our Age. Associated workshops and lectures aimed at secondary school pupils.

L   spring/summer term   **The Grand Tour**
Dulwich Picture Gallery, London SE21
☎ 081-693 6911
A tour of Europe via the pictures in the gallery, explaining events, costume, inventions and discoveries in 17th-century Europe.

NW   Easter* to Nov   **The Technology of Theatre**
Museum of Science and Industry, Liverpool Road, Manchester
☎ 061-832 2244
Exhibition on sound, lighting, make-up and behind-the-scenes techniques. In celebration of Manchester's year as the City of Drama.

EVENTS
APRIL – 1994

R	DURATION	EVENTS

SW Apr–Sep **D-Day Anniversary Exhibition 'Home Front'**
Portland Museum, 217 Wakeham, Portland, Dorset
☎ 0305 772444
Contact: Mr Harvey Bailey
Portland and its harbour played a major role in the Normandy invasion with military hardware being loaded onto the armada of ships and vessels assembled in the docks. This special exhibition shows how the civilian population and armed services worked together during World War II.

S Apr–Aug* **Canvassing the Clyde**
Glasgow Art Galley and Museum, Kelvingrove, Glasgow G3
☎ 041-357 3929
Stanley Spencer and the Clyde shipyards.

SW 1 Apr–31 Oct **The Life and Times of Sir George Williams**
Guildhall Centre Gallery, Dulverton, Somerset
☎ 0398 24081
Exhibition of the life and times of Sir George Williams, founder of the YMCA movement, who was born near Dulverton.

L to 20 Nov **The Kingdom of Shamba: The Kuba of Zaire**
Museum of Mankind, 6 Burlington Gardens, London W1X 2EX
☎ 071-636 1555

L to Dec 95 **Great Benin**
Museum of Mankind, 6 Burlington Gardens, London W1X 2EX
☎ 071-636 1555

L **Ham House: Re-opening**
Ham House, Ham Street, Richmond, Surrey
☎ 081-940 1950
Ham House, owned by the National Trust, will re-open to the public after a £2 million restoration. It is thought to be the most complete and authentic 17th-century domestic building in Britain.

W 5 Apr–7 May **The Twenty Count (Homage to the world's indigenous cultures)**
Wrexham Library Arts Centre, Rhosddu Road, Wrexham, Clwyd
☎ 0978 261932
This exhibition features a series of images inspired by a prayer belonging to the Sundance teachings of the native Americans, originating from a Lakota Indian creation myth. School Art Workshops each Monday and Tuesday.

EVENTS

APRIL – 1994

R	DURATION	EVENTS
W	8–end May	**Travelling Discovery Centre** Swansea Museum, Victoria Road, Swansea SA1 1SN ☎ 0792 653763 This is a touring show from London's Natural History Museum and features many hands-on activities.
SW	10 Apr–19 Jun	**'A Face of War', D-Day Exhibition** Brewers Quay, Hope Square, Weymouth, Dorset ☎ 0305 777622
L	14 Apr–19 Jun	**Colour into Cloth** Crafts Council, 44a Pentonville Road, London N1 9BY ☎ 071-278 7700
M	14 Apr–21 Aug	**Sir Arthur Evans – Centenary Exhibition** Ashmolean Museum, Oxford Contact: Mrs Ann Brown ☎ 0865 278031 Exhibition on the English archaeologist Sir Arthur Evans who made epoch-making explorations and discoveries at Knossos and elsewhere in Crete.
SW	15 Apr–22 May	**Behind the Scenes** Bristol Museum & Art Gallery, Queen's Road, Bristol BS8 1RL ☎ 0272 223571 Results of residency of the artist Rachel Hemming-Bray.
S	20–18 May*	**Nature Preserved – A Tasteful Look at the Art of Taxidermy** Dumfries Museum, The Observatory, Dumfries ☎ 0387 53374
NE	23–16 Sep	**Exhibition 'Siege of York'** Archaeological Resource Centre, St Saviourgate, York YO1 2NN ☎ 0904 654324 Exhibition designed to celebrate the 350th anniversary of the Siege of York, which began on 23 April 1644. Relevant to Key Stage 2 – Tudors and Stuarts, and Key Stage 3 – Making of the United Kingdom.
NE	24 Apr–16 Jul	**350th Anniversary of the Siege of York during the English Civil War** Various venues, York

EVENTS

APRIL – 1994

R	DURATION	EVENTS

NE 27 Apr–29 Aug
Working Days
Abbeydale Industrial Hamlet, Abbeydale Road South, Sheffield S7 3QW
☎ 0742 367731
Features craft demonstrations of traditional Sheffield skills and will include blacksmiths and jewellers.

SW 30 Apr–25 Jun
William Christian Symons (1845–1911)
Victoria Art Gallery, Bridge Street, Bath, Avon
☎ 0225 461111
A retrospective of this artist, whose work is closely related to work by the Newlyn School and the English Impressionist style. Mon–Fri 10.00 am–5.30 pm, Sat 10.00 am–5.00 pm.

NE 30 Apr–26 Jun
How We Used to Live – The Victorians
Cliffe Castle, Spring Gardens Lane, Keighley, W Yorks
☎ 0274 631756

SE 30 Apr–22 May
Victorian St Leonards
Hastings Museum, Cambridge Road, Hastings, East Sussex
☎ 0424 721202

M 30 Apr–3 Jul
Midland Railway 150th Anniversary Exhibition
Derby Industrial Museum, Silk Mill Lane, Derby DE1 3AR
☎ 0332 255308
Major exhibition marking the 150th anniversary of the Midland Railway, with photographs and works from private collections.

NE 30 Apr–26 Jun
In Pursuit of the Spirits: Inuit Printmaking from 1958
Cliffe Castle, Spring Gardens Lane, Keighley, W Yorks
☎ 0274 631756

N 30 Apr–8 May
National Pet Week
☎ 071-255 2424
Nationwide events designed to promote responsible pet ownership. Animal charities and welfare organisations involved.

NW 30–2 May
Saddleworth Canal Festival
Huddersfield Canal Society, 239 Mossley Road, Ashton-under-Lyne, Lancs
☎ 061 339 1332
Festival will mark the bicentenary of the Huddersfield Narrow Canal.

EVENTS

MAY – 1994

| R | DURATION | EVENTS |

MAY

L summer term **Roberto the Storyteller**
Dulwich Picture Gallery, London SE21
☎ 081-693 6911
Roberto tells the stories behind our mythological, biblical and narrative paintings. For junior and secondary school pupils.

SW May–Jun* **D-Day Exhibition**
Royal Armouries, Fort Nelson, Down End Road, Fareham, Hants
☎ 0329 233734
Exhibition highlights artillery used on D-Day.

NW May **Festival of Catalan Culture**
Various venues Manchester
Manchester International Arts, 3 Birch Polygon, Manchester M14 5HX
☎ 061-224 0020
Month-long contemporary arts festival, 'Ona Catalana', featuring 12 Catalan groups. Festival will include theatre, music (flamenco and traditional), street theatre, film programmes and exhibitions.

NE May* to end 1994 **Colour in Mind**
The Colour Museum, Perkin House, 82 Gratton Road, Bradford, W Yorks
☎ 0274 390955
Exhibition on colour symbolism, colour psychology and use of colour in advertising.

W May–mid Jul **The People's Show**
Powysland Museum, The Canal Wharf, Welshpool, Powys
☎ 0938 554656
Exhibition showing collections of ordinary people.

L May–Aug **Indian Paintings in the Howard Hodgkin Collection**
Room 91, British Museum, Great Russell Street, London WC1
☎ 071-636 1555
(Closed May 2)

L May–Aug **Japanese Woodblock Prints 1912–1989**
Rooms 92–94, British Museum, Great Russell Street, London WC1
☎ 071-636 1555

EVENTS
MAY – 1994

R	DURATION	EVENTS

L   May–Jun*   **Sheep Shearing**
Bocketts Farm Park, Young Street, Fetcham, Leatherhead, Surrey
Contact: James Gowing
☎ 0372 363764
There will be sheep shearing over a 6–7-week period throughout May and June.

EA   1   **D-Day Anniversary Event**
Imperial War Museum, Duxford Airfield, Cambridge CB6 4QR
☎ 0223 835000
Aircraft display and military vehicles.

SE   1–2   **'Armies through the Ages'**
Battle Abbey, High Street, Battle, East Sussex
☎ 0424 773792
Covers armies from the Romans to World War II. Admission charge.

N   2–8   **Red Cross Week**
British Red Cross, 9 Grosvenor Crescent, London SW1
☎ 071-235 5454
Week of fundraising with International Red Cross Day on 8 May.

SW   2   **Royal Signals D-Day Photographic Exhibition**
Royal Signals Museum, Blandford, Dorset
☎ 0258 482248

M   4   **Text and Performance**
Shakespeare Centre, Henley Street, Stratford-upon-Avon
☎ 0789 204016
Day School studying Shakespeare's *Measure for Measure*.
Fee: £8

S   5 May–19 Jun   **Medardo Rosso: Impressionist Sculptor**
Scottish National Gallery of Modern Art, Belford Road, Edinburgh
☎ 031-556 8921

S   5 May–10 Jul   **Raphael**
National Gallery of Scotland, The Mound, Edinburgh
☎ 031-556 8921

L   6 May–17 Jul   **Portraits in Disguise**
National Portrait Gallery, London
☎ 071-306 0055

EVENTS

MAY – 1994

R	DURATION	EVENTS

L   6 May–26 Jun

Whitechapel Open
Whitechapel Art Gallery, Whitechapel High Street, London E1
☎ 071-377 0107
Exhibition of work by artists working in East London.

NE   7 May–25 Jun

Miles Richmond – Retrospective Exhibition
Middlesbrough Art Gallery, Middlesbrough Borough Council, PO Box 69, Gurney Street, Middlesbrough, Cleveland
☎ 0642 247445
This show consists of oils, drawings and watercolours spanning the whole of Richmond's career, from his time at the Borough Polytechnic as a pupil of David Bomberg, through the period spent working in Spain to recent landscape and figure studies produced in Yorkshire and Scotland.

M   8

Elvaston Castle Country Park and Working Estate Museum
Borrowash Road, Elvaston, Thulston, Derby
☎ 0332 573799
Display of tree species, wood-turning and wheelwrighting.

EA   10 May–11 Sep*

Surimono II
Fitzwilliam Museum, Cambridge
☎ 0223 332900
Art of Japanese print-making exploring the traditional theme of mother and child.

    10

Origins of the English Civil War
Royal Armouries, HM Tower of London, London
☎ 071-702 0013
Sixth Form day.

M   11

Text and Performance
Shakespeare Centre, Henley Street, Stratford-upon-Avon
☎ 0789 204016
Day School studying Shakespeare's *Richard III*. Fee: £8.

M   12

Shakespeare Workshop
The Shakespeare Centre, Henley Street, Stratford-upon-Avon
☎ 0789 204016
Practical workshop experiencing Shakespeare's *The Comedy of Errors*. Fee: £8.

EVENTS

MAY – 1994

R	DURATION	EVENTS

L   12

Asia and the Arts
Commonwealth Institute, Kensington High Street, London W8
☎ 071-603 4535
Practical sessions and lectures for teachers on music, drama and the arts of Asia. Price: £60 + VAT.

SE   14 May–18 Jun

Wildlife Photographer of the Year
Whitstable Museum and Gallery, Oxford Street, Whitstable, Kent
☎ 0227 276998

W   14 May–18 Jun

Syrcas/Maud Sulter
Wrexham Library Arts Centre, Rhosddu Road, Wrexham, Clwyd
☎ 0978 261932
This exhibition takes as its theme the presence of people of African descent in Europe during the 1930s and 1940s. School Art Workshops each Monday and Tuesday.

M   14–15

A Bunch of Herbs
Sulgrave Manor, Banbury, Oxon
☎ 0295 760205
A celebration of herbs and their uses in history, cooking and medicine. Displays, events, stalls, etc.

N   16–22

National Smile Week
British Dental Health Foundation, Eastlands Court, St Peter's Road, Rugby, CV21 3QP
☎ 0788 546365
Awareness week to promote dental health.

W   16–22

International Animation Festival
St David's Hall, The Hayes, Cardiff
☎ 071-255 1444
Week-long programme to include some 20 screenings and special events. Will feature new work by award-winning animators.

SE   16 May–31 Oct

D-Day Exhibition
Royal Engineers Museum, Prince Arthur Road, Gillingham, Kent
☎ 0634 406397
Models and photographs of the construction of World War II's Mulberry Harbour.

EVENTS

MAY – 1994

R	DURATION	EVENTS

EA 17 May–4 Sep*
The Art of Seeing Nature: British Watercolours 1750–1850
Fitzwilliam Museum, Cambridge
☎ 0223 332900
Exhibition exploring 'The Golden Age of British Watercolours' from the picturesque landscape of the 18th century to the romantic vision of the 19th. Includes work by Constable, Turner, Samuel Palmer and John Ruskin.

L 17 May–31 Oct
D-Day Exhibition
Royal Air Force Museum, Grahame Park Way, London
☎ 081-200 1763
Exhibition of range of aircraft which took part in D-Day including only surviving 'Typhoon' and the Sunderland Flying Boat.

N 17
World Telecommunications Day
☎ 071-630 1981
United Nations awareness day.

L 18
Steaming Days for Schools
Kew Bridge Steam Museum, Green Dragon Lane, Brentford, Middx
☎ 081-452 8567
Day includes lectures on themes such as 'The Victorians' 'Engineering Development', 'Heat and Energy' and 'The Industrial Revolution'.

M 18
Meet the Gardener – Spring into Summer
Ryton Organic Gardens, Ryton-on-Dunsmore, Coventry, CV8 3LG
☎ 0203 303517

O 19
Save the Children 75th anniversary
Head Office, Save the Children Fund, Mary Datchelor House, 17 Grove Lane, London SE5
☎ 071-703 5400
Leaflet describing the history of Save the Children and archive material available.

L 20 May–21 Aug
Prints and Drawings Exhibitions: Printmaking in Germany in the Age of Goethe and the Woodcut Series of William Nicholson
Room 90, British Museum, Great Russell Street, London WC1
☎ 071-636 1555

EVENTS

MAY – 1994

R	DURATION	EVENTS

W   20 May– 5 Jun

Hay-on-Wye Literature Festival, Powys
Various venues Hay-on-Wye, Festival Office, Hay-on-Wye, Powys
☎ 0497 821217
Large literature festival which takes place in the market town of Hay-on-Wye in the Black Mountains of the Welsh Marches. Admission charge.

M   20 May– 5 June

Stars, Stripes and Stitches
Sulgrave Manor, Sulgrave, Banbury, Oxon
☎ 0295 760205
Workshops, demonstrations and exhibitions relating to needlecraft.

M   22

Cotswolds at War Exhibition
GWR Steam Railway, Toddington, Glos
☎ 0242 621405

SE   22 May– 4 Jun

Ramsgate Spring Festival of Arts and Architecture
Ramsgate, Kent
☎ 0843 580994
Classical, jazz and rock music, drama, tours, visual arts, dance workshops, street entertainment, dragon-boat racing.

M   22–23

Spring Engine Rally
The National Waterways Museum, Llanthony Warehouse, Gloucester Docks, Gloucester GL1 2EN
☎ 0452 307009

L   24

Religion and Politics in Tudor England
Royal Armouries, HM Tower of London, London
☎ 071-702 0013
Sixth form day.

L   26 May– 4 Sept

Who's Looking at the Family?
Barbican Art Gallery, Barbican Centre, London EC2
☎ 071-588 9023
The family in photography.

SW   27 May– 12 Jun

Bath International Festival
Bath, Avon
☎ 0225 462231
Theme: Ancient Echoes. Festival includes jazz, opera, concerts, talks and exhibitions.

EVENTS

MAY – 1994

R	DURATION	EVENTS

L   27 May–10 Sept

Regent's Park Open Air Theatre Season
Regent's Park, London NW1
☎ 071-935 5756
The programme is likely to include *A Midsummer Night's Dream* and *Hamlet*.

S   27 May–13 Jun*

Spinners, Weavers and Dyers
Dumfries Museum, The Observatory, Dumfries
☎ 0387 53374

N   28

Forget Me Not Day
Amnesty International
☎ 071-814 6200
A day to remember prisoners of conscience around the world.

SW   28–30

World War II Military Vehicle Rally
Southsea Common.
Contact: Lorraine Gibbison, Portsmouth Tourism (D-Day Office), Civic Offices, Portsmouth
☎ 0705 834800
Over 1,000 vehicles from all over the world will be assembled on Southsea Common.

W   28 May–5 Jun

Making Pottery
Roman Legionary Museum, High Street, Caerleon, Gwent
☎ 0633 423134
Half-term event. Children can make pottery as the Romans used to.

SE   28 May–2 Jun

A Pictorial History of the North American Indian
Hastings Museum, Cambridge Road, Hastings, East Sussex
☎ 0424 721202

NW   28 May–14 Aug*

Africa Explores
Tate Gallery, Liverpool
☎ 051-709 3223
Major survey of twentieth-century African art.

EVENTS

MAY – 1994

R	DURATION	EVENTS

NW 28–30 — **Manchester Ship Canal Centenary Celebration**
The Boat Museum, Dockyard Road, Ellesmere Port L65 4EF
☎ 051-355 5017
Music, entertainments and boat rally to commemorate the centenary of the Manchester Ship Canal.

SW 28–30 — **World War II Military Vehicle Rally**
Southsea Common, Portsmouth, Hants
☎ 0705 230774
Over a thousand vehicles from all over the world.

SE 29–30 — **Jousting and Medieval Entertainment**
Combwell Priory, London Road, Flimwell, Kent
☎ 0580 87754
Jousting, jugglers, fire-eaters and archery.

SE 29–30 — **Normans and Saxons**
Battle Abbey, High Street, Battle, East Sussex
☎ 0424 773792
Event will feature life in a Saxon village, with people dressed traditionally and there will be a small skirmish between the two sides.

NE 29–30 — **Wigfield Farm and Worsborough Mill Open Days**
Worsborough Country Park, Park Road, Worsborough, Barnsley, S Yorks
☎ 0226 774527

W 29 May–4 Jun — **Newport International Festival of Musical Theatre**
Dolman Theatre, Kingsway, Newport, Gwent
☎

SW 30 May–3 Jun — **Royal Marine Museum D-Day Week**
Royal Marine Museum, Southsea, Hants
☎ 0705 819385
Exhibition, practical demonstrations (cook a D-Day meal), fashion show, talks.

NE 30 — **Kendal Medieval Market**
Mrs Buck, 62 Greenside, Kendal
☎ 0539 721154
Market takes place each year on streets of Kendal and includes traditional crafts, displays by lacemakers, farriers etc., as well as featuring medieval instruments and rare animal breeds.

EVENTS

MAY – 1994

R	DURATION	EVENTS

EA 30
D-Day Week
Imperial War Museum, Duxford Airfield, Cambridge CB6 4QR
☎ 0223 835000
As part of the activities, there will be costumed character interpreters of individuals from D-Day, bringing wartime scenes to life.

W 30
Eisteddfod Urdd Gobaith Cymru Youth Festival
Eisteddfod Field, Dolgellau, Gwynedd
☎ 0286 675733

SW end May–mid Sept
The Minack Theatre Summer Season
The Minack Theatre and Exhibition Centre, Porthcurno, Cornwall
☎ 0736 810694
16-week season of plays and musicals at this cliff-top open-air theatre.

SW 31 May–4 Jun
D-Day Anniversary: 'Operation Overlord'
Flavell Hall, Dartmouth, Devon
☎ 0803 832281
Exhibition about Operation Overlord, organised in conjunction with two local museums and schools.

N 31
World No Tobacco Day
United Nations
☎ 071-630 1981
Worldwide United Nations Observance Day.

SW 31
Propaganda Film Evening
D-Day Museum, Southsea
Contact: Lorraine Gibbison, Portsmouth Tourism (D-Day Office), Civic Offices, Portsmouth
☎ 0705 834800
Women and work in World War II and British propaganda in World War II.

SW 31 May–3 Jun
Portsmouth 800 Pageant
Contact: Lorraine Gibbison, Portsmouth Tourism, Civic Offices, Portsmouth
☎ 0705 834800
Starts at 8pm at Southsea Castle, will include a section on the war years in Portsmouth.

EVENTS

JUNE – 1994

| R | DURATION | EVENTS |

JUNE

N June* — **The Blakes Shield, Annual Competition for Natural History and Conservation Projects**
British Naturalists Association, 48 Russell Way, Higham Ferrers, Northants
☎ 0933 314672
Competition is open to groups of young people aged 8–16 years. Will be awarded for a natural history or conservation project which may investigate a wood or pond, or make a study of insects, plants, animals.

L June–Oct — **Greek Gold: Jewellery of the Classical Period**
Rooms 27–28 British Museum, Great Russell Street, London WC1
☎ 071-636 1555
Admission charge.

NE June* — **A Soldier's Life and Fashion Gallery**
Newcastle Discovery, Blandford House, Blandford Square, Newcastle
☎ 091-232 6789

N June* — **Feminist Book Festival**
Temporary contact: The Silver Moon Bookshop, 64–68 Charing Cross Road, London WC2
☎ 071-836 7906
Festival promoting feminist books published over the last year. Catalogue circulated to libraries and bookshops. Events organised at local level.

L June–Aug — **Royal Academy Summer Exhibition**
Royal Academy of Arts, Piccadilly, London W1
☎ 071-439 7438
Major annual exhibition of contemporary art including work by painters, sculptors, printmakers and architects.

L Early June*–Sept — **Prints by R B Kitaj**
V & A, Cromwell Road, London SW7
Education Dept: ☎ 071-938 8638
A selection of Kitaj's prints to complement the Tate Gallery retrospective.

EVENTS
JUNE – 1994

R	DURATION	EVENTS

NE June*
First Nations, A Celebration of North American Indian Life
Archaeological Resource Centre, St Saviourgate, York
☎ 0904 654324
This event aims to illustrate the richness and diversity of the many different cultures of the North American Indian through a variety of mediums including dance, song, storytelling, craft and photography. Will take place in a number of venues, e.g. York City Art Gallery, Hospitium and Impressions Gallery of Photography.

N 1–7
UK Volunteers Week
The Volunteer Centre UK, 29 Lower Kings Road, Berkhamsted, Herts HP4 2AB
☎ 0442 873311
Week involving organisations who involve volunteers of all ages.

SW 1–4
D-Day Anniversary
Weymouth Bay, Weymouth, Dorset
☎ 0305 772444
Display by World War II and D-Day veteran coastal patrol vessel 'Medusa' in Weymouth Bay and Harbour. Also parade, military bands, convoy of World War II vehicles, etc, on 2 June. 4 June tribute including display of tanks by the Bovington Museum.

SE 2–5
Dickens Festival
Various venues, Rochester, Kent
☎ 0634 843666
A Victorian celebration with thousands of people in Victorian costume. Guided walks and tours.

M 3 Jun–27 Aug
Stamford Shakespeare Company Season
Rutland Open Air Theatre, Tolethorpe Hall, Little Casterton, Stamford, Lincs
☎ 0780 54381
Performances of *Romeo and Juliet*, *As You Like It* and *The Merchant of Venice*.

NW 3–5
The Great Garden and Countryside Festival
Holker Hall & Gardens, Cark in Cartmel, Grange-over-Sands, Cumbria LA11 7PL.
☎ 05395 58328
Festival will include hands-on displays of traditional crafts such as stonewalling, exhibits of willow basket makers and beekeepers.

EVENTS

JUNE – 1994

R	DURATION	EVENTS

SW 4 — **French Market**
Portsmouth City Centre
Contact: Lorraine Gibbison, Portsmouth Tourism (D-Day Office),
Civic Offices, Portsmouth
☎ 0705 834800

SW 4-5 — **'The Longest Day' Military Vehicle Rally**
Bovington tank Museum, Wareham, Dorset.
☎ 0929 493329

N 5 — **World Environment Day: United Nations Awareness Day**
☎ 071-630 1981
The General Assembly has urged governments and United Nations organisations to mark World Environment Day with activities reaffirming their concern for the preservation and enhancement of the environment.

SW 5 — **D-Day Celebrations, Portsmouth**
Contact: Lorraine Gibbison, Portsmouth Tourism (D-Day Office),
Civic Offices, Portsmouth
☎ 0705 834800
The celebrations will include the unveiling of statue of Roosevelt and Churchill, flypast by historic US, British and French aircraft and a flotilla of historic vessels and ships from the Allied Forces.

N 6-13 — **Action Aid Week**
Hamlyn House, Macdonald Road, London N19
☎ 071-281 4101
Fundraising and awareness week in aid of the Third World charity Action Aid.

SW 7 — **Propaganda Film Evening at D-Day Museum, Southsea**
Contact: Lorraine Gibbison, Portsmouth Tourism (D-Day Office),
Civic Offices, Portsmouth
☎ 0705 834800
Women and Work in World War II and British propaganda in World War II.

EVENTS

JUNE – 1994

R	DURATION	EVENTS

L 7 **Impact of the English Civil War**
Royal Armouries, HM Tower of London, London
☎ 071-702 0013
Sixth form day.

M 8 **Meet the Gardener – Summer in the Garden**
Ryton Organic Gardens, Ryton-on-Dunsmore, Coventry CV8 3LG
☎ 0203 303517

SW 8–22 **Sidmouth International Festival of Folk Arts**
Manor Pavilion, Manor Road, Sidmouth, Devon
The Festival Office, 6 East Street, Sidmouth
☎ 0395 515134
Two-week festival of the performing arts with participants from all over the world.

NE 9 **South Asia and the National Curriculum**
Commonwealth Institute, Bradford
☎ 0274 530251
Lectures and practical sessions for teachers on India, Pakistan, Sri Lanka and Bangladesh. Talks cover History, Geography, English and Technology and are complementary to the National Curriculum.

EA 10–26 **Aldeburgh Festival of Music and the Arts**
Aldeburgh Foundation, High Street, Aldeburgh, Suffolk IP15 5AX
☎ 0728 452935
Annual arts festival founded by Benjamin Britten, which includes opera, concerts, literary events and exhibitions.

EA 11–12 **Sheep Shearing**
Park Farm, Snettisham, King's Lynn, Norfolk
☎ 0485 542425

SW 11–12 **American Indian Weekend**
American Museum in Britain, Claverton Manor, Bath, Avon
☎ 0225 460503
Exhibition of American Indian artefacts and dancing. Open daily 2.00–5.00pm, grounds 12.00–6.00pm.

SW 13–19 **Woodland Crafts Week**
Exmoor National Park, Exmoor House, Dulverton TA22 9HL
☎ 0398 23665
Events will include charcoal-making (ancient and modern), leather-tanning and the tannery industry, making iron tools, making stakes and doing forestry the modern way.

EVENTS

JUNE – 1994

R	DURATION	EVENTS

M 13–19 **Weaving, Spinning and Dyeing Exhibition**
Elvaston Castle Country Park, Borrowash Road, Elvaston, Derby
☎ 0332 573799
Exhibition of work by the Derby Guild of Weavers, Spinners and Dyers.

N 14 **Drinkwise Day**
☎ 071-383 3833
Annual campaign by the Health Education Authority to warn about the dangers of excessive drinking.

L 15 **Pugin**
Victoria & Albert Museum, Cromwell Road, London SW7
Education Dept: ☎ 071-938 8638
Examples of the work of architect, designer and writer, A W N Pugin (1812–52). Includes examples of his furniture, wallpaper, ceramics and jewellery as well as designs for the Catholic Church and the New Palace of Westminster.

L 15 **Propaganda Film Evening at D-Day Museum, Southsea**
Details as on 7 June above.

L 15 Jun–4 Sep **Friedrich to Hodler: A Romantic Tradition**
National Gallery, Trafalgar Square, London WC2
☎ 071-839 3321
Visiting exhibition from the Oskar Reinhart Foundation.

L 15–4 Sep* **R B Kitaj: A Retrospective**
Tate Gallery, Millbank, London SW1P 4PG
☎ 071-887 8000

SW 17 **Shakespeare in the Park**
Killerton House, Broadclyst EX5 3LE
☎ The Administrator: 0392 881345

S 17 Jun–31 Jul **Annie Leibovitz: Photographs 1970–90**
Scottish National Portrait Gallery, 1 Queen Street, Edinburgh
☎ 031-556 8921

L 17 Jun–4 Sep **BP Portrait Award, Annual Exhibition**
National Portrait Gallery, St Martin's Place, London WC2
☎ 071-306 0055

EVENTS

JUNE – 1994

R	DURATION	EVENTS

SE 18–25
Dickens Festival
Contact: Mrs Downes-Powell, 64 Pierremont Avenue, Broadstairs, Kent
☎ 0843 861045
Week-long festival features a stage version of Dickens' *A Tale of Two Cities* and talks on Victorian life. Living history with people dressed in Victorian costume.

SW 18–26
Lyn and Exmoor Festival
Exmoor National Park, Exmoor House, Dulverton, Somerset
☎ 0398 23665
Annual festival which celebrates the countryside and the arts. In 1994 the theme is 'Forty Years Ago' marking the establishment of Exmoor National Park in 1954. Some of the outdoor events will mark the changes in the countryside over the last 40 years, for example, farming and forestry. There will also be walks and some evening entertainment.

M 19–20
Medieval Weekend
Warwick Castle, Warwick CV34 4QU
☎ 0926 495421
Armoured knights, minstrels, recreation of everyday medieval life, and falconry.

EA 19 Jun–17 Jul
Historical Re-creation of Tudor Life
Kentwell Hall, Long Melford, Suffolk
☎ 0787 310207

SW 21
Propaganda Film Evening at D-Day Museum, Southsea
Details as on 7 June above.

L 22
Technology in Asia
Commonwealth Institute, London W8
☎ 071-603 4535
Conference for teachers looking at technology and its use and effect in Asia.

SE 22 Jun–10 Jul
Polesden Lacey Open Air Theatre
Polesden Lacey, Great Bookham, Surrey
Contact Ms Jennifer Johns, National Trust. ☎ 0372 453401

EVENTS
JUNE – 1994

R	DURATION	EVENTS

L 22–24

The Schools Fair
Wembley Conference Centre
Details from: News International Exhibitions, PO Box 495, Virginia Street, London
☎ 071-782 6872
Annual event targeted at 16+ group looking for long-term career counselling, advice on higher education courses, etc.

L 22 Jun– 19 Jul

South Bank Photography Show
South Bank Centre, London SE1
☎ 071-921 0631
Annual photography competition open to anyone over 16 who either lives or works in London. A hundred winning entries are chosen for display in the South Bank Centre.

SE 23–25

Dover's Roman Festival
White Cliffs Experience, Market Square, Dover, Kent
☎ 0304 210101
This festival features a number of attractions including a Roman market. Schools' days on 23 and 24 June.

L 23 Jun– 29 Aug

Bonnard at The Villa Le Bosquet
Hayward Gallery, South Bank Centre, London SE1
☎ 071-928 3144

L 23–29 Aug

Prints after Nicolas Poussin
Courtauld Institute Galleries, Somerset House, London WC2
☎ 071-873 2526

SE 25 June

Roman Festival
White Cliffs Experience, Market Square, Dover, Kent
Contact: Ms Johnson ☎ 0304 214566

W 25 Jun– 30 Jul

Lesley Sanderson
Wrexham Library Arts Centre, Rhosddu Road, Wrexham, Clwyd
☎ 0978 261932
Sanderson's drawings confront the viewer with strong images which challenge traditions of representation and provoke thought on the stereotyping of race and gender. Schools' Art Workshops each Monday and Tuesday.

EVENTS

JUNE – 1994

R	DURATION	EVENTS

SE 25 **Brilliance of Youth**
Petworth, Sussex
Contact: Music for Youth ☎ 081-870 9624
Youth music festival performed by winners of Music for Youth's annual competition.

M 25–26 **Early Summer National Organic Gardening Weekend**
Ryton Organic Gardens, Ryton-on-Dunsmore, Coventry CV8 3LG
☎ 0203 303517

L 29 June then monthly **Gainsborough: The Linley Portraits**
Dulwich Picture Gallery, London SE21
☎ 081-693 6911
Monthly lecture by Dr Ann Sumner, Keeper of Dulwich Picture Gallery. 2.00pm.

L 30 **Centenary of the Opening of Tower Bridge**
Bridgemaster, Tower Bridge, London SE1
☎ 071-407 0922
Tower Bridge was opened on 30 June 1894 by the Prince of Wales.

JULY

S July–Sep* **New Perspectives: The Italian Renaissance**
Burrell Collection, Pollok Country Park, Glasgow G43
☎ 041-649 7151
Pictures from the Burrell Collection and other sources on the Glasgow area.

SW July **Indian Art Exhibition**
Bristol Museum and Art Gallery, Queen's Road, Bristol BS8 1RL
☎ 0272 223571
Selection from important loan collection of Indian painting.

L July **From a National Bank to a Central Bank: Bank of England Tercentenary Exhibition**
Bank of England Museum, Bartholomew Lane, London EC
☎ 071-601 5545

EVENTS

JULY - 1994

R	DURATION	EVENTS

L   1 Jul–13 Aug   **Disrupted Borders**
Photographer's Gallery, 5 Great Newport Street, London WC2
☎ 071-831 1772
International exhibition bringing together the work of 13 artists who explore new definitions of race, class and sexuality in Europe.

S   1–4 Sep   **The Romantic Spirit in German Art 1790–1990**
Scottish National Gallery of Modern Art, Belford Road, Edinburgh
☎ 031-556 8921

SW   2–13 Aug   **Recent British Sculpture**
Victoria Art Gallery, Bridge Street, Bath, Avon
☎ 0225 461111
Open Mon–Fri 10.00 am–5.30 pm, Sat 10.00 am–5.00 pm.

NE   2–20 Aug   **Bashir Makhoul – Paintings, Installations and Video Works**
Middlesbrough Art Gallery, Middlesbrough Borough Council, PO Box 69, Gurney Street, Middlesbrough, Cleveland
☎ 0642 247445
'Al Hejara' is the first substantial showing of a body of work by the artist Bashir Makhoul, following the success of numerous exhibitions both here and abroad. His work can be seen and interpreted at several levels, from political and polemic narrative to minimal and conceptual art.

SE   2–14 Aug   **William Christian Symons, Painter, 1845–1911**
Hastings Museum, Cambridge Road, Hastings, East Sussex
☎ 0424 721202
Retrospective of the artist whose work is closely related to work by the Newlyn School and the English Impressionist style.

NE   2–3   **Battle of Marston Moor**
Midway between York and Wetherby, N Yorks
☎ 0532 591070
Re-enactment of the 1644 battle. There is also an attempt to break the world record of a costumed re-enactment involving 8,000 people. In aid of Barnado's

M   2–10   **Living History 1780**
Sulgrave Manor, Sulgrave, Banbury, Oxon
☎ 0295 760205
People in costume will demonstrate scenes from daily life in Georgian times.

EVENTS

JULY – 1994

R	DURATION	EVENTS

SE   2–23   **Chaucer Festival**
Various venues, Canterbury and London
Contact: Mr Philippe Wibrotte ☎ 0227 470379
There will be summer 'Canterbury Tales' tours from London to Canterbury on 2, 9 and 16 July at a cost of £25.

SW   3   **Sheep to Jumper**
Farmer Giles Farmstead, Teffont, Salisbury, Wilts SP3 5QY
☎ 0722 716338
Demonstrations of sheep shearing, carding, etc.

SW   4–23*   **Tall Ships Exhibition**
Brewers Quay, Hope Square, Weymouth, Dorset
☎ 0305 777622

L   5–9   **National Festival of Music for Youth**
South Bank Centre, London SE1
Contact: Music for Youth ☎ 081-870 9624
Performed by winners of Music for Youth's annual competition.

L   7–4 Sep   **Retrospective of Elizabeth Fritch**
Crafts Council, 44a Pentonville Road, London N1 9BY
☎ 071-278 7700

L   7   **Teaching about Nigeria**
Commonwealth Institute, London W8
☎ 071-603 4535
Conference for teachers providing up-to-date information and resources about Nigeria and ways of teaching about the country in the National Curriculum.

L   7–2 Oct   **Belgian Post-Impressionists**
Royal Academy of Arts, Piccadilly, London W1
☎ 071-439 7438

L   8 Jul–11 Sep   **Franz Kline**
Whitechapel Art Gallery, London E1
☎ 071-377 0107
The work of Franz Kline (1910–62), leader of the New York School and a radical figure in post-war abstraction.

EVENTS
JULY – 1994

R	DURATION	EVENTS

EA   8–10   **Sheep Shearing**
Park Farm, Snettisham, King's Lynn, Norfolk
☎ 0485 542425

NW   8–10   **Thameside Canals Festival**
Huddersfield Canal Society, 239 Mossley Road, Ashton-under-Lyne, Lancs
☎ 061-339 1332

SE   16   **Jousting Tournament**
Hever Castle and Gardens, Hever, Kent
Contact: Mrs Claire Prout ☎ 0732 865224

M   16–18 Sep   **The Art of Chaos**
Derby Industrial Museum, Silk Mill Lane, Derby DE1 3AR
☎ 0332 255308
Graphics produced by equations developed for the Chaos Theory.

M   20   **Meet the Gardener – Flowers and Fruit**
Ryton Organic Gardens, Ryton-on-Dunsmore, Coventry CV8 3LG
☎ 0203 303517

SE   23   **Longbow Warfare**
Hever Castle and Gardens, Hever, Kent
Contact: Mrs Claire Prout ☎ 0732 865224

W   21–mid Nov   **Civil War in Montgomeryshire**
Powysland Museum, The Canal Wharf, Welshpool, Powys
☎ 0938 554656
Exhibition covering history of Civil War, which only reached Montgomeryshire in 1644.

M   23–30 Aug   **The Canals of Wales**
The National Waterways Museum, Llanthony Warehouse, Gloucester Docks, Gloucester GL1 2EN
☎ 0452 307009
History of the canals which put Wales in the forefront of the Industrial Revolution.

W   23–24   **Country Fayre**
Penrhyn Castle, Bangor, Wales
☎ 0248 353048
The show features rare breeds, spinning and weaving, and has numerous craft tents.

EVENTS
JULY – 1994

R	DURATION	EVENTS

W 23–24 **Display by Ermine Street Guard and Roman Cavalry**
Roman Legionary Museum, High Street, Caerleon, Gwent
☎ 0633 423134
20–30 people put on a display, dressed in full Roman regalia.

W 23–28 Aug **Roman Summer Days**
Roman Legionary Museum, High Street, Caerleon, Gwent
☎ 0633 423134
Theme to be announced. Activities include playing Roman games, painting, dressing in Roman costumes and archaeology. There will be a dig on National Archaeology Day.

SW 24 Jul–30 Jan **Chinese Dinosaur Exhibition**
Royal Albert Memorial Museum, Queen Street, Exeter, Devon
☎ 0392 265858
Dinosaur exhibition featuring huge skeletons and moving models. Associated lectures and activities. Open Tue–Sat 10.00am–5.30pm.

SW 25–29 **D-Day Exhibition, Mountbatten Gallery**
Portsmouth Tourism (D-Day Office), Civic Offices, Portsmouth.
Contact: Lorraine Gibbison ☎ 0705 834800

S 25–19 Aug **The Scottish Schools Design Awards**
Smith Art Gallery, Dumbarton Road, Stirling FK8 2RQ
☎ 0786 471917
A touring exhibition from the Design Council.

SE 30 **Jousting Tournament**
Hever Castle and Gardens, Hever, Kent
Contact: Mrs Claire Prout ☎ 0732 865224

M 30 Jul–3 Sept **Holidays**
Cheltenham Museum, Cheltenham, Glos.
☎ 0242 237431
Exhibition on the growth of holidays and tourism.

NW 30–13 Aug **Wordsworth Summer Conference**
Wordsworth Trust, Dove Cottage, Grasmere
☎ 05394 35544

EVENTS

AUGUST – 1994

R	DURATION	EVENTS

AUGUST

L   Aug*   **The Picture Postcard – Exhibition to Mark 100th Anniversary**
Church Farmhouse Museum, Greyhound Hill, Hendon, London NE4 4JR Contact: Gerard Roots
☎ 081-203 0130

SW   1–31*   **Mask Exhibition**
Brewers Quay, Hope Square, Weymouth, Dorset
☎ 0305 777622

S   1–5*   **Operation Skylark – Environmental Play Scheme**
Smith Art Gallery, Dumbarton Road, Stirling FK8 2RQ
☎ 0786 471917 (8–12-year-olds)

L   5 Aug–23 Oct   **Drawings from the NPG Collection**
National Portrait Gallery, St Martin's Place, London WC2
☎ 071-306 0055

M   6–7   **Late Summer National Organic Gardening Weekend**
Ryton Organic Gardens, Ryton-on-Dunsmore, Coventry CV8 3LG
☎ 0203 303517

W   6 Aug–10 Sep   **Six Voices from Spain**
Wrexham Library Arts Centre, Rhosddu Road, Wrexham, Clwyd
☎ 0978 261932
Exhibition of contemporary sculpture by six leading Spanish artists. Schools Art Workshops each Monday and Tuesday.

SE   6   **Longbow Warfare**
Hever Castle and Gardens, Hever, Kent
Contact: Mrs Claire Prout ☎ 0732 865224

SW   7   **'The Taming of the Shrew'**
Killerton House, Broadclyst EX5 3LE
☎ 0392 881345

EVENTS

AUGUST – 1994

R	DURATION	EVENTS

SW 7
Normandy Veterans' Association Reunion
Naval Memorial, Southsea
Contact: Lorraine Gibbison, Portsmouth Tourism (D-Day Office), Civic Offices, Portsmouth
☎ 0705 834800
Drumhead Service and March past.

S 11–23 Oct
Monet to Matisse: Landscape Painting in France 1874–1914
National Gallery of Scotland, The Mound, Edinburgh
☎ 031-556 8921

SE 13
Jousting Tournament
Hever Castle and Gardens, Hever, Kent
Contact: Mrs Claire Prout ☎ 0732 865224

L 13–21
Flight Activities Week
Royal Air Force Museum, Grahame Park Way, Hendon, London
☎ 081-200 1763
Activities will include parachute drops, helicopter rides, kite building and workshop on 'flight'.

S 14 Aug–3 Sep
Edinburgh International Festival
Edinburgh Festival Society, 21 Market Street, Edinburgh EH1 1BW
☎ 031-226 4001
World's largest festival of the arts attracting many international stars.

S 16–5 Nov
Visions of the Ottoman Empire
Scottish National Portrait Gallery, 1 Queen Street, Edinburgh
☎ 031-556 8921

SE 20
Longbow Warfare
Hever Castle and Gardens, Hever, Kent
Contact: Mrs Claire Prout ☎ 0732 865224

SE 20–25 Sep
The Chemistry Set
Hastings Museum, Cambridge Road, Hastings, East Sussex TN34 1ET
☎ 0424 721202
Crafts Council showing how to use patination on metals, jewellery making and sculpture.

EVENTS

SEPTEMBER – 1994

R	DURATION	EVENTS

SE 27 — **Jousting Tournament**
Hever Castle and Gardens, Hever, Kent
Contact: Mrs Claire Prout ☎ 0732 865224

SW 28 — **Sheep to Jumper**
Farmer Giles Farmstead, Teffont, Salisbury, Wilts SP3 5QY
☎ 0722 716338
Demonstrations of sheep shearing, carding, etc.

SEPTEMBER

NE Sep–Dec* — **The Victorians**
Sheffield Industrial Museum, Off Alma Street, Sheffield S3 8RY
☎ 0742 722106
Exhibition follows Victorian life, industry, social and labour history.

SE Sept* — **Celebration of the End of Shelling in Dover**
White Cliffs Experience, Market Square, Dover, Kent
☎ 0304 210101

W Sep–Oct* — **Schools' Week**
Roman Legionary Museum, High Street, Caerleon, Gwent
☎ 0633 423134
A complete timetable of events for schools; visiting museum, amphitheatre, fortress and barracks. Only five schools per day, so early booking essential.

NE Sep* — **Home and Dry: Clothes for Safety and Comfort**
Gallery of English Costume, Platt Hall, Manchester
☎ 061-236 5244
A look at clothing from a child's perspective.

NE Sep* — **Boddington's Manchester Festival of Arts and Television**
Festival Office, Central Library, St Peter's Square, Manchester M2 5PD
☎ 061-234 1944

NW 3–4 — **Huddersfield Canals Festival**
Huddersfield Canal Society, 239 Mossley Road, Ashton-under-Lyne, Lancs
☎ 061-339 1332
Marks the bicentenary of the Huddersfield Narrow Canal.

EVENTS

SEPTEMBER – 1994

R	DURATION	EVENTS

M   3–4

Grand Medieval Tournament
Warwick Castle, Warwick CV34 4QU
☎ 0926 495421
Grand jousting tournament, foot combat display, long-bow archery, etc.

SW   4–9 Oct

Sarah Newman, Prints and Ceramics
Brewers Quay, Hope Square, Weymouth, Dorset
☎ 0305 777622
Exhibition and demonstrations.

M   5–9

Science in the World Around Us
British Association Annual Festival of Science at Loughborough University of Technology.
British Association for the Advancement of Science, Fortress House, 23 Savile Row, London W1X 1AB
For details contact: ☎ 071-494 3326
During the five days there will be debates, exhibitions, talks, hands-on activities and workshops covering areas such as the Environment, Crime and Communication, Living and Health, The World in Perspective.

M   10 Sep

Exploitation Earth
Cheltenham Museum, Cheltenham, Glos
☎ 0242 237431
Exhibition examining pollution and green issues.

SW   11–12

Country Craft Festival
Farmer Giles Farmstead, Teffont, Salisbury, Wilts SP3 5QY
☎ 0722 716338
Festival features demonstrations of country crafts such as weaving, spinning and knitting.

EA   13 Sep*– early 95

Chinese Ceramics: Recent and Rare
Fitzwilliam Museum, Cambridge
☎ 0223 332900
Exhibition of Chinese ceramics.

NW   14 Sep– 4 Dec

Barbara Hepworth Exhibition
Tate Gallery, Liverpool
☎ 051-709 3223
First full retrospective since the death of the artist in 1975, including over 90 sculptures and 20 drawings.

EVENTS

SEPTEMBER – 1994

R	DURATION	EVENTS
L	15–30 Oct	**Conrad Felix Miller, Graphics and Works on Paper** Courtauld Institute Galleries, Somerset House, London WC2 ☎ 071-873 2526
L	15–13 Nov	**2010 Textiles and New Technology** Crafts Council, 44A Pentonville Rd, London N1 9BY ☎ 071-270 7700
L	15 Sep– 14 Dec*	**The Glory of Venice: Art in the 18th Century** Royal Academy of Arts, Piccadilly, London W1 ☎ 071-439 7438
W	17 Sep– 22 Oct	**Polish Roots, British Soil** Wrexham Library Arts Centre, Rhosddu Road, Wrexham, Clwyd ☎ 0978 261932 Three generations of artists of Polish background who have lived in Britain. Schools' Art Workshops each Monday and Tuesday.
W	17 Sep– 9 Oct*	**Cardiff Festival of Music** St David's Hall, The Hayes, Cardiff CF1 2SH ☎ 0222 342611 Festival with opera, theatre, exhibitions and jazz. Theme: Women in the Arts.
SW	17 Sep– 16 Oct	**Exhibition: Prints from Wood** Royal Cornwall Museum, River Street, Truro, Cornwall Major exhibition of 20th-century print-making, supported by displays of historical prints and work of contemporary print-makers from Cornwall. Open Mon–Fri 10.00 am–5.00 pm.
M	21	**Meet the Gardener – Harvest Question Day** Ryton Organic Gardens, Ryton-on-Dunsmore, Coventry CV8 3LG ☎ 0203 303517
L	23 Sep– 8 Jan 95	**Prints and Drawings Exhibitions: Pre-Raphaelite Drawings and Artistic Circles; the Medal in Britain 1880–1918** Room 90, British Museum, Great Russell Street, London WC1

EVENTS

SEPTEMBER – 1994

R	DURATION	EVENTS

L   23 Sep–20 Nov

Miquel Barcelo
Whitechapel Art Gallery, London E1
☎ 071-377 0107
Work by the most celebrated Spanish artist of his generation, Miquel Barcelo (born 1956).

SE   24–12 Nov

Sea Monsters
Whitstable Museum and Gallery, Oxford Street, Whitstable, Kent
☎ 0227 276998
Exhibition coincides with the opening of the Channel Tunnel.

M   24–25*

Great Grandfather's Harvest
Elvaston Working Estate Museum, Elvaston, Derby
☎ 0332 573799

M   24

Dr Johnson Birthday Celebrations
Market Square, Lichfield, Staffs
☎ 0543 264972
Dr Samuel Johnson (1709–84), English lexicographer, critic and poet.

SE   24–30

Frontline Britain
Various venues, Dover, Kent
Contact: Mr Alex Summers ☎ 0304 381699

L   29 Sep–11 Dec

A Bitter Truth
Art and the First World War
Barbican Art Gallery, Barbican Centre, London WC2
☎ 071-588 9023
International survey commemorating the 80th anniversary of the outbreak of hostilities. Man Ray, Paul Nash, Picasso, Schiele and Kandinsky are among the artists featured.

L   29 Sep–Jan 95

Serious Games: The Romatic Spirit in German Art
Hayward Gallery, South Bank Centre, London SE1
☎ 071-928 3144
Traces the romantic movement in German art from Friedrich to Max Ernst.

EVENTS
OCTOBER – 1994

| R | DURATION | EVENTS |

OCTOBER

SW Mid Oct–Dec **Quay Talks**
Brewers Quay, Hope Square, Weymouth, Dorset
☎ 0305 777622
Series of talks during the autumn, covering subjects such as the history of embroidery, life and works of Barnes Wallace. More suitable for sixth form students.

M 3–7 **Schools Recycling/Composting Week**
Ryton Organic Gardens, Ryton-on-Dunsmore, Coventry CV8 3LG
☎ 0203 303517

EA 4 Oct– 18 Dec* **New York, New York**
Fitzwilliam Museum, Cambridge
☎ 0223 332900
New York views in prints from 1880 to 1980, the earliest prints showing the city before the skyscrapers were built.

L 7 Oct **Women's Photography Festival**
Photographer's Gallery, 5 Great Newport Street, London WC2
☎ 071-831 1772
Includes the work of Dorothy Bohm from her early black-and-white documentary work to recent colour photography in Venice and Egypt.

SW 7–16 **Cheltenham Festival of Literature**
Festival Office, Cheltenham Borough Council, Town Hall, Imperial Square, Cheltenham, Glos
☎ 0242 521621
Held at various venues around Cheltenham, usually during the first two weeks of October. An established festival of literature and related events including book exhibitions, play readings, and literary lectures.

M 8–10 **Tudor Living History, 1580**
Sulgrave Manor, Sulgrave, Banbury, Oxon
☎ 0295 760205
People in period costume act out daily life in Tudor times.

EVENTS

OCTOBER – 1994

R	DURATION	EVENTS

L   11, 18, 25 Oct and 1, 8, 15 Nov   **National Portrait Gallery Lectures**
National Gallery, Trafalgar Square, London WC2
☎ 071-389 1771
Professor Francis Haskell lectures on 'The Dispersal of the Art Collections of Charles I and his Courtiers'.

L   12 Oct–8 Jan 95*   **James McNeill Whistler**
Tate Gallery, Millbank, London SW1P 4PG
☎ 071-887 8000
American painter and etcher.

S   12–9 Nov*   **Holidays**
Dumfries Museum, The Observatory, Dumfries
☎ 0387 53374

L   14 Oct–Jan 95   **Sitwell Exhibition**
National Portrait Gallery, St Martin's Place, London WC2
☎ 071-306 0055

SE   15–20 Nov   **Survey of Seaside Architecture**
Hastings Museum, Cambridge Road, Hastings, East Sussex
☎ 0424 721202

L   19 Oct   **Making and Meaning: The Early Michelangelo**
National Gallery, Trafalgar Square, London WC2
☎ 071-839 3321
Examines how two early panel paintings, 'The Manchester Madonna' and 'The Entombment', were created by the artist. Admission free.

M   19   **Meet the Gardener – Putting the Garden to Bed**
Ryton Organic Gardens, Ryton-on-Dunsmore, Coventry CV8 3LG
☎ 0203 303517

SW   22–4 Dec   **Singer and Friedlander**
Bristol Museum and Art Gallery, Queen's Road, Bristol BS8 1RL
☎ 0272 223571
The pick of the entries from the *Sunday Times* Singer and Friedlander watercolour exhibition.

SW   22–20 Nov   **Wildlife Photography**
Bristol Museum and Art Gallery, Queen's Road, Bristol BS8 1RL
☎ 0272 223571
Prize-winning photographs from the annual competition.

EVENTS

OCTOBER – 1994

R	DURATION	EVENTS

L   22*   **Amnesty International Annual Youth Conference**
London and Edinburgh
Amnesty International, 99–119 Rosebery Avenue, London EC1
Contact: Piers Bannister ☎ 071-278 6000
Conference will include number of speakers covering all aspects of Human Rights. Workshops will be on subjects such as 'Racism in the UK' and 'Death Penalty'. Open to ages 13–19. Admission charge in region of £3.50.

M   23   **National Apple Day**
Ryton Organic Gardens, Ryton on Dunsmore, Coventry CV8 3LG
☎ 0203 303517

W   29 Oct– 10 Dec   **Welsh Local Arts**
Wrexham Library Arts Centre, Rhosddu Road, Wrexham, Clwyd
☎ 0978 261932
Work by young artists from Clwyd. Schools' Art Workshops each Monday and Tuesday.

NOVEMBER

L   Nov*   **Peter Collinson Exhibition**
Church Farmhouse Museum, Greyhound Hill, Hendon, London NE4 4JR
☎ 081-203 0130
Exhibition to mark the 300th anniversary of the birth of the botanist and naturalist Peter Collinson.

L   Nov–Feb 95   **Contemporary Artists Inspired by Ancient Egypt**
Room 25, British Museum, Great Russell Street, London WC1
☎ 071-636 1555

SW   Nov*   **Chemistry Week 1994 – Hands-on Activities**
The Exploratory, Bristol Old Station, Temple Meads, Bristol BS1 6QU
☎ 0272 252008

SW   Nov*   **Victorian Festival**
Dover Gaol, Dover Town Hall, Biggin Street, Dover, Kent
☎ 0304 201200
Range of activities with Victorian theme, including lectures, visits round the gaol, brass rubbing, etc.

EVENTS

NOVEMBER – 1994

R	DURATION	EVENTS
L	2	**Steaming Days for Schools** Kew Bridge Steam Museum, Green Dragon Lane, Brentford, Middx ☎ 081-452 8567 Days will include talks on themes such as 'The Victorians', 'Engineering Development', 'Heat and Energy' and 'The Industrial Revolution'.
L	7–9*	**Schools Prom, Royal Albert Hall** Contact: Music for Youth ☎ 081-870 9624 Concert by winners of Music for Youth annual competition.
L	18 Nov– 12 Feb	**Christina Rossetti** National Portrait Gallery, St Martin's Lane, London WC1 ☎ 071-306 0055 Exhibition on the poet Christina Rossetti (1830–1894).
L	18 Nov– 14 Jan	**Jerome Liebling** Photographer's Gallery, 5 Great Newport Street, London WC2 ☎ 071-831 1772 American post-war photographer. Work includes photographs of New York in the 40s and recent work in rural Massachusetts.
M	19 Nov onwards	**Jack Tithey Retrospective** Derby Industrial Museum, Silk Mill Lane, Derby DE1 3AR ☎ 0332 255308 Retrospective exhibition of Jack Tithey, official photographer for Rolls-Royce.
L	24 Nov– 22 Jan	**What is Jewellery?** Crafts Council, 44a Pentonville Road, London N1 9BY ☎ 071-278 7700
L	25 Nov– 21 Jan	**Nick Waplington** Photographer's Gallery, 5 Great Newport Street, London WC2 ☎ 071-831 1772 Large-scale, panoramic photographs of famous sites around the world.

DECEMBER

L	Dec–Apr 95	**Byzantine Art from British Collections** Rooms 27–28, British Museum, Great Russell Street, London WC1 ☎ 071-636 1555 Admission charge.

EVENTS

DECEMBER – 1994

R	DURATION	EVENTS

SE   3–4   **Dickensian Christmas**
Various venues, Rochester, Kent
Contact: Mrs Dena Oakford ☎ 0634 843666

W   10 Dec–28 Jan   **Asturias: New Art**
Wrexham Library Arts Centre, Rhosddu Road, Wrexham, Clwyd
☎ 0978 261932
The best art of young artists from the Asturias region of Spain. Schools' Art Workshops each Monday and Tuesday.

M   17–Jan 95   **A Green Thought in a Green Shade**
Middlesbrough Art Gallery Middlesbrough Borough Council, PO Box 69, Gurney Street, Middlesbrough, Cleveland TS1 1EL
☎ 0642 247445
A selection of works of art from the permanent collection of Middlesbrough Art Gallery, bringing a distinctive approach which will encourage viewing in a way different from the conventional, and linking the Gallery with wider community interests. Art works have been selected bearing in mind the concept of 'green' and relating the visual material to the written word where appropriate under the general inspiration of the lines for the poem by Andrew Marvell:
> 'Meanwhile the Mind, from pleasure less,
> Withdraws into its happiness . . .
> Annihilating all that's made
> To a green Thought in a green Shade'.

N   **1994 Dates to be announced**

A list of educational events taking place in National Trust houses is available from the National Trust. Contact: Schools' Department or Press Office ☎ 071-222 9251

N   A list of special events taking place at English Heritage properties is available from English Heritage ☎ 071-973 3459.

EVENTS

DATES TO BE ANNOUNCED

R	DURATION	EVENTS

The following events may take place at the National Maritime Museum in Greenwich, London, but are subject to funding. (As we go to press no dates have been announced.)
- Display about the Titanic in Summer 94
- Display about ocean liners in 1994
- Underwater Archaeology Exhibition, possibly from May to September. Contact: Press Office or Schools Programme. ☎ 081-858 4422.

L

Slade Lectures
National Gallery, Trafalgar Square, London WC2
☎ 071-389 1771
Juliet Wilson-Bareau, Slade Professor at Oxford University, lectures on Goya. Dates to be announced.

SW

The Other Classroom – New Hands-on Activity for Schools
Mary Rose Trust, College Road, HM Naval Base, Portsmouth
PO1 3LX
☎ 0705 750521
Date to be announced.

SW

Perception 'A' Level Talk – Prof Richard Gregory
The Exploratory, Bristol Old Station, Templemeads, Bristol
BS1
☎ 0272 252008

L

Summer 94 – Special Effects Exhibition
Museum of the Moving Image (MOMI), South Bank, Waterloo, London SE1 8XT
☎ 071-401 2636
Date to be announced.

EVENTS

ANNIVERSARIES – 1994

R	DURATION	EVENTS

1994: ANNIVERSARIES/SPECIAL YEAR

United Nations International Year of the Family
Manchester: City of Drama 1994
Lisbon: the European City of Culture (from March 94)

Manchester Ship Canal centenary
British Diabetic Association Year (60th Anniversary)
Abbey National 50th Anniversary (formed by the merger of the Abbey Road and the National)
Year of the London Taxi ☎ 071-286 1046
Save the Children – 75th Anniversary
Red Cross – 75th Anniversary
Glyndebourne Diamond Jubilee
70th Anniversary of Wembley Stadium
Centenary of the opening of Tower Bridge
Centenary of Blackpool Tower
50th Anniversary of the D-Day Landings
75th Anniversary of the end of World War I
Young Women's Christian Association centenary
150th Anniversary of the birth of the composer Rimsky-Korsakov
150th Anniversary of the birth of St Bernadette of Lourdes (Jan)
50th Anniversary of the death of painter Edvard Munch
60th Anniversary of the death of British composer Edward Elgar
Centenary of the death of Adolph Sax, inventor of the saxophone

1995

NW 1995 **Modern British Painting**
Tate Gallery, Liverpool
☎ 051-709 3223
From the Tate collection.

NW 1995 **Video Positive**
☎ Tate Gallery: 051-709 3223
International video festival held every two years in Liverpool, various venues. Date to be announced.

L 1995 **Bi-centenary of the poet Keats**
Keats House (Wentworth Place), Keats Grove, Hampstead, London NW3 2RR
☎ 071-435 2062/794 6829
Dates and events to be announced.

EVENTS

JANUARY – 1995

R	DURATION	EVENTS

JANUARY

L   Jan–Apr*

Impressionism in Britain
Barbican Art Gallery, Barbican Centre, London EC2
☎ 071-588 9023
Major survey of artists including Sickert, Steer, and Rothenstein.

    1

J Edgar Hoover
100th anniversary of the birth of the director of the FBI.

    16

Prohibition began in the United States in 1920

    20

Federico Fellini
Italian film director, famous for his film *La Dolce Vita*, born in 1920.

    24

Lord Randolph Churchill
100th anniversary of the death of the politician and father of Sir Winston Churchill.

L   27 Jan–18 Mar

Contemporary Photography from Northern Ireland
Photographer's Gallery, 5 Great Newport Street, London WC2
☎ 071-831 1772
New work from Northern Ireland over the past ten years.

FEBRUARY

NE   Feb

Jorvik Viking Festival
Various venues, York
Jorvik Viking Festival Office, Clifford Chambers, 4 Clifford Street, York YO1 1RD
☎ 0904 611944
Colourful festival with a Viking theme.

L   Feb–Apr

Contemporary Furniture – Craft and Design
Crafts Council, 44A Pentonville Road, London N1 9BY
☎ 071-278 7700

EVENTS

FEBRUARY – 1995

R	DURATION	EVENTS

W 4 Feb– 18 Mar

Antinomies: Work by Evelyn Williams
Wrexham Library Arts Centre, Rhosddu Road, Wrexham, Clwyd
☎ 0978 261932
Williams' large-scale drawings express sadness, fear, anger, helplessness and isolation and explore the consolation and support people find in one another. Schools' Art Workshops each Monday and Tuesday.

18

George Peabody
200th anniversary of the birth of American merchant and philanthropist who donated £2.5 million for building workmen's tenements in London.

MARCH

2

Sir Thomas Bodley
450th anniversary of the birth of the diplomat who bequeathed his fortune and book collection to Oxford University and after whom the Bodleian library is named.

S 25 Mar– 22 Apr

In Touch with the Past
Dumfries Museum, The Observatory, Dumfries
☎ 0387 53374

26

David Lloyd George
50th anniversary of Liberal Prime Minister 1916–22.

27

Wilhelm Rontgen
150th anniversary of the birth of the physicist who discovered X rays and received the Nobel Prize for Physics in 1901.

APRIL

SW 8 Apr– 20 May

Wheels
Bristol Museum and Art Gallery, Queen's Road, Bristol BS8 1RL
☎ 0272 223571
AMC touring interactive exhibition.

ADVERTISERS

ADVERTISERS INDEX

Action Aid	15
Aerospace Museum	295
Blackpool Tower Works	398
Brook Advisory Centre	29
Bryn Bach Park	530
Cabinet War Rooms	163
Carberry Tower	497
Central School of Drama	144
Christian Aid	36
Computers and Dyslexia	14
Cornwall County Council	145
Development Education Association	44
The Engineering Council	51
The Exploratory	446
Forge Mill Needle Museum	308
Forty Hall Museum	188
Ironbridge Gorge	310
Kingswood Centre	294
Kirkham Minibuses	14
Knights Caverns	541
Lords Tours	216
Minority Rights Group	14
Museum of Automata	371
National Children's Bureau	14
National Museum of Wales	525
National Society's RE Centre	144
Oakwood Leisure Ltd	547
Oxfam	75
Parham House and Gardens	231
Pump House	421
Routledge	143
Royal Navy Submarine Museum	144
Scottish Nuclear Ltd	520
Scottish Schools	145
Scottish Ski Tours	519
Sportspages	145
Teachers Assurance	13
The Ulster American Folk Park	487
UNICEF	93
Wembley Stadium Tour	259
Whizz-Kidz	111

COMMENTS & SUGGESTIONS

Dear Reader,

Please complete the form below to help develop the next edition of *The Resourceful Teacher's Handbook*. Please photocopy the form if you wish to comment on more than one organisation. Thank you in advance for your interest and help.

Gill FitzHugh
Editor

A. Please complete the details about the organisation/individual below.

Name ....

Address ....

....

Telephone ....

B. Please say which section of the book the comment refers to:

Visits in ☐   Visits out ☐   Annual events ☐

C. Please write your comment below:

....
....
....
....
....
....

D. Please make suggestions for any further sections you would like included in the book:

....

E. Please complete your details in the section below with your personal details:

Name .... Job Title ....

School/Organisation name and address ....

....

School/Organisation telephone ....

Please note that all information is given on the understanding that the details supplied may be used without further reference to the contributor and that the editor's decision is final. Please send the information to Gill FitzHugh, *The Resourceful Teacher's Handbook*, c/o Pan Macmillan, 18–21 Cavaye Place, London SW10 9PG.